Lecture Notes of the Institute
for Computer Sciences, Social Informatics
and Telecommunications Engineering   286

More information about this series at http://www.springer.com/series/8197

Shuai Han · Liang Ye · Weixiao Meng (Eds.)

Artificial Intelligence for Communications and Networks

First EAI International Conference, AICON 2019
Harbin, China, May 25–26, 2019
Proceedings, Part I

 Springer

Editors
Shuai Han
Harbin Institute of Technology
Harbin, China

Liang Ye
Harbin Institute of Technology
Harbin, China

Weixiao Meng
Harbin Institute of Technology
Harbin, China

ISSN 1867-8211　　　　　　　ISSN 1867-822X (electronic)
Lecture Notes of the Institute for Computer Sciences, Social Informatics
and Telecommunications Engineering
ISBN 978-3-030-22967-2　　　　ISBN 978-3-030-22968-9 (eBook)
https://doi.org/10.1007/978-3-030-22968-9

This Springer imprint is published by the registered company Springer Nature Switzerland AG
The registered company address is: Gewerbestrasse 11, 6330 Cham, Switzerland

Preface

We are delighted to introduce the proceedings of the first edition of the 2019 European Alliance for Innovation (EAI) International Conference on Artificial Intelligence for Communications and Networks (AICON). This conference brought together researchers, developers, and practitioners from around the world who are leveraging and developing artificial intelligence technology for communications and networks. The theme of AICON 2019 was "Artificial Intelligence for Communications and Networks: Applying Artificial Intelligence to Communications and Networks."

The technical program of AICON 2019 consisted of 93 full papers, including six invited papers in oral presentation sessions during the main conference tracks. The conference tracks were: Track 1—AI-Based Medium Access Control; Track 2—AI-based Network Intelligence for IoT; Track 3—AI-enabled Network Layer Algorithms and Protocols; Track 4—Cloud and Big Data of AI-enabled Networks; Track 5—Deep Learning/Machine Learning in Physical Layer and Signal Processing; and Track 6—Security with Deep Learning for Communications and Networks. Aside from the high-quality technical paper presentations, the technical program also featured four keynote speeches and four invited talks. The four keynote speeches were by Prof. Moe Win from the Laboratory for Information and Decision Systems, Massachusetts Institute of Technology, USA, Prof. Mohsen Guizani from the Department of Computer Science and Engineering, Qatar University, Qatar, Prof. Guoqiang Mao from the Center for Real-Time Information Networks, University of Technology Sydney, Australia, and Prof. Byonghyo Shim from the Department of Electrical and Computer Engineering, Seoul National University, South Korea. The invited talks were presented by Prof. Jinhong Yuan from the University of New South Wales, Australia, Prof. Shui Yu from the University of Technology Sydney, Australia, Prof. Bo Rong from the Communications Research Centre, Canada, and Prof. Haixia Zhang from Shandong University, China.

Coordination with the steering chair, Imrich Chlamtac, the general chairs, Xuemai Gu and Cheng Li, and the executive chairs, Qing Guo and Hsiao-Hwa Chen, was essential for the success of the conference. We sincerely appreciate their constant support and guidance. It was also a great pleasure to work with such an excellent Organizing Committee team and we thank them for their hard work in organizing and supporting the conference. In particular, we thank the Technical Program Committee, led by our TPC co-chairs, Prof. Shuai Han and Prof. Weixiao Meng, who completed the peer-review process of technical papers and compiled a high-quality technical program. We are also grateful to the conference manager, Andrea Piekova, for her support and all the authors who submitted their papers to the AICON 2019 conference.

We strongly believe that the AICON conference provides a good forum for all researchers, developers, and practitioners to discuss all scientific and technological aspects that are relevant for artificial intelligence and communications. We also expect that future AICON conferences will be as successful and stimulating as indicated by the contributions presented in this volume.

May 2019

Shuai Han
Liang Ye
Weixiao Meng

Organization

Steering Committee

Imrich Chlamtac   University of Trento, Italy

Organizing Committee

General Chairs

Xuemai Gu   Harbin Institute of Technology, China
Cheng Li   Memorial University of Newfoundland, Canada

Executive Chairs

Qing Guo   Harbin Institute of Technology, China
Hsiao-Hwa Chen   National Cheng Kung University, Taiwan

Program Chairs

Shuai Han   Harbin Institute of Technology, China
Weixiao Meng   Harbin Institute of Technology, China

Sponsorship and Exhibits Chair

Rose Hu   Utah State University, USA

Local Chair

Shuo Shi   Harbin Institute of Technology, China

Workshop Chairs

Yahong Zheng   Missouri University of Science and Technology, USA
Shaochuan Wu   Harbin Institute of Technology, China

Publicity and Social Media Chairs

Zhensheng Zhang   Retired
Lin Ma   Harbin Institute of Technology, China

Publications Chair

Liang Ye   Harbin Institute of Technology, China

Web Chairs

Xuejun Sha   Harbin Institute of Technology, China
Chenguang He   Harbin Institute of Technology, China

Posters and PhD Track Chair

Chau Yuen   Singapore University of Technology and Design,
                                        Singapore

Panels Chair

Xianbin Wang   University of Western Ontario, Canada

Demos Chair

Yi Qian   University of Nebraska Lincoln, USA

Tutorials Chair

Mugen Peng   Beijing University of Posts and Telecommunications,
                                        China

Conference Manager

Andrea Piekova   EAI

Technical Program Committee

Deyue Zou	Dalian University of Technology, China
Fan Jiang	Memorial University of Newfoundland, Canada
Lingyang Song	Peking University, China
Bo Rong	Communications Research Center, Canada
Wei Li	Northern Illinois University, USA
Xi Chen	Flatiron Institute, Simons Foundation, USA
Baoxian Zhang	University of China Academy of Sciences, China
Jalel Ben-Othman	University of Paris 13, France
Jun Shi	Harbin Institute of Technology, China
Ruiqin Zhao	Northwestern Polytechnical University, China
Feng Ye	University of Dayton, USA
Tao Jiang	Huazhong University of Science and Technology, China
Hossam Hassanein	Queen's University, Canada
Ruofei Ma	Harbin Institute of Technology, China
Jun Zheng	Southeast University, China
Wei Shi	Carleton University, Canada
Kun Wang	Nanjing University of Posts and Telecommunications, China
Xianye Ben	Shandong University, China
Shiwen Mao	Auburn University, USA
Mianxiong Dong	Muroran Institute of Technology, Japan
Wei Xiang	James Cook University, Australia
Yulong Gao	Harbin Institute of Technology, China

Contents – Part I

AI-Based Medium Access Control

Contents – Part II

Cloud and Big Data of AI-Enabled Networks

AI-Based Network Intelligence for IoT

Deep Learning/Machine Learning in Physical Layer and Signal Processing

Dual-Mode OFDM-IM by Encoding All Possible Subcarrier Activation Patterns

Xiaoping Jin, Zheng Guo, Mengmeng Zhao, Ning Jin[✉],
and Dongxiao Chen

Key Laboratory of Electromagnetic Wave Information Technology
and Metrology of Zhejiang Province, College of Information Engineering,
China Jiliang University, Hangzhou, China
{jxp1023, jinning1117}@cjlu.edu.cn,
guozheng311@sina.com, z_meng_meng@163.com

Abstract. In traditional orthogonal frequency division multiplexing with index modulation (OFDM-IM), when the subcarrier activation patterns (SAPs) is not a power of 2, part of SAPs will not be used. This will result in low transmission efficiency and low bit error rate (BER) performance. We have proposed a new scheme namely bit-padding dual-mode orthogonal frequency division multiplexing (BPDM-OFDM). It exploits all of the possible SAPs to convey data to obtain a better BER performance. Meanwhile, the BPDM-OFDM uses the dual-mode orthogonal frequency division multiplexing (DM-OFDM) to improve the transmission efficiency. In addition, a subcarrier interleaving technique is adopted to further improve the BER performance and the idea of hard limit algorithm, which is applied to the log-likelihood ratio detector (LLR-HL) to reduce the detection complexity. Significant performance improvement of the proposed scheme, in terms of transmission rate, detection complexity and BER performance, over the traditional OFDM-IM scheme has been validated through theoretical analysis and extensive simulations.

Keywords: OFDM-IM · BPDM-OFDM · Transmission efficiency ·
Bit-padding · LLR-HL detector

1 Introduction

Index modulation (IM) is one of the promising transmission schemes for next-generation wireless communication systems due to its advantages [1]. It utilizes the indices of the building blocks of the corresponding communication systems to convey additional information bits in contrast to traditional modulation schemes that rely on the modulation of the amplitude/phase/frequency of a sinusoidal carrier signal for transmission [2]. In orthogonal frequency division multiplexing with index modulation (OFDM-IM) system, a subset of subcarriers in an OFDM block is activated to convey constellation symbols, the indices of the active subcarriers can be used to convey additional information [3].

In the OFDM-IM system, the active subcarriers are selected by the incoming data [4]. The correct determination of a subcarrier activation pattern (SAP) is essential for

S. Han et al. (Eds.): AICON 2019, LNICST 286, pp. 3–15, 2019.
https://doi.org/10.1007/978-3-030-22968-9_1

the correct detection of the associated information bits. Different mapping and detection techniques have been proposed, which indicate two major problems.

First of all, the detectors suffer from the possibility of detecting an invalid SAP since not all of the possible SAPs are used in OFDM-IM. By now, a look-up table mapping method and a combinatorial mapping method are mainly proposed [5]. But the two methods share a common disadvantage that they cannot make full use of all SAPs, unless the number of the SAPs is a power of 2. In this case, a method of using unequal-length of index bits to exploit all SAPs is proposed [6], but it is difficult for detection and the BER performance decreases. By changing the number of information bits corresponding to the traditional amplitude phase modulation, and the information bits carried by the OFDM block maintain constant, the literature [7] proposed an equiprobable subcarrier activation method which is easy for detection, whereas the transmission efficiency is not improved compared with the traditional OFDM-IM system. In this paper, to achieve a better BER performance and higher transmission efficiency, we propose a constructed index bits mapping method which use the concept of bit-padding (BP) [8] to build an equal-length bits transmission scheme for dual-mode OFDM (BPDM-OFDM).

The second problem is how to reduce the detection complexity while maintaining high transmission efficiency. In [9], a dual-mode method is proposed to improve transmission efficiency, but the log-likelihood ratio (LLR) detection algorithm which is adopted has high complexity, especially under high order modulation [10]. In our BPDM-OFDM system, a reduced-complexity approximate optimal LLR detector based on the hard limit algorithm (LLR-HL) is employed, in which the modulation symbol is detected by directly calculation instead of traversing all constellation points after the active subcarriers are obtained [11].

It is shown via computer simulation that, under additive white Gaussian noise (AWGN) channels and frequency-selective Rayleigh fading channels, our proposed BPDM-OFDM achieves an overall better BER performance. And there is an increase of 1 bit/s/Hz in transmission efficiency and a much lower detection complexity achieved compared to the traditional OFDM-IM.

The rest of the paper is summarized as follows. In Section II, the system model of BPDM-OFDM is presented. In Section III, the constructed index bits mapping method, which is the main concept of BPDM-OFDM system, are introduced. The performance of BPDM-OFDM compared with OFDM-IM is analyzed in Section IV. Finally, Section V concludes the paper.

2 Methods

The number of subcarriers of OFDM-IM system is set as N, which is equal to the fast Fourier transform (FFT). A total of m information bits enter the OFDM-IM transmitter for the transmission of each OFDM block. These m bits are then split into g groups each containing p bits, i.e., $m = pg$. Each group of p-bits is mapped to an OFDM subblock. The number of subcarriers of each subblock is n, where $n = N/g$. Suppose that the number of active subcarriers of each group is k, the number of SAPs is given by the binomial coefficient $C(n, k)$. The specific SAP of a subblock is determined by mapping a p_1-bit data code, where $p_1 = \lfloor \log_2 C(n,k) \rfloor$ and $\lfloor \cdot \rfloor$ is the floor function. A data segment of $p_2 = k \log_2 M$ bits is used such that k data codes of length $\log_2 M$ bits are mapped onto the M-QAM signal constellation to determine the data symbols that are transmitted over the active subcarriers. Therefore, a total of p bits ($p = p_1 + p_2$) are mapped to an OFDM subblock of n subcarriers. This traditional OFDM-IM scheme is shown in Fig. 1.

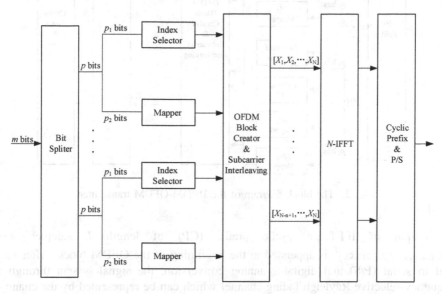

Fig. 1. The block diagram of the traditional OFDM-IM transmitter

As the OFDM-IM transmitter in Fig. 1, if the value of $C(n,k)$ is not a power of 2, there are always some SAPs that cannot be used. For example, for $n = 4$ and $k = 2$, the number of all possible SAPs is 6. Assume $p_1 = 2$ bits, the $2^{p_1} = 4$ SAPs are used. That means there are 2 invalid SAPs. In order to improve the transmission efficiency, we propose a constructed index bits mapping method to make use of all possible SAPs. Instead of the Index Selector and Mapper in Fig. 1, the p_1 bits will be processed by Backward Selection or Padding '1' module according to the decimal value of p_1 bits. The detailed process will be discussed in Sect. 3. After the Backward Selection or Padding '1' module, the constructed index bits are generated. Meanwhile, the p_2 bits are split into two parts and then modulated by the M_A and M_B order modulator, respectively. The value of M_A is equal to that of M_B, whereas the constellation points of M_A mapper and M_B mapper are different in amplitude and phase. This is called dual-mode index modulation (DM-IM) techniques. The block diagram of the above-mentioned scheme, which is called BPDM-OFDM transmitter is given in Fig. 2.

The transmitter combines g subblocks to form an OFDM symbol group. The N symbols are interleaved for the purpose of improving the error performance at low SNR region [12]. Then IFFT operation of point N is carried out to obtain the time domain transmitted signal $x = [x_1, x_2, \ldots, x_N]^T$, where $(\cdot)^T$ represents transpose operation. At

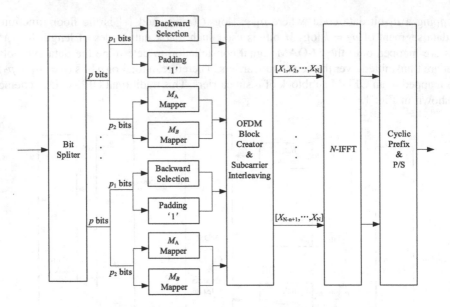

Fig. 2. The block diagram of the BPDM-OFDM transmitter

the output of IFFT, a cyclic prefix (CP) of length L samples $x = [x_{N-L+1}, \ldots, x_{N-1}, x_N]^T$ is appended to the beginning of the OFDM block. After parallel to serial (P/S) and digital-to-analog conversion, the signal is sent through a frequency-selective Rayleigh fading channel which can be represented by the channel impulse response (CIR) coefficients $h_T = [h_T(1) \ldots h_T(v)]^T$, in which $h_T(\sigma), \sigma = 1, \ldots, v$ are the cyclic symmetric complex Gauss random variable with $CN(0, \frac{1}{v})$ distribution, v represents the length of CIR. Supposing that the channel remains constant during the transmission of an OFDM block and the CP length L is larger than v, the coefficient of transfer function of frequency domain channel is the N-point FFT transform of h_T, which is represented as

$$\mathbf{H} = [H_1, H_2, \ldots, H_N]^T = \frac{1}{\sqrt{N}} FFT(\bar{h}_T) \tag{1}$$

where $\bar{h}_T = [h_T(1), \ldots, h_T(v), 0, \ldots, 0]^T$, $\frac{1}{\sqrt{N}} FFT(\cdot)$ represents FFT operation of point N.

At the receiver, after the CP removal operation and serial-to-parallel conversion, the FFT operation of point N and de-interleaving are performed to obtain the received signal $\mathbf{Y} = [Y_1, Y_2, \ldots, Y_N]^T$, where

$$Y_n = H_n X_n + W_n, 1 \leq n \leq N \tag{2}$$

In which W_n is the white Gaussian noise follows $CN(0, N_0)$ distribution.

In order to reduce the computational complexity, we use a low complexity log-likelihood ratio (LLR) algorithm to calculate the constellation diagram where the active symbols belonged. The basic idea is as follows: First, posterior probability is calculated according to formula (3), in which $1 \leq n \leq N$, $S_A(j) \in M_A$, $S_B(j) \in M_B$. If the sign of γ_n is positive, the subcarrier transmits the symbol modulated by M_A-QAM; if the sign of γ_n is negative, the subcarrier transmits the symbol modulated by M_B-QAM. Thus, the corresponding SAP is obtained.

$$\gamma_n = \ln(\frac{\sum_{j=1}^{M_A} \Pr(X_n = S_A(j)|Y_n)}{\sum_{j=1}^{M_B} \Pr(X_n = S_B(j)|Y_n)}) \tag{3}$$

Then, we determine the corresponding modulation symbol [11] of each subcarrier according to HL algorithm. Firstly, break the M-QAM symbols into N_1-PAM and N_2-PAM, where $M = N_1 \times N_2$. Then calculate the values of modulation symbols carried by the received signal Y_l of each subcarrier according to formula (4) and formula (5), in which $s_l = R(s_l) + j * I(s_l)$, $u_1 = R(Y_l)$, $u_2 = I(Y_l)$, and $R(\cdot)$ represents retrieving the real part, $I(\cdot)$ represents getting the imaginary part, $\min(\cdot)$, $\max(\cdot)$, $\text{round}(\cdot)$ represent the minimum, maximum and round values, respectively. It is unnecessary to search modulation symbols when using HL algorithm. So the computational complexity can be greatly reduced, especially in the condition of high order modulation.

$$R(s_l) = \min[\max(2\text{round}(\frac{u_1 + 1}{2}) - 1, -N_1 + 1), N_1 - 1] \tag{4}$$

$$I(s_l) = \min[\max(2\text{round}(\frac{u_2 + 1}{2}) - 1, -N_2 + 1), N_2 - 1] \tag{5}$$

3 The Constructed Index Bits Mapping Method

The constructed index bits mapping method includes the Backward Selection mode and the Padding '1' mode. The main idea is described as follows: a total of m information bits enter the OFDM-IM transmitter for the transmission of each OFDM block, these m bits are split into g groups each containing p bits, i.e., $m = pg$. Select the first p_1 bits of the incoming p bits and convert the value of p_1 into a decimal number Z. Then, we compare the value of Z with $C(n, k) - 2^{p_1} - 1$. According to the results of the comparison, the algorithm decides to choose one of the two modes, Backward Selection or Padding '1'. The block diagram of the transmitter is given in Fig. 2.

(1) **Backward Selection:**
   If $0 \leq Z \leq C(n, k) - 2^{p_1} - 1$, select one more bit after the first p_1 bits, so the index bits become a length of $p_1 + 1$ bits sequence, then take the next step according to the $(p_1 + 1)$-th bit. This is called Backward Selection.
   (a) If the $(p_1 + 1)$-th bit is '0', the index value Z^I is equal to Z.

(b) If the $(p_1 + 1)$-th bit is '1', the index value Z^I is equal to $Z + 2^{p_1}$.

(2) **Padding '1':**

If $Z > C(n, k) - 2^{p_1} - 1$, padding '0' or '1' after p_1 bits, then the index bits of p_1 turn into $p_1 + 1$ bits. The index value Z^I is equal to Z. This is called Padding '1'.

We take $p_1 = 2, n = 4, k = 2$ as an example for each subblock, which is shown in Table 1. If the numeric value in the active subcarrier is '1', it indicates that the corresponding subcarrier is activated, and '0' indicates that the subcarrier is not activated.

Table 1. Constructed index bits mapping method when $p_1 = 2, n = 4, k = 2$

Index bit	Z	$C(n, k)$ $-2^{p_1} - 1$	Backward Selection or Padding '1'	Constructed index bits	Index value Z^I	Sequences J	Active subcarrier
00	0	1	Backward Selection	000	0	$\{1, 0\}$	[1, 1, 0, 0]
				001	4	$\{3, 1\}$	[0, 1, 0, 1]
01	1	1	Backward Selection	010	1	$\{2, 0\}$	[1, 0, 1, 0]
				011	5	$\{3, 2\}$	[0, 0, 1, 1]
10	2	1	Padding '1'	101	2	$\{2, 1\}$	[0, 1, 1, 0]
11	3	1	Padding '1'	111	3	$\{3, 0\}$	[1, 0, 0, 1]

If the $p_1 = 2$ information bits of the data stream are '00', its decimal value is 0, that is, $Z = 0$. And $C(n, k) - 2^{p_1} - 1 = 6 - 2^2 - 1 = 1$, so $0 \le Z \le C(n, k) - 2^{p_1} - 1$ is derived, according to the algorithm, the one more bit after the first p_1 bits of the data stream will be selected. The '0' or '1' should be padded into the sequence after original index bits to form the new index bits sequence, which we named the Constructed Index Bits: If the subsequent bit is '0', the $Z^I = 0$ is obtained by converting the new index bits '000' into decimal form; If the subsequent bit is '1', the $Z^I = 4$ is obtained by converting the new index bits '001' to decimal plus 2^{p_1}, then $Z^I = Z + 2^{p_1} = 4$.

If the two information bits of the data stream are '10', its decimal value is 2. $C(n, k) - 2^{p_1} - 1 = 6 - 2^2 - 1 = 1, 2 \ge 1$. Therefore, according to the algorithm, the information bit '1' will be padded after the original index bits '10', we get a new index bits '101'. Then the new index bits sequence '101' is converted to the decimal form 2, that is $Z^I = 2$.

Each subblock adopts the bit-padding technique mentioned above, in the meantime a total of p_2 bits are sent to the M_A mapper and M_B mapper.

$$p_2 = k \log_2 M_A + (n - k) \log_2 M_B \tag{6}$$

where M_A and M_B represent the modulation order. It is clear that the length of subcarrier indices of each OFDM-IM subblock are equal after bit-padding process, meanwhile the number of bits which carried in each subblock will be $p = (p_1 + 1) + p_2$ or $p = p_1 + p_2$. Because of Backward Selection, the former is 1 larger than the latter.

According to the value of Z^I, we use the combinational method to obtain the corresponding SAP as shown in formula (2) [5]. Among them, $c_k > \ldots > c_1 \ge 0$, which c_k represents the position corresponding to the activation of the subcarrier in each subblock. The number of active subcarriers satisfies $C(c_k, k) \leq Z^l$ and $C(c_{k-1}, k-1) \leq Z^l - C(c_k, k)$, etc. Then the serial number of active subcarriers finally is $J+1$, $J = \{c_k, \ldots, c_1\}$.

$$Z^l = C(c_k, k) + \ldots + C(c_2, 2) + C(c_1, 1) \tag{7}$$

As an example, when $n = 4, k = 2, C(4, 2) = 6$, the algorithm, which finds the lexicographically ordered sequences for all possibilities, can be explained as follows: start by choosing the maximal c_k that satisfies $C(c_{k-1}, 2) \leq 5$ and then choose the maximum c_{k-1} that satisfies $C(c_{k-1}, 1) \leq 5 - C(c_k, 2)$ and so on. The following sequences J can be calculated as:

$$
\begin{aligned}
5 &= C(3,2) + C(2,1) \rightarrow J = \{3,2\} \\
4 &= C(3,2) + C(1,1) \rightarrow J = \{3,1\} \\
3 &= C(3,2) + C(0,1) \rightarrow J = \{3,0\} \\
2 &= C(2,2) + C(1,1) \rightarrow J = \{2,1\} \\
1 &= C(2,2) + C(0,1) \rightarrow J = \{2,0\} \\
0 &= C(1,2) + C(0,1) \rightarrow J = \{1,0\}
\end{aligned}
\tag{8}
$$

4   Results and Discussion

4.1   Transmission Efficiency

The number of data bits carried in each subblock of traditional OFDM-IM and the proposed BPDM-OFDM are as below:

OFDM-IM:

$$p = p_1 + p_2 = \lfloor \log_2 C(n, k) \rfloor + k \log_2 M$$

BPDM-OFDM:

a. Backward Selection:

$$p = (p_1 + 1) + p_2 = \lfloor \log_2 C(n, k) \rfloor + 1 + k \log_2 M_A + k \log_2 M_B$$

b. Padding '1':

$$p = p_1 + p_2 = \lfloor \log_2 C(n, k) \rfloor + k \log_2 M_A + k \log_2 M_B$$

The comparison of the number of transmission data bits in each subblock between BPDM-OFDM and OFDM-IM systems for $n = 4, k = 2$ are shown in Table 2.

Table 2. Comparison of the number of data bits at $n = 4, k = 2$

Modulation mode	OFDM-IM	BPDM-OFDM (Backward Selection)	BPDM-OFDM (Padding '1')
BPSK	4	7	6
QPSK	6	11	10

Spectrum efficiency is calculated with $\rho = \frac{g(p_1 + p_2)}{N+L}$. with BPSK, the spectrum efficiency of OFDM-IM is 0.89 bit/Hz, and the spectrum efficiency of BPDM-OFDM is 1.56 bit/s/Hz or 1.33 bit/s/Hz; With QPSK modulation, the spectrum efficiency of OFDM-IM is 1.33 bit/Hz, and the spectrum efficiency of BPDM-OFDM is 2.45 bit/s/Hz or 2.22 bit/s/Hz. From the comparison it can be concluded that BPDM-OFDM system obtains higher spectrum efficiency.

4.2 Complexity Analysis

The total computational complexity of the detectors of OFDM-IM and BPDM-OFDM systems, in terms of real multiplications, are shown in Table 3.

Table 3. Complexity analysis

Model	Detection algorithm	Complexity	Example: $n, k, M = (4, 2, 4)$
OFDM-IM	ML	$O(2CM^k)$	196
BPDM-OFDM	ML	$O(6n^2 M_A M_B)$	1536
	LLR+ML	$O(6nM_A + 6n(M_A + M_B))$	288
	LLR-HL	$O(9n + 6n(M_A + M_B))$	228

In Table 3, $C = 2^{p_1}$ is the total number of active subcarrier index combinations, and $M_A = M_B = M$ is the order of modulation.

As shown in Table 3, the complexity of ML detection algorithm increases quadratically with the number of subcarriers N, and increases linearly with modulation order. When the transmitting terminal is equipped with dozens or even hundreds of subcarriers, the detection complexity of ML detector will be so large that makes it become impractical. In our proposed LLR-HL algorithm, the posterior probability is used to judge the dual-mode modulation constellation space. HL algorithm which can directly calculates modulation symbol is used to replace the full-search ML detection, so the LLR-HL detection algorithm can greatly reduce the complexity of detection and eliminate the problem that the complexity increases exponentially with N.

4.3   BER Analysis

In this subsection, simulation is carried out under AWGN channel and frequency-selective channel for the BPDM-OFDM with QPSK modulation and OFDM-IM with 16QAM modulation to ensure they have the same spectrum efficiency. In all simulations, we assumed the following system parameters: $N = 128$, $n = 4$, $k = 2$ and $L = 16$. The comparison of BER performance between OFDM-IM and BPDM-OFDM systems using different detection algorithms are shown in Figs. 3, 4 and 5.

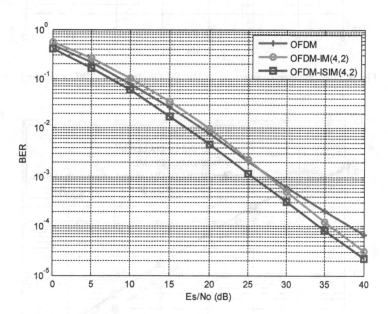

Fig. 3. Performance comparison of OFDM-IM with/without interleaving

As shown in Fig. 3, under BPSK modulation, the OFDM-IM with subcarrier interleaving (OFDM-ISIM) has obvious advantages over OFDM-IM and OFDM at medium to high SNR. At a BER value of 10^{-3}, the performance gap between OFDM-ISIM and OFDM-IM is about 7 dB. Therefore, we employ the subcarrier

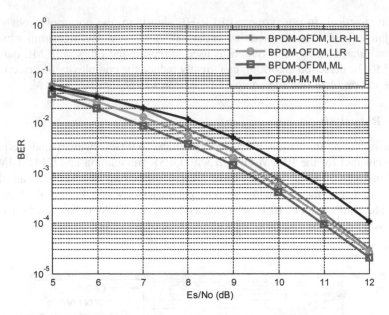

Fig. 4. Performance comparison of BPDM-OFDM over AWGN channel

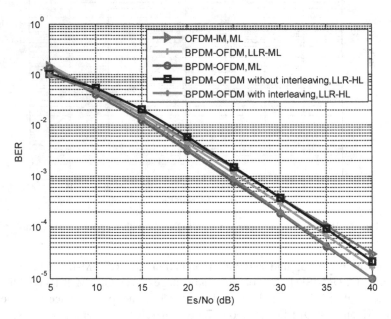

Fig. 5. Performance comparison of BPDM-OFDM over frequency-selective channels

interleaving to BPDM-OFDM, and the BER performance between BPDM-OFDM with/without interleaving is shown in Fig. 5.

As shown in Fig. 4, the proposed BPDM-OFDM achieves approximately 1 dB better than the BER performance of OFDM-IM when using the ML detection. When the LLR detection is used, there is about 0.1 dB performance loss comparing to the ML detection in the low SNR region. Considering the complexity of LLR detection is still high, the LLR-HR detection method is also compared. The BER performance of the proposed LLR-HL detection scheme is very close to that of the LLR detection. As we explained before, LLR uses the posterior probability to reduce the detector's search times, and LLR-HL can directly calculate the modulation symbols according to the real part and imaginary part of the received information after the modulation constellation diagram is decided. Although the LLR-HL detection exhibits a slight BER performance loss compared to ML detection, it achieves a great decrease in computational complexity.

As shown in Fig. 5, the performance of BPDM-OFDM is about 2 dB at the BER 10^{-3}, which shows better performance than that of OFDM-IM. The reason is that under the same spectrum efficiency, BPDM-OFDM adopts QPSK modulation while OFDM-IM adopts 16QAM modulation with higher order. At a BER value of 10^{-3}, the LLR-HL algorithm without interleaving in BPDM-OFDM exhibits about 2 dB loss with ML algorithm. However, the BER performance of LLR-HL detection algorithm could reach the similar performance of ML detection with the interleaving technique.

5 Conclusion

In this paper, a novel BPDM-OFDM scheme has been presented based on dual-mode modulation with bit-padding and subcarrier interleaving techniques. The BPDM-OFDM system is proposed for exploiting all of the possible SAPs to convey data in order to improve transmission efficiency and BER performance in contrast with the traditional OFDM-IM system. A low complexity LLR-HL detection algorithm instead of ML detection is employed, which reduces the detection complexity distinctly. It is shown via computer simulation that the performance of BPDM-OFDM outperforms the traditional OFDM-IM. In follow-up research work, the lower order modulation method in OFDM-IM can be studied to further improve the system error performance and spectral efficiency [14]. The Gray-coded index mapping method was already reported to be used to reduce the index error rate of dual-mode system [14]. The structure of the dual-mode system has yet to be further improved.

Declarations
Availability of Data and Materials

Algorithm 1 Iteration LLR-HL Calculation for BPDM-OFDM

Require: Received signal Y_n, channel coefficient H_n, noise energy N_0, constellation sets M_A, M_B, $M = N_1 \times N_2$, and their sizes of OFDM subblock l, number of subcarriers modulated by mapper A per subblock k;

Ensure: γ_n is LLR of n-th subcarrier;

1: $\Delta_1 = -\dfrac{1}{N_0}|Y_n - H_n S_A(j)|^2$

2: $\Delta_2 = -\dfrac{1}{N_0}|Y_n - H_n S_B(q)|^2$

3: **for** ($j = 2; j \le M_A; j++$) **do**

4: $T_1 = -\dfrac{1}{N_0}|Y_n - H_n S_A(j)|^2$

5: $T_2 = \max\{\Delta_1, T_1\} + f(|\Delta_1 - T_1|)$

6: $\Delta_2 = T_2$

7:**end for**

8:**for** ($q = 2; j \le M_B; q++$) **do**

9: $T_1 = -\dfrac{1}{N_0}|Y_n - H_n S_B(q)|^2$

10: $T_2 = \max\{\Delta_2, T_1\} + f(|\Delta_2 - T_1|)$

11: $\Delta_2 = T_2$

12:**end for**

13: $\gamma_n = \ln(k) - \ln(n-k) + \Delta_1 - \Delta_2$

14: **return** γ_n

15: **If** $\gamma_n > 0$ $D = \dfrac{H_n \times Y_n}{\|H_n\|^2}$

    Else $D = \dfrac{W}{(1+\sqrt{3}) \times \exp(-j \times \pi \times 0.75)}$

16: $u_1 = real(D), u_2 = imag(D)$

17: $R(s_l) = \min[\max(2round(\dfrac{u_1+1}{2})-1, -N_1+1), N_1-1]$

References

1. Cheng, X., Zhang, M., Wen, M., Yang, L.: Index modulation for 5G: striving to do more with less. IEEE Wirel. Commun. **25**(2), 126–132 (2018)
2. Basar, E., Wen, M., Mesleh, R., Di Renzo, M., Xiao, Y., Haas, H.: Index modulation techniques for next-generation wireless networks. IEEE Access **5**, 16693–16746 (2017)
3. Abu-Alhiga, R., Haas, H.: Subcarrier-index modulation OFDM. In: 2009 IEEE 20th International Symposium on Personal, Indoor and Mobile Radio Communications, Tokyo, pp. 177–181 (2009)
4. Başar, E.: Multiple-input multiple-output OFDM with index modulation. IEEE Signal Process. Lett. **22**(12), 2259–2263 (2015)
5. Başar, E., Aygölü, Ü., Panayırcı, E., Poor, H.V.: Orthogonal frequency division multiplexing with index modulation. IEEE Trans. Signal Process. **61**(22), 5536–5549 (2013)
6. Siddiq, A.I.: Low complexity OFDM-IM detector by encoding all possible subcarrier activation patterns. IEEE Commun. Lett. **20**(3), 446–449 (2016)
7. Wen, M., Zhang, Y., Li, J., Basar, E., Chen, F.: Equiprobable subcarrier activation method for OFDM with index modulation. IEEE Commun. Lett. **20**(12), 2386–2389 (2016)
8. Yang, Y., Aissa, S.: Bit-padding information guided channel hopping. IEEE Commun. Lett. **15**(2), 163–165 (2011)
9. Mao, T., Wang, Q., Wang, Z.: Generalized dual-mode index modulation aided OFDM. IEEE Commun. Lett. **21**(4), 761–764 (2017)
10. Zheng, B., Chen, F., Wen, M., Ji, F., Yu, H., Liu, Y.: Low complexity ML detector and performance analysis for OFDM with in-phase/quadrature index modulation. IEEE Commun. Lett. **19**(11), 1893–1896 (2015)
11. Rajashekar, R., Hari, K.V.S., Hanzo, L.: Reduced-complexity ML detection and capacity-optimized training for spatial modulation systems. IEEE Trans. Commun. **62**(1), 112–125 (2014)
12. Başar, E.: OFDM with index modulation using coordinate interleaving. IEEE Wirel. Commun. Lett. **4**(4), 381–384 (2015)
13. Nambi, S.A., Giridhar, K.: Lower order modulation aided BER reduction in OFDM with index modulation. IEEE Commun. Lett. **22**(8), 1596–1599 (2018)
14. Li, X., Wang, H., Guan, N., Lai, W.: A dual-mode index modulation scheme with gray-coded pairwise index mapping. IEEE Commun. Lett. **22**(8), 1580–1583 (2018)

Energy Efficiency Optimization Based SWIPT in OFDM Relaying Systems

Dan Huang[1], Weidang Lu[2], and Mengshu Hou[1(✉)]

[1] University of Electronic Science and Technology of China,
Chengdu 610054, China
mshou@uestc.edu.cn
[2] Zhejiang University of Technology, Hangzhou 310023, China

Abstract. The rapid development of the information and communication industry has brought huge energy consumption, which also reduces the energy efficiency. In this article, we integrate the cooperative relaying technology into a SWIPT-OFDM system, and focus on the system energy efficiency maximization problem. More specifically, the relay node uses the DF protocol to forward information from the base station to the user. The objective function is to maximize the energy efficiency of the system, in which the system fixed circuit power consumption, target rate, and total system power limit are all considered. At first we derive a non-convex fractional expression, after a complex mathematical transformation, a new objective function is obtained, and then we propose an efficient policy to optimize the subcarrier and power allocation for obtaining the optimal energy efficiency. Simulation results show that the proposed algorithm can not only converge after several iterations, but also achieve higher energy efficiency.

Keywords: Energy efficiency · SWIPT · DF relay · OFDM · Resource allocation

1 Introduction

The artificial intelligence (AI) industry is developing rapidly now, AI technology has been applied in many fields [1], and the wireless communication industry is no exception. Applying AI technology to the wireless communications industry can bring better service to the users, however the power consumption has also increased dramatically, which leads to the low energy efficiency [2, 3]. Therefore, how to effectively improve energy efficiency has become a hard problem in wireless communication networks.

SWIPT technology is considered as an effective way to increase energy efficiency.

In [4], the authors applied SWIPT technology to multiple-input multiple-output (MIMO) system, and adopted the time-switching (TS) method to achieve SWIPT, and then found the optimal policy for power allocation and TS ratio which can maximize energy efficiency. Reference [5] considered the energy efficiency maximization problem in Cloud-Based cellular network, where the authors jointly optimized the subcarrier and power allocation, and obtained the optimal energy efficiency.

S. Han et al. (Eds.): AICON 2019, LNICST 286, pp. 16–23, 2019.
https://doi.org/10.1007/978-3-030-22968-9_2

Compared with wired channel, wireless channel has fading effect because of its open propagation space and time-varying characteristics [6]. The transmission signal has often undergone severe attenuation or distortion when it reaches the user. Cooperative relay technology can improve the reliability of information transmission and system capacity, and is widely used in wireless communication networks [7]. The two most common protocols of cooperative relay technology are the amplify-and-forward (AF) protocol and decode-and-forward (DF) protocol [8]. When the distance between base station and relay node is very close and the channel quality is good, the performance of DF protocol is better than that of AF protocol [9]. So in this article, we use the DF protocol at the relay node to forward information to the user.

Inspired by the above literature, in this article, we investigate the energy efficiency maximization problem based on SWIPT in DF relay OFDM systems, where the energy efficiency is maximized by optimizing subcarrier allocation and power allocation.

2   System Model and Problem Formulation

2.1   System Model

We consider a downlink OFDM system, which consists of one base station, one relay node, and one user, as shown in Fig. 1. The set of subcarriers can be expressed as $\mathbf{N} = \{1, 2, 3, \ldots, N\}$, the total transmit power is set to P.

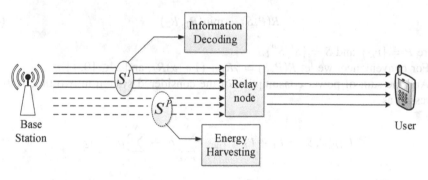

Fig. 1. System model

The transmission time from base station to user is equally divided into two time slots.

In the first time slot, the base station transmits information to the relay node, and the relay node utilizes a part of the subcarriers, which are denoted as S^I, for information decoding, and utilizes the rest of subcarriers, which are denoted as S^P, to perform energy harvesting. Let h_n represent the channel power gain on subcarrier $n(n \in \mathbf{N})$, and p_n denotes the power allocated on subcarrier n, the noise power is set as σ_n^2.

In the second time slot, the relay node forwards the information to the user by using the energy harvested in the first time slot. The channel power gain on subcarrier n' is denoted by $g_{n'}$, and the power on the subcarrier n' is $p_{n'}$, and the noise power is $\sigma_{n'}^2$.

Therefore, the rate received by the relay node in the first time slot can be expressed as

$$R_1 = \frac{1}{2} \sum_{n \in S^I} \ln(1 + \frac{h_n p_n}{\sigma_n^2}) \tag{1}$$

And the energy harvested by the relay node can be written as

$$Q = \xi \sum_{n \in S^P} (h_n p_n + \sigma_n^2) \tag{2}$$

where ξ denotes the energy harvesting conversion efficiency.

In the second time slot, the rate from relay node to user can be expressed as

$$R_2 = \frac{1}{2} \sum_{n'=1}^{N} \ln(1 + \frac{g_{n'} p_{n'}}{\sigma_{n'}^2}) \tag{3}$$

After two time slots, the achievable rate from base station to user with the help of relay node can be given as

$$R(P, S) = \min(R_1, R_2) \tag{4}$$

where $P = \{p_{n'}\}$ and $S = \{S^I, S^P\}$.

For convenience, we let $R(P, S) = \alpha R_1 + (1 - \alpha) R_2$, and $\alpha \in \{0, 1\}$.

And the sum of power consumption of the considered system in two time slots is expressed as

$$U_{TP}(P, S) = P_B + P_R + P_u + \sum_{n=1}^{N} p_n + \sum_{n'=1}^{N} p_{n'} - Q \tag{5}$$

where P_B, P_R and P_u represent the fixed circuit power consumption at base station, relay node and user, respectively.

So we can easily get the mathematical formula of the system energy efficiency, where the energy efficiency is the ratio of system rate to the total power consumption [10], as shown below

$$E_{eff}(P, S) = \frac{R(P, S)}{U_{TP}(P, S)} \tag{6}$$

2.2   Problem Formulation

With the goal of maximizing energy efficiency under some constraints, and this is formulated as

$$\textbf{P1}: \max_{p_{n'}, S^P, S^I} E_{eff}(P, S)$$

$$s.t. \; C1: R_1 = \frac{1}{2} \sum_{n \in S^I} \ln(1 + \frac{h_n p_n}{\sigma_n^2}) \geq R_T$$

$$C2: R_2 = \frac{1}{2} \sum_{n'=1}^{N} \ln(1 + \frac{g_{n'} p_{n'}}{\sigma_{n'}^2}) \geq R_T$$

$$C3: P_B + P_R + P_u + \sum_{n=1}^{N} p_n \leq P, (p_n \geq 0) \tag{7}$$

$$C4: \xi \sum_{n \in S^P} (h_n p_n + \sigma_n^2) \geq \sum_{n'=1}^{N} p_{n'}$$

$$C5: S^I + S^P = \mathbf{N}$$

$$C6: S^I \cap S^P = \varnothing$$

where R_T is the target rate of the system, C1 and C2 give the target rate constraints, C3 represents the total power limit of the system. C4 indicates that the energy required for relay node to forward information to the user comes from Q. C5 and C6 are constraints of subcarrier set.

3   Optimal Solution

In this part, we maximize energy efficiency $E_{eff}(P, S)$ by optimizing the power $p_{n'}$ and the subcarrier allocation (S^I, S^P).

We define the maximum energy efficiency of the system as q^*, i.e.,

$$q^* = \frac{R(P^*, S^*)}{U_{TP}(P^*, S^*)} = \max_{p_{n'}, S^P, S^I} \frac{R(P, S)}{U_{TP}(P, S)} \tag{8}$$

The maximum energy efficiency q^* is obtained only when the following formula is established [11]:

$$\max_{p_{n'}, S^P, S^I} R(P, S) - q^* U_{TP}(P, S)$$

$$= R(P^*, S^*) - q^* U_{TP}(P^*, S^*) = 0 \tag{9}$$

Inspired by (9), we convert the original objective function into the following formula by introducing a parameter q.

$$\mathbf{P2}: \max_{P_{n'},S^P,S^I} R(P,S) - qU_{TP}(P,S)$$

$$s.t.\ C1, C2, C3, C4, C5, C6 \tag{10}$$

Therefore, the Lagrangian function of (10) can be written as

$$
\begin{aligned}
L(P,S) = &\{\frac{\alpha}{2}\sum_{n\in S^I}\ln(1+\frac{h_np_n}{\sigma_n^2}) + \frac{(1-\alpha)}{2}\sum_{n'=1}^{N}\ln(1+\frac{g_{n'}p_{n'}}{\sigma_{n'}^2}) \\
& - q[P_B + P_R + P_u + \sum_{n=1}^{N}p_n + \sum_{n'=1}^{N}p_{n'} - \xi\sum_{n\in S^P}(h_np_n+\sigma_n^2)]\} \\
& + \beta_1[\frac{1}{2}\sum_{n\in S^I}\ln(1+\frac{h_np_n}{\sigma_n^2}) - R_T] + \beta_2[\frac{1}{2}\sum_{n'=1}^{N}\ln(1+\frac{g_{n'}p_{n'}}{\sigma_{n'}^2}) - R_T] \\
& + \beta_3[P - \sum_{n=1}^{N}p_n - P_B - P_R - P_u] + \beta_4[\xi\sum_{n\in S^P}(h_np_n+\sigma_n^2) - \sum_{n'=1}^{N}p_{n'}]
\end{aligned}
\tag{11}
$$

First, subgradient method is applied to obtain the optimal dual variable $\{\beta_1^*, \beta_2^*, \beta_3^*, \beta_4^*\}$.

$$\Delta\beta_1 = \frac{1}{2}\sum_{n\in S^I}\ln(1+\frac{h_np_n}{\sigma_n^2}) - R_T \tag{12}$$

$$\Delta\beta_2 = \frac{1}{2}\sum_{n'=1}^{N}\ln(1+\frac{g_{n'}p_{n'}}{\sigma_{n'}^2}) - R_T \tag{13}$$

$$\Delta\beta_3 = P - \sum_{n=1}^{N}p_n - P_B - P_R - P_u \tag{14}$$

$$\Delta\beta_4 = \xi\sum_{n\in S^P}(h_np_n+\sigma_n^2) - \sum_{n'=1}^{N}p_{n'} \tag{15}$$

Then we are divided into two steps to get the optimal solution and we rewrite (11) as

$$L(P,S) = L - (q+\beta_3)(P_B + P_R + P_u) - \beta_1 R_T - \beta_2 R_T + \beta_3 P \tag{16}$$

where

$$L = \frac{\alpha}{2} \sum_{n \in S^l} \ln(1 + \frac{h_n p_n}{\sigma_n^2}) + \frac{(1 - \alpha)}{2} \sum_{n'=1}^{N} \ln(1 + \frac{g_{n'} p_{n'}}{\sigma_{n'}^2}) - q \sum_{n=1}^{N} p_n - q \sum_{n'=1}^{N} p_{n'}$$
$$+ q\xi \sum_{n \in S^P} (h_n p_n + \sigma_n^2) + \frac{\beta_1}{2} \sum_{n \in S^l} \ln(1 + \frac{h_n p_n}{\sigma_n^2}) + \frac{\beta_2}{2} \sum_{n'=1}^{N} \ln(1 + \frac{g_{n'} p_{n'}}{\sigma_{n'}^2}) \quad (17)$$
$$- \beta_3 \sum_{n=1}^{N} p_n + \beta_4 \xi \sum_{n \in S^P} (h_n p_n + \sigma_n^2) - \beta_4 \sum_{n'=1}^{N} p_{n'} .$$

In this paper, we equally allocate power in the first time slot, and optimize the power in the second time slot. So we get the derivative of L with respect to $p_{n'}$

$$\frac{\partial L}{\partial p_{n'}} = (1 - \alpha + \beta_2) \frac{g_{n'}}{2(\sigma_{n'}^2 + g_{n'} p_{n'})} - q - \beta_4 \quad (18)$$

Let (18) be equal to 0, and we can get the optimal $p_{n'}^*$

$$p_{n'}^* = [\frac{(1 - \alpha + \beta_2)}{2(q + \beta_4)} - \frac{\sigma_{n'}^2}{g_{n'}}]^+ \quad (19)$$

Next substituting (19) into (17), and we can get the optimal subcarrier set (S^{l*}, S^{P*}) in the first time slot.

$$L = \sum_{n'=1}^{N} \{\frac{(1 - \alpha)}{2} \ln(1 + \frac{g_{n'} p_{n'}^*}{\sigma_{n'}^2}) + \frac{\beta_2}{2} \ln(1 + \frac{g_{n'} p_{n'}^*}{\sigma_{n'}^2}) - q p_{n'}^* - \beta_4 p_{n'}^* \}$$
$$+ \sum_{n \in S^l} F + \sum_{n=1}^{N} \{\xi(q + \beta_4)(h_n p_n + \sigma_n^2) - q p_n - \beta_3 p_n\} \quad (20)$$

where

$$F = \frac{\alpha}{2} \ln(1 + \frac{h_n p_n}{\sigma_n^2}) + \frac{\beta_1}{2} \ln(1 + \frac{h_n p_n}{\sigma_n^2}) - \xi(q + \beta_4)(h_n p_n + \sigma_n^2) \quad (21)$$

From the above equation, we can know that S^l can be obtained by finding all subcarrier which can make F positive, as shown below

$$S^{l*} = \arg \max_{S^l} \sum_{n \in S^l} F \quad (22)$$

$$S^{P*} = \mathbf{N} - S^{l*} \quad (23)$$

Thus we get the optimal resource allocation of an iterative process, and the maximum energy efficiency can be obtained by multiple iterations of q.

4 Simulation Results

In the simulation, we set the initial value of q to 0, the total number of subcarriers $N = 32$, the fixed circuit power consumption $P_B = P_R = P_u = 0.02\,\text{W}$, and R_T is set to 8 bps/Hz. For convenience, we let $\xi = 1$, and the noise power of the two time slots are equal to $-80\,\text{dbm}$. Both the distance from the base station to the relay node and the distance from the relay node to the user are set to 1 m.

Figure 2 shows that our proposed algorithm can achieve maximum energy efficiency after four iterations. After each iteration, the value of energy efficiency will increase, and eventually it will not change after reaching the maximum value. Moreover, the trend of energy efficiency is also different with different total transmission power P.

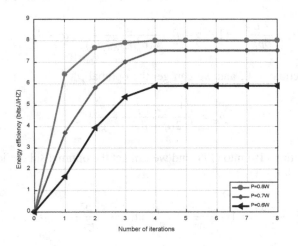

Fig. 2. Energy efficiency versus the number of iterations

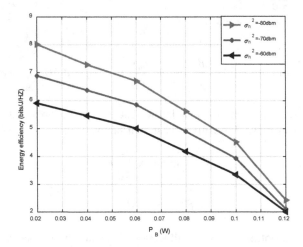

Fig. 3. P_B versus energy efficiency

Figure 3 depicts the fixed circuit power consumption at base station P_B versus energy efficiency. Obviously, the energy efficiency decreases with the increase of P_B. The reason is that the increase of P_B will lead to the increase of total power consumption.

5 Conclusion

In this paper, we formulate the energy efficiency maximization problem in SWIPT-OFDM system with DF protocol, in which the system target rate and fixed power consumption are taken into consideration. By using dual method and iterative method, the optimization problem is solved. Our simulation results demonstrate the effectiveness of the proposed algorithm.

Acknowledgement. This work was supported in part by the National Natural Science Foundation of China under Grants 61871348, by the Project funded by China Postdoctoral Science Foundation under Grant 2017M612027.

References

1. Liu, J., et al.: Artificial intelligence in the 21st century. IEEE Access **6**, 34403–34421 (2018)
2. Kobayashi, M., Murakami, R., Kizaki, K., Saruwatari, S., Watanabe, T.: Wireless full-duplex medium access control for enhancing energy efficiency. IEEE Trans. Green Commun. Netw. **2**(1), 205–221 (2018)
3. Manjate, J.A., Hidell, M., Sjödin, P.: Can energy-aware routing improve the energy savings of energy-efficient ethernet? IEEE Trans. Green Commun. Netw. **2**(3), 787–794 (2018)
4. Tang, J., So, D.K.C., Zhao, N., Shojaeifard, A., Wong, K.: Energy efficiency optimization with SWIPT in MIMO broadcast channels for internet of things. IEEE Internet Things J. **5**(4), 2605–2619 (2018)
5. Zhao, Y., Leung, V.C.M., Zhu, C., Gao, H., Chen, Z., Ji, H.: Energy-efficient sub-carrier and power allocation in cloud-based cellular network with ambient RF energy harvesting. IEEE Access **5**, 1340–1352 (2017)
6. Nguyen, T.T., Oh, H.: A receiver for resource-constrained wireless sensor devices to remove the effect of multipath fading. IEEE Trans. Ind. Electron. **65**(7), 6009–6016 (2018)
7. Varshney, N., Jagannatham, A.K., Hanzo, L.: Asymptotic SER analysis and optimal power sharing for dual-phase and multi-phase multiple-relay cooperative systems. IEEE Access **6**, 50404–50423 (2018)
8. Dashti, M., Mokari, N., Navaie, K.: Uplink radio resource allocation in AF and DF relay-assisted networks with limited rate feedback. IEEE Trans. Veh. Technol. **64**(7), 3056–3074 (2015)
9. Singh, K., Gupta, A., Ratnarajah, T.: Energy efficient resource allocation for multiuser relay networks. IEEE Trans. Wirel. Commun. **16**(2), 1218–1235 (2017)
10. Zhang, Z., Li, Y., Huang, K., Zhou, S., Wang, J.: Energy efficiency analysis of cellular networks with cooperative relays via stochastic geometry. China Commun. **12**(9), 112–121 (2015)
11. Ng, D.W.K., Lo, E.S., Schober, R.: Energy-efficient resource allocation for secure OFDMA systems. IEEE Trans. Veh. Technol. **61**(6), 2572–2585 (2012)

An Efficient Resource Allocation Algorithm for LTE Uplink VMIMO Systems

Yang Cai, Shaojun Qiu, Jia Cai, Wenchi Cheng, and Xiaofeng Lu[✉]

State Key Laboratory of Integrated Service Networks,
Xidian University, Xi'an, China
luxf@xidian.edu.cn

Abstract. In this paper, we focus on the joint user grouping and the resource block (RB) allocation algorithm for LTE uplink virtual MIMO systems. Considering the user grouping and joint resource allocation, we construct a VMIMO transmission system model. Based on this system model, we formulate maximizes the sum of system's capacity with the system constrains, which is a complexity optimization problem. Further, to reduce the computational complexity, especially in the case of large number of users and resources, an efficient branch search algorithm using revised simplex method based on bi-direction 0-1 pivot (SM_BD0-1P) is proposed. We evaluate the proposed joint resource allocation algorithms in LTE uplink scenarios and the results show that it achieves good tradeoff between performance and complexity and has better system throughput than the existing algorithms for LTE uplink virtual MIMO systems.

Keywords: VMIMO · User grouping · System throughput · RB allocation · SC-FDMA

1 Introduction

Multiple-input multiple-output (MIMO) communication can obtain multiuser spatial diversity gain [1, 2, 20], which also has the high energy consumption. Thus, the VMIMO-SC-FDMA is proposed for LTE uplink system to achieve the high spectrum efficient performance [3–5, 14, 18, 19]. Further, some works have been performed about the efficient algorithm solving the joint resource allocation in [6–9, 11–13].

In the above articles, the main differences of the algorithms include: whether the number of resources allocated to the user group is flexible, and the calculation of the user group capacity is different. In [13], the number of the resource allocated to user group is fixed, and in [9, 12], the number of the resource allocated to user group is flexible. We also need pay attention on the metric matrix of user grouping for virtual

This work was supported in part by the Key Research and Development Plan of Shaanxi Province (2018ZDCXL-GY-04-06), in part by the National Natural Science Foundation of China under Grants U1705263, 61371127, 61401347, 61572389, 61671347 and 61771368, in part by the Zhongshan Project (Grant No. 180809162197874) and in part by the Young Elite Scientists Sponsorship Program By CAST (2016QNRC001).

S. Han et al. (Eds.): AICON 2019, LNICST 286, pp. 24–34, 2019.
https://doi.org/10.1007/978-3-030-22968-9_3

MIMO systems. Most of these proposed metric matrixes are derived from the channel capacity [6, 9–11]. In [8], the receive SINR after MMSE equalization and Shannon capacity is used as the user schedule metric. In [9], similar method is adopted for uplink virtual MIMO system with ZF/MMSE/MMSE-SIC linear receiver. However, considering the actual communication systems, BER or SER under given system throughput is usually used as the performance metric at physical layer. In [12, 13], BER is used as a grouping optimization metric, where the BER is evaluated after MMSE linear multiuser equalization. The BER metric in [11] is presented when BPSK is used for modulation and maximal ratio combining is employed for diversity combination.

In comparison with the existing works, our main contributions are as follows: We construct a VMIMO-SC-FDMA transmission system model considering the user grouping and joint resource allocation. Then, we formulate the maximal throughput with BER constraint problem under different transmission constraints to an optimization problem. And then, we propose an efficient branch search algorithm for the optimization problem by using revised simplex method based on bi-direction 0-1 pivot (SM_BD0-1P). As the user and resource numbers increase, the search space becomes very large so that traditional branch-and-bound algorithm is too complex to work efficiently. So, we propose a rapid branch search algorithm using revised simplex method where the search direction is the steepest descent branch with 0-1 pivot. The simulation results have shown the proposed algorithm has better system throughput for LTE uplink virtual MIMO systems.

The rest of this paper is organized as follows. Section 2 gives a brief description of the uplink SC-FDMA multiuser-MIMO system model and presents the optimization object. In Sect. 3, we propose a rapid branch search algorithm for the optimization problem. Simulation results are presented in Sect. 4 and conclusions are drawn in Sect. 5.

2 System Model and Problem Formulation

2.1 System Model

Consider a virtual MIMO uplink system with one base station (BS) where the BS and users are equipped with N_r receive antennas and one transmit antenna, respectively, as shown in Fig. 1.

For an uplink SC-FDMA system with K active users, we write the set of the user groups as:

$$G = \{G_1, \cdots, G_i, \cdots, G_{|G|}\} \tag{1}$$

where $G_i = \{k_1, k_2, \cdots, k_m\}, 1 \leq k_1 < \cdots < k_m \leq K$ is i-th element in the set G.

Assuming the i-th user group G_i scheduled in c-th consecutive subcarriers, the received signal vector before MIMO detector can be written as:

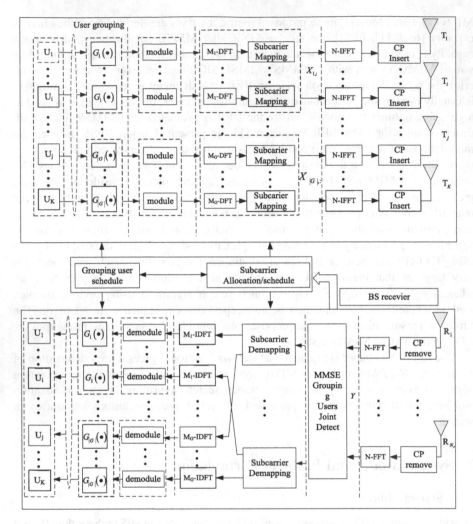

Fig. 1. Block diagram of virtual MIMO for LTE uplink system [12]

$$Y_{i,c} = H_{i,c}X_{i,c} + n_{i,c'} \tag{2}$$

where $H_{i,c}$ is the $N_r \times |U_{G_l}|$ virtual MIMO channel matrix, $X_{i,c}$ is the $|U_{G_l}| \times 1$ transmitting signal vector, $n_{i,c}$ is the $N_r \times 1$ zero-mean additive white Gaussian noise (AWGN) vector with covariance matrix $E\left\{n_{i,c}n_{i,c}^H\right\} = \sigma^2 I_{N_r}$.

At the BS, take the MMSE detector as an example, the detection result can be given as:

$$X_{i,c}^{\mathrm{MMSE}} = \left(\sigma^2 \mathbf{I}_{N_r} + \mathbf{H}_{i,c}^H \mathbf{H}_{i,c}\right)^{-1} \mathbf{H}_{i,c}^H \mathbf{Y}_{i,c} \tag{3}$$

After the subcarrier de-mapping and user de-grouping, the receive data for different users is restored.

2.2 Problem Formulation

According to [12], we can get the user grouping metric matrix based on the above system model. Then, we get the spectral efficiency of user group after MMSE equalization and adaptive modulation (AM) as:

$$R_{G_l}^{\text{MMSE}} = \sum_{k \in U_{G_l}} floor\left(\log_2\left(1 - \frac{1.5SNR_k}{\ln\left(5\text{BER}^{\text{target}}\right)}\right)\right) \tag{4}$$

where $\text{BER}^{\text{target}}$ is the upper bound of the BER for the AWGN channel.

Assume N_{rb} consecutive RBs in LTE uplink is available to allocate to users, similar to [12], we obtain the resource pattern matrix T as:

$$T_{N_{RB} \times J} = \begin{array}{cc} \textit{pattern} & \begin{array}{cccc} 1 & 2 & \cdots & J \end{array} \\ & \begin{bmatrix} 0 & 1 & \cdots & 1 \\ 0 & 0 & \cdots & 1 \\ \cdots & \cdots & \cdots & \cdots \\ 0 & 0 & \cdots & 1 \end{bmatrix} \begin{array}{c} RB_1 \\ RB_2 \\ \cdots \\ RB_{N_{rb}} \end{array} \end{array} \tag{5}$$

In addition, we can obtain the metric matrix M,

$$M_{N_{rb} \times |G|} = \begin{array}{cc} \textit{group index} & \begin{array}{cccc} 1 & 2 & \cdots & |G| \end{array} \\ & \begin{bmatrix} m_{1,1} & m_{1,2} & \cdots & m_{1,|G|} \\ m_{2,1} & m_{2,2} & \cdots & m_{2,|G|} \\ \cdots & \cdots & \cdots & \cdots \\ m_{N_{rb},1} & m_{N_{rb},2} & \cdots & m_{N_{rb},|G|} \end{bmatrix} \begin{array}{c} RB_1 \\ RB_2 \\ \cdots \\ RB_{N_{rb}} \end{array} \end{array}, \tag{6}$$

where the elements $\{m_{i,j}\}$ are calculated according to Eq. (4).

Thus, the transmission rate for i-th user group at j-th resource pattern can be written as:

$$\eta_{i,j} = sum(M(:,i). \times T(:,j)) \tag{7}$$

Define the resource allocation vector $\mathbf{I}$ as: $\mathbf{I} = \left[I_{1,1}, \cdots, I_{|G|,1}, I_{1,2}, \cdots, I_{|G|,2}, \cdots, I_{i,j}, \cdots, I_{|G|,J}\right]^T$, where $I_{i,j} = \{0, 1\}, i = 1, \cdots |G|, j = 1, \cdots, J$, and let the transmission rate vector $\boldsymbol{\eta}$ as $\boldsymbol{\eta} = [\eta_{1,1}, \cdots, \eta_{|G|,1}, \eta_{1,2}, \cdots, \eta_{|G|,2}, \cdots, \eta_{i,j}, \cdots, \eta_{|G|,J}]^T$

Then, we write the optimization problem as

$$\arg\max_{\mathbf{I}} \{\boldsymbol{\eta}^T \mathbf{I}\} \tag{8}$$

subject to

$$\text{AC1:} \qquad C_1 \mathbf{I} \le 1_{N_{RB} \times 1} \qquad\qquad (8a)$$

$$\text{AC2:} \qquad C_2 \mathbf{I} \le 1_{K \times 1} \qquad\qquad (8b)$$

$$\text{AC3:} \qquad I_{i,j} = \{0, 1\}, i = 1, \cdots |G|, j = 1, \cdots, J \qquad\qquad (8c)$$

where $C_1 = T \otimes 1_{1 \times |G|}$, $C_2 = 1_{1 \times J} \otimes B$.

The objectives in problem (8) is to maximize the total throughput. AC1 is to ensure that each RB can only be allocated to one user group, AC2 is to ensure that each user can occupy one resource pattern at most.

As described above, computing burden of this problem increases heavily with the number of users, RBs and grouping users. Then, we design an algorithm reduce computational complexity.

3   Proposed Algorithm

The optimization problem (8) is typical binary integer programming problem. So it is suitable to be converted to Office Assignment Problem (OAP) [15] and use a linear programming (LP)-based branch-and-bound (BNB) algorithm to solve the problem. However, branch-and-bound algorithm is too complex and not practical when user and resource number become large.

3.1   Proposed Algorithm to the Optimization Problems

In order to reduce the algorithm complexity, we convert the optimization problem (8) to following normalized form

$$\min \quad \mathbf{C}^{\mathrm{T}} \mathbf{x} \qquad\qquad (9)$$

subject to

$$\mathbf{A}\mathbf{x} \le \mathbf{b} \\ x_i = \{0, 1\}, (\mathbf{b})_i = 1 \qquad\qquad (9a)$$

Where, $\mathbf{x}$ is the solution variable vector which represents the persons are assigned to the office or not, $\mathbf{C}$ is weight vector for assignment, $\mathbf{A}$ is equality or inequality constraint matrix, and $\mathbf{b}$ is equality or inequality limit vector.

For optimization problem (9), we propose a revised simplex method based on bi-direction 0-1 pivot (SM_BD0-1P) for efficient branch search of the solution. The flow chat providing the detailed description of the proposed algorithm is shown in Fig. 2.

The search space of the revised simplex method based on 0-1 pivot is shown in Fig. 2, where $\{X_B, X_N\}$ is the basic feasible variable set and $\{X_B, X_N\}_{(i,j)}$ represents the j-th node in level i of the branch-tree. The number of nodes in layer i is $\frac{n!}{(n-i)!}$. In each node, X_N is the non-basic variable set, X_B is the basic variable set, and $\{+m\}$ represents x_m enter the basic variable set. As leaving variable is one and only, they are not marked in the tree nodes.

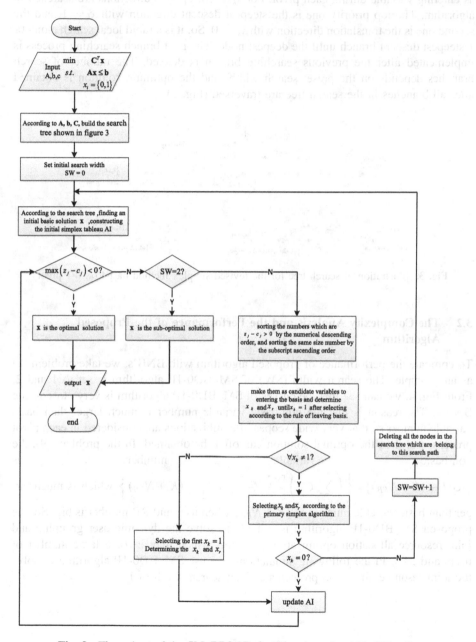

Fig. 2. Flow chart of the SM_BD0-1P algorithm (search width SW = 2)

The algorithm is put forward on the basis of the simplex algorithm [16]. The initial basis variable is artificial variable set. The branch search determination makes use of $\Delta f = f - f_0 = -(z_k - c_k)x_k$. Only the non-basic variable with $z_k - c_k > 0$ is selected as entering variable during each pivot. For $x_k \in \{0, 1\}$, two directions are searched in algorithm. The top priority one is the steepest descent direction with $x_k = 1$, and the second one is the translation direction with $x_k = 0$. So, it is a rapid local search along 0-1 steepest descent branch until the deepest node. The next branch searching process is implemented after the previous searching branch is deleted. The number of search branches depends on the preset search width, and the optimum solution is obtained after all branches in the search tree are traversed (Fig. 3).

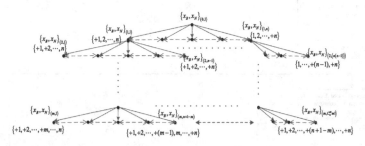

Fig. 3. illustration of search tree for the revised simplex method based on 0-1 pivot

3.2 The Complexity Analysis and the Performance of the Proposed Algorithm

To compare the performance of proposed algorithm with BNB's, we take problem (8) as an example. The search width (SW) of SM_BD0-1P algorithm is set to 1 and 2. From Fig. 4, we can see that the curves of SM_BD0-1P algorithm is very close to the BNB's. The reason is that the non-basic variable number is much larger than basic variable number so that very wide scopes of combinations are considered in each pivot process, and then the optimal solution can often be obtained. In the problem (9), the non-basic   variable   number   is

$$\{|G|J - (K + N_{RB})\} = \left\{ \left(\sum_{m=1}^{N_r} C_K^m \right) \left[\frac{N_{RB}(N_{RB} + 1)}{2} + 1 \right] - (K + N_{RB}) \right\}$$ which is much lar-

ger than basic variable number of $\{K + N_{RB}\}$ when user and RB number is big. So, the proposed SM_BD0-1P algorithm is suitable to solve the dynamic user grouping and joint resource allocation optimization problems which may involve large number of users and RBs. In the following simulations, we use SM_BD0-1P algorithm to solve the joint resource allocation problems and set search width to 1.

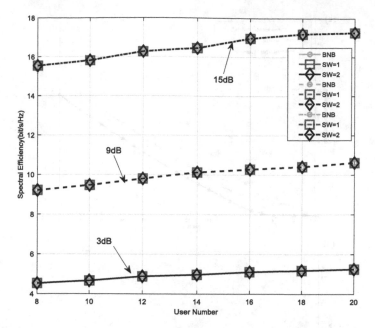

Fig. 4. Performance comparison between BNB and SM_BD0-1P with different user numbers

4 Simulation Results

4.1 Overall Simulation Design

To evaluate the performance of the proposed algorithm, we conduct the simulations based on LTE uplink and list the simulation parameters in Table 1. In addition, we adopt the pedestrian test environment channel A as suggested by ITU-R M.1225 [17].

Table 1. Simulation parameters

Channel parameters	Channel model: ITU Ped-A	Carrier frequency: 2 GHz
	Sampling frequency: 1.92 MHz	Maximum doppler shift: 10 Hz
Simulation parameters	FFT size: 128	Modulation: 16-QAM
	N_{RB}: 6	N_{sc}^{RB}: 12
	OFDM symbols per frame: 14	RB configure: 12×7
	Number of users: 20	MIMO detector: MMSE
	UE transmit antenna number: 1	BS receive antenna number: 4
	TTI duration: 1 ms	Simulation frames: 1000

4.2 Simulation Results of the Throughput Performance

For comparison purpose, three joint resource allocation algorithms with user grouping are implemented in this section. First one is the algorithm proposed in [9], denoted as

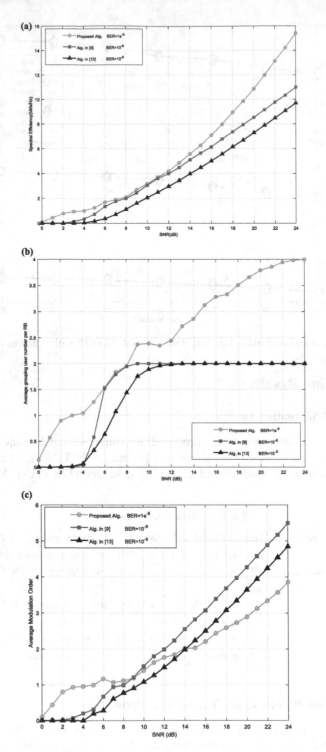

Fig. 5. (a) Spectral efficiency versus SNR for different algorithms using AM technique (b) Average grouping user number versus SNR for different algorithms using AM technique (c) Average modulation order versus SNR for different algorithms using AM technique

'Alg. in [9]'; second one is the algorithm proposed in [13], denoted as 'Alg. in [13]'; last one is the algorithm proposed in this paper, denoted as 'Proposed Alg.'.

To evaluate the proposed algorithm in actual systems, we simulate the algorithm using Eq. (4). For ease of comparison, we modify algorithms in [9, 13] by using AM technique. The results are shown in Fig. 5(a), (b) and (c). As expected, the proposed algorithm achieves the highest spectral efficiency due to the multiuser diversity gain and the joint resource allocation gain. The results of average user grouping number and modulation order per RB are shown in Fig. 5(b) and (c) respectively. Given a BER constraint, the spectral efficiency increases with the increasing of SNR, which dues to adaptive modulation and adaptive user grouping on each RB.

The average user grouping number can be considered as spatial multiplex gain in the system. In the low SNR region, mobile users cannot work normal in 'Alg. in [9]' and 'Alg. in [13]' due to the BER constraints while they can work under single-user mode in proposed algorithm. On the other hand, in the high SNR region, mobile users work under 2-user group mode in 'Alg. in [9]' and 'Alg. in [13]' while they can work under multi-user group mode which is up to 4. At the same time, the modulation order increases with the increasing increase of SNR. Though the modulation order growth rate of proposed algorithm is slower than that of the 'Alg. in [9]' and 'Alg. in [13]', the joint growth rate from spatial multiplex and modulation order of proposed algorithm is faster than other two algorithms, which is shown in Fig. 5(a).

5 Conclusions

In this paper, we investigate the dynamic user grouping and joint resource allocation in uplink SC-FDMA systems. Through the consideration of both system throughput and the receive signal detection performance, we derive the dynamic user grouping criteria and propose adaptive resource allocation algorithm for Shannon capacity and actual throughput with AM techniques. The simulation results demonstrate that the proposed algorithm attain better system throughput than conventional algorithm.

References

1. Panda, K.G., Agrawal, D., Hossain, A.: Virtual MIMO in wireless sensor network - a survey. In: 2016 Online International Conference on Green Engineering and Technologies (IC-GET), Coimbatore, pp. 1–4 (2016)
2. Cheng, W., Zhang, H., Liang, L., Jing, H., Li, Z.: Orbital-angular-momentum embedded massive MIMO: achieving multiplicative spectrum-efficiency for mmWave communications. IEEE Access 6, 2732–2745 (2018)
3. Mondal, B., Thomas, T.A., Ghosh, A.: MU-MIMO system performance analysis in LTE evolution. In: 21st Annual IEEE International Symposium on Personal, Indoor and Mobile Radio Communications, Istanbul, pp. 1510–1515 (2010)
4. Sesia, S., Toufik, I., Baker, M.: Introduction to LTE-advanced. In: LTE - The UMTS Long Term Evolution: From Theory to Practice. Wiley (2011)
5. 3GPP TSG RAN1 #46, R1-062074: Link simulation results for uplink virtual MIMO, Tallinn, Estonia, August 2006

6. Hongzhi, Z., Song, M., Fengwei, L., Youxi, T.: A suboptimal multiuser pairing algorithm with low complexity for virtual MIMO systems. IEEE Trans. Veh. Technol. https://doi.org/10.1109/tvt.2013.2297517

7. Cheng, W., Zhang, X., Zhang, H.: Full-duplex spectrum-sensing and MAC-protocol for multichannel nontime-slotted cognitive radio networks. IEEE J. Sel. Areas Commun. 33(5), 820–831 (2015)

8. 3GPP TSG-RAN1 #46, R1-062052: UL system analysis with SDMA, Tallinn, Estonia, August 2006

9. Fan, J., Li, G.Y., Yin, Q., Peng, B., Zhu, X.: Joint user pairing and resource allocation for LTE uplink transmission. IEEE Trans. Wirel. Commun. 11(8), 2838–2847 (2012)

10. Fan, B., Wang, W., Lin, Y., Huang, L., Zheng, K.: Spatial multi-user pairing for uplink virtual-MIMO systems with linear receiver. In: IEEE WCNC, Budapest, pp. 1–5, April 2009

11. Liang, J., Liang, Q.: Channel selection in virtual MIMO wireless sensor networks. IEEE Trans. Veh. Technol. 58(5), 2249–2257 (2009)

12. Lu, X., Ni, Q., Li, W., Zhang, H.: Dynamic user grouping and joint resource allocation with multi-cell cooperation for uplink virtual MIMO systems. IEEE Trans. Wirel. Commun. 16(6), 3854–3869 (2017)

13. Ruder, M.A., Ding, D., Dang, U.L., Vasilakos, A.V., Gerstacker, W.H.: Joint user grouping and frequency allocation for multiuser SC-FDMA transmission. Phys. Commun. 8, 91–103 (2013)

14. 3GPP: TSG-RAN EUTRA, rel.10, TR 36.213, December 2010

15. http://www.mathworks.co.uk/help/optim/examples/binary-integer-programming.html. Accessed Dec 2012

16. Murty, K.G.: Linear Programming. Wiley, New York (1983)

17. Recommendation ITU-R M.1225: Guidelines for evaluation of radio transmission technologies for IMT-2000, International Telecommunication Union (1997)

18. Zhang, X., Cheng, W., Zhang, H.: Heterogeneous statistical QoS provisioning over airborne mobile wireless networks. IEEE J. Sel. Areas Commun. 36(9), 2139–2152 (2018)

19. Cheng, W., Zhang, W., Jing, H., Gao, S., Zhang, H.: Orbital angular momentum for wireless communications. IEEE Wirel. Commun. 26(1), 100–107 (2019)

20. Yang, Y., Cheng, W., Zhang, W., Zhang, H.: Mode modulation for wireless communications with a twist. IEEE Trans. Veh. Technol. 67(11), 10704–10714 (2018)

Research on UAV Swarm Interference Based on Improved Invasive Weed Optimization Algorithm

Lijiao Wang[✉], Yanping Liao, and Xiaoming Luan

Harbin Engineering University, Harbin 150001, Heilongjiang,
People's Republic of China
15546223529@163.com

Abstract. With the continuous development of Unmanned Aerial Vehicle (UAV) technology, autonomous control systems and communication technologies, the combat mode of UAV has gradually shifted from single-platform to multi-platform operation adapting to complex battlefield environment, i.e. the mode of operation has gradually developed to 'swarm'. On this basis, UAV swarm carried jamming equipment can conduct large-scale cooperative jamming on radar. UAV swarm, with low launch power, can be deployed in the enemy depth and thus obtain the advantages of distance and spatial distribution. This paper focuses on the formation of effective cooperative jamming beams for UAV swarm. Due to the application background of UAVs, the distance between the UAV array antennas is much larger than the half-wavelength, resulting in the occurrence of grating lobes and the energy is difficult to concentrate. And the above problems are solved through sparse array synthesis, which use improved invasive weed optimization (IIWO) algorithm to optimize position of UAVs. And the simulation results show that sparse array synthesis can solve the problem of energy concentration and grating lobes.

Keywords: Invasive weed optimization algorithm · Radar interference · UAV swarm

1 Introduction

With the increasing complexity of modern battlefield environment, radar electronic warfare, as an important part of electronic warfare, influences the outcome of the war [1]. As the radar adopts various anti-interference measures such as low sidelobe level, pulse compression and so on, the corresponding challenge to radar jammer is put forward [2]. Traditional high-power concentrated jamming has disadvantages such as large cross-section area, large transmitting signal power and relatively remote distance to the enemy, which will lead to problems such as easy detection by the enemy radar, negative impact on the equipment of the own side and poor electromagnetic compatibility [3]. Under this circumstance, a specific combat pattern for UAV swarm is raised, namely using UAV swarm carrying jamming equipment to carry out close-range main lobe jamming on target radar. UAV swarm cooperative jamming has many advantages such as large number, small volume, small cross-section area and so on.

S. Han et al. (Eds.): AICON 2019, LNICST 286, pp. 35–46, 2019.
https://doi.org/10.1007/978-3-030-22968-9_4

With the continuous development of aircraft technology, Unmanned Aerial Vehicles (UAVs) have become the focus of research in the world. The UAV is the aircraft without a human pilot, the flight of UAV may operate with various degrees of autonomy: either under remote control by a human operator or autonomously by onboard computers [4]. And with the fast development of UAV, the combat mode of UAV has gradually shifted from single-platform to multi-platform operation adapting to complex battlefield environment, i.e. the mode of operation has gradually developed to 'swarm'. The UAV swarm has a great advantage in pattern of operation, mainly focus on the following aspects: (1) The advantage of low-cost, UAV swarm can be equipped a large number UAVs. (2) The advantage of scale quantity, a large number of low-cost UAV swarm have launched saturation attack on the enemy, making it difficult for the enemy to effectively defend and even the risk of failure of its air defense system. The United States NPS (Naval Postgraduate School) has experimented with UAV swarm, an Aegis Combat System confronts a swarm of UAVs consisting of 5 to 10, the result of the simulation is that 2.8 of every 8 UAVs can effectively break through air defense interceptions. If the number of UAVs is expanded to 20 and 50, the interceptor system can only intercept 7 or so, which greatly improving the UAV's penetration capability [5]. (3) The advantage of combat effectiveness, the UAV swarm has the advantage of cost and quantity scale, which will inevitably bring the advantage of combat effectiveness. (4) The superiority of the system, the UAV swarm system has a strong "self-healing" ability. If some UAVs are shot down by enemy fire, the team adapts by reconfiguring optimally continue the mission with the surviving assets [6].

This paper uses UAV swarm carrying jamming equipment for interfering to the enemy radar. However, under the background of UAVs, Using UAVs to focus on one direction interference has following problems, including: ① The energy of a UAV array element is difficult to concentrate and the power is not enough. Therefore, this paper proposes to use the UAV swarm to carry antenna to form antenna array to send interference signals. ② Because of the volume of the UAV itself, spacing between adjacent UAV require 30–50 m, but the signal frequency is usually at GHz. And it will result in the occurrence of grating lobes and the interference energy is difficult to be concentrated. To solve above problems, this paper proposed to consider the UAVs as the sparse array to focus on the interference energy to concentrate energy.

For the sparse array synthesis problem, evolutionary optimization algorithms have been considered and successfully applied to this problem. And the various approaches have been developed such as genetic algorithm (GA) [7], ant colony optimization (ACO) [8], simulated annealing algorithm (SA) [9], particle swarm optimization (PSO) [10] and so on. The invasive weed optimization (IWO) algorithm is popular of evolutionary optimization algorithms and it is getting much attention due to its efficiency and simplicity. And it has been successfully applied to several optimization problems, such as antenna design [11] and array synthesis [12]. This paper selects IWO algorithm to optimize the position of UAV swarm, and two problems that weak local search ability and slow convergence speed in this algorithm were improved, i.e. the standard deviation formula was improved to enhance the convergence speed and the hill climbing method was improved the local search ability. On the basis of the above improvement, the improved invasive weed optimization (IIWO) algorithm was proposed and selected to optimize the position of UAV swarm along with array optimization models.

The paper is structured as follows: Sect. 1 is the introduction part of this article; Sect. 2 is the signal model and optimal model of the UAVs array antenna; Sect. 3 introduces the IIWO algorithm; Sect. 4 is the simulation results.

2 Signal Model Based on UAVs

In this model, suppose the UAV is used to carry antenna array element, every UAV carries identical antennas working together as a single big UAVs antenna array. The radio frequency power from the UAV is fed to the individual array element with the specific excitation relationship through the device controlled by a computer system, so that the radio waves from the separate UAV array element add together to increase the radiation in a desired direction, while cancelling to suppress radiation in undesired directions. And the interference model of UAV swarm is show in the Fig. 1.

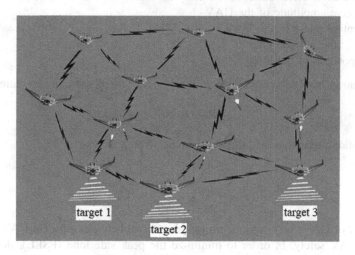

Fig. 1. UAVs interference model

In the practical, for safety reasons, the distance between adjacent UAV elements is 30 to 50 m, but the working frequency is usually GHz, which means that the distance is very small. For this problem, this paper puts forward the sparse array to solve it. Sparse array means that the distances between adjacent UAV elements are different and not constrained in $\lambda/2$. The UAV element positions are randomly distributed within the UAVs aperture [13].

Compared to linear and other planar arrays, circular array can provide 360° azimuth and better controls main lobe direction, at the same time, beam shape, antenna gain and mutual coupling performance maintenance or basically maintain owing to the symmetry of the circular array. These advantages make circular antenna array has been widely used in the field of sonar, radar and satellite communication system [14]. So circular UAVs antenna array is discussed to analyze the problem.

The radiation pattern of an individual antenna element is $f(\theta, \varphi)$, θ and φ are respectively the elevation angle and azimuth angle. Assuming that the array element is an ideal omnidirectional antenna element, the result is that $f(\theta, \varphi) = 1$. The conventional array synthesis is based on the product principle of the directional diagram. Total field radiated by this array in xy plane is expressed as follows:

$$F(\theta, \varphi) = \sum_{n=1}^{N} I_n e^{j[kR \sin \theta \cos(\varphi - d_n) + \beta_n]} \tag{1}$$

The radiation pattern of the entire array is only related to the array factor $F(\theta, \varphi)$. Where

N: the number of UAVs
λ: the wavelength
R: the radius of the circular UAVs array antenna
I_n: incentive amplitude of the UAV
β_n: incentive phase of the UAV
$k = 2\pi/\lambda$: the wavenumber
d_n: the position of the UAV

When the array main lobe is pointed in the (θ_0, φ_0), the phase can be written as:

$$\beta_n = -kR \sin \theta_0 \cos(\varphi_0 - d_n) \tag{2}$$

If the elevation angle $\theta = 90°$, then (1) maybe written as:

$$F(\varphi) = \sum_{n=1}^{N} I_n e^{jkR[\cos(\varphi - d_n) - \cos(\varphi_0 - d_n)]} \tag{3}$$

The number of UAVs is N, and the minimum interval between adjacent UAVs is dc to make the UAV safety. In order to minimize the peak side lobe (PSLL), the optimal model is proposed:

$$\begin{aligned} & find \ \boldsymbol{d} = [d_1, d_2, \ldots, d_N] \\ & \min \ \{PSLL(\boldsymbol{d})\} \\ & s.t. \ \ d_{i+1} - d_i \geq dc \ 1 \leq i \leq N - 1 \end{aligned} \tag{4}$$

The PSLL is expressed:

$$PSLL = \max \left| \frac{AF(\theta_{sl}, \varphi_{sl})}{\max(AF(\theta, \varphi))} \right| \tag{5}$$

Where the denominator is the maximum of the main beam in the direction, and $(\theta_{sl}, \varphi_{sl})$ is the sidelobe region excluding the main beam. The optimization model of formula (3) shows that by optimizing the position of the UAVs can get a good result for interference. And the optimization of location problem is a typical global optimization problem, therefore, using the intelligent optimization algorithm to solve it.

3 Proposal Algorithm

Mehrabian and Lucas proposed the invasive weed optimization (IWO) algorithm for solving continuous optimization problems in 2006 [15]. Each invading weed takes the unused resources in the field and grows to the weed and produces new seeds, independently. The number of new seeds produced by each weed depends on the fitness of that weed in the colony. Those weeds that have better adoption to the environment and take more unused resources grow faster and produce more seeds. The new produced seeds are randomly spread over the field and grow to the weeds. And only those weeds with better fitness can survive and produce new seeds.

3.1 Classical Invasive Weed Optimization Algorithm (IWO)

IWO algorithm is a swarm intelligence optimization algorithm [16]. It mimics the process of colonizing and distributing behavior of weeds. Each weed in the algorithm is a latent solution for the position of the UAVs. Each weed corresponds to a fitness value determined by the fitness function. The algorithm is composed of the following parts:

1. Reproduction. Each member of the weeds is allowed to produce seeds depending on its own, as well as the colony's lowest and highest fitness, so that the number of seeds produced by a weed increases linearly from lowest possible seed for a weed with worst fitness to the maximum number of seeds for a plant with best fitness.
2. Spatial Distribution. Weed seeds produced by normal distribution spread around his father generation. The standard deviation for a particular iteration can be given as follows:

$$\sigma = \frac{(iter_{max} - iter)^n}{(iter_{max})^n} \left(\sigma_{initial} - \sigma_{finial}\right) + \sigma_{finial} \tag{6}$$

Where

$\quad$ n: non-linear harmonic factor
$\quad$ $iter_{max}$: maximum number of evolution
$\quad$ σ_{inital}: maximum standard deviation
$\quad$ σ_{finial}: minimum standard deviation

3. Competitive Exclusion. The weeds in a colony will reproduce fast and all the produced plants will be included in the existing colony, until the number of plants in the colony reaches a maximum value P_{max}. The steps 1 to 3 are repeated until the maximum number of iterations has reached.

3.2   Improved Invasive Weed Optimization Algorithm (IIWO)

Over the past decades, the IWO method has been widely applied to array synthesis. And this algorithm allows all of possible candidates to participate in the reproduction process. The disadvantages of the IWO are that weak local search capability in the late iteration, slow convergence speed, and easy to fall into local optimum [17]. Therefore, this paper improves the algorithm for the above problems.

(1) Improvement of standard deviation formula

In the standard algorithm, the standard deviation in the process of spatial diffusion is only related to iteration. In this paper, the standard deviation formula is improved that not only related to iteration, but also related to the fitness value of the individual. The formula is as follows:

$$\sigma_n = \frac{|f - f_{best}|}{f_{best}} * \sigma \tag{7}$$

Where, f is the fitness value of the current individual, and f_{best} is the best fitness value in the current iteration, σ is the standard deviation, σ_n is the improved standard deviation. In the process of seed diffusion, the standard deviation function not only changes with the change of iteration times, but also is related to the fitness value of the individual. The larger the fitness value of the individual, the smaller of standard deviation will be, i.e. the seeds produced by individuals with better fitness are distributed in a smaller range, while the seeds of individuals with poor fitness are distributed in a larger range. In this way, the convergence speed of the algorithm can be improved and better computing effect can be obtained.

(2) Improvements to local search

As a global search algorithm, one of the disadvantages of the IWO is that weak local search capability in the late iteration. In this case, the hill climbing method can be combined with IWO to improve the local search capability. The main idea of the hill climbing algorithm is: take the adjacent point and the current point for comparison each time, take the better of the two as the next step of climbing [18]. The algorithm firstly should have an initial point which can be obtained by the final result of IWO algorithm, then in the initial position around the calculation of random point fitness value, compared with the initial point, in order to better as a new initial point, repeated operation, until find meet the conditions of point, no change or several iterations ends operations.

The flow chart representing the IIWO algorithm is been shown in Fig. 2.

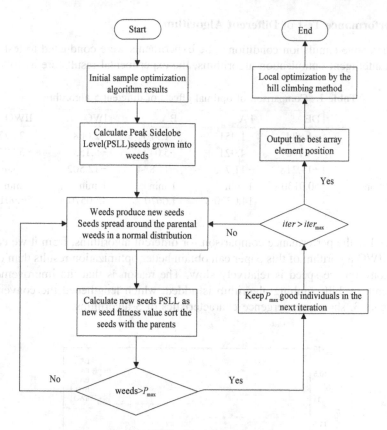

Fig. 2. IIWO algorithm flow chart

4 Simulation Result

This algorithm is simulated and tested in MATLAB-2016 software. The distance between adjacent UAV elements is 30 to 50 m. At the same time, the number of experimental clusters of UAVs is $N = 50$, and the signal frequency is set to 3.5 GHz, the iterations of algorithm is 100, and the radar is in the 150° direction of the UAVs. Under the above conditions, the experiment is conducted. Compare the following results:

1. The experiments give the performance of the differential evolution (DE), firefly algorithm (FA), bat algorithm (BA), invasive weed optimization (IWO) algorithm and improved invasive weed optimization (IIWO) algorithm.
2. The experiments give the performance of the IIWO algorithm.
3. The simulation experiments are conducted to solve the problems of position offset.

4.1   Performance Test of Different Algorithm

Under the above simulation conditions, the experiments were conducted to test under different intelligent optimization algorithms, the experimental results are as follows.

Table 1. Comparison of optimal effects of different 5 algorithm

Index	DE	FA	BA	IWO	IIWO
5	−1.824	−1.951	−1.970	−2.068	−2.573
10	−4.778	−4.921	−5.047	−5.155	−5.896
50	−11.218	−11.733	−11.834	−12.502	−13.404
Optimization of time (50)	50.0130 s	1 min 14.0370 s	1 min 1.0670 s	1 min 45.0570 s	1 min 56.9010 s

Table 1 is the performance comparison for different algorithms, from it we can see that the IIWO algorithm of this paper can obtain better optimization results than others, but its convergence speed is relatively slow. The reason is that the improvement of local search by hill climbing algorithm is added, which lengthened the convergence time. Figure 3. shows convergence characteristics of 5 algorithms.

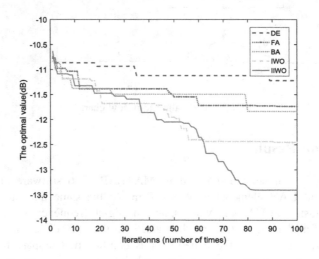

Fig. 3. Convergence characteristics of 5 algorithms (50 Array elements)

4.2   Performance Test of IIWO

Under the same simulation conditions, select IIWO algorithm for simulation, and the results are shown as follows. Figure 4 is the Normalized radiation patterns with IIWO algorithms, Fig. 5 is the distribution map of UAVs after IIWO algorithm optimization, and Fig. 6 is the fitness value convergence characteristic curve and its average curve of five independent simulation experiments of IIWO algorithm, from which it can be seen that the IIWO algorithm has relatively stable convergence.

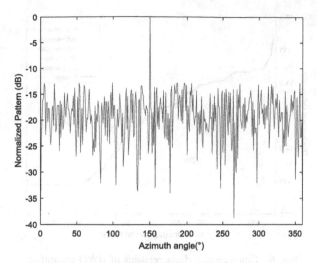

Fig. 4. Normalized radiation pattern of IIWO algorithm

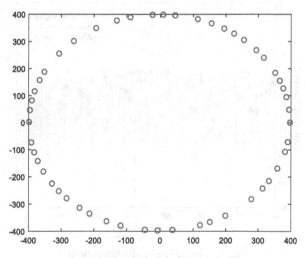

Fig. 5. The distribution of UAVs

4.3 Performance Test of the Simulation Under Position Offset

There will be a variety of factors in the flying process of UAV swarm, which will lead to the problem of position offset. And the simulation experiments are conducted to solve the problems of position offset. The basic simulation parameters are as follows: the number of UAVs $N = 50$; the number of offset $N_o = 15$; the maximum offset distance $d_{max} = 20\,\text{m}$; the excursion position and angle are randomly set, and the results are shown as follows (Fig. 7).

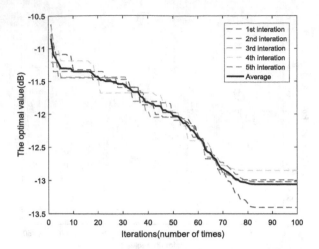

Fig. 6. Convergence characteristics of IIWO algorithm

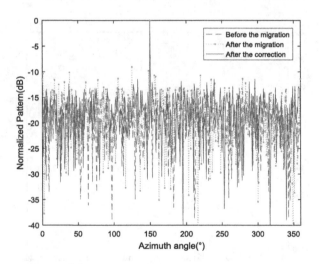

Fig. 7. Normalized radiation pattern

According to the simulation results, the PSLL value before offset is −13.1227 dB, and it drops to −9.0462 dB after offset, the value reaches −11.4374 dB by IIWO algorithm correct. This optimization algorithm can be used to effectively adjust the position of UAV at any time to form a better interference beam. Figure 8 is shows the UAV distribution before and after the offset and after the correction.

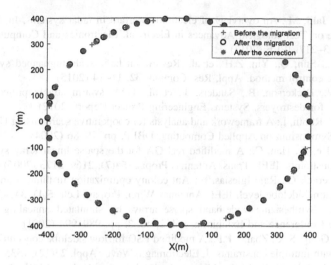

Fig. 8. The distribution of UAVs

5   Conclusions

As an emerging and combat pattern, UAV swarm is exerting immeasurable influences on future wars. This paper analyzes on the advantages of the UAV swarm and the concept of cooperative interference, on the basis of this puts forward the specific model and implementation scheme, i.e. it is using UAV swarm carry jamming equipment to conduct large-scale cooperative jamming on radar. This paper researches the layout scheme of UAV swarm cooperative interference combined with the actual situation of UAV swarm, and presents the optimization model, and selects IIWO algorithms to optimize the position of UAV swarm along with array optimization models. The simulation experiments are conducted to solve the problems of position offset which may occur in the actual interference process, and the correction experiments are analyzed by the IIWO algorithm. Through the analysis of the above results, the proposed implementation scheme can achieve expected result in the actual simulation, and can solve the problem of energy concentration and grating lobes.

Acknowledgments. This work is supported partially by the National Key Research and Development Program of China (2016YFC0101700), by National Natural Science Foundation of China 61301201, Heilongjiang Postdoctoral Research Foundation LBH-Q14039.

References

1. Chen, X.: Research on active distributed jamming of radar system. University of Electronic Science and Technology of China (2007)
2. Li, X.: Research on modern radar jamming technology. University of Electronic Science and Technology of China (2011)

3. Butt, F.A., Jalil, M.: An overview of electronic warfare in radar systems. In: International Conference on Technological Advances in Electrical, Electronics and Computer Engineering, pp. 213–217. IEEE (2013)
4. Liang, X.L., Sun, Q., Yin, Z.H., et al.: Review on large-scale unmanned system swarm intelligence control method. Appl. Res. Comput. **32**, 11–14 (2015)
5. Pham, L.V., Dickerson, B., Sanders, J., et al.: UAV swarm attack: protection system alternatives for destroyers. Systems Engineering Project Report (2012)
6. Vincent, P., Rubin, I.: A framework and analysis for cooperative search using UAV swarms. In: ACM Symposium on Applied Computing, DBLP, pp. 79–86 (2004)
7. Chen, K., He, Z., Han, C.: A modified real GA for the sparse linear array synthesis with multiple constraints. IEEE Trans. Antennas Propag. **54**(7), 2169–2173 (2006)
8. Quevedo-Teruel, O., Rajo-Iglesias, E.: Ant colony optimization in thinned array synthesis with minimum sidelobe level. IEEE Antennas Wirel. Propag. Lett. **5**(1), 349–352 (2006)
9. Trucco, A.: Synthesizing wide-band sparse arrays by simulated annealing. In: Oceans MTS/IEEE Conference and Exhibition, vol. 2, no. 3, pp. 989–994 (2001)
10. Zhang, S., Gong, S.X., Zhang, P.F.: A modified PSO for low sidelobe concentric ring arrays synthesis with multiple constraints. J. Electromagn. Waves Appl. **23**(12), 1535–1544 (2009)
11. Mallahzadeh, A.R., Es'haghi, S., Alipour, A.: Design of an E-shaped MIMO antenna using IWO algorithm for wireless application. Progr. Electromagn. Res. PIER **90**, 187–203 (2009)
12. Roy, G.G., Das, S., Chakraborty, P., Suganthan, P.N.: Design of non-uniform circular antenna arrays using a modified invasive weed optimization algorithm. IEEE Trans. Antennas Propag. **59**(1), 110–118 (2011)
13. Yin, S.: Research on synthesis and optimization algorithm of sparse antenna arrays. Harbin Institute of Technology (2016)
14. Luan, X.M., Shang, X.R.: The optimization of sparse concentric ring array using differential evolution algorithm. In: Proceedings First International Conference on Electronics Instrumentation and Information Systems, pp. 682–687 (2017)
15. Mehrabian, A.R., Lucas, C.: A novel numerical optimization algorithm inspired from weed colonization. Ecol. Inform. **1**(4), 355–366 (2006)
16. Karimkashi, S., Kishk, A.: Invasive weed optimization and its features in electromagnetics. IEEE Trans. Antennas Propag. **58**(4), 1269–1278 (2010)
17. Hua-Ning, W.U., Liu, C., Xie, X.: Pattern synthesis of planar antenna arrays based on invasive weed optimization algorithm. J. Nav. Univ. Eng. (2015)
18. Selvaraj, J., Abd Rahim, N., Tan, C.Y.: Improvement of hill climbing method by introducing simple irradiance detection method. In: IET International Conference on Clean Energy and Electrical Systems, pp. 1–5 (2014)

Sparse Decomposition Algorithm Based on Joint Sparse Model

Qiyun Xuan[1], Si Wang[2], Yulong Gao[1(✉)], and Junhui Cheng[1]

[1] Harbin Institute of Technology, Harbin, China
hitxuanqiyun@126.com, ylgao@hit.edu.cn,
2278752273@qq.com
[2] Shanghai Institute of Satellite Engineering, Shanghai, China
soleyoyo@sina.com

Abstract. Orthogonal Matching Pursuit (OMP) algorithm is the most classical signal recovery algorithm in compressed sensing. It is also applicable to the Joint Sparse Model (JSM) of distributed compressive sensing. However, OMP algorithm suffers from high computational complexity and poor anti-noise ability without considering the correlation between signals. Therefore, by combining the characteristics of the JSM-1 and JSM-2 models, we propose the corresponding joint sparse decomposition algorithms, named JSM1-OMP and JSM2-OMP. The JSM2-OMP algorithm can be viewed as improvement of the JSM1-OMP algorithm. Furthermore, a better JSM-OMP algorithm is proposed by modifying the JSM2-OMP algorithm. The simulation experiments demonstrate the effectiveness of the proposed algorithms.

Keywords: OMP · JSM · JSM1-OMP algorithm · JSM2-OMP algorithm · JSM-OMP algorithm

1 Introduction

Compressed sensing (CS) [1, 2] is a new signal sampling theory for finding sparse solutions of underdetermined linear systems. On the premise that the signal is sparse or sparsely represented, a signal is sampled at a sampling rate much lower than the Nyquist theorem, and then the original signal is accurately reproduced by a nonlinear recovery algorithm. Sparse decomposition is initially used for compressed sensing because the signal is sparse or sparsely decomposable.

Now that there are many recovery algorithms, and they can be summed up into three major categories. The first type of algorithm is the well-known convex relaxation algorithm. The traditional convex relaxation algorithm is to convert the l_0 norm into a l_1 norm, commonly used Lasso algorithm [3], the Basis Pursuit (BP) algorithm [4]. Greedy iterative algorithm is the second most commonly used sparse decomposition algorithm. In [5], Mallat first introduced the concept of redundant dictionary and applied its flexibility instead of a relatively fixed orthogonal basis to propose an algorithm that is still widely used today, namely the Matching Pursuit (MP) algorithm. Orthogonal Matching Pursuit (OMP) was first proposed by Mallat. Gilbert and Tropp later further demonstrated this algorithm and proved its theoretical convergence [6].

S. Han et al. (Eds.): AICON 2019, LNICST 286, pp. 47–56, 2019.
https://doi.org/10.1007/978-3-030-22968-9_5

The representation results obtained by the above two algorithms are single form, and the representation form affects the effect of sparse decomposition. Therefore, one begans to exploit a variety of sparse representations to represent a signal. Elad and Yavneh pointed out that the joint sparse representation is superior to a single sparse representation, and proposed a random orthogonal matching pursuit (RandOMP) algorithm. In [7], Zhang proposed a combined algorithm based on the forward greedy algorithm, but the backward steps adaptively point to the direction with the smallest residual. The last kind of recovery algorithm is a sparse decomposition algorithm based on sparse Bayesian models, such as relevance vector machine (RVM) [8]. In [9], supposing that the hyperparameters in the prior distribution of estimators are La-place prior distributions, a hierarchical Bayesian model is proposed. In this work, sparse coefficients are treated as implicit parameters in the hyperparameter estimation process. And then, the minimum mean-squared error estimate is also used as the optimal metric to obtain the optimal solution under the Bayesian framework [10].

Distributed Compressed Sensing (DCS) extends the compressive sensing of a single signal to a multi-signal model [11], making full use of the correlation between multiple signals and creating joint recovery conditions further reduce the number of measurements required for successful recovery. Baron proposed three signal models for different scenarios, called JSM-1, JSM-2, and JSM-3 [12]. Corresponding signal recovery methods are also different for different joint sparse models. How to study the exact and appropriate recovery method based on the specific joint sparse model is the focus of the distributed compressive sensing.

The rapid development of 5G has gradually turned the massive antenna system (Massive MIMO) into the mainstream of wireless communication. At the same time, distributed processing of multi-antenna signals has gradually become a research hotspot in the field of communications. In this paper, we extend the single measurement model to a multiple measurement model. When the transmitted signal reaches different receiving antennas through different channels, the signals will come with different amplitudes due to multipath fading, but the position of the spectrum remains unchanged, and sparse coefficient positions remain unchanged. Therefore, the signal received by different receiving antennas in a Massive MIMO system shares the same frequency spectrum, but the non-zero amplitude is different. This multiple measurement frame signal structure is basically the same as the JSM-2 model [13]. In addition, we often use the JSM-1 model to represent the actual corresponding signal when we consider the correlation between signal locations. Both of these models are commonly used for modelling multi-antenna sparse signals.

To deal with the mentioned deficiencies, we fully consider the correlation of signals and propose an improved sparse decomposition algorithm for each model. We will introduce the relevant system model in the second section, and describe the three improved algorithms proposed in the third section. Finally, simulation experiments are performed to verify the effectiveness of our proposed algorithms.

2 System Mode

Compressive sensing can be expressed as $Y = \Phi x$, where $x \in R^{N \times 1}$ is the original signal to be observed. Sparsity or compressibility is one of the two preconditions for the application of compressed sensing theory. Consider a real-valued signal X of length N, denoted as $X(n), n \in [1, 2, \ldots, N]$. Combined with the signal theory, X can be represented by a set of base $\Psi \in [\psi_1, \psi_2, \ldots, \psi_n, \ldots, \psi_N]$ linear combinations

$$X = \Psi\Theta = \sum_{i=1}^{N} \psi_i \theta_i \tag{1}$$

where $\theta_i = \langle X, \psi_i \rangle$, $\Psi \in R^{N \times N}$. When signal X has only K non-zero values on a certain transform basis, it is said to be K-sparse on this basis. The basis Ψ is the sparse basis of signal X. Then, $Y = \Phi x = \Phi\Psi\Theta = A^{CS}\Theta$, $A^{CS} = \Phi\Psi \in R^{M \times N}$. The fundamental task of compressive sensing is to solve the sparse coefficient vector from the representation

$$\Theta = \arg\min_{\theta} \| \theta \|_0 \ s.t. y = A^{CS}\Theta \tag{2}$$

Distributed compressed sensing originates from the simultaneous sparse compression sensing of multiple signals. The model expression is written as

$$y_j = \varphi_j x_j, \quad j \in \{1, 2, \ldots, J\} \tag{3}$$

Multiple signals have the following expression

$$X = \begin{bmatrix} x_1 \\ x_2 \\ \cdots \\ x_J \end{bmatrix}, \ Y = \begin{bmatrix} y_1 \\ y_2 \\ \cdots \\ y_J \end{bmatrix}, \ \varphi = \begin{bmatrix} \varphi_1 \\ \varphi_2 \\ \cdots \\ \varphi_J \end{bmatrix} \tag{4}$$

where, $X \in R^{JN}, Y \in R^{\bar{M} \cdot JN}, \varphi \in R^{\bar{M} \cdot JN}, \overline{M} = \sum_{j \in \wedge} M_j, Y = \varphi X^T$. Both the JSM-1 and JSM-2 models can be represented as

$$x_j = z_c + z_j \quad j \in \{1, 2, \cdots, J\} \tag{5}$$

where $z_c = \Psi \cdot \Theta_c, \|\Theta_c\|_0 = K_c, z_j = \Psi \cdot \Theta_j, \|\Theta_j\|_0 = K_j$.

For all original signals $x_j, j \in \{1, 2, \cdots, J\}$, z_c is the sparse common part, and the sparsity of z_c over the sparse base Ψ is k_c; z_j is the unique part of each original signal, and the sparsity on the same sparse base Ψ is k_j. In JSM-1, each signal contains two parts. The signal constructed by this model is mostly affected by the global environment, and the local environment affects the local signal. For example, a sensor network is distributed over a forest to measure temperature, where sunlight is the global influence, while shades of leaves, water flow, and animal activity can all be considered as local influences. In contrast, signals under the JSM-2 model only contains the second part.

The joint sparse decomposition optimization algorithm proposed in this paper is based on the two models to solve the corresponding sparse coefficient vector.

3 Description of the Proposed Method

3.1 JSM1-OMP Algorithm

First define the signal to be decomposed is $X = [x_1, x_2, \cdots, x_J]$, J is the number of antennas, $x_j \in \mathbb{R}^M$ is the signal received by the antenna j, $x_j(m)$ is the mth sample of x_j, dictionary is $D \in \mathbb{R}^{M \times N}$ and X can be sparsely represented on the dictionary D.

Considering characteristics of JSM-1 model, we propose the JSM1-OMP algorithm by exploiting the correlation of signals. We estimate the common part of certain signal as the common part of other signals, and then calculate the unique part for each signal. Finally, we sum over the common part and the unique part to recovery the signals. The specific process is summarized as follows.

(1) Parameter initialization: The number of antennas is J, the antenna receiving sample is $X = [x_1, x_2, \cdots, x_J]$, the dictionary is D, the common sparsity is K_c, and the specific part of sparsity is K_j.

(2) The OMP algorithm is used to sparsely decomposes a certain signal. Here, we select the first signal, and the sparsity is set as the common sparsity K_c so that the common sparse coefficients of all signals are obtained, i.e.

$$\theta_c = OMP(x_1, D, K_c) \tag{6}$$

where θ_c is the sparsity of the common coefficient, then the common sparse signal is computed by $z_c = D\theta_c$.

(3) To find the unique part of each signal, we subtract the common sparse portion obtained by Step (2) from each signal

$$x'_j = x_j - D\theta_c \tag{7}$$

(4) Calculate the unique sparse coefficients of each signal, and use the OMP algorithm to sparsely decompose the unique sparse signal of each channel. The sparsity is $K_j, j \in \{1, 2, \cdots, J\}$. The dictionary D is still used and the solution process is

$$\theta_j = OMP(x'_j, D, K_j) \tag{8}$$

(5) Calculate the sparse coefficient of each signal and add the common sparse coefficient and the unique sparse coefficient

$$\theta'_j = \theta_c + \theta_j \quad j \in \{1, 2, \cdots, J\} \tag{9}$$

(6) Recovery multiple antenna samples

$$\hat{x}_j = D\theta'_j \quad j \in \{1, 2, \cdots, J\} \tag{10}$$

A simple explanation is given for the complexity of the proposed method. First, for the JSM1-OMP algorithm, the sparse decomposition of the first step exploits the OMP algorithm, and the complexity is the same as the case in which an OMP algorithm is used for an antenna with the same sparsity. Then, when the common sparse coefficient is used as a prior condition to solve the special sparse coefficients, the complexity is same as the case in which all the antenna signals use the OMP algorithm. Therefore, the JSM1-OMP possesses lower computational complexity. We use three receiving antennas as an example and assume that the sparsity of the same component is K_c, the sparsity of different components is K_1, K_2, K_3, and the size of the dictionary is $M \times N$. The algorithm complexity of using OMP is $O((4K_c + K_1 + K_2 + K_3)MN)$, The complexity of JSM1-OMP is $O((K_c + K_1 + K_2 + K_3)MN)$.

3.2   JSM2-OMP Algorithm

The JSM2-OMP algorithm is an extension of the OMP algorithm under the JSM-2 model. The OMP algorithm under this model is optimized based on the structural characteristics. The core idea of the algorithm is to require the participation of all signals to find the index of the coefficient position, rather than just a single signal at a time. The signal residuals are respectively summed with the dictionary and then summed as a condition for finding the sparse position index. Specific steps are offered as follows.

(1) Parameter initialization: count $l = 1$, Sub-dictionaries $T_0 = []$, Residual $r_{j0} = x_j (j = 1, 2, \cdots, J)$, atomic index set $t_0 = []$, The maximum number of iterations $interNum = K$.

(2) Select the position index of the atom that most closely matches the signal

$$i_l = \arg \max_{i=1,2,\cdots,N} \left(\sum_{j=1}^{J} |d_i^H r_{j,l-1}| \right) \tag{11}$$

(3) Combine the atomic index found in step 2 with the previous index set

$$t_l = t_{l-1} \cup i_l \tag{12}$$

(4) Merge the atom corresponding to the index found in step 2 with the previously selected atom set

$$T_l = T_{l-1} \cup d_l \tag{13}$$

(5) Solve residuals

$$r_{j,l} = y_j - T_l((T_l^H T_l)^{-1} T_l^H y_j) \tag{14}$$

(6) The end of the algorithm is judged: if $l >$ interNum is satisfied, then step 7 is performed, if not, then return to step 2.
(7) Find sparse coefficients

$$\theta_j' = (T_l^H T_l)^{-1} T_l^H x_j \tag{15}$$

(8) Recovery multiple antenna receive signals

$$x_j' = D\theta_j' \tag{16}$$

The complexity of the JSM2-OMP algorithm is mainly reflected in the steps of summing residuals and the inner product of atoms which coincides with the OMP algorithm. Therefore, the two algorithms are the same complexity. Taking the sparse decomposition of J antenna signals as an example, we assume that the sparsity of each antenna signal is K, and the size of the dictionary is $M \times N$. The complexity of the two algorithms is both $O(JKMN)$

3.3 JSM-OMP Algorithm

The core of this algorithm is to add JSM2-OMP algorithm in the framework of JSM1 model. Considering the characteristics of these two models, in the JSM1-OMP algorithm, the first step of solving the common coefficient sparseness can be replaced with the JSM2-OMP algorithm. By doing so, the sparse locations can be found more accurately and errors can be reduced more effectively. We call the improved algorithm JSM-OMP algorithm. The basic flow of this algorithm is basically the same as that of JSM1-OMP. It differs only when the second step is to solve common sparse coefficients

$$\theta_c = \text{JSM2\_OMP}(X, D, K_c) \tag{17}$$

We have already analyzed that the complexity of the JSM2-OMP is the same as that of the OMP. In the first step, the JSM-OMP is used. The complexity of the algorithm is the same as the OMP algorithm. When estimating the sparse coefficients of different compositions, all OMP algorithms are used, and their complexity is also the same. Therefore, the total complexity of the JSM-OMP algorithm is the same as that of the OMP algorithm. Taking the sparse decomposition of four antenna signals as an example, the total complexity of these two algorithms can be expressed as $O((4K_c + K_1 + K_2 + K_3 + K_4)MN)$.

4 Numerical Simulations

To illustrate the performance of the proposed algorithm, we first compare it with the traditional OMP algorithm, and then analyze the performance of the JSM-OMP algorithm and the JSM1-OMP algorithm. The simulation experiments use the actual signal model and the signal RMSE to measure the performance of the algorithm. RMSE can be defined as

$$RMSE = \sqrt{\frac{1}{N}\sum_{n=1}^{N}[x(n) - \hat{x}(n)]} \tag{18}$$

4.1 Sparse Decomposition Effect Simulation of JSM-1 Model Signal

Specific simulation parameters are set as follows. Dictionary is Fourier basis. The number of rows is $M = 256$, columns is $N = 256$. The number of antennas is 6, the common sparsity is 6, the unique sparsity is set to be the same as 2, each sample is a different frequency sample combination, and all sample frequencies have the same part and different parts. Signal-to-noise ratio is set to $(-15 \sim 25)$ dB. The results are shown in Fig. 1. It is observed that their sparse decomposition performance is basically similar for different SNR. Especially when the SNR is large, it is not difficult to understand because the essence of the JSM1-OMP algorithm is the OMP algorithm. Therefore, the algorithm's sparse decomposition performance should be similar to the OMP algorithm, so its advantages are mainly reflected in the reduced complexity.

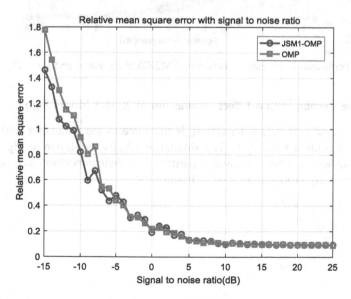

Fig. 1. Performance comparison between JSM1-OMP algorithm and OMP algorithm

4.2   Sparse Decomposition Effect Simulation of JSM-2 Model Signal

Specific simulation parameters are set as follows. Dictionary is Fourier basis. The number of rows is $M = 256$, Columns is $N = 256$.The number of antennas is 10, the sparsity is $K = 7$. Each signal is a combination of signals of different frequencies, and the same signal frequency of different antennas has different coefficients. The SNR is set to $(-15 \sim 25)$ dB.

The simulation results are illustrated in Fig. 2. It can be seen that the recovery performance of JSM2-OMP is better than that of OMP. This advantage is especially obvious at low signal-to-noise ratios because the JSM2-OMP algorithm makes full use of the correlation between signals.

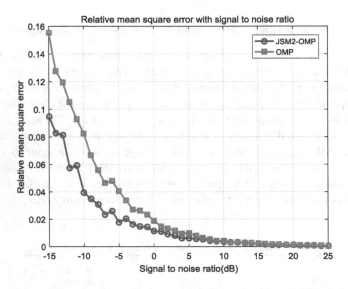

Fig. 2. Performance comparison between JSM2-OMP algorithm and OMP algorithm

4.3   Sparse Decomposition Effect Simulation of JSM-1 Model Signal

The specific simulation parameter setting is the same as the parameter setting in the JSM1-OMP algorithm simulation. The simulation results are shown in Fig. 3. Simulation results show that our improved algorithm has obvious performance advantages over the previously proposed JSM1-OMP algorithm.

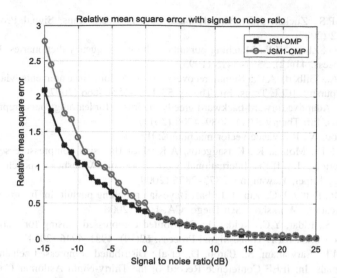

Fig. 3. Performance comparison between JSM-OMP algorithm and JSM1-OMP algorithm

5 Conclusions

We first introduce JSM-1 and JSM-2. Then, based on the structural characteristics of these two models, we propose JSM1-OMP and JSM2-OMP algorithm. The two algorithms are compared with the traditional sparse decomposition algorithm OMP in terms of complexity and sparse decomposition performance under multi-antenna conditions. In terms of complexity, we find that JSM1-OMP is superior to OMP, and JSM2-OMP is the same as OMP. When it comes to sparse decomposition performance, JSM1-OMP is similar to OMP, while JSM2-OMP is much better than OMP, especially in low SNR cases. Then, combining JSM-1 model with JSM2-OMP algorithm, we propose another joint sparse decomposition algorithm, namely JSM-OMP. This algorithm compensates for the defects of OMP in finding common sparse coefficients and makes the decomposition performance of the algorithm much improved compared to JSM1-OMP.

Acknowledgment. This work is supported by National Natural Science Foundation of China (NSFC) (Grant No. 61671176) and Civil Space Pre-research Program during the 13th Five-Year Plan (B0111).

References

1. Donoho, D.L.: Compressed sensing. IEEE Trans. Inf. Theory **52**(4), 1289–1306 (2006)
2. Baraniuk, R.: Compressive sensing. IEEE Signal Process. Mag. **24**(4), 118–121 (2007)
3. Tibshirani, R.: Regression Shrinkage and Selection via the Lasso. J. Roy. Stat. Soc. **73**(3), 267–288 (2011)

4. Huggins, P.S., Zucker, S.W.: Greedy basis pursuit. IEEE Trans. Signal Process. **55**(7), 3760–3772 (2007)
5. Mallat, S.G., Zhang, Z.F.: Matching pursuits with time-frequency dictionaries. IEEE Trans. Signal Process. **41**(12), 3397–3415 (1993)
6. Tropp, J.A., Gilbert, A.C.: Signal recovery from random measurements via orthogonal matching pursuit. IEEE Trans. Inf. Theory **53**(12), 4655–4666 (2007)
7. Zhang, T.: Adaptive forward-backward greedy algorithm for learning sparse representations. IEEE Trans. Inf. Theory **57**(7), 4689–4708 (2011)
8. Karatzoglou, A.: Relevance vector machine (2015)
9. Babacan, S.D., Molina, R., Katsaggelos, A.K.: Fast Bayesian compressive sensing using Laplace priors. In: IEEE International Conference on Acoustics, Speech and Signal Processing, Taipei, Taiwan, pp. 2873–2876 (2009)
10. Schniter, P., Potter, L.C., Ziniel, J.: Fast Bayesian matching pursuit. In: Information Theory and Applications Workshop, San Diego, CA, USA (2008)
11. Patterson, S., Eldar, Y.C., Keidar, I.: Distributed compressed sensing for static and time-varying networks. IEEE Trans. Signal Process. **62**(19), 4931–4946 (2014)
12. Duarte, M.F., Sarvotham, S., Baron, D., et al.: Distributed compressed sensing of jointly sparse signals. In: IEEE Conference Record of the Thirty-Ninth Asilomar Conference on Signals, Systems and Computers, Pacific Grove, California, USA, pp. 1537–1541 (2005)

Millimeter Wave Massive MIMO Channel Estimation and Tracking

Yanwu Song, Shaochuan Wu$^{(\boxtimes)}$, Wenbin Zhang, and Huafeng Zhang

Harbin Institute of Technology, Harbin 150001, Heilongjiang, China
scwu@hit.edu.cn

Abstract. With the rapid development of 5G, massive MIMO technology has become one of the most important technologies in 5G. However, while massive MIMO technology could provide reliable performance guarantee, with the number of antennas increases, the problem of channel estimation has also become more complicated. To solve this problem, we propose a channel state estimation and tracking algorithm based on particle filter, when considering the temporal correlation between the millimeter wave narrowband block fading channels. A channel state model including channel gain, the angle of arrival, and the angle of departure has been established. A performance comparison is carried out, in terms of normalized mean square error, considering massive MIMO channel estimation, for different algorithms. We also take into account the performance affected by signal to noise ratio and the number of antennas. Numerical results show that the performance can be considerably improved in the case of a large number of antennas over the conventional scheme. Furthermore, this algorithm also has better performance under traditional MIMO conditions.

Keywords: Millimeter wave · Massive MIMO · Channel tracking ·
Particle filter

1 Introduction

With the rapid development of 5G technology, millimeter wave technology has become a research hotspot in 5G related technologies, because millimeter wave can provide lower delay and higher transmission rate for the applications in 5G [10]. However, millimeter wave has higher frequency band compared with traditional microwave communication. In this case, millimeter wave has a shorter wavelength, which is much smaller than the size of obstacles. Therefore millimeter has limited scatterings and higher path loss during transmission, which also makes the millimeter wave channel sparse [6]. Compared with the traditional communication technology with a lower carrier frequency range, millimeter wave technology has higher cost and power consumption.

In order to overcome the above shortcomings of millimeter wave, massive multiple-input multiple-output (MIMO) technology can be used to provide huge

© ICST Institute for Computer Sciences, Social Informatics and Telecommunications Engineering 2019
Published by Springer Nature Switzerland AG 2019. All Rights Reserved
S. Han et al. (Eds.): AICON 2019, LNICST 286, pp. 57–69, 2019.
https://doi.org/10.1007/978-3-030-22968-9_6

gain for communication systems [8]. Setting tens or even hundreds of antenna elements at the base station can provide sufficient array gain and path gain for the communication system, with high spectral efficiency and energy efficiency [5]. Since the wavelength of the millimeter wave is short, and the antenna unit spacing of the uniform linear array (ULA) is half the wavelength, the transmitter and the receiver can use a large-scale antenna array for information transmission under the condition of the limited antenna array size. The great path gain of massive MIMO technology can meet the stringent performance requirements in 5G [9].

Beamforming technology is one of the most important technologies of massive MIMO. Because beamforming technology can provide huge beam gain for communication systems to overcome the severe path loss problems caused by millimeter wave and the hardware limitations in massive MIMO systems [5]. Whether analog beamforming, digital beamforming, or hybrid analog beamforming, the transmit beamforming vector and the receive combiner vector need to be designed based on channel state information (CSI). Therefore, the design of a good beamforming structure needs to be obtained through effective channel estimation.

In general, channel estimation can be divided into two ways: implicit channel estimation and explicit channel estimation. In the implicit channel estimation process, the transmitter and the receiver do not need to know the complete channel state information, and the beamforming can be performed iteratively through the pre-designed beamforming codebook, under certain standard conditions [1]. However, in this way, the massive MIMO communication system needs to bear higher complexity costs, which is not able to meet the stringent performance requirements of the millimeter wave communication system. For explicit channel estimation, Alkhateeb proposed an adaptive algorithm for estimating the channel, which uses a beamforming vector with different beamwidths at different stages to search for the paths [2]. The authors of [11] proposed an algorithm to estimate the angles of arrival (AoA) and angles of departure (AoD) of the beam by using extended Kalman filter, and achieved good results. The algorithm is still worth continuing to improve when the number of antennas is large.

The contributions of this paper are mainly in two aspects. First, we propose a channel estimation and tracking algorithm that can be applied to multi-antenna MIMO, where the number of antennas of massive MIMO can sometimes be as many as hundreds. The traditional MIMO channel estimation algorithm can only work when the number of antennas is small. Second, our proposed algorithm also has a good performance when the number of antenna is small, especially in the case of high signal to noise ratio (SNR).

The rest part of the paper is organized as follows. Section 2 illustrates the channel model and the temporal correlated of millimeter wave MIMO channel. Section 3 gives the expression of the observation and presents our algorithm for channel estimation and tracking. In Sect. 4, performance analysis is presented comparing our method with traditional one. Then, Sect. 5 concludes this paper.

2 System Structure and Channel Model

This section introduces the millimeter wave MIMO channel model. A channel model of the millimeter wave can be established in the angle domain, the expression of the channel matrix $\mathbf{H}$ is

$$\mathbf{H} = \sum_{n=1}^{N} \alpha_n \mathbf{a}_r \left(\phi_{n,A} \right) \mathbf{a}_t^H \left(\phi_{n,D} \right), \tag{1}$$

where N is the number of paths, α_n is the paths gain, $\mathbf{a}_r \left(\phi_{n,A} \right)$ and $\mathbf{a}_t \left(\phi_{n,D} \right)$ represent the array response vectors of AoA and AoD, respectively. The $\phi_{n,A}$ and $\phi_{n,D}$ denote AoAs and AoDs of N independent paths. Assume that the ULA model is deployed at the transmitter and the receiver. Then, the expressions of the array response vectors in the AoA and AoD are

$$\mathbf{a}_r \left(\phi_{n,A} \right) = \frac{1}{\sqrt{N_r}} \left[1, e^{j \frac{2\pi}{\lambda} d \cos(\phi_{n,A})}, \cdots, e^{j(N_r - 1) \frac{2\pi}{\lambda} d \cos(\phi_{n,A})} \right]^T \tag{2}$$

and

$$\mathbf{a}_t \left(\phi_{n,D} \right) = \frac{1}{\sqrt{N_t}} \left[1, e^{j \frac{2\pi}{\lambda} d \cos(\phi_{n,D})}, \cdots, e^{j(N_t - 1) \frac{2\pi}{\lambda} d \cos(\phi_{n,D})} \right]^T, \tag{3}$$

where λ is the wavelength of the carrier and d is the distance between transmit antennas.

The following is a signal model for a millimeter wave massive MIMO system. For simplicity, assume that the pilot $\mathbf{x}$ to be transmitted is $\mathbf{1}$. The received signal expression can be expressed as

$$\begin{aligned} \mathbf{y} &= \mathbf{w}^H \mathbf{H} \mathbf{f} + \mathbf{v} \\ &= \sum_{n=1}^{N} \alpha_n \mathbf{w}^H \mathbf{a}_r \left(\phi_{n,A} \right) \mathbf{a}_t^H \left(\phi_{n,D} \right) \mathbf{f} + \mathbf{v}, \end{aligned} \tag{4}$$

where the vectors $\mathbf{w}$ and $\mathbf{f}$ represent the combiner vector and the beamforming vector at the receiver and the transmitter, respectively. The received signal expression for a specific path will be further introduced in the Sect. 3, and its form will be further simplified.

2.1 Temporal Correlated Millimeter Wave MIMO Channel Model

Now we consider narrowband block-fading channel state model in the millimeter wave massive MIMO system [4]. In this channel model, parameters are stable in the same block and have the temporal correlation in adjacent blocks. First, we define a channel state vector at block k as

$$\mathbf{x}[k] = \left[\alpha_R[k], \alpha_I[k], \phi_A[k], \phi_D[k] \right]^T, \tag{5}$$

where $\alpha_R[k]$ and $\alpha_I[k]$ represent the real and imaginary parts of the corresponding path gain of the same path respectively, $\phi_A[k]$ and $\phi_D[k]$ are AoA and AoD of the corresponding path. Assume that the path gain in the channel matrix at different blocks is subject to the first-order Gauss Markov model, as shown below

$$\alpha_i [k + 1] = \rho \alpha_i [k] + \varsigma [k], \tag{6}$$

where $\rho \in [0, 1]$ is the time correlation coefficient, which follows Jakes' model [7] according to $\rho = J_0 (2\pi f_D T)$. The $J_0 (\cdot)$ is the zeroth order Bessel function of first kind, and the f_D and T denote the maximum Doppler frequency and channel block length, respectively. The subscript i indicates the real or imaginary part of the path gain, $\varsigma [k] \sim \mathcal{N} \left(0, \frac{1-\rho^2}{2}\right)$ represents excitation noise between adjacent states. In the adjacent channel blocks, the corresponding AoA and AoD state update models are

$$\phi [k + 1] = \phi [k] + n. \tag{7}$$

$\phi [k] \in (-\pi, \pi]$ represents the AoA or AoD of the path in the channel, and n represents state excitation noise.

Through the path gain between the adjacent channel blocks and the state update model of AoA and AoD, we can conclude that the corresponding channel state vector equation of the millimeter wave massive MIMO system can be expressed as follows

$$\mathbf{x} [k + 1] = \mathbf{F} \mathbf{x} [k - 1] + \mathbf{u} [k - 1], \tag{8}$$

where $\mathbf{F} = diag ([\rho, \rho, 1, 1])$ and $\mathbf{u} [k] \sim \mathcal{CN} (0, \Sigma_u)$, $\Sigma_u = diag([\frac{1-\rho^2}{2}, \frac{1-\rho^2}{2}, \sigma_A^2, \sigma_D^2])$ represents the noise during the update of different state variables.

3   Observation and Channel Tracking

3.1   Observation

In order to complete the implementation of dynamic channel estimation and tracking algorithm, the corresponding observation equation is needed. We define $\Phi_A = \cos \phi_A - \cos \overline{\phi_A}$, $\Phi_D = \cos \phi_D - \cos \overline{\phi_D}$, where $\overline{\phi_A}$ represents the beam direction controlled by the combiner, and $\cos \overline{\phi_D}$ represents the direction of the beamforming vector at the transmitter. A simplified expression can be get as follows

$$\mathbf{w}^H (\overline{\phi_A}) \mathbf{a}_r (\phi_A) = \frac{1}{N_r} \frac{1 - e^{j N_r k d \Phi_A}}{1 - e^{j k d \Phi_A}}. \tag{9}$$

Similarly, we can get a simplified expression of $\mathbf{a}_t^H (\phi_D) \mathbf{f} (\overline{\phi_D})$. Then received signal can be simplified as

$$\mathbf{y} = \sum_{i=1}^{I} \frac{\alpha_i}{N_r N_t} \frac{1 - e^{j N_r k d \Phi_{A,i}}}{1 - e^{j k d \Phi_{A,i}}} \frac{1 - e^{-j N_t k d \Phi_{D,i}}}{1 - e^{-j k d \Phi_{D,i}}} + \mathbf{v}. \tag{10}$$

The transmitter transmit the known training symbols through the beamforming vector at the transmitter, and the final received signal can be obtained by using the combiner vector at the receiver. Section 2 has introduced the millimeter wave dynamic channel state model. Therefore, in the training phase, we pre-designed the corresponding beamforming matrix $\mathbf{F}$ and the combiner matrix $\mathbf{W}$, which are expressed as

$$\mathbf{W} = [\mathbf{w}_1, \mathbf{w}_2, \cdots, \mathbf{w}_N],$$
$$\mathbf{F} = [\mathbf{f}_1, \mathbf{f}_2, \cdots, \mathbf{f}_N], \tag{11}$$

where each column of $\mathbf{F}$ and $\mathbf{W}$ represents a beamforming control vector in a specified direction. The final expression of the received signal that can be obtained is

$$\mathbf{Y} = \mathbf{W}^H \mathbf{H} \mathbf{F} + \mathbf{V}$$
$$= \begin{bmatrix} \mathbf{w}_1^H \mathbf{H} \mathbf{f}_1 & \mathbf{w}_1^H \mathbf{H} \mathbf{f}_2 & \cdots & \mathbf{w}_1^H \mathbf{H} \mathbf{f}_N \\ \mathbf{w}_2^H \mathbf{H} \mathbf{f}_1 & \mathbf{w}_2^H \mathbf{H} \mathbf{f}_2 & \cdots & \mathbf{w}_2^H \mathbf{H} \mathbf{f}_N \\ \vdots & \vdots & \ddots & \vdots \\ \mathbf{w}_N^H \mathbf{H} \mathbf{f}_1 & \mathbf{w}_N^H \mathbf{H} \mathbf{f}_2 & \cdots & \mathbf{w}_N^H \mathbf{H} \mathbf{f}_N \end{bmatrix} + \mathbf{V}. \tag{12}$$

We select the elements on the diagonal we want to get

$$y_n = \mathbf{w}_n^H \mathbf{H} \mathbf{f}_n + v$$
$$= \sum_{i=1}^{I} \mathbf{w}_n^H \alpha_i \mathbf{a}_r(\phi_{i,A}) \mathbf{a}_t^H(\phi_{i,D}) \mathbf{f}_n + v$$
$$= \alpha_n \mathbf{w}_n^H \mathbf{a}_r(\phi_{n,A}) \mathbf{a}_t^H(\phi_{n,D}) \mathbf{f}_n +$$
$$\sum_{i \neq n} \alpha_i \mathbf{w}_n^H \mathbf{a}_r(\phi_{i,A}) \mathbf{a}_t^H(\phi_{i,D}) \mathbf{f}_n + v. \tag{13}$$

For (13), due to the determinism of the main lobe direction of beamforming, consider the latter two parameters as a new noise v_n. Let $\mathbf{f}_n = \mathbf{a}(\bar{\phi}_{n,D})$, $\mathbf{w}_n = \mathbf{a}(\bar{\phi}_{n,A})$, by using the conclusion of (10), we can get

$$y_n = \frac{\alpha_n}{N_r N_t} \frac{1 - e^{jN_r kd\Phi_A}}{1 - e^{jkd\Phi_A}} \frac{1 - e^{-jN_t kd\Phi_D}}{1 - e^{-jkd\Phi_D}} + v_n$$
$$= h(\mathbf{x}[k]) + v_n. \tag{14}$$

In this way, the millimeter wave dynamic channel state model and the observation model of the system have been established. Next, we are going to present a algorithm to estimation and tracking the channel state under the state-space model.

3.2   Particle Filter Based Channel Tracking

Now, the state-space model of the channel through the state model (8) and the observation model (14) have been established. Here we can try to obtain the estimation of the channel state parameters by using the Bayesian estimation idea. The idea of Bayesian estimation can be expressed as estimating the hidden channel state information by prediction and correction. Prediction refers to estimating the channel state of the current block by using the channel state estimation of the previous block in consideration of the temporal correlation of the adjacent blocks. Correction means that the estimated current channel state is corrected based on the observation value of the current block, so that it is more likely to close to the true channel state. The idea of Bayesian estimates is shown in Fig. 1.

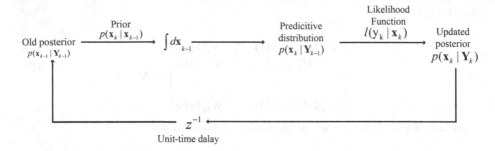

Fig. 1. The idea of Bayesian estimation.

In order to use Bayesian estimation, the state model (8) and the observation model (14) is needed. (8) expresses the changing relationship of channel parameters between adjacent blocks, and (14) expresses the relationship between the channel state and the received signal at a certain block. Bayesian estimates have a variety of specific forms, such as Kalman filter, extended Kalman filter, unscented Kalman filter, particle filter, etc., and their application scenarios are different. The algorithm in [11] tracking the AoA and AoD of the channel by extended Kalman filter. Extended Kalman filter can be used to estimate parameters for slightly nonlinear systems with Gaussian noise, therefore authors of [11] use it to estimate the AoA and AoD of channel. With the number of MIMO antennas increases, the nonlinearity of the system will be further improved. It will be difficult to solve the channel state estimation problem of massive MIMO by using extended Kalman filter. At the same time, since the channel characteristics of massive MIMO do not have an ideal model, the actual noise may not be described by simple Gaussian noise. Therefore, it is considered to estimate the channel of massive MIMO with particle filter [3]. Particle filter has a good performance when processing nonlinear systems with non-Gaussian noise.

We give the specific content of our algorithm in Algorithm 1, and then give some definitions of symbols. $x_{k,pre}$ is the predicted value for the $\mathbf{x}$ state at k block, and $y_{k,pre}$ is the observed value for the $\mathbf{x}$ state predictor at k block. It is worth noting that the $y_{k,pre}$ here is a plural. $x_k^{(i)} \sim p(x_k)$ represents the particle $x_k^{(i)}$ extracted from the posterior distribution $p(x_k)$ at k block. $w_k^{(i)}$ is the weight of the corresponding particle.

Algorithm 1. Particle Filter based Channel Tracking.

Require: Observation $= \{y_1, y_2, \cdots, y_n\}$. Initial value of channel state x_0.
Ensure: x_k as the estimation of channel state.
1: Initialization: $w_0^{(i)} = \frac{1}{N}$, $x_0^{(i)} \sim p(x_0)$
2: **for** each blocks $k = 1, 2, 3, \cdots$ **do**
3:    **for** each particle $i = 1, 2, 3, \cdots, N$ **do**
4:      State predict: $x_{k+1,pre}^{(i)} = \mathbf{F}x_k^{(i)} + u_k$
5:      Observation predict: $y_{k+1,pre}^{(i)} = h\left(x_{k+1}^{(i)}\right) + v_{k+1}$
6:      Weights update: $e_{k+1}^{(i)} = |y_{k+1,pre} - y_{k+1}|^2$,
7: $$w_{k+1}^{(i)} = \frac{1}{2\pi N_0} e^{-\frac{e_{k+1}^{(i)}}{2N_0}}$$
8:    **end for**
9:    $x_{k+1} = \sum_{i=1}^{N} w_{k+1}^{(i)} x_{k+1,pre}^{(i)}$
10:    Resample: $x_{k+1}^{(i)} \sim p(x_{k+1})$, $w_{k+1}^{(i)} = \frac{1}{N}$
11: **end for**

When the channel is estimated by particle filter, the diversity of particles may gradually disappear over time. Therefore, we try to maintain the diversity of the particles by resampling after the estimation is completed at each blocks. The specific method is drawing a set of N discrete random variables $\left\{I^{(1)}, I^{(2)}, \cdots, I^{(N)}\right\}$ that take values in the corresponding set $\{1, 2, \cdots, N\}$ with probabilities $P\left(I^{(s)} = i\right) = w_k^{(i)}$. Then let $w_k^{(i)} = \frac{1}{N}$. When using particle filtering, the selection of the importance distribution $q\left(\mathbf{x}_k | y_k\right)$ is critical. In this algorithm, the left side of the particles of the previous moment are multiplied by the state transition matrix $\mathbf{F}$ and then the disturbance according to the statistics of the state transition noise $\mathbf{u}[k]$ is added.

By observing the algorithm table, It is easy to know that the complexity of particle filter increases linearly with the increase of the number of particles, and the requirement of storage also increases linearly with the increase of the number of particles. Therefore, particle filter's complexity and storage requirements are improved compared to extended Kalman filter.

4 Performance Analysis

In order to further verify the reliability of channel estimation and tracking of the algorithm in millimeter wave massive MIMO system, we carried out a series of simulation experiments and obtained the conclusion based on the corresponding simulation results.

The number of ULA antennas used at the transmitter and receiver are N_t, N_r respectively. ULA at the transmitter and receiver both are based on an analog beamforming structure. The number of RF chain is one. Pilots is transmitted under the channel model of millimeter wave narrowband block-fading. Since the channel of millimeter wave MIMO is sparse, different paths under the channel can be more easily distinguished. Assume that there is only one path falls within the main lobe, and the weak signals in the side lobes are treated as noise. The time correlation coefficient between adjacent channel blocks is $\rho = 0.995$, $\sigma_A^2 = \sigma_D^2 = \frac{0.5}{180}\pi^2$. The proposed algorithm is been simulated with using $N = 1000$ as the number of particles. For the sake of easy, assume only consider one path in the channel model. For each point in the figures, we simulate 100 blocks.

Compare our proposed algorithm (Abbreviated as PF) with the extended Kalman filter (Abbreviated as EKF) described in [11], and use the normalized mean square error (NMSE) $\frac{\mathbb{E}(\|\hat{\mathbf{x}}-\mathbf{x}\|_F^2)}{\mathbb{E}(\|\mathbf{x}\|_F^2)}$ (where $\hat{\mathbf{x}}$ is the estimation of $\mathbf{x}$) of the channel state as the evaluation criterion.

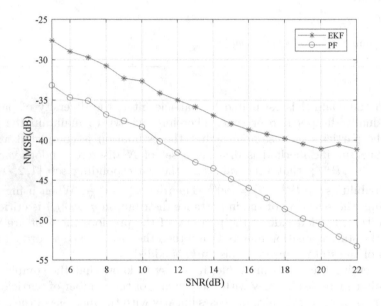

Fig. 2. NMSE of $\mathbf{x}$ versus SNR, $N_t = N_r = 16$.

First, consider the case where the NMSE of both algorithm changes with SNR from 5 dB to 22 dB when the number of transmitting antennas $N_t = 16$ and the receiving antennas $N_r = 16$. From Fig. 2, it can be seen that the system has strong linearity due to the small number of transmitting and receiving antennas. Therefore the EKF has achieved good results in estimating and tracking the channel in this case. However, it is easy to find that the performance of the proposed algorithm is still better than EKF at all range of SNR. The difference between the two algorithms' NMSE is further widened with the increase of SNR. The difference is only about 5 dB when SNR = 5 dB, but the difference is about 12 dB when SNR = 22 dB. Moreover, EKF reaches the performance limit when SNR = 20 dB, and the NMSE curve tends to be gentle. And the estimated value of both algorithm is more closer to the real situation with the SNR increases.

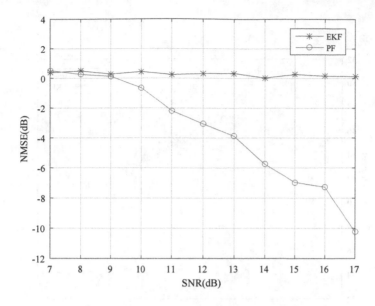

Fig. 3. NMSE of **x** versus SNR, $N_t = N_r = 64$.

Considering that the number of antennas for massive MIMO can be as high as hundreds, we have the simulation with $N_t = N_r = 64$. Figure 3 shows the NMSE of both algorithm changes with SNR from 7 dB to 17 dB. It can be seen from Fig. 3 that the EKF is almost completely unable to estimate the state of the channel in this case, especially the estimation of AoA and AoD. We present simulation results of the tracking of AoA and AoD over time by EKF and PF under $N_t = N_r = 64$ and SNR = 20 dB, which are shown in Figs. 4 and 5, respectively.

We also consider the case where the NMSE of both algorithm changes with number of transmitting antennas N_t and the receiving antennas N_r from 4 to 64 when the SNR = 20 dB. It can be seen from the Fig. 6 that the processing capability of the EKF for the channel state is limited to the case where the number of antennas is less than 32. When the number of antennas exceeds 32, the estimation and tracking ability of the channel state cannot meet the basic requirements. The PF algorithm still has good ability to estimate and track channels when the number of antennas is more than 32.

The reason why EKF does not perform well under these conditions is extended Kalman filter can only handle a certain degree of nonlinear system. From the basic principle of EKF, due to the nonlinear tracking of EKF is mainly approximated to the true value by first-order partial derivative of the Jacobian matrix. Therefore, when the degree of nonlinearity is high, the EKF cannot track the dynamically changing parameter information very well. While particle filter can handle any nonlinear problem. With the number of transmitting antennas

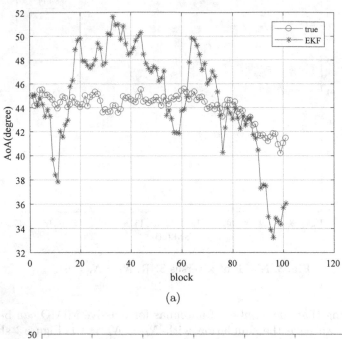

(a)

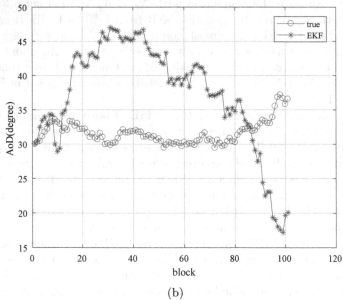

(b)

Fig. 4. EKF, AoA and AoD changes with blocks, SNR = 20 dB, $N_t = N_r = 64$.

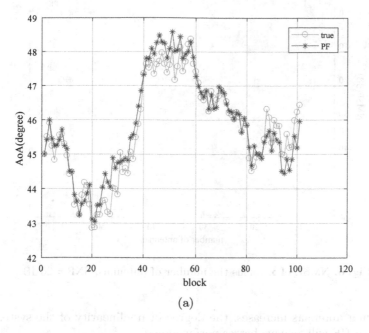

(a)

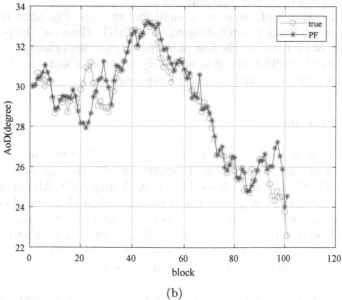

(b)

Fig. 5. PF, AoA and AoD changes with blocks, SNR = 20 dB, $N_t = N_r = 64$.

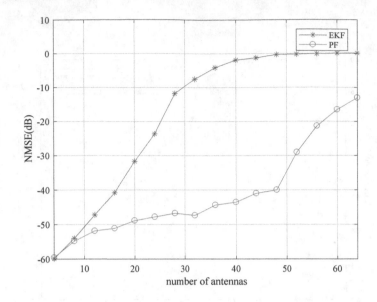

Fig. 6. NMSE of **x** versus the number of antennas, SNR = 20 dB.

and receiving antennas increases, the degree of nonlinearity of the system also increases, so PF will achieve better performance.

When the number of antennas is small and the signal to noise ratio is low, the PF has only a limited gain compared to the EKF. However, the performance improvement of PF comes at the cost of increased complexity and storage. Therefore, in practical applications, it is necessary to make a suitable choice among the two algorithms according to specific requirements.

5   Conclusions

In this paper, we propose a estimation and tracking algorithm based on particle filter, which can solve the problem of estimating and tracking the channel state of massive MIMO including channel gain, AoA and AoD. Although the algorithm has higher complexity than the traditional algorithm, the algorithm still has these advantages: This algorithm has better performance under traditional MIMO conditions, especially when the SNR is limited. This algorithm can be extended with the number of antennas increases, and have a great performance improved by tracking the AoA and AoD of channel.

Acknowledgment. This research was supported by the National Science Foundation of China (Under Grant: 61671173).

References

1. IEEE standard for information technology-telecommunications and information exchange between systems-local and metropolitan area networks-specific requirements-part 11: wireless LAN medium access control (MAC) and physical layer (PHY) specifications amendment 3: enhancements for very high throughput in the 60 GHz band. IEEE Std 802.11ad-2012 (Amendment to IEEE Std 802.11-2012, as amended by IEEE Std 802.11ae-2012 and IEEE Std 802.11aa-2012), pp. 1–628, December 2012. https://doi.org/10.1109/IEEESTD.2012.6392842
2. Alkhateeb, A., Ayach, O.E., Leus, G., Heath, R.W.: Channel estimation and hybrid precoding for millimeter wave cellular systems. IEEE J. Sel. Top. Signal Process. 8(5), 831–846 (2014). https://doi.org/10.1109/JSTSP.2014.2334278
3. Arulampalam, M.S., Maskell, S., Gordon, N., Clapp, T.: A tutorial on particle filters for online nonlinear/non-gaussian Bayesian tracking. IEEE Trans. Signal Process. 50(2), 174–188 (2002). https://doi.org/10.1109/78.978374
4. He, J., Kim, T., Ghauch, H., Liu, K., Wang, G.: Millimeter wave MIMO channel tracking systems. In: 2014 IEEE Globecom Workshops (GC Wkshps), pp. 416–421, December 2014. https://doi.org/10.1109/GLOCOMW.2014.7063467
5. Hur, S., Kim, T., Love, D.J., Krogmeier, J.V., Thomas, T.A., Ghosh, A.: Millimeter wave beamforming for wireless backhaul and access in small cell networks. IEEE Trans. Commun. 61(10), 4391–4403 (2013). https://doi.org/10.1109/TCOMM.2013.090513.120848
6. Pi, Z., Khan, F.: An introduction to millimeter-wave mobile broadband systems. IEEE Commun. Mag. 49(6), 101–107 (2011). https://doi.org/10.1109/MCOM.2011.5783993
7. Proakis, J.G.: Digital Communications, 4th edn. McGraw Hill, Boston (2000)
8. Rappaport, T.S., et al.: Millimeter wave mobile communications for 5G cellular: it will work! IEEE Access 1, 335–349 (2013). https://doi.org/10.1109/ACCESS.2013.2260813
9. Rappaport, T.S., Xing, Y., MacCartney, G.R., Molisch, A.F., Mellios, E., Zhang, J.: Overview of millimeter wave communications for fifth-generation (5G) wireless networks–with a focus on propagation models. IEEE Trans. Antennas Propag. 65(12), 6213–6230 (2017). https://doi.org/10.1109/TAP.2017.2734243
10. Torkildson, E., Madhow, U., Rodwell, M.: Indoor millimeter wave MIMO: feasibility and performance. IEEE Trans. Wirel. Commun. 10(12), 4150–4160 (2011). https://doi.org/10.1109/TWC.2011.092911.101843
11. Zhang, C., Guo, D., Fan, P.: Tracking angles of departure and arrival in a mobile millimeter wave channel. In: 2016 IEEE International Conference on Communications (ICC), pp. 1–6, May 2016. https://doi.org/10.1109/ICC.2016.7510902

Deep Learning-Based Space Shift Keying Systems

Yue Zhang, Xuesi Wang, Jintao Wang$^{(\boxtimes)}$, Yonglin Xue, and Jian Song

Tsinghua University, Beijing 100084, People's Republic of China
dearyovela@gmail.com, wangjintao@tsinghua.edu.cn

Abstract. To handle the performance degradation of space shift keying (SSK) systems under practical non-Gaussian channels, we propose a deep neural network model in which an auto-encoder (AE) is developed to design proper constellations and corresponding demodulation. With full knowledge of channel statistics, the transmitter and receiver are jointly optimized in our scheme. By representing the SSK system as an AE, we consider the cross-entropy loss function for antenna index and formulate the overall pipeline using deep learning techniques. Moreover, our implementation can be adopted in several noise conditions successfully. Results confirm that our model outperforms the maximum likelihood (ML) detection scheme in terms of block error rates (BLER).

Keywords: Space shift keying (SSK) · Deep learning · Neural network

1 Introduction

With the increasing varieties of communication scenarios, information transmission at high speed and reliability has become a main design goal in current communication systems [1]. Owing to the diversity and multiplexing gain in different transmission paths, research on multiple-input multiple-output (MIMO) system has aroused much attention. Spatial modulation (SM) is one promising MIMO techniques that transmits data symbol only on one antenna selected from an antenna group at each time slot [2,3]. When the antenna transmits a pulse instead of a symbol, SM reduces to space shift keying (SSK), in which the information is transmitted only by the index of the activated antenna. In SSK, only one antenna is activated at each transmission and thus only one radio frequency (RF) chain is required. Meanwhile, the problem of inter-channel interference (ICI) is circumvented naturally.

In SM and SSK systems, AWGN is usually considered as the channel model, whose closed-form expression can be explained as mathematical analytic formula directly. Consequently, the design of receiver discrimination schemes is simplified, leading to improvement of algorithm effectiveness. With full knowledge of

Supported by the National Key Research and Development Program of China (Grant No. 2017YFE011230).

S. Han et al. (Eds.): AICON 2019, LNICST 286, pp. 70–78, 2019.
https://doi.org/10.1007/978-3-030-22968-9_7

channel statistics, maximum likelihood (ML) detection scheme can demodulate the index of the activated antenna at the receiver side. The optimal transmitted bit streams can be recovered based on the code book. In practical communication scenarios, however, with the coexistence of complex interferences such as filtering, channel fading and other non-linear effects, the channel noise deviates from Gaussian distribution and exhibits non-Gaussian characteristics [4]. Motivated by the irritable performance degradation [5], the SSK system under such non-Gaussian practical channels requires much investigation.

Inspired by the strong learning ability from data, the neural network (NN) structure has been widely used in nonlinear function fitting [7]. The abstract features learned from neural networks together with the strengths of nonlinear approximations can process multiple types of data recovery problems in computer vision (CV) [8] and nature language processing (NLP) [9]. Moreover, neural networks have already been extended to communication systems including modulation recognition [11], channel estimation [12], channel decoding [13] and CSI feedback [14]. Generally, the communication system is considered as a black box with an end-to-end deep learning architecture [15], and all functionalities are embedded in several layers where the performance can be enhanced jointly. Similar with the training regimes in supervised learning, after back propagation and updates of parameters, the NN implementations learn efficient representations of data and achieve excellent performance.

Taken into consideration those work, in this paper, we present a deep learning based framework in SSK system. The contributions of this paper can be summarized as follows:

1. By characterizing the transmitter and receiver into an auto-encoder (AE), we design a novel end-to-end framework of SSK system. The implementations can be jointly optimized and finally we obtain convincing results competitive with current state-of-art ML methods.
2. We evaluate the adaptability of our proposed framework and verify the robustness with practical noise interferences. The system under consideration is composed of a rayleigh fading channel with white noise while suffering from a high power radar pulse interferences simultaneously. Our DL-based SSK framework can be applied directly and achieve reliable results.

The remainder of the paper is organized as follows. Section 2 describes our DL-based SSK model, including a brief introduction of SSK system. In Sect. 3, the simulation results are provided. The adaptability will be analyzed as well. Finally Sect. 4 concludes the paper.

2   System Model

2.1   SSK System

The SSK system model is composed of N_t transmit antennas and N_r receive antennas. A sequence of independent bit streams $\mathbf{b} = \{b_1, b_2, \cdots, b_k\}$ enters a channel encoder and the corresponding output $\mathbf{c} = \{c_1, c_2, \cdots, c_n\}$ is generated, where k and n represent the input and output dimensions of channel encoder, respectively. The sequence $\mathbf{c}$ then be modulated as the constellation point $\mathbf{x} = [x_1, x_2, \cdots, x_{N_t}]^T$, where $\mathbf{x}$ corresponds to transmission information of $m = \log_2(N_t)$ bits. The power limit can thus be represented as

$$\mathbb{E}_x(\mathbf{x}^H \mathbf{x}) = 1. \tag{1}$$

Hence, the received signal is

$$\mathbf{y} = \sqrt{\rho}\mathbf{H}\mathbf{x} + \boldsymbol{\zeta}, \tag{2}$$

where $\mathbf{H}$ is an $N_r \times N_t$ wireless communication channel matrix, and is combined with an independent identically distributed (i.i.d) additive white Gaussian noise (AWGN) denoted as $\boldsymbol{\zeta} = [\zeta_1, \zeta_2, \cdots, \zeta_{N_r}]^T$. ρ is the average signal to noise ratio (SNR) at each receive antenna. $\mathbf{H}$ and $\boldsymbol{\zeta}$ are subject to i.i.d complex Gaussian distribution, respectively.

Futhermore, SSK maps a set of m-bit information to symbol $\mathbf{x}_j$, which will then be transmitted through the j-th antenna. The symbol itself contains no information, while its position in the constellation point $\mathbf{x}$ indeed reflects the actual message. The one-hot vector $\mathbf{x}$ determines the index of the activated antenna which is thus defined as

$$\mathbf{x}_j \doteq [0, 0, \cdots, 1, \cdots, 0, 0]^T, \tag{3}$$

where 1 (the pulse) is the j-th element. The simplified received signal in Eq. 2 can be formulated as

$$\mathbf{y} = \sqrt{\rho}\mathbf{h}_j + \boldsymbol{\zeta}, \tag{4}$$

in which $\mathbf{h}_j$ refers to the j-th column vector of channel transmission matrix $\mathbf{H}$. According to the prior that the probability of the signal input is equal, we adopt the optimal ML detector as

$$\hat{j} = \arg\max_j P_{\mathbf{Y}}(\mathbf{y} \mid \mathbf{x}_j, \mathbf{H}) = \arg\max_j \|\mathbf{y} - \sqrt{\rho}\mathbf{h}_j\|_F^2, \tag{5}$$

$$P_{\mathbf{Y}}(\mathbf{y} \mid \mathbf{x}_j, \mathbf{H}) = \frac{\exp(-\|\mathbf{y} - \sqrt{\rho}\mathbf{h}_j\|_F^2)}{\pi^{N_r}}, \tag{6}$$

where $\|\cdot\|_F$ refers to the Frobenius norm of vectors and $\hat{j}$ is the discriminated index of the activated antenna.

In practical communication scenarios, where a distant noise with high power appears occasionally with a certain probability and contaminates the original transmitted signal, the overall channel noise deviates from Gaussian distribution and exhibits non-Gaussian characteristics. In this paper, we consider the interference of radar signals, which has caused widespread concern in the next generation of wireless communication system [11]. The transmitted signal can then be mathematically expressed as

$$\mathbf{y} = \sqrt{\rho}\mathbf{h}_j + \boldsymbol{\zeta} + \boldsymbol{\omega}, \tag{7}$$

where ζ remains to be AWGN and ω is the subject to the Gaussian distribution $\mathcal{N}(0, \sigma_\omega^2)$ with the probability of occurrence w:

$$\omega \sim \begin{cases} \mathcal{N}(0, \sigma_\omega^2) & w \\ 0 & 1 - w \end{cases}. \tag{8}$$

Notice that σ_ω^2 is supposed to be a higher variance compared to AWGN.

2.2   Deep Learning-Based Model

Based on the above introduction, here we consider the deep learning-based SSK system in which the number of transmit antenna $N_t = 4$ and the number of receive antenna $N_r = 1$. To prevent confusion we denote the DL-based model as SSK-NN in the following sections. In conventional system, the activated antenna transmits a pulse and the entire information is conveyed through the antenna index. For our SSK-NN model, the activated antenna transmits a learned modulation constellation instead. The overall pipeline is represented in Fig. 1.

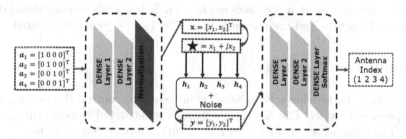

Fig. 1. The SSK-NN overall pipeline. The transmitter end adopts $\mathbf{a}_i$ as the input vector and the training samples for the neural network. In the receiver end, the received signal $\mathbf{y}$ will then be discriminated through two full-connected layers and finally classified by a softmax function.

The transmitter end adopts $\mathbf{a}_i$ as the input vector and the training samples for the neural network. The dimension of $\mathbf{a}$ equals to the number of transmit antenna $N_t = 4$. Since each transmission activates only one antenna, $\mathbf{a}$ is associated with corresponding one-hot vector. The modulation unit is constructed with a three-layers AE where two fully-connected layers and one normalization layer can generate a two-dimension output $\mathbf{x}$. The normalization layer ensures the output constellation points satisfying the power limit and thus to meet the design requirements of communication physical layer. We then treat the two components of $\mathbf{x}$ as two values of I/Q paths and convert $\mathbf{x}$ to a constellation point. Therefore, immediately after the AE modulating a one-hot vector to the corresponding symbol, the activated antenna will transmit it through its own transmission path. Moreover, in the receiver end, the received signal $\mathbf{y}$ will then be discriminated through two full-connected layers and finally classified by a softmax function:

$$S_i = \frac{\exp(V_i)}{\sum_j \exp(V_j)},\tag{9}$$

where V_i represents the output of the i-th neurons in the former layer. The cross-entropy loss will be calculated as

$$\text{Loss} = -\sum_{i=1}^{N_t} S_i \ln(S_i),\tag{10}$$

which then guides the back propagation and stochastic gradient descent (SGD) methods to update parameters in dense layers. Once the training process is completed, the obtained class number (the largest S_i) can predict the antenna index.

Specifically, our SSK-NN system has no strict requirement on the number of N_r in practical design. For simulation convenience, we choose $N_r = 1$ in this paper. Since the training process only makes use of $\mathbf{a}$ and $\mathbf{y}$, the NN architecture remains valid even though there is no channel analytic formula given. Overall, the communication system is considered as a black box with an end-to-end deep learning architecture and the parameters of NNs can be jointly optimized.

3   Simulation Results

In this section, we provide several simulation results to confirm the performance of our proposed model. The NN architecture is constructed through the system model. The parameters of the network structure are provided in Table 1.

Table 1. Network structure

Layers	Output dimensions
Dense+ReLu	4
Dense	2
Normalization	2
·Channel+Noise	2
Dense+ReLu	2
Dense+ReLu	2
Dense+Softmax	4

To meet the power limit, the noise layer is represented with a definite variance $\sigma = (2RE_b/N_0)^{-1}$, where E_b/N_0 refers to the ratio of energy per bit E_b and noise power spectral density N_0. The communication rate of the system is $R = 1$ and the fixed energy constraint is $\|\mathbf{x}\|_2^2 = 2$ (the dimension of the output constellation). We measure the SSK-NN performance using block error rate (BLER), i.e. $P(\hat{j} \neq j)$ and compare the trained neural networks with ML detection methods. Without loss of generality, the training set consists of 1000 samples and is trained for 150 epoches. The code is implemented in PyTorch.

3.1 The Baseline Model

Based on Fig. 1, the transmitter consists of a three-layers feed forward NN, the channel is represented by an fixed-variance additive noise layer and the receiver is implemented as a feed forward NN as well. The AE is trained end-to-end using Adam [16] on the set of all possible messages, i.e. four kinds of **a**. The cross-entropy loss function is used and the learning rate is set as 0.001. Training is completed at a fixed value $E_b/N_0 = 7$ dB and testing is done at the SNR ranging from -2 dB to 10 dB. The BLER comparison is provided in Fig. 2. Notice that in AWGN channels, the ML detection is optimal theoretically. The similar performance provided above indeed verifies the feasibility of our deep learning method.

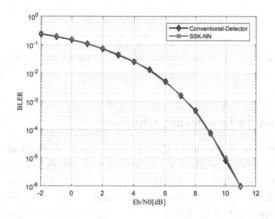

Fig. 2. $N_t = 4$ and $N_r = 1$. Trained at $\text{SNR} = 7$ dB.

3.2 The Transmission Model

Considering the time-invariant channel following a standard complex Gaussian distribution $\mathcal{CN}(0,1)$. The power limit of **y** will still be satisfied owing to the fixed unit variance. In addition, the AWGN still exists. The considered channel is represented by a multiplier matrix **H** combined with the additive layer. The AE is trained end-to-end using Adam optimizer at a fixed $\text{SNR} = 7$ dB and a learning rate 0.001 as well. The BLER comparison is presented in Fig. 3. Specifically, there is a consistent performance gain in a wide testing SNR range, from -2 dB to 10 dB. Our SSK-NN optimizes the AE with respect to the transmission channel and outperforms the ML detection, getting benefit from the adaptive constellation design.

In practical communications, the training process needs to be conducted first. Then the desirable demodulation performance can be obtained over the entire range of noises just after a quick parameter fine-tuning adjustment. For a more convincing comparison, the constellation needs to be examined with some higher-order modulation schemes, applying a channel code for instance. Discussion of these topics is out of the scope of this paper and left to our further research.

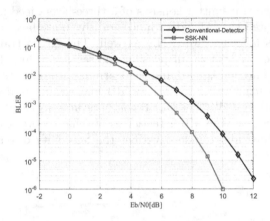

Fig. 3. $N_t = 4$ and $N_r = 1$. Complex Gaussian channels are considered. Trained at SNR $= 7$ dB.

3.3 Adaptability in Interfering Channels

Since the training process regards the channel as a black-box, only the signal input **x** and the received symbol **y** are concerned, which suggests the experiments on non-Gaussian channels worthy a try. We recall the radar interferences introduced in Sect. 2. The non-Gaussian channel model we focus here can be mathematically represented as Eq. 7. Following the above channel design approach, the expression of non-Gaussian radar interferences noise is consistent with the AWGN. The additional noise layer with the fixed variance σ_ω^2 will be added to the NN structure. The training SNR of AWGN is set to be 7 dB while the SNR of radar interferences is 5 dB of higher power. The possibility of interferences occurrence is 0.01, which implies the sporadic and unpredictable of such non-Gaussian scenarios. We still adopt the Adam optimizer with learning rate 0.001 and the BLER results are shown in Fig. 4. Considering the NN implementation and the traditional ML scheme of non-Gaussian noise in the case of 5 dB, both of them have some degradation with respect to the ideal channel setting. Obviously, the SSK-NN outperforms ML at the whole SNR testing ratio. The neural network utilizes its ability to simulate nonlinear degradation and achieve the optimization for communication under non-Gaussian channels.

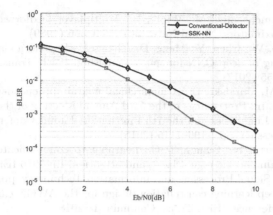

Fig. 4. $N_t = 4$ and $N_r = 1$. Complex Gaussian channels are considered. Trained at SNR = 7 dB with 5 dB radar noises.

4   Conclusion

In this paper, we propose an ene-to-end neural network implementation of SSK system. We develope an AE to design proper constellation points and the corresponding demodulation scheme is obtained simultaneously. The advantages in simulating non-linear functions of deep learning method is taken to overcome the non-Gaussian interference in communication scenarios. The results are analyzed and the comparison convinces that our model presents competitive performance with strong adaptability under non-Gaussian interference.

The lightweight network constructed in SSK system can be expanded to more complicated communication scenarios with more sophisticated network structure. We will continue to investigate for further applications.

References

1. Shafi, M., et al.: 5G: a tutorial overview of standards, trials, challenges, deployment, and practice. IEEE J. Sel. Areas Commun. **35**(6), 1201–1221 (2017)
2. He, L., Wang, J., Song, J.: Spatial modulation for more spatial multiplexing: RF-chain-limited generalized spatial modulation aided mmWave MIMO with hybrid pre-coding. IEEE Trans. Commun. **66**(3), 986–998 (2018)
3. Jaganathan, J., Ghrayeb, A., Szczecinski, L., Ceron, A.: Space shift keying modulation for MIMO channels. IEEE Trans. Wirel. Commun. **8**(7), 3692–3703 (2009)
4. Shahi, S., Tuninetti, D., Devroye, N.: On the capacity of the AWGN channel with additive radar interference. IEEE Trans. Commun. **66**(2), 629–643 (2018)
5. Ikki, S.-S., Mesleh, R.: A general framework for performance analysis of space shift keying (SSK) modulation in the presence of Gaussian imperfect estimation. IEEE Commun. Lett. **16**(2), 228–230 (2012)
6. Goodfellow, I., Bengio, Y., Courville, A.: Deep Learning. MIT Press, Cambridge (2016)

7. Horinik, K., Stinchcombe, M., White, H.: Multiplayer feedforward networks are universal approximators. Neural Netw. **2**(5), 359–366 (1989)
8. Zhang, K., Zuo, W., Chen, Y., Meng, D., Zhang, L.: Beyond a Gaussian denoiser: residual learning of deep CNN for image denoising. IEEE Trans. Image Process. **26**(7), 3142–3155 (2017)
9. Li, J., Luong, M., Jurafsky, D.: A hierarchical neural autoencoder for paragraphs and documents. In: Proceedings of the 53rd Annual Meeting of the Association for Computational Linguistics and the 7th International Joint Conference on Natural Language Processing, pp. 1106–1115 (2015)
10. O'Shea, T., Karra, K., Clancy, T.-C.: Learning to communicate: channel auto-encoders, domain specific regularizers, and attention. In: 2016 IEEE International Symposium on Signal Processing and Information Technology, pp. 223–228 (2016)
11. Alberge, F.: Deep learning constellation design for the AWGN channel with additive radar interference. IEEE Trans. Commun. 1 (2018)
12. He, H., Wen, C., Jin, S., Li, G.-Y.: Deep learning-based channel estimation for beamspace mmWave massive MIMO systems. IEEE Wirel. Commun. Lett. **7**(5), 852–855 (2018)
13. Gruber, T., Cammerer, S., Hoydis, J., Brink, S.-T.: On deep learning-based channel decoding. In: 2017 51st Annual Conference on Information Sciences and Systems, pp. 1–5 (2017)
14. Wen, C., Shih, W., Jin, S.: Deep learning for massive MIMO CSI feedback. IEEE Wirel. Commun. Lett. **7**(5), 748–751 (2018)
15. O'Shea, T., Hoydis, J.: An introduction to deep learning for the physical layer. IEEE Trans. Cogn. Commun. Netw. **3**(4), 563–575 (2017)
16. Kingma, D., Ba, J.: Adam: a method for stochastic optimization. arXiv preprint arXiv: 1412.6980 (2014)
17. Samuel, N., Diskin, T., Wiesel, A.: Deep MIMO detection. In: 2017 IEEE 18th International Workshop on Signal Processing Advances in Wireless Communications, pp. 1–5 (2017)

Non-orthogonal Multiple Access Enabled Power Allocation for Cooperative Jamming in Wireless Networks

Yuan Wu[1], Weicong Wu[2], Daohang Wang[2], Kejie Ni[2], Li Ping Qian[2,3(✉)], Weidang Lu[2], and Limin Meng[2]

[1] State Key Laboratory of Internet of Things for Smart City and Department of Computer and Information Science, University of Macau, Zhuhai, Macau SAR
[2] College of Information Engineering, Zhejiang University of Technology, Hangzhou 310023, China
lpqian@zjut.edu.cn
[3] National Mobile Communications Research Laboratory, Southeast University, Nanjing 210096, China

Abstract. In this work, we investigate the non-orthogonal multiple access (NOMA) enabled power allocation for cooperative jamming under a two-user downlink scenario. In particular, we consider that there exists a malicious eavesdropper overhearing the data transmission of the mobile user (MU) with a stronger channel power gain. Meanwhile, exploiting the simultaneous transmission in NOMA, we consider that the other MU with a weak channel power gain provides cooperative jamming to the eavesdropper for enhancing the secure throughput of the stronger MU. In particular, we formulate a power allocation problem to maximize the secure throughput of the strong MU while satisfying the throughput requirement of the weak MU. Despite the non-convexity of the formulated problem, we provide an efficient algorithm to compute the optimal solution (i.e., the power allocations for the two users). Numerical results are provided to validate the effectiveness of our proposed algorithm and the performance of our optimal power allocation scheme.

Keywords: Non-orthogonal multiple access · Cooperative jamming · Power allocation

1 Introduction

Non-orthogonal multiple access (NOMA), which allows mobile users (MUs) to simultaneously use a same frequency channel for data transmission and further adopts the principle of successive interference cancellation (SIC) to mitigate the MUs' co-channel interference, has been considered as one of the enabling technologies for the fifth generation (5G) cellular systems [1,2]. Compared with the conventional orthogonal multiple access (OMA), NOMA has been expected

S. Han et al. (Eds.): AICON 2019, LNICST 286, pp. 79–93, 2019.
https://doi.org/10.1007/978-3-030-22968-9_8

to significantly improve the spectrum efficiency and the system throughput, and thus has attracted lots of research efforts. Many studies have been devoted to analyzing the potential performance advantage of NOMA [3,4], and NOMA has been exploited for many potential applications, e.g., heterogeneous cellular systems and mobile data offloading [5,6]. In particular, the proper radio resource allocation plays a critical role to reap the benefits of NOMA, and thus has attracted lost of interests for different network paradigms [7–11].

In addition to the improvement on spectrum efficiency and throughput, the simultaneous data transmissions of different MUs over a same frequency channel can also yield an important benefit, namely, the cooperative jamming to encounter the overhearing of some potential eavesdropper. Specifically, let us consider that a downlink NOMA scenario in which the base station (BS) uses NOMA to simultaneously transmit to a group of MUs. There exists a malicious eavesdropper who intentionally overhears the transmission of a targeted MU. Thanks to NOMA, the BS's transmissions to other MUs provide the cooperative jamming to the eavesdropper, which thus improves the secrecy level of the targeted MU. In this work, we thus investigate this cooperative jamming provided by NOMA via proper power allocation. Our detailed contributions in this work can be summarized as follows.

- We consider a representative scenario in which the BS uses NOMA to send data to two different MUs, i.e., one MU with a strong channel power gain and the other with a weak channel power gain, and there exists a malicious eavesdropper who intentionally overhears the strong MU's data. Thanks to NOMA, the BS's transmission to the weak MU provides a cooperative jamming to the eavesdropper and thus helps enhance the secure throughput for the strong MU. To analytically study this problem, we formulate an optimal power allocation problem that aims at maximizing the strong MU's secure throughput while satisfying the throughput requirement of the weak MU and the total power capacity of the BS.
- We use the secrecy-outage probability based on the physical layer security [12,13] to quantify how secure it is for the strong MU's transmission. Despite the non-convexity of the formulated power allocation problem, we identify the monotonic property via a vertical decomposition and thus propose an efficient layered-algorithm to compute the optimal solution. To further reduce the complexity, we exploit the hidden unimodal property with the respective to the secrecy-outage level and propose a low-complexity to compute the solution.
- We provide extensive numerical results to validate the effectiveness of our proposed algorithm and the performance advantage of the optimal cooperative jamming in enhancing the user's secure throughput.

The remainder of this paper is organized as follows. In Sect. 2, we present the system model and problem formulation. We focus on analyzing the most general case of the formulated problem in Sect. 3 and propose an efficient algorithm to compute the optimal solution. Numerical results are provided in Sect. 4, and conclusions are given in Sect. 5.

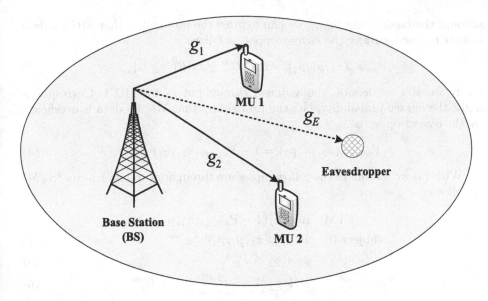

Fig. 1. System model

2   System Model and Problem Formulation

2.1   System Model and Formulation

We consider a two-user downlink NOMA scenario as shown in Fig. 1, in which the BS uses NOMA to simultaneously send data to two MUs. We use g_1, g_2, and g_E to denote the channel power gains from the BS to MU 1, MU 2, and the eavesdropper, respectively. For the sake of easy presentation, we assume that $g_1 \geq g_2$, meaning that MU 1 has a stronger downlink channel power gain than MU 2. Meanwhile, there exists a malicious eavesdropper who intentionally overhears the BS's data transmission to MU 1 (i.e., the strong user). Exploiting NOMA, the transmission to MU 2 provides a cooperative jamming to the eavesdropper for enhancing the security of MU 1's transmission. Let p_1 and p_2 denote the BS's transmit-powers to MU 1 and MU 2, respectively. Thus, based on the physical layer security [12,13], the secure throughput from the BS to MU 1 can be given as

$$R_1^{\text{sec}} = \left[W \log_2(1 + \frac{p_1 g_1}{n_1}) - W \log_2(1 + \frac{p_1 g_E}{n_E + p_2 g_E}) \right]^+, \qquad (1)$$

in which W denotes the channel bandwidth, n_1 and n_E denote the power of the background noise, respectively. Here, function $[x]^+$ denotes $\max(x, 0)$. In particular, the accurate value of g_E may not be available, since the eavesdropper may intentionally hide its location information. Thus, similar to [13], we assume that g_E follows an exponential distribution with the mean equal θ. Taking into account the randomness in g_E, we can express the probability that MU 1's data cannot be overheard by the eavesdropper as follows

$$P_{\text{secure}}(x_1, p_1, p_2) = \Pr\{R_1^{\text{sec}} \geq x_1 | R_1^{\text{sec}} \geq 0\}, \tag{2}$$

where variable x_1 denotes the assigned throughput x_1 for MU 1. Correspondingly, the outage probability, i.e., the probability that MU 1's data is overheard by the eavesdropper is

$$P_{\text{outage}}(x_1, p_1, p_2) = 1 - P_{\text{secure}}(x_1, p_1, p_2). \tag{3}$$

With (3) we formulate the following secure throughput maximization (STM) as follows.

$$(\text{STM}) \quad \max x_1 \left(1 - P_{\text{outage}}(x_1, p_1, p_2)\right)$$

$$\text{subject to:} \quad P_{\text{outage}}(x_1, p_1, p_2) \leq \epsilon^{\max}, \tag{4}$$

$$p_1 + p_2 \leq P_B^{\text{tot}}, \tag{5}$$

$$W \log_2 \left(1 + \frac{p_2 g_2}{p_1 g_2 + n_2}\right) \geq R_2^{\text{req}}, \tag{6}$$

$$\text{variables:} \quad x_1, p_1, \text{ and } p_2.$$

In Problem (STM), the objective function denotes MU 1's secure throughput. Constraint (4) limits the secure-outage probability for MU 1's transmission no greater than the required secrecy-requirement $\epsilon^{\max}$. Constraint (5) means that the BS's total power consumption for both MUs cannot exceed the budget of P_B^{tot}, and finally, constraint (6) means that MU 2 can reach its throughput requirement R_2^{req}.

2.2   Analysis of the Secrecy-Outage Probability

To solve Problem (STM), we firstly derive the analytical expression of $P_{\text{outage}}(x_1, p_1, p_2)$ as follows.

Proposition 1. *The analytical expression of the outage probability* $P_{\text{outage}}(x_1, p_1, p_2)$ *can be given in the following four cases:*

- *(Case-I) when* $x_1 > W \log_2(1 + \frac{p_1 g_1}{n_1})$, *then we have*

$$P_{\text{outage}}(x_1, p_1, p_2) = 1. \tag{7}$$

- *(Case-II) when* $W \log_2(1 + \frac{p_1 g_1}{n_1}) \geq x_1 \geq W \log_2(1 + \frac{p_1 g_1}{n_1}) - W \log_2(1 + \frac{p_1}{p_2})$ *and* $p_2 \geq \frac{n_1}{g_1}$, *then we have*

$$P_{\text{outage}}(x_1, p_1, p_2) = e^{-\frac{1}{\theta}M}, \tag{8}$$

where parameter M *is given by:*

$$M = \frac{n_E}{p_1} \frac{1}{\frac{1}{(1 + \frac{p_1 g_1}{n_1}) 2^{-\frac{x_1}{W}} - 1} - \frac{p_2}{p_1}}. \tag{9}$$

- *(Case-III)* when $W \log_2(1 + \frac{p_1 g_1}{n_1}) - W \log_2(1 + \frac{p_1}{p_2}) \geq x_1$ and $p_2 \geq \frac{n_1}{g_1}$, we have

$$P_{outage}(x_1, p_1, p_2) = 0. \tag{10}$$

- *(Case-IV)* when $W \log_2(1 + \frac{p_1 g_1}{n_1}) \geq x_1 \geq W \log_2(1 + \frac{p_1 g_1}{n_1}) - W \log_2(1 + \frac{p_1}{p_2})$ and $p_2 < \frac{n_1}{g_1}$, then we have

$$P_{outage}(x_1, p_1, p_2) = \frac{e^{-\frac{1}{\theta}M} - e^{-\frac{1}{\theta}\frac{g_1 n_E}{n_1 - g_1 p_2}}}{1 - e^{-\frac{1}{\theta}\frac{g_1 n_E}{n_1 - g_1 p_2}}}, \tag{11}$$

with parameter M given in (9) before.

Proof. Based on (2), we have

$$P_{secure}(x_1, p_1, p_2) = \frac{\Pr\{R_1^{sec} \geq x_1\}}{\Pr\{R_1^{sec} \geq 0\}}. \tag{12}$$

In particular, based on (1), we can derive $\Pr\{R_1^{sec} \geq 0\}$ as

$$\Pr\{R_1^{sec} \geq 0\} = \begin{cases} 1, & \text{when } p_2 \geq \frac{n_1}{g_1} \\ 1 - e^{-\frac{1}{\theta}\frac{g_1 n_E}{n_1 - g_1 p_2}}, & \text{when } p_2 < \frac{n_1}{g_1} \end{cases} \tag{13}$$

In particular, (13) is consistent with the intuition, namely, R_1^{sec} is always positive when p_2 is sufficiently large (i.e., MU 2 provides a sufficiently large jamming to the eavesdropper).

To derive $\Pr\{R_1^{sec} \geq x_1\}$ (with $x_1 \geq 0$), we consider:

$$W \log_2(1 + \frac{p_1 g_1}{n_1}) - W \log_2(1 + \frac{p_1 g_E}{n_E + p_2 g_E}) \geq x_1$$

$$\Longleftrightarrow \frac{n_1 + p_1 g_1}{n_1} 2^{-\frac{x_1}{W}} - 1 \geq \frac{p_1 g_E}{n_E + p_2 g_E} \tag{14}$$

$$\Longleftrightarrow \frac{n_E}{p_1 g_E} \geq \frac{1}{(1 + \frac{p_1 g_1}{n_1}) 2^{-\frac{x_1}{W}} - 1} - \frac{p_2}{p_1} \tag{15}$$

Notice that the equivalence between (14) and (15) requires $x_1 \leq W \log_2(1 + \frac{p_1 g_1}{n_1})$. Otherwise (i.e., $x_1 > W \log_2(1 + \frac{p_1 g_1}{n_1})$), there always exists $\Pr\{R_1^{sec} \geq x_1\} = 0$ according to (1), which leads to Case-I in Proposition 1.

In the next, we consider $x_1 \leq W \log_2(1 + \frac{p_1 g_1}{n_1})$ for Case-II, Case-III, and Case-IV.

In particular, let us first consider the case that $p_2 \geq \frac{n_1}{g_1}$ (i.e., the case of $\Pr\{R_1^{sec} \geq 0\} = 1$ in Eq. (13)). Then, we have

$$\Pr\{R_1^{sec} \geq x_1\} = 1 \text{ when } p_2 \geq \frac{n_1}{g_1} \text{ and}$$

$$x_1 \leq W \log_2(1 + \frac{p_1 g_1}{n_1}) - W \log_2(1 + \frac{p_1}{p_2}). \tag{16}$$

As a result, we have $P_{outage}(x_1, p_1, p_2) = 0$, which corresponds to Case-III in Proposition 1.

In addition, we have

$$\Pr\{R_1^{sec} \geq x_1\} = \Pr\{g_E \leq M\} \text{ when } p_2 \geq \frac{n_1}{g_1},$$

and

$$W \log_2(1 + \frac{p_1 g_1}{n_1}) \geq x_1 \geq W \log_2(1 + \frac{p_1 g_1}{n_1}) - W \log_2(1 + \frac{p_1}{p_2}),$$

where parameter M is given in Eq. (9) (notice that M can be derived from (15)). As a result, we have

$$P_{outage}(x_1, p_1, p_2) = e^{-\frac{1}{\theta}M}, \tag{17}$$

which corresponds to Case-II in Proposition 1.

Finally, when $p_2 < \frac{n_1}{g_1}$, i.e., the case of $\Pr\{R_1^{sec} \geq 0\} = 1 - e^{-\frac{1}{\theta}\frac{g_1 n_E}{n_1 - g_1 p_2}}$ in Eq. (13), then we again have

$$\Pr\{R_1^{sec} \geq x_1\} = \Pr\{g_E \leq M\} \text{ when } p_2 < \frac{n_1}{g_1},$$

and

$$W \log_2(1 + \frac{p_1 g_1}{n_1}) \geq x_1 \geq W \log_2(1 + \frac{p_1 g_1}{n_1}) - W \log_2(1 + \frac{p_1}{p_2}).$$

As a result, we have

$$P_{outage}(x_1, p_1, p_2) = \frac{e^{-\frac{1}{\theta}M} - e^{-\frac{1}{\theta}\frac{g_1 n_E}{n_1 - g_1 p_2}}}{1 - e^{-\frac{1}{\theta}\frac{g_1 n_E}{n_1 - g_1 p_2}}} \tag{18}$$

which corresponds to Case-IV in Proposition 1. Notice that based on (9), there always exists $M < \frac{g_1 n_E}{n_1 - g_1 p_2}$.

We thus finish the proof of Proposition 1.

To solve Problem (STM), we need to consider the above four cases given in Proposition 1, and the maximum secure throughput V^* of Problem (STM) can be given as:

$$V^* = \max\{V^{I*}, V^{II*}, V^{III*}, V^{IV*}\}, \tag{19}$$

where $V^{I*}, V^{II*}, V^{III*}$, and V^{IV*} denote MU 1's maximum secure throughput under Case-I, Case-II, Case-III, and Case-IV, respectively. It is noticed that Case-I is a trivial case since $V^{I*} = 0$. In the following, due to the limited space in the paper, we focus on solving Problem (STM) under the most difficult case, i.e., Case-IV. The other two cases, i.e., Case-II and Case-III, can solved in a similar manner.

3   Optimization Problem Under Case IV

In this section, we focus on solving Problem (STM) under Case-IV. We introduce an auxiliary variable ϵ which denotes the secrecy-outage probability of MU 1, i.e.,

$$\epsilon = \frac{e^{-\frac{1}{\theta}M} - e^{-\frac{1}{\theta}\frac{g_1 n_E}{n_1 - g_1 p_2}}}{1 - e^{-\frac{1}{\theta}\frac{g_1 n_E}{n_1 - g_1 p_2}}} \tag{20}$$

according to (11).

Thus, based on (20), we can derive the following secrecy-based throughput for MU 1:

$$\hat{x}_1^{IV}(\epsilon, p_1, p_2) = W \log_2(1 + \frac{p_1 g_1}{n_1}) - W \log_2(1 + \frac{p_1 z_{(\epsilon, p_2)}}{n_E + p_2 z_{(\epsilon, p_2)}}), \tag{21}$$

where parameter $z_{(\epsilon, p_2)}$ is given by:

$$z_{(\epsilon, p_2)} = -\theta \ln \left(\epsilon + (1 - \epsilon)e^{-\frac{1}{\theta}\frac{g_1 n_E}{n_1 - g_1 p_2}} \right). \tag{22}$$

Notice that $z_{(\epsilon, p_2)}$ is always positive, since $p_2 \leq \frac{n_1}{g_1}$ holds in Case-IV. The secrecy-based throughput $\hat{x}_1^{IV}(\epsilon, p_1, p_2)$ can be treated as the maximum throughput of MU 1, under the given transmit-powers (p_1, p_2) as well as the given level of the secrecy-outage ϵ.

An observation on $\hat{x}_1^{IV}(\epsilon, p_1, p_2)$ is as follows.

Lemma 1. *There always exists*

$$\hat{x}_1^{IV}(\epsilon, p_1, p_2) > W \log_2(1 + \frac{p_1 g_1}{n_1}) - W \log_2(1 + \frac{p_1}{p_2}),$$

meaning that $\hat{x}_1^{IV}(\epsilon, p_1, p_2)$ is compatible with the conditions of Case- IV in Proposition 1.

Proof. Based on (21), we can analytically express $\hat{x}_1^{IV}(\epsilon, p_1, p_2)$ as follows:

$$\begin{aligned}
\hat{x}_1^{IV}(\epsilon, p_1, p_2) &= W \log_2(1 + \frac{p_1 g_1}{n_1}) - W \log_2(1 + \frac{p_1 z_{(\epsilon, p_2)}}{n_E + p_2 z_{(\epsilon, p_2)}}) \\
&> W \log_2(1 + \frac{p_1 g_1}{n_1}) - W \log_2(1 + \frac{p_1}{p_2}).
\end{aligned}$$

We thus finish the proof of Lemma 1.

Based on Lemma 1, we can obtain the equivalent form of Problem (STM) under Case-IV as follows:

$$\begin{aligned}
\text{(STM-E-IV):} \quad &\max \hat{x}_1^{IV}(\epsilon, p_1, p_2)(1 - \epsilon) \\
\text{subject to:} \quad &p_2 \leq \frac{n_1}{g_1}, \tag{23} \\
&0 \leq \epsilon \leq \epsilon^{\max}, \tag{24} \\
&\text{constraints } (5), (6), \text{ and } (21). \\
\text{variables:} \quad &p_1, p_2, \text{ and } \epsilon.
\end{aligned}$$

Notice that constraint (23) comes from the condition of Case-IV. However, directly solving Problem (STM-E-IV) is still difficult since Problem (STM-E-IV) is a non-convex optimization problem [14].

To tackle with this difficulty, we exploit a vertical decomposition as follows. Suppose that the values of (p_2, ϵ) are given in advance. We firstly aim at finding the corresponding optimal p_1 (as a response to (p_2, ϵ)), which corresponds to solving the following optimization problem:

$$(\text{STM-E-IV-Sub}) \quad V_{(p_2,\epsilon)}^{\text{IV-Sub}} = \max \frac{n_1(n_E + p_2 z_{(\epsilon,p_2)}) + p_1 g_1(n_E + p_2 z_{(\epsilon,p_2)})}{n_1(n_E + p_2 z_{(\epsilon,p_2)}) + p_1 n_1 z_{(\epsilon,p_2)}}$$

$$\text{variable: } 0 \leq p_1 \leq \min \left\{ p_2(2^{\frac{R_2^{\text{req}}}{W}} - 1)^{-1} - \frac{n_2}{g_2}, P_B^{\text{tot}} - p_2 \right\}. \qquad (25)$$

In particular, we can analytically solve Problem (STM-E-IV-Sub) based on the following result.

Proposition 2. *Given (p_2, ϵ), the optimal solution of Problem (STM-E-IV-Sub) can be analytically given by:*

$$p_{1,(p_2)}^{IV*} = \begin{cases} p_2(2^{\frac{R_2^{\text{req}}}{W}} - 1)^{-1} - \frac{n_2}{g_2}, & \text{if } p_2 \leq p_2^{IV,Tr} \\ P_B^{\text{tot}} - p_2, & \text{else} \end{cases} \qquad (26)$$

where $p_2^{IV,Tr} = \frac{2^{\frac{R_2^{\text{req}}}{W}} - 1}{2^{\frac{R_2^{\text{req}}}{W}}}(P_B^{\text{tot}} + \frac{n_2}{g_2})$, *if the following condition holds:*

$$\frac{n_1(n_E + p_2 z_{(\epsilon,p_2)}) + p_{1,(p_2)}^{IV*} g_1(n_E + p_2 z_{(\epsilon,p_2)})}{n_1(n_E + p_2 z_{(\epsilon,p_2)}) + p_{1,(p_2)}^{IV*} n_1 z_{(\epsilon,p_2)}} > 1. \qquad (27)$$

Otherwise (namely, (27) does not hold), then Problem (STM-E-IV-Sub) is infeasible.

Proof. The key of the proof is to show that the first order derivative of the objective function of Problem (STM-E-IV-Sub) is increasing in p_1. Therefore, for the sake of clear presentation, we introduce the following three auxiliary parameters:

$$A = n_1(n_E + p_2 z_{(\epsilon,p_2)}), \qquad (28)$$

$$B = g_1(n_E + p_2 z_{(\epsilon,p_2)}), \qquad (29)$$

$$C = n_1 z_{(\epsilon,p_2)}. \qquad (30)$$

With the above defined A, B, and C, we can derive

$$\frac{d}{dp_1}\left(\frac{A + Bp_1}{A + Cp_1}\right) = \frac{A(B - C)}{(A + Cp_1)^2}. \qquad (31)$$

We next focus on proving that $B > C$, namely, $g_1(n_E + p_2 z_{(\epsilon,p_2)}) > n_1 z_{(\epsilon,p_2)}$ always holds. The details are as follows. Based on (22) and $p_2 < \frac{n_1}{g_1}$, we can make the following derivations:

$$g_1(n_E + p_2 z_{(\epsilon,p_2)}) > n_1 z_{(\epsilon,p_2)}$$

$$\Longleftrightarrow \frac{g_1 n_E}{n_1 - g_1 p_2} \geq z_{(\epsilon,p_2)} = -\theta \ln\left(\epsilon + (1-\epsilon)e^{-\frac{1}{\theta}\frac{g_1 n_E}{n_1 - g_1 p_2}}\right)$$

$$\Longleftrightarrow e^{-\frac{1}{\theta}\frac{g_1 n_E}{n_1 - g_1 p_2}} \leq \epsilon + (1-\epsilon)e^{-\frac{1}{\theta}\frac{g_1 n_E}{n_1 - g_1 p_2}}$$

$$\Longleftrightarrow e^{-\frac{1}{\theta}\frac{g_1 n_E}{n_1 - g_1 p_2}} \leq e^{-\frac{1}{\theta}\frac{g_1 n_E}{n_1 - g_1 p_2}} + (1 - e^{-\frac{1}{\theta}\frac{g_1 n_E}{n_1 - g_1 p_2}})\epsilon.$$

With $p_2 < \frac{n_1}{g_1}$, we have $e^{-\frac{1}{\theta}\frac{g_1 n_E}{n_1 - g_1 p_2}} < 1$, meaning that the above inequality always holds. As a result, $B > C$ always holds, which finishes the proof. Since the objective function of Problem (STM-E-IV-Sub) is increasing in p_1, it gives us the optimal solution in (26). Meanwhile, condition 27 is used to guarantee that $\hat{x}_1^{IV}(\epsilon, p_{1,(p_2)}^{IV*}, p_2) \geq 0$.

As a result, we can analytically express $V_{(p_2,\epsilon)}^{IV\text{-Sub}}$ as follows:

$$V_{(p_2,\epsilon)}^{IV\text{-Sub}} = \frac{n_1(n_E + p_2 z_{(\epsilon,p_2)}) + p_{1,(p_2)}^{IV*} g_1(n_E + p_2 z_{(\epsilon,p_2)})}{n_1(n_E + p_2 z_{(\epsilon,p_2)}) + p_{1,(p_2)}^{IV*} n_1 z_{(\epsilon,p_2)}}. \tag{32}$$

3.1 Proposed Algorithm to Find the Optimal (p_2, ϵ)

Based on (32), we then continue to find the optimal (p_2, ϵ), which corresponds to solving the following problem:

$$\begin{aligned}
\text{(STM-E-IV-Top):} \quad &\max (1-\epsilon)W \log_2\left(V_{(p_2,\epsilon)}^{IV\text{-Sub}}\right) \\
\text{subject to:} \quad &0 \leq p_2 \leq \min\{P_B^{tot}, \tfrac{n_1}{g_1}\}, \\
\text{constraints:} \quad &(32) \text{ and } (24), \\
\text{variables:} \quad &(p_2, \epsilon).
\end{aligned}$$

An important observation of Problem (STM-E-IV-Top) is that p_2 falls within a fixed interval $p_2 \in [0, \min\{P_B^{tot}, \frac{n_1}{g_1}\}]$, and ϵ falls within a fixed interval $\epsilon \in [0, \epsilon^{max}]$. Therefore, to solve Problem (STM-E-IV-Top), we can perform a two-dimensional linear-search (2DLS) on (p_2, ϵ) within $[0, \min\{P_B^{tot}, \frac{n_1}{g_1}\}] \times [0, \epsilon^{max}]$ (with small step-sizes Δ_ϵ and Δ_p). The details are shown in the following 2DLS-Algorithm. Notice that the overall complexity in solving Problem (STM) under Case-IV is just $\frac{\epsilon^{max}}{\Delta_\epsilon} \frac{\min\{P_B^{tot}, \frac{n_1}{g_1}\}}{\Delta_p}$.

Let $(p_2^{IV*}, \epsilon^{IV*})$ denote the output of our 2DLS-Algorithm. Then, we have $p_1^{IV*} = p_{1,(p_2^{IV*})}^{IV*}$ (according to (26)), and $x_1^{IV*} = \hat{x}_1^{IV}(\epsilon^{IV*}, p_1^{IV*}, p_2^{IV*})$ (according to (21)). Thus, the maximum secure throughput of MU 1 under Case-IV is $V^{IV*} = x_1^{IV*}(1 - \epsilon^{IV*})$.

Sub-Algorithm: to solve top-problem (STM-E-IV-Sub) and find ($V^{IV\text{-}Sub}_{(p_2^{cur},\epsilon^{cur})}$)

1: **Input:** p_2^{cur} and ϵ^{cur}.
2: Set $p^{IV*}_{1,(p_2^{cur})}$ according to (26).
3: **if** constraint(27) holds **then**
4:     Set $V^{IV\text{-}Sub}_{(p_2^{cur},\epsilon^{cur})}$ according to (32).
5: **else**
6:     Set $V^{IV\text{-}Sub}_{(p_2^{cur},\epsilon^{cur})} = 1$.
7: **end if**
8: **Output:** $V^{IV\text{-}Sub}_{(p_2^{cur},\epsilon^{cur})}$ and $(1 - \epsilon^{cur})W \log_2 \left(V^{IV\text{-}Sub}_{(p_2^{cur},\epsilon^{cur})} \right)$.

2DLS-Algorithm: to solve top-problem (STM-E-IV-Top) and output V^{IV*} and the corresponding ($p_2^{IV*}, \epsilon^{IV*}$)

1: **Initialization:** Set step-size Δ_ϵ and Δ_p as a small number. Set CBV $= 0$ and CBS $= \emptyset$.
2: Set $p_2^{cur} = \Delta_p$, $\epsilon^{cur} = \Delta_\epsilon$.
3: **while** $p_2^{cur} \leq \min\{P_B^{tot}, \frac{n_1}{g_1}\}$ **do**
4:     **while** $\epsilon^{cur} \leq \epsilon^{max}$ **do**
5:         Use Sub-Algorithm to compute $V^{IV\text{-}Sub}_{(p_2^{cur},\epsilon^{cur})}$.
6:         **if** $(1 - \epsilon^{cur})W \log_2 \left(V^{IV\text{-}Sub}_{(p_2^{cur},\epsilon^{cur})} \right) >$ CBV **then**
7:             Set CBV $= (1 - \epsilon^{cur})W \log_2 \left(V^{IV\text{-}Sub}_{(p_2^{cur},\epsilon^{cur})} \right)$.
8:             Set CBS $= (p_2^{cur}, \epsilon^{cur})$.
9:         **end if**
10:         Update $\epsilon^{cur} = \epsilon^{cur} + \Delta_\epsilon$.
11:     **end while**
12:     Update $p_2^{cur} = p_2^{cur} + \Delta_p$.
13: **end while**
14: **Output:** $V^{IV*} =$ CBV and $(p_2^{IV*}, \epsilon^{IV*}) =$ CBS.

3.2   A Low-Complexity Algorithm Based on the Brent's Method

To further reduce the complexity of 2DLS-Algorithm, we identify the following property. Specifically, support that the value of p_2 is given in advance, we enumerate $\epsilon \in [0, \epsilon^{max}]$ with a small step-size Δ_ϵ. The corresponding results are shown in Fig. 2 below. Notice that for each given (p_2, ϵ), we can use (26) to compute $p^{IV*}_{1,(p_2)}$ and obtain the corresponding secure throughput $(1 - \epsilon)W \log_2 \left(V^{IV\text{-}Sub}_{(p_2,\epsilon)} \right)$. Specifically, the left subplot shows the case when $p^{IV*}_{1,(p_2)} = p_2(2^{\frac{R_2^{req}}{W}} - 1)^{-1} - \frac{n_2}{g_2}$, and the right subplot shows the case when $p^{IV*}_{1,(p_2)} = P_B^{tot} - p_2$.

As shown in both subplots, with the respectively given p_2, the secure throughput is always unimodal in ϵ. Such a phenomenon is consistent with the intuition, namely, neither a too large ϵ nor a too small ϵ will be beneficial to the secure throughput. A too large ϵ (meaning a too weak secrecy-level) will directly reduce the secure throughput. In comparison, a too small ϵ (meaning a too strict secrecy-level) will require larger a larger power consumption, which consequently limits the secure throughput due to (5). Thanks to this hidden unimodal property, we can use the Brent's method [15] to find ϵ^* under given p_2. The Brent's method is a numerical algorithm that jointly exploits the golden-section search and the parabolic interpolation, with the objective of efficiently finding the optimum of a single-variable function. In particular, for the unimodal function [15], the Brent's method is guaranteed to find its global optimum within a given interval. Due to the limited space in this paper, we skip the detailed operations of the Brent's method here. Interested readers can refer to [15] for the details. In particular, we emphasize within each round of the iteration in this Brent's method, we need to Sub-Algorithm to compute the value of $V^{\text{IV-Sub}}_{(p_2^{\text{cur}},\epsilon)}$ under the given ϵ (which is being currently evaluated in the Brent's method) as well as the given p_2^{cur}. Therefore, based on the output of the Brent's, we can further execute a linear-search of $p_2 \in [0, \min\{P_B^{\text{tot}}, \frac{n_1}{g_1}\}]$, which leads to the proposed LSBM-Algorithm. Here, "LSBM" means linear-search and the Brent's method.

Although it is technically challenging to prove the unimodal property of the secure throughput of MU 1 with respect to ϵ, our following numerical results in Tables 1 and 2 show that our proposed LSBM-Algorithm can achieve the result almost same (with a negligible relative error) as our 2DLS-Algorithm. In the meantime, thanks to exploiting the Brent's method, LSBM-Algorithm can significantly reduce the computational time compared with 2DLS-Algorithm.

LSBM-Algorithm: to solve top-problem (STM-E-IV-Top) and find $(p_2^{\text{IV}*}, \epsilon^{\text{IV}*})$

1: **Initialization:** Set step-size Δ_p as a small number. Set CBV $= 0$.
2: Set $p_2^{\text{cur}} = \Delta_p$.
3: **while** $p_2^{\text{cur}} \leq \min\{P_B^{\text{tot}}, \frac{n_1}{g_1}\}$ **do**
4:    Use the Brent's method to compute $V^{\text{IV-Sub}}_{(p_2^{\text{cur}},\epsilon^{\text{cur}})}$ and ϵ^{cur}.
5:    **if** $(1 - \epsilon^{\text{cur}})W \log_2\left(V^{\text{IV-Sub}}_{(p_2^{\text{cur}},\epsilon^{\text{cur}})}\right) > $ CBV **then**
6:       Set CBV $= (1 - \epsilon^{\text{cur}})W \log_2\left(V^{\text{IV-Sub}}_{(p_2^{\text{cur}},\epsilon^{\text{cur}})}\right)$ and $(p_2^*, \epsilon^*) = (p_2^{\text{cur}}, \epsilon^{\text{cur}})$.
7:    **end if**
8:    Update $p_2^{\text{cur}} = p_2^{\text{cur}} + \Delta_p$.
9: **end while**
10: **Output:** $V^{\text{IV}*} = $ CBV and $(p_2^{\text{IV}*}, \epsilon^{\text{IV}*})$.

---

4   Numerical Results

We present the numerical results in this section. Figure 2 validates the unimodal property of the secure throughput in ϵ under the given p_2. Specifically, the left subplot shows the case when $p_2 \leq p_2^{\text{IV,Tr}}$, which leads to $p_{1,(p_2)}^{\text{IV}*} = p_2(2^{\frac{R_2^{\text{req}}}{W}} - 1)^{-1} - \frac{n_2}{g_2}$, The right subplot shows the case when $p_2 > p_2^{\text{IV,Tr}}$, which

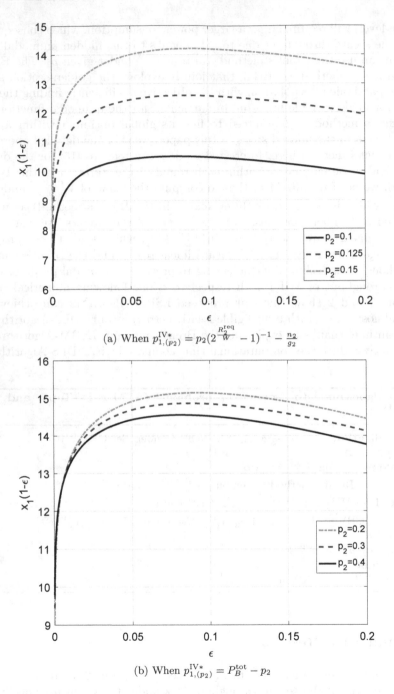

(a) When $p_{1,(p_2)}^{\mathrm{IV}*} = p_2(2^{\frac{R_2^{\mathrm{req}}}{W}} - 1)^{-1} - \frac{n_2}{g_2}$

(b) When $p_{1,(p_2)}^{\mathrm{IV}*} = P_B^{\mathrm{tot}} - p_2$

Fig. 2. Illustration of hidden unimodal property of the secure throughput in ϵ under the given p_2. We set $W = 10\mathrm{MHz}$, $P_B^{\mathrm{tot}} = 2\mathrm{W}$, $R_2^{\mathrm{req}} = 1\mathrm{Mbits}$, $n_1 = 1*10^{-6}$, $n_2 = 1*10^{-6}$, $n_E = 1*10^{-6}$, $\theta = 1*10^{-7}$, and $\epsilon^{\max} = 0.2$. In addition, the randomly generated channel power gains from the BS to the two MUs are $\{g_i\} = \{1.9330 * 10^{-6}, 1.9047 * 10^{-6}\}$.

thus leads to $p_{1,(p_2)}^{\mathrm{IV}*} = P_B^{\mathrm{tot}} - p_2$. As explained before in Sect. 3.2, when we enumerate ϵ, the corresponding MU 1's secure throughput (under different given p_2) always increases firstly and then gradually decreases, i.e., showing the unimodal property.

Tables 1 and 2 show the performance comparison between our proposed 2DLS-Algorithm and LSBM-Algorithm. In particular, the results show that LSBM-Algorithm can achieve approximately the same result as 2DLS-Algorithm($\Delta_p = 0.001, \Delta_\epsilon = 0.001$), while consuming a significantly less computation time. Such an advantage essentially stems from that we exploit the unimodal property of the secure throughput with respect to ϵ, which thus saves the operation of the linear-search in ϵ.

Table 1. 2-MU Scenario: We fix $W_i = 10\,\mathrm{MHz}$, and $\epsilon^{\mathrm{max}} = 0.2$

With $\theta = 1*10^{-7}$	$P_B^{\mathrm{tot}} = 1\,\mathrm{W}$	$P_B^{\mathrm{tot}} = 3\,\mathrm{W}$	$P_B^{\mathrm{tot}} = 5\,\mathrm{W}$	$P_B^{\mathrm{tot}} = 7\,\mathrm{W}$	$P_B^{\mathrm{tot}} = 9\,\mathrm{W}$	Ave. error
2DLS-Algorithm	10.7024, 2.6259 s	17.8531, 2.3464 s	20.9709, 2.1135 s	22.8431, 2.1369 s	22.9778, 2.0802 s	0.0023%
LSBM-Algorithm	10.7026, 0.1833 s	17.8535, 0.1717 s	20.9711, 0.1585 s	22.8436, 0.2006 s	22.9788, 0.2287 s	
With $\theta = 2*10^{-7}$	$P_B^{\mathrm{tot}} = 1\,\mathrm{W}$	$P_B^{\mathrm{tot}} = 3\,\mathrm{W}$	$P_B^{\mathrm{tot}} = 5\,\mathrm{W}$	$P_B^{\mathrm{tot}} = 7\,\mathrm{W}$	$P_B^{\mathrm{tot}} = 9\,\mathrm{W}$	Ave. error
2DLS-Algorithm	8.8601, 2.4043 s	14.4397, 2.4194 s	16.9766, 2.4750 s	18.2725, 2.3883 s	18.3641, 2.4481 s	0.0021%
LSBM-Algorithm	8.8603, 0.2390 s	14.4404, 0.2243 s	16.9768, 0.2878 s	18.2727, 0.2250 s	18.3643, 0.2086 s	

Table 2. 2-MU Scenario: We fix $W_i = 16\,\mathrm{MHz}$, and $\epsilon^{\mathrm{max}} = 0.2$

With $\theta = 1*10^{-7}$	$P_B^{\mathrm{tot}} = 1\,\mathrm{W}$	$P_B^{\mathrm{tot}} = 3\,\mathrm{W}$	$P_B^{\mathrm{tot}} = 5\,\mathrm{W}$	$P_B^{\mathrm{tot}} = 7\,\mathrm{W}$	$P_B^{\mathrm{tot}} = 9\,\mathrm{W}$	Ave. error
2DLS-Algorithm	17.4824, 1.9048 s	28.7146, 2.0574 s	33.5533, 1.9295 s	36.5498, 2.1404 s	38.4497, 2.2434 s	0.0017%
LSBM-Algorithm	17.4827, 0.1969 s	28.7152, 0.1781 s	33.5538, 0.1757 s	36.5503, 0.1983 s	38.4501, 0.2026 s	
With $\theta = 2*10^{-7}$	$P_B^{\mathrm{tot}} = 1\,\mathrm{W}$	$P_B^{\mathrm{tot}} = 3\,\mathrm{W}$	$P_B^{\mathrm{tot}} = 5\,\mathrm{W}$	$P_B^{\mathrm{tot}} = 7\,\mathrm{W}$	$P_B^{\mathrm{tot}} = 9\,\mathrm{W}$	Ave. error
2DLS-Algorithm	14.4187, 2.3016 s	23.1039, 2.4512 s	27.1639, 2.5397 s	29.2377, 2.5824 s	30.5101, 2.5057 s	0.0014%
LSBM-Algorithm	14.4191, 0.2444 s	23.1046, 0.2471 s	27.1640, 0.2482 s	29.2380, 0.2811 s	30.5101, 0.2683 s	

Figure 3 shows the impact of MU 2's throughput requirement R_2^{req}. We set $W = 10\mathrm{MHz}$, $n_1 = 1*10^{-6}$, $n_2 = 1*10^{-6}$, $n_E = 1*10^{-6}$, $\theta = 1*10^{-7}$, and $\epsilon^{\mathrm{max}} = 0.2$. In addition, the randomly generated channel power gains from the BS to the two MUs are $\{g_i\} = \{1.9330*10^{-6}, 1.9047*10^{-6}\}$. As shown in Fig. 3, the MU 1's maximum secure throughput gradually decreases when R_2^{req} increases, which is consistent with the intuition. Corresponding, the corresponding ϵ^* gradually decreases, meaning that a stronger secrecy-level is provided to avoid a significant loss in the secure throughput.

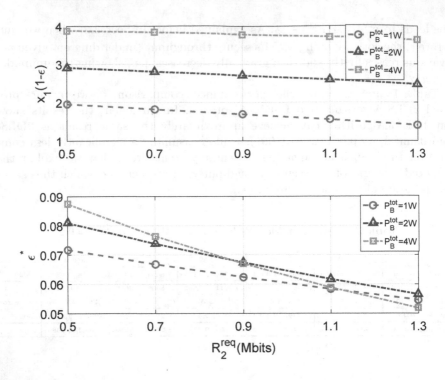

Fig. 3. Impact of MU 2's throughput requirement R_2^{req}.

5 Conclusion

In this paper, we have investigated the optimal power allocation for cooperative jamming in NOMA systems under a two-user downlink scenario. Specifically, exploiting the two MUs' simultaneous transmissions in NOMA, we use the BS's transmission to MU 2 (i.e., the MU with a weak channel power gain) to provide a jamming to the eavesdropper who intentionally overhears the BS's transmission to MU 1 (i.e., the MU with a strong channel power gain). To study this cooperative jamming, we have formulated a power allocation problem to maximize the secure throughput of MU 1 while satisfying the throughput requirement of MU 2. Despite the non-convexity of the above formulated problem, we have provided two efficient algorithms to compute the optimal solution. In addition, Numerical results have been provided to validate the effectiveness of our proposed algorithms and the performance of our proposed cooperative jamming scheme in NOMA.

Acknowledgement. This work was supported in part by the National Natural Science Foundation of China under Grant 61572440, in part by the Zhejiang Provincial Natural Science Foundation of China under Grants LR17F010002 and LR16F010003, and in part by the open research fund of National Mobile Communications Research Laboratory, Southeast University (No. 2019D11).

References

1. Liu, Y., Qin, Z., Elkashlan, M., Ding, Z., Nallanathan, A., Hanzo, L.: Non-orthogonal multiple access for 5G and beyond. Proc. IEEE **105**(12), 2347–2381 (2017)
2. Dai, L., et al.: Non-orthogonal multiple access for 5G: solutions, challenges, opportunities, and future research trends. IEEE Commun. Mag. **53**(9), 74–81 (2015)
3. Zhang, Z., Sun, H., Hu, R.Q.: Downlink and uplink nonorthogonal multiple access in a dense wireless network. IEEE J. Sel. Areas Commun. **35**(17), 2771–2784 (2017)
4. Ding, Z., Fan, P., Poor, H.V.: Impact of user pairing on 5G nonorthogonal multiple access. IEEE Trans. Veh. Technol. **65**(8), 6010–6023 (2016)
5. Ding, Z., et al.: Application of non-orthogonal multiple access in LTE and 5G networks. IEEE Commun. Mag. **55**(2), 185–191 (2017)
6. Wu, Y., Chen, J., Qian, L., Huang, J., Shen, X.: Energy-aware cooperative traffic offloading via device-to-device cooperations: an analytical approach. IEEE Trans. Mob. Comput. **16**(1), 97–114 (2017)
7. Zhang, Y., Wang, H., Zheng, T., Yang, Q.: Energy-efficient transmission design in non-orthogonal multiple access. IEEE Trans. Veh. Technol. **66**(3), 2852–2857 (2017)
8. Zhang, S., Di, B., Song, L., Li, Y.: Sub-channel and power allocation for non-orthogonal multiple access relay networks with amplify-and-forward protocol. IEEE Trans. Wirel. Commun. **16**(4), 2249–2261 (2017)
9. Qian, L., Wu, Y., Zhou, H., Shen, X.: Joint uplink base station association and power control for small-cell networks with non-orthogonal multiple access. IEEE Trans. Wirel. Commun. **16**(9), 5567–5582 (2017)
10. Wu, Y., Qian, L., Mao, H., Yang, X., Shen, X.: Optimal power allocation and scheduling for non-orthogonal multiple access relay-assisted networks. IEEE Trans. Mob. Comput. **17**(11), 2591–2606 (2018)
11. Wu, Y., Ni, K., Zhang, C., Qian, L., Tsang, D.H.K.: NOMA assisted multi-access mobile edge computing: a joint optimization of computation offloading and time allocation. IEEE Trans. Veh. Technol. **67**(12), 12244–12258 (2018)
12. Zhang, N., Cheng, N., Lu, N., Zhang, X., Mark, J.W., Shen, X.: Partner selection and incentive mechanism for physical layer security. IEEE Trans. Wirel. Commun. **14**(8), 4265–4276 (2015)
13. Yue, J., Ma, C., Yu, H., Zhou, W.: Secrecy-based access control for device-to-device communication underlaying cellular networks. IEEE Commun. Lett. **17**(11), 2068–2071 (2013)
14. Boyd, S., Vandenberghe, L.: Convex Optimization. Cambridge University Press, England (2004)
15. Brent, R.P.: Chapters 3–4 in Algorithms for Minimization Without Derivatives. Prentice-Hall, Englewood Cliffs (1973)

Joint Time-Frequency Diversity in the Context of Spread-Spectrum Systems

Qiuhan Teng[1,2] , Xuejun Sha[1(✉)] , and Cong Ma[1]

[1] Harbin Institute of Technology, Harbin 150001, Heilongjiang, China
shaxuejun@hit.edu.cn
[2] The 54th Research Institute of China Electronics Technology Group
Corporation, Shijiazhuang, China

Abstract. We discuss a new method for realizing the diversity in spread-spectrum communications over fast-fading multipath channels. Maximum Ratio Combining (MRC) can add the synchronized tributary signals in the weighted approach to obtain the maximum diversity gain. The signal distortion caused by the Doppler shift broadened spectrum cannot be eliminated. The diversity receiver used in existing systems suffers from significant performance degradation due to the rapid channel variations encountered under fast fading. We show that the Doppler spread caused by temporal channel variations actually provides other versatile means that can be further utilized to resist fading. This paper proposes a receiving method based on time-frequency cooperative processing. Joint time-frequency representation is a powerful tool. With precise synchronization and channel estimation, even the relatively small Doppler spread encountered in practice can be used for significant diversity gains by our approach. The framework is suitable for multiple mobile wireless multiple access systems and can provide significant performance improvements over existing systems.

Keywords: Time-frequency representation · Diversity · Doppler ·
Fast-fading · Multipath

1 Introduction

The signal fading caused by the channel causes the power of the received signal to fluctuate, and the performance of the receiver is significantly reduced, which is a major factor limiting improvements of wireless communication systems. Diversity is used to mitigate the degradation of error performance caused by unstable fading of the wireless channel. Its main idea is to transmit the same data over multiple independent fading paths. Since the probability of the independent path experiencing deep fading at the same time is small, the degree of fading of the received signal is reduced after proper merging.

After obtaining signals over multiple independent paths at the receiving end, branch signals which have been adjusted the phase and delay are weighted and linearly added to obtain the maximum gain. Three basic combination methods are formed owing to the different selection of weighting factors: selection combining, maximum ratio

S. Han et al. (Eds.): AICON 2019, LNICST 286, pp. 94–107, 2019.
https://doi.org/10.1007/978-3-030-22968-9_9

combining and equal gain combining. Among them, the maximum ratio combining method is the most effective. However, the increased mobility of cellular users leads to the fast fading of channel. The Doppler shift makes the spectrum of the signal broaden, which cannot be eliminated by maximum ratio combining [1].

Therefore, this paper proposes a diversity receiving method based on time-frequency cooperative processing. Joint time-frequency representation (TFR) is a powerful tool for processing time-varying signals and fast fading channels. With precise synchronization and channel estimation, this method can still produce significant gains even with relatively small Doppler spread.

2 Preliminaries

2.1 Time-Frequency Representation

Time-frequency representation (TFR) is a powerful tool for analyzing time-varying signals and time-varying systems. It processes non-stationary signals by blocking the time domain, and obtains two-dimensional signals that are parameterized by time and frequency. TFR is well suited for processing signals transmitted over time-varying channels and is also suitable for processing time-varying channels themselves [2].

A typical time-frequency analysis algorithm is the short-time Fourier transform (STFT) proposed by Gabor in 1946 [3]. Fourier transform (FT) is the basic tool of analysis in the frequency domain. The signal is multiplied by the time-limited window function before the Fourier transform, assuming that the non-stationary signal is stationary in the duration of the window function. By moving the window function on the time axis, multiple sets of partial spectrum of the signal can be obtained. By analyzing the difference between partial spectrum at different times, the time-varying characteristics of the signal can be obtained.

The TFR selected in this paper is the STFT which is defined for a signal $r(t)$ as

$$STFT_r(t,f) = \int_{-\infty}^{\infty} r(t')\eta^*(t'-t)e^{-j2\pi ft'}\,dt' \tag{1}$$

for a given window function $\eta(t)$ with a short time width.

2.2 Channel and Signal Models

Taking the spread spectrum signal in CDMA system as an example, the influence of Doppler shift on signal distortion is analyzed as follows. This paper assumes that in the case of single user, the spreading code used is M sequence. Under the premise of precise synchronization and channel estimation, inter symbol interference can be ignored.

The baseband signal $r(t)$ at the receiving end of one of the paths can be expressed as (see Fig. 1):

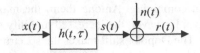

Fig. 1. Mobile wireless channel: linear time-varying system.

$$r(t) = s(t) + n(t) = \int_0^\infty h(t, \tau)x(t - \tau)d\tau + n(t) \qquad (2)$$

where $h(t, \tau)$ is the channel function, and $n(t)$ is zero-mean, complex, circular AWGN with power spectral density N_0.

2.3   Fading and Diversity

Clarke proposed the Rayleigh channel model for describing the small-scale fading channel, which is a narrow-band channel statistical model. The statistical characteristics of the field strength of the transmitting signal and the received signal are based on scattering, which coincides with the characteristics of the shortwave channel. Therefore, it is widely used in channel modeling of shortwave channels [4]. In this paper, the Sum-Of-Sinusoid (SOS) method is taken as an example to study the characteristics of shortwave channels in the joint time-frequency domain.

Diversity is a way to overcome channel fading. It separates the received signals into uncorrelated multipath signals which carry the same information, and then combines and outputs the respective branch signals by combining techniques. Consequently, the probability of deep fading is greatly reduced at the receiving end.

Independent signals in multiple paths obtained by diversity at the receiving end can mainly adopt three different forms of combining techniques, which are maximum ratio combining (MRC), equal gain combining (EGC) and selective combining (SC) [5]. This article discusses the MRC approach, in which the weighting coefficients of each branch must match the channel. MRC achieves the best performance, maximizing the SNR after combining. As the number of receiving antennas increases, the performance of MRC is improved.

3   Joint Time-Frequency Diversity

The increasing mobility of cellular users makes the fast-fading characteristics of the channel more obvious, and consequently the Doppler shift broadens the original spectrum of the signal. MRC does not solve the problem of signal distortion caused by spectrum extension, so that additional techniques are required. In this paper, a time-frequency diversity receiving method is presented, which can further improve the performance by reducing the Doppler shift component on the basis of ensuring the diversity gain.

3.1 Time-Frequency Characteristics of Small-Scale Fading Channels

Assume that the carrier frequency of the signal in the channel is 10 MHz, the maximum Doppler shift is 200 Hz, the number of multipath is four, the delay is 0 ms, 1 ms, 3 ms and 5 ms respectively, and the loss power of each path is −6.96 dB, −6.49 dB, −4.70 dB, and −6.27 dB respectively, the path amplitude distribution and simulated time-frequency distribution characteristics of the channel are shown below (see Fig. 2 (a) and (b)).

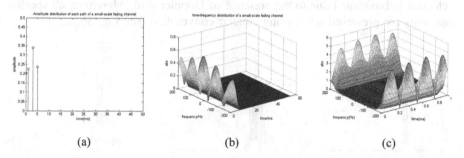

(a)   (b)   (c)

Fig. 2. Time-frequency distribution of small-scale fading channels.

In order to analyze the characteristics of the multipath channel, multiple mixed paths are separated. The time-varying spectrum and the time-varying power spectrum of the fast-fading channel of the single path in the time-frequency domain are given. A reasonable length of the time window and the frequency window are set in the optimal region. The window function is uniformly set to the Hamming window and the time window length of STFT is set to Odd(N/4), where N is the number of sampling points, and Odd means taking an odd number to obtain a better time-frequency resolution. The time-frequency diagram of the narrowband channel is obtained through simulation (see Fig. 2(c)).

The partial channel in the time window can be regarded as non-time-varying in joint time-frequency domain although the channel is always time-varying. Diversity is performed in units of time window to reduce the influence of fast-fading on the signal, which lays a foundation for the proposed diversity receiving method based on time-frequency cooperative processing.

3.2 Frequency Diversity

After complete synchronization of each signal, the time domain expression of the output signal obtained by MRC is

$$y_{MRC}(n) = \sum_{i=1}^{N_R} h_i^*(n) r_i(n) \tag{3}$$

According to the convolution theorem in the frequency domain, the above equation is equivalent to

$$Y_{MRC}(\omega) = \frac{1}{2\pi} \sum_{i=1}^{N_R} H_i^*(\omega) * R_i(\omega) \tag{4}$$

When the Eq. (4) is realized by the circular convolution, it is possible to gain the same effect shown in the Eq. (3) by the MRC. In the fading channel, the spectrum through the channel is broadened due to the presence of Doppler shift. Moreover, all spectral components are preserved when using circular convolution (see Fig. 3(c)).

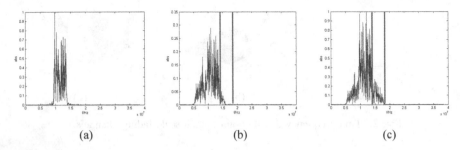

(a)   (b)   (c)

Fig. 3. Comparison chart of spectrum.

In order to weaken the influence of Doppler shift and further improve the performance of MRC, this paper proposes an improved method based on MRC. $H_i^*(\omega)$ and $R_i(\omega)$ are the FFT-transformed frequency domain sequences corresponding to the channel estimation conjugate sequence $h_i^*(n)$ and the received signal sequence $r_i(n)$ of one signal respectively. $H_i^*(\omega)$ and $R_i(\omega)$ are respectively shifted by 1/2 sequence length in the positive direction, and then linear convolution is used to implement Eq. (4).

After the linear convolution of each signal is completed, the results in frequency domain are obtained, which are recorded as $Y_i(\omega), \omega = 1, 2, 3, \cdots, 2N - 1$. The first $N - 1$ terms of $Y_i(\omega)$ is deleted, and $Y_i(\omega), \omega = N, N+1, \cdots, 2N - 1$ are reserved as the frequency domain sequence of each signal after truncation (see Fig. 4(b)). Signals of all branches are combined after the above operations, and then the IFFT transform is conducted to obtain the time domain sequence.

It may be desirable to set the signal sequence received by one of the paths to $[r_1, r_2, r_3]$, the channel estimation conjugate sequence to $[h_1^*, h_2^*, h_3^*]$, and the corresponding FFT-transformed frequency domain sequence to be recorded as $[R_1, R_2, R_3]$ and $[H_1, H_2, H_3]$. See Appendix for the results of the linear convolution and truncation and the results of the circular convolution.

Comparing the results in Appendix with the spectrum information (see Fig. 3), it can be found that the above method can remove part of the high-frequency Doppler component away from the center frequency, that is, the area inside the red line in Fig. 3 (c). However, comparing Fig. 3(a) and (b), it is found that the truncation operation also

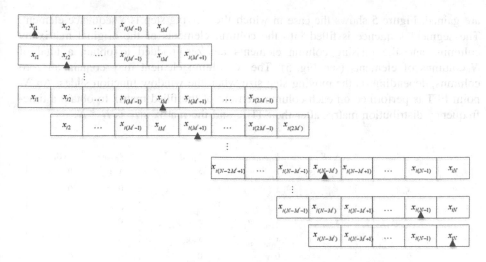

Fig. 4. Schematic diagram of the calculation process of STFT.

brings about partial distortion loss. In order to compensate for the distortion loss caused by the truncation operation, an attempt is made to implement the above method in the time-frequency domain.

3.3   Optimal Time-Frequency Receiver Structures

The frequency domain diversity and puncturing frequency operation described above can remove part of high-frequency Doppler components, which weakens the influence of the Doppler shift on MRC. However, linear convolution and truncation operations also introduce partial distortion loss to the signal. To compensate for the distortion loss of the signal, maximum ratio combining by STFT is proposed in this section. The operation of overlap, decomposition and addition of STFT can alleviate the distortion of the signal, and the window function can reduce the spectrum leakage.
The discrete form of STFT is

$$STFT_{r_i}(m,n) = \sum_{k=-\infty}^{\infty} r_i(k)g(k\Delta t - m\Delta t)e^{-j2\pi(n\Delta f)k}, n = \{1,2,\cdots,N\}, m$$
$$= \{1,2,\cdots,M\} \tag{5}$$

where $r_i(n)$ is a sampling sequence of a signal to be analyzed; $g(m)$ is the sampling sequence of the window function; N is the length of the sample sequence of the signal to be analyzed; M is the length of the sample sequence of the window function(odd), and $M' = (M+1)/2$.
   The signal is segmented by the window function, and the sequence $x_i(n)$ to be analyzed is marked as $x_{in}g_m$ by elements obtained from segment of window function sequence $g(m)$ (see Fig. 4). $x_{i1}, x_{i2}, x_{i3}, \ldots\ldots, x_{iN}$ are considered as the center of the window in order, let the window slide, and then multiple groups of segment sequences

are gained. Figure 5 shows the case in which the moving step is a sequence element. The segment sequence is filled into the column elements of the original matrix by columns, and the missing column elements are zero-padded to obtain a total of N columns of elements (see Fig. 5). The N column element may contain all zero columns, depending on the moving step size when the window function slides. An N-point FFT is performed on each column element of the filled matrix to obtain a time-frequency distribution matrix after the STFT, and the matrix size is $N * N$.

$$\begin{bmatrix}
x_{i1}g_{M'} & x_{i2}g_{M'} & \cdots & x_{iM'}g_{M'} & x_{i(M'+1)}g_{M'} & \cdots & x_{i(N-M'+1)}g_{M'} & \cdots & x_{i(N-1)}g_{M'} & x_{iN}g_{M'} \\
x_{i2}g_{M'+1} & x_{i3}g_{M'+1} & \vdots & x_{i(M'+1)}g_{M'+1} & x_{i(M'+2)}g_{M'+1} & \vdots & x_{i(N-M'+2)}g_{M'+1} & \vdots & x_{iN}g_{M'+1} & 0 \\
x_{i3}g_{M'+2} & x_{i4}g_{M'+2} & \vdots & x_{i(M'+2)}g_{M'+2} & x_{i(M'+3)}g_{M'+2} & \vdots & x_{i(N-M'+3)}g_{M'+2} & \vdots & 0 & 0 \\
\vdots & \vdots & \vdots & \vdots & \vdots & \vdots & \vdots & \vdots & \vdots & \vdots \\
x_{i(M'-1)}g_{2M'-2} & x_{iM'}g_{2M'-2} & \vdots & x_{i(2M'-2)}g_{2M'-2} & x_{i(2M'-1)}g_{2M'-2} & \vdots & x_{i(N-1)}g_{2M'-2} & \vdots & 0 & 0 \\
x_{iM'}g_{2M'-1} & x_{i(M'+1)}g_{2M'-1} & \vdots & x_{i(2M'-1)}g_{2M'-1} & x_{i(2M')}g_{2M'-1} & \vdots & x_{iN}g_{2M'-1} & \vdots & 0 & 0 \\
0 & 0 & \vdots & 0 & 0 & \vdots & 0 & \vdots & 0 & 0 \\
0 & 0 & \vdots & 0 & 0 & \vdots & 0 & \vdots & 0 & 0 \\
\vdots & \vdots & \vdots & \vdots & \vdots & \vdots & \vdots & \vdots & \vdots & \vdots \\
0 & 0 & \vdots & 0 & 0 & \vdots & 0 & \vdots & 0 & 0 \\
0 & 0 & \vdots & x_{i1}g_1 & x_{i2}g_1 & \vdots & x_{i(N-2M'+2)}g_1 & \vdots & x_{i(N-M')}g_1 & x_{i(N-M'+1)}g_1 \\
0 & 0 & \vdots & x_{i2}g_2 & x_{i3}g_2 & \vdots & x_{i(N-2M'+3)}g_2 & \vdots & x_{i(N-M'+1)}g_2 & x_{i(N-M'+2)}g_2 \\
\vdots & \vdots & \vdots & \vdots & \vdots & \vdots & \vdots & \vdots & \vdots & \vdots \\
0 & 0 & \vdots & x_{i(M'-3)}g_{M'-3} & x_{i(M'-2)}g_{M'-3} & \vdots & x_{i(N-M'-2)}g_{M'-3} & \vdots & x_{i(N-4)}g_{M'-3} & x_{i(N-3)}g_{M'-3} \\
0 & 0 & \vdots & x_{i(M'-2)}g_{M'-2} & x_{i(M'-1)}g_{M'-2} & \vdots & x_{i(N-M'-1)}g_{M'-2} & \vdots & x_{i(N-3)}g_{M'-2} & x_{i(N-2)}g_{M'-2} \\
0 & x_{i1}g_{M'-1} & \vdots & x_{i(M'-1)}g_{M'-1} & x_{iM'}g_{M'-1} & \vdots & x_{i(N-M')}g_{M'-1} & \vdots & x_{i(N-2)}g_{M'-1} & x_{i(N-1)}g_{M'-1}
\end{bmatrix}$$

Fig. 5. Calculation matrix of STFT.

The time-frequency distribution matrix of each signal sample sequence $r_i(n)$ and channel estimation conjugate sequence $h_i^*(n)$ is calculated by STFT time-frequency analysis method, and is recorded as $R_i(t, \omega)$ and $H_i(t, \omega)$. The time-frequency distribution matrices $R_i(t, \omega)$ and $H_i(t, \omega)$ are linearly convoluted in columns. The convoluted matrix is denoted as $S_i(t, \omega)$, and the matrix size is $(2N - 1) * N$.

Suppose the element of row k and column j of matrix $R_i(t, \omega)$ is $r_i^j(k)$, the element of row k and column j of matrix $H_i(t, \omega)$ is $h_i^j(k)$, the element of row k and column j of matrix $S_i(t, \omega)$ is $s_i^j(k)$, the convolution operation satisfies the following equation:

$$s_i^j(k) = \sum_{\tau=1}^{N} r_i^j(\tau)h_i^j(k - \tau) \tag{6}$$

The column element of matrix $S_i(t, \omega)$ is $s_i^j(n), n = 1, 2, 3, \cdots, 2N - 1$. The first $N - 1$ of each column element $s_i^j(n), n = 1, 2, 3, \cdots, N - 1$ is deleted and the remaining N elements $s_i^j(n), n = N, N+1, \cdots, 2N - 1$ are the truncated matrix column elements. The new matrix is denoted as S_{inew}.

The truncated convolution matrix S_{inew} gained by each operation is linearly superposed to obtain the matrix S_{sum}. The inverse short-time Fourier transform (ISTFT) of the matrix S_{sum} is applied to obtain the reconstructed time domain sequence $x_{re}(n)$ of the signal.

In summary, the steps of the diversity method of time-frequency coordinated processing can be summarized as follows (see Fig. 6):

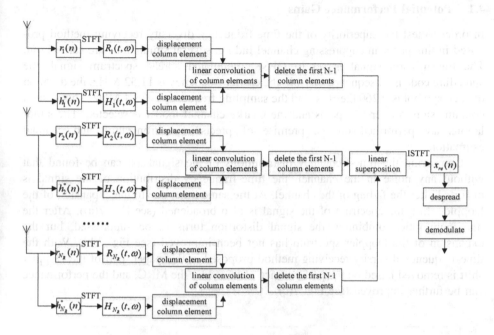

Fig. 6. Implementation flowchart.

(1) The multi-path signals received by the N antennas are subjected to synchronization processing and channel estimation to obtain multiple signals to be processed $(r_i(n))$ and channel estimation conjugate sequences $(h_i^*(n), i = 1, 2, \cdots, N_R)$. The lengths of $r_i(n)$ and $h_i^*(n)$ are both N;

(2) The time-frequency distribution matrix of $r_i(n)$ and $h_i^*(n)$ is calculated by STFT, which is denoted as $R_i(t, \omega)$ and $H_i(t, \omega)$. The matrix size is $N * N$;

(3) The column elements of the time-frequency distribution matrices $R_i(t, \omega)$ and $H_i(t, \omega)$ are circumferentially shifted by 1/2 sequence length in the positive direction. $R_i(t, \omega)$ and $H_i(t, \omega)$ are then linearly convolved in columns. The convoluted matrix is denoted as $S_i(t, \omega)$ and the matrix size is $(2N - 1) * N$. The first $N - 1$ terms of each column of matrix are deleted and the new matrix is denoted as S_{inew}. The matrix size is $N * N$;

(4) The truncated convolution matrix S_{inew} obtained from each path are linearly superposed to get the matrix S_{sum}. The matrix S_{sum} is subjected to an inverse short-time Fourier transform (ISTFT) to obtain a time domain sequence $x_{re}(n)$ of the reconstructed signal, which is to be demodulated.

4 Discussion

In this section, we present the practical feasibility and potential gains of the diversity receiving method based on joint time-frequency processing and determine the optimal window function overlap rate.

4.1 Potential Performance Gains

In order to test the superiority of the time-frequency diversity receiving method proposed in this paper in suppressing channel fading, several simulations are carried out. The transmission signal is set to QPSK modulated spread spectrum signal, the spreading code is M sequence of 7-bit, the carrier frequency is 11.52 MHz, the duration of each symbol is 0.26042e−6 s, and the sampling frequency is 38.4 MHz. This system contains signals over two paths and the Clarke channel model is selected. The simulations are performed on the premise of precise synchronization and channel estimation.

Comparing the time-frequency distributions of the signals, it can be found that without any noise in the channel, the time-frequency distribution of the signal is distorted after the fading of the channel. At the same time, due to the expansion of the Doppler shift, the spectrum of the signal is also broadened (see Fig. 7(a)). After the maximum ratio combining, the signal distortion turns to be suppressed, but the expansion of the Doppler spectrum has not been improved (see Fig. 7(b)). With the time-frequency diversity receiving method proposed in this paper, part of the Doppler shift is removed based on the performance obtained by the MRC, and the performance can be further improved (see Fig. 7(c)).

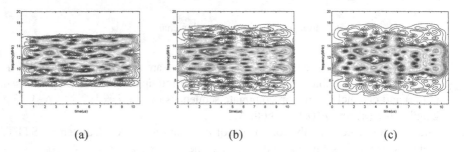

(a)   (b)   (c)

Fig. 7. Time-frequency distribution of each signal.

Using the bit error rate (BER) as the test index, the comparison of different methods is obtained. (see Fig. 8). It can be found that when MRC is implemented by linear convolution and the removal of partial Doppler shift, the BER increases due to large distortion loss. Nevertheless, with the method proposed in this paper, the distortion is alleviated, and partial Doppler shift is removed. Compared with MRC, the bit error rate can be further reduced and the performance can be further improved.

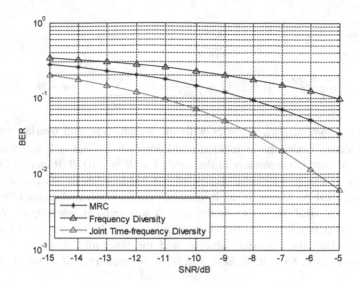

Fig. 8. BER-SNR

4.2   Optimal Window Function Parameter

It can be known from the Heisenberg uncertainty principle that a window function which has both the arbitrary small time width and the arbitrary small bandwidth does not exist. In order to get the best performance of the proposed method, it is necessary to find the optimal window function parameters. An important issue related to the process of the overlap segment is the degree of correlation between the segment sequences, which can be defined by a relatively flat noise power spectrum over the window bandwidth [6]. It is a function of the overlap rate r, which can be measured by

$$c(r) = \frac{\sum_{n=0}^{rN-1} g(n)g(n+(1-r)N)}{\sum_{n=0}^{N-1} g^2(n)} \tag{7}$$

When multiple independent measurements are conducted on K identical distribution variables, the relationship between the mean variance and the single variance of multiple measurements can be expressed by the following equation:

$$\frac{\sigma_{Avg}^2}{\sigma_{Mean}^2} = \frac{1}{K} \tag{8}$$

Thus, for the sequence after overlap truncation, Welch [6] gives another form of the above formula:

$$\frac{\sigma_{Avg}^2}{\sigma_{Mean}^2} = \frac{1}{K}[1 + 2 \cdot \frac{K-1}{K} \sum_{i=1,i\in N}^{ir-(i-1)>0} c^2(ir-(i-1))]$$

$$= \frac{1-r}{L/N-r} \cdot [1 + 2 \cdot (1 - \frac{1-r}{L/N-r}) \cdot \sum_{i=1,i\in N}^{ir-(i-1)>0} c^2(ir-(i-1))]$$

(9)

It can be seen that $\sigma_{Avg}^2/\sigma_{Mean}^2$ varies with the length, type and overlap rate of the window function. Under the simulation conditions set in Sect. 4.1, the above three parameters are changed separately in the case of $SNR = -10dB$. It can be found that the BER hardly changes with the change of the window length. As the overlap rate increases, the BER decreases. When it increases continuously and reaches the optimal overlap rate, the BER begins to flatten and almost remains unchanged. When the window function is taken from the Hamming window, the rectangular window, the triangular window, the Gaussian window and the Blackman window, the optimal overlap ratio is 75%, 85%, 85%, 80% and 80%, respectively, all of which are about 80%.

5 Conclusion

In wireless mobile communication, the movement of the users leads to the intensified signal fading and the decrease of the receiving end performance. The MRC can add the synchronized tributary signals in the weighted approach to obtain the maximum diversity gain. However, the signal distortion caused by the Doppler shift can't be eliminated. In this paper, a time-frequency diversity receiving method is proposed. Each branch signal is analyzed in the time-frequency domain and weighted. Some high-frequency Doppler components are removed by truncation and subtraction, and the branches are combined by summation. The overlapping decomposition and averaging processing of the time-frequency analysis can reduce the effective noise bandwidth and alleviate the distortion loss caused by windowing and frequency clipping. In summary, the time-frequency diversity receiving method can obtain additional performance gain by suppressing the Doppler shift on the basis of ensuring the original performance gain of the MRC. As the overlap rate increases, the BER decreases. When it increases to 80% of the optimal overlap rate, the BER begins to flatten.

Declaration. This work is supported partially by the fund of Science and Technology on Communication Networks Laboratory under grand (No. SXX18641X027) and the National Natural Science Foundation General Program of China (No. 61671179).

Appendix

$$R_1 = r_1 + r_2 + r_3 \tag{10}$$

$$R_2 = r_1 + r_2 e^{-j\frac{2\pi}{3}} + r_3 e^{-j\frac{4\pi}{3}} \tag{11}$$

$$R_3 = r_1 + r_2 e^{-j\frac{4\pi}{3}} + r_3 e^{-j\frac{8\pi}{3}} \tag{12}$$

$$H_1 = h_1^* + h_2^* + h_3^* \tag{13}$$

$$H_2 = h_1^* + h_2^* e^{-j\frac{4\pi}{3}} + h_3^* e^{-j\frac{4\pi}{3}} \tag{14}$$

$$H_3 = h_1^* + h_2^* e^{-j\frac{4\pi}{3}} + h_3^* e^{-j\frac{8\pi}{3}} \tag{15}$$

The results obtained by circularly convolving sequences $[R_1, R_2, R_3]$ and $[H_1, H_2, H_3]$ are as follows:

$$
\begin{aligned}
R_3 H_2 + R_1 H_1 + R_2 H_3 &= (r_1 + r_2 e^{-j\frac{4\pi}{3}} + r_3 e^{-j\frac{8\pi}{3}})(h_1^* + h_2^* e^{-j\frac{4\pi}{3}} + h_3^* e^{-j\frac{4\pi}{3}}) \\
&+ (r_1 + r_2 + r_3)(h_1^* + h_2^* + h_3^*) \\
&+ (r_1 + r_2 e^{-j\frac{2\pi}{3}} + r_3 e^{-j\frac{4\pi}{3}})(h_1^* + h_2^* e^{-j\frac{4\pi}{3}} + h_3^* e^{-j\frac{8\pi}{3}}) \\
&= 3r_1 h_1^* + r_2 h_1^* + r_3 h_1^* + r_1 h_2^* + r_2 h_2^* + r_3 h_2^* + r_1 h_3^* + r_2 h_3^* + r_3 h_3^* \\
&+ (r_1 h_2^* + r_2 h_1^*)e^{-j\frac{2\pi}{3}} + (r_1 h_2^* + r_2 h_1^* + r_1 h_3^* + r_3 h_1^*)e^{-j\frac{4\pi}{3}} \\
&+ (r_3 h_1^* + r_2 h_3^* + r_3 h_2^* + r_1 h_3^*)e^{-j\frac{8\pi}{3}} + 2r_2 h_2^* e^{-j2\pi} + 2r_3 h_3^* e^{-j4\pi} \\
&+ (r_2 h_3^* + r_3 h_2^*)e^{-j\frac{10\pi}{3}}
\end{aligned} \tag{16}
$$

$$
\begin{aligned}
R_3 H_3 + R_1 H_2 + R_2 H_1 &= (r_1 + r_2 e^{-j\frac{4\pi}{3}} + r_3 e^{-j\frac{8\pi}{3}})(h_1^* + h_2^* e^{-j\frac{4\pi}{3}} + h_3^* e^{-j\frac{8\pi}{3}}) \\
&+ (r_1 + r_2 + r_3)(h_1^* + h_2^* e^{-j\frac{2\pi}{3}} + h_3^* e^{-j\frac{4\pi}{3}}) \\
&+ (r_1 + r_2 e^{-j\frac{2\pi}{3}} + r_3 e^{-j\frac{4\pi}{3}})(h_1^* + h_2^* + h_3^*) \\
&= (r_1 h_2^* + r_2 h_1^* + r_1 h_3^* + r_2 h_3^* + 2r_3 h_3^* + r_3 h_2^* + r_3 h_1^*)e^{-j\frac{4\pi}{3}} \\
&+ 3r_1 h_1^* + r_2 h_1^* + r_3 h_1^* + r_1 h_2^* + r_1 h_3^* + r_3 h_3^* e^{-j\frac{16\pi}{3}} \\
&+ (2r_2 h_2^* + r_2 h_3^* + r_3 h_2^* + r_1 h_2^* + r_2 h_1^*)e^{-j\frac{2\pi}{3}} \\
&+ (r_1 h_3^* + r_2 h_2^* + r_3 h_1^*)e^{-j\frac{4\pi}{3}} + (r_2 h_3^* + r_3 h_2^*)e^{-j4\pi}
\end{aligned} \tag{17}
$$

$$
\begin{aligned}
R_3H_1 + R_1H_3 + R_2H_2 &= (r_1 + r_2 e^{-j\frac{4\pi}{3}} + r_3 e^{-j\frac{8\pi}{3}})(h_1^* + h_2^* + h_3^*) \\
&\quad + (r_1 + r_2 + r_3)(h_1^* + h_2^* e^{-j\frac{4\pi}{3}} + h_3^* e^{-j\frac{8\pi}{3}}) \\
&\quad + (r_1 + r_2 e^{-j\frac{2\pi}{3}} + r_3 e^{-j\frac{4\pi}{3}})(h_1^* + h_2^* e^{-j\frac{2\pi}{3}} + h_3^* e^{-j\frac{4\pi}{3}}) \\
&= (r_2 h_1^* + 2r_2 h_2^* + 2r_2 h_3^* + r_1 h_2^* + r_2 h_2^* + r_3 h_2^* + r_1 h_3^* + r_3 h_1^*)e^{-j\frac{4\pi}{3}} \\
&\quad + 3r_1 h_1^* + r_1 h_2^* + r_1 h_3^* + r_3 h_1^* + 2r_2 h_1^* + r_1 h_2^* e^{-j\frac{2\pi}{3}} + r_3 h_2^* e^{-j2\pi} \\
&\quad + (r_3 h_1^* + r_3 h_2^* + r_3 h_3^* + r_1 h_3^* + r_2 h_3^* + 2r_3 h_3^*)e^{-j\frac{8\pi}{3}}
\end{aligned}
\tag{18}
$$

The sequences $[R_1, R_2, R_3]$ and $[H_1, H_2, H_3]$ are circumferentially shifted by 1/2 sequence length in the positive direction to obtain sequences $[R_3, R_1, R_2]$ and $[H_3, H_1, H_2]$. The results of linear convolution of the sequences C and D and truncation are as follows:

$$
\begin{aligned}
R_3H_2 + R_1H_1 + R_2H_3 &= (r_1 + r_2 e^{-j\frac{4\pi}{3}} + r_3 e^{-j\frac{8\pi}{3}})(h_1^* + h_2^* e^{-j\frac{4\pi}{3}} + h_3^* e^{-j\frac{4\pi}{3}}) \\
&\quad + (r_1 + r_2 + r_3)(h_1^* + h_2^* + h_3^*) \\
&\quad + (r_1 + r_2 e^{-j\frac{2\pi}{3}} + r_3 e^{-j\frac{4\pi}{3}})(h_1^* + h_2^* e^{-j\frac{4\pi}{3}} + h_3^* e^{-j\frac{8\pi}{3}}) \\
&= 3r_1 h_1^* + r_2 h_1^* + r_3 h_1^* + r_1 h_2^* + r_2 h_2^* + r_3 h_2^* + r_1 h_3^* + r_2 h_3^* + r_3 h_3^* \\
&\quad + (r_1 h_2^* + r_2 h_1^*)e^{-j\frac{2\pi}{3}} + (r_1 h_2^* + r_2 h_1^* + r_1 h_3^* + r_3 h_1^*)e^{-j\frac{4\pi}{3}} \\
&\quad + (r_3 h_1^* + r_2 h_3^* + r_3 h_2^* + r_1 h_3^*)e^{-j\frac{8\pi}{3}} + 2r_2 h_2^* e^{-j2\pi} \\
&\quad + 2r_3 h_3^* e^{-j4\pi} + (r_2 h_3^* + r_3 h_2^*)e^{-j\frac{10\pi}{3}}
\end{aligned}
\tag{19}
$$

$$
\begin{aligned}
R_3H_1 + R_1H_3 &= (r_1 + r_2 e^{-j\frac{4\pi}{3}} + r_3 e^{-j\frac{8\pi}{3}})(h_1^* + h_2^* + h_3^*) \\
&\quad + (r_1 + r_2 + r_3)(h_1^* + h_2^* e^{-j\frac{4\pi}{3}} + h_3^* e^{-j\frac{8\pi}{3}}) \\
&= 2r_1 h_1^* + r_1 h_2^* + r_1 h_3^* + r_3 h_1^* + r_2 h_1^* \\
&\quad + (r_2 h_1^* + 2r_2 h_2^* + r_2 h_3^* + r_1 h_2^* + r_3 h_2^*)e^{-j\frac{4\pi}{3}} \\
&\quad + (r_3 h_1^* + r_3 h_2^* + r_3 h_3^* + r_1 h_3^* + r_2 h_3^* + r_3 h_3^*)e^{-j\frac{8\pi}{3}}
\end{aligned}
\tag{20}
$$

$$
\begin{aligned}
R_3H_3 &= (r_1 + r_2 e^{-j\frac{4\pi}{3}} + r_3 e^{-j\frac{8\pi}{3}})(h_1^* + h_2^* e^{-j\frac{4\pi}{3}} + h_3^* e^{-j\frac{8\pi}{3}}) \\
&= r_1 h_1^* + (r_1 h_2^* + r_2 h_1^*)e^{-j\frac{4\pi}{3}} + (r_2 h_2^* + r_3 h_1^* + r_1 h_3^*)e^{-j\frac{8\pi}{3}} \\
&\quad + (r_3 h_2^* + r_2 h_3^*)e^{-j4\pi} + r_3 h_3^* e^{-j\frac{16\pi}{3}}
\end{aligned}
\tag{21}
$$

References

1. Sayeed, A.M., Aazhang, B.: Joint multipath-Doppler diversity in mobile wireless communications. IEEE Trans. Commun. **47**(1), 123–132 (1999)
2. Boashash, B., Azemi, G., Khan, N.A.: Principles of time-frequency feature extraction for change detection in non-stationary signals: applications to newborn EEG abnormality detection. Pattern Recogn. **48**(3), 616–627 (2015)
3. Portnoff, M.: Time-frequency representation of digital signals and systems based on short-time Fourier analysis. IEEE Trans. Acoust. Speech Signal Process. **28**(1), 55–69 (2003)
4. Cho, Y.S.: MIMO-OFDM Wireless Communications with MATLAB. Wiley, Hoboken (2010)
5. Agrawal, D.P., Zeng, Q.A.: Introduction to Wireless and Mobile Systems, 4nd edn (2016)
6. Welch, P.D.: The use of fast Fourier transform for the estimation of power spectra: a method based on time averaging over short, modified periodograms. IEEE Trans. Audio Electroacoust. **15**(2), 70–73 (1967)

Design of Radar-Communication Integrated Signal Based on OFDM

Tianqi Liang[1]([✉]), Zhuoming Li[1,2], Mengqi Wang[1], and Xiaojie Fang[1]

[1] School of Electronics and Information Engineering,
Harbin Institute of Technology, Harbin, China
1418816805@qq.com, zhuoming@hit.edu.cn
[2] Peng Cheng Laboratory, Shenzhen 518000, China

Abstract. With the development of information technology, the electromagnetic environment is becoming more and more complex, and the demand for bringing together electronic devices of different functions is urgently increasing. Among them, the radar-communication integration is a research hotspot. The current radar-communication integration research mainly focuses on the integrated signal design. Due to the similarity between OFDM signals and phase-encoding radars, it is possible to apply OFDM to radar. Aiming at the problem that the randomness of communication data affects the detection capability of OFDM radar, this paper proposes an integrated OFDM radar-communication signal design based on P4 cyclic shift code. And we verified communication BER and radar range and velocity performance for multi-target of the integrated system. The transmitting end carries out an integrated signal design that is consistent with the communication OFDM signal. The degree of system integration is high, and it achieves communication functions without reducing radar detection capability. For the high PAPR problem, we introduce CE-OFDM signals, and derive a radar signal processing algorithm based on FFT demodulation. This paper provides a theoretical basis for applications of OFDM-based integrated signals and it is an effective integrated scheme.

Keywords: Radar-communication integration · OFDM · P4 code · CE-OFDM

1 Introduction

The development of modern science has enriched various electronic devices but has also caused increasingly complex electromagnetic environment. Electronic equipment brings serious electromagnetic interference to each other, and the maintenance of equipment is also more time-consuming and labor-intensive. In this background, the integrated design of electronic equipment is very necessary. The high degree of similarity between the hardware of the radar equipment and the communication equipment and the sharing of software resources have brought an opportunity to the integrated design of the radar-communication [1]. Among them, the application of OFDM signals to radar for integrated shared waveform design is an option.

© ICST Institute for Computer Sciences, Social Informatics and Telecommunications Engineering 2019
Published by Springer Nature Switzerland AG 2019. All Rights Reserved
S. Han et al. (Eds.): AICON 2019, LNICST 286, pp. 108–119, 2019.
https://doi.org/10.1007/978-3-030-22968-9_10

Shi et al. proposed three different robust radar waveform design standards based on power minimization [2, 3]. Sit et al. proposed a MIMO-OFDM joint radar-communication system and proposed a system-level interference cancellation algorithm [4]. Herschfelt and Bliss develop and simulate a joint system for a sample multiple access channel [5]. Dokhanchi et al. use phase-modulated continuous wave (PMCW) waveform to modulate a communication stream and effect of joint radar-communication system (JRC) [6]. And they design a vehicle JRC system [7]. Xu et al. introduced FBMC technology into the integrated system, and proposed an m-sequence filter bank multi-carrier (MS-FBMC) integrated radar-communication signal based on m-sequence precoding [8]. The above references don't solve the impact of randomness of communication data on radar detection capability.

Aiming at the influence of randomness of communication data on OFDM detection capability, this paper designs a OFDM radar-communication integrated signal design based on P4 cyclic shift code. This paper discusses the ambiguity function, PAPR, and reception algorithm of the integrated signal. At the same time, it introduced CE-OFDM to solve the problem of excessive PAPR. Through simulation analysis, we discuss the velocity resolution and range resolution of the radar system, the bit error rate of the communication system, and verify the rationality of the integrated signal proposed in this paper.

2 Analysis of Radar-Communication Integration Based on OFDM Signal

In this chapter, we combine the waveform design theory of radar signals, and propose the design criteria of shared waveforms. At the same time, we give a schematic diagram of the system based on OFDM radar-communication integration, and introduce its working principle. It provides guidance for theoretical derivation and simulation analysis.

2.1 Radar Waveform Design Guidelines

The guidelines for measuring the detection capability of radar signals are mainly ambiguity function and interception factors. The output of the radar signal through the matched filter is given by

$$
\begin{aligned}
y(t; F_D) &= \int_{-\infty}^{+\infty} x(s) \exp(j2\pi F_D s) x^*(s - t) ds \\
&= \hat{A}(t, F_D)
\end{aligned}
\tag{1}
$$

We consider the output of the matched filter with the waveform x(t) when the input is a Doppler shift response x(t)exp $(j2\pi F_D t)$. We assume that the filter has unity gain and is designed to peak at zero. A fuzzy function can be defined as

$$
A(t, F_D) = |\hat{A}(t, F_D)|
\tag{2}
$$

By analyzing the ambiguity function, we can evaluate the detection capabilities of radar signals, such as resolution, side lobe performance, and Doppler and range ambiguity. The design should be as close as possible to the ambiguity function, which is characterized by a single central peak, while other energy is evenly distributed in the delayed Doppler plane, which can improve the target resolution.

Another important performance parameter of radar is the intercept factor. The interception factor γ is defined as the ratio of the maximum range of the radar signal that can be received by the interceptor to the maximum detected range of the intercepted radar. Obviously, the smaller the γ, the better. Moreover, γ is inversely proportional to the time-width bandwidth product. Therefore, the pulse compression radar with a large time-width and wide-band product characteristic has a low probability of interception. When designing a radar signal, the time-width bandwidth product should be set as large as possible.

2.2   System Schematic Diagram of OFDM Radar

Based on the architecture of the traditional radar-communication integrated system, this paper gives a schematic diagram of the OFDM radar-communication integrated system. It can be seen in Fig. 1.

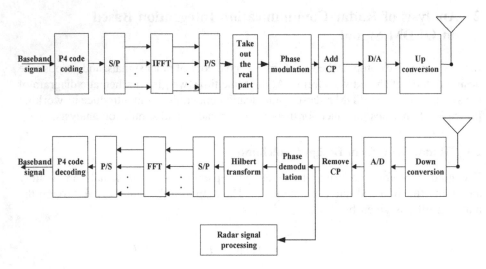

Fig. 1. The schematic diagram of the OFDM radar-communication integrated system.

The radar-communication integrated system adds a P4 code coding map based on the original OFDM system, maps the random bit data into a P4 code sequence, and uses the phase randomness of the P4 code cyclic shift sequence to represent the data information. The receiving end adds a radar signal processing module, which adopts an FFT demodulation receiving algorithm, and the communication part adopts a conventional OFDM demodulation algorithm. The whole system uses software radio technology, so the hardware part before the A/D converter is shared, and the radar signal processing function will be realized by software, and the degree of integration is very high.

3 OFDM Shared Signal Waveform Design

Based on the above system schematic diagram, we derive and simulate the OFDM shared signal waveform. Based on the derivation of the fuzzy function of OFDM signal, it introduces the P4 cyclic code to simulate the ambiguity function, and proposes the CE-OFDM method to reduce PAPR, and analyzes its influence on the ambiguity function.

3.1 Ambiguity Function of OFDM Signal

The signal design of this paper starts from the classical OFDM signal, and its transmitted signal form is given by

$$s(t) = rect(t) \sum_{k=0}^{N-1} C_k \exp\{j2\pi(k\Delta f + f_c)t\} \tag{3}$$

where $rect(t)$ is a window function, N is the number of subcarriers, C_k is the subcarrier amplitude, Δf is the carrier spacing, f_c is the carrier frequency.

When the signal encounters a target with a distance of R and a relative radar radial velocity of v, the echo signal received by the receiver is given by

$$r(t) = rect(t\gamma - \tau) \sum_{l=0}^{N-1} C_l \exp\{j2\pi(l\Delta f + f_c)(t\gamma - \tau)\} \tag{4}$$

where γ is the stretching factor, τ is the delay, and c is the speed of light. The echo signal is down-converted to obtain the baseband signal and brought into the ambiguity function formula simplification. Due to the orthogonality of the subcarriers, we take the main part of the energy to get

$$
\begin{aligned}
\chi_M(\tau, f_d) = \exp\{j2\pi f_c\tau\} \sum_{k=0}^{N-1} \exp\{j2\pi k\Delta f\tau\} C_k C_k^* \\
\sin c(\pi(f_c - k\Delta f)(1 - \gamma)T_d) \\
\exp\{j\pi(f_c - k\Delta f)(\gamma - 1)T_a\}
\end{aligned} \tag{5}
$$

where $T_d = T_{max} - T_{min}$, $T_a = (T_{max} - T_{min})/2$, $T_{min} = \max(0, \tau)$, $T_{max} = \min(T_s, T_s/\gamma + \tau)$.

When $\tau = 0$, $f_d = 0$, ambiguity function reaches the maximum; $\tau \neq 0$, $f_d = 0$, ambiguity function becomes range ambiguity function; $\tau = 0$, $f_d \neq 0$, ambiguity function becomes velocity ambiguity function. Range resolution is inversely proportional to bandwidth, and we can obtain the combined high resolution of range and Doppler by pulse compression.

3.2 Design of OFDM Shared Signal Based on P4 Complementary Code

Since the signal and echo forms given above cannot carry random information, we introduce the P4 code commonly used in radar. The P4 code is defined as

$$\phi_m = \frac{2\pi}{M}(m-1)\frac{(m-1-M)}{2} \tag{6}$$

where M is the number of P4 code bits, and m is the current bit.

A prominent feature of the P4 code is that its cyclic shift can constitute a complementary set. The sum of the autocorrelation functions of the complementary set is a side lobe of zero and the main lobe is a function of the sum of the peaks. If the complementary code generated by cyclically shifting the P4 code is combined with the OFDM signal, the shared signal can have communication capabilities.

To this end, we chose the P4 complementary code for shared signal design. The sequential shift sequence of the P4 code can form a P4 complementary code set, taking the 4-bit P4 code as an example, and the complementary code set is given by

$$\phi_1 = \left\{0, \frac{5}{4}\pi, \pi, \frac{5}{4}\pi\right\} \qquad \phi_2 = \left\{\frac{5}{4}\pi, \pi, \frac{5}{4}\pi, 0\right\}$$

$$\phi_3 = \left\{\pi, \frac{5}{4}\pi, 0, \frac{5}{4}\pi\right\} \qquad \phi_4 = \left\{\frac{5}{4}\pi, 0, \frac{5}{4}\pi, \pi\right\} \tag{7}$$

We can make $\phi_1\ \phi_2\ \phi_3\ \phi_4$ represent different data information respectively, and think that the probability of occurrence of symbols is the same. Then, when the receiver performs the coherent integration processing of the pulses, the side lobes cancel each other due to the complementary code characteristics of the P4 code. Therefore, the side lobes of the ambiguity function at this time will also be very low, and the more the cumulative number of pulses, the more obvious the effect. At this point, the expression of the integrated signal is given by

$$y(n,m) = \sum_{m=1}^{M} rect(t-(M-1)T_s)\sum_{k=0}^{N-1}\exp\left(j\varphi_{k,m}\right)\exp\left\{j2\pi k\frac{n}{N}\right\}$$

$$\varphi_{k,m} = \frac{2\pi}{N}(k-1+c_m-1)\frac{(k-1-N+c_m-1)}{2} \tag{8}$$

$$c_m \in \{1,2,3\ldots,N\}$$

where each OFDM chip signal represents a communication symbol, and c_m is a sequence number representing a communication symbol obtained by bit mapping of the data information. The phase modulated on each subcarrier in each chip signal is determined by the equations of the cm and P4 codes, and cm determines the shift of the modulated P4 code sequence in each chip. Thus different shifts can represent different data information.

Use (5) to write the main lobe formula of the ambiguity function

$$\chi_M(\tau, f_d) = \sum_{k=0}^{N-1} \exp\{j2\pi(f_c + k\Delta f)\tau\} \sum_{l=0}^{M-1}\sum_{m=0}^{M-1} C_{k,l}C_{k,m}^*$$

$$T_d \sin c(\pi(f_c - k\Delta f)(1 - \gamma)T_d)$$

$$\exp\{j\pi(f_c - k\Delta f)(\gamma - 1)T_a\}$$

$$(9)$$

where $C_{k,l}$, $C_{k,m}$ are the lth symbol and the kth symbol on the kth subcarrier in the OFDM signal, respectively. P4 code ambiguity function zero Doppler plane simulation results are shown in Fig. 2.

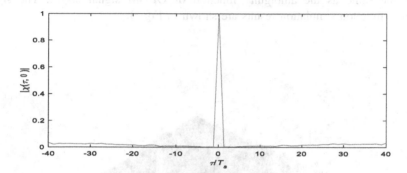

Fig. 2. Improved P4 code zero Doppler plane.

Figure 2 is a range ambiguity function obtained by accumulating 1024 pulses using a 32-bit P4 code. It can be seen that the main lobe is narrow and the side lobes are low. Therefore, the radar detection capability of the integrated signal designed by this method is hardly reduced.

3.3 Method for Reducing PAPR of Shared Signals

Too high PAPR is an unavoidable problem for OFDM systems, and integrated systems are also facing this problem. The traditional clipping method has a small change to the ambiguity function due to the clipping ratio (CR), but has a great influence on BER. To this end, we introduce CE-OFDM to solve the problem of excessive PAPR.

The CE-OFDM method combines OFDM technology with angle modulation or frequency modulation to produce a constant envelope signal that allows the amplifier to operate in saturation and maximize energy efficiency. The PAPR of the signal can be as high as 0 dB. For the sake of discussion, let's take angle modulation as an example. In the CE-OFDM-PM signal, the angle signal should be proportional to the real part of the OFDM signal. We construct the real OFDM signal and combine the angle modulation to obtain the formula of the CE-OFDM-PM signal. It is given by

$$y(t) = A \exp\left(jh_p \sum_{n=1}^{2N} \left\{ \Re[X(n)] \cos\left(j2\pi \frac{n}{T_s} t \right) \right.\right.$$
$$\left.\left. - \Im[X(n)] \sin\left(j2\pi \frac{n}{T_s} t \right) \right\} \right) \tag{10}$$

where h_p is the angle modulation index, and T_s is the OFDM symbol duration, which is reciprocal with the subcarrier spacing to ensure orthogonality.

In the echo signal of the CE-OFDM-PM signal, the effects of delay and Doppler shift will all be applied to the angle signal, so the ambiguity function of CE-OFDM is exactly the same as the ambiguity function of OFDM signal above. The signal ambiguity function simulation results are shown in Fig. 3.

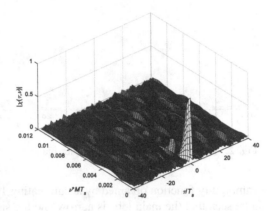

Fig. 3. Ambiguity function graph of CE-OFDM signal modulated by P4 code.

It can be seen that the side lobes are undulating, but not very prominent, and the width of the main lobe is narrow. Therefore, the CE-OFDM signal can be considered as a suitable radar detection signal, which can be directly subjected to pulse compression processing. However, the disadvantage of this method is that the angle demodulation has a threshold effect, which requires that the SNR of the demodulator is greater than 10 dB, which will affect the detection range of the radar.

4   Design and Simulation Analysis of OFDM Integrated Signal Reception Algorithm

4.1   OFDM Integrated Signal Receiving Algorithm Based on FFT Demodulation

Taking a single pulse signal as an example, after down-conversion, A/D conversion, phase demodulation, and Hilbert transform, the expression of the baseband signal entering the radar processing module is given by

$$s(n) = rect\left(\frac{n}{N\Delta f}\left(1 - \frac{2v}{c}\right) - \tau\right)\sum_{m=0}^{N-1}[\exp(j\varphi_m)$$

$$\exp\left\{j2\pi m\Delta f \frac{n}{N\Delta f}\left(1 - \frac{2v}{c}\right)\right\}$$

$$\exp\left\{-j2\pi f_c \frac{n}{N\Delta f}\frac{2v}{c}\right\}$$

$$\exp\left\{-j2\pi(f_c + m\Delta f)\frac{n}{N\Delta f}\frac{2R}{c}\right\}$$

(11)

where n is the number of samples, and the other parameters have the same meaning as above. If the above formula is rewritten as a matrix, the sampled data before entering the radar signal processing module is given by

$$\mathbf{s} = \psi\xi\boldsymbol{\beta}(\mathbf{a}\otimes\boldsymbol{\varphi})$$

(12)

The meaning of each parameter is as follows

$$\psi = \exp\left\{-j2\pi f_c \frac{2R}{c}\right\}$$

(13)

$$\xi = diag\{1 \quad \gamma \quad \gamma^2 \quad \cdots \quad \gamma^{N-1}\}$$

(14)

$$\boldsymbol{\beta} = \begin{bmatrix} 1 & 1 & 1 & \cdots & 1 \\ 1 & \beta & \beta^2 & & \beta^{N-1} \\ 1 & \beta^2 & \beta^4 & & \beta^{2(N-1)} \\ & & & \ddots & \vdots \\ 1 & \beta^{N-1} & \beta^{2(N-1)} & \cdots & \beta^{(N-1)^2} \end{bmatrix}$$

(15)

$$\mathbf{a}^T = \begin{bmatrix} 1 & a & a^2 & \cdots & a^{N-1} \end{bmatrix}$$

(16)

$$\boldsymbol{\varphi}^T = [\exp\{j\varphi_0\} \quad \exp\{j\varphi_1\} \quad \cdots \quad \exp\{j\varphi_{N-1}\}]$$

(17)

The derivation of the range output and velocity output of the formula is summarized as the following algorithm:

Step 1: Each pulse is down-converted, sampled, and demodulated data is stored in a matrix S, and each column of the matrix represents a pulse.

Step 2: Multiply each column in the matrix S by the Hadamard multiplication by the corresponding transmission data, and store the result in the original position.

Step 3: Perform an IFFT transformation on each column of the matrix S, and store the result in the original position, and the result is a range output.

Step 4: Perform FFT transformation on each row of the matrix S, and the result is the speed output.

4.2 Integrated System Simulation and Performance Analysis for Reducing PAPR of Shared Signals

Based on the above shared signal design, we simulated the integrated system, and the system parameter settings are shown in Table 1.

Table 1. System parameter setting.

Symbol	Parameter	Value
B	Bandwidth	6.4 MHz
N	Number of subcarriers	16
Δf	Carrier spacing	400 kHz
T_s	Symbol duration	2.5 μs
M	Number of pulse	1024
T_{PRI}	Pulse repetition time	3.125 μs
f_c	Carrier frequency	10 GHz
δR	Range resolution	25 m
δv	Velocity resolution	4.7 m/s

Suppose the radar scattering area of two targets is 1 m^2, their distance from the radar is 100 m and 200 m, respectively, and their velocity is 200 m/s and 300 m/s. The range output and velocity output are shown in Fig. 4.

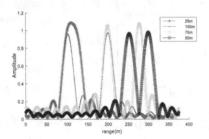 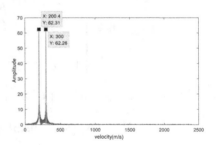

Fig. 4. Radar detection capability simulation results. Among them, the left figure shows the range output of the radar, and the right figure shows the velocity output of the radar.

It can be seen from the figure that the velocity and range of the two targets can be accurately distinguished, and the amplitude attenuation caused by the Doppler shift hardly affects the target recognition. The left image also shows the range display of the radar with two targets separated by 25 m, 50 m and 75 m. It is apparent from the figure that the two targets are indistinguishable when they are separated by 25 m. In the case of 50 m and 75 m, it is still distinguishable.

Using the system parameter, to achieve a Doppler shift of Δf, the target's velocity of motion should be 2500 m/s. We assume that the target position is 100 m and the

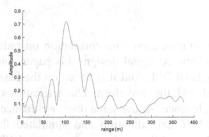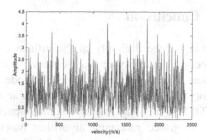

Fig. 5. Simulation results of radar detection capability under large Doppler shift. Among them, the left figure shows the range output of the radar, and the right figure shows the velocity output of the radar.

velocity is 2500 m/s, so the range output and velocity output at this time are shown in Fig. 5.

It can be seen that the range output has a very high secondary peak at 125 m, and the velocity is completely indistinguishable.

BER of CE-OFDM systems. We assume that the channel is a constant reference channel and the noise is white Gaussian noise. Considering the frequency offset produced by the channel, the signal will produce an additional phase after entering the angle demodulator. Due to the orthogonality and periodicity of the carrier, the problem of the symbol error rate of the CE-OFDM system can be reduced to the problem of the symbol error rate of the portion related to the number of bits of P4 cyclic code [11].

Using above analysis, we use the 16-bit P4 code to simulate the system BER based on the original parameters. The result is shown in Fig. 6.

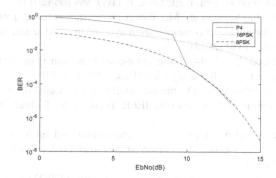

Fig. 6. BER under 16-bit P4 code white Gaussian noise channel.

As can be seen from the figure, due to the threshold effect of the angle modulation, the BER is high before the SNR is 10 dB. Under high SNR conditions, the BER of the design signal is close to the BER of 8PSK, and there is no loss in communication performance.

5 Conclusion

Aiming at the difficulty of the influence of communication data correlation on radar detection capability in radar-communication integrated signal design, this paper constructs shared signal with P4 cyclic code and CE-OFDM. And it is based on the basic theory of ambiguity function of radar signal and the waveform characteristics of OFDM. In this way, we solved the impact of relevance. At the same time, we deduced the integrated receiving algorithm based on FFT demodulation and simulated the corresponding radar range and velocity detection capability and communication BER, and obtained good results.

The radar-communication integrated system based on OFDM signal not only reduces the performance of the radar system, but also has the capability of high-speed communication, and the degree of integration is high, which is an effective and feasible integrated solution. It is also necessary to improve the clutter filtering and Doppler processing operations of the radar receiving algorithm in this system, so that the integrated system has better performance. Moreover, we need to improve the application of this radar-communication integrated system in SAR radar in the follow-up work.

References

1. Chen, X.B., Wang, X.M., Cao, C. (eds.): Techniques Analysis of Radar-Communication Integrating Waveform. China Academy of Electronics and Information Technology, Beijing, China (2013)
2. Garmatyuk, D., Schuerger, J., Kauffman, K.: Multifunctional software-defined radar sensor and data communication system. IEEE Sens. J. **11**(1), 99–106 (2011)
3. Shi, C.G., Wang, F., Sellathurai, M.: Power minimization-based robust OFDM radar waveform design for radar and communication systems in coexistence. IEEE Trans. Signal Process. **66**(5), 1316–1330 (2018)
4. Chalise, B.K., Himed, B.: Dual-function radar-communication using GPS gold codes. In: International Conference on Radar Systems (Radar 2017) (2017)
5. Sit, Y.L., Nuss, B., Zwick, S.: On mutual interference cancellation in a MIMO OFDM multiuser radar-communication network. IEEE Trans. Veh. Technol. **67**(4), 3339–3348 (2018)
6. Herschfelt, A., Bliss, D.W.: Joint radar-communications waveform multiple access and synthetic aperture radar receiver. In: 2017 51st Asilomar Conference on Signals, Systems, and Computers (2017)
7. Dokhanchi, S.H., Bhavani Shankar, M.R., Stifter, T. (eds.): OFDM-based automotive joint radar-communication system. In: Accepted to be Presented at IEEE Radar Conference (RadarConf), Oklahoma, OK (2018)
8. Dokhanchi, S.H., Bhavani Shankar, M.R., Nijsure, Y.A. (eds.): Joint automotive radar-communications waveform design. In: Proceeding IEEE International Symposium on Personal, Indoor and Mobile Radio Communications, Montreal, QC, Canada (2017)
9. Xu, W.W., Wang, C., Cui, G.F. (eds.): The M-sequence encoding method for radar-communication system based on filter bank multi-carrier. In: 2017 9th International Conference on Advanced Infocomm Technology (ICAIT) (2017)

10. Li, Z.Q., Mei, J.J., Hu, D.P. (eds.): Peak-to-Average Power Ratio Reduction for Integration of Radar and Communication Systems Based on OFDM Signals with Block Golay Coding. Air Force Early Warning Academy, Wuhan, China (2014)
11. Azurdia-Meza, C.A., Lee, K., Lee, K.: PAPR reduction by pulse shaping using Nyquist linear combination pulses. IEICE Electron. Express 9(19), 1534–1541 (2012)
12. Ziemer, R.E., Tranter, W.H.: Principles of Communications: Systems, Modulation, and Noise. Wiley, Hoboken (2015)

A Multicast Beamforming Algorithm to Improve the Performance of Group Service for Multicell B-TrunC System

Zheming Zhang[1,2], Chengwen Zhang[1(✉)], Yutao Liu[2], and Bin Wang[1]

[1] The School of Electronics and Information Engineering,
Harbin Institute of Technology, Harbin, China
zcw@hit.edu.cn
[2] Science and Technology on Communication Networks Laboratory,
Shijiazhuang, China

Abstract. With the increasing demand for the command and dispatch service of private network communication system, broadband trunking communication (B-TrunC) system and its standards are improving steadily. In order to improve the performance of group service of B-TrunC system, we propose a system model with same-frequency multicell coordination for group users and a multicast beamforming algorithm based on the system model. The proposed system model combines multicell coordination and same-frequency scheduling. The multicast beamforming optimization problem is a non-deterministic polynomial hard (NP-hard) problem. The mathematical model of the proposed algorithm is obtained according to direction of departure (DOD) of group users and max-min fairness (MMF) principle; the optimal approximate solution of transmitting multicast beamforming weight vector, which maximizes the least received SNR of group users, is obtained on the basis of semidefinite relaxation (SDR). Theoretical analysis and simulation results show that the proposed multicast beamforming algorithm based on same-frequency multicell coordination can significantly improve the SNR of cell-edge users and increase the group user channel capacity. As the group user angle interval decreases or the base station antenna number increases, the performance of the proposed algorithm is further improved.

Keywords: B-TrunC system · Multicast beamforming ·
Multicell coordination · Same-frequency scheduling · Group service

1 Introduction

As an important part of wireless communication, private network communication system with the core business of public service and public safety is developing rapidly around the world. Industry users urgently need private network to provide broadband

This paper is sponsored by the National Natural Science Foundation of China (No. 61771169 and 61831002), the funds of Science and Technology on Communication Networks Laboratory (No. XX17641X011-04) and the Postdoctoral Science-Research Foundation of Heilongjiang (Grant No. LBH-Q11108).

S. Han et al. (Eds.): AICON 2019, LNICST 286, pp. 120–131, 2019.
https://doi.org/10.1007/978-3-030-22968-9_11

services such as high-speed data, images and video. The broadbandization of private network communication system is imperative and urgent. The researches on B-TrunC system, which is based on 4G core technology, have received extensive attention in recent years [1]. Group service is the core business of B-TrunC system. The improvement of the performance of group service has important theoretical significance and application value for promoting the development of B-TrunC system.

Nowadays, the group service of the B-TrunC system adopts inter-frequency scheduling method in different base stations. The same frequencies will be distributed to the same group users in same base station but the different frequencies will be distributed to the same group users in different base stations. This method has short-comings in group user handover delay, cell-edge user performance, and group user channel capacity, etc. Thus, in this paper, a system model with same-frequency multicell coordination for group users and a multicast beamforming algorithm combined multicell coordination and same-frequency scheduling is studied to improve the performance of group service of B-TrunC system.

Beamforming technology can make full use of the spatial domain resources and improve the energy efficiency of wireless communication system [2, 3]. A lot of research results have been achieved on point-to-point single-user beamforming [4]. The research on multicast beamforming for group users has received increasing attention with the increasing demand for multicast services [5, 6]. The difficulty of multicast beamforming for group users is that no matter which beamforming principle is adopted, the optimization of beamforming weight vector is a non-deterministic polynomial hard (NP-hard) problem [7]. The optimal solution can be obtained by sequential quadratic programming (SQP) but with high computational complexity [8]. The semi-definite relaxation (SDR) algorithm can reduce the computational complexity with little performance loss. Reference [9] proposes a multicast beamforming algorithm based on unicast, which improves the performance of zero-forcing method and minimum mean square error method. In [10], the problem of multicast beamforming with perfect and imperfect channel status information (CSI) is studied based on an iterative approach. However, the above studies on beamforming only consider the case of group users in a single base station without considering in multiple base stations cenarios.

The performance for cell-edge users in the group service of B-TrunC system directly affects the overall performance. Multicell coordination can improve the performance for cell-edge users, and further improve the overall performance for group users. In [11], a multi-point coordination scheduling method is adopted to reduce the interference between users in different base stations and improve the performance for cell-edge users. However, the spatial domain resources are not fully utilized, since it uses frequency division multiplexing for the same group users of different base stations.

In order to improve the performance of group service of B-TrunC system, a system model with same-frequency multicell coordination for group users is studied and a multicast beamforming algorithm combined multicell coordination and same-frequency scheduling for B-TrunC system is proposed. The multicast beamforming algorithm based on max-min fairness (MMF) principle fully utilizes the spatial domain resources. The optimal solution of the algorithm is a NP-hard problem and the optimal approximate solution is obtained by semidefinite relaxation.

2 System Model and Optimization Problem

In order to evaluate the performance of the proposed system model and the multicast beamforming algorithm, the system model of the proposed same-frequency multicell coordination (SFMC) is shown in Fig. 1(a); the system model of the original private network non-cooperation (OPNN) is shown in Fig. 1(b); the system model of the original multimedia broadcast/multicast service single frequency network (OMBSFN) with omnidirectional antenna is shown in Fig. 1(c).

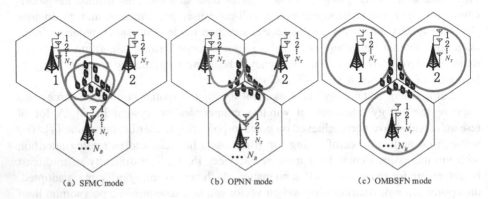

| (a) SFMC mode | (b) OPNN mode | (c) OMBSFN mode |

Fig. 1. System model of three modes

As is shown in Fig. 1(a), there are N_B base stations. Each base station adopts uniform linear array with N_T array elements. And there are M single-antenna users per base station, and all belong to the same group. According to the characteristics that the group users of private network are concentrated and the angle information is easily obtained, the channel model adopts the direction of departure (DOD) mode in this paper. The downlink between the i-th base station and the k-th user in the j-th base station can be expressed as

$$
\begin{aligned}
\mathbf{h}_{i,<j,k>} &= \mathbf{a}_{i,<j,k>}\, \mathbf{g}_{i,<j,k>}\,1 \\
&= [\, h_1^{i,<j,k>} \quad h_2^{i,<j,k>}\,1 \quad \cdots \quad h_{N_T}^{i,<j,k>} \,]^T
\end{aligned}
\tag{1}
$$

Where $\mathbf{a}_{i,<j,k>}$ is a $N_T \times d_k$ dimensional steering matrix; $\mathbf{g}_{i,<j,k>}$ is a $d_k \times 1$ dimensional independent identically distributed complex Gaussian matrix with zero-mean unit-variance per element; d_k is the corresponding DOD multipath number of emission array. In uniform linear array, it can be expressed as:

$$
\mathbf{a}_{i,<j,k>} = \frac{1}{\sqrt{d_k}} \times [\mathbf{a}(\theta_1^{i,<j,k>}), \cdots, \mathbf{a}(\theta_{d_k}^{i,<j,k>})]
\tag{2}
$$

$$
\mathbf{a}(\theta) = [1, e^{j2\pi \frac{d\sin\theta}{\lambda}}, \cdots, e^{j2\pi(N_T-1)\frac{d\sin\theta}{\lambda}}]^T
\tag{3}
$$

Where d is the antenna array element interval; λ is the wavelength of carrier; θ is the DOD. Suppose $\hat{\theta}_{i,<j,k>}$ is the DOD central angle between the i-th base station and the k-th user in the j-th base station, angle expansion is $\Delta\psi_k$, then we have $\theta_{d_k}^{i,<j,k>} = \hat{\theta}_{i,<j,k>} + \rho\Delta\psi_k$, $\rho \in [-1, 1]$.

The transmitting beamforming weight vector of the i-th base station is $\mathbf{w}_i = [w_1\ w_2\ \cdots\ w_{N_T}]^T$ which is a N_T-dimensional column vector; s is the transmitting signal; n is Gaussian noise. Then the received signal of the k-th user in the j-th base station can be expressed as

$$
\begin{aligned}
r_{<j,k>} &= \sum_{i=1}^{N_B} \mathbf{h}_{i,<j,k>}^H\ \mathbf{w}_i s + n \\
&= \mathbf{h}_{j,<j,k>}^H\ \mathbf{w}_j s + \sum_{i=1,i\neq j}^{N_B} \mathbf{h}_{i,<j,k>}^H\ \mathbf{w}_i s + n
\end{aligned}
\tag{4}
$$

In (4), the received signals of the user consist of two parts, one is from the base station which is the user located and the other is from other base stations. In this system model, different base stations use the same time-frequency resources to transmit the same group service information. Cell-edge user can receive signals sent by multiple base stations simultaneously. The SNR of all the received signals of the user can be expressed as

$$
\begin{aligned}
SNR_{SFMC<j,k>} &= \sum_{i=1}^{N_B} \left|\mathbf{w}_i^H \mathbf{h}_{i,<j,k>}\right|^2 \\
&= \left|\mathbf{w}_j^H \mathbf{h}_{j,<j,k>}\right|^2 + \sum_{i=1,i\neq j}^{N_B} \left|\mathbf{w}_i^H \mathbf{h}_{i,<j,k>}\right|^2
\end{aligned}
\tag{5}
$$

In private network communication system, the performance of group service must be guaranteed for all users in the same group. In order to ensure the performance of the group user with the worst received signal, the max-min fairness (MMF) beamforming principle is adopted, which is to maximize the least SNR of the users in the group. Constrain the transmitting power of each base station to be P, then the mathematical model for the multicast beamforming optimization problem with same-frequency multicell coordination is derived as

$$
\begin{aligned}
&\max_{w_1\cdots w_{N_B}} \quad \min_{<j,k>} \left(\sum_{i=1}^{N_B} \left|\mathbf{w}_i^H \mathbf{h}_{i,<j,k>}\right|^2\right) \\
&\qquad\qquad j \in \{1,\cdots,N_B\}, k \in \{1,\cdots,M\} \\
&s.t. \qquad \mathbf{w}_i^H \mathbf{w}_i = P \quad \forall i = 1,\cdots,N_B
\end{aligned}
\tag{6}
$$

From (6), this optimization problem is a NP-hard problem and cannot be solved directly. In this paper, a multicast beamforming algorithm based on semi-definite relaxation is proposed. The algorithm description will be given in the next section.

From Fig. 1(b), in the original private network, the same group users located in different base stations are assigned different subcarriers, and the user only receive signals sent by its own base station. The received SNR of the k-th user in the j-th base station is expressed as

$$SNR_{OPNN<j,k>} = \left| \mathbf{w}_j^H \mathbf{h}_{j,<j,k>} \right|^2 \tag{7}$$

As is shown in Fig. 1(c), the original MBSFN mode with omnidirectional antenna doesn't adopt beamforming technology. The received SNR of the k-th user in the j-th base station is expressed as

$$SNR_{OPNN<j,k>} = \sum_{i=1}^{N_B} \left| \mathbf{w}_0 \mathbf{h}_{i,<j,k>} \right|^2 = \left| \mathbf{w}_0 \mathbf{h}_{j,<j,k>} \right|^2 + \sum_{i=1,i\neq j}^{N_B} \left| \mathbf{w}_0 \mathbf{h}_{i,<j,k>} \right|^2 \tag{8}$$

Where $\mathbf{w}_0 = \sqrt{P/N_T} \cdot I_{N_T}$, the power is evenly distributed among the N_T antennas, and the signal propagates evenly in each direction. Power is wasted since the CSI is not utilized.

By comparing (5) (7) (8), it can be inferred that SNR_{SFMC} is greater than SNR_{OPNN} and SNR_{OMBSFN} under the same base station transmitting power.

The group user channel capacity is defined as the average channel capacity of all the group users. Since the same group users receive the same information, the group user channel capacity in the three modes is defined as follows:

The proposed same-frequency multicell coordination (SFMC) mode:

$$C_{SFMC} = \frac{1}{N_B \times M} \sum_{j=1}^{N_B} \sum_{k=1}^{M} \log_2 (1 + \left| \mathbf{w}_j^H \mathbf{h}_{j,<j,k>} \right|^2 + \sum_{i=1,i\neq j}^{N_B} \left| \mathbf{w}_i^H \mathbf{h}_{i,<j,k>} \right|^2) \tag{9}$$

The original private network non-cooperation (OPNN) mode:

$$C_{OPNN} = \frac{1}{N_B \times M} \sum_{j=1}^{N_B} \sum_{k=1}^{M} \log_2 (1 + \left| \mathbf{w}_j^H \mathbf{h}_{j,<j,k>} \right|^2) \tag{10}$$

The original MBSFN (OMBSFN) with omnidirectional antenna mode:

$$C_{OMBSFN} = \frac{1}{N_B \times M} \sum_{j=1}^{N_B} \sum_{k=1}^{M} \log_2 (1 + \left| \mathbf{w}_0 \mathbf{h}_{j,<j,k>} \right|^2 + \sum_{i=1,i\neq j}^{N_B} \left| \mathbf{w}_0 \mathbf{h}_{i,<j,k>} \right|^2) \tag{11}$$

By comparing (9) (10) (11), it can be inferred that the proposed SFMC mode has a larger group user channel capacity than the other two modes under the same base station transmitting power. This is because the group user in SFMC mode can receive the signals from multiple base stations by multicast beamforming.

3 Multicast Beamforming Algorithm Based on SDR

In order to obtain the optimal approximate solution of the NP-hard problem, a same-frequency multicell coordination multicast beamforming algorithm based on semidefinite relaxation is proposed. Specific steps of the algorithm are as follows:

(1) Transforming the mathematical models

Suppose $\mathbf{W}_i = \mathbf{w}_i\mathbf{w}_i^H$, $\mathbf{H}_{i,<j,k>} = \mathbf{h}_{i,<j,k>}\,\mathbf{h}_{i,<j,k>}^H$, then by the property of matrix we can derived that

$$\left|\mathbf{w}_i^H \mathbf{h}_{i,<j,k>}\right|^2 = \mathbf{w}_i^H \mathbf{h}_{i,<j,k>}\,\mathbf{h}_{i,<j,k>}^H\,\mathbf{w}_i = tr(\mathbf{w}_i\mathbf{w}_i^H \mathbf{h}_{i,<j,k>}\,\mathbf{h}_{i,<j,k>}^H)$$
$$= tr(\mathbf{W}_i\mathbf{H}_{i,<j,k>}) = vec(\mathbf{H}_{i,<j,k>}^T)^T vec(\mathbf{W}_i) \tag{12}$$

$$\mathbf{w}_i\mathbf{w}_i^H = tr(\mathbf{W}_i) = vec(\mathbf{I}_N)^T vec(\mathbf{W}_i) \tag{13}$$

Where $vec(..)$ means vectorized representation of matrix columns. Substituting (12) (13) into (6), the optimization problem of (6) is transformed into:

$$\max \quad \min_{<j,k>} \left\{ \sum_{i=1}^{N_B} tr(\mathbf{W}_i\mathbf{H}_{i,<j,k>}) \right\} \quad j \in \{1,\cdots,N_B\}, k \in \{1,\cdots,M\} \tag{14}$$

$$s.t. \quad tr(\mathbf{W}_i) = P,\ rank(\mathbf{W}_i) = 1,\ \mathbf{W}_i \geq 0,\quad \forall\, i = 1,\cdots,N_B$$

Where $\mathbf{W}_i \geq 0$ means that the matrix $\mathbf{W}_i$ is a semi-definite matrix.

(2) Relax the restrictions and turn the problem into a typical SDP problem

Compared with the standard form of SDP problem, the mathematical model in (14) only adds the restriction that $rank(\mathbf{W}_i) = 1$. We ignore this restriction first and (14) is re-written as

$$\max \quad \min_{<j,k>} \left\{ \sum_{i=1}^{N_B} tr(\mathbf{W}_i\mathbf{H}_{i,<j,k>}) \right\} \quad j \in \{1,\cdots,N_B\}, k \in \{1,\cdots,M\} \tag{15}$$

$$s.t. \quad tr(\mathbf{W}_i) = P,\quad \mathbf{W}_i \geq 0,\qquad \forall\, i = 1,\cdots,N_B$$

At this point, the optimization problem has been transformed into a SDP problem. For the convenience of solving, we suppose $t = \min_{<j,k>}\left\{\sum_{i=1}^{N_B} tr(\mathbf{W}_i\mathbf{H}_{i,<j,k>})\right\}$, and substitute it into (15), then (15) is re-written as

$$\max \quad t$$

$$s.t. \quad \sum_{i=1}^{N_B} tr(\mathbf{W}_i \mathbf{H}_{i,<j,k>}) \geq t, \quad \forall j = 1, \cdots, N_B, \quad \forall k = 1, \cdots, M \quad (16)$$

$$tr(\mathbf{W}_i) = P, \mathbf{W}_i \geq 0, \quad \forall i = 1, \cdots, N_B$$

$$t \geq 0$$

In order to transform the inequations into equations, we introduce a free variable $s_{<j,k>}$, and substitute (12) (13) into (16), then we have

$$\min \quad -t$$

$$s.t. \quad -t - s_{<j,k>} + \sum_{i=1}^{N_B} vec(\mathbf{H}_{i,<j,k>}^T)^T vec(\mathbf{W}_i) = 0, \quad \forall j = 1, \cdots, N_B, \quad \forall k = 1, \cdots, M$$

$$vec(I_N)^T vec(\mathbf{W}_i) = P, \mathbf{W}_i \geq 0, \quad \forall i = 1, \cdots, N_B$$

$$t \geq 0, s_{<j,k>} \geq 0, \quad \forall j = 1, \cdots, N_B, \quad \forall k = 1, \cdots, M$$

$$(17)$$

(3) Optimization tool

We use SeDuMi to get $\mathbf{W}_i$. SeDuMi is an optimization tool to solve the SDP problem.

The dual format of SDP is given as:

$$\min \quad \mathbf{c}^T \mathbf{x}$$

$$s.t. \quad \mathbf{A}_{eq}\mathbf{x} = \mathbf{b}_{eq}$$

$$\mathbf{A}_q\mathbf{x} = \mathbf{b}_q \quad (18)$$

$$\mathbf{F}(\mathbf{x}) = \mathbf{F}_0 + \sum_{i=1}^{n} x_i \mathbf{F}_i \geq 0$$

Let $\mathbf{x} = [t, s_{<1,1>}, s_{<1,2>}, \cdots, s_{<N_B,M>}, vec(\mathbf{W}_1), vec(\mathbf{W}_2), \cdots, vec(\mathbf{W}_{N_B})]$.

Compare the coefficient of the relaxed model in (17) with the dual format of SDP in (18), and then we can obtain:

$$\mathbf{c}^T = [-1, zeros(1, M \times N_B + N_T^2 \times N_B)] \quad (19)$$

$$\mathbf{b}_q = [zeros(1, M \times N_B), P \times ones(1, N_B)]^T \quad (20)$$

$$\mathbf{A}_q = \begin{bmatrix} \mathbf{A}_1 & \mathbf{A}_2 \\ \mathbf{A}_3 & \mathbf{A}_4 \end{bmatrix} \quad (21)$$

Where:

$$\mathbf{A}_1 = \begin{bmatrix} -1 & -1 & 0 & \cdots & 0 \\ -1 & 0 & -1 & \cdots & 0 \\ \vdots & \vdots & \vdots & \ddots & \vdots \\ -1 & 0 & 0 & \cdots & -1 \end{bmatrix} \tag{22}$$

$$\mathbf{A}_2 = \begin{bmatrix} vec(\mathbf{H}^T_{1,<1,1>})^T & vec(\mathbf{H}^T_{2,<1,1>})^T & \cdots & vec(\mathbf{H}^T_{N_B,<1,1>})^T \\ vec(\mathbf{H}^T_{1,<1,2>})^T & vec(\mathbf{H}^T_{2,<1,2>})^T & \cdots & vec(\mathbf{H}^T_{N_B,<1,2>})^T \\ \vdots & \vdots & \ddots & \vdots \\ vec(\mathbf{H}^T_{1,<N_B,M>})^T & vec(\mathbf{H}^T_{2,<N_B,M>})^T & & vec(\mathbf{H}^T_{N_B,<N_B,M>})^T \end{bmatrix} \tag{23}$$

$$\mathbf{A}_3 = zeros[N_B, M \times N_B + 1] \tag{24}$$

$$\mathbf{A}_4 = \begin{bmatrix} vec(I_{N_T})^T & 0 & \cdots & 0 \\ 0 & vec(I_{N_T})^T & \cdots & 0 \\ \vdots & \vdots & \ddots & \vdots \\ 0 & 0 & \cdots & vec(I_{N_T})^T \end{bmatrix} \tag{25}$$

$$K.l = (M+1) \times N_B \tag{26}$$

$$K.s = N_T \tag{27}$$

Where, the dimension of $\mathbf{A}_1$ is $(M \times N_B) \times (M \times N_B + 1)$; the dimension of $\mathbf{A}_2$ is $(M \times N_B) \times (N_B \times N_T^2)$; the dimension of $\mathbf{A}_3$ is $N_B \times (M \times N_B + 1)$; the dimension of $\mathbf{A}_4$ is $N_B \times (N_B \times N_T^2)$; $K.l$ represents the number of equality constraints; $K.s$ represents the order of LMI (Linear Matrix Inequality). Substitute the above parameters into the optimization tool, SeDuMi function, and the optimal solution $\mathbf{x}$ is obtained, and then we choose the $s + 2 + (i - 1) \times N_T^2$ column to the $s + 1 + i \times N_T^2$ column of $\mathbf{x}$ as $vec(\mathbf{W}_i)$. Then, we can obtain the matrix $\mathbf{W}_i$ by converting $vec(\mathbf{W}_i)$.

(4) Randomization and choosing the relatively optimal solution

Due to the condition that rank$(\mathbf{W}_i) = 1$ was ignored in (15), the $\mathbf{W}_i$ we obtained may not meet the restriction rank$(\mathbf{W}_i) = 1$. If the rank of the obtained $\mathbf{W}_i$ is 1, we decompose $\mathbf{W}_i$ according to the form $\mathbf{W}_i = \mathbf{w}_i\mathbf{w}_i^H$, then $\mathbf{w}_i$ is the exact solution. If the rank of the obtained $\mathbf{W}_i$ is not 1, we need to use the randomizing method to get the optimal approximate solution that satisfies rank$(\mathbf{W}_i) = 1$. The randomizing method we used in this paper is as follows:

We decompose each matrix $\mathbf{W}_i$ $(\forall i = 1, \cdots, N_B)$ and get $\mathbf{W}_i = \mathbf{U}_i \Sigma_i \mathbf{U}_i^H$; $\mathbf{U}_i$ and Σ_i are corresponding eigenvector and eigenvalue matrix. Let $\mathbf{w}_i = \mathbf{U}_i \Sigma_i^{1/2} \mathbf{e}_i$, where $\mathbf{e}_i \in C^{N_T \times 1}$, its q-th element $[\mathbf{e}_i]_q = e^{j\theta_{i,q}}$ is a random variable uniformly distributed on the unit circle, which means $\theta_{i,q}$ is a random variable that is evenly distributed within $[0, 2\pi)$.

A set of candidates of transmitting multicast beamforming weight vector $\mathbf{w}_i$ are obtained by the method above. And then these vectors are scaled up to reach $\|\mathbf{w}_i\|_2^2 = P,$

which is the constraint of the base station transmitting power. The transmitting multicast beamforming weight vector with the max least SNR selected from these candidate vectors is used as the optimal approximate solution.

4   Simulation Analysis

The simulation parameters of the proposed SFMC mode, the OPNN mode and the OMBSFN mode (omnidirectional antenna) are shown in Table 1.

Table 1. Simulation parameters

Parameters	Value
Number of base stations (N_B)	3
Number of single base station antennas (N_T)	4
Number of single base station users (M)	5
Group user angle interval	$2°$

The comparison of the least received SNR and the group user channel capacity in the three modes are shown in Figs. 2 and 3 respectively. Figure 2 shows that under the same transmitting power of base station, the least received SNR of group users in the proposed SFMC mode is 4 dB and 2 dB higher than that of OPNN mode and OMBSFN mode. Figure 3 shows that compared with OPNN mode and OMBSFN mode, the group user channel capacity in the proposed SFMC mode is significantly improved. This is because the SFMC mode adopts the proposed multicast beamforming algorithm, the spatial domain resources are fully utilized and the cell-edge users can receive the same information from multiple base stations.

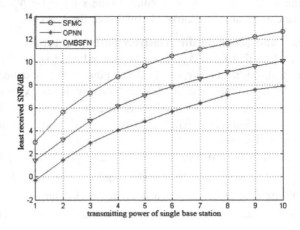

Fig. 2. Least received SNR of group users in the three modes

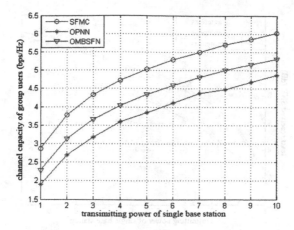

Fig. 3. Group user channel capacity in the three modes

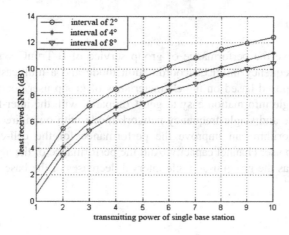

Fig. 4. The performance of the proposed algorithm and the group user angle interval

The relationships between the group user angle interval, the base station antenna number and the performance of the proposed SFMC algorithm are shown in Figs. 4 and 5 respectively. As is shown in Fig. 4, the smaller the group user angle interval is, the better performance the proposed algorithm has. Because the group user angle interval is smaller, the beam lobes are more concentrated by using the multicast beamforming algorithm based on DOD. Thus, the energy will be more concentrated, which leads to the larger the received SNR of the group users. From Fig. 5, the larger the base station antenna number is, the better performance the proposed algorithm has. When the base station antenna number increases from 2 to 4, the SNR is significantly improved. When the base station antenna number increases from 4 to 8, the SNR increases slowly. Therefore, the proposed algorithm can achieve great performance improvement without requiring too many transmitting antennas.

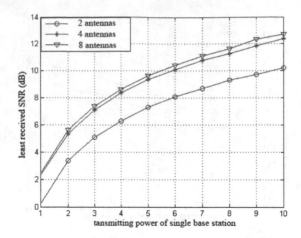

Fig. 5. The performance of the proposed algorithm and the base station antenna number

5 Conclusion

In order to improve the performance of group service of B-TrunC system, a system model of same-frequency multicell coordination mode and a multicast beamforming algorithm are proposed based on the characteristics of group user concentrated distribution and the angle information easy to get. Compared with the inter-frequency non-coordination mode and single frequency network mode with omnidirectional antenna, the proposed algorithm can improve the performance for the cell-edge users and increase the group user channel capacity. And the performance of the algorithm will be further improved as the group user angle interval decreases or the base station antenna number increases.

References

1. Li, S.-Q., Chen, Z., Yu, Q.-Y., Meng, W.-X., Tan, X.-Z.: Toward future public safety communications – the broadband wireless trunking project in China. IEEE Veh. Technol. Mag. **8**(2), 55–63 (2013)
2. Tervo, O., Tran, L.-N., Chatzinotas, S.: Energy-efficient joint unicast and multicast beamforming with multi-antenna user terminals. In: 18th IEEE International Workshop on Signal Processing Advances in Wireless Communications, pp. 1–5. IEEE, Sapporo (2017)
3. Zhou, L., Zheng, L., Wang, X.: Coordinated multicell multicast beamforming based on manifold optimization. IEEE Commun. Lett. **21**(7), 1673–1676 (2017)
4. Han, S., Chih-Lin, I., Xu, Z., et al.: Large-scale antenna systems with hybrid analog and digital beamforming for millimeter wave 5G. IEEE Commun. Mag. **53**(1), 186–194 (2015)
5. Christopoulos, D., Chatzinotas, S., Ottersten, B.: Sum rate maximizing multigroup multicast beamforming under per-antenna power constraints. Mathematics **62**(19), 3354–3359 (2014)
6. Zhang, H., Jiang, Y., Sundaresan, K., et al.: Wireless multicast scheduling with switched beamforming antennas. IEEE/ACM Trans. Netw. **20**(20), 1595–1607 (2012)

7. Karipidis, E., Sidiropoulos, N.D., Luo, Z.Q.: Quality of service and max-min fair transmit beamforming to multiple cochannel multicast groups. IEEE Trans. Signal Process. **56**(3), 1268–1279 (2008)
8. Jordan, M., Senst, M., Ascheid, G., et al.: Long-term beamforming in single frequency networks using semidefinite relaxation. In: IEEE 67th Vehicular Technology Conference, pp. 275–279. IEEE, Singapore (2008)
9. Silva, Y.C.B., Klein, A.: Linear transmit beamforming techniques for the multigroup multicast scenario. IEEE Trans. Veh. Technol. **58**(8), 4353–4367 (2009)
10. Demir, O.T., Tuncer, T.E.: Multi-group multicast beamforming for simultaneous wireless information and power transfer. In: 23rd European Signal Processing Conference, pp. 1356–1360. IEEE, Nice (2015)
11. Xiang, Z., Tao, M., Wang, X.: Coordinated multicast beamforming in multicell networks. IEEE Trans. Wirel. Commun. **12**(1), 12–21 (2012)

Neural Networks in Hybrid Precoding for Millimeter Wave Massive MIMO Systems

Jing Yang[1] , Kai Chen[1], Xiaohu Ge[1(✉)] , Yonghui Li[2], and Lin Tian[3]

[1] School of Electronic Information and Communications,
Huazhong University of Science and Technology, Wuhan, Hubei, China
xhge@mail.hust.edu.cn
[2] School of Electrical and Information Engineering,
University of Sydney, Sydney, Australia
[3] Beijing Key Laboratory of Mobile Computing and Pervasive Devices,
Institute of Computing Technology, Chinese Academy of Sciences, Beijing, China

Abstract. Neural networks have been applied to the physical layer of wireless communication systems to solve complex problems. In millimeter wave (mmWave) massive multiple-input multiple-output (MIMO) systems, hybrid precoding has been considered as an energy-efficient technology to replace fully-digital precoding. The way of designing hybrid precoding in mmWave massive MIMO systems by multi-layer neural networks has not been investigated. Based on further decomposing the baseband precoding matrix, an idea is proposed in this paper to map hybrid precoding structure to a multi-layer neural network. Considering the deterioration in the throughput and energy efficiency of mmWave massive MIMO systems, the feasibility of the proposed idea is analyzed. Moreover, a singular value decomposition (SVD) based decomposing (SVDDE) algorithm is proposed to evaluate the feasibility of the proposed idea. Simulation results indicate that there is an optimal number of users which can minimize the performance deterioration. Moreover, the simulation results also show that slight deterioration in the throughput and energy efficiency of mmWave massive MIMO systems is caused by further decomposing the baseband precoding matrix. In other words, further decomposing the baseband precoding matrix is a feasible way to map the hybrid precoding structure to a multi-layer neural network.

Keywords: Neural networks · Millimeter wave · Massive MIMO · Hybrid precoding

This work was supported by the National Key Research and Development Program of China under Grant 2017YFE0121600.

S. Han et al. (Eds.): AICON 2019, LNICST 286, pp. 132–145, 2019.
https://doi.org/10.1007/978-3-030-22968-9_12

1 Introduction

The design and optimization of the fifth generation (5G) wireless communication system become challenging, due to the expectation of satisfying the key performance indicators (KPIs) in 5G usage scenarios, such as 100 Mbit/s user experienced data rate, 10 Gbit/s peak data rate, 1 millisecond (ms) over-the-air latency and $10^6/\text{km}^2$ connectivity density [1,2]. Combining the millimeter wave (mmWave) communication and massive multiple-input multiple-output (MIMO) technology is a feasible solution to meet the KPIs [3]. Meanwhile, the signal processing of baseband units (BBUs) becomes more complicated in 5G base stations (BSs) [4]. In this case, it is intractable to optimize the real-time hybrid precoding in multi-user mmWave massive MIMO systems [5,6]. Neural networks, one of the technologies in artificial intelligence (AI), have shown the great application value to solve complex and intractable problems in image recognition, automatic control and healthcare [7–9]. Therefore, it is attractive to apply neural networks to design hybrid precoding for multi-user mmWave massive MIMO systems.

Some studies have already investigated the application of neural networks for the physical layer of wireless communication systems. The work in [10] proposed a procedure to predict channel characteristics of mmWave massive MIMO systems, based on convolutional neural networks. Moreover, the predicted results in [10] showed the well matching with the real channel characteristics. In the channel estimation of mmWave massive MIMO systems, the estimation with the help of neural networks was better than the state-of-the-art compressed sensing algorithms [11]. In addition to the channel estimation, neural networks were also used for the modulation classification of raw IQ samples, which achieved competitive accuracy [12]. Considering the unmanageable joint optimization problem of the coverage and capacity in mmWave massive MIMO systems, the authors in [13] enhanced the service coverage and the spectrum efficiency by applying neural networks to solve the joint optimization problem. Combining the distributed massive MIMO with neural networks, more accurate results of user positioning had been achieved [14], which paves the way for network operators to provide better context-aware communication services. It is emerging in designing the physical layer of 5G wireless communication systems by neural networks. The work in [15] provided a comprehensive survey of applications which uses multi-layer neural networks to solve problems in cellular networks. Based on the results in [15], the existing studies, related to the application of neural networks in the physical layer of cellular networks, is divided into five categories, i.e., signal detection, modulation classification, error correction, interference alignment management and anti-jamming. Applications of neural networks in wireless communication systems remain to be explored.

Precoding is one of the key technologies in the physical layer of massive MIMO systems to improve the spectrum efficiency. Considering the high cost of radio frequency (RF) chains in mmWave band for fully-connected precoding, hybrid precoding is proposed in mmWave massive MIMO systems [16]. The topology of the fully-connected phase shifter network in hybrid precoding structure is similar to neural networks. To our knowledge, studies related to design hybrid precoding by multi-layer neural networks have not appeared in the available literature. Inspired by this vacancy in knowledge, the objective of this paper is proposing an idea to map the hybrid precoding structure to multi-layer neural networks. The idea is based on the further decomposition of the baseband precoding matrix in hybrid precoding. Furthermore, an SVD-based decomposing (SVDDE) algorithm is proposed to evaluate the feasibility of the proposed idea. The simulation results show that the performance deterioration in the throughput and energy efficiency of mmWave massive MIMO systems can be caused when the baseband precoding matrix in hybrid precoding is further decomposed. In this case, modeling the hybrid precoding structure as multi-layer neural networks is feasible in mmWave massive MIMO systems.

The rest of this paper is outlined as follows. Section 2 describes the system model. In Sect. 3, an idea is proposed to map hybrid precoding to a multi-layer neural network. Moreover, the feasibility of the proposed idea is analyzed. Section 4 provides the simulation results. Finally, conclusions are drawn in Sect. 5.

2   System Model

As shown in Fig. 1, K single antenna users are served by the mmWave massive MIMO system with fully-connected hybrid precoding. The BS is equipped with N_T antennas and N_{RF} RF chains. Moreover, the values of K, N_T and N_{RF} satisfy $K \leq N_{RF} \leq N_T$. The phase shifter network in Fig. 1 contains $N_T N_{RF}$ phase shifters (PSs). The baseband precoding matrix is denoted as $\mathbf{F}_{BB} \in \mathbb{C}^{N_{RF} \times K}$ and the RF precoding matrix is denoted as $\mathbf{F}_{RF} \in \mathbb{C}^{N_T \times N_{RF}}$. The downlink channel matrix $\mathbf{H} \in \mathbb{C}^{N_T \times K}$ is $\mathbf{H}^H = [\mathbf{h}_1, \cdots, \mathbf{h}_k, \cdots, \mathbf{h}_K]^H$, where $\mathbf{h}_k$ is the downlink channel vector between the BS and the k-th user. The received signal at the k-th user is given as

$$y_k = \mathbf{h}_k^H \mathbf{F}_{RF} \mathbf{F}_{BB} \mathbf{s} + n_k, \tag{1}$$

where $\mathbf{s}$ is $K \times 1$ transmitted signal vector $\mathbf{s} = [s_1, \cdots, s_k, \cdots, s_K]^T$ for K users satisfying $\mathbb{E}[\mathbf{ss}^H] = \mathbf{I}_K$, s_k $(k = 1, \cdots, K)$ is the transmitted signal for the k-th user. $n_k \sim \mathcal{CN}(0, \sigma_n^2)$ is the noise received by the k-th user. $\mathbf{F}_{BB}$ and $\mathbf{F}_{RF}$ satisfy $\|\mathbf{F}_{RF}\mathbf{F}_{BB}\|_F^2 = P_T$ where P_T is the transmission power.

The Saleh-Valenzuela channel model is considered as the mmWave channel model [17] and $\mathbf{h}_k$ is given as

$$\mathbf{h}_k = \sqrt{\frac{N_T \xi_k}{L}} \sum_{l=1}^{L} g_l^k \mathbf{a}(\theta_l), \tag{2}$$

where L is the total number of multipath between the BS and K users. The large-scale fading coefficient is denoted as $\xi_k = \frac{1}{d_k^\alpha}$, where α is the path loss exponent of mmWave and d_k is the distance between the BS and the k-th user [18]. $g_l^k \sim \mathcal{CN}(0, \sigma_{g,l}^2)$ is the complex gain of signals at the l-th multipath [19].

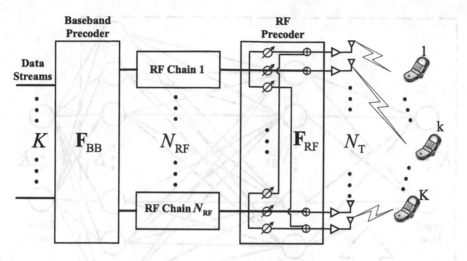

Fig. 1. The mmWave massive MIMO system with fully-connected hybrid precoding structure.

The array response vector $\mathbf{a}\,(\theta_l)$ of the uniform linear array (ULA) in Fig. 1 is written as

$$\mathbf{a}\,(\theta_l) = \frac{1}{\sqrt{N_T}}\left[1, e^{j\frac{2\pi}{\lambda}d_T\sin(\theta_l)}, \cdots , e^{j(N_T-1)\frac{2\pi}{\lambda}d_T\sin(\theta_l)}\right]^{\mathrm{T}}, \qquad (3)$$

where θ_l is the azimuth angle of signals at the l-th multipath, λ is the wavelength of mmWave, d_T is the inter-antenna spacing.

3   The Neural Network in Hybrid Precoding

3.1   The Mapping of a Multi-Layer Neural Network

Most of the studies related to neural networks are training software-based neural networks. Few works have been done in training hardware-based neural networks to achieve learning [20]. In fully-connected hybrid precoding structure (Fig. 1), the phase shifter network has similar topology to neural networks. Furthermore, the baseband precoding processing in BBUs is described as the matrix-vector multiplication $\mathbf{F}_{BB}\mathbf{s}$, which is similar to the mathematic model of neural networks, i.e., the multiplication between weight matrices and input data vectors. It is reasonable to map the hybrid precoding structure in Fig. 1 to a one-layer neural network in Fig. 2a.

The essence of precoding is the signal processing between the input data streams and antennas array. The input data streams and antennas array are treated as the input layer and output layer, respectively, for the equivalent neural network in Fig. 2. In Fig. 2a, the hybrid precoding structure in mmWave massive MIMO systems is mapped to a single-hidden-layer neural network, whose weight

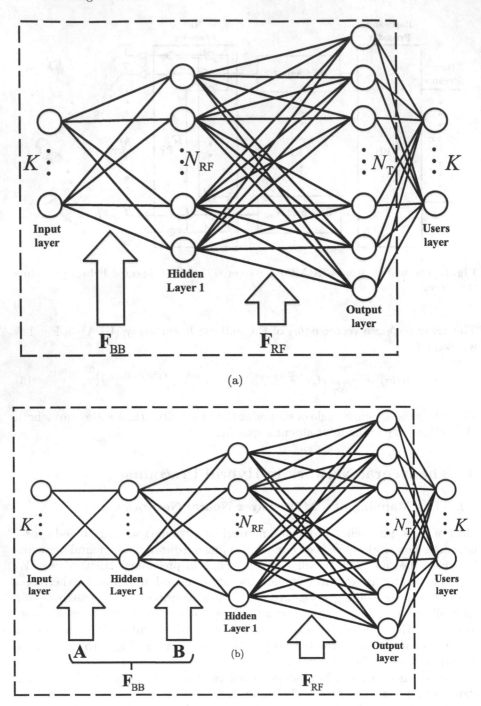

Fig. 2. Hybrid precoding structure in mmWave massive MIMO system is mapped to (a) a one-layer neural network; (b) a multi-layer neural network.

matrices are $\mathbf{F}_{BB}$ and $\mathbf{F}_{RF}$. In hybrid precoding, the digital precoding can adjust both the amplitude and phase of signals and the RF precoding can only change the phase of signals, which implies that the mapped neural network in Fig. 2a has two weight matrices with different properties. There is no denying that multi-layer neural networks commonly have better performance than one layer neural networks. It is reasonable to map the hybrid precoding structure to a multi-layer neural networks. More than two weight matrices are needed in mapping the hybrid precoding structure to a multi-layer neural network. In addition to matrices $\mathbf{F}_{BB}$ and $\mathbf{F}_{RF}$, new weight matrices have to be obtained.

Hybrid precoding is proposed by decomposing fully-digital precoding into a digital baseband precoding and an analog RF precoding. Inspired by the decomposition of fully-digital precoding, an idea that mapping the hybrid precoding structure to a multi-layer neural network is proposed. The baseband precoding matrix $\mathbf{F}_{BB}$ is first decomposed into two new sub-matrices. These new sub-matrices are treated as new weight matrices for a two-layer neural network in Fig. 2b. Different from software-based neural networks and hardware-based neural networks, the equivalent neural network in Fig. 2b is a software-hardware hybrid neural network which consists of a software-based neural network in BBUs and a hardware-based neural network in the phase shifter network. Software-based neural networks have been widely implemented. In contrast, the implementation of hardware-based neural networks still has knotty technical problems. One formidable challenge for implementations of the hardware-based neural network in Fig. 2 is to achieve learning in the phase shifter network. Considering that the software-hardware hybrid neural network has not been implemented, we only investigate the feasibility of the proposed idea.

Considering that the proposed idea is based on further decomposing $\mathbf{F}_{BB}$, we speculate on the feasibility of the proposed idea by using existing methods, due to the difficulty of implementing the software-hardware hybrid neural network. The proposed idea is feasible at the case that the performance deterioration, caused by the decomposition of $\mathbf{F}_{BB}$, is slight in the throughput and energy efficiency of mmWave massive MIMO systems. Considering a widely used approach to decompose $\mathbf{F}_{BB}$, the decomposition algorithm should be proposed and the impact of further decomposing $\mathbf{F}_{BB}$ on the throughput and energy efficiency of mmWave massive MIMO systems with hybrid precoding structure has to be analyzed. The throughput and energy efficiency of mmWave massive MIMO systems is derived in the following.

The received signal-to-interference-plus-noise ratio (SINR) at the k-th user is calculated as

$$SINR_k = \frac{\left|\mathbf{h}_k^H \mathbf{F}_{RF} \mathbf{F}_{BB,\,k} \mathbf{F}_{BB,\,k}^H \mathbf{F}_{RF}^H \mathbf{h}_k\right|^2}{\sigma_n^2 + \sum_{i=1,i\neq k}^{K} \left|\mathbf{h}_k^H \mathbf{F}_{RF} \mathbf{F}_{BB,\,i} \mathbf{F}_{BB,\,i}^H \mathbf{F}_{RF}^H \mathbf{h}_k\right|^2}, \tag{4}$$

where $\mathbf{F}_{\mathrm{BB},\,k}$ is the k-th column vector of $\mathbf{F}_{\mathrm{BB}}$. Thus, the throughput for the BS to simultaneously serve K users is presented by

$$R_{\mathrm{sum}} = W \sum_{k=1}^{K} \log_2 \left(1 + SINR_k\right), \tag{5}$$

where W is the bandwidth.

In Fig. 1, the mmWave massive MIMO system with hybrid precoding structure consists of power amplifiers (PAs), the phase shifter network, RF chains and BBUs. The total power consumption of the mmWave massive MIMO system is

$$P_{\mathrm{total}} = P_{\mathrm{PA}} + N_{\mathrm{T}} N_{\mathrm{RF}} P_{\mathrm{PS}} + N_{\mathrm{RF}} P_{\mathrm{RF}} + P_{\mathrm{BB}}, \tag{6}$$

where $P_{\mathrm{PA}} = \frac{P_{\mathrm{T}}}{\eta_{\mathrm{PA}}}$ is the power of PAs, η_{PA} is the efficiency of PAs [21,22]. The power consumption of the phase shifter network is $N_{\mathrm{T}} N_{\mathrm{RF}} P_{\mathrm{PS}}$, where P_{PS} is the power of a single PS. The power consumption of RF chains is $N_{\mathrm{RF}} P_{\mathrm{RF}}$, where P_{RF} is the power of one RF chain. The power consumed by BBUs can be obtained by

$$P_{\mathrm{BB}} = W \frac{\Delta}{L_{\mathrm{BS}}} + \frac{W}{W_{\mathrm{c}} T_{\mathrm{c}}} \frac{\Omega}{L_{\mathrm{BS}}}, \tag{7}$$

where the first term is the power consumption of the multiplication $\mathbf{F}_{\mathrm{BB}}\mathbf{s}$ in precoding processing, Δ is the number of floating-point operations for the multiplication $\mathbf{F}_{\mathrm{BB}}\mathbf{s}$. The second term in (7) is the power consumption of the precoding algorithm used in BBUs, Ω is the number of floating-point operations for the precoding algorithm. The coherence bandwidth and coherence time of mmWave frequency are denoted as W_{c} and T_{c}, respectively. The typical values of W_{c} and T_{c} in mmWave massive MIMO systems are 100 MHz and $35\,\mu\mathrm{s}$, respectively [23,24]. L_{BS} is defined as the computation efficiency of BBUs, whose typical value is 12.8 GFLOPS/W [25].

Based on (5) and (6), the energy efficiency of the mmWave massive MIMO system with hybrid precoding structure is denoted as

$$\eta_{\mathrm{EE}} = \frac{R_{\mathrm{sum}}}{P_{\mathrm{total}}}. \tag{8}$$

3.2   The Decomposition Based on SVD

Assuming that the BS has the perfect channel state information (CSI), the near-optimal baseband precoding matrix for maximizing the R_{sum} is equivalent zero-forcing (ZF) precoding [5] which is given by

$$\mathbf{F}_{\mathrm{BB}}^{\mathrm{opt}} = \mathbf{H}_{\mathrm{eq}}^{\mathrm{H}} \left(\mathbf{H}_{\mathrm{eq}} \mathbf{H}_{\mathrm{eq}}^{\mathrm{H}}\right)^{-1} \mathbf{D}, \tag{9}$$

where $\mathbf{H}_{\mathrm{eq}} = \mathbf{H}^{\mathrm{H}} \mathbf{F}_{\mathrm{RF}}^{\mathrm{opt}}$ is the $K \times N_{\mathrm{RF}}$ equivalent downlink channel matrix for K users, $\mathbf{F}_{\mathrm{RF}}^{\mathrm{opt}}$ is the optimal RF precoding matrix which can be written as linear combination of $\mathbf{a}\left(\theta_l\right)$, e.g., vectors $\mathbf{a}\left(\theta_l\right)$ with different θ_l as columns of $\mathbf{F}_{\mathrm{RF}}^{\mathrm{opt}}$ [16]. $\mathbf{D}$ is a $K \times K$ diagonal matrix to normalize $\mathbf{F}_{\mathrm{BB}}^{\mathrm{opt}}$. The singular value decomposition (SVD) is widely used to decompose a matrix. Accordingly, the SVD of $\mathbf{F}_{\mathrm{BB}}^{\mathrm{opt}}$ is considered as the decomposition approach to investigate the feasibility of the proposed idea. Define the SVD of $\mathbf{F}_{\mathrm{BB}}^{\mathrm{opt}}$ as $\mathbf{F}_{\mathrm{BB}}^{\mathrm{opt}} = \mathbf{U}\boldsymbol{\Sigma}\mathbf{V}^{\mathrm{H}}$, where $\mathbf{U} = [\mathbf{u}_1, \mathbf{u}_2, \cdots, \mathbf{u}_K]$ is a $N_{\mathrm{RF}} \times K$ left singular vector matrix and $\mathbf{V} = [\mathbf{v}_1, \mathbf{v}_2, \cdots, \mathbf{v}_K]$ is a $K \times K$ right singular vector matrix. $\boldsymbol{\Sigma} = \mathrm{diag}\,(\sigma_1, \sigma_2, \cdots, \sigma_K)$ is a $K \times K$ diagonal matrix containing the nonzero singular values of $\mathbf{F}_{\mathrm{BB}}^{\mathrm{opt}}$ in decreasing order, i.e., $\sigma_1 \geq \sigma_2 \geq \cdots \geq \sigma_K$. Set $\mathbf{A} = \mathbf{U}\boldsymbol{\Sigma}$ and $\mathbf{B} = \mathbf{V}^{\mathrm{H}}$, $\mathbf{F}_{\mathrm{BB}}^{\mathrm{opt}}$ is rewritten as $\mathbf{F}_{\mathrm{BB}}^{\mathrm{opt}} = \mathbf{A}\mathbf{B}$. Decomposing $\mathbf{F}_{\mathrm{BB}}^{\mathrm{opt}}$ into two sub-matrices $\mathbf{A}$ and $\mathbf{B}$, a new hidden layer is added to the equivalent neural network which is a two-layer neural network in Fig. 2b. Moreover, both matrices $\mathbf{A} \in \mathbb{C}^{N_{\mathrm{RF}} \times K}$ and $\mathbf{B} \in \mathbb{C}^{K \times K}$ are treated as the weight matrices for the two-layer neural network.

Combining the mmWave communication and massive MIMO technologies in 5G BSs complicates the real-time signal processing in BBUs. Moreover, the number of floating-point operations in precoding processing has been increased, which increases the power consumption of BBUs [4]. Considering that the power consumption of BBUs has a great impact on the energy efficiency of mmWave massive MIMO systems, the decomposition of $\mathbf{F}_{\mathrm{BB}}^{\mathrm{opt}}$ should not increase the power consumption of BBUs, i.e., not increasing the number of floating-point operations in hybrid precoding. The number of floating-point operations for multiplications $\mathbf{F}_{\mathrm{BB}}\mathbf{s}$ and $\mathbf{A}\mathbf{B}\mathbf{s}$ are $\Lambda_1 = 8N_{\mathrm{RF}}K - 2N_{\mathrm{RF}}$ and $\Lambda_2 = 8\left(N_{\mathrm{RF}}K + K^2\right) - 2\left(N_{\mathrm{RF}} + K\right)$, respectively. The additional number of floating-point operations in hybrid precoding processing is denoted as Φ. When $\mathbf{F}_{\mathrm{BB}}^{\mathrm{opt}}$ is decomposed into two sub-matrices $\mathbf{A}$ and $\mathbf{B}$, $\Phi = \Lambda_2 - \Lambda_1$ and $\Phi > 0$ which indicates that the number of floating-point operations is increased. Therefore, another two matrices $\mathbf{C} \in \mathbb{C}^{N_{\mathrm{RF}} \times m}$ and $\mathbf{D} \in \mathbb{C}^{m \times K}$ have to be constructed to make $\Phi \leq 0$, i.e., the number of floating-point operations in the multiplication $\mathbf{C}\mathbf{D}\mathbf{s}$ is less than or equal to the number of floating-point operations in the multiplication $\mathbf{F}_{\mathrm{BB}}\mathbf{s}$.

The SVD of $\mathbf{F}_{\mathrm{BB}}^{\mathrm{opt}}$ can be rewritten as

$$
\begin{aligned}
\mathbf{F}_{\mathrm{BB}}^{\mathrm{opt}} &= \mathbf{A}\mathbf{B} \\
&= \sum_{i=1}^{K} \mathbf{A}^{(i)}\mathbf{B}_{(i)} \\
&= \sum_{i=1}^{K} \left(\sigma_i \mathbf{u}_i\right) \mathbf{v}_i^{\mathrm{H}}
\end{aligned}
\tag{10}
$$

where $\mathbf{A}^{(i)}$ is the i-th column vector of $\mathbf{A}$ and $\mathbf{B}_{(i)}$ is the i-th row vector of $\mathbf{B}$. Based on (10), $\mathbf{C}$ and $\mathbf{D}$ are constructed as

$$
\mathbf{C} = [\sigma_1 \mathbf{u}_1, \sigma_2 \mathbf{u}_2, \cdots, \sigma_m \mathbf{u}_m]
\tag{11}
$$

and

$$
\mathbf{D} = [\mathbf{v}_1, \mathbf{v}_2, \cdots, \mathbf{v}_m]^{\mathrm{H}},
\tag{12}
$$

where $m \in [1, K]$ is the number of column and row vectors in $\mathbf{C}$ and $\mathbf{D}$. The number of floating-point operations for the multiplication $\mathbf{CD}$s is $\Lambda_3 = 8\left(N_{\mathrm{RF}}m + mK\right) - 2\left(N_{\mathrm{RF}} + m\right)$. Considering the constraint $\Phi \leq 0$, i.e., $\Lambda_3 \leq \Lambda_1$, the value of m satisfies

$$m \leq \frac{N_{\mathrm{RF}}K}{N_{\mathrm{RF}} + K - \frac{1}{4}}. \tag{13}$$

Based on (13), the value of m is smaller than K, which indicates that the multiplication $\mathbf{CD}$ is the approximation of the multiplication $\mathbf{AB}$. Define the square of the Euclidean distance $\|\mathbf{AB} - \mathbf{CD}\|_F^2$ as the error $\|\mathbf{E}\|_F^2$, which is derived as

$$\|\mathbf{E}\|_F^2 = \|\mathbf{AB} - \mathbf{CD}\|_F^2$$
$$= \left\| \sum_{i=m+1}^{K} \left(\sigma_i \mathbf{u}_i\right) \mathbf{v}_i^{\mathrm{H}} \right\|_F^2. \tag{14}$$

Based on (14), the smaller the value of m is, the larger the error will be. Furthermore, the performance deterioration in the throughput of mmWave massive MIMO systems depends on the value of $\|\mathbf{E}\|_F^2$. Considering that the value of m is a positive integer, the maximum value of m is given as

$$m_{\max} = \left\lfloor \frac{N_{\mathrm{RF}}K}{N_{\mathrm{RF}} + K - \frac{1}{4}} \right\rfloor, \tag{15}$$

where $\lfloor x \rfloor$ is the floor function of a real number x, i.e., outputs the greatest integer which is less than or equal to x. When $m = m_{\max}$, $\|\mathbf{E}\|_F^2$ is the smallest. On the contrary, $\|\mathbf{E}\|_F^2$ is the largest for $m = 1$. An SVD-based decomposing (SVDDE) algorithm is proposed in the following to decompose the baseband precoding matrix into two sub-matrices. The proposed SVDDE algorithm is given as follows.

Algorithm 1. SVD-based decomposing (SVDDE)

Require: $\mathbf{F}_{\mathrm{BB}}^{\mathrm{opt}}$ and m
1: Give the SVD of $\mathbf{F}_{\mathrm{BB}}^{\mathrm{opt}}$ and $\mathbf{F}_{\mathrm{BB}}^{\mathrm{opt}} = \mathbf{U}\boldsymbol{\Sigma}\mathbf{V}^{\mathrm{H}}$
2: **for** $i = 1, \cdots, m$ **do**
3:     Select the i-th column vectors of $\mathbf{u}_i$ and $\mathbf{v}_i$ which corresponding to the i-th singular value σ_i
4:     Set $\mathbf{C}^{(i)} = \sigma_i \mathbf{u}_i$ and $\mathbf{D}_{(i)} = \mathbf{v}_i$
5: **end for**
6: Generate matrices $\mathbf{C} = [\sigma_1 \mathbf{u}_1, \sigma_2 \mathbf{u}_2, \cdots, \sigma_m \mathbf{u}_m]$ and $\mathbf{D} = [\mathbf{v}_1, \mathbf{v}_2, \cdots, \mathbf{v}_m]$
7: **return** $\mathbf{F}_{\mathrm{BB}} = \frac{\mathbf{CD}}{\|\mathbf{CD}\|_F}$

3.3   Computational Complexity Analysis

The number of floating-point operations is considered as the computational complexity. One of the input in **Algorithm 1** is the near-optimal baseband precoding matrix $\mathbf{F}_{\mathrm{BB}}^{\mathrm{opt}}$, which is obtained by consuming $K^3 + 9N_{\mathrm{RF}}K^2 + 3N_{\mathrm{RF}}K$ floating-point operations. The SVD, in the first step of **Algorithm 1**, needs $4N_{\mathrm{RF}}^2 K + 22K^3$ floating-point operations [26]. Moreover, the number of floating-point operations in generating two matrices $\mathbf{C}$ and $\mathbf{D}$ is $4N_{\mathrm{RF}}^2 K + 22K^3 + 2mN_{\mathrm{RF}}$. Therefore, the computational complexity of **Algorithm 1** is $\Omega = 9N_{\mathrm{RF}}K^2 + 3N_{\mathrm{RF}}K + 4N_{\mathrm{RF}}^2 K + 23K^3 + 2mN_{\mathrm{RF}}$.

Based on the computational complexity of **Algorithm 1**, the computation power of BBUs is calculated and the total power consumption of the mmWave massive MIMO system is obtained. Therefore, the performance deterioration in the energy efficiency of mmWave massive MIMO systems can be analyzed.

4   Simulation Results

In this section, simulation results are provided to show the impact of decomposing $\mathbf{F}_{\mathrm{BB}}^{\mathrm{opt}}$ on the throughput and energy efficiency of mmWave massive MIMO systems with hybrid precoding structure. The carrier frequency is assumed to be 28 GHz. Moreover, there are 256 antennas and 60 RF chains in the mmWave massive MIMO system. Other default values of parameters in the mmWave massive MIMO system are listed in Table 1.

Table 1. Simulation parameters.

Parameters	Values
Bandwidth W	1 GHz
Transmission Power P_{T}	5 W
Path loss exponent α	4.6
The number of multipath L	20
Efficiency of PAs η_{PA}	38%
Power of a phase shifter P_{PS}	12 mW
Power of an RF chain P_{RF}	57 mW

Figure 3 shows the error $\|\mathbf{E}_2\|_F^2$ with respect to the number of users, considering different numbers of RF chains. The results in Fig. 3 indicate that the value of $\|\mathbf{E}_2\|_F^2$ first decreases with the number of users. However, there is an inflection point, i.e., $K = 20$ for $N_{\mathrm{RF}} = 50$ and $K = 22$ for $N_{\mathrm{RF}} = 70$, where the value of $\|\mathbf{E}_2\|_F^2$ starts increasing instead. Based on the results in Fig. 3, there is an optimal number of users which can minimize the error. It is possible to use multi-layer neural networks to optimize the number of RF chains to minimize the error for different numbers of users.

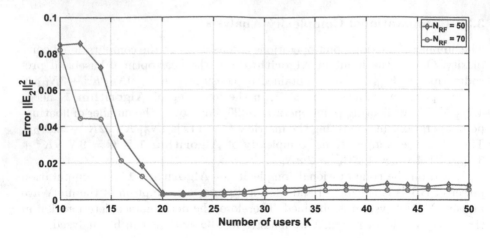

Fig. 3. Error $\|\mathbf{E}_2\|_F^2$ with respect to the number of users.

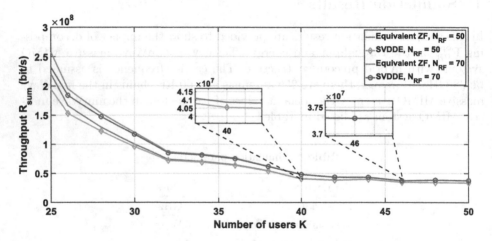

Fig. 4. Throughput with respect to the number of users.

In Fig. 4, the throughput as a function of the number of users is illustrated when different numbers of RF chains is considered. Moreover, the equivalent ZF algorithm is simulated for performance comparison. The results in Fig. 4 indicates that the further decomposition of the baseband precoding matrix, based on the SVDDE algorithm, causes the performance deterioration in the throughput of mmWave massive MIMO systems with hybrid precoding structure. Based on the results in Fig. 4, the gap between the equivalent ZF algorithm and the SVDDE algorithm in terms of the throughput is shrunk when the number of users is increased. Therefore, a slight performance deterioration in the throughput of multi-user mmWave massive MIMO systems is caused by further decomposing the baseband precoding matrix.

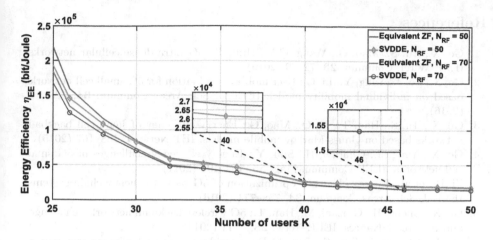

Fig. 5. Energy efficiency with respect to the number of users.

Figure 5 illustrates the energy efficiency with respect to the number of users, considering different numbers of RF chains. Based on the results in Fig. 5, the energy efficiency decreases with the number of users. One of two reasons for the decreasing of the energy efficiency is ascribed to the deterioration of the throughput in Fig. 4. Based on (7), increasing the number of users grows the power consumption on BBUs, which is another reason for the decreasing of the energy efficiency. The gap between the equivalent ZF algorithm and the SVDDE algorithm in terms of the energy efficiency is narrowing with increasing the number of users in Fig. 5. Therefore, a slight performance deterioration in the energy efficiency of multi-user mmWave massive MIMO systems is caused by further decomposing the baseband precoding matrix.

5   Conclusions

In this paper, an idea of further decomposing the baseband precoding matrix is proposed to map the hybrid precoding structure in mmWave massive MIMO systems to a multi-layer neural network. Moreover, an SVDDE algorithm is proposed to evaluate the feasibility of the proposed idea. Simulation results indicated that there is an optimal number of users which can minimize the performance deterioration. The existence of the optimal number of users shows the opportunity of applying multi-layer neural networks to design hybrid precoding. Moreover, simulation results also show that slight performance deterioration in the throughput and energy efficiency of mmWave massive MIMO systems is caused by further decomposing the baseband precoding matrix of hybrid precoding structure. Therefore, it is feasible to map the hybrid precoding structure of mmWave massive MIMO systems to a multi-layer neural network. For the future study, we will investigate the design of hybrid precoding based on software-hardware hybrid neural networks.

References

1. Ge, X., Tu, S., Mao, G., Wang, C.X., Han, T.: 5G ultra-dense cellular networks. IEEE Wirel. Commun. **23**, 72–79 (2016)
2. Ge, X., Ye, J., Yang, Y., Li, Q.: User mobility evaluation for 5G small cell networks based on individual mobility model. IEEE J. Sel. Areas Commun. **34**, 528–541 (2016)
3. Ge, X., Tu, S., Han, T., Li, Q., Mao, G.: Energy efficiency of small cell backhaul networks based on Gauss-Markov mobile models. IET Netw. **4**, 158–167 (2015)
4. Ge, X., Yang, J., Gharavi, H., Sun, Y.: Energy efficiency challenges of 5G small cell networks. IEEE Commun. Mag. **55**, 184–191 (2017)
5. Zi, R., et al.: Energy efficiency optimization of 5G radio frequency chain systems. IEEE J. Sel. Areas Commun. **34**, 758–771 (2016)
6. Ge, X., Cheng, H., Guizani, M., Han, T.: 5G wireless backhaul networks: challenges and research advances. IEEE Netw. **28**, 6–11 (2014)
7. He, K., Zhang, X., Ren, S., Sun, J.: Deep residual learning for image recognition. In: 2016 IEEE Conference on Computer Vision and Pattern Recognition (CVPR), pp. 770–778 (2016)
8. Gao, H., He, W., Zhou, C., Sun, C.: Neural network control of a two-link flexible robotic manipulator using assumed mode method. IEEE Trans. Ind. Inform. **15**, 755–765 (2018)
9. Yu, K.-H., Beam, A.L., Kohane, I.S.: Artificial intelligence in healthcare. Nat. Biomed. Eng. **2**, 719–731 (2018)
10. Bai, L., et al.: Predicting wireless MmWave massive MIMO channel characteristics using machine learning algorithms. Wirel. Commun. Mob. Comput. (2018)
11. He, H.T., Wen, C.K., Jin, S., Li, G.Y.: Deep learning-based channel estimation for beamspace mmwave massive MIMO systems. IEEE Wirel. Commun. Lett. **7**, 852–855 (2018)
12. O'Shea, T., Hoydis, J.: An introduction to deep learning for the physical layer. IEEE Trans. Cogn. Commun. Netw. **3**, 563–575 (2017)
13. Yang, Y., et al.: DECCO: deep-learning enabled coverage and capacity optimization for massive MIMO systems. IEEE Access **6**, 23361–23371 (2018)
14. Prasad, K., Hossain, E., Bhargava, V.K.: Machine learning methods for RSS-based user positioning in distributed massive MIMO. IEEE Trans. Wirel. Commun. **17**, 8402–8417 (2018)
15. Mao, Q., Hu, F., Hao, Q.: Deep learning for intelligent wireless networks: a comprehensive survey. IEEE Commun. Surv. Tutor. **20**, 2595–2621 (2018)
16. Ayach, O.E., Rajagopal, S., Abu-Surra, S., Pi, Z., Heath, R.W.: Spatially sparse precoding in millimeter wave MIMO systems. IEEE Trans. Wirel. Commun. **13**, 1499–1513 (2014)
17. Hao, X., Kukshya, V., Rappaport, T.S.: Spatial and temporal characteristics of 60-GHz indoor channels. IEEE J. Sel. Areas Commun. **20**, 620–630 (2002)
18. Xiang, L., Ge, X., Wang, C.X., Li, F.Y., Reichert, F.: Energy efficiency evaluation of cellular networks based on spatial distributions of traffic load and power consumption. IEEE Trans. Wirel. Commun. **12**, 961–973 (2013)
19. Ge, X., Huang, K., Wang, C.X., Hong, X., Yang, X.: Capacity analysis of a multi-cell multi-antenna cooperative cellular network with co-channel interference. IEEE Trans. Wirel. Commun. **10**, 3298–3309 (2011)
20. Romera, M., et al.: Vowel recognition with four coupled spin-torque nano-oscillators. Nature **563**, 230–234 (2018)

21. Ge, X., et al.: Spatial spectrum and energy efficiency of random cellular networks. IEEE Trans. Commun. **63**, 1019–1030 (2015)
22. Ge, X., et al.: Energy efficiency optimization for MIMO-OFDM mobile multimedia communication systems with QoS constraints. IEEE Trans. Veh. Technol. **63**, 2127–2138 (2014)
23. Hur, S., et al.: Millimeter wave beamforming for wireless backhaul and access in small cell networks. IEEE Trans. Commun. **61**, 4391–4403 (2013)
24. Mumtaz, S., Rodriguez, J., Dai, L.: mmWave Massive MIMO: A Paradigm for 5G (2016)
25. Bjornson, E., Sanguinetti, L., Hoydis, J., Debbah, M.: Optimal design of energy-efficient multi-user MIMO systems: is massive MIMO the answer? IEEE Trans. Wirel. Commun. **14**, 3059–3075 (2015)
26. Ribeiro, L.N., Schwarz, S., Rupp, M., de Almeida, A.L.F.: Energy efficiency of mmwave massive MIMO precoding with low-resolution DACs. IEEE J. Sel. Top. Signal Process. **12**, 298–312 (2018)

A Reinforcement Learning Based Joint Spectrum Allocation and Power Control Algorithm for D2D Communication Underlaying Cellular Networks

Wentai Chen and Jun Zheng[✉]

National Mobile Communications Research Laboratory, Southeast University,
Nanjing 210096, Jiangsu, People's Republic of China
{wtchen, junzheng}@seu.edu.cn

Abstract. This paper studies the spectrum allocation and power control (SA-PC) problem in device-to-device (D2D) communication underlaying a cellular network. A distributed multi-agent reinforcement learning (MARL) based joint SA-PC algorithm is proposed for performing spectrum allocation and power control for each D2D user in the network. The proposed algorithm uses Q learning, a typical form of reinforcement learning (RL), to select the optimal resource block (RB) and power level for each D2D user. In the Q-learning algorithm, each D2D user is treated as an individual agent and maintains a single-state Q table. Each agent selects an RB and a power level according to its Q table in the learning process. Simulation results show that the proposed Q-learning based joint SA-PC algorithm can achieve good throughput performance.

Keywords: D2D communication · Spectrum allocation · Power control ·
Multi-agent reinforcement learning · Q learning

1 Introduction

Device to device (D2D) communication is one of the promising technologies for future mobile cellular networks. In D2D communication, two mobile devices directly communicate with each other without traversing a base station (BS), which can effectively improve spectral efficiency, increase the system throughput, and reduce the data transmission latency of a network [1]. Usually, D2D communication works in an underlay mode in which D2D users share the spectrum resources of cellular users. While this can effectively improve the network performance, it would on the other hand cause severe interference between D2D users and cellular users. Accordingly, the mitigation of such interference becomes a critical issue in D2D communication. An effective way to address this issue is through efficient resource management, including spectrum allocation and power control. In this context, extensive work has been conducted and a variety of spectrum allocation and/or power control algorithms have been proposed using traditional approaches [2–8]. With recent advances in artificial intelligence (AI), machine learning (ML) is arousing a widespread interest from the

S. Han et al. (Eds.): AICON 2019, LNICST 286, pp. 146–158, 2019.
https://doi.org/10.1007/978-3-030-22968-9_13

community of wireless communication. Considerable work has been conducted in applying this advanced approach to wireless communication in general and D2D communication in particular. But even so, relevant work on resource management for D2D communication is still limited. It is interesting to further explore the application of the advanced ML approach in spectrum allocation and power control for improving the performance of D2D communication, which motivated us to conduct this work.

In this paper, we study the spectrum allocation and power control (SA-PC) problem in D2D communication underlaying a cellular network using the ML approach. A distributed multi-agent reinforcement learning (MARL) based joint SA-PC algorithm is proposed for performing spectrum allocation and power control for each D2D user in the network. Specifically, the proposed algorithm uses Q learning, a typical form of reinforcement learning (RL), to select the optimal resource block (RB) and power level for each D2D user. In the algorithm, each D2D user is treated as an individual agent and maintains a single-state Q table. In the learning process, each agent selects an RB and a power level according to its Q table. Simulation results are shown to evaluate the performance of the proposed Q-learning based joint SA-PC algorithm in terms of the throughput performance.

The rest of the paper is organized as follows. Section 2 reviews related work in the literature. Section 3 describes the system model and formulates the SA-PC problem considered in this paper. Section 4 presents the proposed MARL-based SA-PC algorithm. Section 5 shows simulation results to evaluate the performance of the proposed algorithm. Section 6 concludes the paper.

2 Related Work

Spectrum allocation (SA) and power control (PC) have been extensively studied for D2D communication underlaying cellular networks. A variety of SA-PC algorithms have been proposed in the literature [2–8]. In [2], Cai et al. proposed a capacity oriented resource allocation algorithm (CORAL) for resource allocation in D2D communication. The proposed algorithm introduces the concept of a Capacity-Oriented REstricted (CORE) region for a D2D pair to determine a candidate cellular user set for the D2D pair in resource allocation, which can help increase the system capacity. In [3], Chen et al. proposed a time division scheduling (TDS) resource allocation algorithm to efficiently exploit the downlink spectrum resources of cellular users for D2D communication. In the D2D pair assignment for each timeslot, the proposed algorithm follows a location dispersion principle in order to reduce the interference from D2D users to cellular users and thus can increase the system throughput. In [4], Cai et al. proposed a graph-coloring resource allocation (GOAL) algorithm using a graph-coloring approach and introduced the concept of the interference negligible distance (INS) to identify those D2D pairs which can simultaneously share the same spectrum resources of cellular users, and the concept of the signal to interference ratio limited area (SLA) to identify a set of D2D pairs which cannot share the spectrum resources of a cellular user. In [5], Chen et al.proposeda service-aware resource allocation (SARA) scheme for D2D communication to improve the network performance, which takes into account the different service requirements of D2D users. In [6], Zulhasnine et al.

proposed a centralized heuristic algorithm considering the interference link gain from a D2D transmitter to the BS. The optimization problem is formulated as a Mixed Integer Non-Linear Programming (MINLP) with the synchronized resource allocation of the cellular users and D2D users. In [7], Esmat et al. proposed a two-phase optimization algorithm for adaptive resource allocation, which provides better system throughput than the traditional algorithm by computing a Lagrangian dual decomposition (LDD) problem. In [8], Hsu and Chen proposed a power control and channel allocation algorithm, in which the channel of each user device is reallocated after the first turn of power allocation. The channel reallocation and power control proceed until the transmission power no longer decreases. Simulation results show that the proposed algorithm outperforms the existing algorithms in terms of system capacity.

With recent advances in the ML area, considerable work has been conducted to explore the application of the ML approach in resource management for D2D communication [9–12]. In [9], a Q learning-based algorithm was proposed for the resource allocation in a single-cell scenario with two cellular users and several D2D users whose arrival follows a poison process. In [10], a centralized Q-learning algorithm and a distributed Q-learning algorithm were proposed to solve the power control problem for D2D communication underlying cellular networks. In [11], a power control method based on Classification and Regression Tree (CART) was proposed, which provides a faster convergence than the reinforcement learning methods. In [12], an adaptive resource allocation algorithm was proposed using cooperative reinforcement learning considering the neighboring factor of the D2D users. The proposed algorithm considers the coordination problem between different D2D users and can achieve a better system throughput than some existing reinforcement learning algorithms.

3   System Model and Problem Formulation

In this section, we first describe the system model and then formulate the joint spectrum allocation and power control (SA-PC) problem considered in this paper.

3.1   System Model

We consider a single-cell cellular system consisting of one base station (BS), M cellular users (CUs) and N D2D user (DU) pairs, where a DU pair consists of the transmitter (T_x) of one DU and the receiver (R_x) of another DU. The set of M CUs is denoted by $C = \{C_1, C_2, ..., C_M\}$ and the set of N DU pairs is denoted by $\mathcal{D} = \{D_1, D_2, ..., D_N\}$. There are K orthogonal resource blocks (RBs) in the system, which are denoted by $\mathcal{B} = \{B_1, B_2, ..., B_K\}$. We assume that the DU pairs work in an underlay mode and are allowed to share the uplink transmission resources (i.e., RBs) of the CUs. Each RB is occupied by one CU and can be shared by one or more DU pairs. Either a CU or a DU pair is allowed to occupy only one RB. The system model is illustrated in Fig. 1.

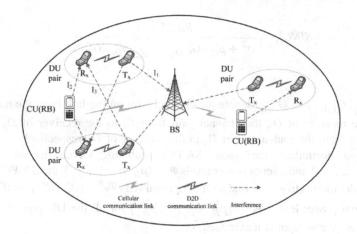

Fig. 1. System model

There exist three types of interferences in the system model, which are illustrated in Fig. 1:

(1) I_1: the interference from the transmitter T_x of a D2D pair to the BS;
(2) I_2: the interference from a CU to the receiver R_x of a D2D pair, where the CU and the DU pair share the same RB;
(3) I_3: the interference from the transmitter T_x of one D2D pair to the receiver R_x of another D2D pair, where the two D2D pairs share the same RB.

3.2 Problem Formulation

In this paper, we consider the joint spectrum allocation and power control problem in D2D communication underlaying a single-cell cellular system shown in Fig. 1. There are two aspects in the SA-PC problem: RB allocation for the DU pairs (i.e., SA) and power assignment for the DU pairs (i.e., PC). For simplicity, we assume that $M = K$ and the RB allocation for the CUs is fixed. Each CU is allocated a different RB.

Before we formulate the power control problem, we first analyze the signal to interference plus noise ratio (SINR) at a CU and at the receiver of a DU, respectively. For a CU that occupies the rth RB, the SINR at the CU is given by

$$SINC_{C_i}^r = \frac{p_{C_i}^r \cdot G_{C_i}^r}{\sigma^2 + \sum_{D_j \in \Phi^r} p_{D_j}^r \cdot G_{D_j}^r}, \quad i=1,2,\ldots,M; j=1,2,\ldots,N \tag{1}$$

where C_i denotes the ith CU, D_j denotes the jth DU pair, Φ^r denotes a set of DU pairs that share the rth RB, $p_{C_i}^r$ and $p_{D_j}^r$ denote the transmission power of C_i and D_j which share the rth RB, respectively, $G_{C_i}^r$ and $G_{D_j}^r$ denote the channel gains on the rth RB from the BS to C_i and D_j, respectively, and σ^2 is the noise variance.

Similarly, for a DU pair that shares the rth RB, the SINR at the receiver of the DU pair is given by

$$SINC_{D_j}^r = \frac{p_{D_j}^r \cdot G_{D_jD_j}^r}{\sigma^2 + p_{C_i}^r \cdot G_{C_iD_j}^r + \sum_{\substack{D_k \in \mathcal{D}^r \\ k \neq j}} p_{D_k}^r \cdot G_{D_kD_j}^r}, \tag{2}$$

where $G_{D_jD_j}^r$, $G_{C_iD_j}^r$, and $G_{D_kD_j}^r$ denote the channel gain on the link from the transmitter of D_j to the receiver of D_j, the channel gain from C_i to the receiver of D_j, and the channel gain from the transmitter of D_k to the receiver of D_j, respectively.

Next we formulate the joint SA-PC problem. Given a set of RBs $\mathcal{B} = \{B_1, B_2, ..., B_K\}$ and a set of power levels $\mathcal{P} = \{p_1, p_2, ..., p_L\}$, the SA-PC problem under consideration is to jointly find a set of optimal RBs $\mathcal{B}_b{}^* = \{B_{D_1}^*, B_{D_2}^*, \cdots, B_{D_N}^*\}$ and a set of optimal power levels $\mathcal{P}_b{}^* = \{p_{D_1}^*, p_{D_2}^*, \cdots, p_{D_N}^*\}$ for all the DU pairs so that the overall system throughput is maximized, i.e.,

Objective: $$\max \sum_{r=1}^{K} \{\log_2(1 + SINR_{C_i}^r) + \sum_{D_j \in \mathcal{D}^r} \log_2(1 + SINR_{D_j}^r)\} \tag{3}$$

subject to $$SINR_{C_i}^r \geq \tau_0, \tag{4}$$

$$p_1 \leq p_{D_j}^r \leq p_L, \quad \forall j, r, \tag{5}$$

where τ_0 denotes the minimum SINR requirement of a CU, constraint (4) ensures the SINR requirement of each CU, and constraint (5) ensures that the transmission power of each DU is limited to the range $[p_1, p_L]$.

4   MARL-Based SA-PC Algorithm

In this section, we first introduce the concept of reinforcement learning and then present an MARL-based algorithm to solve the SA-PC problem formulated in Sect. 3.

4.1   Reinforcement Learning

Reinforcement learning is an important branch of machine learning. A typical RL problem can be modeled as a Markov Decision Process (MDP), which is defined as a decision process that satisfies the Markov property, i.e., the environment's response at time $t + 1$ depends only on the state and action at t, and does not rely on the previous states. An MDP can be represented as a tuple of 5 elements, denoted as $\{S, A, T, R, \gamma\}$:

- S: a finite set of all possible states;
- A: a finite set of actions that can be selected by an agent;
- T: a set of transition probabilities from one state to another;
- R: a reward function to evaluate the action chosen by an agent;
- γ: a discount factor to balance the effect of the future reward and the immediate reward.

In a standard RL process, an agent interacts with the environment in a sequence of episodes, which are denoted by $t = 0, 1, 2, \ldots$ There are three steps in each episode, which are shown in Fig. 2:

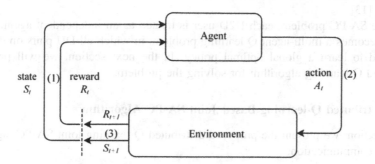

Fig. 2. Standard reinforcement learning process

(1) The agent receives the current state S_t and reward signal R_t.
(2) The agent selects and executes the action A_t.
(3) The environment generates a new reward R_{t+1} and transfers to another state S_{t+1}.

An agent starts learning from an initial state S_0, and continues the episodes until the learning process converges.

In the above learning process, an agent selects its action in each episode according to a policy π, which is given by

$$\pi_t(a \mid s) = P(A_t = a \mid S_t = s), \quad a \in \mathcal{A}, \ s \in \mathcal{S}, \tag{6}$$

where $P(A_t = a \mid S_t = s)$ is the probability of selecting action a in state s. By selecting different actions and updating the current policy in each episode, the agent can make a better decision and reaches the optimal policy π^* after a number of episodes.

Next we introduce a typical form of reinforcement learning: Q learning, which will be used to solve the SA-PC problem. Like other RL methods, Q learning needs no prior knowledge about the environment. In Q learning, an agent learns how to behave based on the previous experience, which is traced by a Q function. The Q function is used to determine the value of an action a in a given state s and is defined

$$Q_t(s, a) = E_\pi[\sum_{i=1}^{\infty} \eta^{i-1} R_{t+i} \mid S_t = s, A_t = a], \tag{8}$$

where $E_\pi(\cdot)$ denotes the expected value of a random variable given that the agent follows the policy π, t denotes the index of the current episode, η is the discount rate, and R_{t+i} is the reward in the $(t + i)$th episode.

In Q learning, the Q function is represented by a two-dimensional table, in which each row represents a state of the environment, and each column represents an action of an agent. The learning process starts with an initial state, and the initial Q table is usually set to all zeros. At each episode, assuming that the current state is $S_t = s$, the agent needs to select the best action $A_t = a$ according to the learned policy. After performing a, the agent will receive a reward R_{t+1}, and the environment will transfer to the next state S_{t+1}. It can be proved by induction that Q learning is able to converge to the optimal values if all the states can be visited infinitely as the learning process proceeds [13].

In the SA-PC problem, each D2D user is treated as an independent agent. In this way, it becomes a multi-agent Q learning problem, in which all DU pairs on different RBs need to learn a global optimal policy. In the next section, we will present a distributed Q-learning algorithm for solving the problem.

4.2   Distributed Q-learning Based Joint SA-PC Algorithm

In this section, we present the proposed distributed Q-learning joint SA-PC algorithm for D2D communication.

A. Component definitions
We first define the components of distributed Q learning, namely agent, action and reward. In the distributed Q learning algorithm, an agent is defined as a DU pair in the cellular system. Thus, there are N agents in the whole system. An action of an agent is defined as the action that a DU pair takes to select a RB from $\mathcal{B} = \{B_1, B_2, ..., B_K\}$ and a power level p from $\mathcal{P} = \{p_1, p_2, ..., p_L\}$. A reward is defined as the overall system throughput including all CUs and all DU pairs. The value of the reward is determined using the following reward function:

$$R = \sum_{r=1}^{K} R^r, \tag{8}$$

where R^r is the reward on the rth RB, which is given by

$$R^r = \begin{cases} \log_2(1+SINR_{C_i}^r) + \sum_{D_j \in \Phi^r} \log_2(1+SINR_{D_j}^r), & SINR_{C_i}^r \geq \tau_0 \\ -1 & \text{otherwise} \end{cases}. \tag{9}$$

According to Eq. (9), if the SINR requirement of C_i cannot be satisfied, i.e., $SINR_{C_i}^r < \tau_0$, the reward is set to -1 as a penalty term, which ensures the priority of C_i.

In a standard Q learning algorithm, an agent needs to transfer between different states by selecting different actions, which usually takes a large number of episodes to converge. Furthermore, it is difficult to define the states in the Q learning algorithm that matches the physical states in the single-cell cellular system [14]. According to [14], we use a single state in the distributed Q learning algorithm and the state formulation is not needed.

B. Algorithm description

The distributed Q learning based SA-PC algorithm is proposed for performing spectrum allocation and power control for the DU pairs in the system. In the algorithm, each agent maintains a single-state Q table of size $(1, K \times L)$. In the learning process, the Q table for a D2D pair is initialized to all zeros. In each episode, each agent (i.e., each DU pair) selects RBs and power levels simultaneously, and then receives a reward and updates its Q table. The learning process continues until all Q tables converge to the same optimal values.

In each episode, an action is selected based on an ε-greedy strategy, which is described as follows:

- Select a random action with a probability ε;
- Select an action according to the maximum Q value of the current state with a probability $(1 - \varepsilon)$.

Here, ε is the threshold of the probability, which decays with the number of episodes as

$$\varepsilon = \varepsilon_{\min} + (\varepsilon_{\max} - \varepsilon_{\min}) \cdot \exp(-h \cdot t), \tag{10}$$

where $\varepsilon_{\max}$ and $\varepsilon_{\min}$ denote the upper limit and the lower limit of ε; h is a decay rate within $[0, 1]$; t is the index of the current episode. At the beginning of learning, ε is set to a value close to 1. Thus, the agent is likely to select a random action that it has not selected before to find more new states of the environment. As the learning process continues, the value of ε decreases accordingly, and thus the agent relies more on the learned policy. The ε-greedy strategy helps an agent explore more states and actions at the beginning of the learning process so that the convergence of Q learning can be ensured [9]. After an action is selected, the Q table is updated based on the following function:

$$Q_{t+1}^j(s,a) = \max\{Q_t^j(s,a), \ r_{t+1} + \gamma \max_{a' \in A} Q_t^j(s',a')\}, \tag{11}$$

where the Q value for D_j in the $(t + 1)$th episode $Q_{t+1}^j(s, a)$ will be updated only when the newly arrived Q value exceeds $Q_{t+1}^j(s, a)$ and γ is the discount factor which varies from 0 to 1. The newly arrived Q value corresponds to the second item in Eq. (11), i.e.,

$$r_{t+1} + \gamma \cdot \max_{a \in A} Q_i^j(s',a'). \tag{12}$$

The pseudo codes of the proposed distributed Q learning based SA-PC algorithm is described in Algorithm 1.

Algorithm 1   Distributed Q-learning based SA-PC algorithm

Input:

$\mathcal{B} = \{B_1, B_2, ..., B_K\}$ {a set of K resource blocks}

$C = \{C_1, C_2, ..., C_M\}$ {a set of M cellular users}

$\mathcal{D} = \{D_1, D_2, ..., D_N\}$ {a set of N D2D users}

$\mathcal{P} = \{p_1, p_2, ..., p_L\}$ {a set of available power levels}

Output:

$\mathcal{B}_o^* = \{B_{D_1}^*, B_{D_2}^*, \cdots, B_{D_K}^*\}$ {optimal RBs for all DU pairs}

$\mathcal{P}_o^* = \{p_{D_1}^*, p_{D_2}^*, \cdots, p_{D_N}^*\}$ {optimal power levels for all DU pairs}

Function:

$Q_t^j(s, a)$,   {Q table for D_j in the tth episode

                            under state s and action a}

Initialize:

for D_j, $j \in \{1, 2, ..., N\}$

initialize $Q_t^j(s, a) = 0$, $a \in \mathcal{A}$

Learning:

for:

select the rth RB, $r \in \{1, 2, ..., K\}$

for:

select D_j, for all the DUs on the rth RB.

for:

select action $a \in \mathcal{A}$ according to the ε greedy strategy

execute a and calculate the reward r_{t+1}

update $Q_t^j(s, a)$ according to Eq. (11)

end for

end for

end for

---

5 Simulation Results

In this section, we evaluate the performance of the proposed distributed Q learning based SA-PC algorithm through simulation results. The simulation experiment was conducted on a simulator developed using python. We consider a single-cell cellular system where the CUs and DU pairs are uniformly distributed. The parameters used in the simulation experiment are listed in Table 1.

In the performance evaluation, we compare the proposed Q-learning based SA-PC algorithm with a Q-learning based PC algorithm and a random allocation algorithm. The PC algorithm only considers the power control for the DU pairs based on Q learning, while assuming that the RBs are randomly allocated to all DU pairs. In the random allocation algorithm, both RBs and power levels are randomly allocated to all DU pairs. Moreover, we use the system throughput and the D2D throughput as the

Table 1. Simulation parameters

Parameter	Value
M	20
N	10–100
K	20
L	5
Cell radius	500 m
p_1, p_2, p_3, p_4, p_5	{1, 6.5, 12, 17.5, 23} dBm
p_c	24 dBm
Noise power	−116 dBm/Hz
Resource block bandwidth	180 kHz
Gain model between user and BS	15.3 + 37.6 lg(d(km)) dB
Gain model between two users	128 + 40 lg(d(km)) dB
Learning rate α	0.9
Discount factor γ	0.9
τ_0	6 dB

performance metrics. The system throughput is defined as the throughput of all CUs and DU pairs in the system, and the D2D throughput is defined as the throughput of all DU pairs in the system.

Figure 3 compares the convergence of the optimal Q values with the distributed Q learning based SA-PC algorithm under $M = 20$, $N = 10$. It can be observed that all the Q values converge to the same optimal values after around 1200 episodes, which proves that an optimal policy can be obtained for the proposed Q learning algorithm. Meanwhile, the updates of different DU pairs are asynchronous, due to the fact that they select their actions independently during the learning process.

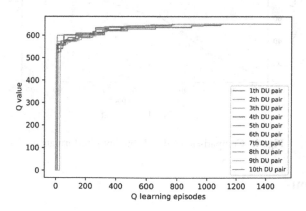

Fig. 3. Convergence of the Q values (M = 20, N = 10)

Figure 4 shows the system throughput and D2D throughput with the proposed SA-PC algorithm, the PC algorithm and the random allocation algorithm, respectively. It is observed that both the system throughput and the D2D throughput increase as the number of DU pairs increases, and all the three algorithms have the same trends over the number of DU pairs. On the other hand, both the system throughput and the D2D throughput with the proposed SA-PC algorithm are larger than those with the PC algorithm and the random allocation algorithm, which demonstrates the superior performance of the proposed SA-PC algorithm.

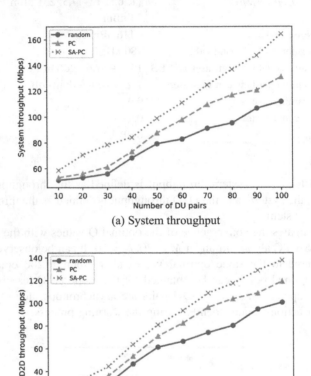

(a) System throughput

(b) D2D throughput

Fig. 4. Comparison of the throughput performance

6   Conclusion

This paper studied the SA-PC problem in D2D communication underlaying a cellular network. A distributed Q-learning based joint SA-PC algorithm was proposed for performing spectrum allocation and power control for each D2D user in the network. The proposed algorithm uses Q learning, a typical form of RL, to select the optimal RB and power level for each D2D user. In the Q-learning algorithm, each DU pair is treated as an individual agent and maintains a single-state Q table. Each agent selects an RB and a power level according to its Q table in the learning process. The objective is to select the optimal RB and power level for each D2D user. Simulation results shows that the proposed Q-learning based joint SA-PC algorithm can achieve better performance than a Q-learning based PC algorithm and a random allocation algorithm in terms of the system throughput and the D2D throughput..

References

1. Asadi, A., Wang, Q., Mancuso, V.: A survey on device-to-device communication in cellular networks. IEEE Commun. Surv. Tutor. **16**(4), 1801–1819 (2014)
2. Cai, X., Zheng, J., Zhang, Y., Murata, H.: A capacity oriented resource allocation algorithm for device-to-device communication in mobile cellular networks. In: Proceedings of IEEE ICC 2014, Sydney, Australia, June 2014
3. Chen, B., Zheng, J., Zhang, Y.: A time division scheduling resource allocation for D2D communication in cellular networks. In: Proceedings of IEEE ICC 2015, London, UK, June 2015
4. Cai, X., Zheng, J., Zhang, Y.: A graph coloring based resource allocation algorithm for D2D communication in cellular networks. In: Proceedings of IEEE ICC 2015, London, UK, June 2015
5. Chen, B., Zheng, J., Zhang, Y., Murata, H.: SARA: a service-aware resource allocation scheme for device-to-device communication underlaying cellular networks. In: Proceedings of IEEE Globecom 2014, Austin, USA, December 2014, pp. 4916–4921 (2014)
6. Zulhasnine, M., Huang, C., Srinivasan, A.: Efficient resource allocation for device-to-device communication underlaying LTE networks. In: Proceedings of 2010 IEEE 6th International Conference on Wireless and Mobile Computing, Networking and Communications (WiMob 2010), Niagara Falls, Canada, pp. 11–13, October 2010
7. Esmat, H., Elmesalawy, M., Ibrahim, I.: Adaptive resource sharing algorithm for device-to-device communications underlaying cellular networks. IEEE Commun. Lett. **20**(3), 530–533 (2016)
8. Hsu, C., Chen, W.: Joint power control and channel assignment for green device-to-device communication. In: Proceedings of 2018 16th International Conference on Pervasive Intelligence and Computing (PiCom 2018), Athens, Greece, pp. 881–884 (2018)
9. Luo, Y., Shi, Z., Zhou, X., Liu, Q., Yi, Q.: Dynamic resource allocations based on q-learning for D2D communication in cellular networks. In: Proceedings of 2014 11th International Computer Conference on Wavelet Active Media Technology and Information Processing (ICCWAMTIP), Chengdu, China, 19–21 December 2014
10. Nie, S., Fan, Z., Zhao, M., Gu, X., Zhang, L.: Q-learning based power control algorithm for D2D communication. In: Proceedings of 2016 IEEE 27th Annual International Symposium on Personal, Indoor, and Mobile Radio Communications (PIMRC 2016), Valencia, Spain, pp. 1–6 (2016)
11. Fan, Z., Gu, X., Nie, S., Chen, M.: D2D power control based on supervised and unsupervised learning. In: Proceedings of 2017 3rd IEEE International Conference on Computer and Communications (ICCC 2017), Chengdu, China, pp. 558–563 (2017)

12. Khan, M.I., Alam, M.M., Le Moullec, Y., Yaacoub, E.: Cooperative reinforcement learning for adaptive power allocation in device-to-device communication. In: Proceedings of 2018 IEEE 4th World Forum on Internet of Things (WF-IoT), Singapore, pp. 476–481 (2018)
13. Sutton, R.S., Barto, A.G.: Reinforcement learning: an introduction. IEEE Trans. Neural Netw. **9**(5), 1054 (1998)
14. Lauer, M., Riedmiller, M.: An algorithm for distributed reinforcement learning in cooperative multi-agent systems. In: Proceedings of 2000 17th International Conference on Machine Learning, San Francisco, CA, pp. 535–542 (2000)

Improved Neural Machine Translation with POS-Tagging Through Joint Decoding

Xiaocheng Feng[1], Zhangyin Feng[1], Wanlong Zhao[2,3,4(✉)], Nan Zou[5], Bing Qin[1], and Ting Liu[1]

[1] Research Center for Social Computing and Information Retrieval,
Harbin Institute of Technology, Harbin 150001, China
[2] Acoustic Science and Technology Laboratory, Harbin Engineering University,
Harbin 150001, China
wlzhao@hrbeu.edu.cn
[3] Key Laboratory of Marine Information Acquisition and Security
(Harbin Engineering University), Ministry of Industry and Information Technology,
Harbin 150001, China
[4] College of Underwater Acoustic Engineering, Harbin Engineering University,
Harbin 150001, China
[5] Harbin University of Commerce, Harbin 150001, China

Abstract. In this paper, we improve the performance of neural machine translation (NMT) with shallow syntax (e.g., POS tag) of target language, which has better accuracy and latency than deep syntax such as dependency parsing. We present three NMT decoding models (independent decoder, gates shared decoder and fully shared decoder) to jointly predict target word and POS tag sequences. Experiments on Chinese-English and German-English translation tasks show that the fully shared decoder can acquire the best performance, which increases the BLEU score by 1.4 and 2.25 points respectively compared with the attention-based NMT model.

Keywords: Neural machine translation ·
Natural language processing · Artificial intelligence

1 Introduction

Neural Machine Translation (NMT) plays an important role in current natural language processing (NLP) community and its performance is usually used as a metric to evaluate the development of artificial intelligence [1]. Recently, deep structure representations (e.g., dependence) are applied to NMT tasks as external features in both encoding and decoding sides, and new architectures have achieved impressive results in translation quality of many language pairs [2–4]. Compared to deep syntax, we favor to shallow structures (e.g., POS tag

© ICST Institute for Computer Sciences, Social Informatics and Telecommunications Engineering 2019
Published by Springer Nature Switzerland AG 2019. All Rights Reserved
S. Han et al. (Eds.): AICON 2019, LNICST 286, pp. 159–166, 2019.
https://doi.org/10.1007/978-3-030-22968-9_14

and chunk) in this work, which have higher accuracy and faster analyzers. We believe that the performance of an NMT system would benefit from POS tag information of target language. Implicit patterns of target language (e.g. word order) could be revealed from the POS tag sequence. For instance, a Chinese POS tagger typically outputs a *"noun"* or *"pronoun"* after an *"adjective"*. A desirable English-Chinese translator should follow this protocol to generate Chinese sentences during the translation procedure. Further, a POS tag is more informative than a chunk or a phrase, and is more concise than combinatory category grammar (CCG) supertag [5], which includes about 500 tags.

Following this direction, our work is to examine the benefit of incorporating POS tags on the target-side. Inspired by the success of multi-task learning in NMT [5–7], we develop three encoder-decoder based NMT architectures to improve the performance of NMT, all of which encode the source language sentence into continuous vectors, and then decode the target language sentence and its POS tag sequence. The difference between these model variations is that they gradually share more parameters in decoding process. Concretely, the first model uses two independent decoders to predict both sequences, and the second one shares partial gated units of those two decoders. As for the third one, the decoding layers are fully shared except for two task-specific softmax functions, which are used for generating different target symbols.

We demonstrate the effectiveness of our architectures on Chinese-English and German-English translation datasets. Experimental results show that our proposed models could improve the performance in contrast to single NMT task with the help of target POS tag sequence prediction. Moreover, our best approach (fully shared decoder) outperforms the attention-based NMT model by an average of 1.8 BLEU points on both datasets. Finally, we show that incorporating source-side POS tags into our architectures could achieve improved performance on German-English translation dataset.

2   Standard NMT Model

In this part, we introduce a conventional encoder-decoder architecture for NMT. Generally, the encoder is a recurrent neural network (RNN) with LSTM [8], whose input is a source sentence $\mathbf{x} = [x_1, ..., x_n]$. The decoder is another LSTM-based RNN, which works in a sequential way and generates a word at each time step. The generation of a word is actually selectively replicating a word from the target vocabulary. The probability of generating the word y_t at the t-th time step is calculated as follows, where $f(\cdot)$ is a non-linear function; s_t is the *decoder state* at the time step t, $t \in [1, T]$; $e_{y_{t-1}}$ is the embedding of y_{t-1}; c_t is the context vector, which is calculated by an *attention* model; W is a linear transformation.

$$p_{\mathbf{y}} = \prod_t^T P(y_t|\mathbf{x}, y_{<t-1}) = \prod_t^T \mathtt{softmax}(f(e_{y_{t-1}}, s_t, c_t)W) \tag{1}$$

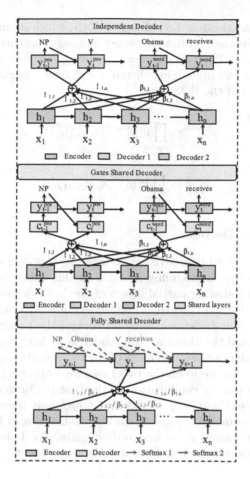

Fig. 1. Architectures of our three NMT models. (Color figure online)

3 Methodology

In this section, we describe the developed neural architectures for NMT. We first introduce a basic multi-task approach, which includes one shared encoder and two different decoders to explicitly model target word and POS tag sequences. Further, we extend two LSTM-based decoders by sharing partial gated neural layers (*input* and *forget*), where the implicit language expression patterns of both sequences are learned. Lastly, we present the third model that shares all decoding layers except for two self-contained softmax functions, where the task-specific and task-related knowledge are modeled together.

3.1 Independent Decoder

An illustration of this model is given in top dashed box of Fig. 1. It shares similar intuition with [6] and [5]. In the multi-task framework [6], the two decoders are two parameter-independent LSTM-based RNN, which input the same source context representations and output the target language sentence and corresponding POS tag sequence. The two decoders predict a different number of target symbols, resulting in two probability distributions over separate target vocabularies for the words and the POS tags:

$$p_{\mathbf{y}}^{word} = \prod_t^T P(y_t^{word}|\mathbf{x}, y_{<t-1}^{word}) \tag{2}$$

$$p_{\mathbf{y}}^{pos} = \prod_t^T P(y_t^{pos}|\mathbf{x}, y_{<t-1}^{pos}) \tag{3}$$

3.2   Gates Shared Decoder

The aforementioned multi-task strategy is a loose coupling of the translated words and the POS tags in decoding process. In this subsection, we propose a tighter integration by sharing partial layers of the both decoders. As we know, the LSTM is a special form of recurrent neural networks (RNNs) with three gated units, *input, output* and *forget*, which could control the passing of information along the sequence and thus improve the modeling of long-range dependencies. Actually, we try to share some gated units of the two decoders in order to capture some implicit knowledge between the two tasks for improving the performance of NMT. Among all our six combinations[1], the best performances are achieved when *input* and *output* units are shared and *forget* unit remains independent. An illustration of this model is given in middle dashed box of Fig. 1. The yellow block represents the shared *input* and *output* gates, the blue and pink blocks represent the task-specific units of both decoders, respectively.

3.3   Fully Shared Decoder

In this part, we develop a fully shared encoder-decoder framework. An overview of this architecture is illustrated in bottom dashed box of Fig. 1. The model learns the same set of parameters for modeling the source sentence and predicting the target word and POS tag sequences. Specifically, the decoder needs to be able to predict two sequences of different symbols. Therefore, we equip the shared LSTM-based decoder with two different linear transformation matrices, $W_{word} \in \mathbb{R}^{d \times l}$ and $W_{pos} \in \mathbb{R}^{d \times f}$, where l is the size of target vocabulary and f is the number of target POS tags.

---

[1] Six combinations (*shared gates / independent gates*): {[*input / forget, output*], [*input, forget / output*], [*input,output / forget*], [*forget / input, output*], [*output / input, forget*], [*forget, output / input*]}.

3.4 Source-Side POS Tags - Shared Embedding

Although our focus is on target-side POS tags, we also experiment with source-side POS tags to show whether the two approaches are complementary. In detail, we follow the previous work [9] and learn a separate embedding for both source-side features such as the word itself and its POS tag. Both feature embeddings are concatenated into one embedding vector which is used in all parts of the encoder model instead of the word embedding [10].

3.5 Training

We used Standford POS tagger [11] to label the corpora instead of using a corpus with gold annotations as in [6]. The final loss was the sum of the losses for the two decoders:

$$loss = -(\log(p_y^{word}) + \log(p_y^{pos})) \tag{4}$$

Models were trained jointly in an alternate manner. We first trained POS tags prediction model and then trained NMT model. The models were optimized using ADADELTA following [9] and all the parameters were initialized randomly with Gaussian distribution. Beam search was adopted for decoding. For brevity, the hyperparameters of the training procedure were given in the published codes[2].

4 Experiments

We conduct experiments on a Chinese-English translation dataset. The training corpora consist of about 1.25 million sentence pairs[3]. We choose the NIST 2002 dataset as our development set, and the NIST 2003, 2004, 2005, 2006 and 2008 datasets as our test sets. Furthermore, we evaluate our model on the IWSLT 2014 translation task of German-English, which consists of sentences-aligned subtitles of TED and TEDx talks. Following the previous study [12], we use 153,000 sentence pairs as training data and extract 6,969 sentence pairs as development set. We also choose dev2010, dev2012, tst2010, tst2011 and tst2012 as test sets, which comprises of about 6,750 sentence pairs.

We compare our models with three strong baselines:

- *RNNSearch*: an in-house implementation of the attention-based NMT system [9] with its default settings.
- *Chunk-Based model*: a chunk-based bi-scale decoder [13] for NMT, in which way, the target sentence is translated hierarchically from chunks to words.
- *CCG Interleaving*: [5] proposed a tight integration in the decoder of the combinatory category grammar (CCG) supertags and the words, where the target sequence includes its CCG supertags as extra tokens.

---

[2] The codes are implemented with Pytorch, which we plan to release to the community.
[3] The corpora includes LDC2002E18, LDC2003E07, LDC2003E14, the Hansards portion of LDC2004T08, and LDC2005T06.

Table 1. Main experimental results on the NIST Chinese-English and IWSLT German-English translation tasks. * means that the model further incorporates the source-side POS tag information.

Model	Chinese-English							German-English	
	N02	*N03*	*N04*	*N05*	*N06*	*N08*	*Ave.*	*Dev*	*Test*
RNNSearch	36.51	33.32	36.15	33.49	29.77	24.95	31.54	24.93	23.80
Chunk-Based model	36.96	33.83	36.47	33.51	29.82	24.91	31.70	26.57	24.25
CCG interleaving	37.34	34.07	36.95	34.79	30.19	25.85	32.37	27.70	25.50
Independent decoder	37.27	33.90	36.83	33.79	30.25	25.39	32.03	26.83	24.45
Independent decoder*	37.06	33.25	36.50	33.51	29.93	25.20	31.67	27.61	25.39
Gates shared decoder	37.43	34.27	37.15	**34.99**	30.39	26.05	32.57	26.90	25.04
Gates shared decoder*	37.12	34.03	36.98	34.08	29.52	25.40	32.01	27.89	26.03
Fully shared decoder	**37.97**	**34.80**	**38.09**	34.73	**30.87**	**26.23**	**32.95**	27.37	25.27
Fully shared decoder*	37.73	34.03	36.98	34.08	29.52	24.40	32.01	**27.95**	**26.05**

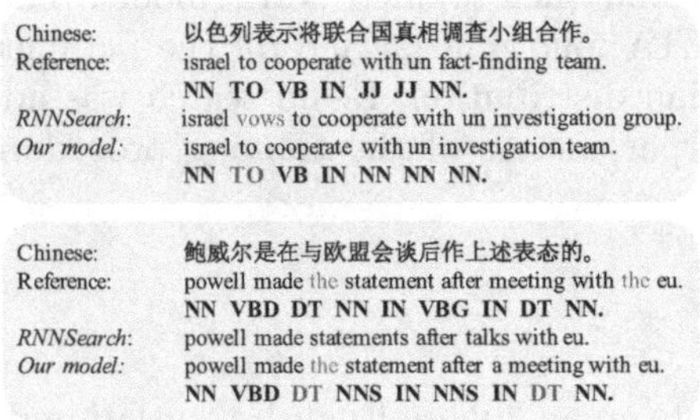

Chinese: 以色列表示将联合国真相调查小组合作。
Reference: israel to cooperate with un fact-finding team.
NN TO VB IN JJ JJ NN.
RNNSearch: israel vows to cooperate with un investigation group.
Our model: israel to cooperate with un investigation team.
NN TO VB IN NN NN NN.

Chinese: 鲍威尔是在与欧盟会谈后作上述表态的。
Reference: powell made the statement after meeting with the eu.
NN VBD DT NN IN VBG IN DT NN.
RNNSearch: powell made statements after talks with eu.
Our model: powell made the statement after a meeting with eu.
NN VBD DT NNS IN NNS IN DT NN.

Fig. 2. Case study on the test set.

Table 1 reports the main results of different models measured in terms of BLEU score[4]. Our proposed models outperform different baselines on all sets, which verify that incorporating POS tags in the target-side is helpful for NMT. Our best model *FSD* (*Fully shared decoder*) gains a 1.4 BLEU score improvement upon the standard NMT baseline on Chinese-English corpora and 2.25 (+POS tags in source-side) BLEU points on German-English corpus. Moreover, we find that our proposed three approaches obtain lower scores when incorporating source-side POS tag information on Chinese-English datasets. We speculate that the definition of POS tag in different family of languages may be different. For example, both English and German belong to the Germanic languages while Chinese belongs to the Sino-Tibetan language family.

Furthermore, we also compare *FSD* with the *RNNSearch* and *Chunk-Based model* baselines by subjective evaluation on Chinese-English datasets. Three human evaluators are asked to evaluate the translations of 100 source sentences randomly sampled from the test sets without knowing which system the trans-

---

[4] ftp://jaguar.ncsl.nist.gov/mt/resources/mteval-v11b.pl

Table 2. Subjective evaluation results

Model	Adequacy	Fluency
RNNSearch	3.31	3.58
Chunk-Based model	3.43	3.65
Fully shared decoder	3.50	3.84

lation is translated by. The evaluator is asked to give 2 scores: adequacy and fluency, which are from 0 to 5, the larger, the better[5]. Table 2 shows that the subjective evaluation results are highly consistent with the results of objective evaluation. *FSD* improves the two baselines on both the translation adequacy and fluency aspects. Specifically, the fluency increases by an average of 0.225, which confirms the assumption in the introduction that incorporating POS tags in target-side can optimize the word order of the generating sentences. Lastly, we give a case study to illustrate the generated results by *FSD*, as shown in Fig. 2, with a comparison to *RNNSearch* on Chinese-English test set. In the first example, *RNNSearch* generates an extra word "vows", which is addressed in FSD through considering the second POS tag "TO" in predicted POS tag sequence. In the second example, the translated English sentence need to add two definite articles "the". This is partially learned in FSD through taking into account the two "DT" tags in predicted POS tag sequence.

5   Conclusion

In this paper, we focus on NMT task and develop three neural architectures for jointly predicting the target sentence and corresponding POS tag sequence. The basic idea is to guide NMT models towards desired behavior through learning implicit knowledge from target POS tag sequence. Experimental results on Chinese-English and German-English translation tasks have demonstrated that the proposed architectures can significantly improve the translation performance with the help of target POS tag sequence prediction.

References

1. LeCun, Y., Bengio, Y., Hinton, G.: Deep learning. Nature **521**(7553), 436 (2015)
2. Bentivogli, L., Bisazza, A., Cettolo, M., et al.: Neural versus phrase-based machine translation quality: a case study (2016)
3. Eriguchi, A., Tsuruoka, Y., Cho, K.: Learning to parse and translate improves neural machine translation (2017)
4. Hashimoto, K., Tsuruoka, Y.: Neural machine translation with source-side latent graph parsing. In: Proceedings of the Conference on Machine Translation, WMT 2017, pp. 125–135. Association for Computational Linguistics (2017)

[5] The value of kappa is 0.65 in 1–5 scale on two dimensions.

5. Nadejde, M., Reddy, S., Sennrich, R., et al.: Predicting target language CCG Supertags improves neural machine translation. In: Proceedings of the Conference on Machine Translation, WMT 2017, vol. 1, pp. 68–79. Association for Computational Linguistics (2017)

6. Luong, M.-T., Le, Q.V., Sutskever, I., Vinyals, O., Kaiser, L.: Multi-task sequence to sequence learning. In: Proceedings of the Conference on Machine Translation, WMT 2016. ICLR (2016)

7. Niehues, J., Cho E.: Exploiting linguistic resources for neural machine translation using multi-task learning. In: Proceedings of the Conference on Machine Translation, WMT 2017, vol. 1, pp. 80–89. Association for Computational Linguistics (2017)

8. Hochreiter, S., Schmidhuber, J.: Long short-term memory. Neural Comput. **9**(8), 1735–1780 (1997)

9. Bahdanau, D., Cho, K., Bengio, Y.: Neural machine translation by jointly learning to align and translate (2014)

10. Mikolov, T., Sutskever, I., Chen, K., Corrado, G.S., Dean, J.: Distributed representations of words and phrases and their compositionality. In: 27th Annual Conference on Neural Information Processing Systems 2013, pp. 3111–3119 (2013)

11. Manning, C., Surdeanu, M., Bauer, J., Finkel, J., Bethard, S., McClosky, D.: The Stanford CoreNLP natural language processing toolkit. In: Proceedings of 52nd Annual Meeting of the Association for Computational Linguistics: System Demonstrations, pp. 55–60 (2014)

12. Ranzato, M., Chopra, S., Auli, M., et al.: Sequence level training with recurrent neural networks. Comput. Sci. (2015)

13. Zhou, H., Tu, Z., Huang, S., et al.: Chunk-based bi-scale decoder for neural machine translation. In: Proceedings of the 55th Annual Meeting of the Association for Computational Linguistics (Short Papers), pp. 580–586. Association for Computational Linguistics (2017)

Distance Measurement Based on Linear Phase Correlation in WiFi CSI

Qingfei Kang$^{(\boxtimes)}$, Liangbo Xie, Mu Zhou, and Zengshan Tian

School of Communication and Information Engineering,
Chongqing University of Posts and Telecommunications, Chongqing 400065, China
S160131065@stu.cqupt.edu.cn, {xielb,zhoumu,tianzs}@cqupt.edu.cn

Abstract. In this paper, we propose a new distance measurement algorithm based on WiFi Channel State Information (CSI). In order to resolve the phase error in traditional commodity WiFi devices, we design a system based on the Universal Software Radio Peripheral (USRP) with GNU Radio to analyze and separate the mixed phase errors. After the calibration of the CSI phase, it is found that the clock divider phase offset (DPO), which is introduced by the random phase offset in the clock, will affect the CSI phase, and a clustering-based method is proposed to remove the effect of DPO. We recover the linear relationships among the subcarriers phase and combine the center subcarrier phase to estimate the distance. In our algorithm, we can complete the distance measurement by using only one frequency band. Experiment results indicate that our algorithm can achieve centimeter-level accuracy in distance measurement.

Keywords: WiFi · CSI phase · GNU Radio · Distance measurement

1 Introduction

The Channel State Information (CSI) exposed by WiFi device, which is measured in channel equalization, is widely used for location as a replacement of Received Signal Strength Indication (RSSI). Due to the difficulty of eliminating CSI phase error, most of the recent WiFi location systems are based on the CSI amplitude as the substitution of RSSI. As we known, Chronos [1] is the first system to use CSI phase for location, however, Chronos only uses the zero-subcarrier to avoid the linear phase error and needs frequency hopping in the device. Splicer [2] combines amplitude with the phase in 10 different bands rather than only use the phase with mixed phase errors to locate the target but it also needs to frequency sweeping. What's more, in order to improve the positioning accuracy the above applications have focused on the distance measurement accuracy and the accuracy of phase plays an important role in distance measurement.

According to previous work [3], most methods conduct a linear transform on the raw CSI phase to remove the linear CSI phase errors, which move the mean

© ICST Institute for Computer Sciences, Social Informatics and Telecommunications Engineering 2019
Published by Springer Nature Switzerland AG 2019. All Rights Reserved
S. Han et al. (Eds.): AICON 2019, LNICST 286, pp. 167–174, 2019.
https://doi.org/10.1007/978-3-030-22968-9_15

of phases on all sub-carriers to zero. After the phase adjustment, the phase slope between the subcarriers, which includes the linear phase caused by the Time-of-Flight (ToF) is also forced to zero. As a result, the linear transform method can't use the phase difference between the subcarriers to estimate the ToF. Recent work [4] subtracts the linear slope value by conducting a linear fitting from the raw CSI phase. But the value can't be used to represent the slope caused by the ToF since the Sampling Frequency Offset (SFO) is mixed with ToF. To remove the SFO, high precise synchronization across the device is needed, SourceSync [5] implement a symbol level synchronizer WiFi system on the customized Field Programmable Gate Array (FPGA) platform, but such mechanisms are not available in the public. Hence, we use Universal Software Radio Peripheral (USRP) to do high precise synchronization, which has a variety of alternative method to synchronize different devices such as Multiple Input Multiple Output (MIMO) Cable and GPS Disciplined Oscillator (GPSDO) or external reference clock. What's more, by using the GNU Radio platform, we can develop our WiFi receiver quickly to collect the physical layer CSI information as we want.

Specifically, by using the synchronization feature of USRP, we can remove the main phase errors in CSI, but we find a new Divider Phase Offset (DPO) caused by the divider in USRP N210, which also exists on the commodity WiFi devices. To address this issue, we propose a strategy to eliminate the DPO and recover the linear phase slope between the subcarriers. After that, we use the accurate phase slope value and combine the zero-subcarrier phase to measure the distance.

The rest of this paper is organized as follows. We first make a overview of our system design in Sects. 2 and 3 describes the phase error calibration method in our system. We evaluate the performance of our system in Sect. 4 and we conclude in Sect. 5.

2   System Design

2.1   Signal Model

To simplify the channel model in [6], we only consider the environment with the single direct propagation path. The channel response $h(f)$ can be simplified as:

$$h(f) = \alpha \cdot e^{-j \cdot 2\pi \cdot f \cdot \tau}, \tag{1}$$

where α represents the amplification factor of amplitude and τ represents the propagation delay of the signal. Since the different subcarriers in the same frequency band undergo the same ToF, the phase difference $\Delta_{m,n}$ between subcarriers m and n can be expressed as:

$$\Delta_{m,n} = -2\pi \cdot (f_m - f_n) \cdot \tau \bmod 2\pi, \tag{2}$$

where f_m and f_n are the frequency of subcarriers m and n in the passband. We conduct that the phase ambiguity between two consecutive subcarriers only occurs when the phase difference between two consecutive subcarriers greater than 2π. In our usual usage, the WiFi signal propagation delay is much smaller than this value. Under such a premise, we can describe Eq. (2) as:

$$\Delta_{m,n} = -2\pi \cdot (f_m - f_n) \cdot \tau, \tag{3}$$

From Eq. (3) we can observe an obvious linear relationship between the phase and subcarriers index after we transform Eq. (3) as:

$$\phi_m = \phi_0 - 2\pi \cdot k \cdot f_s \cdot \tau, \tag{4}$$

where ϕ_m is the phase of the mth subcarrier, k is the index of subcarriers, which ranges from 0 to 53. ϕ_0 represents the phase of the first subcarrier and the f_s is the frequency spacing between two consecutive subcarriers. In order to calculate the distance, we need to get the ToF, which can be obtained by fit the phase slope. In Eq. (4) τ is multiple with k, we take its partial respect to k and obtained the phase slope s:

$$s = -2\pi \cdot f_s \cdot \tau, \tag{5}$$

since the max resolution of the CSI slope that represent ToF is only limited to the sampling period T_s [7] and we take it to Eq. (5) as:

$$s = -2\pi \cdot f_s \cdot (\tau \bmod T_s). \tag{6}$$

According to [1], the zero-subcarrier phase θ with the center frequency f_c can also represent ToF since it won't be affected by the linear phase error and can be express as:

$$\theta = -2\pi \cdot f_c \cdot \left(\tau \bmod \frac{1}{f_c}\right), \tag{7}$$

If we can get the CSI phase without any additional phase error, the slope s in Eq. (6) and the zero-subcarrier θ in Eq. (7) should have the relationship as the picture plotted in Fig. 1.

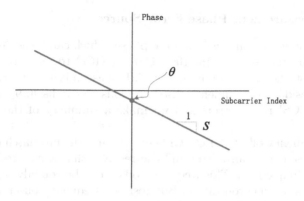

Fig. 1. The CSI phase without phase error in theoretically.

2.2   Distance Measurement

From Eqs. (6) and (7), both the zero-subcarrier phase and the phase slope have
the ambiguity that can't represent the true ToF. Notice that the center frequency
f_c, which defined in the standard should have the fixed value (e.g., 2.412 GHz,
2.417 GHz, 2.422 GHz, etc.). And the sampling period T_s is related to the bandwidth, which should have a value of 20M or 40M in normal usage. We note that
T_s is not an integer multiple of $\frac{1}{f_c}$ and the above ambiguity can be resolved
by the well-known Chinese remainder theorem [8]. We get the initial ambiguity
value of phase slope s and zero-subcarrier θ and combine Eqs. (6) and (7) to
search real ToF τ as described in Fig. 2.

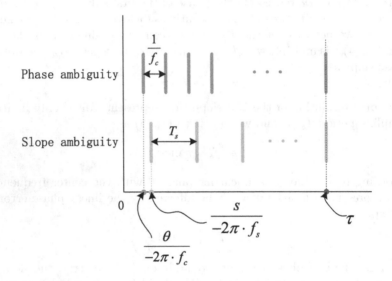

Fig. 2. Resolve phase ambiguity by phase slope and zero-subcarrier phase.

2.3   CSI Measurement Phase Error Source

Generally speaking, we can easily use the phase, which can be achieved from the
CSI reported by the Network Interface Cards (NICs) to measure the distance.
But previous studies have reported the CSI phase mixed with rich hardware
distortions. Besides environment noise, previous researchs [6,9] have resolved
the sources of CSI phase errors and we make a summary of the major phase
error.

Carrier frequency offset (CFO). CFO exists since the mismatch of the crystal
oscillator between the transmitter and the receiver that can't produce the consistent central frequencies. This frequency offset can be roughly removed in the
stage of frequency synchronization. But residual frequency offset remain exists
that will affect the CSI phase heavily.

Sampling frequency offset (SFO). SFO is a difference between the sampling clock of the Analog to Digital Converter (ADC) and the Digital to Analog Converter (DAC), which will cause a difference of sampling period. This error will gradually increase and lead to a rotation error. This rotation error will cause ambiguity in CSI phase that disrupts the linear relationship between subcarrier.

Divider Phase Offset (DPO). DPO is caused by the divider, which doesn't lock the output clock phase. Since any timing shift on the ADC clock is combined with the desired signal at the ADC output. For this reason, the DPO in ADC clock will introduce a phase error to the CSI phase. As we need a sample rate of 20 MHz, which divides from the 100 MHz master clock in USRP N210, we get 5 different slopes in the CSI phase. What's more, DPO also includes a phase offset like CFO if the ADC and frequency mixer use single clock source. As we can see from Fig. 3 the red line represents the phase without phase error, and one blue line represents one packet CSI phase, which mixed with CFO and SFO. If we collet lots of packets and the phase between two blue lines is DPO.

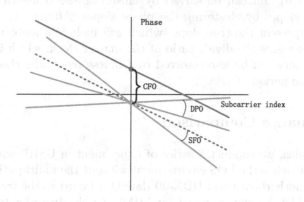

Fig. 3. The CSI phase with phase errors. (Color figure online)

3   Phase Error Calibration

As we known, CFO and SFO are caused by the crystal oscillator mismatch between the transmitter and the receiver. It can be easily resolved when we synchronize transmitter and receiver by using the fantastic feature of USRP. We test this method in USRP N210.

We first collect 50 packets CSI without any synchronization methods with the constant distance. And then we repeat the experiment again by using MIMO Cable for synchronization. We plot the unwrapped CSI phase in Fig. 4.

From Fig. 4(b) we can see the phase has an obvious linear relationship between the subcarrier index compare to Fig. 4(a) since the SFO is removed. And the phase of zero-subcarrier (27th subcarrier) become stable since the CFO is also removed once we synchronize two USRP devices.

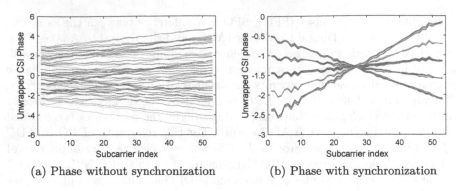

(a) Phase without synchronization   (b) Phase with synchronization

Fig. 4. Effect of synchronization.

We note that DPO will lead to a rotation error, which has a fix rotation values in Fig. 4(b) and can be solved by clustering-based algorithm. We first get 5 different slopes by clustering the phase slopes. After that, we can select one slope to represent the true slope, which will include a ambiguity of $\frac{T_s}{div}$ in Eq. (6). div represents the divide ratio of the master clock, which is a constant. But this ambiguity can be also resolved by Chinese remainder theorem since it only reduces the period of s.

4 Performance Comparison

To verify our idea, we conduct a series of experiment in USRP with a spacious environment, which is the LOS environment without the multi-path distraction. We use N210 motherboard and UBX-40 daughter board as the transmitter and the receiver which be synchronized by MIMO Cable. In order to remove the DPO in frequency mixer, we can only use the center frequency is multiples of the master clock 100M, which means our experiments will limit the test distance to 3 m.

In order to use the zero-subcarrier for distance measurement, we need to get the stable zero-subcarrier phase. We conduct an experiment with the center frequency of 2.4 GHz and we restart the devices 20 times to collect 1000 packets. We find that the phase of zero-subcarrier is much stable with an error less than 0.15 rad, which means that the max error of distance calculated by the zero-subcarrier is less than 0.3 cm. This accuracy has met our requirements.

After we clustering the phase slope, we need to select one slope from 5 slopes to represent the ToF. In order to select the slope with minimal error, we calculate the variance of the 5 different slopes in Fig. 5(a) from the max slope to the min slope and plot the variance in Fig. 5(b). We can find that the minimal slope which plots in red color in Fig. 5(a) has the smallest variance. We repeat this experiment many times and come to the same conclusion. And we find the range of the minimal slope is about 0.00055, which means that the max error of distance calculated by the phase slope is less than 8.4 cm.

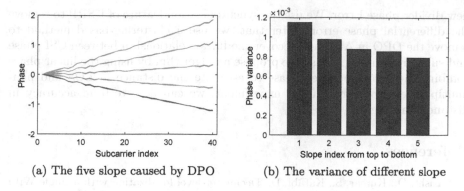

(a) The five slope caused by DPO   (b) The variance of different slope

Fig. 5. Phase slope selection. (Color figure online)

To measure the distance, we fix the transmitter and move the receiver. For each distance, we collect 200 packets CSI. But we can only under the max distance of 3 m since the power of the signal is limited by the hardware. In Fig. 6, we provide detailed statistical results for performance achieved by the algorithm described in Sect. 2 with different distance.

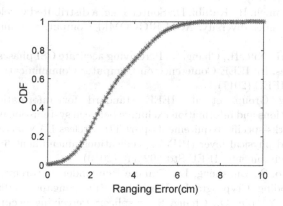

Fig. 6. Distance measurement result.

Compare to the max accuracy system that using WiFi signal [1], our system can achieve the distance error less than 10 cm by using the synchronization feature of USRP, which is superior to the best performance of 26 cm in Chronos.

5   Conclusion

This paper design a new distance measurement system. From the CSI collect by the USRP devices we analysis the mixed phase error in CSI phase and identify a new divider phase Error. We use the synchronization feature of USRP to remove the differential phase error. After that, we use a clustering-based method to remove the DPO in ADC and recover the linear relationship between CSI phase and subcarrier index. At last, we propose an algorithm by using the linear phase combine the zero-subcarrier phase to estimate the distance in LOS and non-multipath environment. In our experiment, we can achieve 6 cm accuracy in distance tracking.

References

1. Vasisht, D., Kumar, S., Katabi, D.: Decimeter-level localization with a single WiFi access point. In: NSDI, vol. 16, pp. 165–178 (2016)
2. Xie, Y., Li, Z., Li, M.: Precise power delay profiling with commodity Wi-Fi. IEEE Trans. Mob. Comput. 18(6), 1342–1355 (2018)
3. Wang, Y., Liu, J., Chen, Y., Gruteser, M., Yang, J., Liu, H.: E-eyes: device-free location-oriented activity identification using fine-grained wifi signatures. In: Proceedings of the 20th Annual International Conference on Mobile Computing and Networking, pp. 617–628. ACM (2014)
4. Kotaru, M., Joshi, K., Bharadia, D., Katti, S.: SpotFi: decimeter level localization using WiFi. In: ACM SIGCOMM Computer Communication Review, vol. 45, pp. 269–282. ACM (2015)
5. Rahul, H., Hassanieh, H., Katabi, D.: SourceSync: a distributed wireless architecture for exploiting sender diversity. ACM SIGCOMM Comput. Commun. Rev. 41(4), 171–182 (2011)
6. Zhuo, Y., Zhu, H., Xue, H., Chang, S.: Perceiving accurate CSI phases with commodity WiFi devices. In: IEEE Conference on Computer Communications, INFOCOM 2017, pp. 1–9. IEEE (2017)
7. IEEE Working Group, et al.: IEEE standard for information technology-telecommunications and information exchange between systems-local and metropolitan area networks-specific requirements-part 11: wireless LAN medium access control (MAC) and physical layer (PHY) specifications amendment 6: wireless access in vehicular environments. IEEE Std 802(11) (2010)
8. Dingyi, P., Arto, S., Cunsheng, D.: Chinese Remainder Theorem: Applications in Computing, Coding, Cryptography. World Scientific, Singapore (1996)
9. Zhu, H., Zhuo, Y., Liu, Q., Chang, S.: π-splicer: Perceiving accurate CSI phases with commodity WiFi devices. IEEE Tran. Mob. Comput. 17(9), 2155–2165 (2018)

A Transfer Learning Method for Aircrafts Recognition

Hongbo Li[✉], Bin Guo, Tong Gao, and Hao Chen

Harbin Institute of Technology, Harbin, People's Republic of China
drbobo@hit.edu.cn

Abstract. An effective method for recognizing aircrafts with different resolutions is proposed. Since training aircraft samples and test aircraft samples are imaging in different resolutions, different satellites and different imaging conditions, they obey different distributions. The Feature Subspace Alignment and Balanced Distribution Adaptation (FSA-BDA) method is proposed to solve this problem. Different from other transfer learning methods, it considers both spatial alignment and probability adaptation, so that, the probability distribution of the source domain data and the target domain data is as consistent as possible in the same feature space. The method first performs FSA, which maps the source domain and the target domain data to a low-dimensional common mapping space through different mapping matrices for preserving the structural information. Secondly, the BDA method is used to properly adapt the marginal probability and the conditional probability through the weight adjustment, which can leverage the importance of the marginal and conditional distribution discrepancies. This paper aims at recognizing three types of aircrafts, which are B52, F15 and F16 aircrafts. The experimental results show that the proposed method is better than several state-of-the-art methods.

Keywords: Aircrafts recognition · Probability adaptation · Transfer learning

1 Introduction

In recent years, computer vision and related technologies have developed rapidly. Image recognition technology has become a hot topic in research. As the number of remote sensing satellites increases, the amount of data on aircraft targets based on optical satellite remote sensing images is also increasing. However, the acquisition time, weather conditions, imaging angles and image spatial resolutions of the aircraft in optical images are usually different. Moreover, due to the different resolutions, the data difference is very large. Therefore, it is necessary to study how to automatically identify aircraft targets based on a small amount of labeled data.

The representative of the earlier aircraft image recognition research is Dudani S A who proved that the aircraft was automatically identified [1]. In [2], a coarse-to-fine strategy is proposed. And the fine matching phase uses the shape feature to complete the matching of the candidate target. A reconstruction-based similarity measure is proposed [3], which transforms the type recognition problem into a reconstruction problem. In recent years, a novel airport detection and aircraft recognition method that

S. Han et al. (Eds.): AICON 2019, LNICST 286, pp. 175–185, 2019.
https://doi.org/10.1007/978-3-030-22968-9_16

is based on the two-layer visual saliency analysis model and support vector machines is proposed for high-resolution broad-area remote-sensing images [4]. The aircraft's landmark detection is used to address the aircraft type recognition problem [5], which needs fewer labeled data and alleviates the work of human annotation. A novel aircraft type recognition framework based on deep convolutional neural networks is proposed [6]. The idea of fine-grained visual classification is proposed, which attempts to make full use of the features from discriminative object parts [7].

However, none of these methods considers the difference between the training sample and the test sample, and some methods require a large number of labeled data. However, in actual situations, the data obtained are often very different due to the different types of satellites, and the data with labels is very rare. In order to solve the problem of large differences in training and test samples, a transfer learning method was proposed.

Aiming at the research goal of this paper, a Feature Subspace Alignment and Balanced Distribution Adaptation (FSA-BDA) algorithm is proposed to solve this problem. The method first performs feature subspace alignment, and obtains a mapping matrix for the source domain data and the target domain data respectively, and maps the source domain and the target domain data to a low-dimensional common mapping space through different mapping matrices. After the spatial alignment is achieved, the BDA [8] method is used to properly adapt the edge probability and the conditional probability through the weight setting, so that their distribution in the same mapping space is as uniform as possible, and a better effect is obtained.

There are two points different from the other transfer learning methods. First, consider both spatial alignment and probability adaptation, so that the distribution of source and target domains in the same mapping space is as uniform as possible. Second, when the proposed method is spatially aligned, two different mapping matrices are used to map the source and target domains respectively, and the structural information in the source data and the target data can be retained.

Due to the good nature of Gabor features, we extract Gabor features to identify aircrafts. We first proposed FSA algorithm which achieves space alignment and then aligned both marginal distribution and conditional distribution by BDA method, so that the new method FSA-BDA which we proposed can increase the accuracy rate of aircrafts recognition.

2   Related Work

According to the definition of transfer learning, it can be divided into multi-task learning, cross-domain learning and learning under different data distribution [9]. According to the label of data in the target domain, the transfer learning can also be divided into supervised transfer learning and transfer learning. In this paper, we pay attention to the difficult unsupervised transfer learning that the target domain is completely unlabeled. About the domain adaptation problem, some methods align the space, projecting source data and target data into a new space, such as SA [10] and SDA [11]. But they do not consider the distribution alignment.

Some methods align distribution. For example, the STL [12] reduces the distance of the conditional probability distribution of the source domain and the target domain, thereby completing the migration learning. TCA [13] adapts marginal distribution, and JDA [14] adapts marginal distribution and conditional distribution at the same time.

However, sometimes it cannot achieve satisfaction effect by only considering space alignment or probability distribution adaptation. Therefore, we propose FSA-BDA algorithm. This method considers both spatial alignment and probability adaptation. First, the data in the source domain and the target domain are mapped to the same feature space, and then the balanced distribution adaptation method is used to simultaneously adapt the two domains which are marginal distribution and conditional distribution according to a certain weight. So this method can achieve a better effect.

3 Proposed Method

The method first performs Feature Subspace Alignment (FSA), which maps the source domain and the target domain data to a low-dimensional common mapping space through different mapping matrices. And then, the BDA [8] is used to properly adapt the edge probability and the conditional probability through the weight setting, so that their distribution in the same mapping space is as uniform as possible.

3.1 Feature Spatial Alignment

For data with different distributions, although they are of the same type, the difference in the characteristic representation of the data causes their spatial distribution inconsistency. The FSA finds the appropriate mapping change by solving the feature representation of the data, and maps the source domain data and the target domain data into a common space through feature transformation. The FSA algorithm can construct a low-dimensional common mapping space. The specific algorithm is as follows.

Suppose the label space $C = \{c_1, c_2, \ldots, c_c\}$. The source domain and the target domain data are $\mathbf{D}_s$ and $\mathbf{D}_t$, respectively, $\mathbf{D}_s \neq \mathbf{D}_t$. And the problem is to get the label $\mathbf{Y}_t$ of the target domain. The source domain $\mathbf{X}_s \in \mathbf{R}^{m \times p}$ contains m samples, and $\mathbf{Y}_s$ is the label of $\mathbf{X}_s$. The target domain $\mathbf{X}_s \in \mathbf{R}^{m \times p}$ contains n samples, and p is the dimension of the sample feature. Learning the transformation matrix $\mathbf{T} = \{\mathbf{t}_1, \mathbf{t}_2, \ldots, \mathbf{t}_d\} \in \mathbf{R}^{p \times d}$ from the above given conditions, the low-dimensional projection of the original data via the transformation matrix is $\mathbf{Z}_s \in \mathbf{R}^{m \times d}$ and $\mathbf{Z}_t \in \mathbf{R}^{n \times d}$, where d is the dimension of the new feature. Mapping function of the two mapping source domains, the mapping of the target domain function. Find the mapping function $\mathbf{T}_s : \mathbf{X}_s \rightarrow \mathbf{Z}_S \in \mathbf{R}^{m \times d}$ of the source domain, the mapping function $\mathbf{T}_t : \mathbf{X}_t \rightarrow \mathbf{Z}_t \in \mathbf{R}^{n \times d}$ of the target domain.

To get the appropriate mapping changes, minimization (1) is able to align data from different fields in the mapping space.

$$F_1 = \sum_{x_i \in D_s} \sum_{x_j \in D_t} \left\| T_s^T x_i - T_t^T x_j \right\|_2^2 W(i,j) \tag{1}$$

Where x_i and x_j are derived from different fields and measure the similarity between x_i and x_j. The similarity matrix $W = \begin{Bmatrix} 0 & W_a^{s,t} \\ W_a^{t,s} & 0 \end{Bmatrix}$ is $(m+n) \times (m+n)$. $W_a(i,j)$ represents the similarity of x_i and x_j.

Similarly, minimizing Eq. (2) can constrain similar data in the source domain to be mapped to similar locations, while unsimilar data is separated in the mapped space.

$$F_2 = \sum_{x_i \in D_s} \sum_{x_j \in D_s} \left\| T_s^T x_i - T_s^T x_j \right\|_2^2 W_s(i,j) \tag{2}$$

Where x_i and x_j come from different domains, and $W_s(i,j)$ measures the similarity between x_i and x_j.

Similarly, minimizing Eq. (3) can constrain similar data in the target domain to be mapped to similar locations, while unsimilar data is separated.

$$F_3 = \sum_{x_i \in D_t} \sum_{x_j \in D_t} \left\| T_t^T x_i - T_t^T x_j \right\|_2^2 W_t(i,j) \tag{3}$$

Where x_i and x_j are from the target domain. If x_i and x_j are neighbors in the original field of the target domain, they should remain in the neighbors in the mapped space, otherwise they should be away from each other in the mapped space.

Define the objective function as:

$$C(T_s, T_t) = F_1 + \alpha F_2 + (1 - \alpha)F_3 \tag{4}$$

Where F_1 can make similar data in different fields be aligned to similar positions in the mapping space, F_2 and F_3 maintain the original manifold structure of each domain data in the low-dimensional mapping space. In order to optimizing $C(T_s, T_t)$, Definition $T^T = [T_S^T, T_T^T]$, $X^T = [X_S^T, X_T^T]$ and expand the equation as follows.

$$\begin{aligned} F_1 &= \sum_{x_i \in D_s} \sum_{x_j \in D_t} \left\| T_s^T x_i - T_t^T x_j \right\|_2^2 W(i,j) \\ &= 2T^T X (P - W) X^T T \\ &= 2T^T X L X^T T \end{aligned} \tag{5}$$

Where P is a diagonal matrix, $P(i,j) = \sum_j W(i,j)$, $L = P - W$.

$$F_2 = \sum_{x_i \in D_s} \sum_{x_j \in D_s} \left\| T_s^T x_i - T_s^T x_j \right\|_2^2 W_s(i,j)$$
$$= 2T^T X (P_s - W_s) X^T T \tag{6}$$
$$= 2T^T X L_s X^T T$$

Where P_s is a diagonal matrix, $P_s(i,j) = \sum_j W_s(i,j)$, $L_s = P_s - W_s$.

$$F_3 = \sum_{x_i \in D_t} \sum_{x_j \in D_t} \left\| T_t^T x_i - T_t^T x_j \right\|_2^2 W_t(i,j)$$
$$= 2T^T X (D_t - W_t) X^T T \tag{7}$$
$$= 2T^T X L_t X^T T$$

Where P_t is a diagonal matrix, $P_t(i,j) = \sum_j W_t(i,j)$, $L_t = P_t - W_t$.

Substituting Eqs. (5), (6) and (7) into (4), by mathematical principles of matrix and regularization, Eq. (8) can be obtained.

$$C(T_S, T_T) = F_1 + \alpha F_2 + (1 - \alpha) F_3$$
$$= T_t X L X^T T + \alpha T^T X L_s X^T T + (1 - \alpha) T^T X L_t X^T T \tag{8}$$

Where α is used to control the contribution of the manifold regularization terms in the two fields. The target vector that needs to be solved in the problem is

$$F^* = \arg_{T_t, T_s} \min F_1 + \alpha F_2 + (1 - \alpha) F_3$$
$$= \arg_{T_t, T_s} \min T_t X L X^T T + \alpha T^T X L_s X^T T + (1 - \alpha) T^T X L_t X^T T \tag{9}$$

Solving the k minimum eigenvalues of (9) gives the obtained mapping function. It can be seen that Eq. (9) is a generalized Rayleigh quotient problem. According to the solution spectrum framework, its solution is the eigenvector corresponding to the largest generalized eigenvalue of Eq. (10).

$$X(L + \alpha L_s + (1 - \alpha) L_t) X^T \tag{10}$$

When $d > 1$, the feature vector corresponding to the first d largest non-zero eigenvalues can be used to form a transformed projection matrix. We can get $Z_S \in F_S D_S$ and $Z_T \in F_T D_T$, which map the two domains to the same space.

3.2 Balanced Distribution Adaptation

After spatial alignment, the BDA [8] method is used to match the edge probability and the conditional probability with different weight ratios, thereby aligning the probability distributions of the features in the same space.

After MA algorithm, the feature space $\chi_S = \chi_T$ and the label space $\mathbf{y}_S = \mathbf{y}_T$, the marginal distribution $P_s(\mathbf{Z}_S) \neq P_t(\mathbf{Z}_T)$ the conditional distribution $P_s(\mathbf{y}_s|\mathbf{Z}_S) \neq P_t(\mathbf{y}_t|\mathbf{Z}_T)$.

The BDA method reduces the difference in marginal distribution and conditional distribution. According to a certain proportion. It can be expressed as follow.

$$D(\mathbf{Z}_S|\mathbf{Z}_T) = (1 - \beta)D(P_s(\mathbf{Z}_S), P_t(\mathbf{Z}_T)) + \beta D(P_s(\mathbf{y}_s|\mathbf{Z}_S), P_t(\mathbf{y}_t|\mathbf{Z}_T)) \qquad (11)$$

Where $\beta \in [0, 1]$ is a balance factor to leverage the different importance of distributions. When $\beta \rightarrow 0$, it means the datasets are more dissimilar, so the marginal distribution is more dominant; when $\beta \rightarrow 1$ it reveals the datasets are similar, so the conditional distribution is more important to adapt. Therefore, the balance factor β can adaptively leverage the importance of each distribution and lead to good results

Using the class conditional distribution $P_t(Z_T|y_t)$ approximate $P_t(y_t|Z_T)$ according to the sufficient statistics when sample sizes are large. In order to compute $P_t(Z_T|y_t)$, we apply prediction on D_t using some base classifier trained on D_s to get the soft labels for D_t. The soft labels may be less reliable, so we iteratively refine them. Using maximum mean discrepancy (MMD) [14] to compute the marginal and conditional distribution divergences Eq. (11) can be represented as:

$$D(\mathbf{Z}_S, \mathbf{Z}_T) = (1 - \beta)\left\|\frac{1}{n}\sum_{i=1}^{n}\mathbf{z}_{s_i} - \frac{1}{m}\sum_{j=1}^{m}\mathbf{z}_{t_j}\right\|_H^2 + \beta\sum_{c=1}^{C}\left\|\frac{1}{n_c}\sum_{z_{s_i}\in Z_S^{(c)}}\mathbf{z}_{s_i} - \frac{1}{m_c}\sum_{z_{s_i}\in Z_T^{(c)}}\mathbf{z}_{t_j}\right\|_H^2$$

$$(12)$$

Where $Z_S^{(c)}$ and $Z_T^{(c)}$ denote the samples belonging to class c in source and target domain, respectively. n_c and m_c, denote the number of samples. And, n and m stand for the number of samples in the source or target domain. H denotes reproducing kernel Hilbert space. By mathematical principles, Eq. (12) can be formalized as follows.

$$\min tr\left(\mathbf{A}^T\mathbf{Z}\left((1 - \beta)\mathbf{K_0} + \beta\sum_{c=1}^{C}\mathbf{K_c}\right)\mathbf{Z}^T\mathbf{A}\right) + \lambda\|\mathbf{A}\|_F^2 \qquad (13)$$
$$s.t.\mathbf{A}^T\mathbf{Z}\mathbf{H}\mathbf{Z}^T\mathbf{A} = I$$

Where λ is the regularization parameter with $\|.\|_F^2$ the Frobenius norm. What's more, $\mathbf{K_0}$ and $\mathbf{K_c}$ are MMD matrices and can be constructed as follows.

$$(\mathbf{K_0})_{ij} = \begin{cases} \frac{1}{n^2} & \mathbf{z}_i, \mathbf{z}_j \in \mathbf{D}_s \\ \frac{1}{m^2} & \mathbf{z}_i, \mathbf{z}_j \in \mathbf{D}_t \\ -\frac{1}{mn} & \text{otherwise} \end{cases} \qquad (14)$$

$$
(K_c)_{ij} =
\begin{cases}
\frac{1}{n_c^2} & \mathbf{z}_i, \mathbf{z}_j \in \mathbf{D}_s^{(c)} \\[4pt]
\frac{1}{m_c^2} & \mathbf{z}_i, \mathbf{z}_j \in \mathbf{D}_t^{(c)} \\[4pt]
-\frac{1}{m_c n_c} & \begin{cases} \mathbf{z}_i \in \mathbf{D}_t^{(c)}, \mathbf{z}_j \in \mathbf{D}_s^{(c)} \\ \mathbf{z}_i \in \mathbf{D}_s^{(c)}, \mathbf{z}_j \in \mathbf{D}_t^{(c)} \end{cases} \\[4pt]
0 & \text{otherwise}
\end{cases}
\tag{15}
$$

Where Z stands for the input data matrix composed of source data and target data, A denotes the transformation matrix, I is the identity matrix, and $H = I - (1/n)\mathbf{1}$.

Denote $\Phi = (\varphi_1, \varphi_2, \cdots, \varphi_d)$ as Lagrange multipliers, then Lagrange function for (13) is

$$
L = tr\left(A^T Z \left((1-\beta)K_0 + \beta \sum_{c=1}^C K_c \right) Z^T A \right) + \lambda \|A\|_F^2 + tr((I - A^T ZHZ^T A)\Phi) \tag{16}
$$

Set derivative $\partial L / \partial A = 0$, the optimization can be derived as a generalized eigen decomposition problem.

$$
\left(Z \left((1-\beta)K_0 + \beta \sum_{c=1}^C K_c \right) Z^T + \lambda I \right) A = ZHZ^T A \Phi \tag{17}
$$

Finally, the optimal transformation matrix A can be obtained by solving this equation and finding its d smallest eigenvectors.

By the FSA-BDA method, the source domain feature data and the target domain feature data can be mapped to the same space, and their distribution is also aligned by the BDA method.

4 Experiment and Analysis

4.1 Data Sets

The data sets are aircrafts with different resolutions under different imaging conditions obtained from open satellite maps. Parts of the dataset images are shown in Fig. 1. And the left of F15 aircrafts, F16 aircrafts and B52 aircrafts is 0.5 m resolution. The right of them is 1 m resolution.

The differences of the aircraft in different resolutions are very large. We use the labeled image in the source domain to identify the unlabeled image in the target domain. There are 200 B52 aircrafts, 180 F15 aircrafts and 210 F16 aircrafts in the source domain which are 0.5 m resolution. There are 125 B52 aircrafts, 125 F15 aircrafts and 125 F16 aircrafts in the source domain which are 1 m resolution.

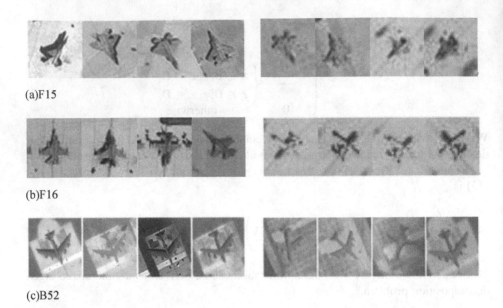

(a)F15

(b)F16

(c)B52

Fig. 1. Parts of the dataset. (a), (b) and (c) shows the three types of aircrafts in images in different resolutions.

4.2 Contrast Methods

The FSA-BDA is compared with five related methods, which are 1-Nearest Neighbor Classifier (NN), Principal Component Analysis(PCA) + NN, Transfer Component Analysis (TCA) + NN [13], Balanced Distribution Adaptation (BDA) + NN [8], Subspace Alignment (SA) + NN [10]. The 1NN classifier is trained on the source domain for identifying target domain ships.

These methods involve the subspace base k or d and the regularization parameters. We set d = k = 110 and $\lambda = 0.6, \alpha = 0.7, \beta = 0.3$ by ten cross-validation. The number of iterations of BDA and the proposed method is set to T = 15. What is more, the classification accuracy is used as an evaluation index, which is calculated as the ratio of the number of correctly identified samples to the total number of input samples in the target domain.

4.3 Experimental Results and Analysis

Results of experiments are discussed in this section. The performance of FSA-BDA algorithm is measured by classification accuracy and MMD distance. The following is the specific description.

Classification Accuracy. The classification accuracy of the three types of aircrafts shown in Table 1 and Fig. 2. The abscissas 1, 2 and 3 represent B52, F15 and F16 aircrafts respectively.

Table 1. Recognition accuracy.

Classification	B52	F15	F16	Average
FSA-BDA	97.6%	96.8%	98.4%	97.6%
JDA	93.6%	92.8%	95.2%	93.9%
TCA	89.6%	88.8%	91.2%	89.9%
SA	88.0%	87.2%	90.4%	88.5%
PCA	78.4%	76.8%	81.6%	78.9%
1NN	75.2%	73.6%	78.4%	75.7%

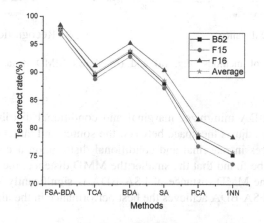

Fig. 2. Recognition accuracy.

The results are reported in Fig. 2 and Table 1 respectively. As illustrated, our method significantly outperforms the existing methods. The average recognition accuracy of the six methods is 97.6%, 93.86%, 89.86%, 88.53%, 78.93% and 75.73%. The accuracy of FSA-BDA on three aircrafts is 97.6%, which performs better than BDA, TCA, SA, PCA and 1NN. PCA and 1NN are traditional methods. SA only considers spatial alignment in adaptive domain problems. BDA minimizes the marginal and conditional allocation differences according to a certain weight between domains, while TCA can only minimize marginal differences. However, neither BDA nor TCA considers space adjustments. FSA-BDA considers spatial alignment and distribution differences. Therefore, theoretical analysis can explain the rationality of experimental results.

MMD Distance. MMD distance [14] is used to verify the distribution suitability of FSA-BDA and the other five methods. As shown in Fig. 3, the MMD distance and the average accuracy of NN, PCA, TCA, BDA, SA, and FSA-BDA increased with the number of iterations are shown. The abscissas stand for iterations.

The proposed method is compared with state-of-the-art methods in Fig. 3. Experiments demonstrate the efficacy of our method. All transfer learning methods can reduce the MMD distance. When only NN is used, the distance between the source domain and the target domain is large. Since TCA minimizes marginal differences, SA

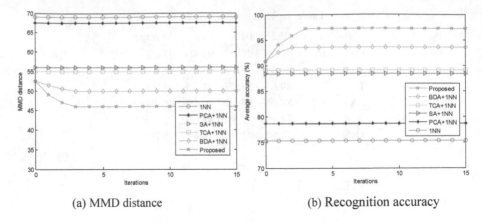

(a) MMD distance   (b) Recognition accuracy

Fig. 3. Performance of methods. Fig. (a) and (b) shows MMD distance and recognition accuracy.

aligns space, and BDA minimizes marginal and conditional distribution differences. FSA-BDA not only adjusts the space between the source and target domains, but also minimizes differences in marginal and conditional distribution according to a certain weight. And it can be found that the smaller the MMD distance, the higher the correct recognition rate. The MMD distance of FSA-BDA is significantly smaller than other methods. It shows FSA-BDA achieves the best performance in the aircrafts recognition problems.

5 Conclusion

In this paper, we propose a method called the Feature Subspace Alignment and Balanced Distribution Adaptation (FSA-BDA) for recognizing aircrafts with different resolutions. This method not only considers spatial alignment, but also considers probabilistic adaptation, so it achieves better results. The feature subspace alignment (FSA) maps the source domain and the target domain data to a low-dimensional common mapping space through different mapping matrices, in order to preserve the structural information in the source data and the target data. The BDA method is used to properly adapt the edge probability and the conditional probability through the weight setting, so that their distribution in the same mapping space is as uniform as possible. Extensive experiments demonstrate that the FSA-BDA method is better than the state-of-the-art transfer learning methods. In the future, we will continue to study the aircraft target recognition problem combined with transfer learning, such as the targets from different sources.

Acknowledgements. This work was supported in part by a grant from the Defense Industrial Technology Development Program (No. JCKY2016603C004).

References

1. Dudani, S.A., Breeding, K.J., McGhee, R.B.: Aircraft identification by moment invariants. IEEE Trans. Comput. **100**(1), 39–46 (1977)
2. Liu, G., Sun, X., et al.: Aircraft recognition in high-resolution satellite images using coarse-to-fine shape prior. IEEE Geosci. Remote Sens. Lett. **10**(3), 573–577 (2013)
3. Wu, Q., Sun, H., Sun, X., et al.: Aircraft recognition in high-resolution optical satellite remote sensing images. IEEE Geosc. Remote Sens. Lett. **12**(1), 112–116 (2015)
4. Zhang, L., Zhang, Y.: Airport detection and aircraft recognition based on two-layer saliency model in high spatial resolution remote-sensing images. IEEE J. Sele. Top. Appl. Earth Obs. Remote Sens. **10**(4), 1511–1524 (2017)
5. Zhao, A., Fu, K., Wang, S., et al.: Aircraft recognition based on landmark detection in remote sensing images. IEEE Geosci. Remote Sens. Lett. **14**(8), 1413–1417 (2017)
6. Zuo, J., Xu, G., Fu, K., et al.: Aircraft type recognition based on segmentation with deep convolutional neural networks. IEEE Geosci. Remote Sens. Lett. **15**(2), 282–286 (2018)
7. Fu, K., Dai, W., Zhang, Y., et al.: MultiCAM: multiple class activation mapping for aircraft recognition in remote sensing images. Remote Sens. **11**(5), 544 (2019)
8. Wang, J., Chen, Y.: Balanced distribution adaptation for transfer learning. In: 2017 IEEE International Conference on Data Mining, pp. 1129–1134 (2017)
9. Pan, S.J., Yang, Q.: A survey on transfer learning. IEEE Trans. Knowl. Data Eng. **22**(10), 1345–1359 (2010)
10. Fernando, B., Habrard, A., Sebban, M., Tuytelaars, T.: Unsupervised visual domain adaptation using subspace alignment. In: Proceedings of the IEEE International Conference on Computer Vision, pp. 2960–2967 (2013)
11. Sun, B., Saenko, K.: Subspace: distribution alignment for unsupervised domain adaptation. In: BMVC, p. 24:1 (2015)
12. Wang, J., Chen, Y., Hu, L., Peng, X., Philip, S.Y.: Stratified transfer learning for cross-domain activity recognition. In: 2018 IEEE International Conference on Pervasive Computing and Communications, pp. 1–10 (2018)
13. Pan, S.J., Tsang, I.W., Kwok, J.T., et al.: Domain adaptation via transfer component analysis. IEEE Trans. Neural Netw. **22**(2), 199–210 (2011)
14. Long, M., Wang, J., Ding, G., Sun, J., Yu, P.S.: Transfer feature learning with joint distribution adaptation. In: Proceedings of the IEEE International Conference on Computer Vision, pp. 2200–2207 (2013)

A New Two-Microphone Reduce Size SMFTF Algorithm for Speech Enhancement in New Telecommunication Systems

Zineddine Guernaz[✉] and Xuanli Wu

School of Electronics and Information Engineering,
Harbin Institute of Technology, Harbin, Heilongjiang, China
zinoudrai@outlook.com, xlwu2002@hit.edu.cn

Abstract. This paper considers the problem of speech enhancement and noise reduction in speech recognition systems and 5G mobile communication systems. The presence of these systems in a noisy environment reduces their effectiveness and makes degradation in their performance. here, we propose a new contribution to resolve noise reduction and speech enhancement problem in these systems by proposing a new algorithm. The proposed two microphones reduce size simplified fast transversal filter (TM-RSMFTF) algorithm is an outcome of the good combination between the well-known forward blind source separation structure and the adaptive algorithm reduce size simplified fast transversal filter properties which is a stable version of fast transversal filter (FTF) algorithms. The proposed algorithm has low computational complexity. The simulation results show a good performances and effectiveness of this new TM-RSMFTF algorithm in comparison with conventional TM-NLMS algorithm and almost similar performances with full-size TM-SFTF in terms of various objectives criteria such as Segmental SNR, System Mismatch, Segmental MSE.

Keywords: Noise reduction · Speech enhancement · TM-RSMFTF

1 Introduction

Nowadays, many applications such as 4G and 5G telecommunication systems, speech recognition systems, VoIP and teleconferencing systems, insist the presence of speech enhancement and acoustic noise reduction methods because these applications are designed for the quiet environment but in real life, the presence of different noise sources corrupt the speech signal causing degradation in the performances of these systems.

In the last decades, a lot of algorithms and techniques have been developed in the literature for speech enhancement with the first goal of raising speech quality such as spectral subtraction techniques [1], Wiener filter [2], minimum mean-square error estimator [3, 4]. We found also the most powerful speech enhancement techniques which are based on the adaptive filter [5]. The coefficients of the adaptive filter can be adjusted automatically by using various adaptive algorithms.

© ICST Institute for Computer Sciences, Social Informatics and Telecommunications Engineering 2019
Published by Springer Nature Switzerland AG 2019. All Rights Reserved
S. Han et al. (Eds.): AICON 2019, LNICST 286, pp. 186–202, 2019.
https://doi.org/10.1007/978-3-030-22968-9_17

Several adaptive algorithms have been proposed, the most popular one is normalized least mean square (NLMS) [5], and it is characterized by low computational complexity and low convergence speed. Another popular algorithms are recursive least square (RLS) algorithms [5], the main drawback of these algorithms is high computation complexity.

Many fast recursive least mean square algorithms have been proposed to resolve the high computational complexity problem such as the fast Kalman [6], fast transversal filter (FTF) [7], and the main drawback of these algorithms is the numerical instability. In the literature, several solutions have been proposed to solve this problem [8, 9].

To solve acoustic noise reduction and speech enhancement problem, a stable version of FTF algorithm, i.e., the simplified FTF algorithm (SMFTF) was proposed in [10]. In this algorithm, the adaptation gain is evaluated by using only the forward prediction variables and discarding the backward prediction and also by adding regularization constant and leakage factor. In the same work, reduce size simplified FTF (R-SMFTF) algorithm was proposed by reducing the size of forward predictor and calculating two likelihood variables, the first one was used to update the transversal filter and the forward predictor order P and the second one was used to update the forward prediction error variance, and this algorithm shows numerical stability and similar performance with FRLS algorithms with low computational complexity $(2L + 5P)$ where L is the length of the adaptive filter, and P is the size of forward predictor.

To reduce more computational complexity for SMFTF and R-SMFTF algorithms, the author in [11] proposed new algorithms similar to SMFTF and R-SMFTF with new relations to calculate the likelihood variables which reduce the computational complexity of simplified FTF algorithm to $6L$ and $2L + 4P$ for reduce size simplified FTF algorithm, respectively.

To reduce noise and enhance speech, several algorithms based on the combination of forward blind source separation structure and various adaptive algorithms have been proposed [12, 13]. In this work, we propose a new two-microphones reduce size simplified fast transversal filter (TM-RSMFTF) algorithm for speech enhancement and noise reduction application. This proposed algorithm obtained by the good combination between the reduce size simplified FTF algorithm and the forward blind sources separation (FBSS) structure.

The low computational complexity and the good performances shown in the simulation results of this new algorithm makes it a good choice for implementation in the 4G and 5G mobile communication and speech recognition systems.

This work is organized as follows. Section 2 presents the simplified model of a convolutive mixture that we used. In Sect. 3, FBSS is described. Section 4 discusses the proposed algorithm and in Sect. 5, we highlight the computational complexity. In Sect. 6, we present simulation results and comparative study of the proposed algorithm with two-microphone algorithms. Finally, we present the conclusion in Sect. 7.

2 The Simplified Model of a Convolutive Mixture

In our work, we consider the situation of two microphones and two uncorrelated signals which are speech signal $s(n)$ and noise signal $b(n)$, we consider that the speech signal is captured by two sensors, and the useful signal is near to the first sensor and the unwanted signal is near to the other sensor, this mixing model [14–17] is shown in Fig. 1.

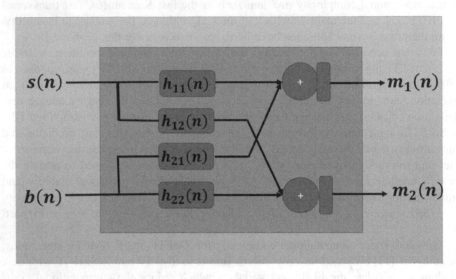

Fig. 1. The mixture model with two microphones

The two convolutive observations we obtained at the output of this mixing model are given by the following equations:

$$m_1(n) = s(n) * h_{11}(n) + h_{21}(n) * b(n), \tag{1}$$

$$m_2(n) = b(n) * h_{22}(n) + h_{12}(n) * s(n), \tag{2}$$

where, $s(n)$ is the source of speech and $b(n)$ is the source of noise, $h_{11}(n)$ and $h_{22}(n)$ represent the impulse responses of each direct channel respectively and they assumed to be identity $(h_{11}(n) = h_{22}(n) = \delta(n))$, $h_{21}(n)$ and $h_{12}(n)$ represent the cross-coupling effects between the 2 channels. The symbol * represents the convolution operation.

3 The Forward Blind Sources Separation (FBSS) Structure

The widely known forward blind source is effectively combined with many different algorithms to reduce noise and enhance the performance of speech. The forward BSS structure is shown in Fig. 2, and the aim of two channels forward BSS is to restore $s(n)$ and $b(n)$ only from the two convolutive observations [16]. For identification of the two real impulse response $h_{12}(n)$ and $h_{21}(n)$, we use the two adaptive filters of the two channel forward BSS structure.

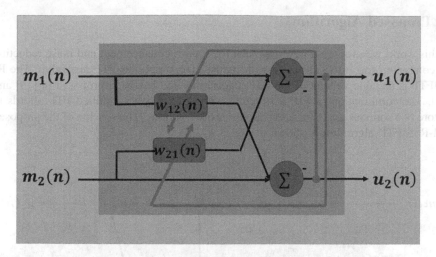

Fig. 2. The forward blind sources separation (FBSS) structure

The two outputs of this structure are given by:

$$u_1(n) = m_1(n) - m_2(n) * w_{21}(n), \tag{3}$$

$$u_2(n) = m_2(n) - m_1(n) * w_{12}(n), \tag{4}$$

where, $(*)$ represents the convolution operation. By inserting (1) and (2) into (3) and (4), we can obtain the two outputs equations $u_1(n)$ and $u_2(n)$ as follows:

$$u_1(n) = b(n) * [h_{21}(n) - w_{21}(n)] + s(n) * [\delta(n) - h_{12}(n) * w_{21}(n)], \tag{5}$$

$$u_2(n) = s(n) * [h_{12}(n) - w_{12}(n)] + b(n) * [\delta(n) - h_{21}(n) * w_{12}(n)]. \tag{6}$$

If we use an optimal assumption for the two adaptive filters $(h_{21}(n) = w_{21}(n))$ and $(h_{12}(n) = w_{12}(n))$, in this situation the two outputs become:

$$u_1(n) = s(n) * [\delta(n) - h_{12}(n) * w_{21}(n)], \tag{7}$$

$$u_2(n) = b(n) * [\delta(n) - h_{21}(n) * w_{12}(n)]. \tag{8}$$

where, $\varphi_1(n)$ and $\varphi_2(n)$ are post filters which are given respectively by:

$$\varphi_1(n) = \delta(n) - h_{12}(n) * w_{21}(n), \tag{9}$$

$$\varphi_2(n) = \delta(n) - h_{21}(n) * w_{12}(n). \tag{10}$$

From (7) and (8), the post filter distorts the output signal, and if the two sensors are closely spaced, the effect of this post filter is critical [18]. To escape the effect of this post filter, we take the situation where two sensors are loosely spaced which has a minimal distortion because of this post filter [13].

4 Proposed Algorithm

In this work, we propose a new approach for speech enhancement and noise reduction by combining the FBSS structure with reduce size simplified FTF algorithm. The R-SMFTF is a stable version of the FTF algorithms, and has been proposed in [10] and [11]. The combination of FBSS structure with reduce size simplified FTF affords to restore two source signals from two mixtures observations. The scheme of the proposed TM-RSMFTF algorithm is shown in Fig. 3.

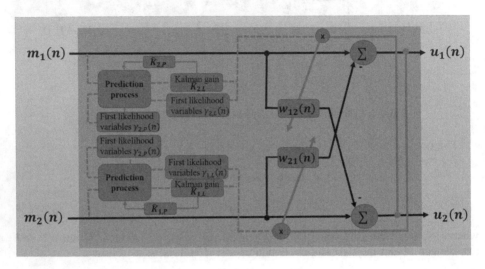

Fig. 3. The proposed TM-RSMFTF algorithm scheme

The two outputs of the TM-RSMFTF algorithm $u_1(n)$ and $u_2(n)$ are given as:

$$u_1(n) = m_1(n) - w_{21}^T(n)M_2(n), \tag{11}$$

$$u_2(n) = m_2(n) - w_{12}^T(n)M_1(n). \tag{12}$$

where, $M_1(n) = [m_1(n), m_1(n-1), \ldots, m_1(n-L+1)]$ and $M_2(n) = [m_2(n), m_2(n-1), \ldots, m_2(n-L+1)]$ are two vectors represent respectively the 2 mixture inputs $m_1(n)$ and $m_2(n)$. The updated equations of the two cross filters tap-weights w_{21} and w_{12} are controlled by the TM-RSMFTF algorithm and they are given as follows, respectively:

$$w_{21}(n) = w_{21}(n-1) + K_1(n)u_1(n), \tag{13}$$

$$w_{12}(n) = w_{12}(n-1) + K_2(n)u_2(n). \tag{14}$$

The two vectors $K_1(n)$ and $K_2(n)$ represent the adaptation gain which are given by:

$$K_1(n) = \gamma_{1,L}(n)\widehat{K_1}(n), \tag{15}$$

$$K_2(n) = \gamma_{2,L}(n)\widehat{K_2}(n). \tag{16}$$

where, the variables $\gamma_{1,L}(n)$ and $\gamma_{2,L}(n)$ which represent the first likelihood variables are used to update the two cross filters tap-weights that will give bellow and $\widehat{K_1}(n)$, $\widehat{K_2}(n)$ are normalized Kalman gain vectors. From [11, 19], the normalized Kalman gain vectors can be calculated by using only the forward predictor $a(n)$, and they are given by:

$$\begin{bmatrix} \widehat{K_1}(n) \\ c_1(n) \end{bmatrix} = \begin{bmatrix} 0 \\ \widehat{K_1}(n-1) \end{bmatrix} + \varphi_1(n) \begin{bmatrix} 1 \\ -a_{1,P} \\ 0_{L-P} \end{bmatrix}, \tag{17}$$

$$\begin{bmatrix} \widehat{K_2}(n) \\ c_2(n) \end{bmatrix} = \begin{bmatrix} 0 \\ \widehat{K_2}(n-1) \end{bmatrix} + \varphi_2(n) \begin{bmatrix} 1 \\ -a_{2,P} \\ 0_{L-P} \end{bmatrix}. \tag{18}$$

where, $c_1(n)$ and $c_2(n)$ are the last unused components of the normalized Kalman gain vectors, and the variables $\varphi_1(n)$ and $\varphi_2(n)$ are given respectively by:

$$\varphi_1(n) = \frac{e_1(n)}{\lambda\alpha_1(n) + c_a}, \tag{19}$$

$$\varphi_2(n) = \frac{e_2(n)}{\lambda\alpha_2(n) + c_a}. \tag{20}$$

where, $0 > \lambda > 1$ is forgetting factor and c_a is small regularization constant use to avoid performing numerical divisions by very small values in the absence of the input signal (silence period). The parameters α_1 and α_2 are the forward prediction errors variance, and they are given by:

$$\alpha_1(n) = \lambda\alpha_1(n-1) + \gamma_{1,P}e_1^2(n), \tag{21}$$

$$\alpha_2(n) = \lambda\alpha_2(n-1) + \gamma_{2,P}e_2^2(n). \tag{22}$$

where, $\gamma_{1,P}$ and $\gamma_{2,P}$ are second likelihood variables that will also give bellow, and they are used to update the forward prediction errors variance. The prediction error $e_1(n)$ and $e_2(n)$ can be be calculated by using the same algorithm and are given by:

$$e_1(n) = m_2(n) - a_{1,P}(n)M_{2,P}(n-1), \tag{23}$$

$$e_2(n) = m_1(n) - a_{2,P}(n)M_{1,P}(n-1).$$ (24)

where, $M_{1,P}(n)$ and $M_{2,P}(n)$ are two vectors that represent the P last simples of the two mixture signals $m_1(n)$ and $m_2(n)$, respectively. $a_{1,P}(n)$ and $a_{2,P}(n)$ are the forward predictors of order P that are calculated by minimizing the criteria $E[e_1^2(n)]$ and $E[e_2^2(n)]$,

$$a_{1,P}(n) = \eta(a_{1,P}(n-1) - \gamma_{1,L}(n)\widehat{K}_{1,P}(n-1)e_1(n),$$ (25)

$$a_{2,P}(n) = \eta(a_{2,P}(n-1) - \gamma_{2,L}(n)\widehat{K}_{2,P}(n-1)e_2(n).$$ (26)

Where $\widehat{K}_{1,P}(n)$ and $\widehat{K}_{2,P}(n)$ are the first P elements of $\widehat{K}_1(n)$ and $\widehat{K}_2(n)$ respectively, and the constant η, which is close to one, is called the leakage factor that allows the forward predictors to return back to zero [10].By saving $\varphi_1(n), \varphi_2(n), e_1(n)$ and $e_2(n)$ in vectors of length $(L+1)$, we can obtain: $\varphi_1(n) = [\varphi_1(n), \varphi_1(n-1), \ldots, \varphi_1(n-L)]^T$, $\varphi_2(n) = [\varphi_2(n), \varphi_2(n-1), \ldots, \varphi_2(n-L)]^T$, $E_1(n) = [e_1(n), e_1(n-1), \ldots, e_1(n-L)]^T$ and $E_2(n) = [e_2(n), e_2(n-1), \ldots, e_2(n-L)]^T$.

The first likelihood variables $\gamma_{1,L}(n)$ and $\gamma_{2,L}(n)$ of the Eqs. (15), (16), (25) and (26) are given by [11]:

$$\gamma_{1,L}(n) = \frac{1}{1 - \psi_1(n)}, \text{ at each period of } N \text{ simples we do: } \gamma_{1,L}(n) = \eta\gamma_{1,L}(n),$$ (27)

$$\gamma_{2,L}(n) = \frac{1}{1 - \psi_2(n)}, \text{ at each period of } N \text{ simples we do: } \gamma_{L,2}(n) = \eta\gamma_{2,L}(n).$$ (28)

where, $\psi_1(n)$ and $\psi_2(n)$ are given by:

$$\psi_1(n) = \psi_1(n-1) - \varphi_1(n)e_1(n) + \varphi_1(n-L)e_1(n-L),$$ (29)

$$\psi_2(n) = \psi_2(n-1) - \varphi_2(n)e_2(n) + \varphi_2(n-L)e_2(n-L).$$ (30)

where, $\varphi_i(n)$ and $\varphi_i(n-L)$ are the first and $(L+1)^{th}$ components of vector $\varphi_i(n)$, respectively. The elements $e_i(n)$ and $e_i(n-L)$ are the first and $(L+1)^{th}$ components of vector $E_i(n)$, respectively $i \in \{1,2\}$.

The second likelihood variables $\gamma_{1,P}(n)$ and $\gamma_{2,P}(n)$ of the Eqs. (21) and (22) are given by [11]:

$$\gamma_{1,P}(n) = \frac{1}{1 - \phi_1(n)}, \text{ at each period of } N \text{ simples we do: } \gamma_{1,P}(n) = \eta\gamma_{1,P}(n),$$ (31)

$$\gamma_{2,P}(n) = \frac{1}{1 - \phi_2(n)}, \text{ at each period of } N \text{ simples we do: } \gamma_{2,P}(n) = \eta\gamma_{2,P}(n).$$ (32)

Where $\phi_1(n)$ and $\phi_2(n)$ are given by:

$$\phi_1(n) = \phi_1(n-1) - \varphi_1(n)e_1(n) + \varphi_1(n-L+P)e_1(n-L+P), \quad (33)$$

$$\phi_2(n) = \phi_2(n-1) - \varphi_2(n)e_2(n) + \varphi_2(n-L+P)e_2(n-L+P). \quad (34)$$

Where $\varphi_i(n-L+P)$ and $e_i(n-L+P)$ are the $(L-P)^{th}$ components of vectors $\varphi_i(n)$ and $E_i(n)$, respectively. $i \in \{1,2\}$. We recall here that the forgetting factor λ is calculating by [10]:

$$\frac{1 + \sqrt{1 + (P+2)\left(\frac{1}{\eta^2} - 1\right)}}{P+2} \geq \lambda > 1. \quad (35)$$

5 Computational Complexity

In this Section, we quantify the computational complexity of the proposed TM-RSMFTF algorithm in comparison with TM-SFTF algorithm and TM-FNLMS algorithm. To highlight the computational complexity of each algorithm, we have calculated the number of multiplications and additions per iteration. We have reported in Table 1 the computational complexity of the proposed TM-RSMFTF algorithm for various size predictor ($P = 1$, 40 and 100), TM-SFTF algorithm, TM-FNLMS algorithm. The length of the real adaptive filter is $L = 128$ and 512.

Table 1. Computational complexity of the proposed algorithm, TM-SFTF, and TM-FNLMS algorithm.

Algorithms		Computational complexity		$L = 128$	$L = 512$
		Multiplications per iteration	Additions per iteration		
TM-RSMFTF	$P = 1$	$6L + 6P + 22$	$6L + 4P + 18$	1586	6194
	$P = 40$			1976	6584
	$P = 100$			2576	7184
TM-SFTF		$12L + 18$	$10L + 14$	2848	11296
TM-FNLMS		$6L + 4$	$6L + 4$	1544	6152

From Table 1, we can observe that the proposed algorithm is less complex than the full-size version (TM-SFTF) by about $4L - 4P$ additions and $6L - 6P$ multiplications and is more complex than the TM-FNLMS algorithm by about $4P$ additions and $6P$ multiplications and it has the same computational complexity of the TM-FNLMS algorithm if $P = 1$ and lower than the TM-SFTF algorithm for any size $P < L$.

6 Simulation Results

In this Section, we present the simulation results of the proposed algorithm described previously, many experiments were performed to evaluate the performance and to show the behavior of the proposed algorithm TM-RSMFTF in comparison with the TM-FNLMS and TM-SFTF algorithm. To evaluate the performance of the proposed algorithm, the following objective criteria are used: Time evolution of the output speech signal $u_1(n)$ with original speech signal, the system mismatch (SM) and segmental mean square error (SegMSE) to evaluate convergence speed and we also used the segmental signal to noise ratio (segSNR) to evaluate the noise reduction performance and Cepstral distance (CD) to evaluate the distortion caused by these techniques in the output speech signal.

6.1 Description of the Used Signals and the Experimental

In this sub-Section, the speech signal that we have used is selected from AURORA database and given in Fig. 4, and the sources noise is stationary noise USASI (United States of America Standard Institute now ANSI) which is correlated signal noise. All these signals are sampled at sampling frequency $F_s = 8$ kHz and coded on 16 bits and given in Fig. 4. For the spaced microphones configuration, we have constructed the impulse responses $h_{21}(n)$ and $h_{12}(n)$ which are given in Fig. 5 according to the model presented in [16]. We note here that for generating the two mixture signals $m_1(n)$ and $m_2(n)$, we have used (1) and (2), and they are shown in Fig. 6. The real filters length is $L = 128$, and the input SNR at the first input $m_1(n)$ is equal to 0 dB and at the second input $m_2(n)$ is equal to -3 dB. Finally, Table 2 summarizes the controlling parameters for each algorithm.

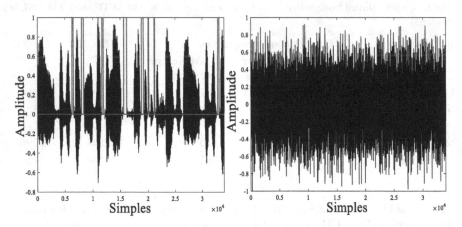

Fig. 4. Original speech signal (in left) with its segmentation (in red) and USASI noise (in right) (Color figure online)

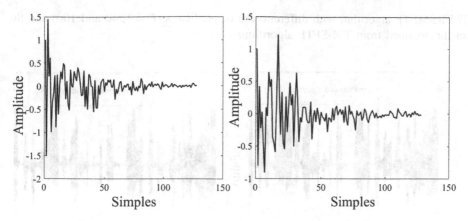

Fig. 5. Examples of simulated impulse responses h_{21}, h_{12}

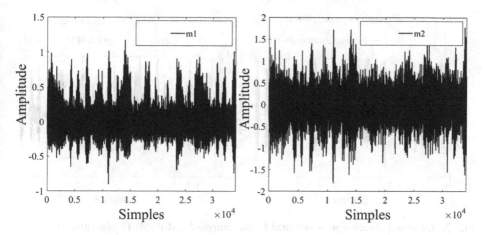

Fig. 6. The mixture signal $m_1(n)$ (in left) and the mixture signal $m_2(n)$ (in right).

Table 2. Controlling parameters for the proposed algorithm, TM-FNLMS and TM-SFTF

TM-FNLMS	TM-SFTF	Proposed TM-RSMFTF algorithm		
$\mu_{21} = 0.7$	$\eta = 0.995$	$P = 1$	$P = 40$	$P = 100$
$\mu_{12} = 0.7$		$\eta = 0.995$	$\eta = 0.999$	$\eta = 0.991$
$C = 0.000001$	$\lambda = 0.5$	$\lambda = 0.7$	$\lambda = 0.5$	$\lambda = 0.5$
	$c_a = 1$	$c_a = 0.1$	$c_a = 0.5$	$c_a = 1$

6.2 Time Evolution of the Output Speech Signal

In order to evaluate the performance of the proposed algorithm TM-RSMFTF, we have given in Fig. 7, the estimated speech signals $u_1(n)$ that are obtained by the proposed

TM-RSMFTF algorithm with different size of predictors (P = 1, 40 and 100) and the results obtained from TM-SFTF algorithm.

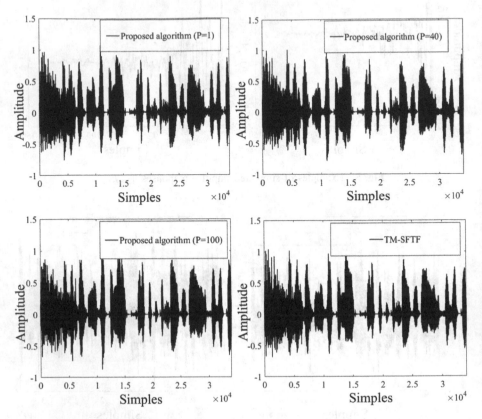

Fig. 7. Estimated speech signals obtained by the proposed TM-RSMFTF algorithm (P = 1, 40 and 100), and The TM-SFTF algorithm.

Based on Fig. 7, it can be observed that the acoustic noise almost entirely reduced from the output speech signals by the proposed algorithm TM-RSMFTF with various size predictor and TM-SFTF algorithm, and from these results we can conclude that the proposed algorithm has good performance to reduce acoustic noise and enhance speech but we cannot judge whom of the 4 algorithms is the best in term of the quality of the estimated output speech and convergence speed that's why we have used different objective criteria such as the system mismatch(SM), mean square error(MSE), segmental signal to noise ratio(segSNR) and Cepstral distance(CD).

6.3   System Mismatch (SM)

In order to evaluate the convergence speed and tracking ability of the proposed algorithm, we used system mismatch criteria (SM). This objective criterion will facilitate quantifying the convergence and tracking ability of any methods. As we are interested in noise reduction and speech enhancement in our TM-FBSS structure so our interest is directed to the estimated speech output $u_1(n)$; and therefore, we concentrate only on the adaptive filter $w_{21}(n)$. The SM of $w_{21}(n)$ is computed by the following equation [11]:

$$SM_{dB} = 20log_{10}\left(\frac{\|h_{21} - w_{21}(n)\|^2}{\|h_{21}\|^2}\right). \tag{36}$$

where, $w_{21}(n)$ and h_{21} are simulated and real impulse responses. We have carried out many experiments of the proposed algorithm TM-RSMFTF with different sizes predictors P, TM-SFTF and conventional TM-NLMS algorithm. The source noise is USASI noise and input SNR at the first input is equal to 0 dB and at the second is equal to -3 dB.

We have given in Fig. 8 the SM criterion evaluation obtained by the proposed algorithm TM-RSMFTF for different size predictor ($P = 1$, 40 and 100), TM-SFTF algorithm and TM-FNLMS algorithm. According to Fig. 8, we noticed that for different size predictor, the proposed algorithm have almost the same performance with the full-size version(TM-SFTF), and this result is obtained by the good choice of the controlling parameters (λ, η, c_a) for each algorithm. We can conclude that the good convergence speed of the proposed algorithm allows us to say that this algorithm is a good choice for noise reduction and speech enhancement applications.

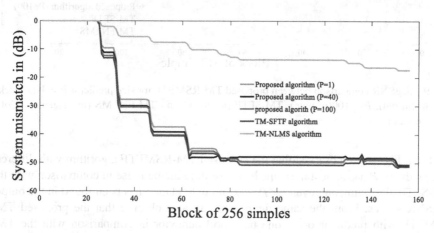

Fig. 8. SM comparison between proposed TM-RSMFTF for size predictor $P = 1$(in green), $P = 40$(in black), $P = 100$(in red), TM-SFTF (in blue) and TM-FNLMS algorithm (in cyan). (Color figure online)

6.4   Signal to Noise Ratio (SNR)

In order to quantify the noise reduction performance of the proposed TM-FRSMFTF algorithm, we have calculated the output SNR of the estimated speech output. The SegSNR criterion is given by the following expression:

$$SNR_{dB} = 10log_{10}\left(\frac{\sum_{k=1}^{Q-1}|s(k)|^2}{\sum_{k=1}^{Q-1}|s(k) - u_1(k)|^2}VAD_K\right). \tag{37}$$

where, $s(n)$ and $u_1(n)$ are respectively the original speech signal and the enhanced signal. The parameter Q is the mean averaging value of the output SNR. The presence of the term VAD (voice activity detector) in (37) means that this objective criterion calculated only during speech signal periods. We have reported in Fig. 9 that the results of SegSNR obtained by the proposed algorithm with different size predictor ($P = 1, 40$ and 100), TM-SFTF algorithm and the TM-FNLMS algorithm.

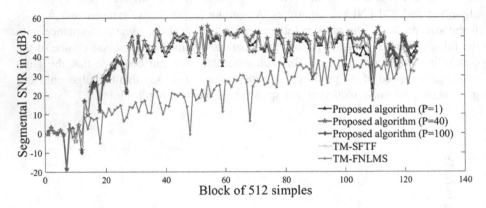

Fig. 9. SegSNR comparison between proposed TM-RSMFTF for size predictor $P = 1$(in black), $P = 40$ (in red), $P = 100$(in blue), TM-SFTF (in green) and TM-FNLMS (in magenta). (Color figure online)

From Fig. 9, we observed that the proposed TM-RSMFTF algorithm with different size predictor P has almost the same behavior in reducing noise in comparison with the TM-SFTF algorithm, and even for $P \ll L$, no degradation has been found in the output SegSNR values. From the same figure, we can also observe that the proposed TM-RSMFTF with predictor order one has good behavior in comparison with the TM-FNLMS algorithm and almost identical to TM-SFTF algorithm. From these results, we can conclude that the proposed TM-RSMFTF algorithm has good behavior in reducing noise.

6.5 Cepstral Distance (CD)

The CD criterion allows evaluating the distortion of the TM-FNLMS algorithm, TM-FRLS, and the proposed TM-FRSMFTF algorithm. This objective criterion is estimated by using the log-spectrum distance between the original speech signal $sp(n)$ and $u_1(n)$, where $u_1(n)$ is the estimated speech signal obtained at the output of the FBSS structure and is given by the following equation [11]:

$$CD_{dB} = \sum_{k=1}^{Q-1} IFFT[((log_{10}(|S(k,\omega)| - log_{10}(|U_1(k,\omega)|)VAD_K)]^2 \quad (38)$$

where, $S(\omega)$ and $U_1(\omega)$ are respectively the short Fourier transform of the original speech signal $s(n)$ and the enhanced one $u_1(n)$ at each frame k, and Q is the mean averaging value of the CD criterion. The presence of the parameter VAD (voice activity detector) in (38) means that we calculate this criterion only during the presence of speech signal periods, and in these periods, VAD takes 1 and when the speech signal is absent VAD takes 0.

We have done our simulation with the same speech signal of Fig. 4 and source noise is USASI with the same controlling parameters in Table 2 and the input SNR at the first input is 0 dB and at the second input is −3 dB. From Fig. 10, we have seen the superiority in less distortion of the proposed algorithm in comparison with the TM-FNLMS algorithm.

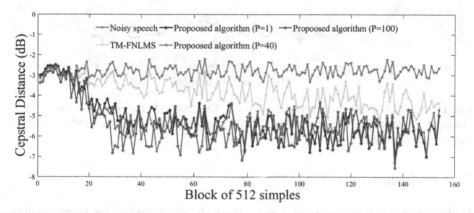

Fig. 10. Cepstral distance evaluation of the proposed algorithm ($P = 1$ in black), ($P = 40$ in red), ($P = 100$ in blue) TM-FNLMS algorithm (in green) and noisy speech (in magenta). (Color figure online)

6.6 Mean Square Error

In order to quantify the convergence of the algorithms i.e. the proposed TM-RSMFTF, TM-FNLMS, and TM-SFTF, we use another objective criterion which calls SegMSE. This SegMSE criterion is given by the following equation:

$$MSE(db) = 20log_{10}\left(\sum_{k=1}^{Q-1} u_1(k)VAD_K\right). \tag{39}$$

where, $u_1(n)$ is the enhanced speech signal, and the parameter Q is the mean averaging value of SegMSE. The *VAD* is voice activity detector used to estimate the SegMSE in absence speech periods.

From Fig. 11, we have confirmed the good speed convergence of the proposed TM-RSMFTF algorithm with different size of predictor ($P = 1$, 40 and 100). We have also confirmed that no retrogression has been seen in SegMSE values in the steady-state regime even for small size predictor. The good choice of the controlling parameters (λ, η, c_a) for each algorithm lead to the same convergence speed performance with the TM-SFTF algorithm. Finally, we confirmed that the good convergence speed of the proposed TM-RSMFTF algorithm allows us to say that this algorithm is a good choice for noise reduction and speech enhancement applications.

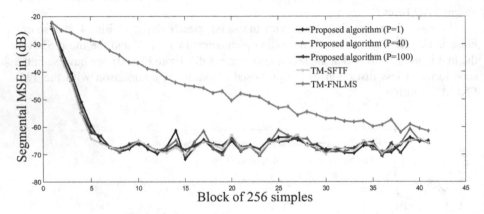

Fig. 11. SegMSE comparison between proposed TM-RSMFTF for size predictor $P = 1$(in black), $P = 40$(in red), $P = 100$(in blue), TM-SFTF algorithm (in green) and TM-FNLMS (in magenta). (Color figure online)

7   Conclusion

In this paper, we have proposed a new robust algorithm applied for speech quality improvement and noise reduction in new telecommunication systems and speech recognition systems. The proposed algorithm is an outcome of the combination of two microphones forward blind source separation structure and the reduce size simplified fast transversal filter which is a stable and robust version of the FTF algorithms.

The proposed TM-RSMFTF algorithm has low computational complexity, which is less than TM-SFTF algorithm, and similar to the TM-NLMS algorithm if $P = 1$. Reducing the size predictor P leads to the reduction of the computation complexity for this algorithm without degradation in its performance even for small size predictor ($P \ll L$) due to the presence of regularization constant and leakage factor and also to the two likelihood variables.

The simulation results confirm this conclusion and also show that the proposed algorithm has almost similar performance with the TM-SFTF algorithm and better than the TM-FNLMS algorithm in term of less distortion on the enhanced speech signal, speed convergence and different objective criteria such as segmental signal to noise ratio (SegSNR), Segmental mean square error (SegMSE) and the system mismatch (SM).

Acknowledgment. This work was supported in part by the National Basis Research Program of China 973 Program under Grant 2013CB329003 and in part by the National Natural Science Foundation of China under Grants 61671179.

References

1. Boll, S.: Suppression of acoustic noise in speech using spectral subtraction. IEEE Trans. Acoust. Speech Sig. Process. **27**(2), 113–120 (1979)
2. Lim, J.S., Oppenheim, A.V.: Enhancement and bandwidth compression of noisy speech. Proc. IEEE **67**(12), 1586–1604 (1979)
3. Ephraim, Y., Malah, D.: Speech enhancement using a minimum mean-square error log-spectral amplitude estimator. IEEE Trans. Acoust. Speech Sig. Process. **33**(2), 443–445 (1985)
4. Zou, X., Zhang, X.: Speech enhancement using an MMSE short time DCT coefficients estimator with supergaussian speech modeling. J. Electron. (China) **24**(3), 332–337 (2007)
5. Haykin, S.: Adaptive Filter Theory, 4th edn. Prentice-Hall, Englewood Cliffs (2002)
6. Ljung, L., Morf, M., Falconer, D.: Fast calculation of gain matrices for recursive estimation schemes. Int. J. Control **27**(1), 1–19 (1978)
7. Cioffi, J., Kailath, T.: Fast, recursive-least-squares transversal filters for adaptive filtering. IEEE Trans. Acoust. Speech Sig. Process. **32**(2), 304–337 (1984)
8. Benallal, A., Gilloire, A.: A new method to stabilize fast RLS algorithms based on a first-order of the propagation of numerical errors. In: International Conference on Acoustics, Speech, and Signal Processing, ICASSP 1988, pp. 1373–1376. IEEE (1988)
9. Slock, D.T.M., Kailath, T.: Numerically stable fast transversal filters for recursive least-squares adaptive filtering. In: Golub, G.H., Van Dooren, P. (eds.) Numerical Linear Algebra, Digital Signal Processing and Parallel Algorithms, vol. 70, pp. 605–615. Springer, Heidelberg (1991). https://doi.org/10.1007/978-3-642-75536-1_49
10. Benallal, A., Benkrid, A.: A simplified FTF-type algorithm for adaptive filtering. Sig. Process. **87**(5), 904–917 (2007)
11. Djendi, M.: New efficient adaptive fast transversal filtering (FTF)-type algorithms for mono and stereophonic acoustic echo cancelation. Int. J. Adapt. Control Sig. Process. **29**(3), 273–301 (2015)
12. Rahima, H., Djebari, M., Mohamed, D.: Blind speech enhancement and acoustic noise reduction by SFTF adaptive algorithm. In: 2017 5th International Conference on Electrical Engineering-Boumerdes (ICEE-B), pp. 1–4. IEEE (2017)
13. Djendi, M.: A new two-microphone Gauss-Seidel pseudo affine projection algorithm for speech quality enhancement. Int. J. Adapt. Control Sig. Process. **31**(8), 1162–1183 (2017)
14. Van Gerven, S., Van Compernolle, D.: Signal separation by symmetric adaptive decorrelation: stability, convergence, and uniqueness. IEEE Trans. Sig. Process. **43**(7), 1602–1612 (1995)

15. Thi, H.L.N., Jutten, C.: Blind source separation for convolutive mixtures. Sig. Process. **45** (2), 209–229 (1995)
16. Djendi, M., Gilloire, A., Scalart, P.: Noise cancellation using two closely spaced microphones: experimental study with a specific model and two adaptive algorithms. In: 2006 IEEE International Conference on Acoustics Speech and Signal Processing Proceedings, vol. 3, p. III. IEEE (2006)
17. Weinstein, E., Feder, M., Oppenheim, A.V.: Multi-channel signal separation by decorrelation. IEEE Trans. Speech Audio Process. **1**(4), 405–413 (1993)
18. Djendi, M., Scalart, P., Gilloire, A.: Analysis of two-sensors forward BSS structure with post-filters in the presence of coherent and incoherent noise. Speech Commun. **55**(10), 975–987 (2013)
19. Arezki, M., Benallal, A., Meyrueis, P., Berkani, D.: A new algorithm with low complexity for adaptive filtering. Eng. Lett. **18**(3), 205 (2010)

Adaptive Beamforming of Vertical Frequency Diverse Array for Airborne Radar

Xuzi Wu[✉] and Yongliang Sun

School of Computer Science and Technology,
Nanjing Tech University, Nanjing 211816, China
xuziwu@njtech.edu.cn

Abstract. To decouple the range-angle-dependent beampattern, a new type of frequency diverse array (FDA) with frequency increment applied across the vertical array elements is proposed, referred to as the vertical frequency diverse array (VFDA). The adaptive algorithm for the design of the receive antenna is also presented to generate a single-maximum beampattern. Simulation results verify the effectiveness. It shows that the proposed approach outperforms the multiple-input multiple-output (MIMO) radar in focusing the transmit energy on the far-field targets.

Keywords: Beamforming · Frequency diverse array · Range-dependent

1 Introduction

Phased-array has been widely used in airborne radar systems for its flexible beam scanning ability. However, the beampattern of the phased-array is range independent. When detecting the ground moving targets, the transmit energy would be distributed broadly in range with the decrease of the elevation angle, resulting in more mainlobe interference. To achieve narrow mainlobe, the enlarged antenna aperture is needed, which is however difficult for the radar with limited antenna size. To overcome this disadvantage, a novel beam scanning array, referred to as the FDA, was presented in [1]. Benefits have been demonstrated by applying the unique range-dependent characteristic of the FDA to different radar tasks, e.g. target localization [2, 3], clutter suppression [4, 5], pattern synthesis [6–9]. In the conventional FDA, a linear frequency increment is always applied across the horizontal elements of the antenna array, providing an increased degrees-of-freedom (DOFs) to design and control the beampattern. However, it may be difficult to implement in actual airborne radar systems due to the range-angle-coupling and time-variant effects on the estimate of the effective covariance matrix.

To decouple the range-angle dependent beampattern, a nonuniform linear array was employed in [7], which may be difficult to implement due to the high accuracy requirement of the transmitter and receiver positions. A logarithmically increasing frequency increment was proposed in [8] to synthesize a nonperiodic beampattern. But it is unable to obtain the closed form expression of the beampattern. In [9], the convex optimization is used to achieve dot-shaped transmit beampattern and better resolution

S. Han et al. (Eds.): AICON 2019, LNICST 286, pp. 203–209, 2019.
https://doi.org/10.1007/978-3-030-22968-9_18

in the range dimension compared with that in [8]. However, the algorithm has a relatively high complexity, which is difficult for the implementation of the multilog-FDA.

In this paper, a new type of FDA with frequency increment used across the vertical array elements is explored. The design algorithm for the receive array configuration is also presented to generate a beampattern with no grating lobes. Compared to the beampattern in the conventional FDA and the MIMO radar, the single-maximum and range-dependent beampattern in the VFDA may be more capable of rejecting clutter and jamming in airborne radar systems.

2 Adaptive Beamforming Algorithm

2.1 The Transmit Beampattern of VFDA

Consider an $(M \times N)$-element planar array antenna with uniform frequency increment Δf across the vertical elements, the signal transmitted by the (m, n)th element is

$$s_{m,n}(t) = \exp(j2\pi f_m t) = \exp\{j2\pi [f_0 + (m-1)\Delta f]t\} \tag{1}$$

where f_0 is the carrier frequency. For a far-field point target located at the azimuth angle φ, elevation angle θ, and range R relative to the $(0, 0)$th element, the signal arriving at the target can be expressed as

$$s_{m,n}(t - R_{m,n}/c) = \alpha_{m,n}\exp\{j2\pi f_m(t - R_{m,n}/c)\} \tag{2}$$

where c is the speed of light, $\alpha_{m,n}$ is a complex weighting factor that represents transmission and propagation effects.

$$R_{m,n} = R - (n-1)d_N \cos\theta \cos\varphi + (m-1)d_M \sin\theta \tag{3}$$

is the range of the target to the (m, n)th element with d_M and d_N representing the vertical and horizontal element spacing, respectively. Taking the narrowband assumption, the VFDA transmit beampattern steered to $(\theta_0, \varphi_0, R_0)$ is given by

$$G_t(t, \theta, \varphi, R) = \sum_{m=1}^{M}\sum_{n=1}^{N} \alpha_{m,n} \exp\left[j2\pi f_m\left(t - \frac{R_{m,n}}{c}\right)\right] \cdot \exp\left[j2\pi f_m \frac{R_0}{c}\right]$$
$$\cdot\exp\left[-j2\pi f_m(n-1) \cos\theta_0 \cos\varphi_0 \frac{d_N}{c}\right] \cdot \exp\left[j2\pi f_m(m-1) \sin\theta_0 \frac{d_M}{c}\right] \tag{4}$$

The approximated expression of $|G_t(t, \theta, \varphi, R)|$ is

$$|G_t(t, \theta, \varphi, R)| \approx \frac{\left|\sin[\pi N(\cos \theta \cos \varphi - \cos \theta_0 \cos \varphi_0) d_N / \lambda_0]\right|}{\sin[\pi(\cos \theta \cos \varphi - \cos \theta_0 \cos \varphi_0) d_N / \lambda_0]}$$
$$\cdot \frac{\left|\sin[\pi M \Delta f t - \pi M \Delta f (R - R_0)/c - \pi M(\sin \theta - \sin \theta_0) d_M / \lambda_0]\right|}{\sin[\pi \Delta f t - \pi \Delta f (R - R_0)/c - \pi(\sin \theta - \sin \theta_0) d_M / \lambda_0]} \quad (5)$$

where $\lambda_0 = c/f_0$. Here we have assumed that the complex weighting factors are all equal to 1,

$$(M - 1)\Delta f \ll f_0 \quad (6)$$

and

$$R \gg \max\left[(M - 1)^2 d_M / \lambda_0, (M - 1)(N - 1) d_N / \lambda_0\right] \quad (7)$$

It can be observed that the phase differences depending on time and range are incorporated into the second term of (5), positioning the multiple maxima at different ranges but the same azimuth angle φ_0. Therefore, the pattern will not keep the 'S'-shaped feature with coupling between the azimuth angle and range. The following task is to synthesize the beampattern with no grating lobes in the range dimension.

2.2 Transmit-Receive Beamforming with no Grating Lobes

A $(Q \times P)$-element receive array collocated with the transmit antenna is considered in this paper. When the signal is received by each element, a set of bandpass filters will be applied to extract the complete transmit signals. We then have the VFDA two-way beampattern

$$G_r(t, \theta, \varphi, R) = \sum_{q=1}^{Q} \sum_{p=1}^{P} \sum_{m=1}^{M} \sum_{n=1}^{N} \exp\left[j2\pi f_m\left(t - \frac{R_{m,n} + R_{q,p}}{c}\right)\right]$$
$$\cdot \exp\left[j4\pi f_m \frac{R_0}{c}\right] \cdot \exp\left[-j2\pi f_m(n - 1)\cos \theta_0 \cos \varphi_0 \frac{d_N}{c}\right]$$
$$\cdot \exp\left[-j2\pi f_m(p - 1)\cos \theta_0 \cos \varphi_0 \frac{d_P}{c}\right] \quad (8)$$
$$\cdot \exp\left[j2\pi f_m(m - 1)\sin \theta_0 \frac{d_M}{c}\right] \cdot \exp\left[j2\pi f_m(q - 1)\sin \theta_0 \frac{d_Q}{c}\right]$$

where $R_{q,p}$ is the range of the target to the (q, p)th receive element. d_Q and d_P are the vertical and horizontal element spacing in the receiver, respectively. Assume $P = N$ and $d_P = d_N$, $|G_r(t, \theta, \varphi, R)|$ can be simplified as

$$|G_r(t,\theta,\varphi,R)|$$

$$\approx \left|\frac{\sin[\pi N(\cos\theta\cos\varphi - \cos\theta_0\cos\varphi_0)d_N/\lambda_0]}{\sin[\pi(\cos\theta\cos\varphi - \cos\theta_0\cos\varphi_0)d_N/\lambda_0]}\right|^2$$

$$\cdot\left|\frac{\sin[\pi M\Delta ft - 2\pi M\Delta f(R - R_0)/c - \pi M(\sin\theta - \sin\theta_0)d_M/\lambda_0]}{\sin[\pi\Delta ft - 2\pi\Delta f(R - R_0)/c - \pi(\sin\theta - \sin\theta_0)d_M/\lambda_0]}\right| \qquad (9)$$

$$\cdot\left|\frac{\sin[\pi Q(\sin\theta - \sin\theta_0)d_Q/\lambda_0]}{\sin[\pi(\sin\theta - \sin\theta_0)d_Q/\lambda_0]}\right|$$

In order to avoid the grating lobes in the range dimension, the adaptive beam-forming algorithm is presented in the following procedure.

Step 1: Ignore the effect of the earth curvature, the maxima of the second term in (9) can be achieved when the phase term satisfies

$$\pi\Delta ft - 2\pi\Delta f(R - R_0)/c - \pi(R/H - R_0/H)d_M/\lambda_0 = a\pi \qquad (10)$$

where a is an integer and H is the platform altitude. Thus, the grating lobes are located at

$$\bar{R} = \frac{\eta + \sqrt{\eta^2 - 8c\Delta fHd_M/\lambda_0}}{4\Delta f}; \bar{R} \in [H, R_{max}], a \neq 0 \qquad (11)$$

where R_{max} is the maximum range of radar.

$$\eta = c\Delta ft + 2\Delta fR_0 - ac + cHd_M/R_0\lambda_0 \qquad (12)$$

Define

$$\sigma = |H/\bar{R} - H/R_0| \qquad (13)$$

and calculate the maximum and minimum value of (13) as σ_{max} and σ_{min}, respectively.

Step 2: For the last term of (9), the pattern peaks are separated by λ_0/d_Q. To avoid the furthest grating lobe from moving into the peaks, we require

$$\lambda_0/d_Q \geq \sigma_{max} + \sigma_{min} \qquad (14)$$

Then, the vertical element spacing d_Q in the receiver should be constrained to

$$0 < d_Q \leq \lambda_0/(\sigma_{max} + \sigma_{min}) \qquad (15)$$

Step 3: Fix d_Q, the beamwidth of the last term in (9) is

$$B_r = 2\lambda_0/Qd_Q \qquad (16)$$

To ensure the nearest grating lobe outside of the main beam, the number of the vertical array elements Q should satisfy

$$B_r = 2\lambda_0/Qd_Q \leq \sigma_{min} \qquad (17)$$

This can be rewritten as

$$Q \geq \text{ceil}\left[\lambda_0/(d_Q\sigma_{min})\right] \qquad (18)$$

where $\text{ceil}[\cdot]$ denotes the nearest integer towards infinity.

3   Simulation Results

In the simulations, an X-band VFDA radar operating at a carrier frequency of $f_0 = 10$ GHz is simulated. The transmit antenna is set with 8×8 elements and the element space is $d_M = d_N = 0.015$ m. The frequency increment is taken as $\Delta f = 2$ KHz. The platform altitude and radar maximum range are $H = 8$ km and $R_{max} = 300$ km, respectively. Assume the target is positioned at $(2°, 90°, 229$ km$)$, it is calculated that there are 2 maxima in the range of $(8$ km, 300 km$)$ except R_0. The maximum and minimum value of σ are $\sigma_{max} = 58 \times 10^{-3}$ and $\sigma_{min} = 16 \times 10^{-3}$, respectively. Based on (14) and (15), the receive antenna is designed with $Q = 6$ vertical array elements and $d_Q = 0.35$ m element space.

Assume $t = 0$, Fig. 1 shows the comparison of the normalized beampatterns generated by the MIMO radar and the VFDA radar, respectively. In Fig. 1(a), it can be observed that the mainlobe is seriously expanded in the range dimension due to the small value of φ_0. For the VFDA, the beamwidth of the pattern is range-dependent and a function of the frequency increment Δf and the number of the vertical array elements M. This generates a different beampattern with energy distributed in smaller range regions, as is shown in Fig. 1(b). By using the proposed algorithm for antenna design, the beampattern with no grating lobes is synthesised in Fig. 1(c). It can be noticed that the azimuth angle of the mainlobe in the VFDA is constant along the range axis, which is different from that in the conventional FDA. This avoids the coupling between angle and range, therefore, is a more capable approach to reject the range-dependent interference and improve the signal-to-interference-plus-noise (SINR) ratio.

4   Conclusion

An Adaptive transmit-receive beamforming algorithm for the VFDA has been proposed to decouple the range-angle-dependent beampattern and suppress the grating lobes in the range dimension. Simulation results show that the proposed approach performs better in focusing the transmit energy on the desired targets, especially in the far-field ranges. And the low complexity of the algorithm is also suitable for the

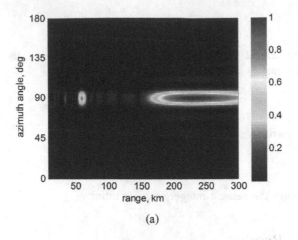

(a)

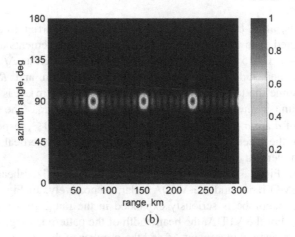

(b)

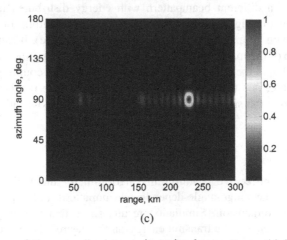

(c)

Fig. 1. Comparison of the normalized transmit-receive beampatterns: (a) MIMO radar with $Q = 6$ and $d_Q = 0.35$ m; (b) VFDA radar with no antenna design where $Q = 6$ and $d_Q = 0.015$ m; (c) VFDA radar with $Q = 6$ and $d_Q = 0.35$ m.

implementation of the VFDA in practice. However, the beampattern of the VFDA is still time-variant, similar to that of the conventional FDA, which is reserved for subsequent research.

References

1. Antonik, P., Wicks, M.C., Griffiths, H.D., et al.: Frequency diverse array radars. In: Proceedings of the IEEE Radar Conference, Verona, pp. 215–217 (2006)
2. Wang, W.-Q., So, H.C.: Transmit subaperturing for range and angle estimation in frequency diverse array radar. IEEE Trans. Sig. Process. 62(8), 2000–2011 (2014)
3. Wang, W.-Q., Shao, H.: Range-angle localization of targets by a double-pulse frequency diverse array radar. IEEE J. Sel. Top. Sig. Process. 8(1), 106–114 (2014)
4. Baizert, P., Hale, T.B., Temple, M.A., et al.: Forward-looking radar GMTI benefits using a linear frequency diverse array. Electron. Lett. 42(22), 1311–1312 (2006)
5. Xu, J., Zhu, S., Liao, G.: Range ambiguous clutter suppression for airborne FDA-STAP radar. IEEE J. Sel. Top. Sig. Process. 9(8), 1620–1631 (2015)
6. Wang, W.-Q.: Cognitive frequency diverse array radar with situational awareness. IET Radar Sonar Navig. 10(2), 359–369 (2016)
7. Sammartino, P.F., Baker, C.J., Griffiths, H.D.: Frequency diverse MIMO techniques for radar. IEEE Trans. Aerosp. Electron. Syst. 49(1), 201–222 (2013)
8. Khan, W., Qureshi, I.M., Saeed, S.: Frequency diverse array radar with logarithmically increasing frequency offset. IEEE Antennas Wirel. Propag. Lett. 14, 499–502 (2015)
9. Shao, H., Dai, J., Xiong, J., et al.: Dot-shaped range-angle beampattern synthesis of frequency diverse array. IEEE Antennas Wirel. Propag. Lett. 15, 1703–1706 (2016)

2D DOA Estimation of PR-WSF Algorithm Based on Modified Fireworks Algorithm

Yanping Liao, Chang Fu[✉], and Emmanuel Milambo Mung'onya

Harbin Engineering University, Harbin 150001, Heilongjiang, China
fuchang08@163.com

Abstract. Two-dimensional direction of arrival (DOA) estimation has more application significance than one-dimensional estimation. However, the increase of computation scale causes serious problems of slow speed of solution and poor real-time performance. Among the common algorithms of two-dimensional direction of arrival (DOA) estimation, the weighted subspace fitting (WSF) algorithm possesses high accuracy, but its complexity in solving process weakens its performance advantage. In addition, the accuracy of WSF is poor under the condition of low signal-to-noise ratio (SNR) and insufficient snapshot number (i.e. threshold). Hence, this paper proposes a PR-WSF algorithm based on modified fireworks algorithm: the radius and number of explosions in fireworks algorithm are initially improved, then the ESPRIT algorithm combined with cramer-rao bound (CRB) is adopted to create a smaller searching space, and finally the pseudo-random noise resampling (PR) algorithm is introduced to improve the "threshold performance. The experimental results show that this algorithm balances the relationship between global search and local search, reduces unnecessary computation, and has better estimation performance at the threshold.

Keywords: 2-D DOA estimation · Weighed subspace fitting ·
Fireworks algorithm · Pseudo-random noise resampling

1 Introduction

Early algorithms of DOA estimation mostly studied one-dimensional parameter performance estimation [1], which mainly estimate the azimuth or pitch angle of the incident signal source in a space plane. Considering the actual needs, however, the information in three-dimensional space can reflect the actual situation more comprehensively. For example, in the actual mobile communication system, users often send and receive signals in multi-dimensional space, thus the multi-dimensional spatial spectrum direction finding can be better applied to the actual environment. Compared with one-dimensional DOA estimation, the two-dimensional one provides more accurate source spatial location information for base stations. The more reliable the information, the stronger the directivity of beamforming, and the more effective the interference is suppressed, so that the signal can be delivered to the target user more accurately. In massive MIMO technology [2], one of the key technologies of the future 5G wireless communication system, the base station terminal needs to estimate the

S. Han et al. (Eds.): AICON 2019, LNICST 286, pp. 210–224, 2019.
https://doi.org/10.1007/978-3-030-22968-9_19

two-dimensional direction of arrival of the source to achieve better space division multiplexing and improve link reliability [3]. In addition, multidimensional spatial spectrum direction finding can make full use of the spatial redundancy of channel and make the angle direction finding performance better. Multidimensional spatial spectrum direction finding can take full advantage of the spatial redundancy of channel and achieve better angle direction finding performance. Therefore, two-dimensional, even multidimensional, direction finding algorithm has been widely studied. The joint estimation of two-dimensional parametric azimuth and elevation angles is a key research topic.

As an important algorithm in DOA estimation, weighted signal subspace fitting algorithm possesses the advantage of more accurate estimation of signal direction [4]. However, due to its non-linear estimation function, it cannot solve the incident direction of signal efficiently, which makes the solving speed a disadvantage of WSF algorithm. Herein multi-dimensional search is normally adopted, which is quite complex, and two parameters – elevation angle and azimuth angle – need to be estimated in two-dimensional DOA estimation. With the increase of the number of signal sources, the dimensions of the matrix increase correspondingly, and the computation needed in the search process increases exponentially, which increases the difficulty of real-time application and cannot meet the real-time requirements in the actual environment. Even with the rapid development of computer hardware, it is still difficult to search DOA of multiple signal sources simultaneously. With the continuous development of intelligent optimization algorithms, they have been applied to the solution of WSF algorithm. Genetic algorithm is adopted to optimize WSF algorithm, which limits the genetic search space and reduces the complexity of WSF algorithm by shortening the genetic length [5]. However, this method may cause poor convergence effect of genetic algorithm and unpredictable poor mutation in the subsequent iteration process. Another algorithm adopts particle swarm optimization (PSO) to optimize WSF [6], which joints ESPRIT algorithm of low complexity and accuracy and particle swarm optimization algorithm, greatly reduces the initialization space of particles and the required particles, and obtained improved computational speed and accuracy compared with the traditional particle swarm optimization. Nevertheless, neither of the above two algorithms can solve the problem of poor threshold performance of WSF algorithm.

With a different search mechanism from the above optimization algorithms, the fireworks algorithm is mainly used to solve optimization problems in continuous space. In an iteration process, the fireworks population will retain more than one individual, while the above algorithms usually retain one only. This explosion mechanism of fireworks algorithm enables a more thorough search in nearby area, which is conducive to improving the convergence speed.

In order to solve the threshold effect of traditional DOA estimation, Gershman proposed a pseudo-random resampling (PR) algorithm [7]. PR technique repeatedly sample the same set of data by artificially generated pseudo-random noise, which can redistribute the noise in the original data and eliminate the unreliable data, thus creating a good operating environment for restoring the performance of DOA estimation algorithm.

Therefore, a PR-WSF algorithm based on improved fireworks algorithm is proposed to solve the problem of large computation, slow solution and poor accuracy in the case of low SNR and insufficient snapshots.

2 Problem Formulation

Suppose the receiving array is uniform square array in the dimension of $M \times N$, where M and N respectively represent number of antennas configured on two adjacent edges, and d stands for spacing of adjacent elements. Q narrow band far-field signals are incident from different azimuth angles $\{\theta_1, \cdots \theta_Q\}$ and pitch angles $\{\varphi_1, \cdots \varphi_Q\}$ at the uniform square array. Therefore, at the moment t, the signal received by URA can be expressed as

$$x_l(t) = \sum_{i=1}^{Q} s_i(t - \tau_{li}) + n_l(t) \quad l = 1, \ldots, MN \tag{1}$$

In this equation, τ_{li} represents the time difference between arrival of signal i' to array element l and its arrival to the reference element, and $n_l(t)$ stands for the noise value received by element l at the moment t.

Since $s_i(t)$ are narrow band far-field incident signals, the signals $x_l(t)$ received by the l-th array element are

$$x_l(t) = \sum_{i=1}^{Q} s_i(t) e^{(-j\omega_0 \tau_{li})} + n_l(t) \quad l = 1, \ldots, MN \tag{2}$$

Write the Eq. (2) in matrix form as

$$\begin{bmatrix} x_1(t) \\ x_2(t) \\ \vdots \\ x_{MN}(t) \end{bmatrix} = \begin{bmatrix} 1 & \cdots & 1 \\ e^{-j\omega_0 \tau_{21}} & \cdots & e^{-j\omega_0 \tau_{2Q}} \\ \vdots & \ddots & \vdots \\ e^{-j\omega_0 \tau_{MN1}} & \cdots & e^{-j\omega_0 \tau_{MNQ}} \end{bmatrix} \begin{bmatrix} s_1(t) \\ s_2(t) \\ \vdots \\ s_Q(t) \end{bmatrix} + \begin{bmatrix} n_1(t) \\ n_2(t) \\ \vdots \\ n_{MN}(t) \end{bmatrix} \tag{3}$$

Therefore, its vector expression can be written as

$$x(t) = As(t) + n(t) \tag{4}$$

where the steering matrix A is a $MN \times Q$ matrix, $x(t) = [x_1(t), \cdots, x_{MN}(t)]^T$ is the vector that receives data of $MN \times 1$, $s(t) = [s_1(t), \cdots, s_Q(t)]^T$ is the vector of narrow band far-field incident signals of $Q \times 1$, and $n(t) = [n_1(t), \cdots, n_{MN}(t)]^T$ is the vector of zero-mean additive Gaussian white noise of $MN \times 1$.

For arbitrary antennas arrays, the phase delay τ_{li} of i-th signal source in l-th array element channel can be expressed as

$$\tau_{li} = \frac{1}{c}(x_l \cos \theta_i \sin \varphi_i + y_l \sin \theta_i \sin \varphi_i + z_l \cos \varphi_i) \tag{5}$$

where θ_i and φ_i respectively represent the azimuth angle and the pitch angle of l-th signal source, (x_l, y_l, z_l) is the space coordinate of l-th array element, and c is speed of light. So, the $M \times N$ steering matrix A can be written as

$$A = [a(\theta_1, \varphi_1), \cdots, a(\theta_Q, \varphi_Q)] \tag{6}$$

where the steering vector $a(\theta_i, \varphi_i) = [1, e^{-j\omega_0\tau_{2i}}, \cdots, e^{-j\omega_0\tau_{MNi}}]^T$.

According to the vector representation of received signals, the data covariance expression under ideal state can be obtained as

$$R = E[x(t)x^H(t)] = AR_sA^H + \sigma_n^2I \tag{7}$$

where $R_s = E[s(t)s^H(t)]$ is the $Q \times Q$ signal data covariance matrix, σ_n^2 is the power value of zero-mean additive Gaussian white noise, and I is the $MN \times MN$ unit diagonal matrix.

In concrete implementation, the result of eigen-decomposition operation on R is

$$R = U\Lambda U^H = \sum_{i=1}^{MN} \lambda_i u_i u_i^H = U_s\Lambda_s U_s^H + U_n\Lambda_n U_n^H \tag{8}$$

where U_s is the signal subspace, and U_n is the noise subspace.

Because the space A of is the same as that of U_s, there is a fitting relationship between them:

$$U_s = A(\theta, \varphi)T \tag{9}$$

where T is a full rank matrix.

Subspace fitting algorithm estimates the DOA of signals by reconstructing the fitting relationship in noisy environment: an estimated value of matrix T is obtained from the equation below, and achieve the best fitting effect with U_s in the least squares sense.

$$\theta, \varphi, \hat{T} = \min\|U_s - A\hat{T}\|_F^2 \tag{10}$$

where the DOA of signals can be obtained

$$(\theta, \varphi) = \min \text{ tr}\{P_A^\perp \hat{U}_s \hat{U}_s^H\} = \max \text{ tr}\{P_A \hat{U}_s \hat{U}_s^H\} \tag{11}$$

Generally, the weight matrix W can be introduced in the Eq. (11) to reach a better fitting result

$$(\theta, \varphi) = \min \text{ tr}\{P_A^\perp \hat{U}_s W \hat{U}_s^H\} = \max \text{ tr}\{P_A \hat{U}_s W \hat{U}_s^H\} \tag{12}$$

The performance of WSF will achieve the best when the weight matrix satisfies

$$W = W_{\text{opt}} = (\hat{\Lambda}_s - \sigma_n^2 I)^2 \hat{\Lambda}_s^{-1} \tag{13}$$

where the diagonal matrix $\hat{\Lambda}_s$ is composed by $\hat{U}_s$'s eigenvalue, σ_n^2 represents the noise power, and I is the $Q \times Q$ unit matrix.

3   PR-WSF Algorithm Based on Modified Fireworks Algorithm

3.1   Fireworks Algorithm

Fireworks algorithm, inspired by fireworks exploding in the night sky, is used to solve global optimization problems of complex functions [8]. The explosion process of fireworks can be viewed as a local search around a certain point from which fireworks explode and fly off sparks. In this algorithm, the goal is to find a point x_i that satisfies $f(x_i) = y$, and fireworks continue to explode in this potential space until a target spark appears near the point x_i.

3.2   The Improvement of Fireworks Algorithm

The Improvement of Explosion Number. The principle of the number of sparks means the closer the particles are to the best fireworks from last explosion, the more sparks will be generated. And best fireworks from the last explosion will produce most sparks. Considering that the number of fireworks explosion should be integer, sparks generated by fireworks explosion can be expressed as

$$s_i = m \cdot \frac{f(\mathbf{X}_i) - y_{\min} + \xi}{\sum\limits_{i=1}^{n} f(\mathbf{X}_i) - y_{\min} + \xi}$$

$$s_i = \begin{cases} s_{\max}, & if \quad s_i > s_{\max} \\ s_{\min}, & if \quad s_i < s_{\min} \\ round(s_i), & others \end{cases} \tag{14}$$

where $s_{\max}$ and $s_{\min}$ are the maximum and minimum spark number respectively.

Since the number of explosions is an integer, the differences in fitness value of the algorithm is not obvious due to the selection of the objective function when solving the specific problem of two-dimensional WSF. That is to say, when the values of $y_{\max}$ and $y_{\min}$ are close, the difference between the maximum and the minimum of s_i is probably less than 1, and the value tends to be the same after rounding, which means all fireworks have the same number of explosions. Therefore, the above equation cannot realize the principle of higher fitness values together with more sparks. It weakens the searching ability of fireworks algorithm near the optimal solution and increases the number of sparks generated near the inferior solution, which is not conducive to the fast convergence of fireworks algorithm. In view of the above problems, the calculation rules for the number of sparks are improved here, and the improved algorithm for number of sparks is

$$s_i = M \cdot (f(\mathbf{x}_i) - y_{\min}) \tag{15}$$

$$M = \frac{s_{\max} - s_{\min}}{y_{\max} - y_{\min}} \tag{16}$$

The Eq. (15) compares the fitness values of all fireworks to the minimum, no longer dividing them from $\sum_{i=1}^{n} f(\mathbf{x}_i) - y_{\min} + \xi$, and amplifies the tiny fitness values. At the same time, in order to guarantee the limit of the number of explosions, M is no longer a fixed value in the Eq. (16). M' value will be determined by the difference between the optimal solution and the worst inferior solution produced by this explosion. The smaller the difference is, the denser the solution will be, so it will take a larger value. On the contrary, the smaller the difference value is, the more dispersed the solution is, so its value should be reduced at this time. According to the above equation, the number of sparks calculated varies greatly, and sparks generated by each iteration are more near the better individuals, which is conducive to the search throughout the space and careful search.

The Improvement of Blast Radius. Consider the process of fireworks explosion as the process of searching for the optimal solution, and the i-th blast radius of firework is

$$A_i = A \cdot \frac{y_{\max} - f(\mathbf{x}_i) + \xi}{\sum_{i=1}^{n} y_{\max} - f(\mathbf{x}_i) + \xi} \tag{17}$$

where A represents the preset maximum blast radius, and $y_{\max} = \max(f(\mathbf{x}_i))$ stands for the maximum value of target function for n fireworks.

The main principle of the Eq. (17) is that when the value of the target function corresponding to fireworks is larger, i.e., the closer to the optimal solution, the smaller the blast radius is. Since there is a greater possibility of the global optimal solution around the particle, it is necessary to give a smaller blast radius, strengthen the search near the particle, and improve the possibility of finding the global optimal solution. But there is a problem that when the firework is the best from the last explosion, $f(\mathbf{x}_i) = y_{\max}$, the result can be substituted into the Eq. (17)

$$A_i = A \cdot \frac{\xi}{\sum_{i=1}^{n} y_{\max} - f(\mathbf{x}_i) + \xi} \tag{18}$$

Since ξ is a minimal constant, it is not difficult to find out that when this fireworks is the best from the last explosion, the result of the above equation is close to 0. However, the better the fitness value of fireworks is, the more fireworks will be produced, so the optimal fireworks should generate the maximum number of sparks. It means that the best fireworks from the last explosion will generate the maximum number of sparks within the radius of zero in this explosion, which is equivalent to the repetition of the previous optimal solution in this explosion and find no other solutions around the fireworks. In the next explosion, for the same fireworks $d(x_i - x_j) = 0$, therefore, the probability of these sparks being selected is zero, and all the repeated solutions will be discarded, which not only increases the calculation of algorithm, but also reduces search opportunities. In view of the above disadvantages of the basic fireworks algorithm, the blast radius will be perfected. The improved equation for calculating the blast radius is shown in (19).

$$A_i = A_t - (A_t - A_{\min}) \times f(x_i)/y_{\max}$$
$$A_t = A \times (T - t + 1)/T \tag{19}$$

In Eq. (19), t represents the iteration number of explosion search, T is the iteration number of preset total search, A_t is the maximum blast radius under the current iteration number, and $A_{\min}$ is the preset minimum blast radius. Obviously, with the increase of t, A_t will gradually decrease and A_i will also decrease, which makes the algorithm focus on global search with a large radius at the beginning, and reduce the radius when the optimal value is found in the later stage. This is conductive to fine search in local areas. Also, it guarantees that under the same search iteration number, the better the particle is, the smaller the explosion radius is, which is conducive to strengthening the search near the current optimal solution and improving the ability of global search.

The Improvement of Search Space. In the solution space of WSF algorithm, ESPRIT algorithm combined with Cramer-Rao bound are used to determine a smaller search space containing the global optimal solution, and then the modified fireworks algorithm is used to solve in this small space to reduce the computational complexity of the algorithm.

Since the ESPRIT algorithm can directly obtain the DOA through calculation without the multi-dimensional search of global extremum [9], the complexity is much lower than that of WSF. Although the distinguishability of ESPRIT algorithm is lower than that of WSF algorithm, it is undeniable that the solutions of ESPRIT algorithm and WSF algorithm are all angle estimates of the DOA, so their solutions are similar. Therefore, ESPRIT is used to solve the coarse estimated value as a center to select the search space. Under the condition of ensuring certain accuracy, if the selection of search space is too large, the fireworks algorithm needs to select more individuals in the initial population, the required blast radius is increased, and more iterations will be needed to realize the global search. However, if the selection of search space is too small, it will not contain the global optimal value. Hence, a suitable search space is crucial for the selection of primary fireworks and blast radius.

CRB is the lower bound of the variance of unbiased estimator in parameter estimation, a parameter related to SNR and the number of snapshots. With the decrease of SNR or number of snapshots, the deviation between coarse estimated value and real value of ESPRIT algorithm increases, and CRB also becomes larger. Therefore, CRB, which is magnified μ times, is taken as the half boundary of the search space, and the search space can be expressed as $[\theta_e - \mu CRB, \theta_e + \mu CRB]$ and $[\varphi_e - \mu CRB, \varphi_e + \mu CRB]$.

3.3   Pseudo-Random Noise Re-sampling Technique

Pseudo-random noise re-sampling technology adopts artificial pseudo-random noise to repeatedly sample the same set of data. This process can reallocate the noise in the original data and eliminate the unreliable data, and then, thus creating a good operating condition for DOA estimation algorithm. The operation procedures can be summarized as follows:

The same group of received data is sampled repeatedly by pseudo-random noise to recreated data matrixes.

Conduct DOA estimation on the newly generated data in parallel, and save the results.

Set the reliability test conditions, screen the estimated results of the previous step to remove the unreliable data, and the remaining reliable data is the final result.

Let the receiving data of original array be X and the number of snapshots be K, then the data matrix after re-sampling can be defined as

$$Y = X + Z \tag{20}$$

where Z represents pseudo-random noise $MN \times K$ matrix, and it has the following features:

$$E[Z] = 0, \quad E[ZZ^H] = \sigma_z^2 NI, \quad E[ZZ^T] = 0 \tag{21}$$

where I represents $MN \times MN$ unit matrix, and σ_z^2 stands for pseudo-random noise power.

Reliability test plays an important role in PR algorithm, and its accuracy in harsh environment directly determines the performance of PR algorithm. DOA estimation is carried out on the data from pseudo-random noise re-sampling, and the results need to be filtrated by reliability tests, so as to eliminate the unreliable data and obtain the reliable data.

In PR algorithm, the essence of reliability tests is the union of azimuth and pitch angle regions of each incident signal DOA. If their sets are set as Θ, Φ respectively, then the condition for reliability test will be that the DOA estimation results of the re-sampled data are all within Θ, Φ. In the PR algorithm, Bartlett algorithm can be used to solve Θ, Φ and can be expressed as [10]

$$\begin{aligned} \Theta &= \bigcup_{p=1}^{P} \left[\theta_p^{max} - \theta_p^{left}, \theta_p^{max} + \theta_p^{right} \right] \\ \Phi &= \bigcup_{p=1}^{P} \left[\varphi_p^{max} - \varphi_p^{left}, \varphi_p^{max} + \varphi_p^{right} \right] \end{aligned} \tag{22}$$

where $\theta_p^{max} (p = 1, \cdots P)$ is the azimuth angle corresponding to the p-th power peak in the algorithm output results, and $\varphi_p^{max} (p = 1, \cdots P)$ is the pitch angle corresponding to the p-th power peak in the algorithm output results. θ_p^{left} and φ_p^{right} are left and right boundaries of the p-th subinterval in Θ. Similarly, θ_p^{left} and φ_p^{right} are left and right boundaries of the p-th subinterval in Φ, and both are consistent with the corresponding angle of 3 dB bandwidth of the peak power in the interval.

The modified fireworks algorithm and pseudo-random noise re-sampling algorithm are adopted to solve the equation of weighted-signal subspace fitting. The global optimal solution of the optimization problem is the DOA estimated value of the signal source. Therefore, in this maximum optimization problem, the corresponding fitness function can be defined as

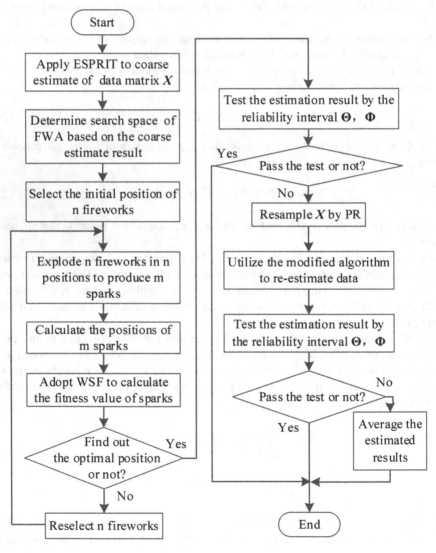

Fig. 1. Algorithm flow chart

$$F(\theta, \varphi) = \text{tr}\left\{ P_A \hat{U}_s W \hat{U}_s^H \right\} \tag{23}$$

The position of the fireworks and sparks (θ_i, φ_i) correspond to a set of angular estimates.

According to the above algorithms, the flowchart of PR-WSF algorithm based on the modified fireworks algorithm is shown in the Fig. 1.

4 Performance Study

4.1 Modified FWA

The simulation model is a 8×8 matrix URA with the spacing between elements $d = \lambda/2$, the two narrow-band signals are incident on the array at azimuth $25°, 35°$ and elevation $10°, 20°$, and the noise is additive Gaussian white noise. To verify the effectiveness of the modified fireworks algorithm, it is compared with FWA WSF, PSO WSF, limited GA WSF [5] and Joint-PSO WSF [6].

The root-mean-square error is defined as

$$RMSE_\theta = \sqrt{\frac{1}{RQ} \sum_{r=1}^{R} \sum_{i=1}^{Q} \left(\hat{\theta}_{i,r} - \theta_i \right)^2}$$

$$RMSE_\varphi = \sqrt{\frac{1}{RQ} \sum_{r=1}^{R} \sum_{i=1}^{Q} \left(\hat{\varphi}_{i,r} - \varphi_i \right)^2} \tag{24}$$

where R is the number of Monte Carlo independent experiments, $\hat{\theta}_{i,r}, \hat{\varphi}_{i,r}$ is the estimate of azimuth and elevation of the i-th incident signal obtained from the r-th Monte Carlo experiment, and θ_i, φ_i is their accurate value.

Figure 2 reveals the comparison of estimation results between FWA WSF and the modified FWA WSF in 300 times of Monte Carlo independent experiments when SNR

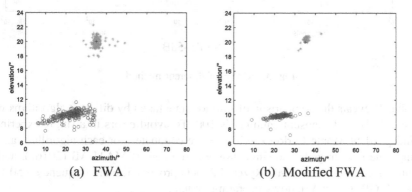

(a) FWA   (b) Modified FWA

Fig. 2. Results of different methods

is −5 dB, and snapshots number is 100, with "+" for the real position of incident signals. Simulation results show that under the same iteration times, the modified fireworks algorithm has a smaller deviation from the real value when solving the WSF algorithm, thus obtains better effects. The modified fireworks algorithm has smaller search space, which makes the results inevitably fall within the range closer to the real value. Combined with the improvement of explosion radius, the modified fireworks algorithm can search accurately in a small range, and the iterative solution process is less likely to fall into local optimum.

Figure 3 shows the performance comparison of different algorithms with different SNRs and snapshot numbers in 500 times of Monte Carlo independent experiments, where SNR goes from −15 dB to 10 dB, and the snapshots from 10 to 1000.

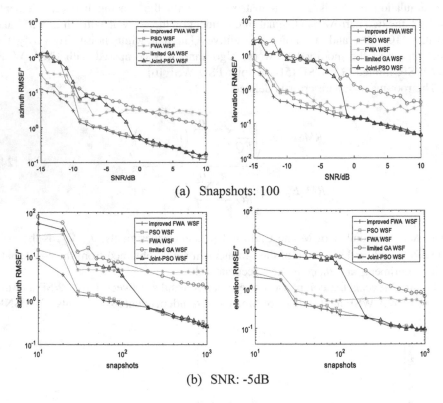

(a) Snapshots: 100

(b) SNR: -5dB

Fig. 3. RMSE of different methods

Table 1 reveals the comparison of solution time taken by different algorithms when SNR is −5 dB, and snapshots number is 100. To avoid errors in a single experiment, 500 independent Monte Carlo experiments are conducted for each algorithm, and the running time is averaged. The simulation environment is MATLAB (2016b), and the computer is configured as AMD Ryzen 3 2200G processor, main frequency 3.50 GHz, memory 8 GB, 64-bit Windows operating system.

Table 1. Comparison of solution time

Algorithm	PSO WSF	FWA WSF	Modified FWA WSF	Joint-PSO WSF	Limited GA WSF
Time for a single solution/s	8.84	5.62	5.70	7.81	9.61
Time for a single iteration/s	0.022	0.056	0.057	0.026	0.032

It can be seen from the above two groups of experiments that the original fireworks algorithm has poor ability to optimize the target function of WSF algorithm, and the incomplete search results lead to great errors in estimation results. The estimation error of limited GA WSF algorithm is apparently higher than that of other algorithms due to the poor convergence performance of the genetic algorithm and the tendency of getting into the local optimum in the iteration process, but the modified algorithm improves the calculation speed obviously. In the case of high SNR and number of snapshots, the mean-square error curve basically overlaps with the PSO WSF algorithm. However, with the decrease of SNR and number of snapshots, the deviation between the initial population and the real value of this algorithm becomes larger, and the same iterative solution process improves the operation speed at the cost of the breakdown accuracy. The accuracy of the modified fireworks algorithm is similar to that of the particle swarm optimization, but the its performance is improved slightly in the region where the threshold effect occurs due to the assistance of coarse estimation of ESPRIT algorithm. The modified explosion strategy improves the search performance of the algorithm, and the overall estimation performance is better than other methods.

When the solution results are similar, the particle swarm optimization algorithm needs 8.84 s, and the modified fireworks algorithm needs 5.70 s. It should be noted that in this experiment, algorithm of particle swarm optimization needs 400 iterations for a single solution process, while the improved fireworks algorithm only needs 100. It can be concluded that algorithm of particle swarm optimization has small amount of calculation and fast single iteration. It takes a long time for the improved fireworks algorithm to calculate a large amount of data in a single iteration in parallel, but its fast convergence speed makes the final solution time less than that of particle swarm optimization algorithm. In conclusion, the modified fireworks algorithm has higher accuracy and faster single solution speed for WSF algorithm.

4.2 PR-WSF Algorithm Based on Improved Fireworks Algorithm

In order to prove the effectiveness of this algorithm, it is compared with POS WSF and WSF algorithm based on improved FWA. The simulation conditions are the same as Sect. 4.1.

Figure 4 shows the performance comparison of each algorithm at different SNRs and snapshot numbers. Simulation results reveals that the algorithm modified by pseudo-random noise re-sampling has better performance than other algorithms when the SNR is lower than −9 db or the number of snapshots is less than 30. However, as the cost of performance improvement, its computational complexity increases significantly, which leads to a decrease in calculation speed. When the SNR and the number of snapshots increase to a certain amount, the algorithm will not take the re-sampling step. At this time, the complexity and speed of the algorithm are approximately equal to the WSF algorithm based on improved FWA.

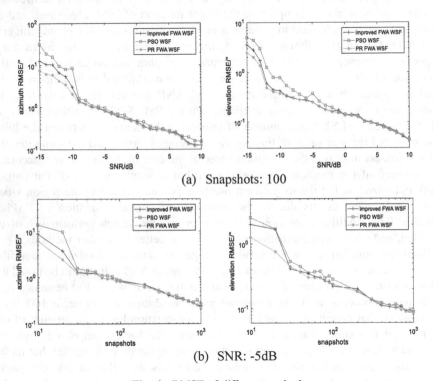

(a) Snapshots: 100

(b) SNR: -5dB

Fig. 4. RMSE of different methods

Figure 5 shows the influence of different re-sampling times on algorithm performance. The re-sampling times are set as 1, 3 and 5 respectively. Simulation results reveals that pseudo-random noise re-sampling can effectively improve the DOA estimation performance under the condition of low SNR and insufficient number of snapshots, and multiple re-samplings can explore the useful information in data more thoroughly and make the results more accurate. However, as re-sampling times increases, the mean-square error decreases gradually. The reason is that in the re-sampling operation, the dynamic pseudo-random noise introduced changes the noise distribution in the original data, and the re-sampled data contains more complex noise information, and the influences on the original data gradually reach the limit. In addition, re-sampling times are directly related to the computational complexity. The more re-sampling times are, the longer the required operation time is needed, and the corresponding solution accuracy is also improved.

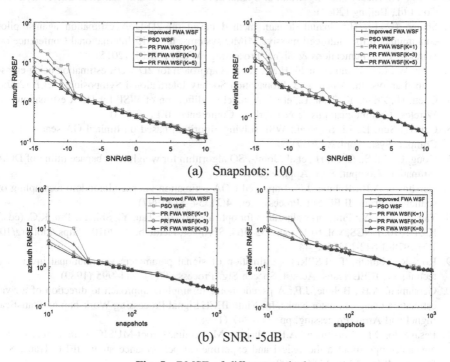

(a) Snapshots: 100

(b) SNR: -5dB

Fig. 5. RMSE of different methods

5   Concluding Remarks

In view of the complexity of WSF algorithm in solving process, which does not meet the real-time, this paper introduces the fireworks algorithm into the solving process, and improves the parameters design of the fireworks algorithm; meanwhile, inspired by literature, a fireworks algorithm with limited search space is proposed. In order to improve the convergence rate of intelligent algorithm, this algorithm adopts limited search space to make fireworks algorithm solve data in parallel while reducing the total amount of data to accelerate the solving process. In addition, the DOA estimation algorithm under the influence of threshold effect is studied, and a PR-WSF algorithm based on improved fireworks algorithm is proposed. With the purpose of improving data utilization, this PR-WSF algorithm combines PR algorithm to resample data, and improves the performance of the algorithm under low SNR and small number of snapshots condition. The simulation study reveals that the proposed PR-WSF algorithm based on improved fireworks algorithm has relatively faster solving speed and higher threshold performance.

References

1. Wang, Y.: Theory and Algorithm of Spatial Spectral Estimation. Tsinghua University Press Co., Ltd., Beijing (2004)
2. Shang, G., Li, H.: Spatial domain method based on 2D-DoA estimation against pilot contamination for multi-cell massive MIMO systems. In: 2015 International Conference on Wireless Communications & Signal Processing (WCSP). IEEE (2015)
3. Diab, W.M.G., Elkamchouchi, H.M.: A novel approach for 2D-DOA estimation using cross-shaped arrays. In: Antennas & Propagation Society International Symposium. IEEE (2008)
4. Chen, H., Zhou, Y., Tian, L., et al.: A novel modification of WSF for DOA estimation. In: Wireless Communications & Networking Conference. IEEE (2013)
5. Cai, L., Sun, L., Li, S., et al.: WSF solving algorithm based on limited GA search space. Comput. Syst. Appl. 8 (2017)
6. Gong, C., Li, S., Chen, H., et al.: Joint-PSO algorithm for weighted subspace fitting of DOA estimation. Comput. Syst. Appl. 9 (2017)
7. Gershman, A.B., Bohme, J.F.: Improved DOA estimation via pseudorandom resampling of spatial spectrum. IEEE Sig. Process. Lett. 4(2), 54–57 (1997)
8. Tan, Y., Zhu, Y.: Fireworks algorithm for optimization. In: Tan, Y., Shi, Y., Tan, K.C. (eds.) ICSI 2010. LNCS, vol. 6145, pp. 355–364. Springer, Heidelberg (2010). https://doi.org/10.1007/978-3-642-13495-1_44
9. Roy, R., Kailath, T.: ESPRIT - estimation of signal parameters via rotational invariance techniques. IEEE Trans. Acoust. Speech Sig. Process. 37(7), 984–995 (1989)
10. Gershman, A.B., Bohme, J.F.: A pseudo-noise resampling approach to direction of arrival estimation using estimator banks. In: Ninth IEEE Signal Processing Workshop on Statistical Signal and Array Processing, pp. 244–247 (1998)
11. Pesavento, M., Gershman, A.B., Haardt, M.: Unitary root-MUSIC with a real-valued eigendecomposition: a theoretical and experimental performance study. IEEE Trans. Sig. Process. 48(5), 1306–1314 (2000)
12. Chen, Z., Gokeda, G., Yu, Y.: Introduction to Direction-of-arrival Estimation, p. 41. Artech House, Boston (2010)

Research on Indoor and Outdoor Seamless Positioning Based on Combination of Clustering and GPS

Jingqiu Ren[1]([✉]), Ke Bao[1], Siyue Sun[2], and Weidang Lu[3]

[1] College of Electrical and Information Engineering,
Northeast Petroleum University, Daqing, China
dqzgh@139.com
[2] Shanghai Engineering Center for Micro-satellites, Shanghai, China
[3] College of Information Engineering, Zhejiang University of Technology,
Hangzhou, China

Abstract. Aiming at the key technical issue which is needed to be solved in seamless positioning, a seamless positioning algorithm based on combination of indoor joint clustering positioning and GPS is proposed in this paper. This algorithm uses GPS satellite positioning technology in outdoor environment and indoor joint clustering positioning algorithm in indoor environment, a switching algorithm is proposed to improve the smoothness of switching when it transit from indoor environment to outdoor one (and vice versa). The experimental results show that the proposed algorithm can meet the requirements of seamless positioning both indoors and outdoors better.

Keywords: Clustering · Gaussian mixture model ·
Seamless positioning · GPS

1 Introduction

With the development of science and technology, the market of location-based services is growing gradually, and the need of improving the positioning precision and reducing the deployment cost of positioning systems is also increasing. Global positioning system (GPS) dominates the future development of location-based services [1]. GPS positioning system has been relatively well done in outdoor positioning technology. In the outdoor environment, the GPS positioning system has been widely used for its features of high positioning accuracy and wide coverage. However, the signal is vulnerable to the influence of propagation factors such as multipath and obstacles, and the GPS positioning system cannot achieve idea positioning result in the complex urban and indoor environment

This work was supported in part by the National Natural Science Foundation of China under Grant (61871348) and open foundation of laboratory (2018JYWXTX02).

S. Han et al. (Eds.): AICON 2019, LNICST 286, pp. 225–239, 2019.
https://doi.org/10.1007/978-3-030-22968-9_20

[2–4]. In indoor positioning technology, infrared, Bluetooth, ultrasound, RFID, WLAN and UWB are often used [5–8]. Literature [9] proposed the indoor positioning scheme that integrates Bluetooth and pedestrian track estimation. This method eliminates the instability of Bluetooth system, but the positioning accuracy needs to be further improved. Literature [10] integrated UWB and inertial measurement unit sensor positioning system by Extended Kalman Filter (EKF) which has better performance on correcting the positioning error, but the error accumulation still exists. Aiming at the deficiency of KNN positioning algorithm in indoor positioning, literature [11] proposed an indoor positioning algorithm based on fuzzy set theory, this algorithm is simple and has more precise positioning accuracy. Literature [12] proposed an indoor positioning algorithm based on geometric and RSS clustering, which has the advantages of fast positioning speed and high positioning accuracy, but the training workload is large. By using Bayesian theory, the study [13] proposed a positioning method based on Received Signal Strength Indication (RSSI), which has a better positioning accuracy. Literature [14] proposed a Fingerprint recognition scheme based on Crowdsourcing and multi-source Fusion based Fingerprint Sensing (CMFS). In order to further improve the positioning accuracy of CMFS, ekf-based Fusion algorithm was adopted to fuse the positioning information between Fingerprint and PDR. Literature [15] has developed a wireless performance evaluation platform LAN (WLAN) positioning system based on fingerprint. In the proposed test bed, several scenes are set to test the indoor and outdoor positioning systems.

However, the positioning range of indoor positioning technology is limited. In order to achieve the smooth transition of indoor and outdoor positioning, accurate seamless indoor and outdoor positioning technology is needed in many cases. In 2011, Naohiko and Shusuke had developed a new type of positioning System, the System used the GPS chipset receiver to realize the Indoor positioning, any equipment of GPS receiver chipsets can be detected Indoor Messaging System (IMES) signals for positioning, assisted GPS/IMES developed network, and on the GPS chip firmware to modify the SET, can according to the movement of the user, smoothly to provide location information of seamless Indoor and outdoor [16]. In [17], a low-power iBeacon technology is proposed to run IO detection and location-based services (LBS) on mobile devices. GPS signal is used to trigger off GPS and turn on bluetooth to enable GPS in outdoor environment, while the iBeacon mode of BlueDetect is enabled in semi-outdoor environment to provide LBS. By comparing the signals of two Bluetooth Low Energy (BLE) beacons on both sides of the building entrance, the seamless connection between semi-outdoor environment and indoor environment is realized. In [18], a switching technique for precise monitoring of SNR changes of GPS satellites is proposed. By selecting the high-altitude satellite behind the user and switching it precisely at the entrance, the energy consumption of the algorithm is low. In [19], a universal seamless localization method combining GNSS pseudo-distance and WLAN received signal strength index (RSSI) based on particle filter was proposed. Gaussian process was used to model the spatial RSSI distribution, and these models were used to predict the RSSI of particle positions, and the point estimation of the RSSI likelihood function was obtained. The results of extended kalman filter are compared with pseudo distance and WLAN position. The algorithm achieves precise and robust seamless positioning. In [20], a modular system is proposed, which currently consists of three positioning modules: GPS, gsm-based positioning system and wifi positioning system. The optimal positioning module is automatically selected based on available radio signals, which can provide seamless positioning in different environments. Wu and Geng et al. combined the differential global positioning system (DGPS) with ultra-wideband (UWB), eliminated the UWB non-line-of-sight error (NLOS) with Kalrnan filter, used particle filter for data fusion of different sensors, and used GPRS communication module for wireless data transmission. The system improves the overall positioning accuracy, which can not only meet the indoor and outdoor seamless positioning, but also has a high positioning accuracy [21]. Cai et al. realized seamless indoor and outdoor positioning and navigation by combining GNSS positioning technology and the combination method of indoor geomagnetic fingerprint nodes to solve the problems such as low precision of indoor and outdoor seamless positioning in the transition point and the inability of smooth automatic switching. Since the indoor geomagnetic positioning accuracy is gradually better than GNSS positioning accuracy from outdoor to indoor, the optimal GDOP conversion range value is obtained through analysis and calculation at two critical points of positioning accuracy for smooth switching. Compared with the positioning accuracy of single GNSS or geomagnetic method, the positioning accuracy is improved [22]. In order to solve the problem of discontinuous positioning and low accuracy of current pedestrian navigation in indoor and outdoor environment, Wang and Guo et al. proposed a pedestrian seamless navigation and positioning method based on beidou/GPS/IMU. When the satellite is unlocked, according to the characteristics of the periodicity of pedestrian walking, a zero-speed detection algorithm with multiple conditions and constraints is designed based on IMU. The extended kalman filter can reduce the divergence of inertial sensor with time, and the positioning accuracy of outdoor pedestrian can reach cm [23]. Hu, Liao et al. proposed the indoor and outdoor seamless positioning algorithm gps-lf based on GPS satellite positioning technology and wifi location fingerprint positioning technology. The gps-lf algorithm USES GPS satellite positioning technology for positioning in the outdoor environment. After entering the room, it switches to the wifi location for fingerprint positioning. Multiple groups of wi-fi signal strength values received by the node to be positioned are matched with the location fingerprint database that has been downloaded to the node in advance to estimate the location of the unknown node [24]. In [25], the smart phone is used as the platform to study the indoor and outdoor seamless positioning technology integrating beidou satellite navigation system, wifi, bluetooth and other technologies, and to design the location service application scheme, providing a new idea for the indoor and outdoor seamless positioning. In [26], an intelligent switching algorithm based on counting and threshold mechanism is proposed, which avoids the calculation waste caused by repeated switching of positioning system, reduces the energy consumption of smart phones, and realizes the seamless connection between GPS and indoor wifi location fingerprint positioning technology. In [27], an indoor and outdoor positioning technology and automatic switching strategy of positioning method are designed to provide continuous positioning services. The alpha-count method was introduced to improve the smoothness and reliability of positioning switch. A prototype indoor and outdoor seamless positioning system UL mobile was built, which integrated GPS and wifi.

In this paper, indoor combined clustering and GPS combined positioning method is adopted, Kalman filtering and clustering combined positioning method is adopted indoors, and GPS positioning is used in outdoor environment. In order to reduce the ping-pong effect, a new algorithm named double threshold switching is proposed. Compared with the traditional NN algorithm and K-means-WKNN algorithm, the clustering joint positioning algorithm in this paper has reduced the average positioning error and achieved the seamless switch positioning between indoor and outdoor positioning effectively.

2   Methodology

2.1   Outdoor Positioning Principle

GPS positioning system is composed of 24 to 32 satellites or space crafts, and the system consists of the space section, ground control section and users [28]. The space section of GPS is composed of 24 working satellites, providing the navigation system with continuous global navigation capability in time. The observation, collection and tracking data of the ground control part can be conducted according to the positioning calculation method after the tracking satellite signal is captured by the user. The principle of GPS positioning is shown in Fig. 1.

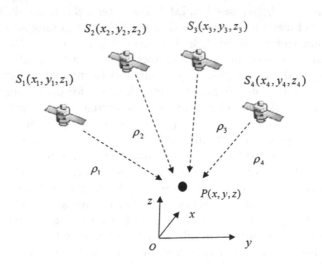

Fig. 1. GPS positioning

P is the position to be measured, the distance from P to four satellites measured by GPS receiver is $\rho_1, \rho_2, \rho_3, \rho_4$ respectively, and the observation equation to solve the position of P is:

$$\begin{cases} \rho_1^2 = (x - x_1)^2 + (y - y_1)^2 + (z - z_1)^2 + c\delta_t \\ \rho_2^2 = (x - x_2)^2 + (y - y_2)^2 + (z - z_2)^2 + c\delta_t \\ \rho_3^2 = (x - x_3)^2 + (y - y_3)^2 + (z - z_3)^2 + c\delta_t \\ \rho_4^2 = (x - x_4)^2 + (y - y_4)^2 + (z - z_4)^2 + c\delta_t \end{cases} \tag{1}$$

Where c is the speed of light and δ_t is the clock difference of the receiver. Due to various types of errors, in order to achieve the positioning accuracy, at least four satellites are needed to be observed simultaneously to achieve the positioning.

2.2 Indoor Positioning Principle

In this algorithm, fingerprint database is established in the offline phase. K-means clustering algorithm and GMM clustering algorithm are used to get the clustering fingerprint database. The Euclidean distance between the test signal and each clustering center is calculated, and the test point is classified into the class with the smallest Euclidean distance value until all test points are classified. The Euclidean distance between the test signal and the clustering fingerprint database was calculated, K positions with the smallest Euclidean distance were selected, the weight was calculated, and the position coordinates were estimated according to the weight. Kalman filter is applied to the estimated position and the positioning result is optimized to obtain the position of the point to be measured. The positioning process is shown in Fig. 2.

K-Means Clustering Algorithm. The K-means clustering algorithm assumes the set $X \sim \{x_1, x_2, \ldots, x_n\}$ that contains N data (objects), and divides this data set into K clustering center sets $C \sim \{c_1, c_2, \ldots, c_K\}$ [29]. If the sample number of class i is N_i, then $N = \sum_{i=1}^{K} N_i$, and the mean value of each class C_i is $\{m_1, m_2, \ldots, m_K\}$, then $m_i = \frac{1}{N} \sum_{n=1}^{N_i} x_n$, i = 1, 2 ... , K. The minimum objective function of K-means clustering algorithm is:

$$J = \sum_{i=1}^{K} \sum_{n=1}^{N_i} \|x_n - m_i\|^2 \tag{2}$$

Gaussian Mixture Model Algorithm (GMM). Gaussian mixture model positioning method can be regarded as a fingerprint probability method. Suppose the entire data set is generated by k Gaussian models, then the model parameters and which Gaussian model is most likely to generate each data point are calculated by EM algorithm, and finally the data points generated by the same Gaussian model are divided into one class. Gaussian mixture model refers

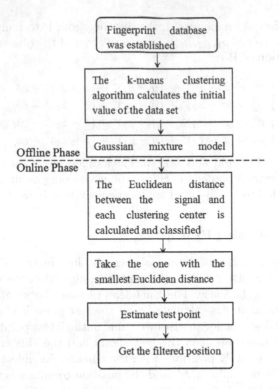

Fig. 2. Position flow chart

to the probability distribution model with the following forms:

$$P\left(x \mid \theta\right) = \sum_{i=1}^{K} \alpha_i \phi\left(x \mid \theta_i\right) \tag{3}$$

In Eq. 3, α_i is the coefficient, $\alpha_i \geq 0$, $\sum_{i=1}^{K} \alpha_i = 1$; X is the observation data, $x = \{x_1, x_2, \ldots, x_n\}$, $\phi\left(x \mid \theta_i\right)$ is the Gaussian distribution density function, $\theta_i = \left(\mu_i, \sigma_i^2\right)$,

$$\phi\left(x \mid \theta_i\right) = \frac{1}{\sqrt{2\pi}\sigma_i} \exp\left(-\frac{(x - \mu_i)^2}{2\sigma_i^2}\right) \tag{4}$$

It's called the ith submodel.

Expectation maximization (EM) algorithm is adopted for the estimation of model parameters [30]. The EM algorithm includes two steps: the expected step (e-step) and the maximum stride length (m-step).In the first iteration, the parameters are initialized, the covariance matrix is set to the identity matrix,The ith gaussian weight coefficient is $\alpha_i = \frac{1}{K}$, the parameter $\hat{\theta}$ that maximizes the logarithmic likelihood function of x is obtained.

$$\hat{\theta} = \arg\ max_\theta p\left(x \mid \theta\right) \tag{5}$$

Step E finds the expected value of the hidden variable from the current parameter and the estimated variable $\hat{\gamma}_{ji}$, $j = 1, 2, \cdots, n$, $i = 1, 2, \cdots, K$.

$$\hat{\gamma}_{ji} = \frac{\alpha_i \phi (x_j \mid \theta_i)}{\sum_{i=1}^{K} \alpha_i \phi (x_j \mid \theta_i)} \tag{6}$$

Step M to obtain the maximum expected logarithmic likelihood function of the observed data.

$$\hat{\mu} = \frac{\sum_{j=1}^{n} \hat{\gamma}_{ji} y_j}{\sum_{j=1}^{n} \hat{\gamma}_{ji}} \tag{7}$$

$$\hat{\sigma}^2 = \frac{\sum_{j=1}^{n} \hat{\gamma}_{ji} (y_j - \mu_i)^2}{\sum_{j=1}^{n} \hat{\gamma}_{ji}} \tag{8}$$

$$\hat{\alpha}_i = \frac{\sum_{j=1}^{n} \hat{\gamma}_{ji}}{n} \tag{9}$$

Repeat these two steps until the change of the mean value of two successive iterations is lower than the threshold value which has been set, and finally obtain the parameter to be estimated.

The Establishment of Signal Fingerprint Database. Multiple WiFi signals can be collected at a certain location in the positioning area, and multiple WiFi signals collected at the same location constitute the feature vector of the signal (RSS). Assuming that there are M WiFi hotspots in the location scene and WiFi signals are collected for N times,the sample data set can be expressed as $I = \{x_i, y_i, f_i\}$, Where $i = 1, 2, \cdots, N$, $f_i = (f_{i1}, f_{i2}, \cdots, f_{iM})$, (x_i, y_i) represents the corresponding position of the vector f_i. The process of fingerprint positioning is shown in Fig. 3.

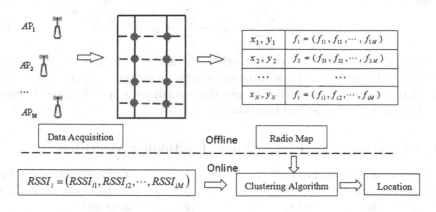

Fig. 3. Fingerprint locating process

In the off-line phase, in order to obtain the global optimal solution, the number of sub-models is first determined, and the above k-means algorithm is used to calculate the initial value of the constructed sample data set model. Then, GMM clustering is used to obtain the fingerprint database S after clustering.

$$S = \{s_1, s_2, \cdots, s_j\} \tag{10}$$

The center of clustering $C_j = \{c_{j1}, c_{j2}, \cdots, c_{jM}\}$, Where j is the number of classes.

Online Positioning Stage. $RSSI_i = (RSSI_{i1}, RSSI_{i2}, \cdots, RSSI_{iM})$ is the collected test signal, $i = 1, 2 \cdots, n$, n is the number of test points. The Euclidean distance D of each test signal $RSSI_i$ and the clustering center value C_j can be expressed as

$$D_{ij} = \sqrt{\sum_{N=1}^{M} (RSSI_{iN} - c_{jN})^2} \tag{11}$$

In this formula, $i = 1, 2 \cdots, n$, j is the number of clustering.

The size of Euclidean distance between each test signal and each cluster center value was compared, and the clustering with the smallest Euclidean distance was selected to classify the test points into the cluster until all the test points were classified.

The Euclidean distance O between the measured signal and the cluster fingerprint database is calculated, K positions with the smallest Euclidean distance are selected, and the weight w_i is calculated, $i = 1, 2 \cdots, K$.

$$w_i = \frac{O_i}{\sum_{i=1}^{K} O_i} \tag{12}$$

The position coordinates are estimated according to the weight values obtained, as follows:

$$\hat{x} = \sum_{i=1}^{K} w_i x_i, \hat{y} = \sum_{i=1}^{K} w_i y_i \tag{13}$$

In this paper, the joint clustering algorithm is used to calculate the location of the measured points, and then Kalman filtering algorithm is used to filter the estimated position coordinates. The position coordinates after Kalman filtering are relatively close to the real coordinates.

2.3   Clustering and GPS Combined Positioning Algorithm

In order to ensure the continuity of positioning service, the positioning method in the positioning area is an important factor to be considered in the positioning process. The seamless positioning scheme in this paper is as follows:

Step 1: when WiFi signal is available and GPS signal cannot be detected, indoor clustering joint positioning algorithm is adopted.
Step 2: when there is WiFi signal and the number of GPS satellites is less than 4, clustering and GPS combined positioning algorithm are adopted.

Step 3: when the number of GPS satellites is greater than or equal to 4, GPS positioning is adopted.

The specific implementation of combined positioning is as follows:
(1) Mean positioning error can be expressed as:

$$E = \sqrt{(\hat{x} - x)^2 + (\hat{y} - y)^2} \tag{14}$$

$(\hat{x}, \hat{y})$ is the estimated position coordinate of the to be measured point, and (x, y) is the true position coordinate of the point to be measured.

The system parameters T of combined positioning are determined by mean positioning error E and Euclidean distance O, which can be expressed as:

$$T = \alpha E + (1 - \alpha) O \tag{15}$$

α is the weighted factor.

(2) Double threshold value h_1, h_2 is used in this paper, when users go from indoor to outdoor. If T is less than the setting threshold h_1, the indoor clustering joint positioning algorithm is adopted. If T is greater than the setting threshold h_1, then GPS positioning is adopted.

(3) When the user walks into the room from outside, if T is larger than the threshold value h_2, GPS positioning is adopted. If T is less than the threshold value h_2, the indoor clustering joint positioning algorithm is adopted.

The flow chart of combined positioning is shown in Fig. 4.

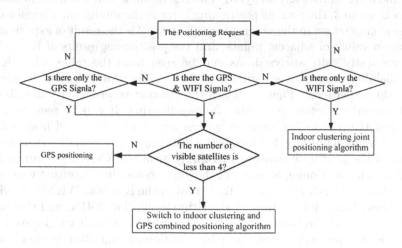

Fig. 4. Combined positioning flow chart

3   Experiments and Analysis

Experiments of indoor cluster joint positioning and combined positioning were carried out based on experimental data. Six AP were arranged in a $20\,\mathrm{m} \times 15\,\mathrm{m}$

Table 1. Cluster number error analysis

Cluster number	3	4	5
Average localization error	1.650	2.820	2.473

Table 2. The number of adjacent points k-value positioning error probability statistics

K	6	7	8	9	10
The error is less than 1 m	18.6	25.7	24.3	33.3	27.1
The error is less than 2 m	72.9	75.7	80.0	78.6	70
The error is less than 3 m	88.6	87.1	90.0	88.6	87.1

room. The RSSI values of 6 wireless access points were sampled at each sampling point. The selected wireless route AP is TP-LINK, and the type number is TL-WR842N, the signal receiver used in the test is samsung Galaxy S7 mobile phone. After reading the signal strength for 50 times, the mean value was taken and the mean value of RSSI was recorded into the fingerprint database. MATLAB software was used to achieve the positioning algorithm, the positioning results and positioning errors of the test points were obtained through experiments.

Table 1 shows the results of the experimental analysis on the value of the number of clusters, and the positioning error results with the number of clusters of 3, 4 and 5 are statistically analyzed. The results show that when the number of clusters is set to 3, the average positioning error is the minimum. Therefore, the number of clusters set in the experiment is 3. Table 2 is the result of experimental analysis on values of adjacent points, and the positioning results of $K = 6, 7, 8, 9, 10$ are statistically analyzed. As can be seen from the table, when $K = 9$, the probability of error less than 1 m is 33.3%. Therefore, K value is selected as 9 in this experiment. Figure 5 shows the cumulative probability distribution of distance errors before and after Kalman filtering. It can be seen from the figure that the positioning accuracy within 2 m can be improved from 75% to 80% after Kalman filtering. Figure 6 is the distance error cumulative distribution function of the joint positioning algorithm, K-means-WKNN algorithm and NN algorithm. The positioning accuracy of the joint positioning algorithm within 2 m is 83%, that of the NN algorithm is 69%, that of the K-means-WKNN algorithm is 66%, that of the joint positioning algorithm within 1 m is 41%, and that of the NN algorithm and the K-means-WKNN algorithm is 32%. It can be seen that the positioning performance of the joint positioning algorithm is significantly better than the other two algorithms.

The positioning error results of the three algorithms are shown in Table 3. The experimental results show that the positioning error of the joint localization algorithm is about 1.6 m, while that of the NN algorithm and the K-means-WKNN algorithm is about 2.2 m. The combined positioning algorithm reduces the average positioning error by 17% compared with the NN algorithm, and the average positioning error by 24% compared with the K-means-WKNN algorithm. The

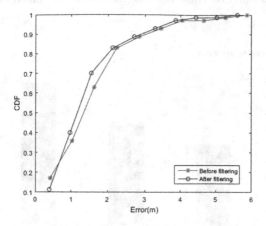

Fig. 5. Comparison before and after Kalman filtering

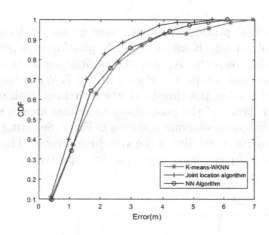

Fig. 6. Cumulative distribution function of distance error

Table 3. Position error results of three algorithms

Algorithm	Mean error	Maximum error	Error minimum
NN algorithm	1.989	6.407	0.119
K-means-WKNN algorithm	2.170	7.289	0.034
Joint location algorithm	1.651	5.879	0.109

error accumulation function converges the fastest, and it has a better positioning effect indoors.

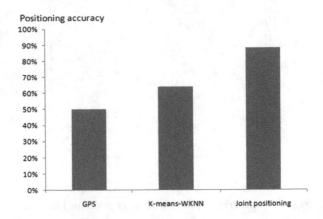

Fig. 7. The precision of the three positioning methods

In the experimental process, 50 points were measured using the clustering joint localization algorithm, K-means-WKNN positioning algorithm and GPS positioning algorithm respectively, and the positioning accuracy of the three positioning methods was obtained as shown in Fig. 7. When the user enters the switching area and reaches the threshold, the switching positioning method is adopted. The plan sketch of the positioning switching area is shown in Fig. 8, and the switching judgment diagram is shown in Fig. 9. Selecting the appropriate threshold can improve the stability of the switching process. The weighted factor $\alpha = 0.6$, the values of h_1 and h_2 re four and six respectively.

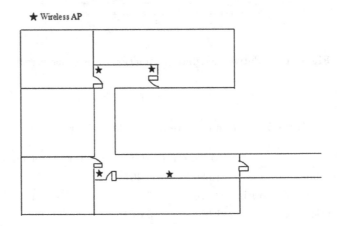

Fig. 8. Plan sketch of positioning switching area and WiFi signal source arrangement

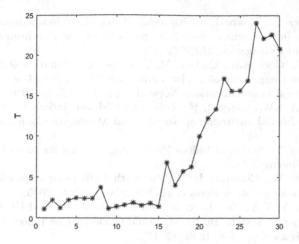

Fig. 9. Switching decision diagram

It can be obtained from the experimental data that GPS positioning cannot achieve high precision positioning indoors. Compared with the K-means-WKNN algorithm, the positioning algorithm proposed in this paper effectively improves the positioning accuracy and realizes seamless positioning indoors and outdoors.

4 Conclusions

The existing single positioning technology cannot meet the needs of the indoor and outdoor positioning at the same time, this paper proposes a method that combines indoor clustering joint positioning with GPS positioning algorithm, the average positioning error in this algorithm is reduced 17% and 24% compared with that of NN algorithm and K-means-WKNN algorithm respectively. This way effectively improves the positioning accuracy and realizes the seamless switching positioning between indoor and outdoor positioning system.

References

1. Mehmood, H., Tripathi, N.K., Tipdecho, T.: Seamless switching between GNSS and WLAN based indoor positioning system for ubiquitous positioning. Earth Sci. Inform. **8**(1), 221–231 (2015)
2. Wei, P.T., Wang, Y.: GPS/INS combined positioning scheme and test data analysis. Mod. Defense Technol. **1**, 69–73 (2018)
3. Lu, W.J., Sun, X.Y., et al.: Research and implementation of GPS pseudo-satellite high-precision indoor positioning technology. Application of Electronic Technology (2018)
4. Zeng, A.M., Yang, Y.X., Jing, Y.F., et al.: Deviation compensation model and performance analysis of GPS fusion positioning system. J. Wuhan Univ. (Inf. Sci. Ed.) (10) (2017)

5. Januszkiewicz, L., Kawecki, J., Kawecki, R., et al.: Wireless indoor positioning system with inertial sensors and infrared beacons. In: European Conference on Antennas and Propagation. IEEE (2016)
6. Varshney, V., Goel, R.K., Qadeer, M.A.: Indoor positioning system using Wi-Fi bluetooth low energy technology. In: Thirteenth International Conference on Wireless and Optical Communications Networks, pp. 1–6. IEEE (2016)
7. Ab Razak, A.A.W., Samsuri, F.: Active RFID-based Indoor Positioning System (IPS) for industrial environment. In: RF and Microwave Conference, pp. 89–91. IEEE (2016)
8. Shi, G., Ming, Y.: Survey of Indoor Positioning Systems Based on Ultra-wideband (UWB) Technology (2016)
9. Xin, L., Jian, W., Chunyan, L.: A Bluetooth/PDR integration algorithm for an indoor positioning system. Sensors **15**(10), 24862–24885 (2015)
10. Yao, L., Wu, Y.W.A., Yao, L., et al.: An integrated IMU and UWB sensor based indoor positioning system. In: International Conference on Indoor Positioning and Indoor Navigation, pp. 1–8. IEEE (2017)
11. Yu, J., Liu, J.: A KNN indoor positioning algorithm that is weighted by the membership of fuzzy set. In: Green Computing and Communications, pp. 1899–1903. IEEE (2013)
12. Peng, J., Li, T., Ge, Z., et al.: An indoor positioning algorithm based on geometry and RSS clustering. In: World Automation Congress 2016, pp. 1–6. IEEE (2016)
13. Zhou, F., Lin, K., Ren, A., et al.: RSSI indoor localization through a Bayesian strategy. In: Advanced Information Technology, Electronic and Automation Control Conference, pp. 1975–1979. IEEE (2017)
14. Zhao, W., Han, S., Hu, R.Q., et al.: Crowdsourcing and multi-source fusion based fingerprint sensing in smartphone localization. IEEE Sens. J. **18**(8), 3236–3247 (2018)
15. Zhao, W., Han, S., Meng, W., et al.: A testbed of performance evaluation for fingerprint based WLAN positioning system. KSII Trans. Internet Inf. Syst. **10**(6), 2583–2605 (2016)
16. Kohtake, N., Shusuke M., et al.: Indoor and outdoor seamless positioning using indoor messaging system and GPS. In: International Conference on Indoor Positioning and Indoor Navigation, pp. 21–23 (2011)
17. Han, Z., Hao, J., Yiwen, L., et al.: BlueDetect: an iBeacon-enabled scheme for accurate and energy-efficient indoor-outdoor detection and seamless location-based service. Sensors **16**(2), 268 (2016)
18. Yungeun, K., Songhee, L., Seokjoon, L., et al.: A GPS sensing strategy for accurate and energy-efficient outdoor-to-indoor handover in seamless localization systems. Mob. Inf. Syst. **8**(4), 315–332 (2012)
19. Toledano-Ayala, M., Richter, P.: Ubiquitous and seamless localization: fusing GNSS pseudoranges and WLAN signal strengths. Mob. Inf. Syst. **2017**, 1–16 (2017)
20. Juraj, M., Peter, B., Jozef, B.: Scalability optimization of seamless positioning service. Mob. Inf. Syst. **2016**, 1–11 (2016)
21. Wu, C., Geng, Q., Liu, J., et al.: Research on precise and seamless positioning technology of hybrid UWB with DGPS. Sens. Microsyst. **831**(3), 74–77 (2012)
22. Cai, J., et al.: A method for seamless indoor and outdoor positioning and smooth transition of GNSS/geomagnetic combination. Bull. Surv. Mapp. (2018)
23. Wang, K.L., Guo, H.: Research on positioning accuracy of indoor and outdoor pedestrian seamless navigation. Comput. Simul. **35**(09), 456–460 (2018)
24. Hu, K., Liao, X.Y., Yu, M., et al.: Research on indoor and outdoor seamless location based on GPS and Wi-Fi location fingerprint. Comput. Eng. 98–103 (2016)

25. Shen, F., Sun, S.Y.: Research and implementation of indoor and outdoor seamless positioning technology integrated with BeiDou. In: Annual Academic Conference of GPS and Ground Professional Committee of Jiangsu Society of Surveying and Mapping Geographic Information and JSCORS Technical Exchange Conference Proceedings (2017)
26. Guo, K.X., Lu, Y.L., Feng, T., et al.: Research on indoor and outdoor seamless positioning technology based on intelligent switching algorithm. Sens. Microsyst. **317**(7), 56–62 (2018)
27. Hu, X.K., Shang, J.G., Gu, F.Q., et al.: Development of indoor and outdoor seamless positioning prototype system integrating GPS and Wi-Fi. Miniat. Microcomput. Syst. **35**(2), 428–432 (2014)
28. Ho, Y.H., Abdullah, S.: Reduced global positioning system (GPS) positioning error by mitigating ionospheric scintillation. In: Wireless Technology Applications, pp. 110–15. IEEE (2014)
29. Li, W.: Analysis of localization algorithm based on k-mean clustering. J. Guangxi Univ. Sci. Technol. **23**(3), 45–482 (2012)
30. Alfakih, M., Keche, M., Benoudnine, H.: Gaussian mixture modeling for indoor positioning WIFI systems. In: International Conference on Control, Engineering Information Technology. IEEE (2015)

Angle-of-Arrival Positioning System Based on CSI Virtual Antenna Array

Lu Yin, Ziyang Wang[✉], Zhongliang Deng, Tianrun Jiang, and Yuan Sun

Beijing University of Posts and Telecommunications, Beijing 100876, China
wangziyang35@bupt.edu.cn

Abstract. Traditional Wi-Fi positioning systems usually use the signal intensity for fingerprint localization. However, the intensity of the received signal varies with time. And it is also easily affected by the indoor multipath environment. This paper presents a positioning system using Channel State Information (CSI) exposed by commodity Wi-Fi chips without any hardware adjustments. The core modules of this system include an Angle of Arrival (AOA) and Time of Flight (TOF) estimating algorithm using CSI, along with a clustering algorithm to identify the direct path in multipath environment. In this paper, we employ affine propagation clustering to avoid disadvantages of traditional K-means algorithm. The experiment results show the proposed system achieves an accuracy of about 1 m in a multipath-rich indoor environment.

Keywords: Indoor positioning · Channel state information · Angle of arrival

1 Introduction

As an important part of pervasive computing and Internet of Things (IOT), location technology is attracting more and more attention. Although Global Navigation Satellite System (GNSS) can provide high precision localization services in outdoor environment, satellite signals will decay due to wall obstructing and so on indoors [1]. As the GNSS is not able to achieve high positioning accuracy, indoor localization technology has received more attention.

In recent years, many indoor positioning technologies have been developed, such as Wi-Fi, Base-station, Ultra-wide bandwidth (UWB) based localization systems [2, 3]. With the development of Multiple-Input Multiple-Output (MIMO) technology, Angle of Arrival (AOA) based systems have been paid much attention. This kind of systems generally estimates the AOA of multipath signal at each wireless Access Point (AP), and then use triangulation method to locate the target. For example, Wang and Ho proposed an AOA-based system using hybrid AOA-TDOA positioning [4], which extends the source range to 90 m and maintains the estimation accuracy. But this system requires preliminary measurement of unique positions. A novel autofocusing approach for Direction of Arrival (DOA) estimation, proposed by Pal and Vaidyanathan, applies modified focusing matrices in the coherent methods for wideband DOA

© ICST Institute for Computer Sciences, Social Informatics and Telecommunications Engineering 2019
Published by Springer Nature Switzerland AG 2019. All Rights Reserved
S. Han et al. (Eds.): AICON 2019, LNICST 286, pp. 240–250, 2019.
https://doi.org/10.1007/978-3-030-22968-9_21

estimation using 8 antennas and exhibits satisfactory performance in comparison to the existing algorithms [5]. While the hardware of the autofocusing algorithm is difficult to deploy.

Channel State Information (CSI) is a kind of Physical layer (PHY) information, which extends Received Signal Strength Indication (RSSI) to frequency domain with phase information per subcarrier per antenna. Thus CSI is a kind of fine-grained information. Zhou used a deterministic CSI fingerprinting method and a threshold-based method separately to detect human presence in an omnidirectional manner [6]. Li Mo measured the CSI of multiple subcarriers in the coherent time of the channel, making it possible to achieve a median accuracy of sub-meter level [7]. However, these systems require strict time synchronization of all APs, which is impossible in commodity Wi-Fi infrastructure.

In this paper, the CSI of subcarrier is used to establish one-dimension Multiple Signal Classification (MUSIC) algorithm [8] in frequency domain. To meet the number requirement of antennas in AOA based system, an AOA and Time of Flight (TOF) joint estimation MUSIC algorithm is applied to expand the number of antennas by using spatial smoothing technique [9, 10]. In addition, affinity propagation clustering method is applied to cluster the paths, and a weight allocation based method is used to recognize Line of Sight (LOS) path. At last, the least square algorithm is used to locate the target with AOA and LOS information of multiple APs.

2 Preliminary

2.1 MUSIC Algorithm

Considering a uniform linear array (ULA) with N antennas, d is the distance of adjacent sensor, M is the number of uncorrelated signal sources ($M < N$), θ_k is the AOA of the kth source. The sampled data vector $x(t)$ obtained at time t by ULA is:

$$x(t) = As(t) + n(t) \tag{1}$$

where A is the $N \times M$ steering matrix, $s(t)$ is the $M \times 1$ signal vector, $n(t)$ is the additive white Gaussian noise vector.

$$A = [a(\theta_1), a(\theta_2), \cdots, a(\theta_M)] \tag{2}$$

$$a(\theta_k) = \left[1, e^{2\pi d \sin \theta_k/\lambda}, \cdots, e^{2\pi(N-1)d\sin\theta_k/\lambda}\right]^T \tag{3}$$

$$s(t) = [s_1(t), \cdots, s_M(t)]^T \tag{4}$$

$$n(t) = [n_1(t), n_2(t), \cdots, n_M(t)]^T \tag{5}$$

where λ is the wavelength of signals, $a(\theta_k)$ is the steering vector of the kth propagation path.

Since the incident signals on each sensor are uncorrelated with the noise, the $N \times N$ covariance of vector $x(t)$ is:

$$
\begin{aligned}
R &= E\left[x(t)x^H(t)\right] \\
&= AE\left[s(t)s^H(t)\right]A^H + E\left[n(t)n^H(t)\right] \\
&= APA^H + \sigma^2 I
\end{aligned}
\tag{6}
$$

where I is an identity matrix and diagonal matrix $P = E[s(t)s^H(t)] \in C^{N \times N}$. Note that the rank of A is M, so is the rank of P, which is less than N, therefore:

$$
\left|APA^H\right| = 0
\tag{7}
$$

For A full rank and P positive definite, APA^H is nonnegative definite. Therefore, R is Hermitian matrix. Conducting the singular-value decomposition (SVD) of R, we have:

$$
R = U_s \Sigma_s U_s^H + U_n \Sigma_n U_n^H
\tag{8}
$$

where $U_s = [u_1, u_2, \cdots, u_M] \in C^{N \times M}$ is the matrix composed of the signal eigenvectors and $U_n = [u_{M+1}, u_{M+2}, \cdots, u_N] \in C^{N \times (N-M)}$ is the matrix composed of the noise eigenvectors. The columns of U_s and U_n span the signal subspace and its orthogonal subspace respectively. According to definitions, $span(U_s) = span(A)$ and $span(U_n) \perp span(A)$. Together with (6) and (7), we have:

$$
RU_n = \sigma^2 U_n
\tag{9}
$$

$$
RU_n = APA^H U_n + \sigma^2 U_n
\tag{10}
$$

Therefore, $APA^H U_n = 0$ and:

$$
U_n^H APA^H U_n = \left(A^H U_n\right)^H PA^H U_n = 0
\tag{11}
$$

Since P is full-rank, $A^H U_n = 0$. Using this property, the AOAs of M signals can be found as:

$$
P_{MUSIC}(\theta) = \frac{1}{a^H(\theta)U_n U_n^H a(\theta)}
\tag{12}
$$

2.2   CSI Phase Correction

Since Wi-Fi network is built based on a burst communication mechanism, each received CSI packet will introduce packet detect delay (PDD). Compared with 10 ns-level mean propagation delay, PDD is much higher [7]. As a result, the acquired CSI phase cannot be used directly. By applying linear least square fitting method, the influence of PDD can be eliminated. We can build the model of CSI phase as [11]:

$$\widehat{\varphi}(s) = \varphi(s) + 2\pi s \Delta f \delta + \beta \tag{13}$$

where $\widehat{\varphi}(s)$ and $\varphi(s)$ are the measured CSI phase and the true CSI phase of the sth subcarrier, respectively. Δf is the frequency interval between subcarriers. δ_i is the PDD of ith packet and β is the phase noise. Let $\psi_i(n, s)$ denote the unwrapped CSI phase from the ith packet at the sth subcarrier of the nth antenna, the optimal slope of unwrapped CSI phase is obtained by:

$$\widehat{\delta}_i = \arg_{\delta_i} \min \sum_{n,s=1}^{N,S} \left(\psi_i(n, s) - \widehat{\varphi}(s) \right)^2 \tag{14}$$

where N denotes the number of antennas and S denotes the number of subcarriers. Then subtract phase offset $\widehat{\delta}_i$ caused by PDD from unwrapped CSI phase and obtain modified CSI phase $\widehat{\psi}_i(n, s)$:

$$\widehat{\psi}_i(n, s) = \psi_i(n, s) - s\widehat{\delta}_i \tag{15}$$

Figure 1 indicates the phase of unwrapped CSI (left) and modified CSI (right). After CSI phase correction, the CSI phase of two consecutive packets match basically in spite of different PDDs.

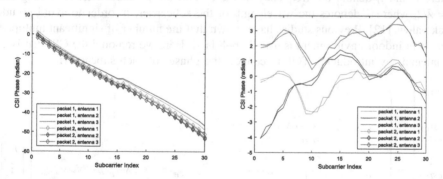

Fig. 1. Comparison of unwrapped CSI phase and modified CSI phase.

3   System Design

The workflow of the positioning system in this paper is illustrated in Fig. 2. The system estimates the AOA and TOF of multipath signals arriving at APs from the target using CSI information obtained from Wi-Fi Network Interface Cards (NICs). Then, the system identifies the most possible direct propagation path from the target to AP based

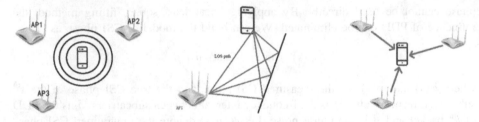

Fig. 2. Workflow of the system: First, collect CSI data from all the APs in range. Then the system estimates the AOA and TOF of all propagation paths from the target to each AP and identify the LOS path between the target and the AP. Finally, the system locates the target with AOA data of multiple APs.

on the weight of each path. Finally, by combining AOAs of all direct paths, the system estimates the target's position.

3.1 Estimating AOA and TOF

Let's denote S as the number of subcarriers of each antenna, and assume that there are L propagation paths. θ_k is the angle between the kth path and the antenna. To the Wi-Fi signal of a propagation path, the largest phase shift between subcarriers introduced by the distance between antennas can be expressed as:

$$\Delta\varphi = 2\pi \times (3-1) \times \left(f_i - f_j\right) \times d \times \sin\theta/c \tag{16}$$

where f_i and f_j denote the frequency of the ith and the jth subcarrier. Assuming that $d = \lambda/2$, where λ denotes the wavelength of the subcarrier, in order to avoid pseudo peak values [12]. Previous studies have shown that the number of significant multipath signals in indoor environment is usually 6–8 [13]. Here we remodel the CSI matrix of N antennas by introducing TOF to connect the phases of each subcarrier:

$$
\begin{bmatrix} csi_{1,1} \\ \vdots \\ csi_{1,S} \\ csi_{2,1} \\ \vdots \\ csi_{2,S} \\ \vdots \\ csi_{N,1} \\ \vdots \\ csi_{N,S} \end{bmatrix}
=
\begin{bmatrix}
1 & \cdots & 1 \\
\vdots & \ddots & \vdots \\
e^{-j2\pi\times(S-1)\Delta f\tau_1} & \cdots & e^{-j2\pi\times(S-1)\Delta f\tau_L} \\
e^{-j2\pi f_1 d\sin\theta_1/c} & \cdots & e^{-j2\pi f_1 d\sin\theta_L/c} \\
\vdots & \ddots & \vdots \\
e^{-j2\pi\times(S-1)\Delta f\tau_1}e^{-j2\pi\times f_1 d\sin\theta_1/c} & \cdots & e^{-j2\pi\times(S-1)\Delta f\tau_1}e^{-j2\pi\times f_1 d\sin\theta_L/c} \\
\vdots & \cdots & \vdots \\
e^{-j2\pi\times f_1\times(N-1)d\sin\theta_1/c} & \cdots & e^{-j2\pi\times f_1\times(N-1)d\sin\theta_L/c} \\
\vdots & \ddots & \vdots \\
e^{-j2\pi\times(S-1)\Delta f\tau_1}e^{-j2\pi\times f_1\times(N-1)d\sin\theta_1/c} & \cdots & e^{-j2\pi\times(S-1)\Delta f\tau_1}e^{-j2\pi\times f_1\times(N-1)d\sin\theta_L/c}
\end{bmatrix}
\begin{bmatrix} \beta_1 \\ \vdots \\ \beta_L \end{bmatrix}
$$

$$\tag{17}$$

where $\beta_k = \alpha_k \times e^{-j2\pi f_1\tau_k}$. We can see that the number of sensors has been expanded to $N \times S$. However, an indoor environment is usually filled with coherent signals, thus the CSI value we obtained from (17) across antennas is not independent. Therefore, the noise subspace will spread to the signal subspace, resulting in the performance degradation of the algorithm. Traditional MUSIC algorithm solves this problem at the cost of the number of antennas [9]. Different from the traditional method, we apply a two-dimensional spatial smoothing method. If we divide the two dimensional array with $N \times S$ sensors into subarrays of size $N_{sub1} \times N_{sub2}$, then the channel frequency response matrices of all subarrays are obtained. Finally we expand the number of sensors to $(N - N_{sub1} + 1) \times (S - N_{sub2} + 1)$. We can conduct two dimensional MUSIC algorithm on the smoothed CSI matrix and get estimated AOA and TOF.

Figure 3 illustrates the simulation results of AOA estimation by both traditional MUSIC algorithm and our modified MUSIC algorithm. It should be mentioned that the modified MUSIC estimator has been shown to perform better than traditional MUSIC estimator with higher precision.

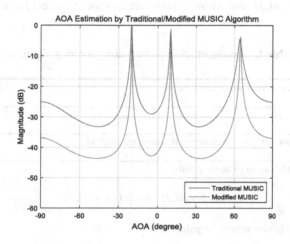

Fig. 3. Comparison between traditional MUSIC algorithm and modified MUSIC algorithm.

3.2 Identifying Direct Path

Typically, there are about 5 significant multipath signals [14]. However, in the actual situation, the number of paths that each AP receives at different times may change, and the number of fixed classes in the clustering algorithm may lead to a decrease in the positioning accuracy. The clustering method used in this paper is affine propagation clustering [15]. Compared to traditional clustering algorithms, such as K-means clustering, affine propagation clustering does not need to select the number of clusters in advance, and the number of paths can be determined adaptively. At the same time, the clustering effect will not be reduced because of the improper selection of the initial cluster center.

We normalize the data in time and angle dimensions, and let similarity $s(i, j)$ denotes the negative squared error (Euclidean distance) between extreme points as similarity:

$$s(i,j) = -\|\Omega_i - \Omega_j\|_2, \forall i, j \neq i \in \{1, 2, \cdots, N_{data}\} \tag{18}$$

where Ω_i and Ω_j are two random extreme points, N_{data} is the number of data points. After calculating the similarity of all extreme points, the similarity is stored as a $N_{data} \times N_{data}$ matrix. Similarly, let $s(k, k)$ denotes the self-similarity:

$$s(k,k) = \frac{\sum\limits_{i,j=1,i\neq j}^{N_{data}} s(i,j)}{N_{data} \times (N_{data} - 1)}, 1 \leq k \leq N_{data} \tag{19}$$

Set the input of clustering algorithm to be matrix $s(i, j)$ and $s(k, k)$. Let $r(i, j)$ and $a(i, j)$ denote the "degree of attraction" sent from i to j and the "degree of belonging" sent from j to i, $r(i, j)$ reflects the degree of suitability of extreme point j being the cluster center of i, $a(i, j)$ shows how appropriate it is for i to select j as the cluster point.

Table 1. Process of affine propagation clustering algorithm

Affine propagation clustering algorithm.
Input: random $s(i,j)$.
Parameter initiation: $a(i,j)=0$; maximum iteration number $M_{iteration}$
1. Calculate $r(i,j)$ between extreme points: $$r(i,j) = s(i,j) - \max\{a(i,j) + s(i,j)\}$$
2. Calculate $a(i,j)$ between extreme points: $$a(i,j) = \min\left\{0, r(i,j) + \sum_{i\neq i,j} \max\{0, r(i,j)\}\right\}$$
3. Calculate $a(k,k)$ of extreme points: $$a(k,k) = \sum_{i\neq j} \max\{0, r(i,j)\}$$
4. $j' = \arg\max\limits_{j\in\{1,2,\cdots,N_{data}\}}\{a(i,j) + r(i,j)\}$, if $i=j'$, select j' as the cluster center, otherwise select i as the cluster center.
5. Repeat step 1-4 until the cluster center no longer changes or reaches the maximum number of iterations.
Output: Classes of all extreme points and corresponding cluster centers.

The process of affine propagation clustering algorithm can be described in Table 1. After path clustering, the system allocates weights to different classes to identify direct path.

The likelihood of the kth propagation path being the LOS path is calculated as [16]:

$$likelihood_k = f(w_c n_k - w_\theta \sigma_{\theta_k} - w_\tau \sigma_{\tau_k} - w_s \bar{\tau}_K) \tag{20}$$

where f(·) is an increasing function, e.g. exp(·). n_k is the number of extreme points of the class representing the kth path. σ_{θ_k} and σ_{τ_k} are the variance of AOAs and TOFs of the kth class, respectively. w_c, w_θ, w_τ and w_s are corresponding weight parameters. The system selects the path with the highest likelihood as the LOS path. Figure 4 illustrates the result of affine propagation clustering. The blue squares with a black circle around them represent the LOS path. It can be seen that among the 6 propagation paths, the system identifies the path with smallest fluctuation in both AOA dimension and TOF dimension.

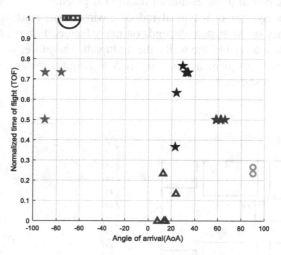

Fig. 4. Result of affine propagation clustering. (Color figure online)

3.3 Localizing the Target by Multiple APs

After obtaining the estimated values of AOA and TOF of LOS paths from multiple APs, AOA based positioning is achievable. Assuming that there are H APs, the position of the target can be estimated by least square method:

$$position = \arg \min_p \sum_{i=1}^{H} \left[\hat{\theta}(i) - \theta(i)\right]^2 \tag{21}$$

where $\hat{\theta}(i)$ and $\theta(i)$ denote the estimated and actual AOA of the ith AP, respectively.

4 Experimental Evaluation

To test the performance of the system, we implement the system using laptop with 3-antenna Intel 5300 Wi-Fi NICs as AP and a mobile phone hotspot as sender. In this paper, $N = 3$, $S = 30$, $N_{sub1} = 2$, $N_{sub2} = 15$. All experiments are conducted as follows:

1. Linux CSI Tool [17] is used to obtain CSI value for each packet.
2. The Intel 5300 NIC works under 802.11n mode and operates in 5 GHz Wi-Fi spectrum with a bandwidth of 40 MHz.
3. The AP operates in monitor mode.

In the test, a coordinate system is set up first. The distance between the test point and the AP is measured by a tape. The angles between the test points and the APs are calculated. Then, keeping the sender at the same position, a set of CSI information of one position is collected. Repeat this step and change the position of the AP, more CSI data will be obtained to establish the fingerprint database. Finally, all CSI data is processed in the server and the estimated position is given.

We deploy the system in a typical indoor environment: student dormitory. The positioning accuracy of the system depends on many factors. For example, the number of the furniture, the material of the walls, the multipath. Therefore, we choose a typical indoor environment of a square area of roughly 5×7 square meters and deploy 3 APs in this area as Fig. 5 shows.

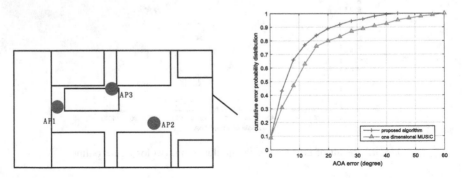

Fig. 5. The space of experimental environment (left) is about 5×7 square meters and it contains furniture, walls and other obstacles. Identify performance of different AOA estimation algorithm (right).

To test the positioning performance, we choose test positions randomly and use the laptop to obtain CSI information at selected AP position. Then, the laptop is moved to the next AP position. The method of calculating the angle estimation error is to find the extreme points closest to the real angle in the space spectrum, and to calculate the absolute value of the difference between the measured value and the actual value. Then we employ a multi-AP joint positioning algorithm to estimate the target position after identifying AOA of LOS path.

Figure 5 indicates that the proposed algorithm has a smaller range of AOA estimation error and is more robust against multipath-rich environment. Figure 6 illustrates that compared with ArrayTrack [18], the proposed algorithm has smaller maximum positioning error and higher positioning accuracy. It is observed that the median positioning error of the proposed system achieves 1.7 m under the condition of 3 APs.

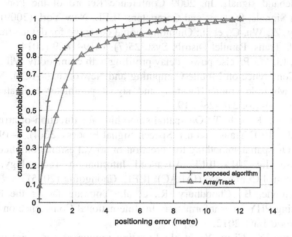

Fig. 6. Positioning performance of different algorithms.

5 Conclusion

In this paper, we design an Angle-of-Arrival positioning system based on CSI virtual antenna array using commodity Wi-Fi NICs such as Intel 5300 with three antennas. After having obtained AOA and TOF by modified MUSIC algorithm, the system employs its phase correction algorithm to eliminate PDD. Affine clustering method is applied identify LOS path. We prototype the system in typical indoor scenario. The result shows that our system achieves a meter level accuracy without any hardware and firmware modifications.

Acknowledgement. This research was supported in part by the National Natural Science Foundation of China under Grant 61801041 and the Fundamental Research Funds for the Central Universities under Grant 2018RC15.

References

1. Razavi, A., Gebre-Egziabher, D., Akos, D.M.: Carrier loop architectures for tracking weak GPS signals. IEEE Trans. Aerosp. Electron. Syst. **44**(2), 697–710 (2008)
2. Han, S., Li, Y., Meng, W., et al.: Indoor Localization with a single Wi-Fi access point based on OFDM-MIMO. IEEE Syst. J. 1–9 (2018)

3. De Angelis, G., Moschitta, A., Carbone, P.: Positioning techniques in indoor environments based on stochastic modeling of UWB round-triptime measurements. IEEE Trans. Intell. Transp. Syst. **17**(8), 2272–2281 (2016)
4. Wang, Y., Ho, K.C.: Unified near-field and far-field localization for AOA and hybrid AOA-TDOA positionings. IEEE Trans. Wirel. Commun. **2**(17), 1242–1254 (2018)
5. Pal, P., Vaidyanathan, P.P.: A novel autofocusing approach for estimating directions-of-arrival of wideband signals. In: 2009 Conference Record of the Forty-Third Asilomar Conference on Signals, Systems and Computers. IEEE, New York (2009)
6. Zhou, Z., Yang, Z., Wu, C., et al.: Omnidirectional coverage for device-free passive human detection. IEEE Trans. Parallel Distrib. Syst. **25**(7), 1819–1829 (2014)
7. Xie, Y., Li, Z., Li, M.: Precise power delay profiling with commodity WiFi. In: 21st Annual International Conference on Mobile Computing and Networking. ACM, New York (2015)
8. Schimidt, R.: Multiple emitter location and signal parameter estimation. IEEE Trans. Antennas Propag. **34**(3), 276–280 (1986)
9. Shan, T., Wax, M., Kailath, T.: On spatial smoothing for direction-of-arrival estimation of coherent signals. IEEE Trans. Acoust. Speech Signal Process. **33**(4), 8–19 (1985)
10. Li S., Lin, B.: On spatial smoothing for direction-of-arrival estimation of coherent signals in impulsive noise. In: 2015 IEEE Advanced Information Technology, Electronic and Automation Control Conference (IAEAC). IEEE, Chongqing (2015)
11. Sen, S., Radunovic, B., Choudhury, R., et al.: You are facing the Mona Lisa: spot localization using PHY layer information. In: International Conference on Mobile Systems. ACM, Low Wood Bay (2012)
12. Wang, C., Zheng, X., Chen, Y., et al.: Locating rogue access point using fine-grained channel information. IEEE Trans. Mob. Comput. **16**(9), 2560–2573 (2017)
13. Czink, N., Herdin, M., Ozcelik, H., et al.: Number of multipath clusters in indoor MIMO propagation environments. Electron. Lett. **40**(23), 1498–1499 (2004)
14. Gjengset, J., Xiong, J., Jamieson, K., et al.: Phaser: enabling phased array signal processing on commodity Wifi access points. In: International Conference on Mobile Computing & Networking. ACM, Maui (2014)
15. Frey, B., Dueck, D.: Clustering by passing messages between data points. Scinece **315**(5814), 972–976 (2007)
16. Joshi, K., Hong, S., Katti, S.: PinPoint: localizing interfering radios. In: nsdi 2013 Proceedings of the 10th USENIX Conference on Networked Systems Design and Implementation, pp. 241–254. USENIX Association, Berkeley (2013)
17. Halperin, D., Hu, W., Sheth, A., et al.: Tool release: gathering 802.11n traces with channel state information. ACM Sigcomm Comput. Commun. Rev. **41**(1), 53 (2011)
18. Jie, X., Kyle, J.: ArrayTrack: a fine-grained indoor location system. In: nsdi 2013 Proceedings of the 10th USENIX Conference on Networked Systems Design and Implementation, pp. 71–84. USENIX Association, Berkeley (2013)

Cross-Sensor Image Change Detection Based on Deep Canonically Correlated Autoencoders

Yuan Zhou[1,2(✉)], Hui Liu[1], Dan Li[1], Hai Cao[1], Jing Yang[2], and Zizi Li[2]

[1] National Ocean Technology Center, Tianjin 300072, China
zhouyuan@tju.edu.cn
[2] Tianjin University, Tianjin 300072, China

Abstract. Change detection for cross-sensor remote sensing images is an important research topic with a wide range of applications in disaster treatment, environmental monitoring and so on. It is a challenging problem as images from various acquisitions have difference in the spatial and spectral domains. Change detection models need effective feature representations to estimate interesting changes, but sometimes the hand-crafted low-level features affect the detection result. In this paper, we propose a novel cross-sensor remote sensing image change detection method based on deep canonically correlated autoencoders (DCCAE). The method extracts abstract and robust features of two multi-spectral images through two autoencoders, and then project them into a common latent space, in which any change detection models can be applied. Our experimental results on real datasets demonstrate the promising performance of the proposed network compared to several existing approaches.

Keywords: Change detection · Cross-sensor ·
Deep canonically correlated autoencoders (DCCAE)

1 Introduction

With the development of satellite technology, images shot by various sensors covering the same geographic area are available now. Accordingly, the considerable volume of remote sensing images makes it possible to study changes taking place on the surface of the earth [10]. Cross-sensor remote sensing image change detection aims to detect changes of interest between two images shot by two types of sensors of the same area graphical area at different times. It is an effective method to solve emergencies that require quickly responses, such as those natural disaster management and assessment [2,4]. Therefore, cross-sensor change detection has become an important issue for the remote sensing community [11].

There exist some works performing general cross-sensor multi-spectral change detection. Post-classification comparison (PCC) derives the classification map of each image independently and compare the maps pixel by pixel to detect changes. Object-based image analysis is considered as an ensemble approach

© ICST Institute for Computer Sciences, Social Informatics and Telecommunications Engineering 2019
Published by Springer Nature Switzerland AG 2019. All Rights Reserved
S. Han et al. (Eds.): AICON 2019, LNICST 286, pp. 251–257, 2019.
https://doi.org/10.1007/978-3-030-22968-9_22

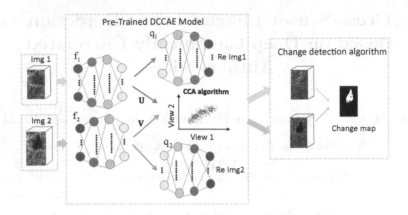

Fig. 1. Schematic diagram of DCCAE-based cross-sensor change detection.

which combines image segmentation and classification in image analysis [1]. The main advantage of object-based change detection is that the change map can avoid the error caused by noise. However, object-based methods heavily relies on the segmentation accuracy of the generations of objects. Michele et al. [7] first used kernel canonical correlation analysis (KCCA)[3] to learn nonlinear spectral feature transformations to enhance the accuracy of the change detection. Yang [9] uses a DNN extension of canonical correlation analysis termed DCCA to perform the spectral alignment. Other methods such as manifold learning and Bayesian nonparametric model are studied on the cross-sensor remote sensing image change detection. However, these methods only learn the low-level hand-crafted features of the images, which may affect the change detection accuracy and limit the applications.

In this paper, we propose a novel cross-sensor remote sensing image change detection method based on deep canonically correlated autoencoders (DCCAE). The method learns abstract and high-level features by exploiting a set of pixel samples belonging to the unchanged areas to train the DCCAE network. Feature transformation is made simultaneously from both sides of the network by maximizing the canonical correlation analysis function and minimizing the reconstruction errors. The two cross-sensor images are projected into a common latent space. In the space, any change detection models such as change vector analysis (CVA) can be used. As far as we know, this is the first time that DCCAE models has been successfully applied for cross-sensor remote sensing image change detection.

2   DCCAE-Based Cross-Sensor Change Detection Method

The framework of the proposed DCCAE-based method, as shown in Fig. 1, is made up of two stages, including joint transformation of spectral domains and change detection methods.

Let X and Y represent a pair of coregistered images acquired by two types of sensors. Here, we assume the images are coregistered geometrically. We select N unchanged pixels corresponding to each position from both images as the training set. Let $\mathbf{X} = [x_1, x_2, ..., x_N] \in \mathbb{R}^{N \times D_x}$ and $\mathbf{Y} = [y_1, y_2, ..., y_N] \in \mathbb{R}^{N \times D_y}$ be the training data matrices, where D_x and D_y represent the spectral dimension of each image, respectively.

DCCAE proposed by Wang et al. [8] is a model consisting of two autoencoders and the CCA algorithm. The encoder network f_1, f_2 and the corresponding decoder network q_1, q_2 are trained to minimize reconstruction errors, which amounts to maximizing the distribution characteristics of the input images [5]. Meanwhile, we project the features to a common latent space by CCA. Projection matrices $\mathbf{U}$ and $\mathbf{V}$ are determined by maximizing the correlation between the learning bottleneck representations $f_1(\mathbf{X}, \theta_1)$ and $f_2(\mathbf{Y}, \theta_2)$, as indicated in Fig. 1. $\{\theta_1, \theta_2\}$ indicate parameters of encoder network and $\{\theta_3, \theta_4\}$ indicate the corresponding parameters of decoder network. The distance between paired feature vectors transformed from unchanged positions is shrunk, and the distance between paired feature vectors transformed from changed positions is enlarged. Mathematically, the DCCAE model optimizes the combination of canonical correlation and the reconstruction errors of the autoencoders:

$$
\underset{\theta_1, \theta_2, \theta_3, \theta_4, \mathbf{U}, \mathbf{V}}{\arg\min} \quad -\frac{1}{N} \text{tr}(\mathbf{U}^T f_1(\mathbf{X}) f_2(\mathbf{Y})^T \mathbf{V})
$$

$$
+ \frac{\lambda}{N} \sum_{i=1}^{N} (||x_i - q_1(f_1(x_i))||^2 + ||y_i - q_2(f_2(y_i))||^2)
$$

$$
s.t. \ \mathbf{U}^T (\frac{1}{N} f_1(\mathbf{X})^T f_1(\mathbf{X}) + r_1 \mathbf{I}) \mathbf{U} = \mathbf{I},
$$

$$
\mathbf{V}^T (\frac{1}{N} f_2(\mathbf{Y})^T f_2(\mathbf{Y}) + r_2 \mathbf{I}) \mathbf{V} = \mathbf{I},
$$

$$
\mathbf{u}_i^T f_1(\mathbf{X}) f_2(\mathbf{Y})^T \mathbf{v}_j = 0, \ \text{for } i \neq j,
$$

(1)

where $\mathbf{U} \in \mathbb{R}^{d_1 \times l}$ and $\mathbf{V} \in \mathbb{R}^{d_2 \times l}$ are the projection matrices, l is the number of projection vectors. λ is a weight that trades off the correlation with reconstruction errors. We use SGD for optimization. The gradient of the DCCAE model is the sum of the gradient for CCA term and the gradient for reconstruction term.

3   Experiments and Results

To validate the effectiveness of the proposed method, it is compared with three methods (CCA [7], KCCA [6] and DCCA [9]).

3.1   Dataset

The performance of the proposed method is evaluated on the Bastrop country complex fire datasets, which is made up four images acquired by three types of

Fig. 2. The Bastrop country complex fire datasets. (a) T1 image (landsat 5, Aug.2011) (b) T2 image (landsat 5, Sep.2011) (c) T2 image (EO-1 ALI, Sep.2011) (d) T2 image (Landsat 8, June.2013).

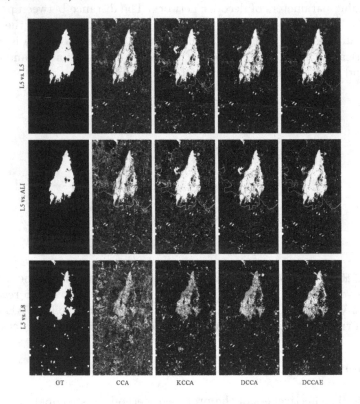

Fig. 3. The ground truth map and change maps generated by the four methods.

sensors. The main cause of surface changes was the fire on September 4, 2011. Figure 2 shows the specific information of the datasets. The size of all the images are 1534×808 pixels with different spectrum channels.

3.2   Experimental Settings

(1) Training Set: To study the impact of samples on the results, the number of training samples N is selected from $\{50, 100, 250, 500, 1000\}$. For fair comparison, the same samples are used for the four methods.

(2) DCCAE Network: The networks f_1, f_2 are built with 3 hidden layers, each of 100 sigmoid units, and an output layer for linear CCA with 7 units. The networks q_1, q_2 are implemented by 3 hidden layers, each of 100 sigmoid units, and an output layer with the same units as the width of input dataset. In the training procedure, the hyper-parameter of DCCAE model with SGD optimization is set as follows: the learning rate is 0.001 and momentum is 0.99, respectively.

(3) Change Detection Algorithm: We use the change vector analysis (CVA) as the change detection algorithm. We randomly selected 40 validation pixels from the changed or unchanged areas to tune the threshold of each binary CVA model in a supervised wayin order to select a proper threshold.

Table 1. OA (standard deviation) comparison of change detection methods.

	CCA-based	KCCA-based	DCCA-based	DCCAE-based
L5 vs. *L5*				
50	84.1(6.3)	91.2(4.7)	90.7(3.8)	**93.4(2.1)**
100	86.2(3.6)	88.9(6.5)	91.6(3.2)	**94.3(1.7)**
250	82.9(7.7)	90.7(3.1)	93.2(1.7)	**93.7(2.9)**
500	85.2(4.3)	90.9(3.1)	93.6(4.2)	**94.4(1.6)**
1000	87.2(3.6)	92.6(3.0)	95.6(1.1)	**96.6(1.8)**
L5 vs. *ALI*				
50	80.0(7.0)	90.2(4.3)	89.4(4.5)	89.9(3.8)
100	78.4(4.8)	91.5(2.2)	92.2(2.6)	**92.9(2.7)**
250	80.0(3.3)	91.2(2.3)	92.6(3.4)	**93.5(2.9)**
500	81.2(5.8)	90.3(4.0)	93.4(2.8)	**94.3(2.4)**
1000	79.3(5.6)	89.8(2.3)	94.6(1.6)	**95.7(2.3)**
L5 vs. *L8*				
50	75.0(3.2)	86.9(5.0)	81.1(7.1)	84.5(3.3)
100	76.8(3.0)	88.5(4.3)	85.9(4.8)	**88.9(2.7)**
250	77.2(3.1)	88.9(3.7)	90.2(1.4)	**90.6(2.8)**
500	76.2(1.9)	91.3(1.7)	92.3(1.1)	**92.9(1.5)**
1000	77.1(3.0)	91.7(1.2)	93.9(2.2)	**94.3(1.2)**

3.3   Evaluation Results

Table 1 presents the OAs of all competitors and the proposed method under different number of training sets. When the number reaches 100, DCCAE-based method can get more accurate change detection results. Figure 3 lists the change detection results of the Bastrop datasets obtained by the CVA algorithm after the projection of the datasets by CCA, KCCA, DCCA and DCCAE. As can be seen, for the L5T1 vs. L5T2 experiment, the proposed DCCAE-based change maps can detect correct burned area effectively. For the L5T1 vs. ALIT2 experiment, DCCAE-based change map shows the least additional other changes. Other change maps include more small water basins. For the L5T1 vs. L5T8 experiment, DCCAE-based change maps miss less internal pixels than other maps.

4   Conclusion

In this paper, we propose a novel change detection method based on deep canonically correlated autoencoders (DCCAE) for cross-sensor change detection. Our experimental results show that the proposed method significantly can effectively detect the interesting changes. Considering the practical application scenarios, future work should address the cross-sensor change detection task in an unsupervised way.

References

1. Gong, M., Zhan, T., Zhang, P., Miao, Q.: Superpixel-based difference representation learning for change detection in multispectral remote sensing images. IEEE Trans. Geosci. Remote Sens. **55**(5), 2658–2673 (2017)
2. Gueguen, L., Hamid, R.: Toward a generalizable image representation for large-scale change detection: application to generic damage analysis. IEEE Trans. Geosci. Remote Sens. **54**(6), 3378–3387 (2016)
3. Lai, P.L., Fyfe, C.: Kernel and nonlinear canonical correlation analysis. Int. J. Neural Syst. **10**(05), 365–377 (2000)
4. Roemer, H., Kaiser, G., Sterr, H., Ludwig, R.: Using remote sensing to assess tsunami-induced impacts on coastal forest ecosystems at the andaman sea coast of thailand. Nat. Hazards Earth Syst. Sci. **10**(4), 729 (2010)
5. Vincent, P., Larochelle, H., Lajoie, I., Bengio, Y., Manzagol, P.A.: Stacked denoising autoencoders: learning useful representations in a deep network with a local denoising criterion. J. Mach. Learn. Res. **11**(Dec), 3371–3408 (2010)
6. Volpi, M., Camps-Valls, G., Tuia, D.: Spectral alignment of multi-temporal cross-sensor images with automated kernel canonical correlation analysis. ISPRS J. Photogramm. Remote. Sens. **107**, 50–63 (2015)
7. Volpi, M., de Morsier, F., Camps-Valls, G., Kanevski, M., Tuia, D.: Multi-sensor change detection based on nonlinear canonical correlations. In: 2013 IEEE International Geoscience and Remote Sensing Symposium (IGARSS), pp. 1944–1947. IEEE (2013)

8. Wang, W., Arora, R., Livescu, K., Bilmes, J.: On deep multi-view representation learning: objectives and optimization. arXiv preprint arXiv:1602.01024 (2016)
9. Yang, J., Zhou, Y., Cao, Y., Feng, L.: Heterogeneous image change detection using deep canonical correlation analysis. In: 2018 24th International Conference on Pattern Recognition (ICPR), pp. 2917–2922. IEEE (2018)
10. Zhang, Z., Vosselman, G., Gerke, M., Tuia, D., Yang, M.Y.: Change detection between multimodal remote sensing data using siamese CNN. arXiv preprint arXiv:1807.09562 (2018)
11. Zhao, W., Wang, Z., Gong, M., Liu, J.: Discriminative feature learning for unsupervised change detection in heterogeneous images based on a coupled neural network. IEEE Trans. Geosci. Remote Sens. **55**(12), 7066–7080 (2017)

An Innovative Weighted KNN Indoor Location Technology

Lu Huang[1,2(✉)], Xingli Gan[1,2], Dan Du[3], Boyuan Wang[1,2],
and Shuang Li[1,2]

[1] The 54th Research Institute of China Electronics Technology Group
Corporation, Shijiazhuang 050081, Hebei, China
18642720668@163.com
[2] State Key Laboratory of Satellite Navigation System and Equipment
Technology, Shijiazhuang 050081, Hebei, China
[3] Pla Army Equipment Department, Shijiazhuang 050081, Hebei, China

Abstract. Aiming at the problem of large fluctuation and low precision of the positioning method based on wireless fingerprint matching, we proposed an improved weighted K nearest neighbor algorithm and compared it with the commonly used machine learning algorithm. At the same time, we designed an innovative fingerprint database construction method and a new matching strategy. We used the particle filter algorithm to realize the fusion of the fingerprint matching localization algorithm and the pedestrian dead reckoning (PDR) algorithm, and eliminated the outliers, thus improving the positioning accuracy. The experimental results show that the average positioning accuracy after fusion is 0.512 m, and the positioning error within 1 m is 93.88%. It satisfies the accuracy requirements of indoor positioning and also verifies the effectiveness of the algorithm.

Keywords: Indoor position · Machine learning · Wireless fingerprint ·
Particle filter

1 Introduction

According to statistics in recent years, 80%–90% of people's lives are in indoor environments, including shopping malls, airports, libraries, and university campuses. At the same time, 70% of mobile phones and 80% of cellular data are transmitted from indoors [1–3]. These have led to a strong interest in indoor positioning based on location-based services and location awareness. In order to make these applications widely accepted, indoor positioning requires an accurate and reliable position estimation scheme. People use the global satellite navigation system outdoors, but indoors, GPS signals can't get accurate positioning results due to factors such as being blocked by buildings, which leads people to spend a lot of time and effort to get into the strange

This research was supported by the project "Indoor hybrid intelligent positioning and indoor GIS technology", which is part to State's Key Project and Development Plan of China, Contract No. 2016YFB0502100 and 2016YFB0502102.

S. Han et al. (Eds.): AICON 2019, LNICST 286, pp. 258–269, 2019.
https://doi.org/10.1007/978-3-030-22968-9_23

environment. The environment greatly reduces the efficiency and even brings about various potential dangers in a special environment.

Due to the complexity of the indoor environment, there are multiple types of interference that make it difficult to obtain accurate positioning results based on traditional methods of arrival time and angle of arrival. Although wireless networks are widely found in indoor environments, the indoor environment is time-varying. Changes in the location of the wireless signal source, the movement of the building, etc. [4–6] will have an impact on the positioning results, and the algorithm based on fingerprint matching can hardly be popularized and used. To solve the above problems, this paper proposes an indoor positioning solution that uses the MEMS sensor in the smart terminal to implement the pedestrian dead reckoning algorithm and uses map information to constrain the calculation results to improve the positioning accuracy [7]. Pedestrian dead reckoning is an equation based on the gait characteristics of pedestrian walking. We use inexpensive self-contained sensors to calculate the relative displacement of pedestrians [8–11]. Figure 1 is the schematic diagram of the pedestrian dead reckoning. The accelerometer's measured values are used to detect the number of steps, and the gyroscopes and magnetometers are used to detect the direction when detecting. When the pedestrian walks one step, the step length and direction of travel estimation algorithm starts to run and the step length in the step and the travel direction are estimated. The position of the pedestrian can be updated according to Eq. 1 [12].

$$\begin{cases} x_{i+1} = x_i + L_i \times cos\theta_i \\ y_{i+1} = y_i + L_i \times sin\theta_i \end{cases} \tag{1}$$

where x_i is the east-west coordinate of the pedestrian in the coordinate system in step i, and y_i is the north-south coordinate of the pedestrian in the coordinate system in step i.

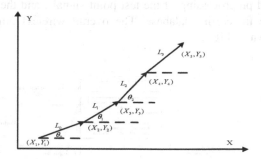

Fig. 1. Schematic diagram of the PDR algorithm

2   Improvement of Wireless Fingerprint Location Algorithm

2.1   Traditional Weighted KNN Algorithm

In the exploration and development of indoor positioning technology, wireless fingerprint matching is the most widely used, most mature and easiest to promote the use of fixed technology. At present, major shopping malls, airports, museums and other large venues have covered wireless networks, these wireless signals can be used to determine the location of pedestrians in the environment and achieve indoor positioning [12–14].

Fingerprint matching technology, also known as scene analysis, is a positioning method based on matching ideas. Through the matching of scene information received in real time in a scene and the information in the fingerprint database, the optimal estimate is obtained. In an indoor environment, especially a large-scale building, radio waves transmit propagation loss, reflection, refraction, diffraction, and multipath propagation during transmission, and a part of energy is absorbed each time the obstacle is touched. Although the indoor environment is complex, the pattern remains basically the same, and the facilities will hardly be moved too much. Therefore, as long as the source does not change, the characteristics of wireless signals formed at a specific location will show a higher degree of particularity [15]. If the feature is correlated with the coordinates of the position, the signal feature can represent the position of the point, which is a necessary condition for the establishment of the position fingerprinting technology.

The WLAN wireless positioning system mainly includes a networking phase, an offline phase, and an online phase. The networking stage includes the establishment of an indoor propagation model and the layout of the AP. The off-line phase includes fingerprint acquisition and database preprocessing. The on-line phase includes the real-time acquisition and preprocessing of the test point signals, and the positioning algorithm matching the fingerprint database. The overall wireless fingerprint matching block diagram shown in Fig. 2.

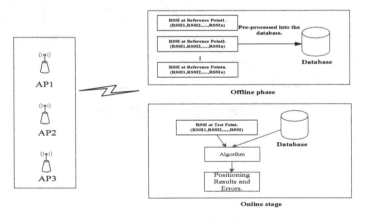

Fig. 2.   Schematic diagram of fingerprint matching

Although the wireless fingerprint matching technology has been used in indoor positioning early, but the accuracy is still far from enough, so this paper proposes an improved weighted K-nearest neighbor algorithm for fingerprint database location, and proposes a new fingerprint construction mode.

Wi-Fi networks exist in almost any building in real life, which allows people to distinguish different locations based on received Wi-Fi signal strength values from various routers. Positioning system based on location fingerprint database usually includes two stages: offline sampling phase and online testing phase [8, 17, 18].

In the off-line sampling phase, unique features of AP hotspots are utilized. Each AP hotspot has its own identifier *BSSID*, and the signal strength value *rssi* received at a known location will be weaker and weaker as the distance increases. Within 10 m, we can still obtain the signal strength value of each AP hotspot broadcast, record the signal strength value RSSI from m different APs at the sampling point, and construct the Wi-Fi fingerprint map radio map, n reference points. The storage structure is as follows:

$$(q_i, r_i) \quad i = 1, 2, \ldots, n$$

Where $q_i = (x_i, y_i)$ q_i is the geographic coordinate of the i position and $r_i = (r_{i1}, r_{i2}, \ldots, r_{im})$ is the signal strength value received from m APs at position i.

In the online measurement phase, the fingerprint information received is collected and recorded at the point to be located, and the location map is calculated using the location estimation algorithm combined with the radio map constructed in the off-line stage as the result of Wi-Fi single-point positioning [19].

This paper uses the improved weighted KNN algorithm to solve the Wi-Fi position. The traditional weighted KNN algorithm first computes the Euclidean distances of the signal strength values of n reference points and positioning points, and then increments the arrangement distance d, and takes the first k values and their coordinates to calculate the coordinates of the positioning point by using Formula as follows:

(1) Find k nearest reference points in radio map

Input: $(q_1, r_1), (q_2, r_2), \ldots, (q_n, r_n)$ of n the reference point, RSSI of the unknown point is r.

Output: k nearest reference points.

Step: Calculate the Euclidean distance between *rssi* and n reference points *rssi* of the unknown point by the formula, and arrange them in ascending order, returning to the first k positions $(q_1, r_1), (q_2, r_2), \ldots, (q_k, r_k)$.

(2) Calculate the coordinates of the current point to be positioned

Input: The information of the nearest neighbor k reference points, including the position coordinates and signal strength values r of each AP received at the position.

Output: The coordinates of the point to be positioned.

Step: Use the formula to calculate the position coordinates

$$q = \sum_{j=1}^{k} \frac{w_j q_j}{\sum_{l=1}^{k} w_l} \tag{2}$$

All weights here are non-negative

$$w_j = d_{(r_i,r)}^{-1}$$

d is the Euclidean distance between the signal strength values and the coordinates of the third position.

The weighted K nearest neighbor algorithm has an adjustment parameter k, which is used to control the calculated position coordinates. When k is equal to 1, the algorithm is equivalent to finding a position coordinate in a list. When the value of k is large, the calculation is performed. The position coordinates are estimated to be near these reference points. Taking into account some of the real factors [20]:

(1) The jittered received signal strength results in a large difference in signal strength at the same location;

(2) AP reliability problem, all APs should be available for a long time or newly added APs will not affect the stability of the system.

(3) The user's body is oriented, and the moisture in the human body will seriously affect the signal strength value received by the user.

2.2   Improved Weighted K Nearest Neighbor Algorithm

The transmission of wireless signals in space will be interfered with by various factors such as buildings, people, and electromagnetic fields. These interferences will cause RSSI obtained by us to be inaccurate and affect the positioning results. Therefore, in response to the various issues raised in the previous section, this paper proposes a series of solutions. First, the maximum value, minimum value, and average value of each AP during a period of time are collected while data is collected in an offline training stage. Moving around within 1 square meter of the sampling point, the body is collecting information in different directions for 30–40 s, and the data file name is set to the position coordinates of the sampling point. In the online phase, new APs are incrementally added and stored in an offline sampling format. The fingerprint information database is updated in real time to enhance the stability of the positioning system. We know that the most important influence on the positioning algorithm is the calculation of weights. The traditional weighted K-nearest neighbor algorithm only uses the Euclidean distance of the signal strength value as the weight, but due to the instability of the signal strength value, the wrong weight distribution will result. As a result, the positioning error increases, so in order to solve this problem.

This paper proposes a new method to optimize the weights, to some extent solve the error caused by the path loss, the specific implementation steps are as follows:

(1) In the off-line sampling phase, in order to solve the indistinguishable problem of searching for the intensity values of many AP hotspots in a fixed area, We used the maximum and minimum values of *BSSID* and *rssi*, and average sampling over a fixed period of time. A radio map we select a number of locations within the building as a sampling reference point, the database storage format: (*BSSID rssi_max rssi_min rssi_mean*).

(2) During the online measurement phase, after using the KNN algorithm to calculate the k nearest neighbor reference points, the concept of the matching ratio is introduced when the weights are assigned, that is, the fingerprint database and the fingerprint of the point to be positioned are respectively determined. The matching degree of the information is calculated by programming to calculate the matching rate of the k position points. The program pseudo code is as follows.

Algorithm: Improved partial pseudocode

```
1 for(ArrayList<Info> table:Table){
2    for(Data d:dtable){
3    for(Info i:table){
4    if(i.getBSSID().equals(d.getBSSID())){
5    if(d.getLevel()<i.getHighestlevel()&&d.getLevel()>i.getLowestlevel()){
6       result[Table.indexOf(table)]++;
7    }
8    }
9 r[Table.indexOf(table)]=((float)result[Table.indexOf(table)]/ (float)table.size())*100;
10 }
```

---

3   WIFI and PDR Integration Scenario

This paper introduces a particle filter algorithm to fuse the improved KNN algorithm with the PDR algorithm. We use the fingerprint matching positioning result as the observation value, and use the PDR algorithm to set the moving direction and the moving step size of the particle, thereby improving the particle renewal speed and positioning accuracy. The positioning algorithm is as follows:

Algorithm: Particle filter fusion

---

1 for each detected step do

2 $k = k + 1$;

3 Prediction-Proposal sampling

4 for each particle i do

5   $l^{(i)} \leftarrow U(a, b)$;

6   $\theta^{(i)} \leftarrow N(\theta_{k-1}, \sigma_\theta)$; // σ_θ the standard deviation of the heading Angle.

7   $step = \begin{bmatrix} \cos(\theta^{(i)}) \\ \sin(\theta^{(i)}) \end{bmatrix} l^{(i)}$;

8   $^{(i)}p_k^n = {}^{(i)}p_{k-1}^n + {}^{(i)}step$;

9 end for

10 $\theta_k \leftarrow \theta_{current}$

Update weights and resampling

   // Initialization:

   $s_0^i \sim p(s_0)$ the apriori distribution

   $\{w_o^i\}_{i=1}^{N_s} = \dfrac{1}{N_s}$, a uniform distribution

11 prediction and Update:

12 $x_k^i \sim q(x_k \mid x_{0:k-1}, z_{1:k})$

13 $w_k^i \propto \dfrac{p(z_k|s_k)p(s_k|s_{k-1})}{q(s_k^i|s_{0:k-1}^i, z_{1:k})} w_{k-1}^i$

The basic algorithm suffers from degeneration; the weights series $w_{k(i=1)}^{i\,(N_s)}$ converges towards a single non-zero value as k increases. The solution is Resampling. We define

14 $N_{s,eff} = \dfrac{1}{\sum_i^{N_s}(w_k^i)^2}$

An effective number of non zero-probability particles. Once a certain threshold is crossed;

   1) Extract a new grid of N_s terms whose weights are higher than a certain threshold.

Of course, some of the new particles appear more than once in the new grid

   2) Assign the new grid/particles series a uniform weight;

15 $\{w_k^i\}_{i=1}^{N_s} = \dfrac{1}{N_s}$

If $N_{s,eff} < N_{th}$ Resample. Else go to 12.

The weight center of all particles is compared with the previous estimated position. In the weight update phase, the position of each particle is compared with that of the previous time, and the weight of the step is too large to reset zero.

4 Experiment and Result Analysis

The test environment size is 20 m × 82 m, as shown in Fig. 3. Four APs are deployed in the scenario, calibrate the reference point position. The reference point spacing is 1 m. The black circle in the figure is the selected reference point. Two different paths were selected for experimentation and 154 reference points were collected.

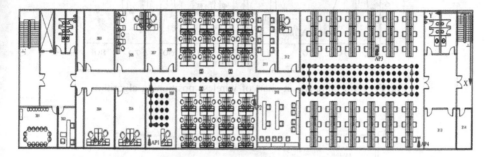

Fig. 3. Diagram of test environment

The position coordinates are used as file names and the contents include the maximum, minimum, and average values of the physical address and signal strength values. The storage format is shown in Fig. 4:

```
556 541 ⅜
08:10:79:76:48:b1    -87 -93  -88
1a:97:ff:03:63:33    -82 -87  -85
14:cf:92:b0:1f:b7    -51 -69  -60
ee:df:3a:45:57:0c    -59 -79  -68
5a:08:6c:82:00:aa    -27 -43  -33
10:2a:b3:79:f2:b6    -49 -63  -55
ec:26:ca:2f:dc:a0    -90 -90  -90
```

Fig. 4. Fingerprint library storage format

In the off-line acquisition phase, the experimenter collects the signal strength values in four directions at each reference point. The duration is about 10 s. The collected information is sent to the server for fingerprint library construction and distributed to each terminal. In the online positioning stage, the user holds the smart terminal, selects a different positioning algorithm to walk on each path, and stores the localized position coordinates in the memory card. In order to verify the validity of the algorithm, the experiment is repeated many times. The experimental results are shown in the Fig. 5 below.

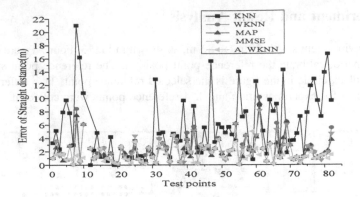

Fig. 5. Error comparison chart of wireless positioning algorithm

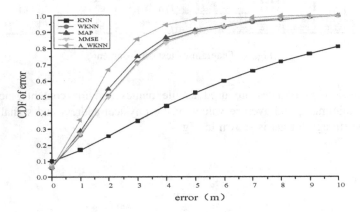

Fig. 6. CDF of wireless positioning algorithm error

From the above Fig. 6, we can see that the traditional KNN algorithm has large fluctuations in positioning error. The traditional WKNN algorithm assigns the weighting error of the fingerprint information assignment of K = 3 reference points to be relatively stable. When the signal intensity value fluctuates, the weight distribution will be inaccurate. The positioning error is still large. The MAP and MMSE localization algorithms based on probability statistical distribution are slightly better than the WKNN algorithm. The improved WKNN algorithm proposed in this paper will assign better weights to different locations, making the overall error stable, and the average error has been improved. The results are shown in the following table. Table 1 is a comparative analysis of five different wireless positioning methods. The comparison data in the table are data collected after many real experiments to ensure the reliability and universality of the data. Experiments verify the effectiveness of the algorithm.

From Table 1, we can see the significant difference in positioning accuracy between the traditional wireless positioning algorithm and the positioning algorithm proposed in this paper. The two deterministic positioning algorithms, KNN and WKNN, have large

Table 1. Comparing the results of different location way.

Compare items	KNN	WKNN	MAP	MMSE	A_WKNN
Maximum error (m)	21.11	9.15	8.71	8.90	7.55
Minimum error (m)	1.58	0.22	0.32	0.30	0.25
Average error (m)	5.90	2.35	2.33	2.19	1.66
Accuracy within 3 m	37.0%	71.6%	68.8%	69.9%	85.6%
Accuracy within 5 m	52.9%	90.7%	89.7%	90.1%	98.7%

fluctuations in error and the average positioning error is 5.90 m and 2.35 m respectively, positioning accuracy within 5 m respectively reached 52.9% and 90.7%. The average positioning errors of the two probabilistic positioning algorithms MAP and MMSE are 2.33 m and 2.19 m, respectively, and the confidence probability that the positioning error is better than 5 m is 89.7% and 90.1%, respectively. The improved averaged positioning error of the weighted KNN algorithm proposed in this paper is 1.66 m, and the confidence probability of 5 m is 98.7%. Compared with the previous algorithms, the average positioning accuracy reaches the expected positioning effect.

In order to further improve the positioning accuracy and stability, this paper uses particle filter algorithm to fuse the improved wireless fingerprint positioning results with PDR, and establishes a stable positioning system. The experimental results are shown in the figure below.

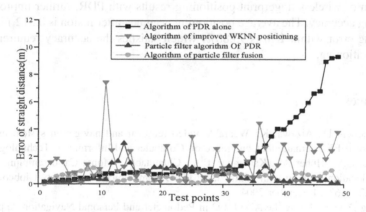

Fig. 7. Comparison chart of positioning error

From Figs. 7 and 8, it can be seen that the traditional PDR positioning algorithm is stable in the early stage of positioning and the error is small. As the cumulative error increases, the error starts to diverge, the average error is 2.1 m, and the positioning accuracy within the error within 1 m is 55.1%. The average position error of the improved wireless fingerprint positioning algorithm is 1.64 m, and the positioning accuracy of the error within 1 m is 40.82%. The average positioning error of the particle filter fusion Wi-Fi and PDR positioning is 0.512 m, and the positioning accuracy of the error within 1 m is 93.88%.

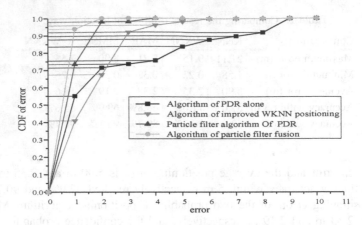

Fig. 8. Error cumulative distribution function of error

5   Conclusion

This paper proposes an improved weighted KNN algorithm aiming at the problems of large fluctuation and low precision in positioning algorithm based on wireless signal fingerprint matching. The experimental comparison is made and the positioning error is significantly improved. Then the particle filter algorithm was introduced to achieve the integration of wireless fingerprint positioning results with PDR, further improving the positioning accuracy. The average positioning accuracy after fusion is 0.512 m, and the positioning error within 1 m is 93.88%, which satisfies the accuracy requirements of indoor positioning.

References

1. Tancharoen, D., Aizawa, K.: Wearable video retrieval and navigation system using GPS data. In: IEEE International Conference on Computer and Information Technology (2010)
2. Záruba, G.V., Huber, M., Kamangar, F.A., Chlamtac, I.: Monte Carlo sampling based in-home location tracking with minimal. In: IEEE Communications Society Globcom, vol. 6, pp. 3624–3629, December 2004
3. Analog Devices: Using the ADXL202 in Pedometer and Personal Navigation Applications. Application Note AN602, Analog Devices
4. Bahl, P., Padmanabhan, V.N.: RADAR: an in-building RF-based user location and tracking system. Microsoft Research (2000)
5. Ma, J., Li, X., Tao, X., Lu, J.: Cluster filtered KNN: a WLAN-based indoor positioning scheme. In: International Symposium on a World of Wireless, Mobile and Multimedia Networks, pp. 1–8, June 2008
6. Youssef, M.A., Agrawala, A., Shankar, A.U.: WLAN location determination via clustering and probability distributions. In: IEEE International Conference on Pervasive Computing and Communications, pp. 143–150, March 2003

7. Saha, S., Chaudhuri, K., Sanghi, D., Bhagwat, P.: Location determination of a mobile device using IEEE 802.11b access point signals. In: Proceedings of IEEE WCNC, New Orleans, Louisiana, USA, March 2003

8. Prasithsangaree, P., Krishnamurthy, P., Chrysanthis, P.K.: On indoor position location with wireless LANs. In: Proceedings of IEEE PIMRC, Lisbon, Portugal, September 2002

9. Jimenez, A., Seco, F., Prieto, C., Guevara, J.: A comparison of pedestrian dead-reckoning algorithms using a low-cost MEMS IMU. In: IEEE International Symposium on Intelligent Signal Processing, pp. 37–42 (2009)

10. Azizyan, M., Constandache, L., Choudhury, R.R.: SurroundSense: mobile phone localization via ambience fingerprinting. In: Proceedings of 15th ACM MobiCom, pp. 261–272 (2009)

11. Rallapalli, S., Qiu, L., Zhang, Y., Chen, Y.-C.: Exploiting temporal stability and low-rank structure for localization in mobile networks. In: Proceedings of 16th ACM MOBICOM, pp. 161–172 (2010)

12. Steinhoff, U., Schiele, B.: Dead reckoning from the pocket. In: Proceedings of 8th IEEE PerCom, pp. 162–170 (2010)

13. Saeidi, C., Fard, A., Hodjatkashani, F.: Full three-dimensional radio wave propagation prediction model. IEEE Trans. Antennas Propag. 60(5), 2462–2471 (2012)

14. Singh, J.M., Narayanan, P.J.: Real-time ray tracing of implicit surfaces on the GPU. IEEE Trans. Vis. Comput. Graph. 16(2), 261–272 (2010)

15. Ahmed, I., Orfali, S., Khattab, T., et al.: Characterization of the indoor-outdoor radio propagation channel at 2.4 GHz. In: GCC Conference and Exhibition, pp. 605–608 (2011)

16. Wang, Y., Liu, W., Zhu, H.: Experimental study on indoor channel model for wireless sensor networks and internet of things. In: IEEE International Conference on ICCT, pp. 624–627 (2010)

17. Liu, K., Liu, X., Li, X.: Guoguo: enabling ne-grained indoor localization via smartphone. In: Proceedings of ACM MobiSys 2013, Taipei, Taiwan, pp. 32–43, June 2013

18. Xiao, J., Wu, K., Yi, Y., Ni, L.: FIFS: fine-grained indoor fingerprinting system. In: Proceedings of IEEE ICCCN 2012, pp. 1–7, August 2012

19. Fadib, F., Katabi, D.: Seeing through walls using WiFi!. In: Proceedings of ACM NSDI 2013, Lombard, IL, April 2013, pp. 75–86 (2013)

20. Liu, H.: Push the limit of WiFi based localization for smartphones. In: Proceedings of ACM Mobicom 2012, Istanbul, Turkey, August 2012, pp. 305–316 (2012)

A Resistance Frequency Offset Synchronization Scheme Based on the Zadoff-Chu Conjugate Sequence

Cong Ma[1,2], Xuejun Sha[1(✉)], Yong Li[2], and Xu Lin[1]

[1] Harbin Institute of Technology, Harbin 150001, Heilongjiang, China
shaxuejun@hit.edu.cn
[2] The 54th Research Institute of China Electronics Technology Group Corporation,
Shijiazhuang, China

Abstract. Zadoff-Chu (ZC) sequences have been used as synchronization sequences in many wireless communication systems because of their perfect correlation properties. However, almost all of these ideal characteristics are based on the assumption of zero carrier frequency offset (CFO). Under large frequency offset circumstances, the perfect autocorrelation property of ZC sequence is destroyed, where the main correlation peak is decreasing while the vice peak is increasing, consequently degrading the timing performance. In this paper, the autocorrelation of the ZC sequence and its conjugate sequence are investigated, and the symmetry between the modulus values of their autocorrelation functions is developed as well. Taking advantage of this symmetry, a novel training sequence composed of ZC sequence and ZC conjugate sequence is proposed. Also proposed is a corresponding synchronization scheme enabling robust timing synchronization based on the ZC sequence and ZC conjugate sequence at the receiver in the presence of large CFO.

Keywords: Zadoff-Chu sequences · Resistance frequency offset · Synchronization method

1 Introduction

In 4G systems, ZC sequences are used as the downlink primary synchronization signals (PSSs) [1,2] by means of replacing the PN sequences which are used in 2G and 3G systems. From a mathematical point of view, ZC sequences indeed have perfect autocorrelation properties [3], but almost all of these characteristics are based on the assumption of zero carrier frequency offset (CFO). However, for a practical wireless communication system, the frequency offset is almost

This work is supported partially by the fund of Science and Technology on Communication Networks Laboratory under grand (No. SXX18641X027) and the National Natural Science Foundation General Program of China (No.61671179).

© ICST Institute for Computer Sciences, Social Informatics and Telecommunications Engineering 2019
Published by Springer Nature Switzerland AG 2019. All Rights Reserved
S. Han et al. (Eds.): AICON 2019, LNICST 286, pp. 270–276, 2019.
https://doi.org/10.1007/978-3-030-22968-9_24

unevitable because of the mismatch between the transmitter and receiver oscillators as well as the impact of Doppler shift [4]. In the cases where the CFO is small, ZC sequence can overcome the effect of CFO by its self-robustness, however, the autocorrelation characteristics of ZC sequence could be destroyed with the gradual increase of CFO [5,6]. Under large frequency offset circumstances, the perfect autocorrelation property of ZC sequence is lost because of the decreasing main correlation peak and the increasing vice peak as well, degrading the time performance consequently as a result. As the carrier frequency increases, the CFO between the transceiver and the receiver becomes increasingly larger. Taking the system with 6 GHz carrier frequency as an example, even if the crystal oscillator with 3 mmp accuracy is used, the CFO of the system is up to 18 kHz. In this case, the traditional ZC sequence can not achieve accurate synchronization as a result.

In order to reduce the impact of CFO, the ZC sequence is replaced by m sequence in 5G system [7], which will, however, lead to the deterioration of peak to average power ratio (PAPR). [8] designs a training sequence with two OFDM symbols each of which is with a cyclic suffix (CS) in addition to the CP. Although this approach can improve the robustness of time synchronization, the addition of cyclic suffix reduces the spectral efficiency of the system. [9] adopts hybrid carrier to combat CFO which can only enhance the resistance frequency offset ability of the signal, but can not solve the timing problem brought by the CFO.

In this paper, a novel training sequence is proposed on the basis of the symmetry characteristics of the autocorrelations between the ZC and its conjugate sequences. Moreover, a novel resistance frequency offset synchronization approach is developed correspondingly, which enables robust time synchronization in the presence of CFO.

2   System Model

In this paper, a base-band equivalent system model where the training sequence is composed of a ZC sequence and its conjugate sequence is considered. Assuming that the training sequence length in the conventional frame structure is N, as shown in Fig. 1(a), in order to ensure that the proposed training sequence does not generate additional overhead, the ZC sequence length N_{zc} used in the proposed scheme is

$$N_{zc} = \lfloor N/2 \rfloor \tag{1}$$

where $\lfloor . \rfloor$ represents the rounding down. According to the frame structure shown in Fig. 1(b), the training sequence can be given by the formula below:

$$X(n) = \begin{cases} ZC(n) & 0 \leq n < N_{zc} \\ ZC^*(n) & N_{zc} \leq n < 2N_{zc} \end{cases} \tag{2}$$

For a communication system adopting the training sequence shown in (2) above, in the cases where frequency offset exists between the transmitter and the receiver, the received signal can be expressed as

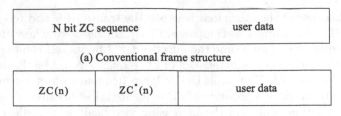

N bit ZC sequence	user data

(a) Conventional frame structure

ZC(n)	ZC*(n)	user data

(b) Proposed frame structure

Fig. 1. Frame structure for different systems.

$$R(n) = X(n) \exp[-j2\pi \frac{\Delta f}{f_s} n] + w(n) \tag{3}$$

where Δf is the frequency offset between the transmitter and receiver, f_s is the baseband sampling rate, and $w(n)$ is the nth additive white gaussian noise (AWGN) sample, respectively.

3   Proposed Synchronization Method

The original definition of a N_{zc}-length Zadoff-Chu sequence is as follows [10]:

$$a_u(n) = \exp[-j2\pi u \frac{n(n+1)/2 + ln}{N_{zc}}] \tag{4}$$

where $u \in \{1, ..., N_{zc} - 1\}$ is the root index of ZC sequence, $n = 0, 1, ..., N_{zc} - 1$, l can be any integer. For the sake of simplicity, l is typically set to 0 in most actual system (such as LTE system). Thus, in the actual system, the ZC sequence used for synchronization is given by

$$ZC_u(n) = \exp[-j \frac{\pi u n(n+1)}{N_{zc}}] \tag{5}$$

Assuming that the transmitter only transmits the ZC sequence, and the receiver correlates the received signal with the sliding local ZC sequence, where the correlation function is:

$$r_{zc}(\tau) = \sum_{n=0}^{N_{zc}-1} R(n-\tau) ZC_u^*(n) \tag{6}$$

where τ is the time offset. Replacing $R(n)$ and $ZC_u(n)$ in (6) without considering the effect of noise, it yields

$$r_{zc}(\tau) = \exp\left[-j \frac{\pi u(\tau^2 - \tau)}{N_{zc}} + j \frac{2\pi \Delta f \tau}{f_s}\right]$$
$$* \sum_{n=0}^{N_{zc}-1} \exp\left[j2\pi n \left(\frac{u\tau}{N_{zc}} - \frac{\Delta f}{f_s}\right)\right] \tag{7}$$

As can be seen from formula (7), the correlation function of the ZC sequence can be expressed as the product of the two separate parts in the presence of the frequency offset. The former part only impacts the phase of the correlation function without affecting the amplitude while the latter one is just the sum of geometric series. In the cases where the time offset is τ, only $N_{zc} - |\tau|$ elements of the summation items could be nonzero. Through the use of geometric series summation formula, the modulus of the ZC sequence correlation function can be written as

$$|r_{zc}(\tau)| = \begin{cases} N_{zc} - |\tau| & \frac{u\tau}{N_{zc}} - \frac{\Delta f}{f_s} \in Z \\ \left| \frac{1-\exp\left[j2\pi(N_{zc}-|\tau|)\left(\frac{u\tau}{N_{zc}} - \frac{\Delta f}{f_s}\right)\right]}{1-\exp\left[j2\pi\left(\frac{u\tau}{N_{zc}} - \frac{\Delta f}{f_s}\right)\right]} \right| & \text{others} \end{cases} \tag{8}$$

where Z represents the set of integers. Similarly, when the transmitter only transmits the conjugate ZC sequence, the modulus of its correlation function can be given by

$$|r_{zc^*}(\tau)| = \begin{cases} N_{zc} - |\tau| & \frac{-u\tau}{N_{zc}} - \frac{\Delta f}{f_s} \in Z \\ \left| \frac{1-\exp\left[j2\pi(N_{zc}-|\tau|)\left(\frac{-u\tau}{N_{zc}} - \frac{\Delta f}{f_s}\right)\right]}{1-\exp\left[j2\pi\left(\frac{-u\tau}{N_{zc}} - \frac{\Delta f}{f_s}\right)\right]} \right| & \text{others} \end{cases} \tag{9}$$

As indicated by (8) and (9), with the gradual increase of the Δf, the modulus of the main correlation peak $|r_{zc}(0)|$(or $|r_{zc^*}(0)|$) will decrease, even as low as to 0 (when $\Delta f = f_s/N_{zc}$). In contrast, some vice peaks will increase for whatever ZC sequence or its conjugate sequence. These changes will destroy the autocorrelation characteristic of the ZC sequence, and degrade its timing synchronization performance. However, by comparing the (8) and (9), it is easy to find that

$$|r_{zc}(\tau)| = |r_{zc^*}(-\tau)| \tag{10}$$

That is to say, for a particular Δf, if the correlation value of ZC sequence has a peak at the position of τ ahead, the correlation value of the ZC conjugate sequence would inevitably have an equal peak at the position of τ lag.

For ZC sequence and ZC conjugate sequence, due to the symmetry between their autocorrelation peaks, the advantage of whose character could be taken in order to achieve the correct synchronization under frequency offset conditions. First and foremost, for the proposed training sequence, the ZC sequence and ZC conjugate sequence are adopted by the receiver for the purpose of sliding correlation. Secondly, each peak position exceeding the threshold respectively is recorded and all of these positions are averaged subsequently. Last but not least, $N_{zc}/2 + 1$ is added to the average position to get the starting position of the user data. In this way, the starting position of the user data can be calculated as follows:

$$P = \frac{\sum_{k=0}^{M_1} I_{zc}(k) + \sum_{k=0}^{M_2} I_{zc^*}(k)}{M_1 + M_2} + N_{zc}/2 + 1 \tag{11}$$

where M_1 and M_2 are the number of over threshold peaks in the two groups of sliding correlation, I_{zc} and I_{zc^*} are the position indexes of the corresponding correlation peaks.

Moreover, whether the 2 sequences have good cross-correlation or not needs to be taken into consideration since the proposed training sequence is composed of ZC sequence and its conjugate sequence as well. With the result of $\exp[-j\pi n(n+1)] = 1$, the ZC conjugate sequence is expressed as

$$
\begin{aligned}
ZC_u^*(n) &= \exp\left[j\frac{\pi un(n+1)}{N_{zc}}\right] \\
&= \exp\left[-j\frac{\pi(-u)n(n+1)}{N_{zc}}\right] \exp[-j\pi n(n+1)] \\
&= ZC_{N_{zc}-u}(n)
\end{aligned}
\tag{12}
$$

Thus, it is shown that ZC conjugate sequences with root exponent u are exactly the ZC sequences with the root exponent $N_{zc} - u$. Given that the cross-correlation between two ZC sequences of different root exponents is quite small [11], the interaction of ZC sequence and ZC conjugate sequence in the sliding correlation could be therefore ignored.

4   Simulation Results

In order to evaluate the performance of the proposed scheme in resistance frequency offset, two groups of sliding correlation values are simulated with $\Delta f = 0\,\text{kHz}$ and $\Delta f = 8\,\text{kHz}$, respectively. The simulation parameters are as follows: $N = 127$, $N_{zc} = 63$, $u = 29$, $f_s = 1\,\text{MHz}$, and the threshold is set to 60% of the maximum autocorrelation value. In the cases where the frequency offset is zero, the maximum of the correlation peaks occurs at the location where the local sequence is exactly aligned with the training sequence, as shown in Fig. 2. In this case, both the conventional method and the proposed method can achieve correct synchronization. Additionally, in the cases where a 8 kHz frequency offset exists between the transmitter and receiver, the autocorrelation value at the correct synchronization position is made no longer the largest. Under such conditions, the traditional single-sequence sliding correlation will place the system synchronization in the wrong position, as shown in Fig. 3, on the contrary, the proposed method can still achieve the correct synchronization.

Figure 4 shows the Monte Carlo simulation results of the relationship between the correct synchronization probability and the frequency offset under the conditions of $\text{SNR} = 10\,\text{dB}$. It can be seen from Fig. 4 that the proposed method can achieve the correct synchronization in the larger frequency offset range in comparison with the traditional method as a result. It should be noted that the correct synchronization probability of the proposed scheme decreases to a certain extent near the 8 kHz CFO, which is due to the close relationship between the two correlation peaks and the threshold in this case. Nevertheless, compared with the traditional scheme, the proposed scheme is still very significant for improving the correct synchronization probability in the case of large CFO.

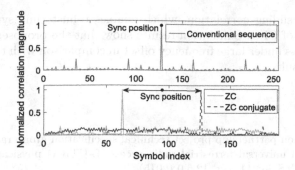

Fig. 2. Training sequence correlation without CFO

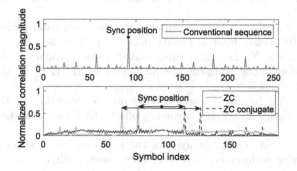

Fig. 3. Training sequence correlation with 8 kHz CFO

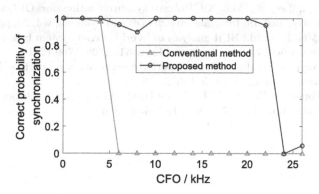

Fig. 4. Correct probability of synchronization when SNR = 10 dB

5   Conclusion

In this paper, a novel training sequence composed of ZC sequence and ZC conjugate sequence is proposed by taking advantage of the symmetry between their autocorrelation peaks. In addition, a corresponding synchronization method is developed by adopting ZC sequence and ZC conjugate sequence respectively for the purpose of sliding correlation, which enables robust time synchronization in the presence of CFO. Simulation results show that the proposed method has better robustness under large frequency offset in comparison with the traditional method as a result.

References

1. 3rd Generation partnership project technical specification group radio access network evolved universal terrestrial radio access (E-UTRA) physical channels and modulation, TS 36.211, ver. 12.6.0 (2015)
2. Hyder, M., Mahata, K.: Zadoff-Chu sequence design for random access initial uplink synchronization in LTE-like systems. IEEE Trans. Wirel. Commun. **16**(1), 503–511 (2016)
3. Frank, R.L., Zadoff, S.A.: Phase shift pulse codes with good periodic correlation properties. IRE Trans. Inform. Theory (Corresp.) **IT–8**, 381–382 (1962)
4. Gul, M.M.U., Ma, X., Lee, S.: Timing and frequency synchronization for OFDM downlink transmissions using Zadoff-Chu Sequences. IEEE Trans. Wirel. Commun. **14**, 1716–1729 (2015)
5. Jun, T., Le, Y.: Improved Zadoff-Chu sequence detection in the presence of unknown multipath and carrier frequency offset. IEEE Commun. Lett. **22**(5), 922–925 (2018)
6. Hua, M., Wang, M., et al.: Analysis of the frequency offset effect on Zadoff-Chu sequence timing performance. IEEE Trans. Commun. **62**(11), 4024–4039 (2014)
7. 3rd Generation partnership project technical specification group radio access network NR physical channels and modulation, TS 38.211, ver. 15.3.0 (2018)
8. Gul, M.M.U., Lee, S., Ma, X.: Robust synchronization for OFDM employing Zadoff-Chu sequence. In: Information Sciences and Systems, vol. 26, pp. 1–6 (2012)
9. Wang, Z., Mei, L., et al.: BER analysis of hybrid carrier system based on WFRFT with carrier frequency offset. Electron. Lett. **51**, 1708–1709 (2015)
10. Chu, D.: Polyphase codes with good periodic correlation properties. IEEE Trans. Inform. Theory (Corresp.) **18**, 531–532 (1972)
11. Sesia, S., Toufik, I., Baker, M.: LTE-The UMTS Long Term Evolution: From Theory to Practice, pp. 145–147. Wiley, Hoboken (2009)

AI-Based Medium Access Control

Compressed Sensing ISAR 3D Imaging Methods Based on OMP Algorithm

Jingcheng Zhao, Zongkai Yang, and Shaozhu Gu$^{(\boxtimes)}$

School of Electronics and Information Engineering,
Beijing University of Aeronautics and Astronautics, Beijing 100191, China
gushaozhu@126.com

Abstract. In the application of three-dimensional imaging inverse synthetic aperture radar, the existing matching tracking-based compression tracking reconstruction algorithm has many problems, such as large computer storage and low computational efficiency. Based on the Orthogonal Matching Pursuit (OMP) algorithm, this paper proposes a dimensionality-compressive sensing reconstruction method Kron OMP based on the sparseness of the Inverse-Synthetic-Aperture-Radar (ISAR) target and the three-dimensional separability of the perceptual matrix. Firstly, a three-dimensional ISAR imaging model is established, and the Kronecker product expression method is used to split the perceptual matrix and transform the 3D reconstruction into a two-dimensional reconstruction problem. Comparing the time and memory consumption of the algorithm, the Kron OMP algorithm reduces the computer memory requirements of the perceptual matrix by more than 95% during the reconstruction process and reduces the computation time by more than 90%. Simulation experiments verify the effectiveness of the algorithm.

Keywords: Compressed sensing · ISAR · OMP · Three-dimensional imaging · Signal reconstruction

1 Introduction

Compared to optical imaging, microwave imaging offers all-weather, all-day, long-range detection and high resolution. Inverse-Synthetic-Aperture-Radar (ISAR) is a high-resolution imaging system [1]. A high resolution of the range is achieved by transmitting a wideband signal, and a high resolution is achieved in the azimuth and pitch directions by inversely synthesizing the aperture. For turntable measurement systems, large-scale sampling of azimuth and pitch directions will consume a large amount of test time, while dense sampling of wideband signals will place higher demands on hardware devices. In 2006, Candes et al. used mathematical derivation to prove that the original signal can be reconstructed by partial Fourier transform coefficients, which lays the theoretical foundation of Compressed Sensing (CS) [2]. Based on these results, Donoho formally proposed the concept of compressed sensing theory and related theoretical framework [3]. The compressed sensing method utilizes the sparseness of the signal, and reconstructs the original signal based on the amount of measured data of the signal is much smaller than that of the traditional sampling

S. Han et al. (Eds.): AICON 2019, LNICST 286, pp. 279–292, 2019.
https://doi.org/10.1007/978-3-030-22968-9_25

method, which breaks through the limitation of the Shannon-Nyquist sampling theorem. After the theory of compressed sensing, Baraniuk first proposed the application of compressed sensing theory to radar imaging in 2007 [4]. Since then, the application of compressed sensing to radar imaging has received extensive attention from scholars at home and abroad, and has achieved a series of research results [5–8]. At present, typical reconstruction algorithms can be divided into three categories: (1) Convex optimization algorithm, which is solved by transforming non-convex problems into convex problems. This type of algorithm requires less measurement and high reconstruction accuracy, but the computational complexity is high and the efficiency is low. (2) Combining algorithms to reconstruct signals by packet detection. Although this type of algorithm is faster, it requires a special structure to be included in the measurement object and the observation matrix is sparse. (3) The greedy algorithm approximates the original signal by selecting the atom most relevant to the original signal. This type of algorithm has low computational complexity and high efficiency, and has become the mainstream algorithm [9]. OMP algorithm is one of the most representative greedy algorithms. It has the advantages of simple implementation, stable performance and low computational complexity. It has been widely studied by scholars. However, the compressed sensing algorithm reduces the sampling rate of the system, improves the imaging quality and reduces the amount of sampled data, while increasing the requirements of the algorithm for computer memory during the reconstruction process. For the OMP reconstruction process in the 3D ISAR scenario, the measurement matrix can easily reach hundreds of GB, and the computer memory cannot store such huge data explicitly. Therefore, it is urgent to study a new method to solve this problem.

At present, the research on the field of ISAR three-dimensional imaging for compressed sensing mainly includes the following contents. In [8], the theory of compressed sensing is applied to the reconstruction process of InISAR two-dimensional image, and then multiple two-dimensional images are synthesized into three-dimensional images by conventional restoration method. However, this single processing method is insufficient, and the premise of using this method is different coherence. The antennas have the same sparse support. In [10], InISAR imaging is proposed as a kind of multi-channel ISAR imaging, and combined with sparsity constraints to improve the accuracy of target height estimation. In [11], under the premise of small target size, the perceptual matrix is set to a one-dimensional long vector by means of compressed sensing method, and the target three-dimensional image is reconstructed by OMP method. Reduced sampling rate and reduced sampling time, but increased the need for memory. In [12], based on the 3-dimensional decomposable property of the echo matrix, a dimensionality reduction method is proposed to develop the three-dimensional ISAR problem into two-dimensional calculation. The method uses 2DSL0 method to process the two-dimensional data to reduce the storage capacity. The computational efficiency is improved, but the 2DSL0 method has the problems of low imaging dynamic range and many false scattering points, and this method has high requirements for parameter selection. In [13], a two-dimensional joint super-resolution method is proposed. Based on the echo signal of pulse compression, an imaging algorithm suitable for three-dimensional is proposed, but the algorithm is mainly used for MIMO imaging with low resolution. In [14], the scene segmentation method is used to divide the large scene into several small scenes for imaging separately, and finally the results are stacked in order to obtain the ISAR three-dimensional image in the large scene. The algorithm improves the calculation speed while solving the ISAR three-dimensional imaging problem in large scenes, but it has strict requirements for scene segmentation. Once the scattering point is at the edge of the sub-scene, it will generate a strong reconstruction of nearby sub-scene interference.

In this paper, when the matching tracking algorithm is applied in 3D ISAR imaging, the echo is complex, the data volume is large, and the computational complexity is high, which makes it difficult to calculate. According to the 3D separability of the radar echo sparse dictionary and the compressed measurement matrix, the Kronecker product is utilized. The way to expand the 3D signal to 2D, using Kron OMP processing method, the perceptual matrix of the reconstruction process reduces the computer memory requirements by more than 95%, and shortens the calculation time by 90% the above. The remainder of this paper is organized as follows: Part 2 derives the three-dimensional representation model of the radar echo signal, and Part 3 introduces the process of three-dimensional model expansion to two-dimensional, and introduces the solution to the three-dimensional ISAR compression-aware Kron OMP algorithm. The fourth part is The MATLAB simulation results of simple targets, the fifth part is the FEKO simulation results of complex targets, and the sixth part is the summary of the article.

2 3D ISAR Imaging Model Based on Compressed Sensing

In this paper, the three-dimensional imaging method optimization of the turntable target is studied. For the ISAR imaging of the moving target, after motion compensation, the model can be equivalent to the three-dimensional turntable model. Therefore, this research has universality for ISAR imaging. The schematic diagram of the relationship between radar and turntable targets is as follows:

The target coordinate system X-Y-Z is established with the target center as the coordinate origin, which rotates with the target. Another coordinate system u-v-n is established along the direction of the radar, which is fixed and does not rotate with the target. Radar can get high resolution in range direction by transmitting broadband signals. As shown in Fig. 1, target rotates around n axis with azimuth angle θ and rotates around axis v with pitch angle φ. The azimuth and pitch inverse synthetic aperture scans are used to obtain high resolution in these two directions. The distance between the radar and the turntable target center is R_0. At the moment t, the projection of a point P(X, Y, Z) on the target along the u axis in the u-v-n can be expressed as:

$$R(t) = R_0 + x\cos\theta(t)\cos\varphi(t) - y\sin\theta(t)\cos\varphi(t) + z\sin\varphi(t) \qquad (1)$$

Where, $\varphi(t)$ represents the change of the angle versus time in pitch direction. $\theta(t)$ indicates the change of the angle versus time in azimuth direction. Using stepped frequency radar signal, the initial frequency is set to f_0, the frequency step length is Δf, the frequency bandwidth is B = (N − 1)Δf, and the stepped frequency number is N.

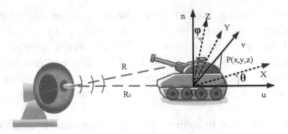

Fig. 1. Relative position between radar and the target on the turntable

Considering the far-field and small-angle observation conditions, after mixing the echo data, the echo data of the m-azimuth, the l-elevation and the n-sampling frequency points can be expressed as follows:

$$s(f_n, \theta_m, \varphi_l) = \sum_{i=1}^{I} \sigma_i \exp\left(-j\frac{4\pi f_n R}{c}\right)$$

$$= \sum_{i=1}^{I} \sigma_i \exp\left(-j\frac{4\pi f_n}{c}(x_i \cos\theta_m \cos\varphi_l - y_i \sin\theta_m \cos\varphi_l + z_i \sin\varphi_l)\right)$$

$$= \sum_{i=1}^{I} \sigma_i \exp\left(-j\frac{4\pi f_n}{c}(x_i - y_i + z_i \varphi_l)\right)$$

$$(2)$$

Where σ_i is the scattering coefficient of the ith ($i = 1,2, \ldots, I$) scattering point in the target space. The frequency of the nth pulse is $f_n = f_0 + (n-1)\Delta f$, $n = 1,2, \ldots, N$. The azimuth and pitch observation angles are discretized. The azimuth angle is $\theta_m = (m-1)\Delta\theta$, where $\Delta\theta$ is azimuth angle sampling interval and the pitch angle is $\varphi_l = (l-1)\Delta\varphi$, $l = 1,2, \ldots, L$, where $\Delta\varphi$ is pitch angle sampling interval. Three-dimensional scattering distribution $\sigma = [\sigma_{p,q,k}]$ $P \times Q \times K$ can be obtained by discrete sampling of the scattering rate function of the object.

$$\begin{cases} x_p = p\Delta x, p = 1,2,\ldots,P \\ y_q = q\Delta y, q = 1,2,\ldots,Q \\ x_k = k\Delta z, k = 1,2,\ldots,K \end{cases} \qquad (3)$$

Where $\Delta x = c/2(P-1)\Delta f$, $\Delta y = \lambda_0/2(Q-1)\Delta\theta$ and $\Delta z = \lambda_0/2(K-1)\Delta\varphi$ respectively represent the resolution of the three dimensions. $P = E_1 N$, $Q = E_2 M$, $K = E_2 L$. E_1, E_2, E_3 are the super-resolution multiples of the three directions, respectively. In case $E_1 = E_2 = E_3 = 1$, the imaging resolution is consistent with the traditional method. $\lambda_0 = c/f_0$ is the initial signal wavelength, in general $\lambda_0 \approx \lambda_n$, therefore, Eq. (2) can be written as:

$$s(n, m, l) = \sum_{P=0}^{P-1} \sum_{Q=0}^{Q-1} \sum_{K=0}^{K-1} \sigma(p, q, k) exp(-2j\pi \frac{p(n-1)}{p})$$

$$exp(-2j\pi \frac{p(n-1)}{p}) exp(-2j\pi \frac{p(n-1)}{p})$$

(4)

When the scattering point distribution $\sigma = [\sigma p, q, k]P \times Q \times K$ is sparse, it can be solved by compressed sensing. Write the formula in the form of a matrix or a vector. $S = [yn, m, l] N \times M \times L$ represents the 3D observation echo matrix and change the matrix into a vector:

$$S_{NML \times 1} = [s(1, 1, 1) \dots s(N, 1, 1) \dots S(N, M, 1) \dots S(N, M, L)]^T$$

(5)

At the same time, the target scattering point distribution is also changed into a vector:

$$\sigma_{PQK \times 1} = [\sigma(1, 1, 1) \dots \sigma(P, 1, 1) \dots \sigma(P, Q, 1) \dots \sigma(P, Q, K)]^T$$

(6)

$\varphi_r = [exp(-2j\pi p(n-1)/P)]_{N \times P}$, $\varphi_c = [exp(-2j\pi p(m-1)/P)]_{M \times Q}$ and $\varphi_v = [exp(-2j\pi p(l-1)/P)]_{L \times K}$ are respectively Fourier dictionaries in distance direction, azimuth direction and pitch direction. Based on the above formula, the relationship between the observed data and the imaging space can be obtained as

$$S_{NML} \times 1 = (\varphi_v \otimes \varphi_c \otimes \varphi r)\sigma_{PQK} \times 1 = \varphi_{NML \times PQK}\sigma_{PQK \times 1}$$

(7)

Where, $\otimes$ represents the Kronecker operator, $\varphi_{NML \times PQK}$ is the sensing matrix. Formula (7) is the Kronecker decomposition for the three-dimensional ISAR imaging. The compressed sensing can recover the original signal with a small number of sampling points under the premise of target sparsity. The observation matrices in the three directions of distance, azimuth and elevation are respectively γ_r, γ_c and γ_v with the sizes $G_{1 \times N}, G_{2 \times M}$ and $G_{3 \times L}$. The imaging formula by compressed sensing can be expressed as:

$$u_{G_1 G_2 G_3 \times 1} = (\gamma_v \varphi_v) \otimes (\gamma_c \varphi_c) \otimes (\gamma_r \varphi_r)\sigma_{PQK \times 1} = \psi_{G_1 G_2 G_3 \times PQK}\sigma_{PQK \times 1}$$

(8)

Among them, $\Theta_v = \gamma_v \varphi_v$, $\Theta_c = \gamma_c \varphi_c$ and $\Theta_r = \gamma_r \varphi_r$ are the compressed sensing dictionary matrix in the pitch direction, the azimuth direction and the distance direction, respectively. $\psi_{G_1 G_2 G_3 \times PQK}$ is the global sensing matrix. Therefore, the compressed sensing solution of this problem can be expressed as the following form:

$$\hat{\sigma} = \min_\sigma \|\sigma\|_0, \text{ s.t.} \|s - \psi s\|_2 \leq \varepsilon$$

(9)

Where, $\|\cdot\|_p$ means the lp norm.

Compressed sensing algorithm greatly reduces the amount of data needed for measurement, reduces the testing time and improves the testing efficiency. However, the requirement of computational resources is greatly increased in the process of algorithm reconstruction. For example, for a matrix of radar echo data size

$61 \times 61 \times 61$, the target space is imaged with 2 times resolution, which means $E1 = E2 = E3 = 2$, the target space mesh size is equal to $121 \times 121 \times 121$, and the resulting perception matrix size is 226981×1771561. Conventional OMP algorithms are difficult to calculate on ordinary computers and small workstations. When the resolution is further increased, the sensing matrix will increase exponentially. The reason for this problem is that the OMP algorithm used to solve the three-dimensional imaging problem in vector, which makes the sensing matrix increase sharply, and it is difficult to express it explicitly in computer memory.

3   Three-Dimensional Reduction Algorithm

In order to solve the problem raised in the second part, this paper improves the OMP algorithm to solve the problem that the matching pursuit compressed sensing method is difficult to calculate in the application of ISAR three-dimensional imaging. The method flow is shown in the following figure (Fig. 2).

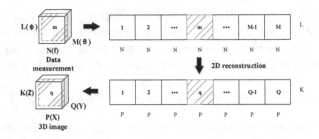

Fig. 2. Kron OMP ISAR 3D imaging flow chart

Firstly, we need to change three-dimensional echo data into two-dimensional form along a certain plane [13]. Because the test space and target space studied in this paper are cubic distribution, the range-pitch slice is chosen to change. In practice, it can be changed in the direction with more test points, and better optimization results can be obtained. Then Kron OMP algorithm is used to solve the two-dimensional reconstruction problem. In the process of solving the problem, the scattering matrix of the target needs to be arranged in two-dimensional form $\widehat{g}_{PQ \times K}$. Finally, the two-dimensional scattering coefficient distribution obtained by the solution can be rearranged into three-dimensional. At this point, Eqs. (8) and (9) can be expressed as

$$U_{G_1 G_2 G_3} = (\Theta_c \otimes \Theta_r)\widehat{g}_{PQ \times K}\Theta_v^T \tag{10}$$

$$\widehat{g} = \min_g \|g_0\|, \text{s.t.} \left\| U - (\Theta_c \otimes \Theta_r)\widehat{g}_{PQ \times K}\Theta_{v2}^T \right\| \leq \varepsilon \tag{11}$$

The details for solving the formula (11) using the Kron OMP algorithm are shown in Table 1. The key of the algorithm is to avoid the explicit storage of the huge vector and to store two dictionary matrices, which greatly reduces the demand for computer memory.

The steps of 3D ISAR imaging algorithm based on OMP are as follows.

Input: $\Theta_v, \Theta_c, \Theta_r$ measurement vector in CS method $u_{G_1 G_2 G_3 \times 1}$, scattering sparsity of target K

Output: 3-D scattering distribution of Target

Kron OMP process steps:

(1) Let $A = \Theta_c \otimes \Theta_r$, $B = \Theta_v$, residual signal vector $r = u_{G_1 G_2 G_3 \times 1}$, index set $\Omega = \emptyset$, empty matrix φ for saving estimation vector, iteration times k = 1;

(2) Find the index ii in sensing matrix ψ, which is the index of the column that has the largest correlation with residual signal vector r. The specific method is to arrange the residual signal vector r into two-dimensional matrix $R_{NM \times K}$. Calculate $y^H r = (\Theta_v \otimes \Theta_c \otimes \Theta_r)^H r = (\Theta_c \otimes \Theta_r)^H R_{NM \times K} \Theta_v^* = A^H R_{NM \times K} B^*$, and record the row number and column number of the maximum;

(3) According to the row and column number acquired in step (2), find the corresponding column vector in ψ. $\omega_k = B(:,col) \otimes A(:,row)$, update index set $\Omega = \Omega \bigcup \{ii\}$, update the matrix $\varphi = [\varphi, \omega_k]$;

(4) Estimation by least square method $\hat{\sigma} = \left(\omega_k^H \omega_k\right)^{-1} \omega_k^H r$;

(5) Updating residual signals $r = u - \omega_k \hat{\sigma}$, update k = k+1;

(6) Determine whether k > K is valid, if it is valid, stop iteration, otherwise, repeat steps (2)–(5);

(7) Rearrange the result $\hat{\sigma}$ into three dimensions, and output the 3-D scattering distribution of Target.

Through the above algorithm, we can solve the computational difficulty problem of ISAR three-dimensional using compressed sensing. The original method needs to perceive matrix memory O(MNLPQK). After adopting the new method, only O (MNPQ+LK) size data need to be stored, and the demand for memory is reduced by more than 95%.

4   MATLAB Simulation Results

The computer is Windows7 system and the processor is Intel(R) Xeon(R) X5650. The two processors have a clock speed of 2.67 GHz and 2.66 GHz respectively, and the installed memory is 48.0 GB. The MATLAB version is MATLABR2015b, and the radar transmission frequency stepping signal is set. The simulation parameters are shown in Table 1.

Table 1. Simulation parameter setting

Sampling frequency range	10 GHz – 11.5 GHz
Sampling frequency points number	61
Sampling azimuth range	$-4.3° \sim 4.3°$
Sampling azimuth points number	61
Sampling pitch angle range	$-4.3° \sim 4.3°$
Sampling pitch points number	61

The target consists of 9 scattering points. The echo data is generated according to the point scattering model. The target scattering point distribution and FFT imaging results are shown in Fig. 3. The FFT imaging results are calculated by the ifftn function in MATLAB. It can be seen that the method is imaged. The results have large side lobes and the imaging dynamic range is small. The measured compression ratio d defining the distance, azimuth and pitch directions is N/P, M/Q, L/K, respectively. Assuming that the target scattering point number is known, Fig. 4 shows the CS imaging result of the Kron OMP algorithm in the three-dimensional measurement compression ratio d = 1, where the red circle represents the target point position set during the simulation. The imaging target space uses a super resolution of E1 = E2 = E3 = 2 times. At this time, the perceptual matrix of the original OMP algorithm will reach thousands of GB, and the ordinary workstation cannot explicitly store the matrix data, and thus cannot be calculated. The Kron OMP algorithm can be used to image the target under the parameter by Kronecker multiplication integral solution. The

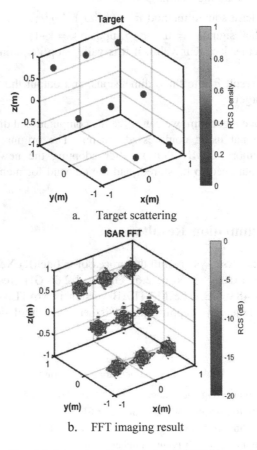

a.   Target scattering

b.   FFT imaging result

Fig. 3. Simulated target scattering point and FFT imaging results

specific consumption time and memory comparison are shown in Table 2. Compared with the FFT imaging results, the Kron OMP algorithm has no side lobes and the imaging dynamic range is larger.

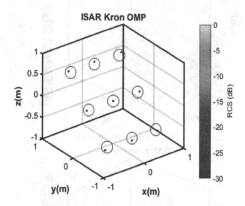

Fig. 4. CS Kron OMP imaging results by simulation when compression ratio d = 1 (Color figure online)

Table 2. Comparison of original OMP and Kron OMP algorithm

Algorithm name	OMP (d = 1)	OMP (d = 3)	Kron OMP (d = 1)	Kron OMP (d = 3)
Time consumption/s	/	6.449	5.860	0.159
Memory consumption/GB	/	9.511	0.812	0.011

Figure 5 shows the CS imaging results of the original OMP algorithm and the Kron OMP algorithm in the three-dimensional measurement compression ratio d = 3, where the red circle represents the target point position set at the time of simulation. The imaging target space adopts super-resolution of E1 = E2 = E3 times. At this time, the time consumed by the sampling and the amount of processed data are greatly reduced, and the memory consumed by the sensing matrix is greatly reduced. Comparing the imaging results of OMP algorithm and Kron OMP algorithm, the improved algorithm imaging results are basically consistent with the original algorithm results, and the original model can be restored better.

Comparing the OMP algorithm and the Kron OMP algorithm in Table 2 with respect to time and memory consumption, the new algorithm can significantly reduce the requirements of the ISAR compression-sensing 3D imaging for hardware memory systems. In this example, the Kron OMP algorithm is used for different data volumes. Computer memory requirements have dropped by more than 95%, and time has also been reduced by more than 90%.

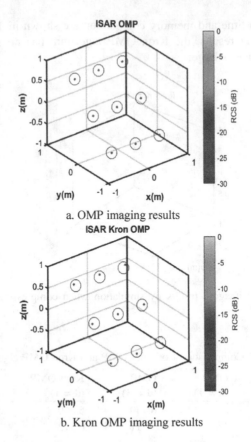

a. OMP imaging results

b. Kron OMP imaging results

Fig. 5. CS Kron OMP imaging results by simulation when compression ratio d = 3 (Color figure online)

5   FEKO Simulation Results

This simulation is simulated by the 2017 version of FEKO software. FEKO software is a 3D full-wave electromagnetic simulation software. The simulation parameters are set in Table 2. The target model is shown in Fig. 6, which is a 45° oblique view of the model and a side view. The measured compression ratio d defining the distance, azimuth and pitch directions is N/P, M/Q, L/K, respectively. Set the target sparsity K = 100. Figure 7 shows the 3D imaging of the FFT algorithm. The FFT imaging results are calculated by the ifftn function in MATLAB. It can be seen that the imaging results have large side lobes and imaging. The dynamic range is small. Figure 8 shows the CS imaging results of the Kron OMP algorithm when the compression ratio d = 1 is measured in three dimensions. The imaging target space uses double super resolution. At this time, the perceptual matrix of the original OMP algorithm will reach thousands of GB, and the ordinary workstation cannot explicitly store the matrix data, and thus cannot be calculated. The Kron OMP algorithm can be used to image the

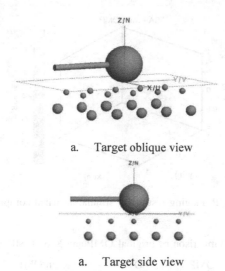

a.   Target oblique view

a.   Target side view

Fig. 6. Simulation target model

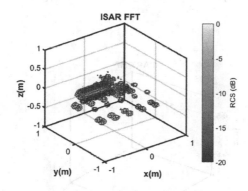

Fig. 7. FFT imaging results by simulation when compression ratio d = 1

target under the parameter by Kronecker multiplication solution. The specific consumption time and memory comparison are shown in Table 3. Compared with the FFT imaging results, the Kron OMP algorithm has no side lobes and the imaging dynamic range is larger.

Figure 9 shows the CS imaging results of the original OMP algorithm and the Kron OMP algorithm when the three-dimensional measurement compression ratio is d = 3. At this time, the time consumed by the sampling and the amount of processed data are greatly reduced, and the memory consumed by the sensing matrix is greatly reduced. Comparing the imaging results of OMP algorithm and Kron OMP algorithm, the improved algorithm imaging results are basically consistent with the original algorithm results, and the original model can be restored well.

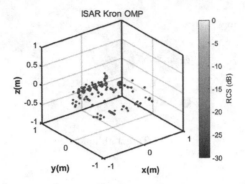

Fig. 8. CS Kron OMP imaging results by simulation when compression ratio d = 1

Table 3. Comparison of original OMP and Kron OMP algorithm

Algorithm name	OMP (d = 1)	OMP (d = 3)	Kron OMP (d = 1)	Kron OMP (d = 3)
Time consumption/s	/	70.982	131.394	4.666
Memory consumption/GB	/	9.511	0.812	0.011

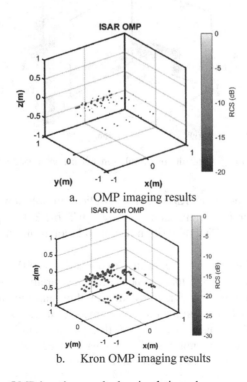

a.   OMP imaging results

b.   Kron OMP imaging results

Fig. 9. CS Kron OMP imaging results by simulation when compression ratio d = 3

Comparing the OMP algorithm and the Kron OMP algorithm in Table 3 with respect to time and memory consumption, the new algorithm can significantly reduce the requirements of the ISAR compression-aware 3D imaging for the hardware memory system. In this example, the Kron OMP algorithm is used for different data volumes. Computer memory requirements have dropped by more than 95%, and time has also been reduced by more than 90%.

6   Conclusion

Compressed sensing method applied to the field of ISAR three-dimensional imaging will bring about the problem of large storage capacity and low computational efficiency. The original OMP algorithm often cannot calculate because the memory consumption of the sensing matrix is too large. In this paper, based on the OPR algorithm, the prior information of sparseness in the spatial domain is used. Based on the OMP algorithm, based on the 3D separability of the perceptual matrix, the Kron OMP method based on the OMP method for ISAR compressed sensing 3D imaging is proposed. The feasibility of the new algorithm is verified by MATLAB simulation and FEKO simulation results. Comparing the time and memory consumption of the two algorithms, the new algorithm reduces the memory requirements of the computer by more than 95% and the time is also more than 90%.

References

1. Fan, H.L.: Research on imaging and Jamming of inverse synthetic aperture radar. University of Electronic Science and Technology of China, Xian (2006)
2. Candes, E.J., Romberg, J., Tao, T.: Robust uncertainty principles: exact signal reconstruction from highly incomplete frequency information (2006)
3. Donoho, D.L.: Compressed sensing. IEEE Trans. Inf. Theory **52**(4), 1289–1306 (2006)
4. Baraniuk, R., Steeghs, P.: Compressive radar imaging. In: Radar Conference (2007)
5. Qiu, W., Zhao, H.Z., Chen, J.J., et al.: High-resolution radar one-dimensional imaging based on smoothed 1 (0) norm. J. Electron. Inf. Technol. **33**(12), 2869–2874 (2011). Dianzi Yu Xinxi Xuebao
6. Zhang, S.S., Zhang, Y.Q.: Adaptive compressed sensing for high-resolution ISAR imaging. In: Proceedings of EUSAR 2016 11th European Conference on Synthetic Aperture Radar. VDE, pp. 1–4 (2016)
7. Larsson, C.: Compressive sensing methods for radar cross section ISAR measurements. In: 2016 4th International Workshop on Compressed Sensing Theory and its Applications to Radar, Sonar and Remote Sensing (CoSeRa), pp. 237–241 (2016)
8. Zhao, J., Zhang, M.: Performance 3-D ISAR imaging in compact antenna test range via compressed sensing. In: 2017 17th IEEE International Conference on Communication Technology Proceedings, ICCT, 2017 October, pp. 736–740 (2018)
9. Zhu, X.X., Hu, W.H., Guo, B.F.: Overview of ISAR imaging technology based on compressed sensing. Aerodyn. Missile J. (03), 84–89 (2018)
10. Liu, Y., Li, N., Wang, R., Deng, Y.: Achieving high-quality three-dimensional In ISAR imageries of maneuvering target via super-resolution ISAR imaging by exploiting sparseness. IEEE Geosci. Remote Sens. **11**(4), 828–832 (2014)

11. Wei, Q.: Research on multi-dimensional radar imaging method based on compressed sensing. National University of Defense Technology (2014)
12. Qiu, W., Martorella, M., Zhou, J., et al.: Three-dimensional inverse synthetic aperture radar imaging based on compressive sensing. IET Radar Sonar Navig. **9**(4), 411–420 (2015)
13. Wang, D., Ma, X., Chen, A.L., et al.: High-resolution imaging using a wideband MIMO radar system with two distributed arrays. IEEE Trans. Image Process. **19**(5), 1280–1289 (2010)
14. Lü, M., Li, S., Chen, W., et al.: Fast ISAR imaging method based on scene segmentation. J. Syst. Eng. Electron. **28**(6), 1078–1088 (2017)

Ambiguity Function Analysis of Radar-Communication Integrated Waveform Based on FDM and TDM Technologies

Hongzhi Men[1,2], Zhiqun Song[2(✉)], and Guisheng Liao[1]

[1] School of Electronics Engineering Xi'an, Xi'an 710126, China
[2] The 54th Research Institute of CECT, Shijiazhuang 050081, Hebei, China
zhiqunsy@163.com

Abstract. In this letter, we propose a novel radar-communication integration signal, which employs the linear frequency modulation (LFM) signal modulated by digital symbols is divided from time and frequency domain to achieve radar detection and data communication. By analyzing its ambiguity function, we confirm its feasibility of applying in radar-communication integration system.

Keywords: Radar-communication integration · LFM · TDM · Ambiguity function

1 Introduction

The more and more complex electronic environment and scenarios require the electronic system smaller size, more function, lower consumption and greater capacity. Hence, the concept of the integrated electronic systems is proposed to meet a variety of applications, especially the integrated radar-communication system. The concept of the radar-communication integration is proposed in recent few decades, whose existing researches mainly focus on the waveform design. Now it is a research hot-spot to employ multiple resources and technologies to form a integrated waveform for high data rate, long distance, reliable communication and high measurement accuracy, high resolution radar detection.

Over the last few decades, several design approaches have been proposed to design integrated radar-communication signal [1]. The key difference between these approaches is how the radar signal and communication data are combined. These methods can be summarized as resource reuse method, waveform multiplexing method and technologies fusion method. The integrated signal design is mainly supported by the spread spectrum (SS) technology [2,3], linear frequency modulation (LFM) [4-6], and the orthogonal frequency division multiplexing (OFDM) [7-9]. In the existing SS-based [2,3] and LFM-based [4-6] design

© ICST Institute for Computer Sciences, Social Informatics and Telecommunications Engineering 2019
Published by Springer Nature Switzerland AG 2019. All Rights Reserved
S. Han et al. (Eds.): AICON 2019, LNICST 286, pp. 293-307, 2019.
https://doi.org/10.1007/978-3-030-22968-9_26

schemes, particular technology carriers modulated by digital symbols are used for radar and communication pulses, the envelop of integrated signal and digital symbols presenting radar waveform and information data respectively. However, SS-based and LFM-based approaches cannot meet the demand of transmitting a large number of data, because the SS-technology makes equivalent available bandwidth of radar and communication great decrease under the condition of the same system bandwidth. In recent years, OFDM waveform also has been introduced to design integrated waveforms for higher transmission rate due to its frequency orthogonality and high order number of modulation symbols. While, peak-to-average ratio, frequency deviation and easily broken orthogonality limit its application in the design of integrated signals.

Considering the above issues, this paper proposes a novel design scheme of radar-communication integrated waveform. In the design scheme, the key parameters of LFM carrier are modulated by communication sequences, the time division factor L and frequency selection sequences.

The rest of the manuscript is organized as follows. In Sect. 2, we introduce the basic principles of the LFM signal. In Sect. 3, we first describe the design scheme and mathematical expression of the integrated signal, and then analyze its ambiguity function performance. Section 4 presents the simulation results of the proposed integrated waveform. Finally, Sect. 5 ends up with conclusion.

Notation: $(\cdot)^*$ is the conjugate of a complex number; $|a|$ is the modulus value of the variable a.

2   A Novel Integrated Signal

2.1   Waveform Generation

In the radar-communication integration system, we suppose that the bandwidth, the time period and the pulse width are represented by B, T and T_s, respectively. To describe the design scheme of the integrated signal, we propose two key parameters, time division factor N and frequency division factor L. The signal bandwidth is divided into N sub-bands, and the signal pulse width T_s is divided into L sub-signal periods. Hence, the bandwidth and time period of the sub-signals are $\tilde{B} = B/N$ and $T_t = T_s/L$, respectively.

The proposed integrated waveform is a special sub-signal sequence, i.e.,

$$s(t) = \{s_1(t), s_2(t), \cdots, s_L(t)\} = \sum_{k=0}^{L-1} s_k(t), \tag{1}$$

where the kth sub-signal is

$$\begin{aligned} s_k(t) &= s_k \exp[j2\pi f_k(t - kT_t) + j\pi\mu(t - kT_t)^2]\text{rect}(\frac{t - kT_t}{T_t}) \\ &= P_k \exp[j2\pi(f_k - \mu kT_t)t + j\pi\mu t^2]\text{rect}(\frac{t - kT_t}{T_t}) \end{aligned} \tag{2}$$

where the variable $P_k = s_k \exp[-j2\pi f_k kT_t + j\pi\mu(kT_t)^2]$. In the expression of the sub-signal $s_k(t)$, the function $\text{rect}(x)$ is

$$\text{rect}(x) = \begin{cases} 1, 0 \le x \le 1; \\ 0, \text{else.} \end{cases} \tag{3}$$

Moreover, the variables s_k and f_k are respectively on behalf of the transmitted symbol and initial frequency of the LFM carrier, which are decided by the current communication information. The communication information bit-stream is divided into blocks with $\log_2(N) + \log_2(M)$ bits, i.e.,

$$X_k = \{\underbrace{x_1, x_2, \cdots, x_{\log_2(M)}}_{q_k}, \underbrace{y_1, y_2, \cdots, y_{\log_2(N)}}_{p_k}\}. \tag{4}$$

Thereinto, the first $\log_2(M)$ bits are used to select the transmitted symbol s_k from M-ary modulation signal set, i.e., $s_k = A_k \exp(j\theta_{q_k})$. The second $\log_2(N)$ bits are used to select one sub-carrier $f_k = f(p_k)$ from the initial frequency set. L blocks are spliced together to constitute the integrated signal waveform. In Fig. 1, we illustrate the modulator diagram of the integrated waveform for the integrated radar-communication system.

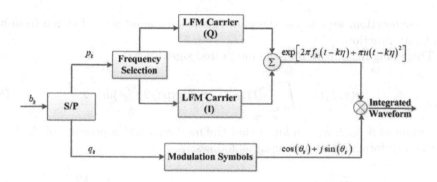

Fig. 1. Modulator

2.2 Spectrum of Waveform

The frequency spectrum of the integrated signal can be calculate as

$$\int_{-\infty}^{+\infty} s(t) \exp(-j2\pi ft)dt$$

$$= \sum_{k=0}^{L-1} P_k \int_{kT_t}^{(k+1)T_t} \exp[j2\pi(f_k - f - \mu kT_t)t + j\pi\mu t^2]dt \tag{5}$$

$$= \sum_{k=0}^{L-1} P_k \exp\left(-j\pi\mu\xi^2\right) \int_{kT_t}^{(k+1)T_t} \exp\left[j\pi\mu(t + \xi)^2\right] dt,$$

where the variable $\xi = (f_k - f - k\mu\eta)/\mu$. To acquire an accurate theory result, Fresnel integral can be applied,

$$
\int_{kT_t}^{(k+1)T_t} \exp\left[j\pi\mu(t+\xi)^2\right] dt
$$

$$
= \int_{\sqrt{2\mu}(kT_t+\xi)}^{\sqrt{2\mu}[(k+1)T_t+\xi]} \exp\left(j\frac{\pi x^2}{2}\right) dt
$$

$$
= \int_{\sqrt{2\mu}(kT_t+\xi)}^{\sqrt{2\mu}[(k+1)T_t+\xi]} \cos\left(\frac{\pi x^2}{2}\right) dt + j \int_{\sqrt{2\mu}(kT_t+\xi)}^{\sqrt{2\mu}[(k+1)T_t+\xi]} \sin\left(\frac{\pi x^2}{2}\right) dt
$$

$$
= [\mathcal{C}(\nu_1) - \mathcal{C}(\nu_2)] + j\,[\mathcal{S}(\nu_1) - \mathcal{S}(\nu_2)]
$$

(6)

where the variable $x = \sqrt{2\mu}(t+\xi)$, $\nu_1 = \sqrt{2\mu}[(k+1)T_t+\xi]$ and $\nu_2 = \sqrt{2\mu}(kT_t+\xi)$, and the Fresnel integral function is

$$
\mathcal{C}(\nu) = \int_0^\nu \cos\left(\frac{\pi x^2}{2}\right) dt, \quad \mathcal{S}(\nu) = \int_0^\nu \sin\left(\frac{\pi x^2}{2}\right) dt.
$$

(7)

3 Ambiguity Function

In this subsection, we analyze the performance of the integrated signal from its ambiguity function.

The ambiguity function of the integrated signal is

$$
\chi(\tau, f_d) = \left| \int_{-\infty}^{\infty} s(t)\,[s(t-\tau)]^* \exp\left(j2\pi f_d t\right) dt \right|^2.
$$

(8)

According to Sect. 2, we can know that the mathematical expression of the integrated waveform can be presented as follows,

$$
s(t) = \sum_{k=0}^{L-1} P_k \exp[j2\pi(f_k - \mu kT_t)t + j\pi\mu t^2]\mathrm{rect}(\frac{t - kT_t}{T_t}).
$$

(9)

To calculate the ambiguity function in (8), we first simply the integral function,

$$
s(t-\tau) = \sum_{k=0}^{L-1} P_k Q_k \exp[j2\pi(f_k - \mu kT_t - \mu\tau)t + j\pi\mu t^2]
$$

(10)

where $Q_k = \exp\left[-j2\pi(f_k - \mu kT_t)\tau + j\pi\mu\tau^2\right]$. Hence, the equation in (8) can be written as

$$
\chi(\tau, f_d) = \left| \int_{-\infty}^{\infty} \sum_{k=0}^{L-1}\sum_{l=0}^{L-1} s_k(t)s_l^*(t-\tau) \exp\left(j2\pi f_d t\right) dt \right|^2.
$$

(11)

In the following, we discuss the values of the delay τ and the Doppler frequency shift f_d to calculate the ambiguity function of integrated waveform.

$$\chi(\tau, f_d) = \begin{cases} \textbf{C1}, \tau = 0, f_d = 0; \\ \textbf{C2}, \tau = 0, f_d \neq 0; \\ \textbf{C3}, \tau \neq 0, f_d = 0; \\ \textbf{C4}, \tau \neq 0, f_d \neq 0. \end{cases} \tag{12}$$

C1:

$$\chi(\tau, f_d) = \left| \sum_{k=0}^{L-1} \int_{kT_t}^{(k+1)T_t} |s_k|^2 dt \right|^2 = (T_t)^2 \sum_{k=0}^{L-1} |s_k|^2. \tag{13}$$

C2:

$$\chi(\tau, f_d) = \left| \sum_{k=0}^{L-1} \int_{kT_t}^{(k+1)T_t} \exp\left(j2\pi f_d t\right) dt \right|^2$$

$$= \left| \frac{\sin(\pi f_d T_t)}{\pi f_d} \right|^2 \left| \sum_{k=0}^{L-1} |s_k|^2 \exp\left[j\pi f_d(2k+1)T_t \right] \right|^2. \tag{14}$$

C3:

$$\chi(\tau, f_d) = \begin{cases} 0, & |\tau| \geq T_s; \\ \textbf{C}_3^1, & -T_s < \tau < 0, |\tau| = KT_t + \Delta t; \\ \textbf{C}_3^2, & 0 < \tau < T_s, |\tau| = KT_t + \Delta t. \end{cases} \tag{15}$$

C$_3^1$:

$$\chi(\tau, f_d) = \left| \sum_{k=0}^{L-K-1} \int_{kT_t}^{(k+1)T_t - \Delta t} f_1(t) dt + \sum_{k=0}^{L-K-2} \int_{(k+1)T_t - \Delta t}^{(k+1)T_t} f_2(t) dt \right|^2, \tag{16}$$

where the integral functions $f_1(t)$ and $f_2(t)$ have the following expressions,

$$f_1(t) = s_k(t) \left[s_{k+K+1}(t - \tau) \right]^*, $$
$$f_2(t) = s_k(t) \left[s_{k+K+2}(t - \tau) \right]^*. \tag{17}$$

Thus, we can know that

$$\int_{kT_t}^{(k+1)T_t - \Delta t} f_1(t) dt$$

$$= P_k P_{k+K+1}^* Q_{k+K+1}^* \int_{kT_t}^{(k+1)T_t - \Delta t} \exp(j2\pi f_k^1 t) dt$$

$$= P_k P_{k+K+1}^* Q_{k+K+1}^* Y_k^1 \sin\left[\pi f_k^1(T_t - \Delta t) \right] / (\pi f_k^1), \tag{18}$$

where the variables f_k^1 and Y_k^1 are

$$f_k^1 = f_k - f_{k+K+1} + \mu(K+1)T_t + \mu\tau,$$
$$Y_k^1 = \exp\{ j\pi f_k^1 [(2k+1)T_t - \Delta t] \}; \tag{19}$$

and

$$\int_{(k+1)T_t-\Delta t}^{(k+1)T_t} f_2(t)dt$$

$$=P_k P_{k+K+2}^* Q_{k+K+2}^* \int_{(k+1)T_t-\Delta t}^{(k+1)T_t} \exp(j2\pi f_k^2 t)dt \qquad (20)$$

$$=P_k P_{k+K+2}^* Q_{k+K+2}^* Y_k^2 \sin(\pi f_k^2 \Delta t)/(\pi f_k^2),$$

where the variables f_k^2 and Y_k^2 are

$$f_k^2 = f_k - f_{k+K+2} + \mu(K+2)T_t + \mu\tau,$$
$$Y_k^2 = \exp\{j\pi f_k^2[(2k+2)T_t - \Delta t]\}. \qquad (21)$$

Thus, the ambiguity function under the above conditions in $\mathbf{C}_3^1$ is

$$\chi(\tau, f_d)$$

$$=\left| \sum_{k=0}^{L-K-1} P_k P_{k+K+1}^* Q_{k+K+1}^* Y_k \sin\left[\pi f_k^1(T_t - \Delta t)\right]/(\pi f_k^1) \right. \qquad (22)$$

$$\left. + \sum_{k=0}^{L-K-2} P_k P_{k+K+2}^* Q_{k+K+2}^* Z_k \sin(\pi f_k^2 \Delta t)/(\pi f_k^2) \right|^2.$$

$\mathbf{C}_3^2$:

$$\chi(\tau, f_d) = \left| \sum_{k=0}^{L-K-1} \int_{kT_t}^{(k+1)T_t-\Delta t} f_3(t)dt + \sum_{k=0}^{L-K-2} \int_{(k+1)T_t-\Delta t}^{(k+1)T_t} f_4(t)dt \right|^2 \qquad (23)$$

where the integral functions $f_3(t)$ and $f_4(t)$ have the following expressions,

$$f_3(t) = s_{k+K+1}(t)\left[s_k(t-\tau)\right]^*,$$
$$f_4(t) = s_{k+K+2}(t)\left[s_k(t-\tau)\right]^*. \qquad (24)$$

Thus, we can know that

$$\int_{kT_t}^{(k+1)T_t-\Delta t} f_3(t)dt$$

$$=P_{k+K+1}P_k^* Q_k^* \int_{kT_t}^{(k+1)T_t-\Delta t} \exp(j2\pi f_k^3 t)dt \qquad (25)$$

$$=P_{k+K+1}P_k^* Q_k^* Y_k^3 \sin\left[\pi f_k^3(T_t - \Delta t)\right]/(\pi f_k^3),$$

where the variables f_k^3 and Y_k^3 are

$$f_k^3 = f_{k+K+1} - f_k - \mu(K+1)T_t - \mu\tau,$$
$$Y_k^3 = \exp\{j\pi f_k^3[(2k+1)T_t - \Delta t]\}; \qquad (26)$$

and

$$\int_{(k+1)T_t - \Delta t}^{(k+1)T_t} f_4(t)dt$$

$$= P_{k+K+2} P_k^* Q_k^* \int_{kT_t}^{(k+2)T_t - \Delta t} \exp(j2\pi f_k^4 t)dt \tag{27}$$

$$= P_{k+K+2} P_k^* Q_k^* Y_k^4 \sin \left[\pi f_k^4 (T_t - \Delta t) \right] / (\pi f_k^4),$$

where the variables f_k^4 and Y_k^4 are

$$f_k^4 = f_{k+K+2} - f_k - \mu(K+2)T_t - \mu\tau, \tag{28}$$
$$Y_k^4 = \exp\{j\pi f_k^4 [(2k+2)T_t - \Delta t]\};$$

Thus, the ambiguity function under the above conditions in $\mathbf{C_3^2}$ is

$$\chi(\tau, f_d)$$

$$= | \sum_{k=0}^{L-K-1} P_k P_{k+K+1}^* Q_{k+K+1}^* Y_k^3 \sin \left[\pi f_k^3 (T_t - \Delta t) \right] / (\pi f_k^3) \tag{29}$$

$$+ \sum_{k=0}^{L-K-2} P_k P_{k+K+2}^* Q_{k+K+2}^* Y_k^4 \sin(\pi f_k^4 \Delta t) / (\pi f_k^4) |^2.$$

C4:

$$\chi(\tau, f_d) = \begin{cases} 0, & |\tau| \ge T_s; \\ \mathbf{C_4^1}, & -T_s < \tau < 0, |\tau| = KT_t + \Delta t; \\ \mathbf{C_4^2}, & 0 < \tau < T_s, |\tau| = KT_t + \Delta t. \end{cases} \tag{30}$$

C$_4^1$:

$$\chi(\tau, f_d) = \left| \sum_{k=0}^{L-K-1} \int_{kT_t}^{(k+1)T_t - \Delta t} h_1(t)dt + \sum_{k=0}^{L-K-2} \int_{(k+1)T_t - \Delta t}^{(k+1)T_t} h_2(t)dt \right|^2$$

where the integral functions $h_1(t)$ and $h_2(t)$ have the following expressions,

$$h_1(t) = s_k(t) \left[s_{k+K+1}(t - \tau) \right]^* \exp(j2\pi f_d t), \tag{31}$$
$$h_2(t) = s_k(t) \left[s_{k+K+2}(t - \tau) \right]^* \exp(j2\pi f_d t).$$

Thus, we can know that

$$\int_{kT_t}^{(k+1)T_t - \Delta t} h_1(t)dt$$

$$= P_k P_{k+K+1}^* Q_{k+K+1}^* \int_{kT_t}^{(k+1)T_t - \Delta t} \exp(j2\pi \tilde{f}_k^1 t)dt \tag{32}$$

$$= P_k P_{k+K+1}^* Q_{k+K+1}^* Z_k^1 \sin \left[\pi \tilde{f}_k^1 (T_t - \Delta t) \right] / (\pi \tilde{f}_k^1),$$

where the variables $\tilde{f}_k^1$ and Z_k^1 are

$$
\begin{aligned}
\tilde{f}_k^1 &= f_k - f_{k+K+1} + \mu(K+1)T_t + \mu\tau + f_d, \\
Z_k^1 &= \exp\{j\pi\tilde{f}_k^1[(2k+1)T_t - \Delta t]\};
\end{aligned}
\tag{33}
$$

and

$$
\begin{aligned}
&\int_{(k+1)T_t-\Delta t}^{(k+1)T_t} h_2(t)dt \\
&= P_k P_{k+K+2}^* Q_{k+K+2}^* \int_{(k+1)T_t-\Delta t}^{(k+1)T_t} \exp(j2\pi\tilde{f}_k^2 t)dt \\
&= P_k P_{k+K+2}^* Q_{k+K+2}^* Z_k^2 \sin(\pi\tilde{f}_k^2 \Delta t)/(\pi\tilde{f}_k^2),
\end{aligned}
\tag{34}
$$

where the variables $\tilde{f}_k^2$ and Z_k^2 are

$$
\begin{aligned}
\tilde{f}_k^2 &= f_k - f_{k+K+2} + \mu(K+2)T_t + \mu\tau + f_d, \\
Z_k^2 &= \exp\{j\pi\tilde{f}_k^2[(2k+2)T_t - \Delta t]\}.
\end{aligned}
\tag{35}
$$

Thus, the ambiguity function under the above conditions in $\mathbf{C}_4^1$ is

$$
\begin{aligned}
&\chi(\tau, f_d) \\
&= \Big| \sum_{k=0}^{L-K-1} P_k P_{k+K+1}^* Q_{k+K+1}^* Z_k^1 \sin\left[\pi\tilde{f}_k^1(T_t - \Delta t)\right]/(\pi\tilde{f}_k^1) \\
&\quad + \sum_{k=0}^{L-K-2} P_k P_{k+K+2}^* Q_{k+K+2}^* Z_k^2 \sin(\pi\tilde{f}_k^2\Delta t)/(\pi\tilde{f}_k^2)\Big|^2.
\end{aligned}
\tag{36}
$$

$\mathbf{C}_4^2$:

$$
\chi(\tau, f_d) = \left| \sum_{k=0}^{L-K-1} \int_{kT_t}^{(k+1)T_t-\Delta t} h_3(t)dt + \sum_{k=0}^{L-K-2} \int_{(k+1)T_t-\Delta t}^{(k+1)T_t} h_4(t)dt \right|^2
\tag{37}
$$

where the integral functions $h_3(t)$ and $h_4(t)$ have the following expressions,

$$
\begin{aligned}
h_3(t) &= s_{k+K+1}(t)\left[s_k(t-\tau)\right]^* \exp(j2\pi f_d t), \\
h_4(t) &= s_{k+K+2}(t)\left[s_k(t-\tau)\right]^* \exp(j2\pi f_d t).
\end{aligned}
\tag{38}
$$

Thus, we can know that

$$
\begin{aligned}
&\int_{kT_t}^{(k+1)T_t-\Delta t} h_3(t)dt \\
&= P_{k+K+1}P_k^* Q_k^* \int_{kT_t}^{(k+1)T_t-\Delta t} \exp(j2\pi\tilde{f}_k^3 t)dt \\
&= P_{k+K+1}P_k^* Q_k^* Z_k^3 \sin\left[\pi\tilde{f}_k^3(T_t - \Delta t)\right]/(\pi\tilde{f}_k^3),
\end{aligned}
\tag{39}
$$

where the variables $\tilde{f}_k^3$ and Z_k^3 are

$$\tilde{f}_k^3 = f_{k+K+1} - f_k - \mu(K+1)T_t - \mu\tau + f_d,$$
$$Z_k^3 = \exp\{j\pi \tilde{f}_k^3[(2k+1)T_t - \Delta t]\};$$

(40)

and

$$\int_{(k+1)T_t - \Delta t}^{(k+1)T_t} h_4(t)dt$$
$$= P_{k+K+2} P_k^* Q_k^* \int_{kT_t}^{(k+2)T_t - \Delta t} \exp(j2\pi \tilde{f}_k^4 t)dt$$
$$= P_{k+K+2} P_k^* Q_k^* Z_k^4 \sin\left[\pi \tilde{f}_k^4 (T_t - \Delta t)\right]/(\pi \tilde{f}_k^4),$$

(41)

where the variables $\tilde{f}_k^4$ and Z_k^4 are

$$\tilde{f}_k^4 = f_{k+K+2} - f_k - \mu(K+2)T_t - \mu\tau + f_d,$$
$$Z_k^4 = \exp\{j\pi \tilde{f}_k^4[(2k+2)T_t - \Delta t]\};$$

(42)

Thus, the ambiguity function under the above conditions in $\mathbf{C}_4^2$ is

$$\chi(\tau, f_d)$$
$$= |\sum_{k=0}^{L-K-1} P_k P_{k+K+1}^* Q_{k+K+1}^* Z_k^3 \sin\left[\pi \tilde{f}_k^3 (T_t - \Delta t)\right]/(\pi \tilde{f}_k^3)$$
$$+ \sum_{k=0}^{L-K-2} P_k P_{k+K+2}^* Q_{k+K+2}^* Z_k^4 \sin(\pi \tilde{f}_k^4 \Delta t)/(\pi \tilde{f}_k^4)|^2.$$

(43)

4   Simulation Results and Performance Analysis

In the simulations, we set the key parameters of the proposed integrated signal as pulse period $T = 100\,\mu s$, pulse width $T_s = 10\,\mu s$, the initial frequency $f_0 = 0\,MHz$, frequency division factor $N = 64$, and the sampling rate $f_s = 4B\,MHz$.

From Figs. 2, 3, 4, 5, 6, 7, 8, 9, 10 and 11, we can know that

1. The ambiguity function of the proposed integrated signal must have the best performance, when the appropriate time division factor L is used in the simulations;
2. The proposed integrated-signal with orthogonal f_k sequence has better ambiguity function compare to the integrated-signal with no orthogonal f_k sequence;
3. The proposed integrated-signal with orthogonal f_k sequence requires larger bandwidth compared with the integrated-signal with no orthogonal f_k sequence.

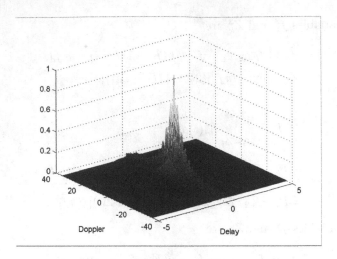

Fig. 2. Ambiguity function of integrated signal with orthogonal f_k sequence time division factor $L = 5$

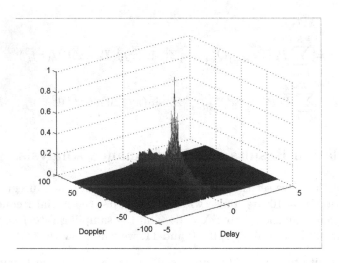

Fig. 3. Ambiguity function of integrated signal with orthogonal f_k sequence time division factor $L = 10$

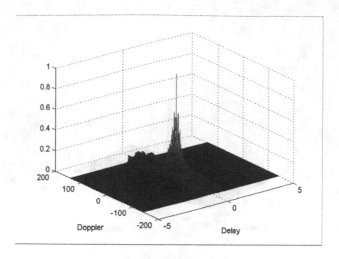

Fig. 4. Ambiguity function of integrated signal with orthogonal f_k sequence time division factor $L = 20$

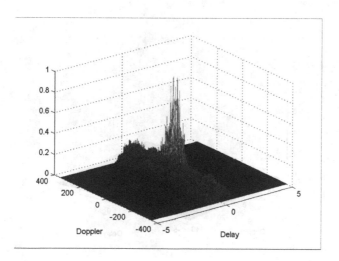

Fig. 5. Ambiguity function of integrated signal with orthogonal f_k sequence time division factor $L = 50$

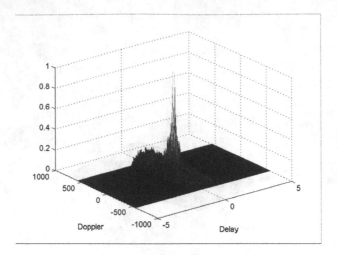

Fig. 6. Ambiguity function of integrated signal with orthogonal f_k sequence time division factor $L = 80$

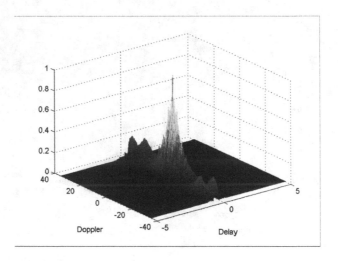

Fig. 7. Ambiguity function of integrated signal with no orthogonal f_k sequence time division factor $L = 5$

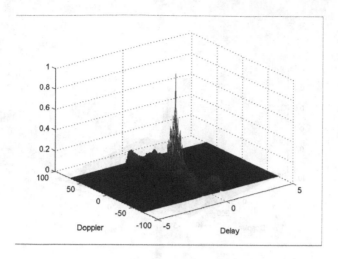

Fig. 8. Ambiguity function of integrated signal with no orthogonal f_k sequence time division factor $L = 10$

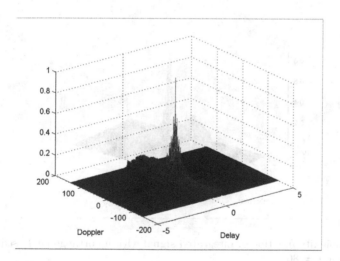

Fig. 9. Ambiguity function of integrated signal with no orthogonal f_k sequence time division factor $L = 20$

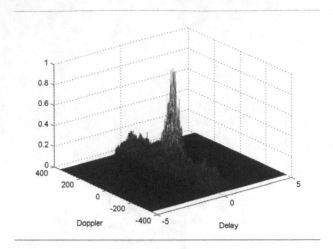

Fig. 10. Ambiguity function of integrated signal with no orthogonal f_k sequence time division factor $L = 50$

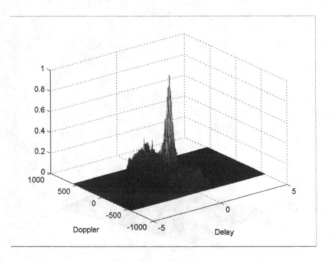

Fig. 11. Ambiguity function of integrated signal with no orthogonal f_k sequence time division factor $L = 80$

5   Summary

In this paper, we first extrapolate the key characteristics of LFM signal when it is employed in the radar system. Then a novel radar-communication integration waveform is proposed to realize the detection and communication at the same time. Moreover, its important performance, ambiguity function, is derived, which shows its feasibility of application in the radar-communication integrated system. Given the length of this journal, other important performance, including detection performance and bits error rate, will not be described in this paper.

References

1. Lou, H., et al.: Waveform design and analysis for radar and communication integration system. In: IET International Radar Conference 2015, Beijing, China, October 2015
2. Xu, S.J., Chen, B., Zhang, P.: Radar-communication integration based on DSSS techniques. In: IEEE International Conference on Signal Processing, Beijing, China (2006)
3. Xu, S.J., Chen, B., Zhang, P.: Integrated radar and communication based on DS-UWB. In: IEEE International Conference on Ultra-Wideband and Ultra-Short Impulse Signals (2006)
4. Michael, N., et al.: Co-designed radar-communication using linear frequency modulation waveform. IEEE Aerosp. Electron. Syst. Mag. **31**(10), 28–35 (2016)
5. Zhao, Z., Jiang, D.: A novel integrated radar and communication waveform based on LFM signal. In: 5th International Conference on Electronics Information and Emergency Communication (ICEIEC) (2015)
6. Chen, X., Wang, X., Xu, S., Zhang, J.: A novel radar waveform compatible with communication. In: International Conference on Computational Problem-Solving (ICCP) (2011)
7. Hu, L., Du, Z.S., Xue, G.R.: Radar-communication integration based on OFDM signal. In: IEEE International Conference on Signal Processing, Communications and Computing (ICSPCC), August 2014
8. Chen, K., Liu, Y., Zhang, W.: Study on integrated radar-communication signal of OFDM-LFM based on FRFT. In: IET International Radar Conference, vol. 16, no. 1, pp. 1–6 (2015)
9. Lou, H., et al.: A novel signal model for integration of radar and communication. In: IEEE International Conference on Computational Electromagnetics (ICCEM), February 2016

Transmission Quality Improvement Algorithms for Multicast Terrestrial-Satellite Cooperation System

Yuandong Zhang[1,2,3] and Liuguo Yin[1,2,3]([✉])

[1] School of Information Science and Technology,
Tsinghua University, Beijing 100084, China
`yinlg@tsinghua.edu.cn`
[2] Beijing National Research Center for Information Science and Technology,
Beijing 100084, China
[3] Key Laboratory of EDA, Research Institute of Tsinghua University in Shenzhen,
Shenzhen 518057, China

Abstract. In this paper, we investigate a terrestrial-satellite multicast beamforming cooperative system to optimize the problem of low expenses and high capacity requirements of ground users. Different from the point-to-point link-based terrestrial network, we design the terrestrial and satellite beamforming vectors cooperatively based on the required contents of users in order to realize more reasonable resource allocation. The satellite and base stations provide service cooperatively for ground users within coverage, and during transmission, both the satellite and the base stations use the multicast beamforming technique to improve the system performance, and the user group scheduling, resource allocation and beamforming design are considered jointly. Based on this architecture, we first formulate a joint optimization problem to maximize the system capacity performance, and we design the beamforming vectors of the base stations and the satellite cooperatively on the basis of user group scheduling and power constraints. Then we extend the problem into a more realistic scene that the link delay of satellite is larger than it of base stations, this may influence the joint optimization timeliness of condition changes. So we propose a two phases optimization algorithm that we optimize terrestrial-satellite system jointly in the first phase and optimize terrestrial part independently in the second phase. The simulation results show that, the proposed algorithm gains more than 38% of capacity improvement compared with maximum ratio transmission (MRT) method.

Keywords: Terrestrial-satellite cooperation system · Multicast ·
Beamforming design · Resource allocation · User group scheduling

This work was supported by the National Natural Science Foundation of China (NSFC, 91538203 and 61871257), the new strategic industries development projects of Shenzhen City (JCYJ20170307145820484), the Joint Research Foundation of the General Armaments Department and the Ministry of Education (6141A02033322), and the Beijing Innovation Center for Future Chips, Tsinghua University.

1   Introduction

In recent years, the number of smart mobile terminals shows a trend of rapid growth, especially mobile phones and mobile tablets. The market statistics in [1] represents that the global smart mobile phones account for 55% in all kinds of mobile terminals, and nearly 2.75 billion people have more than one phone. Meanwhile, other reports indicate that, with the increasing number of mobile terminal users, the requirement of mobile service such as music, video, mobile TV etc. develop rapidly [2]. In [2], it is estimated that, by 2019, the video service ratio will ascend to 72% of total mobile service, which was only 55% in 2014. The consequent situation of mobile service increment is the explosive growth of mobile data flow. In 2014, the mobile data flow was about 2.5EB and it was predicted to reach 24.3EB in 2019. It can be noticed that the wireless communication and wireless service nowadays present a new trend and challenge the traditional service techniques. On the one hand, the traditional communication is connection centric but the developing trend of communication is content centric. Compared with the content centric communication, the basis requirement of connection centric communication is the connection link that the efficiency and resource utilization ratio are low. The current communication system cannot satisfy the demand of date traffic. On the other hand, for the content centric requirement, the user-desired contents may be requested by many users at the same time such as famous video clips, live sports competitions, focus news and so on. So how to satisfy the complex content requirement and the communication link requirement simultaneously is the principal problem [3]. Compared with the traditional point-to-point transmission method, the point-to-multipoint transmission using multicast technique could provide services of the same contents for more users in the same time without extra resource and improve the system performance and network capacity [4]. Furthermore, under the multicast transmission condition, how to consume the cost of power, frequency, bandwidth etc. and obtain more communication efficiency and higher quality of service (QoS) is another focus problem [5]. Thus, the low expenses high capability multigroup multicast beamforming transmission technique plays a more important role in content centric wireless communication gradually.

In the previous literatures, the multicast beamforming technique was first proposed in wireless communication networks in [6]. The researchers designed an adaptive transmit antenna array to solve the multicast problem of system performance, but they assumed the channel information of transmitter was perfect that ignored many constraints in actual scene. Later in [7], an optimization problem of multicast beamforming for one group was first proposed. In this literature, beamforming design problem was considered to improve the performance of the system. The authors proved the relations between the max-min-fair (MMF) problem and the quality of service (QoS) problem. But the single group scene didn't consider the interference. The literature [8] extended the problem in [7] to multigroup scene. The optimization problem based on the relation between MMF problem and QoS problem was solved. In [9] the authors built a multiuser multichannel multiple-input-single-output (MISO) cognitive radio network model, they proposed two explicit searching algorithm based method to solve the suboptimal channel allocation problem and obtained significant improvement in achievable sum rate. But this method solved problem with dividing it into subproblems, that might influence the result. In [10] a non-orthogonal multiple access (NOMA) based multimedia multicast beamforming Terrestrial-Satellite Network model was built. The users in the model was divided into base station users and satellite users, meanwhile the satellite and the base stations were equipped with multi-antennas and could serve group users based on their required content. This work improved the scene from ground network to the satellite, but the division of users was simple. So, these works were meaningful that brought a new area of wireless communication and improved the performance, but they still have some small defects that could not afford the requirement recently.

To enhance these weaknesses, two stage cooperative multicast transmission was proposed in [11], in which the method aimed to guarantee a practical coverage ratio with the minimum base station power. Later, in [12], a joint beamforming design problem was considered to maximize signal-to-interference plus noise ratio in multiple multicast groups. Although these works optimized different objective functions, the limitations were similar. Optimization goal in [11] was limited by the power rate of base stations, and in [12] it was constrained by per-cell power. And to make the optimization problem more realistic, the researchers discussed better user access and more efficiency resource allocation to improve the system ability. In [13], a three-tier heterogeneous cellular network was proposed. The users were assumed to access more than one base station. However, the paper finally solved the problem of the single base station, and optimized user association and power allocation separately. The performance might not be the best. Later in [14], the authors focused on a joint beamforming, user scheduling and power allocation method. They improved the system ability in optimizing the limitations cooperatively, but they only considered the intercell interference. The researchers in [15] separated the operation of wireless powered communication networks into two phases that namely the wireless energy transfer (WET) phase and wireless information transfer (WIT) phase. And in [14], a two phases cooperative NOMA system was proposed. Based on the time division, the users could combines the signals that received from the two phases by using the maximal-ration combining (MRC) technology. These papers gave new thinking that the user scheduling and resource allocation efficiency of time division were two important concerns in improving communication ability.

Motivated by this, in this paper, we consider a downlink multicast beamforming terrestrial-satellite cooperative system in which satellite and base stations provide service corporately for ground users within coverage. In this model, during the transmission, the users are divided into groups based on their requirement, and the system optimize the user group scheduling jointly with the resource allocation. The satellite and the base stations are all equipped with multi-antennas and reuse the same bandwidth, so they could provide the multicast service for ground users. We first formulate the problem to optimize the system capacity performance under the constraints of power allocation and user group scheduling. Then we design the beamforming vectors and solve the optimization problem by using the max-min-fair problem. Later we extend the problem into a more realistic scene that we consider the influence of the satellite and base station link delay, in order to decrease the influence for the joint optimization of base stations and satellite, and we propose an iterative algorithm to improve the system capacity performance based on two optimization phases.

The rest of the paper is organized as follows. In Sect. 2, the system model and the problem formulation are presented. In Sect. 3, the relaxation of user group scheduling and max-min-fair function, and the Lagrange Dual Method are adopted to solve the joint optimization problem. Finally the numerical results and simulation results are discussed in Sect. 4 and the conclusions are presented in Sect. 5.

2   System Model and Problem Formulation

2.1   System Model

Figure 1 shows a Terrestrial-Satellite Cooperative System model of multicast multigroup downlink architecture. In this system a satellite and I_B base stations serve ground users cooperatively. All users are under coverage of the satellite, and could access more than one base stations according to their requirement. Then we divide these users into J_G groups totally based on their desired contents. Under this circumstance, the satellite not only provides the desired contents to the users but also promotes the quality of service of the bottleneck users. In this paper, we assume the satellite to be a low earth orbit (LEO) satellite. Further more, we assume that each base station has A_B antennas, the satellite has A_S antennas, the maximum user number is M_U, the satellite and the base stations use the same spectrum during entire transmission, so the interference appears in different groups of one base station, different groups of different base stations and satellite.

It is denoted that $\omega_{i,j}$ is the beamforming vector for base station i group j, and $\|\omega_{i,j}\|^2 = P_{B,i,j}$ which is the transmission power of group j in base station i. $x_{B,i,j}$ is the multicast signal serving group j, and $E[|x_{B,i,j}|^2] = 1$. Therefore, the transmission signal of base station i can be written as

$$s_{B,i} = \sum_{j=1}^{J_B} \omega_{i,j} x_{B,i,j} \tag{1}$$

For the satellite, the transmission signal can be written similarly as

$$s_S = \sum_{j=1}^{J_S} \nu_j x_{S,j} \tag{2}$$

where ν_j is the beamforming vector for group j, and $\|\nu_j\|^2 = P_{S,j}$ which is the transmission power of group j. $x_{S,j}$ is multicast signal serving group j, and $E[|x_{S,j}|^2] = 1$.

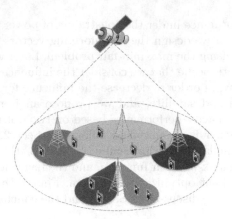

Fig. 1. The terrestrial-satellite cooperate network.

Then the received signal of base station user K in group J of base station I is

$$y_{I,J,K} = \sum_{i=1}^{I_B} h_{i,I,J,K}^H \omega_{i,I,J} x_J + g_{I,J,K}^H \nu_J x_J$$

$$+ \sum_{\substack{j=1 \\ j \neq J}}^{J_G} \left(\sum_{i=1}^{I_B} h_{i,I,J,K}^H \omega_{i,I,j} x_j + g_{I,J,K}^H \nu_j x_j \right) + n_{I,J,K} \quad (3)$$

where $h_{i,I,J,K}$ is the channel from base station i to the user K in base station I group J, $g_{I,J,K}$ is the channel from satellite to the user K in base station I group J. $\omega_{i,I,J}$ is the beamforming vector from base station i to group J of base station I, and ν_j is the beamforming vector from satellite to group j. $n_{I,J,K}$ is the AWGN noise. x_j is the required multicast signal of group j that $E[|x_j|^2] = 1$.

So the SINR of user K of group J in base station I is

$$\gamma_{I,J,K} = \frac{|\sum_{i=1}^{I_B} h_{i,I,J,K}^H \omega_{i,I,J} + g_{I,J,K}^H \nu_J|^2}{\sum_{\substack{j=1 \\ j \neq J}}^{J_G} |\sum_{i=1}^{I_B} h_{i,I,J,K}^H \omega_{i,I,j} + g_{I,J,K}^H \nu_j|^2 + \sigma_n^2} \quad (4)$$

Based on Shannon's Theorem, the capacity can be calculated by

$$R_{I,J,K} = \log_2(1 + \gamma_{I,J,K}) \quad (5)$$

where $R_{I,J,K}$ is the capacity of user K in group J from base station I including the signal from base stations, and the satellite.

Although, the user group scheduling should be considered in multicast transmission. So the SINR of user K of group J in base station I could be rewritten as

$$\gamma_{I,J,K_u} = \frac{u_J|\sum_{i=1}^{I_B} h_{i,I,J,K}^H \omega_{i,I,J} + g_{I,J,K}^H \nu_J|^2}{\sum_{\substack{j=1 \\ j \neq J}}^{J_G} u_j|\sum_{i=1}^{I_B} h_{i,I,J,K}^H \omega_{i,I,j} + g_{I,J,K}^H \nu_j|^2 + \sigma_n^2} \quad (6)$$

where the group J is served if $u_J = 1$, otherwise $u_J = 0$.

Then the capacity could be written as

$$R_{I,J,K} = \log_2(1 + \gamma_{I,J,K_u}) \tag{7}$$

2.2 Problem Formulation

Expression (7) gives the formulation of the capacity, but in wireless communication that the channel condition of different users relate to many reasons such as place, time, environment, weather, and so on. So we should notice that the SINR of each group is decided by the user who under the poorest channel condition. Considering the power limit, we can formulate the optimization problem (OP) as

$$(OP) \quad \max_{\{\omega_j\}_{j=1}^{J_G}, \{\nu_j\}_{j=1}^{J_G}, u} \quad \log(1 + \min_{I,J,K} \gamma_{I,J,K_u})$$

$$s.t.\ C1: P_{B,I} = \sum_{j=1}^{J_G} u_j \|\omega_{i,I,J}\|^2 \leq P_{B,i,I,max}\ I \in [1, I_B]$$
$$C2: P_S = \sum_{j=1}^{J_G} u_j \|\nu_j\|^2 \leq P_{S,max}$$
$$C3: u_j \in \{0,1\}, j = 1, \dots, J_G$$

where $C1$ and $C2$ are the maximum transmission power constraints for the base stations and the satellite, and $C3$ is the user group scheduling constraints.

3 Algorithm Development

We formulate the optimization problem in Sect. 2 based on the power constraints, but the optimization problem cannot be solved directly. Firstly, the function of the optimization problem is non-convex because of the γ_{I,J,K_u} in $R_{I,J,K}$. Secondly, the constraints $C3$ is a $0-1$ variable which is non-convex. So in this section, we first relax the optimization problem into the convex form, and then we expand the solution into a complex scenario to improve the system performance under the scenario that the link delay of satellite optimization is larger than it in base station optimization.

3.1 Relaxation and Solution of the Optimization Problem (OP)

The user group scheduling factor $u_j = 1$ when the group is under served and $u_j = 0$ otherwise, so combining the property of the beamforming vector ω and ν we could say that $u_j = 0$ if and only if $\omega = 0$ and $\nu = 0$. That means if the group is under service, the beamforming vector is absolutely non-zero. This lead to the reformulation of (OP):

$$(OP') \quad \max_{\{\omega_j\}_{j=1}^{J_G}, \{\nu_j\}_{j=1}^{J_G}} \quad \log(1 + \min_{I,J,K} \gamma_{I,J,K})$$

$$s.t.\ C1: P_{B,I} = \sum_{j=1}^{J_G} \|\omega_{i,I,J}\|^2 \leq P_{B,i,I,max}\ I \in [1, I_B]$$
$$C2: P_S = \sum_{j=1}^{J_G} \|\nu_j\|^2 \leq P_{S,max}$$

We suppose (u^*, Ω^*) and Ω^* as the optimal solutions of the problem (OP) and (OP'), in which $\Omega^* = [\omega^*, \nu^*]$. So the relationship between them is

$$u^* = \mathcal{F}(\Omega^*); \qquad u^*\Omega^* = \Omega^* \tag{8}$$

where $\mathcal{F}x$ indicates that the value of it is one if $x \neq 0$ and zero otherwise. Referring to [13], we could prove the relation between (OP) and (OP').

Proof. Necessity part:
We assume Φ_1 and Φ_2 as the feasible sets of (OP) and (OP'). Using (8) we have

$$\log(1 + \min_{I,J,K} \gamma_{I,J,K_u}(u^*, \Omega^*)) = \log(1 + \min_{I,J,K} \gamma_{I,J,K}(\Omega^*))$$

$$\geq \log(1 + \min_{I,J,K} \gamma_{I,J,K}(\Omega)), (u^*, \Omega^*) \in \Phi_1 \Omega^* \in \Phi_2$$

So for any $(\hat{u}, \hat{\Omega}) \in \Phi_1$ there exists $\bar{\Omega} \in \Phi_2$ that satisfies

$$\log(1 + \min_{I,J,K} \gamma_{I,J,K_u}(\hat{u}, \hat{\Omega})) = \log(1 + \min_{I,J,K} \gamma_{I,J,K}(\bar{\Omega}))$$

Then we obtain

$$\log(1 + \min_{I,J,K} \gamma_{I,J,K_u}(u^*, \Omega^*)) \geq \log(1 + \min_{I,J,K} \gamma_{I,J,K_u}(\hat{u}, \hat{\Omega}))$$

Proof. Sufficiency part:
Similarly, using (8) we have

$$\log(1 + \min_{I,J,K} \gamma_{I,J,K}(\Omega^*)) = \log(1 + \min_{I,J,K} \gamma_{I,J,K_u}(u^*, \Omega^*))$$

$$\geq \log(1 + \min_{I,J,K} \gamma_{I,J,K_u}(u, \Omega))$$

For any $\bar{\Omega} \in \Phi_2$ there exists $(\hat{u}, \hat{\Omega}) \in \Phi_1$ that satisfies

$$\log(1 + \min_{I,J,K} \gamma_{I,J,K}(\bar{\Omega})) = \log(1 + \min_{I,J,K} \gamma_{I,J,K_u}(\hat{u}, \hat{\Omega}))$$

Then we obtain

$$\log(1 + \min_{I,J,K} \gamma_{I,J,K}(\Omega^*)) \geq \log(1 + \min_{I,J,K} \gamma_{I,J,K}(\bar{\Omega}))$$

So we know that, the Eq. (8) and the relation between (OP) and (OP') are valid.

After relaxing the user group scheduling factors, by the monotonicity of logarithm function referring to [6], the problem could be rewritten as

$$(DOP) \quad \max_{\{\omega_j\}_{j=1}^{J_G}, \{\nu_j\}_{j=1}^{J_G}} \quad \min_{I,J,K} \gamma_{I,J,K}$$

$$s.t. \ C1: P_{B,I} = \sum_{j=1}^{J_G} ||\omega_{i,I,J}||^2 \leq P_{B,i,I,max} \ I \in [1, I_B]$$
$$C2: P_S = \sum_{j=1}^{J_G} ||\nu_j||^2 \leq P_{S,max}$$

But according to [17] it is still non-convex, so we couldn't solve it in a direct and simple way. We introduce an auxiliary variable t into (DOP), the problem can be written as the equivalent formulation below.

$$(DOP_t) \quad \max_{\{\omega_j\}_{j=1}^{J_G}, \{\nu_j\}_{j=1}^{J_G}, t} \quad t$$

$$\text{s.t. } C1: \gamma_{I,J,K} \geq t$$
$$C2: P_{B,I} = \sum_{j=1}^{J_G} ||\omega_{i,I,J}||^2 \leq P_{B,i,I,max} \; I \in [1, I_B]$$
$$C3: P_S = \sum_{j=1}^{J_G} ||\nu_j||^2 \leq P_{S,max}$$

Then we use the trace matrix $|h^H \omega|^2 = tr(hh^H \omega \omega^H)$ and $||\omega||^2 = tr(\omega \omega^H)$ to reformulate (DOP_t) as follow,

$$(DOP_X) \quad \max_{\{X_j\}_{j=1}^{J_G}, t} \quad t$$

$$\text{s.t. } C1: t(\sum_{\substack{j'=1 \\ j \neq j}}^{J_G} tr(Q_{I,J,K} X_j) + \delta_N^2) - tr(Q_{I,J,K} X_J) \leq 0$$
$$C2: X_J \geq 0 \; J \in [1, J_G]$$
$$C3: P_{B,I} = \sum_{j=1}^{J_G} tr(A_{B,i} X_j) \leq P_{B,i,I,max} \; I \in [1, I_B]$$
$$C4: P_S = \sum_{j=1}^{J_G} tr(A_S X_j) \leq P_{S,max}$$
$$C5: rank(X_J) = 1 \; J \in [1, J_G]$$

where

$$\Omega_{joint,J} = \left[\omega_{1,I,J}^H, \omega_{2,I,J}^H, \ldots, \omega_{I_B,I,J}^H, \nu_J^H \right]^H, \; X_J = \left[\Omega_{joint,J} \Omega_{joint,J}^H \right]$$

$$h_{joint,I,J,K} = \left[h_{1,I,J,K}^H, \ldots, h_{I_B,I,J,K}^H, g_{I,J,K}^H \right]^H, \; Q_{I,J,K} = h_{joint,I,J,K} h_{joint,I,J,K}^H$$

$$A_{B,I} = Diag\{Z_B, Z_S\}, Z_B = I_{A_B \times A_B}, Z_S = 0_{A_S \times A_S}$$

$$A_S = Diag\{Z_B, Z_S\}, Z_B = 0_{A_B \times A_B}, Z_S = I_{A_S \times A_S}$$

and $X_J \geq 0$ means the matrix X_J is positive semi-definite. It is obviously that if we want to optimize ω and ν, we should satisfy $X_J \geq 0$ and $rank(X_J) = 1$.

In (DOP_X), the power constrains could be rewrite as $\sum_{i=1}^{I_B} P_{B,i} + P_S = \sum_{j=1}^{J_G} tr(X_j) \leq \sum_{i=1}^{I_B} P_{B,i,I,max} + P_{S,max}$. It is clearly that if the power constrains of base stations and satellite are all satisfied, the inequation above is obviously satisfied. So we introduce another auxiliary parameter $\Delta_P \geq 0$ and a total power auxiliary variable P_{AUX} into the total power constrain as $\sum_{j=1}^{J_G} tr(X_j) + \Delta_P = P_{AUX}$. Then we can relax (DOP_X) without rank-1 constrains as

$$(DOP_{X_{\Delta P}}) \quad \max_{\{X_j\}_{j=1}^{J_G}, t, \Delta P} \quad t$$

$$s.t. \ C1: t(\sum_{\substack{j'=1 \\ j \neq j}}^{J_G} tr(Q_{I,J,K}X_j) + \delta_N^2) - tr(Q_{I,J,K}X_J) \leq 0$$

$$C2: X_J \geq 0 \ J \in [1, J_G]$$

$$C3: P_{B,I} = \sum_{j=1}^{J_G} tr(A_{B,i}X_j) \leq P_{B,i,I,max} \ I \in [1, I_B]$$

$$C4: P_S = \sum_{j=1}^{J_G} tr(A_S X_j) \leq P_{S,max}$$

$$C5: \sum_{j=1}^{J_G} tr(X_j) + \Delta_P = P_{AUX}$$

$$C6: \Delta_P \geq 0$$

It is proved or quoted in [17] that if $P_{AUX} \geq \sum_{i=1}^{I_B} P_{B,i,I,max} + P_{S,max}$, the optimization problem $(DOP_{X_{\Delta P}})$ is equal to (DOP_X) because the constrains $C5$ and $C6$ in $(DOP_{X_{\Delta P}})$ is invalid under this condition. In multicast beamforming scene, references [4] and [8] considered max-min fare problem and QoS problem are two main problems. In QoS problem, the beamforming vectors ω and ν are optimized to minimum the total power for all served users. Same as the relaxation above, the QoS problem can be written as

$$(DOP_Q) \quad \min_{\{X_j\}_{j=1}^{J_G}} \sum_{j=1}^{J_G} tr(X_j)$$

$$s.t. \ C1: (\sum_{\substack{j'=1 \\ j \neq j}}^{J_G} tr(Q_{I,J,K}X_j) + \delta_N^2) - tr(Q_{I,J,K}X_J) \leq 0$$

$$C2: X_J \geq 0 \ J \in [1, J_G]$$

$$C3: P_{B,I} = \sum_{j=1}^{J_G} tr(A_{B,i}X_j) \leq P_{B,i,I,max} \ I \in [1, I_B]$$

$$C4: P_S = \sum_{j=1}^{J_G} tr(A_S X_j) \leq P_{S,max}$$

Here we define $DOP_{X_{\Delta P}}(P_{B,i,I,max}, P_{S,max}, P_{AUX})$ to represent optimization problem $DOP_{X_{\Delta P}}$, and we know that (X_j^*, t^*, Δ_P^*) is the solution of the optimization problem. Same as the definition above, the QoS problem can be written as $DOP_Q(P_{B,i,I,max}, P_{S,max})$, and the solution is (X_j^*). According to the $C5$ in $(DOP_{X_{\Delta P}})$, the constraint could be rewritten as $DOP_{X_{\Delta P}}(P_{B,i,I,max}, P_{S,max}, DOP_Q(P_{B,i,I,max}, P_{S,max}) + \Delta_P^*)$, so we could establish relationship between the relaxed problem $DOP_{X_{\Delta P}}$ and the relaxed problem DOP_Q as follow:

$$t^* = DOP_{X_{\Delta P}}\left(P_{B,i,I,max}, P_{S,max}, DOP_Q\left(t, P_{B,i,I,max}, P_{S,max}\right) + \Delta_P^*\right)$$

$$P_{AUX} - \Delta_P^* = DOP_Q\left(DOP_{X_{\Delta P}}\left(P_{B,i,I,max}, P_{S,max}, P_{AUX}\right), P_{B,i,I,max}, P_{S,max}\right)$$

to simplify the equation, we use P to represent $(P_{B,i,I,max}, P_{S,max})$:

$$t^* = DOP_{X_{\Delta P}}\left(P, DOP_Q\left(t, P\right) + \Delta_P^*\right),$$

$$P_{AUX} - \Delta_P^* = DOP_Q\left(DOP_{X_{\Delta_P}}\left(P, P_{AUX}\right), P\right) \tag{9}$$

which is proved in [16].

The optimization problem DOP_Q is a standard SDP problem [7]. Previous researchers solved standard SDP problems with SeDuMi, CVX and so on. Here we choose SeDuMi [18] to calculate the SDP function. From [7] we know that, since $DOP_{X_{\Delta_P}}$ and DOP_Q are monotonically nondecreasing in t and P_{AUX}, optimization problem $DOP_{X_{\Delta_P}}$ could be solved based on the relation in Eq. (9). So we can use the bisection search over t with given P as follow:

Initialize: $[t_L, t_U]$, end condition ϵ

    Step 1: Set $t = \frac{t_L + t_U}{2}$, solve the opitmization
            problem $DOP_Q(t, P_{B,i,I,J}, P_{S,I,J})$.
    Step 2: If problem $DOP_Q(t, P_{B,i,I,J}, P_{S,I,J})$
            is infeasible, or the optimum solution
            is greater than P_{AUX}, set $t_U = t$;
            otherwise $t_L = t$.
    Step 3: If $|t_U - t_L| \leq \epsilon$, terminate. If not, repeat
            previous steps.

First, we set two initial values t_L and t_U that the solution of $t = DOP_{X_{\Delta_P}}$ $(P_{B,i,I,max}, P_{S,max}, P_{AUX})$ is located in $[t_L, t_U]$. Then, let $t = \frac{t_L + t_U}{2}$ and try to solve the optimization problem $DOP_Q(P_{B,i,I,max}, P_{S,max})$ with SeDuMi function tools. Next, if problem $DOP_Q(P_{B,i,I,max}, P_{S,max})$ is infeasible, or the optimum solution is greater than P_{AUX}, set $t_U = t$; if not, set $t_L = t$. Finally, if $|t_U - t_L| \leq \epsilon$, terminate the repetition and output the calculation results. If not, repeat previous steps until satisfying the end conditions.

As for the values of t_L and t_U, because of the physical meaning of the optimization problem, the lower bound $t_L = 0$ is obviously. By analysing the problem $t = DOP_{X_{\Delta_P}}$, we could find that when the system only serves one user in one group, the interference is zero and the t reaches t_U. Under this condition, the optimization problem could be written as

$$\max_{\{\omega_j\}_{j=1}^{J_G}, \{\nu_j\}_{j=1}^{J_G}} \frac{|h_{joint,I,J,K}^H \Omega_{joint,J}|^2}{\delta^2} \tag{10}$$

which we consider the only served user is $u_{I,J,K}$. Then we use the Cauchy-Schwartz inequality, the optimal beamforming vector could be written as

$$\Omega_{joint,J} = \sqrt{P_{AUX}} \frac{h_{joint,I,I,K}}{||h_{joint,I,I,K}||} \tag{11}$$

so the SINR $\gamma_{I,J,K}$ equal to $\frac{P_{AUX}||h_{joint,I,I,K}||^2}{\delta^2}$. The only one user $u_{I,J,K}$ condition could be extend to more users condition, then the SINR could be written as

$$\min_{I,J,K} \frac{P_{AUX}||h_{joint,I,I,K}||^2}{\delta^2} \tag{12}$$

and it equals to the upper bound t_U. By confirming the lower bound and upper bound t_L and t_U, we could calculate the optimal solution with a small enough ϵ.

After calculating the optimization problem $DOP_{X_{\Delta_P}}$ and DOP_Q, we notice that these two problems are constrain-relaxed. To ensure the beamforming vectors ω and ν are existent and the solution of X_J is valid, we constraint X_J as a positive semi-definite matrix and $rank(X_J) = 1$. But in problem $DOP_{X_{\Delta_P}}$ and DOP_Q, we drop the rank-1 constraint and relaxed them, it means that when we optimize $DOP_{X_{\Delta_P}}$ and DOP_Q, the result cannot always satisfy the constraint of rank-1. Previous researchers discussed these questions in [19]. They found that the Gaussian randomization method could give the highest accuracy in multicast beamforming system conditions [20]. In this case, we generate candidate beamforming vectors and choose the best performance beamforming vectors to solve the relaxed optimization problem. We know from [19] that we can generate a Gaussian random vector μ with zero-mean and unit-variance, which $\mu \sim CN(0, I)$. So based on the solution X_J, we perform the eigenvalue decomposition that $X_J = U_J \Sigma_J U_J^H$. For the beamforming vector, assumed in group J, can be calculated by $\Omega_{joint,J} = U_J \Sigma_J^{\frac{1}{2}} \mu_J$, where $\mu_J \sim CN(0, I)$ and $E[\Omega_{joint,J} \Omega_{joint,J}^H] = X_J$. But we should notice, when we choose the best performance beamforming vector for the optimization problem, the corresponding power constraints should be adjusted. Because not all the original power constraints satisfy the new method and there may exist some original available power constraints unused. To solve this question, we introduce a new optimal power scaling factor p_F into total power constraints. Accordingly, the original optimization problem $DOP_{X_{\Delta_P}}$ and DOP_Q could be reformulated as following:

$$(DOP_{p_F}) \quad \max_{\{p_{F,j}\}_{j=1}^{J_G}, t, \Delta_P} \quad t$$

$$s.t. \ C1: t \leq \frac{p_{F,j} |\sum_{i=1}^{I_B} h_{i,I,J,K}^H \omega_{i,I,J} + g_{I,J,K}^H \nu_J|^2}{\sum_{\substack{j=1 \\ j \neq J}}^{J_G} p_{F,j} |\sum_{i=1}^{I_B} h_{i,I,J,K}^H \omega_{i,I,J} + g_{I,J,K}^H \nu_J|^2 + \sigma_N^2}$$

$$C2: P_{B,I} = \sum_{j=1}^{N_G} p_{F,j} ||\omega_{i,I,J}||^2 \leq P_{B,i,I,max} \qquad I \in [1, I_B]$$

$$C3: P_S = \sum_{j=1}^{J_G} p_{F,j} ||\nu_j||^2 \leq P_{S,max}$$

$$C4: \sum_{j=1}^{J_G} p_{F,j} ||\Omega_{joint,j}||^2 + \Delta_P = P_{AUX}$$

$$C5: p_{F,J} \geq 0 \qquad J \in [1, J_G]$$

Then, the optimization problem DOP_Q could be reformulated as

$$(DOP_{Q_F}) \quad \min_{\{p_{F,j}\}_{j=1}^{J_G}} \sum_{j=1}^{J_G} p_{F,j} ||\Omega_{joint,j}||^2$$

$$s.t. \ C1: \sum_{\substack{j=1 \\ j \neq J}}^{J_G} p_{F,j} |\sum_{i=1}^{I_B} h_{i,I,J,K}^H \omega_{i,I,J} + g_{I,J,K}^H \nu_J|^2 + \sigma_N^2$$

$$\leq p_{F,j} |\sum_{i=1}^{I_B} h_{i,I,J,K}^H \omega_{i,I,J} + g_{I,J,K}^H \nu_J|^2$$

$$C2: P_{B,I} = \sum_{j=1}^{N_G} p_{F,j} ||\omega_{i,I,J}||^2 \leq P_{B,i,I,max} \qquad I \in [1, I_B]$$

$$C3: P_S = \sum_{j=1}^{J_G} p_{F,j} ||\nu_j||^2 \leq P_{S,max}$$

$$C4: p_{F,J} \geq 0 \qquad J \in [1, J_G]$$

Same as the relation of (9), we have

$$t^* = DOP_{p_F}\left(P, DOP_{Q_F}\left(t, P\right) + \Delta_P^*\right),$$

$$P_{AUX} - \Delta_P^* = DOP_{Q_F}\left(DOP_{p_F}\left(P, P_{AUX}\right), P\right) \tag{13}$$

which the constraint $C1$ in DOP_{p_F} is nonconvex, so we cannot solve the optimization problem DOP_{p_F} directly. Observing the optimization problem DOP_{Q_F}, we know that it is a standard linear formulation. So we could refer the method above to solve the optimization problem using the relation between DOP_{p_F} and DOP_{Q_F}. Similarly, the optimal beamforming vector is $p_{F,J}\Omega_{joint,J}$ and the upper bound of optimum solution t_U could be calculate as $\min\limits_{I,J,K} \frac{P_{AUX}\|h_{joint,I,I,K}\|^2}{\delta^2}$. Finally, we summarize the optimization algorithm as Algorithm 1.

Algorithm 1. Joint Terrestrial-Satellite Beamforming Design Algorithm

---
1: **Initialization:** $[t_L, t_U]$, end condition ϵ.
2: **while** $|t_U - t_L| \geq \epsilon$ **do**
3:    Set $t = \frac{t_L + t_U}{2}$ and solve the optimization problem $DOP_{Q_F}(\mathbf{P})$.
4:    **if** $DOP_{Q_F}(\mathbf{P})$ infeasible **or** $DOP_{Q_F}(\mathbf{P}) \geq P_{AUX}$ **then**
5:        set $t_U = t$
6:    **else**
7:        set $t_L = t$
8:    **End If**
9: **End While**
10: Generate candidate beamforming vectors and choose the best performance beam-forming vector to solve the optimization problem DOP_{p_F}.

3.2   Expand Power Optimization of Base Stations

In the last subsection, we relax the (OP) into convex form and solve it. But in the actual scene, we cannot always optimize the base stations and satellite jointly. Because the link delay of satellite is much larger than that of base stations, when the channel condition or the requirement of users change, the optimization of base stations could match it in time but the satellite may not. That means joint optimization of satellite and base stations might not always match up to the changes. Considering this, we divide the optimization of transmission into two phases. The joint optimization of satellite and base stations is in the first phase, and in the second phase we optimize the power of base stations to better satisfy the need of users.

The first phase is illustrate in the last subsection. We notice that $\omega = \omega_0 P$ where $||\omega_0|| = 1$, so we could rewrite the extend optimization problem (EP) as

$$(EP) \max_{P_{B,I}} \min_{I,J,K} \gamma_{I,J,K}$$

$$s.t.\ C1: P_{B,I} = \sum_{j=1}^{N_G} ||\omega_{i,I,J_0}\sqrt{P_{B,i,I,J}}||^2 \leq P_{B,i,I,max}\ I \in [1, I_B]$$

in which $\omega_{i,I,J_0}\sqrt{P_{B,i,I,J}} = \omega_{i,I,J}$. Same as the method before, we can get:

$$(EP_t) \max_{P_{B,I},t} t$$

$$s.t.\ C1: \gamma_{I,J,K} \geq t$$
$$C2: P_{B,I} = \sum_{j=1}^{N_G} ||\omega_{i,I,J_0}\sqrt{P_{B,i,I,J}}||^2 \leq P_{B,i,I,max}\ I \in [1, I_B]$$

To solve this problem, we use the Lagrange Dual Method to transmit (EP_t) into the dual problem. Then the Lagrange function of the (EP_t) is:

$$\mathcal{L}(P_{B,I}, t, \eta) = t - \eta_1(t - \gamma_{I,J,K}) - \eta_2(\sum_{j=1}^{N_G} ||\omega_{i,I,J_0}\sqrt{P_{B,i,I,J}}||^2 - P_{B,i,I,max}) \quad (14)$$

the dual function is

$$\theta(\eta) = \sup\mathcal{L}(P_{B,I}, t, \eta) \quad (15)$$

Then the corresponding dual optimization of (EP_t) is

$$(EP_{DUAL}) \min \theta(\eta)$$

$$s.t.\ C1: \eta_l \geq 0 \qquad\qquad l = \{1, 2\}$$
$$C2: \sum_{l=\{1,2\}} \eta_l = 1$$

The optimal solutions must satisfy the Karush-Kuhn-Tucher (KKT) condition, we have

$$\frac{\partial \mathcal{L}}{\partial P_{B,I}} = 0 \quad (16)$$

So, the optimal solution of base station transmission power allocation could be calculated as

$$P_{B,i,I,J} = \left(\frac{4(1-\eta_1)\sum_{i=1}^{I_B} h_{i,I,J,K}^H \omega_{i,I,J_0} g_{I,J,K}^H \nu_J}{2\eta_2 \sum_{\substack{j=1 \\ j \neq J}}^{J_G} |\mathcal{I}|^2 - 4(1-\eta_1)\sum_{i=1}^{I_B} h_{i,I,J,K}^H{}^2 \omega_{i,I,J_0}^2}\right)^2 \quad (17)$$

where $\mathcal{I} = \sum_{i=1}^{I_B} h_{i,I,J,K}^H \omega_{i,I,j} + g_{I,J,K}^H \nu_j$.

Then we put the optimal solution into the dual problem (EP_{DUAL}), and use the subgradient method to update the Lagrange multipliers iteratively.

$$\eta_1[t+1] = \max\left\{\eta_1[t] - \delta_{\eta_1}[t+1](t - \gamma_{I,J,K}), 0\right\} \quad (18)$$

$$\eta_2[t+2] = \max\left\{\eta_2[t] - \delta_{\eta_2}[t+1]\left(\sum_{j=1}^{N_G}||\omega_{i,I,J_0}\sqrt{P_{B,i,I,J}}||^2 - P_{B,i,I,max}\right), 0\right\} \quad (19)$$

where we denote t as the iteration step, and δ is the step length for the iteration. So we obtain all the factors we need. And the expand power optimization of base stations algorithm is exhibited below.

Initialize: $\eta_l[0]$, $l = 1, 2$

Repeat: 1. Update SINR according to (4)

2. For $I = [1, I_B]$, $J = [1, J_G]$, update $P_{B,i,I,J}$ according to (17)

3. Update η_l according to (18) and (19)

4. If $P_{B,I}$ converge, end.

So the complete joint optimization algorithm of phase division under the consideration of link delay is described in Algorithm 2.

Algorithm 2. Phase Division Joint Optimization Algorithm

1: **Initialize:**$\eta_l[0]$, $l = 1, 2$
2: Design the beamforming vectors according to **Algorithm 1**
3: **while** $P_{B,I}$ converge **do**
4:     **Update** SINR according to (4)
5:     **for** $I =1$ to I_B **do**
6:         **for** $J =1$ to J_G **do**
7:             **Update** $P_{B,i,I,J}$ according to (17)
8:         **End For**
9:     **End For**
10:     **Update** η_l according to (18) and (19)
11:     $t = t + 1$
12: **End While**

---

4   Performance Evaluation

In this section, we use the MATLAB software to simulate and evaluate the proposed algorithm and then present the result. The proposed system model is a downlink communication network that the satellite, base stations and ground mobile terminals work cooperatively. The satellite is a LEO with $1000\,\mathrm{km}$ from the ground, the maximum power is $40\,\mathrm{W}$, and the carrier frequency is set as $2\,\mathrm{GHz}$, the AWGN power σ_n is set as $-134\,\mathrm{dBm}$. The maximum constraint power of the base stations $P_{B,i,I,max}$ is set as $43\,\mathrm{dBm}$. The gain of mobile terminal is $0\,\mathrm{dbi}$. The transmission gain of the satellite and the base station are $50\,\mathrm{dBi}$ and $18\,\mathrm{dBi}$. The terrestrial channel is set as Rayleigh channel, the satellite channel is set as Rician channel.

Figures 2, 3 and 4 shows the influence of base station number, group size and group number. The blue lines in these figures represent the optimal capacity of Algorithm 1, the purple lines represent the capacity that only served by the base

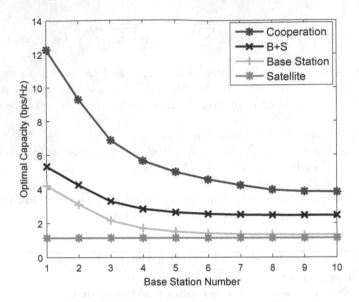

Fig. 2. Influence of base station number on optimal capacity. (Color figure online)

stations, the red lines represent the capacity that only served by the satellite, and the black lines are the sum capacity of base stations and satellite.

In Fig. 2, we set $A_B = 2$, $A_S = 5$, $M_U = 5$ and $J_G = 2$. We could observe from Fig. 2 that when the base station number rises, the optimal capacity decreases. When there is only one base station, the capacity of blue line is about 2.9 times to the purple line and about 2.3 times to the black line. When the number of base station comes to 10, the capacity of blue line declines to 150% of the black line. This is because when the number of base station increases, the interference between base stations has a greater impact on the SINR and capacity, but the positive effect of the Algorithm 1 is notable.

In Fig. 3 we set $A_B = 2$, $A_S = 5$, $I_B = 2$ and $J_G = 2$. And in Fig. 4 we set $A_B = 2$, $A_S = 5$, $I_B = 2$ and $M_U = 5$. It is obviously that the speed of decrease of the capacity in Fig. 3 is much slower than it in Fig. 4. That means the influence of the interference that brought by the group number is greater than by the group size. In Fig. 3 the capacity of algorithm 1 nearly keeps the 60% increment to the capacity in black line, so we find that the group size influence the capacity but play a minor role in our proposed algorithm. In Fig. 4 when the group number raises from 1 to 3, not only the cooperative capacity decreases about 77%, but also the capacity of purple line and red line decrease very fast. Combining the Figs. 2, 3 and 4, the problem that how to design the number of base station, the group size and group number according to the requirement of users is a complex but important question. But it is beyond the scope of this paper.

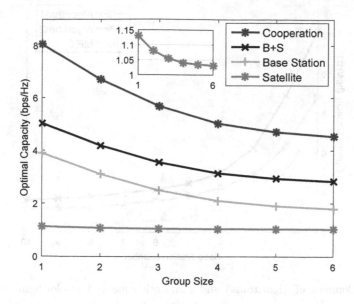

Fig. 3. Influence of group size on optimal capacity. (Color figure online)

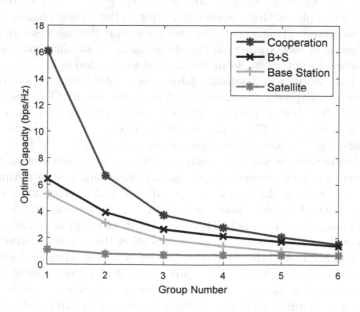

Fig. 4. Influence of group number on optimal capacity. (Color figure online)

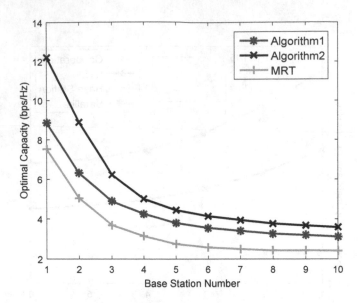

Fig. 5. Compare of Algorithms 1 and 2 and other method. (Color figure online)

In Fig. 5 we compare the capacity of Algorithms 1 and 2 and other method in [21] that the beamforming vectors is calculated by maximum ratio transmission (MRT). We set $A_B = 2$, $A_S = 5$, $M_U = 5$ and $J_G = 2$. And we divide the program into two phases that the user condition in the second phase is different from the first phase. This simulate the real scene that the link delay of satellite is larger than it of base station, so the optimization of satellite may not catch up with the change of users. So in the first phase we design the beamforming vectors of base stations and satellite jointly, in second phase we optimize the capacity under the power constraints of base stations only. The results show that when the number of base station is 1 and 2, the capacity increment of algorithm 2 is 41% and 37% compared with Algorithm 1. When the number of base station gets higher, the percent of capacity keeps nearly 15%. Because when the interference is not very complex with a small base station number, the improvement in the second phase play an important role in optimization. As the number of base station raises, the influences of interference get higher, the improvement of second phase optimization decreases but still important. The purple line in Fig. 5 is the MRT method that we could find that, our joint optimization algorithm of beamforming design effect the capacity of system more markable than MRT. And the simulation results show that when the base station number is 1, 2 or bigger than 7, the improvement of blue line is about 29%, but when the number is 6, the capacity improvement of Algorithm 1 is 38%. And the improvement of Algorithm 2 is about 60% compared with MRT method. So the suitable base station number could improve the capacity markable.

5 Conclusion

In this paper, we proposed a multicast beamforming terrestrial-satellite cooperation system, in which satellite and base stations provide service cooperatively for
ground users. By formulating and solving optimization problem under the constraints of user group scheduling, resource allocation and beamforming design,
we improved the system capacity performance. When the scene is more realistic, we optimized the problem in two phases that we designed the beamforming
vectors of base station and satellite jointly in the first phase, obtained the power
allocation result in the second phase because of the optimization link delay of
satellite is larger than it of base station. The simulation results showed that,
comparing with other methods, the proposed algorithm in this paper was better
in performance especially when the factors such as base station number, group
size and group number were suitable for the hole system. The proposed algorithm of beamforming design, optimization of resource allocation and user group
scheduling in this paper gained more than 38% of capacity improvement.

References

1. Ericsson mobility report (2018). https://www.ericsson.com/en/mobility-report
2. Cisco.: Cisco visual networking index: global mobile data traffic forecast update
   2014–2019. Whitepaper (2015)
3. Sinky, H., Khalfi, B., Hamdaoui, B., Rayes, A.: Responsive content-centric delivery
   in large urban communication networks: a LinkNYC use-case. IEEE Trans. Wirel.
   Commun. 17(3), 1688–1699 (2018)
4. Xiao, L., Dai, H., Ning, P.: Jamming-resistant collaborative broadcast using unco-
   ordinated frequency hopping. IEEE Trans. Inf. Forensics Secur. 7(1), 297C–309
   (2012)
5. Lin, B., Fei, Z., Zhang, Y.: UAV communications for 5G and beyond: recent
   advances and future trends. IEEE Internet Things J. 6(2), 2241–2263 (2019)
6. Sun, Y., Liu, K.: Transmit diversity techniques for multicasting over wireless
   networks. In: 2004 IEEE Wireless Communications and Networking Conference,
   Atlanta, GA, USA (2004)
7. Sidiropoulos, N., Davidson, T., Luo, Z.: Transmit beamforming for physical-layer
   multicasting. IEEE Trans. Signal Process. 54(6), 2239–2251 (2006)
8. Karipidis, E., Sidiropoulos, N., Luo, Z.: Convex transmit beamforming for downlink
   multicasting to multiple co-channel groups. In: 2006 IEEE International Conference
   on Acoustics Speech and Signal Processing Proceedings, Toulouse (2006)
9. Dadallage, S., Yi, C., Cai, J.: Joint beamforming, power, and channel allocation in
   multiuser and multichannel underlay MISO cognitive radio networks. IEEE Trans.
   Veh. Technol. 65(5), 3349–3359 (2016)
10. Zhu, X., Jiang, C., Kuang, L., Ge, N., Lu, J.: Non-orthogonal multiple access based
    integrated terrestrial-satellite networks. IEEE J. Sel. Areas Commun. 35(10),
    2253–2267 (2017)
11. Zhou, Y., Liu, H., Pan, Z., Tian, L., Shi, J., Yang, G.: Two-stage cooperative mul-
    ticast transmission with optimized power consumption and guaranteed coverage.
    IEEE J. Sel. Areas Commun. 32(2), 274–284 (2014)

12. Hsu, G., Liu, B., Wang, H., Su, H.: Joint beamforming for multicell multigroup multicast with per-cell power constraints. IEEE Trans. Veh. Technol. **66**(5), 4044–4058 (2017)
13. Ye, Q., Rong, B., Chen, Y., Al-Shalash, M., Caramanis, C., Andrews, J.: User association for load balancing in heterogeneous cellular networks. IEEE Trans. Wirel. Commun. **12**(6), 2706–2716 (2013)
14. Ku, M., Wang, L., Liu, Y.: Joint antenna beamforming, multiuser scheduling, and power allocation for hierarchical cellular systems. IEEE J. Sel. Areas Commun. **33**(5), 896–909 (2015)
15. Yang, K., Yu, Q., Leng, S., Fan, B., Wu, F.: Data and energy integrated communication networks for wireless big data. IEEE Access **4**, 713C–723 (2016)
16. Liu, Y., Ding, Z., Elkashlan, M., Poor, H.: Cooperative nonorthogonal multiple access with simultaneous wireless information and power transfer. IEEE J. Sel. Areas Commun. **34**(4), 938C–953 (2016)
17. Karipidis, E., Sidiropoulos, N., Luo, Z.: Quality of service and max-min fair transmit beamforming to multiple cochannel multicast groups. IEEE Trans. Signal Process. **56**(3), 1268–1279 (2008)
18. Sturm, J.: Using SeDuMi 1.02, a MATLAB toolbox for optimization over symmetric cones. Optim. Methods Softw. **11–12**, 625–C653 (1999)
19. Pennanen, H., Christopoulos, D., Chatzinotas, S., Ottersten, B.: Distributed coordinated beamforming for multi-cell multigroup multicast systems. In: 2016 IEEE International Conference on Communications (ICC), Kuala Lumpur (2016)
20. Jiang, C., Chen, Y., Gao, Y., Liu, K.: Joint spectrum sensing and access evolutionary game in cognitive radio networks. IEEE Trans. Wirel. Commun. **12**(5), 2470C–2483 (2013)
21. Zhao, Z., Chen, W.: An adaptive switching method for sum rate maximization in downlink MISO-NOMA systems. In: GLOBECOM 2017 IEEE Global Communications Conference, Singapore (2017)

Application of Wavelet Analysis Method in Radar Echo Signal Detection

Qiuyue Li[1]([✉]) and Xiangyu Tong[2]

[1] China Agricultural University, Beijing 100083, China
lqyue@cau.edu.cn
[2] Harbin Institute of Technology, Harbin 150001, China
18904809089@163.com

Abstract. In this paper, we focus on several signal detection method and wavelet analysis method for radar echo signal detection. According to the characteristics of signal detection and modern signal processing theory, we have deduced and analyzed the principles of these algorithms in mathematics, which involves more profound knowledge such as higher-order statistics and wavelet, and of course. It is important that we perform wavelet analysis on the echo signals of the HF ground wave radar to remove the weak ionospheric clutter and the method performs well. Wavelet is an important mathematical application method in signal detection.

Keywords: Signal detection · Radar echo · Wavelet

1 Introduction

Signal detection is an important branch of signal processing. It has been widely used in radar, communication, sonar and automatic fault detection. With the advancement of modernization, electronic equipment is becoming more and more diversified, and the electromagnetic environment in communication is becoming more and more complex, which puts forward higher requirements for signal detection algorithm. With the emergence of many theories and methods, such as high-order statistics, adaptive filtering, time-frequency analysis and neural networks, new vitality has been injected into the field of signal detection. The theoretical level and application level of signal detection have been greatly improved, and the performance of signal detection has been greatly improved. In this paper, we analyze the principle of correlation detection algorithm, and study the source of higher-order statistics and the principle of signal detection based on bispectrum analysis. At the same time, we also perform wavelet processing on the echo signals of high-frequency ground wave radar, which shows the effect of wavelet on signal processing.

© ICST Institute for Computer Sciences, Social Informatics and Telecommunications Engineering 2019
Published by Springer Nature Switzerland AG 2019. All Rights Reserved
S. Han et al. (Eds.): AICON 2019, LNICST 286, pp. 327–333, 2019.
https://doi.org/10.1007/978-3-030-22968-9_28

2 Signal Detection Method

2.1 Correlation Detection

Correlation detection is a technology developed in the 1960s. The earliest practical correlation detection system was realized by using tape recorder technology such as Bennett of Bell Laboratory in 1953. In 1961, Weinreb's article described the use of autocorrelation to extract periodic signals from random noise. Since then, a lot of work has been done and this technology has been widely used.

The correlation detection mainly carries on the correlation analysis to the signal and the noise, and the correlation function R(t) is the main physical quantity of the correlation analysis. The values of deterministic signals at different times are generally highly correlated. As for the interference noise, because of its strong randomness, the correlation of the values at different times is generally poor. Using this difference, the deterministic signal is distinguished from the interference noise.

Correlation detection includes autocorrelation method and cross correlation method. autocorrelation method measures the correlation before and after a random process by autocorrelation function, while cross correlation method measures the correlation between two random processes by cross correlation function. Compared with autocorrelation method, the stronger the ability of cross-correlation method to extract signals, the more thorough the noise suppression. Generally, cross-correlation is based on the repetition period or known frequency of the received signal, which sends out the same reference signal as the frequency of the signal to be measured at the receiving end, and correlates the reference signal with the input signal mixed with noise. The cross-correlation function is expressed as formula (2.1).

$$R_{xy}(\tau) = \lim_{T \to 0} \frac{1}{T} \int_0^T x(\tau)y(t - \tau)dt \qquad (2.1)$$

Let the signal to be measured be x(t) = S(t) + n(t), where S(t) is the characteristic signal and n(t) is the noise. If y(t) is the reference signal and $R_{xy}(\tau)$ is the cross-correlation function of x(t) and y(t), then the cross-correlation function is formula (2.2):

$$\begin{aligned} R_{xy}(\tau) &= E[x(t)y(t - \tau)] \\ &= E[S(t)y(t - \tau)] + E[n(t)y(t - \tau)] \\ &= R_{Sy}(\tau) + R_{ny}(\tau) \end{aligned} \qquad (2.2)$$

If n(t) is not related to y(t), then $R_{ny}(\tau) = 0$. Therefore, $R_{xy}(\tau) = R_{Sy}(\tau)$, in which $R_{Sy}(\tau)$ is the cross-correlation function of S(t) and reference signal y(t).

2.2 Signal Detection Based on Higher Order Statistics

High-order statistics contain a lot of rich information that second-order statistics do not have, so the application of high-order statistics in signal detection can achieve higher performance than second-order statistics in signal detection.

Let the random variable X have a probability density function f(x), the character-istic function is defined as formula (2.3):

$$\Phi(\omega) = \int_{-\infty}^{\infty} f(x)e^{j\omega x}dx = E\{e^{j\omega x}\} \tag{2.3}$$

The eigenfunction is also called the first eigenfunction. The second eigenfunction is defined as formula (2.4):

$$\Psi(\omega) = \ln[\Phi(\omega)] \tag{2.4}$$

K-order moment m_k of random variable x, such as k-order derivative of first characteristic function of random variable at origin, as formula (2.5):

$$m_k = \Phi^k(\omega)|_{\omega=0} \tag{2.5}$$

The k-order derivative of the second characteristic function of a random variable at the origin is equal to the k-order cumulant kc of the random variable x, as formula (2.6):

$$c_k = \Psi^k(\omega)|_{\omega=0} \tag{2.6}$$

Let $\{x(n)\}$ be a k-order stationary process with zero mean, then the k-order moments of the process are defined as formula (2.7):

$$m_{kx}(\tau_1, \tau_2, \ldots, \tau_{k-1}) = mom\{x(n), x(n+\tau_1), \ldots, x(n+\tau_{k-1})\} \tag{2.7}$$

The k-order cumulant is defined as formula (2.8):

$$c_{kx}(\tau_1, \tau_2, \ldots, \tau_{k-1}) = cum\{x(n), x(n+\tau_1), \ldots, x(n+\tau_{k-1})\} \tag{2.8}$$

The most common high-order spectrum is the third-order spectrum (bispectrum) as formula (2.9):

$$B_x(\omega_1, \omega_2) = \sum_{\tau_1=-\infty}^{\infty} \sum_{\tau_2=-\infty}^{\infty} c_{3x}(\tau_1, \tau_2)e^{-j(\omega_1\tau_1 + \omega_2\tau_2)} \tag{2.9}$$

When the detected signal is detected, the given data is divided into K segments, each segment contains M observation samples, namely N = KM, and the average value of each segment is subtracted from the data. If necessary, add zero to each segment of data to meet the requirement of the general length M of FFT. Next, calculate the DFT coefficient, as formula (2.10).

$$Y^{(i)}(\omega) = \frac{1}{M} \sum_{n=0}^{M-1} y^{(i)}(n) \exp(-j2\pi n\omega/M)$$
$$\omega = 0, 1, \ldots, M/2, i = 1, 2, \ldots, K \tag{2.10}$$

Continue to calculate the triple correlation of DFT coefficients as formula (2.11):

$$b_i(\omega_1,\omega_2) = \frac{1}{A_0^2} \sum_{k_1=-L_1}^{L_1} \sum_{k_2=-L_2}^{L_1} Y^{(i)}(\omega_1+k_1)Y^{(i)}(\omega_2+k_2)Y^{(i)}(-\omega_1-k_1-\omega_2-k_2)$$

$$i = 1,2,\ldots,K,$$
$$0 \le \omega_2 \le \omega_1,$$
$$\omega_1 + \omega_2 \le f_s/2,$$
$$M = (2L_1+1)N$$

(2.11)

From this, we can get the bispectrum estimation of the measured data, which is showed as formula (2.12):

$$B_D(\overline{\omega_1},\overline{\omega_2}) = \frac{1}{K}\sum_{i=1}^{K} b_i(\overline{\omega_1},\overline{\omega_2})$$

$$\overline{\omega_1} = \left(\frac{2\pi f_s}{N_0}\right)\omega_1, \overline{\omega_2} = \left(\frac{2\pi f_s}{N_0}\right)\omega_2$$

(2.12)

2.3 Signal Detection Based on Wavelet Transform

Wavelet analysis is a kind of time-frequency analysis. It is the development of Fourier analysis, but it is better than Fourier analysis. Although Fourier analysis is widely used as a classical method, it has its own shortcomings, that is, it can not express the most critical time-frequency localization properties of signals. In order to analyze and process non-stationary signals, short-time Fourier transform and wavelet transform are generated. The window width of the wavelet transform is adjustable. It has the ability to characterize the local characteristics of signals in both time and frequency domains, and has the characteristics of multi-resolution analysis.

Wavelet transform is defined as follows: Let $\Psi(t) \in L^2(R)$, whose Fourier transformation satisfies admissible condition (2.13):

$$\int_R \frac{|\Psi(\omega)|^2}{\omega} d\omega < \infty$$

(2.13)

$\Psi(t)$ is called the wavelet generating function. The scaling and translation of the wavelet generating function are carried out. The scaling factor is a and the translation factor is τ. If the scaling function is $\Psi_{a,\tau}(t)$, the scaling factor of the wavelet generating function is as formula (2.14):

$$\Psi_{a,\tau}(t) = a^{-\frac{1}{2}}\Psi\left(\frac{t-\tau}{a}\right), a > 0, \tau \in R$$

(2.14)

$\Psi_{a,\tau}(t)$ is called a wavelet basis function. Expansion of any function $f(t) \in L^2(R)$ on wavelet basis is called continuous wavelet transform of function f(t). Its expression is as formula (2.15):

$$WT_f(a, \tau) = \frac{1}{\sqrt{a}} \int_R f(t) \Psi^* \left(\frac{t - \tau}{a}\right) dt \qquad (2.15)$$

Reference formula (2.14), formula (2.15) can be written in the form of inner product as formula (2.16).

$$WT_f(a, \tau) = \int_{-\infty}^{+\infty} f(t) \Psi_{a,\tau}^*(t) = \langle f(t), \Psi_{a,\tau}(t) \rangle \qquad (2.16)$$

It can be seen from the formula that when scale a increases, the whole f (t) is observed with extended $\Psi(t)$ waveform, whereas when scale a decreases, the local f(t) is measured with compressed $\Psi(t)$ waveform. In a certain scale or within a certain scale, the intensity of the wavelet coefficients of the signal is larger. Therefore, the wavelet coefficients can be used as the object of signal detection.

Next we take the high-frequency ground wave radar echo signal with a large number of ionospheric clutter as an example, and use the processing of different wavelet bases to compare the wavelet to help the data detection processing (Figs. 1 and 2).

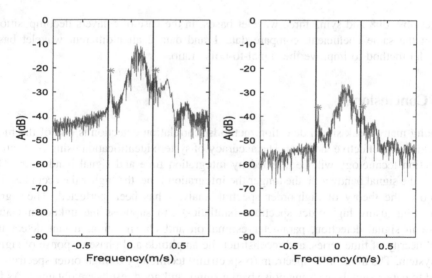

Fig. 1. Comparison before and after wavelet processing

Observing and comparing the radar echo spectrum and the spectrogram obtained by processing the data 1 and data 2 using two wavelet bases, the signal-to-noise ratio of the unprocessed signal is calculated to be 10.1. After processing the data 1 by the wavelet method, the haar wavelet base improves the signal miscellaneous The ratio is 2.06, and the signal-to-noise ratio improved by sym8 wavelet is 0.12. After processing data 2 by wavelet method, the haar wavelet base improves the signal-to-noise ratio to 1.97, and the sym8 wavelet improves the signal-to-noise ratio to 1.09. Then continue to

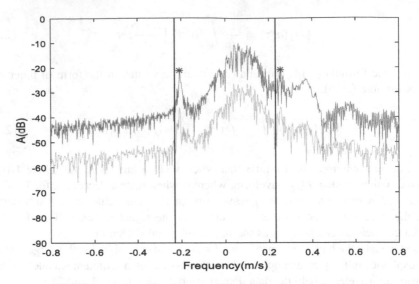

Fig. 2. Visual comparison before and after wavelet processing

select db9, db8 and sym5 three wavelet bases, in the case of 5 layers decomposition, select the same coefficient, compare data 1 and data 2 after different wavelet basis wavelet method to improve the signal-to-noise ratio.

3   Conclusion

Among many weak signal detection methods, correlation detection is one of the most common and effective methods. The accuracy of system identification using correlation detection technology will be affected by integration time and signal bandwidth. The wider the signal bandwidth, the longer the integration time, the higher the accuracy. Up to now, the theory of high-order spectral analysis has been perfected. The signal processing using high-order spectrum (statistics) can suppress the unknown Gauss noise in signal detection, parameter estimation and classification. It can detect the nonlinearity of time series, and reconstruct the amplitude and phase response of signal or system. The third-order spectrum (bispectrum) technology of high-order spectrum is used to detect signals in strong noise background, and good results are obtained. As for the detection method of wavelet coefficients, we can choose the wavelet coefficients in a single scale as the object of study, or we can enhance the strength of the useful signals by averaging the wavelet coefficients in several scales in a certain scale range, that is, the method of coefficient accumulation.

References

1. Cohen, L.: Time-frequency Distributions-A Review. Proc. IEEE **77**(7), 941–981 (1989)
2. Shu-jun, X., Ying, W.: The detection of transient signals based on gabor transform. IEEE Proc. ICSP **I**, 259–262 (2006)
3. Williams, C.: Robust chaotic communications exploiting waveform diversity part 1: correlation detection and implicit coding. IEEE J. **2**(10), 1213–1222 (2008)
4. Lili, T., Gang, W.: Least mean square adaptive echo cancellation algorithm based on high-order statistics. Control Theory Appl. **17**(6), 911–914 (2000)
5. Lin, I.S., Weiner, A.M.: Selective correlation detection of photonic ally generated ultra wideband RF signals. IEEE J. **26**(15), 2692–2699 (2008)
6. Ball, J.E., Tolley, A.: Low SNR radar signal detection using the continuous wavelet transform (CWT) and a Morlet wavelet. In: Radar Conference, RADAR 2008. IEEE (2008)
7. Wang, F.-T., Chang, S.-H.: Signal detection with a shift invariant noise model based on wavelet bases. In: Oceans 2004, MTTS/IEEE Techno-Ocean 2004 (2004)

Chinese News Keyword Extraction Algorithm Based on TextRank and Topic Model

Ao Xiong and Qing Guo$^{(\boxtimes)}$

Beijing University of Posts and Telecommunications, Beijing 100876, China
xiongao@bupt.edu.cn, guoqingbupt@163.com

Abstract. TextRank tends to choose frequent words as keywords of a document. In fact, some infrequent words can also be keywords. In order to improve this situation, a Chinese news keyword extraction algorithm LDA-TextRank based on TextRank and LDA topic model is proposed. The algorithm is a single document, unsupervised algorithm. It defines the diffusivity of two candidate words, constructs a new weight formula, and improves the weight of the edges in the text graph. At the same time, it combines with the LDA topic model, and the damping factor in TextRank is adjusted by calculating the word's topic relevance of the document. The experiment was carried out on the Chinese corpus. The results show that compared with TextRank, LDA-TextRank has an improvement in Precision, Recall and F1-measure.

Keywords: Keyword extraction · TextRank · LDA topic model

1 Introduction

Keywords are the summary of an article or a document. Keywords can be defined as a set of words or phrases that can summarize the topic of the article [1]. Keywords have important practical values in many fields, such as text classification and clustering, literature information retrieval, recommendation systems, etc. In most cases, however, the document does not provide keywords, so it is necessary to design an algorithm that automatically extracts keywords.

The algorithm of keyword extraction can be classified into the supervised and the unsupervised. As for the supervised algorithms, Witten et al. designed the KEA [2] system and proposed an algorithm for keyword extraction using Naïve Bayesian machine learning method. The algorithm only uses two features: word's TF-IDF (Term Frequency-Inverse Document Frequency) and its first occurrence in the document. The algorithm has to train a large number of labeled corpus to get the model. Turney et al. [1] designed a keyword extraction algorithm based on C4.5 decision tree and GenEx system based on the genetic algorithm to extract keywords. For unsupervised algorithms, Sparck [3] first proposed the concept of IDF (Inverse Document Frequency). Salton et al. [4] discussed the application of Term Frequency-Inverse Document Frequency (TF-IDF) in the field of information retrieval. Since then TF-IDF was regarded by scholars as a simple and basic algorithm for keyword extraction. TF-IDF treats the document as a Bag of Words (BOW) model, which means the order of words does not affect the results of the algorithm. In 2004, TextRank algorithm was proposed by

S. Han et al. (Eds.): AICON 2019, LNICST 286, pp. 334–341, 2019.
https://doi.org/10.1007/978-3-030-22968-9_29

Mihalcea et al. [5]. The algorithm originates from Google's PageRank algorithm for page ranking [6]. The words in the document are regarded as nodes, and the number of co-occurrences in the fixed-length window is used as the weight of the edges between the nodes, thus establishing the relation between the words. By constructing a text network to iterate, the score of each node is finally obtained, and the keywords are determined according to the scores.

At present, TextRank has been widely studied and various keyword extraction algorithms based on TextRank have been proposed. For example, Gu et al. [7] use only the TF of the candidate words to construct the weight between the nodes, and brings the factor of whether the candidate word is in the title to weight the final score. Since the IDF of the candidate word is not used, the computational complexity of the algorithm is reduced accordingly. Li et al. [8] mine the corpus of Wikipedia, calculate the TF-IDF of each term and convert them into vectors. Each element in the vector is its TF-IDF, and the cosine similarity of two vectors is used to represent the weight of the edge. The algorithm utilizes the information of Wikipedia, and improves the performance of TextRank in short documents. In addition, the first N words, whether the word is in the first sentence of a paragraph can also be used for keyword extraction [9]. Recent years, the LDA [10] topic model has also aroused attention in keyword extraction. For example, Liu [11] has carried out a systematic study on keyword extraction. The LDA topic model is combined with the TextRank algorithm. By calculating the scores of words in different topics, and finally weighting according to the topic weights, the scores of candidate words are obtained.

Based on TextRank, this paper introduces the concept of diffusivity, constructs a new formula for edge weights, and introduces the LDA topic model into TextRank to calculate the topic relevance of each word in the document, thereby changing the jump probability of the damping factor term and increasing the score of the word with high relevance of the topic. The experiment uses the open sourced jieba[1] package as the word segmentation tool, and compares the proposed algorithm with TextRank on the Chinese corpus.

The rest is organized as follows. In Sect. 2, the proposed algorithm will be described in detail. In Sect. 3, experiments and results will be shown. Section 4 will conclude the work.

2 Algorithm Description

2.1 Diffusivity Between Two Candidate Words

For a Chinese document, we have first to segment it into words using jieba, which an open sourced word segmentation tool for Chinese. After that, we need to filter out unwanted words based on part of speech (POS) and stop words. Finally, we only keep verbs, nouns and non-stop words as candidate words, each of which could probably be keywords. Additionally, we need also segment the document into sentences according to punctuations like full stop, ellipsis, exclamation mark, etc.

---

[1] https://pypi.org/project/jieba/.

Some statistics need to be done as followings.

- For each candidate word W_i, count the number of sentences containing W_i as N_i;
- For each pair of candidate words (W_i, W_j), count the number of sentences that contain both W_i and W_j as N_{ij}.

The definition of the diffusion of two candidate words is as follows.

$$u_{ij} = \frac{N_i + N_j - 2N_{ij} + 0.5}{N + 0.5} \tag{1}$$

where N represents the total number of sentences of the text.

The diffusivity of two words indicates how dispersed the two words are in the article. 0.5 here is a smoothing factor, which avoids that u_{ij} could be zero. From its definition, two following conclusions can be got.

- $u_{ij} = u_{ji}$.
- If words W_i and W_j always appear in the same sentences, which results in $N_i = N_j = N_{ij}$, thus u_{ij} would be close to zero.

2.2   Relation Between Two Candidate Words

Compared with TextRank, the proposed algorithm calculates the relation between two candidate words in a little more complicated way. First, as in TextRank, we need to define a co-occurrence window length $l(l \geq 2)$ and count the times of every pair of words W_i and W_j where they co-occur within the window length l, denoted as c_{ij}. Then we define the relation between words W_i and W_j as the following

$$w_{ij} = c_{ij} \cdot u_{ij} \tag{2}$$

Equation (2) shows that the relation between two candidate words is a balance of co-occurrence time and diffusivity.

Considering that the non-candidate words can provide the distance information to judge the relation between the two words, the words in the co-occurrence would also contains non-candidate words [11].

Then a graph would be built where all the candidate words are set as nodes in the graph and the relation between two candidate words are set as the edge weight. It should be noted that the graph is non-directed.

2.3   Bringing in LDA Topic Model

LDA (Latent Dirichlet Allocation) model was first proposed by Blei et al. in 2003 in order to build a document topic model [10]. The model is a generation model in which for each document d, it can be represented as a Multinomial distribution of K topics. At the same time, the words in the topic and vocabulary also satisfy a Multinomial distribution, which is the Dirichlet prior distribution with hyperparameters α or β. Therefore, for a document d, it can be regarded as extracting a topic from the topic distribution θ, and extracting a word from the word distribution φ corresponding to the topic, repeating N times, that is, generating an article containing N words. The joint distribution can be obtained by Eq. (3).

$$p(\theta, z, w|\alpha, \beta) = p(\theta|\alpha) \prod_{n=1}^{N} p(z_n|\theta)p(w_n|z_n, \beta) \tag{3}$$

The LDA model can be trained by Gibbs Sampling algorithm [12]. Then parameter θ and φ would be estimated. Supposing there are K topics, we could get the estimated probability of word w in topic k, $p(w|k)$ via φ, and estimated probability of topic k in document d, $p(k|d)$ via θ. Hence the relevance between word w and document d could be calculated by Eq. (4).

$$p(w|d) = \sum_{k=1}^{K} p(w|k)p(k|d) \tag{4}$$

The equation of TextRank model can be defined as shown below

$$S(W_i) = (1 - p) + p \cdot \sum_{W_j \in In(W_i)} \frac{c_{ji}}{\sum_{W_k \in Out(W_j)} c_{jk}} S(W_j) \tag{5}$$

where p is a damping factor, which guarantees that the algorithm can reach convergence. It means each node in the graph can be reached by the probability of p through other nodes connected to it and by the probability of $1-p$ through any other nodes in the graph. $In(W_i)$ represents the set of nodes that point to W_i and $Out(W_i)$ represents the set of nodes pointed to by W_i. Since the graph is an undirected graph, $In(W_i)$ and $Out(W_i)$ means the same set.

In the proposed algorithm, we replace c_{ij} in Eq. (5) with w_{ij} in Eq. (2). After experiments, we found that the following equation would get better results.

$$S(W_i) = (1 - d) \cdot \exp(p(W_i|d)) + d \cdot \sum_{W_j \in In(W_i)} \frac{w_{ji}}{\sum_{W_k \in Out(W_j)} w_{jk}} S(W_j) \tag{6}$$

In Eq. (6), the damping factor varies according to different words. Every node in the graph is required to give an initial score which is often a small value between 0 and 1 and then its score would be calculated iteratively according to Eq. (6). The process would stop until the maximum number of iterations is reached or the scores reach to a convergence. Particularly, some candidate words in the document may not be in the LDA topic model. Here we use the average $p(W_i|d)$ of other candidate words in that document to replace it.

2.4   Getting Keywords

First, we need to train the LDA topic model using the corpus. For every word W_i in document d, we have to calculate $p(W_i|d)$ in Eq. (4) and for every pair of word W_i and W_j we have to calculate w_{ij} in Eq. (2). Then we initialize all the nodes' scores to a value close to zero and calculate the score of each node in the graph iteratively according to Eq. (6). When the iteration repeats 100 times or the scores reach to a convergence, the iteration stops. Finally, we rank the words by their scores and pick the words with highest scores as keywords.

3   Experiment and Results

3.1   Corpus and Evaluation

The corpus in the experiment is the news articles released in September 2017 from *South Daily*. Every news article would be given several keywords by the editor. We take these words as reference keywords. 500 articles with no less than 5 reference keywords are randomly chosen as the test corpus.

Precision (P), Recall (R) and F1-measure $(F1)$ is used to evaluate the experiment [13]. Their definitions are as follows

$$P = \frac{|A \cap B|}{|A|}, R = \frac{|A \cap B|}{|B|}, F1 = \frac{2PR}{P+R} \tag{7}$$

where A is the set of keywords extracted by the algorithm, B is the set of the reference keywords and $|A|$ is the number of elements in A.

3.2   Results

We name the proposed algorithm LDA-TextRank. After experiments, we found that in different co-occurrence window length l and damping factor p, LDA-TextRank outperforms in Precision, Recall and F1-measure compared to TextRank. When $l = 10$, $d = 0.5$ and topic number $K = 50$, they both perform their best. In this condition, experiments are conducted when number of keywords varies from 1 to 15.

Figure 1 shows that when the number of extracted keywords is small, the Precision curve of LDA-TextRank is above that of TextRank. Figures 2 and 3 show that when the keywords number is small, the Recall curves and F1-measure curves of two algorithm almost overlap. However, when the keywords number increases, LDA-TextRank performs better than TextRank. Particularly, F1-measure reaches the peak at the number of 5. This is because most documents in the corpus have 5 reference keywords. Figure 4 shows that the TextRank's curve is inside the LDA-TextRank's curve, which means at the same Precision (or Recall), LDA-TextRank's Recall (or Precision) is higher than TextRank's. In conclusion, the results show that LDA-TextRank outperforms TextRank.

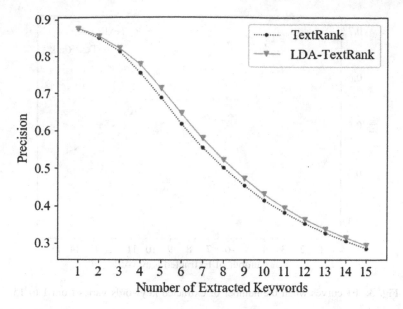

Fig. 1. Precision curves when the number of extracted keywords varies from 1 to 15

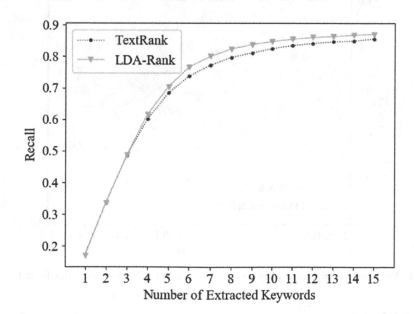

Fig. 2. Recall curves when the number of extracted keywords varies from 1 to 15

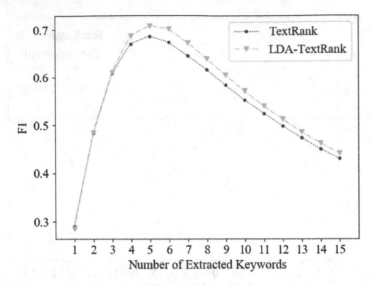

Fig. 3. F1 curves when the number of extracted keywords varies from 1 to 15

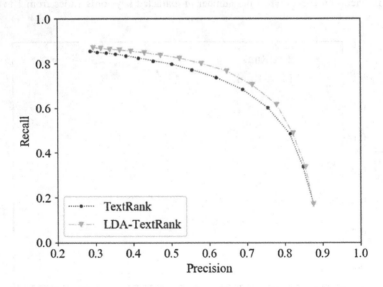

Fig. 4. Precision-Recall curves when the number of extracted keywords varies from 1 to 15

4   Conclusion

The paper optimizes the TextRank algorithm by bringing the concept of diffusivity and integrate LDA topic model in the proposed algorithm. Hence the algorithm actually extracts keywords in the level of the whole text instead of only within a co-occurrence window and integrating the topic model would allow the algorithm to catch some important topic words in a document properly. Results show that the proposed algorithm outperforms TextRank in Precision, Recall and F1-measure.

References

1. Turney, P.D.: Learning algorithms for keyphrase extraction. Inf. Retrieval **2**(4), 303–336 (2000)
2. Frank, E., Paynter, G.W., Witten, I.H., et al: Domain-specific keyphrase extraction. In: 16th International Joint Conference on Artificial Intelligence (IJCAI 99), pp. 668–673. Morgan Kaufmann Publishers Inc., San Francisco (1999)
3. Sparck Jones, K.: A statistical interpretation of term specificity and its application in retrieval. J. Documentation **28**(1), 11–21 (1972)
4. Wu, H., Salton, G.: A comparison of search term weighting: term relevance vs. inverse document frequency. In: Proceedings of the 4th Annual International ACM SIGIR Conference on Information Storage and Retrieval, pp. 30–39. ACM Press, New York (1981)
5. Mihalcea, R., Tarau, P.: TextRank: bringing order into text. In: Proceedings of the 2004 Conference on Empirical Methods in Natural Language Processing, pp. 404–441. ACL, Stroudsburg (2004)
6. Wu, X., Kumar, V., Quinlan, J.R., et al.: Top 10 algorithms in data mining. Knowl. Inf. Syst. **14**(1), 1–37 (2008)
7. Gu, Y.R., Xu, M.X.: Keyword extraction from News articles based on PageRank algorithm. J. Univ. Electron. Sci. Technol. China **46**(5), 777–783 (2017)
8. Li, W., Zhao, J.: TextRank algorithm by exploiting Wikipedia for short text keywords extraction. In: 2016 3rd International Conference on Information Science and Control Engineering (ICISCE), pp. 683–686. IEEE, Piscataway (2016)
9. Siddiqi, S., Sharan, A.: Keyword and keyphrase extraction techniques: a literature review. Int. J. Comput. Appl. **109**(2), 18–23 (2015)
10. Blei, D.M., Ng, A.Y., Jordan, M.I.: Latent Dirichlet allocation. J. Mach. Learn. Res. **3**(Jan), 993–1022 (2003)
11. Liu, Z.Y.: Research on Keyword Extraction Using Document Topical Structure. Tsinghua University, Beijing (2011)
12. Casella, G., George, E.I.: Explaining the Gibbs sampler. Am. Stat. **46**(3), 167–174 (1992)
13. Powers, D.M.: Evaluation: from precision, recall and F-measure to ROC, informedness, markedness and correlation. J. Mach. Learn. Technol. **2**(1), 37–63 (2011)

An Adaptive Threshold Decision Algorithm in Non-cooperative Signal Detection

Ziheng Li[✉], Shuo Shi, and Xuemai Gu

Harbin Institute of Technology, Harbin, China
liziheng@stu.hit.edu.cn, {crcss,guxuemai}@hit.edu.cn

Abstract. As the communication environment becomes more and more complex, it becomes more meaningful to detect and capture useful signals accurately. In this paper, we mainly focus on several typical burst signal detection algorithms in wireless communication networks. We analyze the signal energy detection algorithm, preamble detection, and frequency domain detection algorithms, then perform simulations for them. Above these, responding to non-cooperative communications, an adaptive threshold decision algorithm based on projection method is designed. Finally, we come to a conclusion, that each algorithm is suitable for burst signal detection, having its own advantages and disadvantages in different environments. And our decision algorithm is effective.

Keywords: Signal detection · Burst · Energy · Projection

1 Instruction

Now is an era of information technology. With the rapid development of economic globalization, the demand for information transmission and information exchange in various countries is increasing day by day. Communication information technology is developing in an unprecedented situation. Information transmission technology is affecting and changing people's production methods and lifestyles, and has gradually become an important driving force for modern economic development. It has also become a key factor in enhancing the comprehensive strength of countries and improving their competitiveness.

As one of the key technologies in information transmission, signal detection technology has been widely studied by scholars because of its important position. On the one hand, modern communication signals have the characteristics of adaptively adjusting their own parameters according to different communication environments, and thus the signals themselves will have more and more complex and varied forms. On the other hand, under the premise that the signal prior information is known, it will be affected by various factors of space during the transmission process, and frequency offset, attenuation, distortion.

When studying signal detection problems, the burst signal detection under cooperative conditions is relatively simple, and a matched filter is usually used as the detection structure. For non-cooperative correspondents, maybe lack most of the prior information, but burst signals often have two stable characteristics. First, the burst signal has obvious time continuity. Although the duration of the burst is unknown, it

S. Han et al. (Eds.): AICON 2019, LNICST 286, pp. 342–349, 2019.
https://doi.org/10.1007/978-3-030-22968-9_30

will certainly last for a period of time from the beginning to the end, which can be observed. The second characteristic is that most burst signals are band-pass, that is to say, most of the energy of burst signals in the spectrum is concentrated together. Most of detection algorithms utilize these characteristics of burst signals, and then perform corresponding operations according to the subsequent different signal processing requirements.

2 Signal Detection Algorithm

The current common burst signal detection algorithms mainly include time domain detection algorithm, frequency domain detection algorithm and so on. Energy detection algorithm is a more intuitive algorithm of time domain detection algorithm, it determines whether the signal into the receiver by using the energy of the received signal. The result is decided by observation on the sample value of the signal for a certain period of time and the calculation of the energy size. If the value is greater than a certain threshold, the signal will be determined to enter and the receiver notified to start the synchronization process. Preamble detection is based on the pilot sequence of the signal itself, then operate again on the local preamble correlation using the already known fixed signal format, to define the arrival time of the received signal accurately.

In addition, there are other frequency detection algorithms such as power detection, frequency spectrum detection. This paper mainly studies and analyzes several signal detection algorithms in wireless networks based on the Gaussian white noise channel model.

2.1 Energy Detection

The energy detection algorithm usually measures the average energy of a signal over a period of time to determine whether a signal arrives. It does not require prior information of the signal to be detected, also because of its low computational complexity has it become the most commonly used signal detection algorithm in an actual system. Method A directly measures the total energy of the received signal over a period of time and then compares it with the decision threshold to determine the presence of a signal. The principle of the algorithm and the block diagram works as follows formula (1) and Fig. 1:

$$Z(d) = \sum_{k=0}^{L-1} |r(d+k)|^2 \tag{1}$$

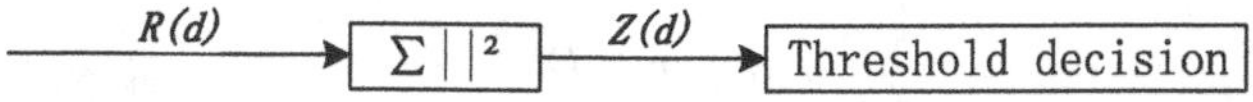

Fig. 1. Flow diagram of method A

Simulate this algorithm, we can get the result as Fig. 2. From this figure, it is obvious to find when useful signal reach.

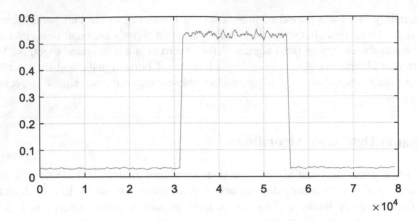

Fig. 2. Simulation result of method A

Method B is an improvement based on method A, which uses the ratio of the signal shift correlation to the energy of the signal itself as a decision statistic, a kind of relative threshold algorithm [1]. This algorithm performs better but has a slightly higher complexity than method A. The principle and block diagram work as follows Fig. 3 and formula (2):

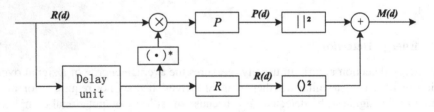

Fig. 3. Flow diagram of method B

$$P(d) = \sum_{m=0}^{L-1} r(d+m)r*(d+m+D)$$

$$R(d) = \sum_{m=0}^{L-1} r(d+m+D)r*(d+m+D)$$

$$= \sum_{m=0}^{L-1} |r(d+m+D)|^2$$

$$M(d) = \frac{|P(d)|^2}{|R(d)|^2}$$

(2)

From Fig. 4 we can get when useful signal arrive, statistics decision generate a peak value. And we can get the simulation as Fig. 4.

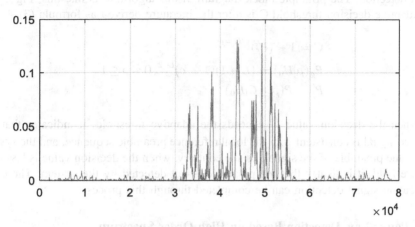

Fig. 4. Result of method B

2.2 Signal Detection Using Preamble

In wireless network communication, the receiving end can detect the communication signal by detecting and capturing the preamble sequence added before the data is effectively transmitted, and can also utilize the preamble sequence to initial capture the bit timing. In a wireless communication system, the power of the received signal is greatly affected by the transmission distance and various fading. Therefore, the signal detection performance has a crucial influence on the overall communication. Because the received signal level is unknown and time-varying, the fixed-threshold signal detection scheme often cannot obtain good detection performance, so that the detection probability decreases or the false alarm probability increases, while the unknown power of interference and interference power changes will affect the detection performance.

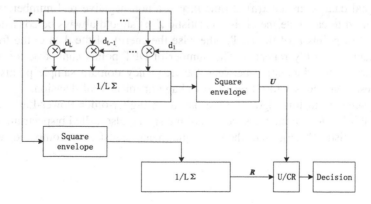

Fig. 5. Flow diagram of preamble detection

These situations are more suitable for using adaptive signal detection algorithm to detect the signal in the preamble to complete the wireless communication network signal detection. The principle block diagram of this algorithm is like this, Fig. 5.

Adaptive decision threshold C is after the literature derived as formula (3)

$$
\begin{aligned}
C &= 1 - (P_f')^{1/(L-1)} \\
P_\rho(\rho|H_0) &= (L-1)(1-\rho)^{L-2}, 0 \le \rho \le 1 \\
P_f' &= P(\rho \ge C|H_0)
\end{aligned}
\tag{3}
$$

When the decision value $\frac{U}{CR}$ exceeds the adaptive threshold, it indicates that the received signal is consistent with the local reference preamble sequence, and the system detects the preamble of the signal; on the contrary, when the decision value is less than the threshold, it indicates that the preamble is not detected by the system. The communication signal detection can be completed through this process.

2.3   Power-Law Detection Based on High-Order Spectrum

Frequency domain signal detection algorithm means to transform the signal to the frequency domain, and then calculate the decision statistic to determine the presence of the signal. Frequency-domain decision statistics usually use higher-order statistics [2] or the spectrum obtained by DFT. This algorithm usually has higher computational complexity, but it has still a good detection quality at a lower SNR. These signal detection algorithms are mainly the algorithms based on DFT Power-Law [3, 4], and an optimization called high-order spectrum Power-Law detection algorithm [5]. The decision statistics used in the Power-Law algorithm based on the DFT transform are some transformation of the amplitude spectrum and can be described as the formula (4):

$$
Z(n) = \sum_{k=0}^{N-1} X_k^v(n)
\tag{4}
$$

Where $X_k^v(n)$ represents the k-th amplitude square value of the P-point DFT result of the signal data sequence $x(n)$ at time n, v is a non-negative real number, The data length N used to calculate the decision statistic $Z(n)$ should always be consistent with the number of points P of the DFT, otherwise the energy of the data in the frequency domain cannot be truly reflected. The number of DFT points cannot be too small as well, otherwise the fluctuation between the frequency domain sample points will be great. These conditions will all result in leakage or mistake of decision.

Improvements to this algorithm are based on higher-order Power-Law detectors, using the third-order cumulated spectrum of the signal, also called bispectrum, replaces judgment statistic $X_k^v(n)$, and then the judgment statistic is compared with the threshold. The Fourier transform of each piece of data is recorded as $X^{(i)}(w)$, its bispectrum estimation is shown as formula (5):

$$B_{xx}^{(i)}(\omega_1, \omega_2) = M^2 X^{(i)}(\omega_1) X^{(i)}(\omega_1 + \omega_2) \tag{5}$$

Calculate the decision statistic and we give an example like Fig. 6.

$$Z(n) = \sum_{j=1}^{N} \sum_{i=1}^{K} \left| B_{xx}(\omega_{1j}, \omega_{2i}) \right|^{\nu}$$

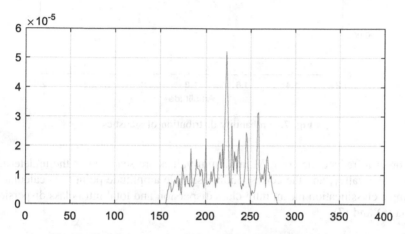

Fig. 6. Simulation result of bispectrality Power-Law detection

3 An Adaptive Threshold Decision Algorithm Based on Projection Method

In the above research on the signal detection algorithm, it is found that the existing threshold decision algorithm has a performance degradation when the signal-to-noise ratio is low, resulting in a false judgment. In many simulation experiments, we found that, when there is a burst signal in a period of time, the magnitude of the decision statistic obtained by various signal detection algorithms shows a bimodal distribution. These conditions are in line with the idea of separating single-peak subclasses by projection method in pattern recognition, so an adaptive threshold decision algorithm based on projection method is designed.

The basic steps of the algorithm are as follows. Obtain the judgment statistic $S(n)$ by the detection algorithm, divide the amplitude N segments by the same length, and calculate the probability density p_i of each segment separately. Look for the number of peaks in the probability distribution. If the probability distribution shows a single peak, then there is only noise during this period. If there are two or more peaks, find the minimum point between every two peaks, as Fig. 7.

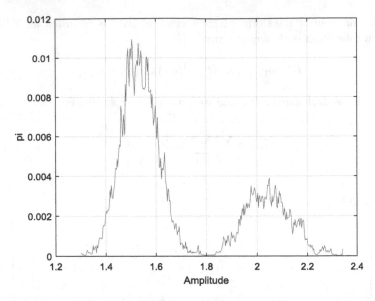

Fig. 7. Probability distribution of statistics

In order to reduce the error, M minimum values are searched as the undetermined data near the valley, and the corresponding sample amplitude point x_i is calculated as the sample classification mean, intra-class dispersion and total intra-class dispersion as formula (6) and (7).

$$m_j^i = \frac{1}{N_j} \sum_{x \in X_j} x, i = 1, 2, \ldots, M; j = 1, 2. \tag{6}$$

$$S_j^i = \sum_{x \in X_j} (x - m_j^i)^2 \qquad , i = 1, 2, \ldots M; j = 1, 2. \tag{7}$$
$$S_w^i = \sum S_j^i$$

Since the entire data set only needs to be divided into two categories, the value of j is taken as 2. Subsequent calculation of the minimum value of the dispersion Sw within the total class, as shown in formula (8).

$$S = \min(S_w^i), i = 1, 2, \ldots, M \tag{8}$$

Finally, the magnitude corresponding to the dispersion S in the smallest total class is selected as the adaptive threshold Z calculated by the algorithm, and the threshold decision is performed by using Z.

4 Conclusion

In this paper, we analyze and theoretically simulate several burst signal detection algorithms. Among them, the energy detection algorithm works faster and easier, has a very good detection effect when the channel conditions are good. The preamble sequence-related detection has been widely used in cooperative communication, and due to its correlation, it can still achieve better results when the channel is poor. Compared with the energy detection algorithm, the bispectrality Power-Law detection algorithm has a larger amount of computation and higher computational complexity, takes a while to accumulate data, but at the cost of this, its detection performance is quite excellent. When the channel environment is very bad, the burst signal can still be detected more accurately. For non-cooperative signal detection, our proposed adaptive threshold decision algorithm also achieves good results in simulation, and can improve signal detection performance when the channel environment is degraded, but the real-time performance needs to be improved.

References

1. Chen, H.-H., Sim, H.-K.: Orthogonal decision-feedback detector for asynchronous multiuser CDMA systems. IEEE Trans. Commun. 8(42), 1963–1972 (2001)
2. Colonnese, S., Sxarano, G.: Transient signal detection using higher order moments. IEEE Trans. Signal Process. 47(2), 515–520 (1999)
3. Wang, Z., Willett, P.: All-purpose and plug-in power-law detectors for transient signals. IEEE Trans. Signal Process. 49(11), 2454–2466 (2001)
4. Kirsteins, I.P., Mehta, S.K.: Power-law processors for detection unknown signals in colored noise. In: IEEE Processing ICASSP, vol. 1, pp. 483–486
5. Xiong, S., Wu, Y.: The detection of transient signals based on gabor transform. In: IEEE Processing ICSP, vol. I, pp. 259–262 (2006)
6. Huang, C., Liu, Y., Chen, L.: Time-frequency joint analysis for peak power of microwave burst signal. In: IEEE International Symposium on Microwave, Antenna, Propagation and EMC Technologies for Wireless Communications, Chengdu, pp. 202–205 (2013)

Trajectory Optimization Under Constrained UAV-Aided Wireless Communications with Ground Terminals

Kun Chen[1,2(✉)], Hong Lu[1,2], Xiangping Bryce Zhai[1,2], Congduan Li[3],
Yunlong Zhao[1,2], and Bing Chen[1,2]

[1] Nanjing University of Aeronautics and Astronautics, Nanjing 211106, China
Chan_Kun@126.com, luh.lewis@gmail.com,
{blueicezhaixp,zhaoyunlong,cb_china}@nuaa.edu.cn
[2] Collaborative Innovation Center of Novel Software Technology and
Industrialization, Nanjing 210032, China
[3] Sun Yat-Sen University, Guangzhou 510275, China
licongd@mail.sysu.edu.cn

Abstract. Using the unmanned aerial vehicles (UAV) to form a communication platform is of great practical significance in future wireless networks. This article investigates the flight trajectory optimization problem with minimum energy consumption when the UAVs are mobile servers and communicate with the ground terminals (GT). The proposed trajectory considers the features of conventional paths as well, i.e., the channel quality and energy saving. Numerical results show that our approach outperforms the other schemes in terms of the throughput of data and the features of the UAV.

Keywords: Unmanned aerial vehicle · Energy optimization · Wireless networks · Mobile server · Trajectory optimization

1 Introduction

The use of unmanned aerial vehicles (UAVs) as communication platforms is of great practical significance in future wireless networks. For example, UAVs can be utilized as mobile relays to help information exchange between far-apart ground users [15]. UAV can be viewed as mobile base stations (BSs) where a UAV is dispatched as a BS to serve a group of users on the ground [2,3,9,12,13]. UAV technology is becoming more and more sophisticated where the weight of drones is getting lighter and the UAV can fly longer and longer. However,

Supported in part by the National Natural Science Foundation of China under Grants No. 61701231, No. 61672283, in part by six talent peaks project in Jiangsu Province under Grant No. XYDXXJS-031, in part by Hundred Talents Program of Sun Yat-Sen University under Grant No. 76150-18841214.

S. Han et al. (Eds.): AICON 2019, LNICST 286, pp. 350–362, 2019.
https://doi.org/10.1007/978-3-030-22968-9_31

the energy consumption of UAV is still a challenge. For the UAV-aided wireless communication system, UAVs cannot guarantee long-term data transmission with the limited energy. The UAVs need return to the depot for battery charging or exchanging which will cause service interruptions. This severely hinders the practical implementation of UAV-enabled communications.

For the UAV-enabled multiuser communication networks, a novel cyclical multiple access scheme is proposed in [10] where the UAV periodically serves each of the ground users along its cyclical trajectory via TDMA. In [13], a joint user scheduling, power control, and trajectory optimization problem is investigated for a multi-UAV enabled multiuser system. The problem of joint caching and resource allocation is investigated in [5] for a network of cache-enabled unmanned aerial vehicles (UAVs) that service wireless ground users over the LTE licensed and unlicensed (LTE-U) bands. The problem of proactive deployment of cache-enabled UAVs for optimizing the quality-of-experience (QoE) of wireless devices in a cloud radio access network is studied in [4].

Via energy-efficient trajectory designs [14], the UAV endurance problem remains improvable. For the endurance issue, we mainly optimize the UAV trajectory to save the UAV's energy consumption. In this article, we focus on the fixed-wing UAVs. Even though the reduction of the link distance saves the communication power, the UAV systems are subject to additional propulsion power consumption for maintaining the UAV aloft and supporting its mobility (if necessary), which is usually much higher than the communication power consumption. The purpose of this article is minimizing the propulsion power consumption of the UAV by optimizing the flight path. The proposed trajectory considers the features of conventional paths, when the UAV flies straight over the GT's center. UAV starts to communicate with the GT after entering the ground terminal communication range. The UAV can also fly beside over the GT's center instead of flying directly above the GT's center.

The main contributions of this article include:

(1) We derive a system model of the data transfer rate. At the same time, we derive a theoretical model for the propulsion energy consumption of fixed-wing UAVs as a function of flying velocity and acceleration.
(2) We optimize the trajectory with minimum energy consumption, which allows the UAV to move away from GT's center point.

The rest of the paper is organized as follows. Section 2 introduces the system model, and defines the UAV's propulsion energy consumption based on a theoretical model. Section 3 describes how to find the path that minimizes the energy and the path planning algorithm is presented for energy minimization. Section 4 reports a set of experimental results to validate the proposed approach. Finally, we conclude the paper and state our future work in Sect. 5.

2   System Model

2.1   Data Rate Model

We aim to optimize the UAV's trajectory so as to minimize its energy consumption. Without loss of generality, we consider a three-dimensional (3D) Cartesian coordinate system where the GT is located at the origin (0, 0, 0). Furthermore, for simplicity, we assume that the UAV flies horizontally at a fixed altitude H. In practice, H could correspond to the minimum altitude required for safety considerations (e.g., terrain or building avoidance) without frequent aircraft ascending and descending. The extensions on varing H will be left as a future work.

Denote the UAV trajectory projected on the horizontal plane as $\mathbf{q}(t) = [x(t), y(t)]^T \in \mathbb{R}^{2 \times 1}$. Thus, the time-varying distance from the UAV to the GT can be expressed as:

$$
\begin{aligned}
d(t) = & \sqrt{H^2 + \|\mathbf{q}(t)\|^2} \\
= & \sqrt{H^2 + x(t)^2 + y(t)^2}.
\end{aligned} \tag{1}
$$

The Doppler effect due to the UAV's mobility is assumed to be perfectly compensated. Therefore, the time-varying channel power gain from the UAV to each GT follows the free-space path loss model [11], which can be given by:

$$
h(t) = \beta_0 d^{-2}(t) = \frac{\beta_0}{H^2 + \|\mathbf{q}(t)\|^2}, \tag{2}
$$

where β_0 denotes the channel power gain at the reference distance $d_0 = 1$ meter (m), whose value depends on the carrier frequency, antenna gain, etc. and $d(t)$ is the link distance between the UAV and the GT at time t. The instantaneous channel capacity from the UAV to the GT in bits/second can be expressed as:

$$
\begin{aligned}
R(t) = & Blog_2 \left(1 + \frac{Ph(t)}{\sigma^2} \right) \\
= & Blog_2 \left(1 + \frac{\gamma_0}{H^2 + \|\mathbf{q}(t)\|^2} \right),
\end{aligned} \tag{3}
$$

where B denotes the channel bandwidth and σ^2 is the white Gaussian noise power at the GT receiver. In the following, we use the unit of bps/Hz to measure the throughput per unit bandwidth, also known as the spectrum efficiency. $\gamma_0 = \beta_0 P / \sigma^2$ is the reference received signal-to-noise ratio (SNR) at $d_0 = 1$ m.

For each GT, the rate $R(t)$ is symmetric and unimodal, which achieves its maximum when the UAV flies closest to the ground terminal (e.g., $x = 0$ and $y = 0$). As an illustration, Fig. 1 plots the instantaneous rate of each GT versus the UAV position x, with $P = 10$ dBm, $\gamma_0 = 80$ dB, $H = 100$ m.

The total amount of information bits that can be transmitted from the UAV to the GT over the duration T is a function of the UAV trajectory $\mathbf{q}(t)$, expressed as:

Data rate in 3D surface map

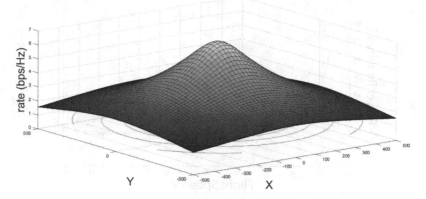

Fig. 1. The illustration of the throughput versus UAV's position.

$$\bar{R}(\mathbf{q}(t)) = \int_0^T Blog_2 \left(1 + \frac{\gamma_0}{H^2 + \|\mathbf{q}(t)\|^2} \right) dt. \tag{4}$$

The issue is the packet loss [1] due to the highly dynamic wireless channels between the GT and the moving UAV. Thus, the trajectory of the UAV should be properly designed.

2.2 UAV Energy Consumption Model

The total energy consumption of the UAV includes two components. The first one is the communication-related energy and the other is the propulsion energy. Note that in practice, the communication-related energy is usually much smaller than the UAV's propulsion energy, e.g., a few watts [6] versus hundreds of watts [7], and thus is less considered in this paper.

Furthermore, for fixed-wing UAVs, the total propulsion energy required is a function of the trajectory $\mathbf{q}(t)$, which is corresponded to the classic aircraft power consumption model known in aerodynamics theory [8]. The function is expressed as:

$$E(\mathbf{q}(t)) = \int_0^T \left[c_1 \|\mathbf{v}(t)^3\| + \frac{c_2}{\|\mathbf{v}(t)\|} \left(1 + \frac{\|\mathbf{a}(t)\|^2 - \frac{\mathbf{a}^T(t)\mathbf{v}(t)^2}{\|\mathbf{v}(t)\|^2}}{g^2} \right) \right] dt \tag{5}$$

$$+ \frac{1}{2} m (\|\mathbf{v}(T)\|^2 - \|\mathbf{v}(0)\|^2).$$

where

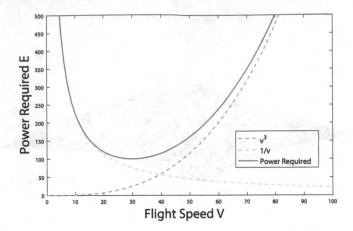

Fig. 2. Typical power required curve versus speed V for a UAV in straight-and-level flight.

$$\mathbf{v}(t) \triangleq \dot{\mathbf{q}}(t), \quad \mathbf{a}(t) \triangleq \ddot{\mathbf{q}}(t), \tag{6}$$

denote the instantaneous UAV velocity and acceleration vectors, respectively. c_1 and c_2 are two parameters related to the aircraft's weight, wing area, air density, etc., $\mathbf{g}$ is the gravitational acceleration with nominal value $9.8\,\mathrm{m/s^2}$ and m is the mass of the UAV including its all payload.

We first consider the special case of steady straight-and-level flight (SLF) with constant speed V, i.e., $\|\mathbf{v}(t)\| = V$ and $\|\mathbf{a}(t)\| = 0$, $\forall t$. In this case, (5) reduces to:

$$\bar{E}_{SLF}(V) = T\left(c_1 V^3 + \frac{c_2}{V}\right). \tag{7}$$

The power consumption of (7) as a function of V is illustrated in Fig. 2, which consists of two terms. The first term, which is proportional to the cube of the speed V, is known as the parasitic power for overcoming the parasitic drag due to the aircraft's skin friction, form drag, etc. The second term, which is inversely proportional to V, is known as the induced power for overcoming the lift-induced drag, i.e., the resulting drag force due to wings redirecting air to generate the lift for compensating the aircraft's weight.

Next, we consider another special trajectory where the UAV flies at a constant speed V but with possibly time-varying headings. In this case, we have $\|\mathbf{v}(t)\| = V$ and $\mathbf{a}^\top(t)\mathbf{v}(t) = 0$, $\forall t$. Thus, (5) reduces to:

$$\bar{E}(V, a(t)) = \bar{E}_{SLF}(V) + \frac{c_2}{V\mathbf{g}^2} \int_0^T a^2(t)\, dt. \tag{8}$$

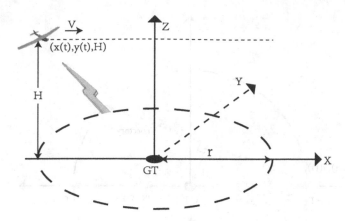

Fig. 3. The illustration of UAV severs the ground terminal.

As we aim to cost the least power of the UAV to satisfy data transmission, the problem is formulated as:

$$\text{minimize } \bar{E}$$
$$\text{subject to } V_{min} \leq \|\mathbf{v}(t)\| \leq V_{max}$$
$$\|\mathbf{a}(t)\| \leq a_{max} \tag{9}$$
$$\bar{R} = R_{req}$$
$$\text{variables : } \mathbf{q}(t), \mathbf{v}(t), \mathbf{a}(t).$$

where V_{min}, V_{max} denote the UAV's slowest speed and fastest speed respectively, a_{max} denotes the UAV's maximum acceleration and R_{req} denotes the volume of the requirement data. This problem is difficult to be directly solved. Firstly, it requires the optimization of the continuous function $\mathbf{q}(t)$, as well as its first- and second-order derivatives $\mathbf{v}(t)$ and $\mathbf{a}(t)$ and the objective function lacks closed-form expressions. In the following, a path planning algorithm is proposed.

3 UAV Trajectory Design

As far as we know, the current conventional approach is the UAV flies straight over the GT's center while UAV starts to communicate with the GT after entering the ground terminal communication range, as shown in Fig. 3. In practice, each GT could correspond to a cluster head that serves as a gateway for a cluster of nearby nodes communicating with the UAV. Conventionally, in this scenario the trajectory of UAV would be designed as straight path.

We consider that when the UAV flies directly above the GT's center. Generally, the channel quality is relatively better at this time. Therefore, the communication time can be reduced in some degree. Although the UAV has long distance trajectory, the overall duration of data transmission is shorter with reliable channel connections. At this time, we term this situation as scenario I.

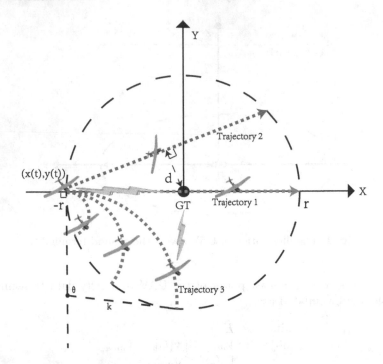

Fig. 4. Three trajectories of the UAV that severs one GT with straight or curve trajectories. The blue trajectory 1 is classic path that cross the GT's center. The red trajectory 2 is the path generated by Algorithm 1. The green curve trajectory 3 is the path generated by Algorithm 2. (Color figure online)

Since there are multiple GTs need to be served, the origin and the destination of the UAV are often related to the position of the GT, so when we design single UAV path, it is not necessary to strictly consider the origin and destination and this research will be discussed in future work.

Intuitively, Scenario I is more suitable for this situation that the UAV and GT need a reliable channel. In other words, Scenario I can be selected to ensure reliable data transmission. But the flight speed at this time is relatively large, so the energy consumption is uncertain which needs to be discussed in detail in the experimental part.

In addition to this, the UAV can fly beside over the GT's center instead of flying directly above the GT's center. At this time, we term this situation as Scenario II. In this situation, UAV can choose straight flight or curve flight, as shown in Fig. 4.

For simplicity, we first study the steady straight-and-level flight. When the UAV flies into the ground terminal communication range, the data transmission rate is not as good as the former Scenario I, leading to a longer communication time between the UAV and the GT. In addition, the UAV's flight distance is shorter at this time. Both of these situations lead the speed of the UAV to be slower. At this point, the energy consumption of the UAV can be calculated by the corresponding energy consumption formula in Sect. 2 with the speed and time variables. Intuitively, the energy consumption of the Scenario II will be less than the former Scenario I and the results will be discussed in the experimental section based on the data transmission model and energy consumption model in Sect. 2. By referring the red trajectory 2 in Fig. 4, the straight trajectory design algorithm is presented as follows:

Algorithm 1. (Straight Tragectory Beside GT's center)

---

1. *Initialization:*
   - Initialize the volume of data $\bar{R}$, height H and communication range r.

2. *Calculate the energy consumption of the trajectory:*
   - Let $d = 0$ m and $l = 0$ then update the trajectory $\mathbf{q}(t)$ of UAV, where

$$x(t) = -\sqrt{r^2 - d^2} + Vt, \quad y(t) = d. \tag{10}$$

   - Calculate the communication time T with the function (4) *and variable* $\mathbf{q}(t)$.

   - Update the speed V of the UAV under the constraints (9):

$$V = \frac{\|\mathbf{q}(t) - \mathbf{q}(0)\|}{T} \tag{11}$$

   - Update the energy consumption $\bar{E}_l(V)$ of the trajectory with the equation (7).

3. *Update the variable d and l:*

$$d = d + l * n, \quad l = l + 1 \tag{12}$$

4. *If a maximum number of iterations has been reached or $d = r$, find the optimal d satisfying:*

$$d = \arg\min_{l \geq 0, l \in \mathbb{Z}} \bar{E}_l(V) \tag{13}$$

   else go to Step 2
   end

At this point, the algorithm of the curve flight trajectory can be obtained by the same reason, by reference the green trajectory 3 in Fig. 4 as shown below:

Algorithm 2. (Curve Tragectory Beside GT's center)

---

1. **Run Algorithm 1, replace the Eqs. (10), (11), (12) and (13) by the following computations:**
   - Let flight radius $k = 0$, $l = 0$ and update the trajectory $\mathbf{q}(t)$ of UAV, where

   $$x(t) = k * cos(\frac{\pi}{2} - \theta(t)), \quad y(t) = k * sin(\frac{\pi}{2} - \theta(t)). \quad (14)$$

   where θ denotes the flight angular of the circle trajectory.
   - Update the speed V and acceleration $a(t)$ of the UAV:

   $$V = \frac{k\theta(t)}{T}, \quad a(t) = \frac{V^2}{k} \quad (15)$$

   - Update the energy consumption $\bar{E}_l(V, a(t))$ of the trajectory with the equation (8)
   - Update flight radius k

   $$k = k + l * n, \quad l = l + 1 \quad (16)$$

2. **Find the optimal k satisfying:**

   $$k = \arg \min_{l \geq 0, l \in \mathbb{Z}} \bar{E}_l(V, a(t)) \quad (17)$$

The variables d and k are very complicated, so these variables are calculated by brute-force method. It is interesting to note that there is a bond of the volume of data, when the curve trajectory performs relatively ideal.

Note that since each iteration of Algorithm the variables are complicated, the time complexity of the proposed algorithm presents an exponential explosion. Furthermore, the trajectory optimization problem can be solved off-line before the UAV dispatch at the ground control station with a high computational capability.

4 Numerical Results

In this section, numerical results are provided to validate the proposed design. The UAV altitude is fixed at $H = 100$ m. The communication bandwidth is $B = 1$ MHz and the noise power spectrum density at the GT receiver is assumed to be $N_0 = -170$ dBm/Hz. Thus, the corresponding noise power is $\sigma^2 = N_0 B = -110$ dBm. We assume that the UAV transmission power is $P = 10$ dBm (i.e., 0.01W), and the reference channel power is $\beta_0 = -50$ dB. As a result, the maximum SNR achieved when the UAV is just above the GT can be obtained as 30 dB. Furthermore, we assume that $c_1 = 9.26 \times 10^{-4}$ and

Table 1. System parameters

Parameter	Value	Parameter	Value	Parameter	Value
H	100 m	B	1 MHZ	σ^2	$-110\,$dBm
P	10 dBm	β_0	$-50\,$dB	V_{em}	30 m/s
c_1	9.26×10^{-4}	c_2	2250	P_{em}	100 W
V_{max}	100 m/s	V_{min}	3 m/s	a_{max}	5 m/s

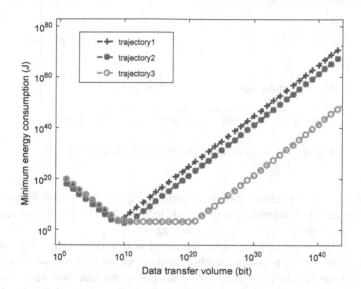

Fig. 5. The figure of minimum energy consumption versus data transfer volume for different trajectories. The blue line is the energy performance of the trajectory 1. The red line is the energy performance of the trajectory 2 generated by Algorithm 1. The green line is the energy performance of the trajectory 3 generated by Algorithm 2. (Color figure online)

$c_2 = 2250$, where these parameters are subject to the flight properties of fixed-wing drones in [8], such that the UAV's energy-minimum speed is $V_{em} = 30\,$m/s as shown in Fig. 2 and the corresponding minimum propulsion power consumption is $P_{em} = 100\,$W. Note that we have $P \ll P_{em}$, thus the UAV transmission power can be less considered.

Based on this situation, when $\bar{R} = 10^9$ bit, $V_{max} = 100\,$m/s, $V_{min} = 3\,$m/s and $a_{max} = 5\,$m/s^2, the energy consumption of the trajectory 1, trajectory 2 and trajectory 3 are $4.0786 \times 10^3\,$J, $2.8364 \times 10^3\,$J and $5.7332 \times 10^3\,$J respectively. The parameters are shown in the Table 1. From this we can find that the energy consumption performance of the trajectory 2 is better than the trajectory 1 and trajectory 3.

At this time, when the amount of data transmitted is relatively small, e.g., $\bar{R} \leq 10^{10}$ bit, the data volume is termed as transmitting a document file, the

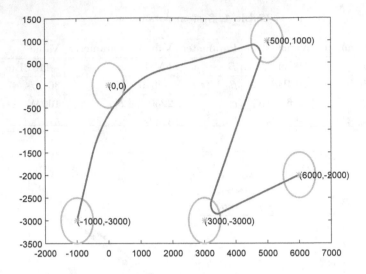

Fig. 6. The trajectory of the UAV which severs 5 GTs.

energy consumption performance is shown in Fig. 5. From this figure, we can find that the energy consumption of red trajectory 2 is the least, and the energy consumption of curve trajectory 3 is the largest.

But when the amount of data transmitted is relatively large, e.g., $\bar{R} \geq 10^{10}$ bit, for example, when real-time high-definition video transmission is required, the data volume is relatively large. At this point, we can find that the energy consumption generated by curve trajectory 3 is the lowest, as showed in Fig. 5, so we can conclude that when there is a large amount of data need to be transmitted, we can choose the curve flight path without passing over the GT's center. The reason is when there is a great deal of data need to be transmitted, the curve trajectory 3 ensures a better channel quality that is the feature of trajectory 1 and also ensures the optimal energy consumption that is the feature of the trajectory 2. Therefore, when these two features are combined, energy consumption performance of the curve trajectory 3 is relatively better especially for massive data. As we mentioned before, when the curve trajectory performs relatively ideal, there is a bond of the volume of data and the bond of the volume is related to the channel quality, e.g. $\bar{R} = 10^{10} bit$ when the transmission power is 0.01W. When the channel quality is reliable, the bond becomes larger, which means the curve trajectory is suitable for massive data transmission especially for reliable channel quality.

Based on the previous scenario, when there are multiple GTs which are severed by the UAV, e.g., 5 GTs are generated randomly and there is a lot of data to be transmitted with reliable channel quality. At this time, the trajectory of the UAV can refer the curve trajectory 3 for minimum energy consumption, as shown in Fig. 6. At this time, compared with the conventional trajectory, this curve trajectory performs better. Since fixed-wing UAV can't hover, so when there are multiple GTs need to be severed, the drone which flies along the conventional trajectory 1 needs to spend extra energy to change direction, and the energy consumption of this hovering steering is very large may even be infinite. But the UAV flies around the GT along the trajectory 3 with smooth turning angles, which achieves a good balance between rate maximization and energy minimization.

5 Conclusion

This paper studies a new trajectory of the UAV which can save more energy for long endurance. By exploiting the conventional trajectory that cross the GT's center and a straight flight path which is beside the GT's center, we design a new trajectory that combines both features of the former trajectories. Specifically, this designed trajectory not only ensures an ideal channel quality but also ensure less energy consumption. Based on these results, a trajectory design algorithm is proposed to jointly optimize the channel quality and energy consumption. Numerical results show that when there is little data to be transmitted, the performance of the curve trajectory is not as ideal as the conventional straight path, but when there is a large amount of data, the curve trajectory performs better, which shows the great potential of this new trajectory. The result in this paper can be further extended by considering the energy efficiency of the UAV.

References

1. Ahmed, N., Kanhere, S.S., Jha, S.: On the importance of link characterization for aerial wireless sensor networks. IEEE Commun. Mag. **54**(5), 52–57 (2016)
2. Bor-Yaliniz, R.I., El-Keyi, A., Yanikomeroglu, H.: Efficient 3-D placement of an aerial base station in next generation cellular networks. In: IEEE ICC, pp. 1938–1883, February 2016
3. Chen, J., Esrafilian, O., Gesbert, D., Mitra, U.: Efficient algorithms for air-to-ground channel reconstruction in UAV-aided communications. In: IEEE Globecom Workshop, pp. 1–6, December 2017
4. Chen, M., Mozaffari, M., Saad, W., Yin, C.: Caching in the sky: proactive deployment of cache-enabled unmanned aerial vehicles for optimized quality-of-experience. IEEE J. Sel. Areas Commun. **35**(5), 1046–1061 (2017)
5. Chen, M., Saad, W., Yin, C.: Liquid state machine learning for resource and cache management in LTE-U unmanned aerial vehicle (UAV) networks. IEEE Trans. Wirel. Commun. **18**(3), 1504–1517 (2019)
6. Desset, C.: Flexible power modeling of LTE base stations. In: IEEE Wireless Communications and Networking Conference (WCNC), pp. 2858–2862, April 2012
7. Franco, C.D., Buttazzo, G.: Energy-aware coverage path planning of UAVs. In: IEEE Interenational Conference on Autonomous Robot Systems and Competitions, pp. 111–117, April 2015
8. Greitzer, E.M., Spakovszky, Z.S., Waitz, I.A.: Thermodynamics and propulsion. MIT Course Notes, July 2016
9. Lyu, J., Zeng, Y., Lim, T.J.: Placement optimization of UAV-mounted mobile base stations. IEEE Commun. Lett **21**(3), 604–607 (2017)

10. Lyu, J., Zeng, Y., Zhang, R.: Cyclical multiple access in UAV-Aided communications: a throughput-delay tradeoff. IEEE Wirel. Commun. Lett. **5**(6), 600–603 (2016)
11. Mengali, U., D'Andrea, A.N.: Synchronization Techniques for Digital Receivers. Springer, New York (1997)
12. Mozaffari, M., Saad, W., Bennis, M., Debbah, M.: Efficient deployment of multiple unmanned aerial vehicles for optimal wireless coverage. IEEE Commun. Lett **20**(8), 1647–1650 (2016)
13. Wu, Q., Zeng, Y., Zhang, R.: Joint trajectory and communication design for multi-UAV enabled wireless networks. IEEE Trans. Wirel. Commun. **17**(3), 2109–2121 (2018)
14. Zeng, Y., Zhang, R.: Energy-efficient UAV communication with trajectory optimization. IEEE Trans. Wirel. Commun. **16**(6), 3747–3760 (2017)
15. Zeng, Y., Zhang, R., Lim, T.J.: Throughput maximization for UAV-Enabled mobile relaying systems. IEEE Trans. Commun. **64**(12), 4983–4996 (2016)

IOT-Based Thermal Comfort Control for Livable Environment

Miao Zang, Zhiqiang Xing$^{(\boxtimes)}$, and Yingqi Tan

North China University of Technology,
Beijing 100144, People's Republic of China
speech@ncut.edu.cn

Abstract. Thermal Comfort Control for indoor environment is an important issue in smart city since it is benefit to people's health and helps to maximize their working productivity and provide a livable environment. In this paper, we present an IOT (Internet of Things) based personal thermal comfort model with automatic regulation. This model employs some environment sensors such as temperature sensor, humidity sensor, etc., to continuously obtain the general environmental measurements. Specially, video cameras are also integrated into the IOT network of sensors to capture the individual's activity and dressing condition, which are important factors affecting one's thermal sensation. The individual's condition image can be mapped into different metabolic rates and different clothing insulations by machine learning classification algorithm. Then, all the captured or converted data are fed into a PMV (Predicted Mean Vote) model to learn the individual's thermal comfort level. In the prediction stage, we introduce the cuckoo search algorithm to solve the air temperature and air velocity with the learnt thermal comfort level, which is convergent rapidly. Our experiments demonstrate that the metabolic rates and clothing insulation have great effect on personal thermal comfort, and our model with video capture helps to obtain the variant values regularly, thus maintains the individual's thermal comfort balance in spite of the variation of activity or clothing.

Keywords: Thermal comfort control · IOT · PMV · Cuckoo search algorithm

1 Introduction

Nowadays, people spend most of their time in enclosed environment, especially for vulnerable senior and younger populations [1]. The indoor environment has great impact on people's health and life comfort. One of the most common requirements of human beings for indoor environment is thermal comfort, which is defined as the subjective satisfaction evaluation for the surrounding thermal environment. It has been reported that thermal comfort is of great importance to health, happiness, creative ability and working efficiency. For these reasons, indoor thermal comfort control by optimal setting has become of increasing concern in both scientific and industrial communities. However, due to the non-linear mapping between various environmental variables and personal preferences, as well as the complexity of thermodynamics of human body, the thermal comfort environment control is still a challenging task.

© ICST Institute for Computer Sciences, Social Informatics and Telecommunications Engineering 2019
Published by Springer Nature Switzerland AG 2019. All Rights Reserved
S. Han et al. (Eds.): AICON 2019, LNICST 286, pp. 363–373, 2019.
https://doi.org/10.1007/978-3-030-22968-9_32

Considering an optimal thermal comfort control system that predicts an individual's thermal comfort in an indoor environment automatically, compares it with the ideal value and makes calibrations in time by adjusting the set point (such as air temperature and air velocity) of an air conditioning system of a building. The key to the system is a thermal comfort model that simulates the individual's thermal sensation accurately. Fanger's PMV model [2, 3] is the dominant model, which has been adopted as an international standard in ISO 7730. It is represented by a heat balance equation describing the heat energy transfer from the body to the environment. Depending on the mean vote of thermal comfort from a group of individuals exposed to certain thermal conditions for some time, the model will consider a PMV index comfortable only when at least 95% of respondents are satisfied to this condition. Here, the thermal vote is scaled into 7 integer levels between −3 and 3 on the ASHRAE scale. Despite being widely accepted, the model appears some limitations in practice. For example, the model often need the user's feedback about his/her activity, and allocate the corresponding assumption constant for this user. This is not convenient for elder or younger people. It is often the same case to obtain user's clothing regularly.

In this work, we propose a thermal comfort control scheme for personal thermal balance adjustment with automation. It captures the capabilities of IOT network to incorporate video camera as well as normal environment sensors together. In which, the video camera is used to capture the individual's activity and clothing condition regularly, which will be converted into metabolic rate and clothing insulation by machine learning algorithm accordingly. Then all the captured or converted data are exploited to learn the PMV index, which reflecting the individual's living habit and thermal comfort preference. At last, the learnt personal PMV index value is used to predict the air temperature and air velocity of the air conditioning system for environment calibration. We derived the solution optimization process for proposed model by Cuckoo Search algorithm, which can be convergent quickly. In the experiment, we analyzed the effect of different factors such as metabolic rate, clothing insulation, and air humidity, on the predicted solution in the thermal comfort model.

The rest of this paper is organized as follows. In Sect. 2, we give a brief introduction to the PMV index equation. Then in Sect. 3, we present the framework of our thermal control system, the optimization algorithm and the procedure of solution determination. Section 4 shows the obtained results and analysis based on our optimal PMV model. Section 5 concludes the paper.

2   PMV Model

PMV is able to predict the average response about thermal sensation of a group of people exposed to certain thermal conditions for a long time. The index can be estimated as a thermal balance function considering the human body as a whole entity, which deals with the following six variables: metabolic rate (M), air temperature (t_a), mean radiant temperature (t_r), air humidity (ϕ_a), air velocity (v_a) and clothing insulation (I_{cl}). Equations (1)–(5) show the function relations with all the variables.

$$PMV = [0.303 \exp(-0.036M) + 0.275]$$
$$* \{M - W - 3.05[5.733 - 0.007(M - W) - P_a]$$
$$- 0.42(M - W - 58.15) - 0.0173M(5.867 - P_a) \tag{1}$$
$$- 0.0014M(34 - t_a) - f_{cl}h_c(t_{cl} - t_a)$$
$$- 3.96 \times 10^{-8}f_{cl}[(t_{cl} + 273)^4 - (t_r + 273)^4]\}$$

Where

$$Pa = \varphi_a \times EXP[16.6536 - 4030.183/(t_a + 235)] \tag{2}$$

$$t_{cl} = 35.7 - 0.028(M - W)$$
$$- I_{cl}\{3.96 \times 10^{-8} \times f_{cl}[(t_{cl} + 273)^4 \tag{3}$$
$$- (t_r + 273)^4] + f_{cl}h_c(t_{cl} - t_a)\}$$

$$h_c = \begin{cases} 2.38(t_{cl} - t_a)^{0.25}, & 2.38(t_{cl} - t_a)^{0.25} > 12.1\sqrt{v_a} \\ 12.1\sqrt{v_a}, & 2.38(t_{cl} - t_a)^{0.25} \leq 12.1\sqrt{v_a} \end{cases} \tag{4}$$

$$f_{cl} = \begin{cases} 1.00 + 1.290I_{cl}, I_{cl} \leq 0.078 \\ 1.05 + 0.645I_{cl}, I_{cl} > 0.078 \end{cases} \tag{5}$$

Most values of these variables are acquired by sensors. However, clothing insulation and human activity are variables not easily accessed since they depend on the individual's current situation at a time. Conventionally, the values related to both variables under different conditions can be found in manuals and standards [4]. Then, the resulting 7 PMV scales are: 0 neutral, ±1 slightly warm/cool, ±2 warm/cool, ±3 hot/cold. Hence, the simplest way to guarantee thermal comfort conditions in a certain environment is to keep PMV index value at 0.

3   Proposed Thermal Comfort Control System

In this section, we present the architecture of our thermal comfort control system, parameter determine approaches for PMV thermal comfort model in detail, followed by the model optimization algorithm.

Figure 1 describes the framework of our personal thermal comfort control system.

The sensors network is composed of several sensors connected together by IOT. In which, the temperature sensor, humidity sensor and air velocity sensor are used to capture the indoor environment information; video camera is used to monitor the individual's personal information, such as activity condition and clothing condition. Then, machine learning method is used to classify the individual's clothing captured and map classification result to the clothing insulation value; similarly, the activity condition is classified into 3 states (sitting, sleeping, and activity) corresponds to the of metabolic rate. Next, the PMV index is calculated by Eqs. (1)–(5) based on the

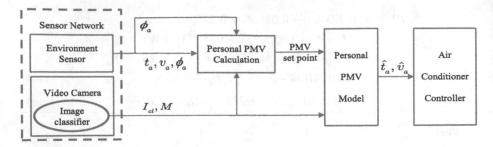

Fig. 1. Schematic illustration of the proposed thermal comfort control system.

obtained factors. The mean value of PMV recorded for a period is used for the individual's personal PMV, which reflecting the individual's living habit and preference. At last, in the prediction stage, we deduce the air temperature and air velocity through the learnt personal PMV by the PMV model. If the system finds a mismatch between predicted air temperature as well as velocity and the measured values, it will adjust the air conditioner controller automatically. The presented system tries to keep the balance between occupant's thermal sensation and expectation by minimizing the mismatch between demand and supply for thermal dynamic mechanics. Thus, it also avoids the energy wastage, and improves the energy efficiency.

3.1 Parameter Determination

PMV model depends on 6 factors actually, including the air temperature t_a, mean radiant temperature t_r, air velocity v_a, comparative air humidity ϕ_a, metabolic rate M, and clothing surface temperature t_{cl}.

Calculation of clothing surface temperature t_{cl} and convective heat transfer coefficient h_c. From Eqs. (1)–(5), we can see PMV model deals with several complex expression. Especially for Eqs. (3) and (4), in which the calculation of two intermediate variables clothing surface temperature t_{cl} and the convective heat transfer coefficient h_c depends on each other. In this paper, we try to calculate the two variables by iteration method.

From Eq. (3), let

$$
\begin{aligned}
F(t_{cl}, h_c) = {}& 35.7 - 0.028(M - W) \\
& - I_{cl}\{3.96 \times 10^{-8} \times f_{cl}[(t_{cl} + 273)^4 \\
& - (t_r + 273)^4] + f_{cl}h_c(t_{cl} - t_a)\} - t_{cl}
\end{aligned}
\tag{6}
$$

Then, Eqs. (3) and (4) is expressed as follows:

$$
\begin{cases}
F(t_{cl}, h_c) = 0 \\
h_c = \begin{cases}
2.38(t_{cl} - t_a)^{0.25} \ \text{when} \quad 2.38(t_{cl} - t_a)^{0.25} > 12.1\sqrt{v_a} \\
12.1\sqrt{v_a} \quad \text{when} \quad 2.38(t_{cl} - t_a)^{0.25} \le 12.1\sqrt{v_a}
\end{cases}
\end{cases}
\tag{7}
$$

Equation (7) is solved by iteration. First, set a search range for the value of t_{cl} in 20 °C–40 °C. Then, for each fixed value of t_{cl}, calculate h_c by Eq. (4); Next, calculate $F(t_{cl}, h_c)$ by Eq. (6). Repeat the above two steps until $F(t_{cl}, h_c)$ approaches to zero.

Obtain metabolic rate M and clothing insulation I_{cl} by image classification. In Fanger's study, three classes of activity condition have been given with the corresponding metabolic rate, as seen in Table 1. Thus the images we captured for activity classification are divided into 3 classes accordingly. An activity classifier is trained first to get the mapping between activity condition in the image and the metabolic rate. Then, given a new image, the classifier is used to predict the corresponding activity condition, and further, find the metabolic rate.

Table 1. Different activity conditions and their metabolic rates.

Activity condition	Metabolic rate (met)
Sitting	1
Activation	2
Sleeping	0.5

The clothing insulation is obtained in the similar method, and 4 classes of clothing have been given with the corresponding clothing insulation, as seen in Table 2.

Table 2. Different clothing and their insulations.

Clothing	Clothing insulation (clo)
Short sleeves, shorts	0.3
Long sleeves, slacks	0.5
Jacket, sweater	0.7
Padded coat	1.0

3.2 Personal PMV Training

By Fanger's model, the best thermal comfort condition is when PMV = 0. But different people have different thermal comfort sensation. The thermal sensation may differ in ages, gender, and health condition, even in physiological and psychological factors. Thus, the optimization goal of PMV = 0 does not fit all the people, especially for vulnerable seniors and youngers.

To find a personal PMV, we capture the indoor air temperature, air humidity, and air velocity by the corresponding sensors, capture the individual's clothing and activity condition, and transfer them into corresponding clothing insulation value and metabolic rate by machine leaning classification algorithm. All the data obtained for a period are feed into the PMV model to calculate the personal PMV values, which reflect the person's living habit and preference. At last, we choose the mean value as the personal PMV for the preceding model prediction, and note it as PMV_0.

3.3   Model Prediction

Among the six factors relevant to PMV index, we can see the indoor temperature t_a and the air velocity v_a can be adjusted by air conditioner. Thus, the issue of thermal comfort control is converted into an optimization issue of t_a and v_a simultaneously given a personal PMV value PMV_0 based on PMV model. From Eq. (1), let $fit(t_a, v_a) = PMV - PMV_0$, then the optimization problem can be formulated as:

$$\begin{cases} \underset{t_a, v_a}{\operatorname{argmin}} |fit(t_a, v_a)| \\ s.t.\ Eq.(2), Eq.(3), Eq.(4), Eq.(5) \end{cases} \tag{8}$$

Equation (8) is a continuous optimization problem. We employ the CS (Cuckoo Search) algorithm [5] to solve this problem. CS algorithm is inspired by the obligate brood parasitism of some cuckoo species laying their eggs in the nests of other host birds. It assumes that the host bird discovers the egg laid by cuckoo with a probability of $P \in [0, 1]$. In this case, the host will throw the egg or abandon the nest to build a new one. Thus, the process of finding the solution of an optimal problem is a cuckoo search process, where each cuckoo nest corresponds to a solution, and the optimal solution is evaluated by fitness function. Then we describe the process of solving Eq. (8) by CS algorithm as follows.

Denote by $X = [X_1, X_2, \ldots, X_i, \ldots, X_N] \in \mathbf{R}^{2 \times N}$ the original research space formed by N cuckoos, where each column $X_i = [x_{1i}, x_{2i}]^T$, $(i = 1, 2, \ldots, N)$, is the ith cukcoo of two dimension. x_{1i} and x_{2i} corresponds to t_a and v_a in Eq. (8) respectively. Assume each cuckoo corresponds to one nest, and each nest a solution. The optimization procedure of CS algorithm is to update the nest X_i^t Iteratively, where t indexes an iteration. In each iteration, there are two steps to update the cuckoos:

① Given the current host nests X^t, get new N Cuckoo nests $X_L \in \mathbf{R}^{2 \times N}$ randomly by Levy flight:

$$X_L = X^t + \alpha \bullet L(\lambda) \tag{9}$$

Where $\alpha = [\alpha_1, \alpha_2] \in \mathbf{R}^{2 \times N}$ is a constant parameter matrix related to the scales of the problem of interest and is often chosen such that the flight step should not be aggressive. Here, we set $\alpha_1 = 1$, and $\alpha_2 = 0.0625$. The product $\bullet$ means entry-wise multiplications. $L(\lambda) \in \mathbf{R}^{2 \times N}$ is the step size matrix of random walk through Levy flight.

Generally, the next location after a random walk only depends on the current location and the Levy step. The Levy step is taken from the Levy distribution, which represented as:

$$L(\lambda) = \frac{U}{|Z|^{\frac{1}{(\lambda-1)}}}, (1 < \lambda < 3) \tag{10}$$

Where U and Z are obtained from a normal distribution $U \sim N(0, \sigma_U^2), Z \sim N(0, 1)$, and

$$\sigma_U(\lambda) = \left[\frac{\Gamma(1+\lambda)\sin\left(\frac{\pi\lambda}{2}\right)}{\lambda\Gamma\left(\frac{1+\lambda}{2}\right)2^{\left(\frac{\lambda-1}{2}\right)}}\right]^{\frac{1}{\lambda}} \tag{11}$$

Then, the original host nests X_i^t and the new generated cuckoo nests X_{Li} will be compared by fitness function $F = fit(\cdot)$ and the better ones will be kept as X_i^{t+1}.

② Next, the host throws the egg of cuckoos away or abandons the nest to build one in a new location randomly. This step commonly use the preference random walk, which make use of the other nests similarity [6]. Thus the new built nests $X_R \in \mathbf{R}^{2 \times N}$ is depicted as:

$$X_R = X^t + \gamma \bullet Heaviside(P - \varepsilon) \bullet (X'' - X''') \tag{12}$$

Where, γ and ε are random obeying uniform distribution, $Heaviside(\cdot)$ is a jump function, which is described as:

$$Heaviside(\theta) = \begin{cases} 1, \theta > 0 \\ 0, \theta < 0 \end{cases} \tag{13}$$

X'' and X''' are two nest arrays, each of them is the result matrix changing the column order of X^t randomly. Then the better solutions will be determined by fitness function similar to step ①. And the best solution is find by ranking. In the experiments, we set $P_a = 0.25$, number of cuckoos $N = 50$, δ is set 0.0001, maximum iteration is 30, t_a and v_a are limited in [15, 32] and [0, 0.5]. We observed that the CS optimization converge rapidly. Figure 2 plots the changing values of the fitness function in the convergence process.

4   Experiments

In this section, we will give the result of proposed thermal control system as well as the results analysis.

4.1   Experimental Settings

In our experiment, we assume the mean radiant temperature t_r is equal to the air temperature t_a. The indoor air velocity v_a is limited not more than 0.5 m/s. We do the experiment 20 times and get 20 solutions for each setup.

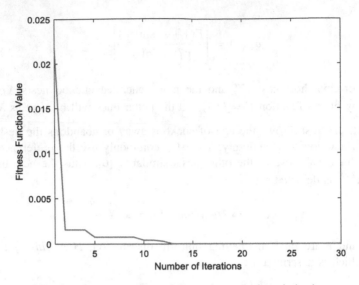

Fig. 2. The convergence of the cuckoo search optimization

4.2 Prediction Results for Thermal Comfort

The number of solutions that satisfied the given thermal comfort requirement is not limited to one. Table 3 gives some examples of predicted result when metabolic rate $M = 1$ met, and clothing insulation $I_{cl} = 0.5$ clo with humidity changing between 20% and 80%. In which, t_a and v_a represent the solution with the air temperature nearest to the mean value. We define Δt_a as the relative variation of the predicted air temperature, which is calculated by:

$$\Delta t_a = \frac{t_{a\,max} - t_{a\,min}}{t_{a\,min}} \times 100\% \tag{14}$$

Where $t_{a\,min}$ and $v_{a\,min}$ is the solution with the minimum value, $t_{a\,max}$ and $v_{a\,max}$ the maximum.

Table 3. Results of the thermal control system with variation of comparative humidity φ_a, keeping metabolic rate $M = 1$ met, and clothing insulation $I_{cl} = 0.5$ clo.

$\varphi_a(\%)$	$t_a(°C)$	$v_a(m/s)$	$\Delta t_a(\%)$
20	27.69	0.24	5.4
30	27.34	0.21	6.5
40	27.00	0.19	6.7
50	26.72	0.18	6.8
60	26.09	0.12	6.9
70	26.66	0.27	7.1
80	26.04	0.18	7.3

From Table 3, we can observe:

(1) With the humidity increase from 20% to 80%, the predicted temperature for thermal comfort will decrease by 6%. While the corresponding air velocity is always changing in the whole given range. This shows that the humidity has a comparatively small effect on the predicted air temperature, and nearly has no effect on the air velocity.

(2) With the humidity increase, the relative variation of the air temperature Δt_a is increasing, which shows that the adjustable scope of air temperature for the thermal control system is enlarged with the increase of humidity.

(3) The solutions being satisfied to a given fitness requirement are more than one, which may provide the adjustment flexibility for our system and the possibility to find a common or similar thermal comfort setting for an indoor environment with more person who have different preferences.

Table 4 gives some examples of predicted result when humidity $\varphi_a = 50\%$ fixed and metabolic rate M and clothing insulation I_{cl} changing in the range of [0.5, 1, 2] met and [0.3, 0.5, 0.7, 1.0] clo respectively.

Table 4. Results of the thermal control system with variation of metabolic rate M and clothing insulation I_{cl}, keeping comparative humidity $\varphi_a = 50\%$.

M(met)	I_{cl}(clo)	$t_a(°C)$	v_a(m/s)	$\Delta t_a(\%)$
0.5	0.3	30.49	0.14	4.51
	0.5	29.95	0.19	4.36
	0.7	29.10	0.17	4.41
	1.0	27.93	0.16	4.45
1	0.3	27.90	0.20	6.64
	0.5	26.76	0.19	6.83
	0.7	25.40	0.16	6.98
	1.0	23.83	0.17	7.04
2	0.3	22.68	0.24	12.65
	0.5	20.76	0.23	13.40
	0.7	18.73	0.21	14.03
	1.0	16.11	0.23	15.40

From Table 4, we can observe:

(1) Keeping the metabolic rate M fixed as 0.5 met, increase the clothing insulation from 0.3 clo to 1.0 clo, the predicted temperature for thermal comfort will decrease by 8.4%, accordingly, the predicted temperature will decrease by 14.6% when M is set 1 met, and 28% when M is 2 met. While the corresponding air velocity is always changing in the given range. This shows that the clothing insulation has a clear effect on the predicted air temperature, and has little effect on the air velocity. Also, the effect is increasing greatly with the increase of metabolic rate.

(2) Keeping the clothing insulation I_{cl} fixed as 0.3 clo, increase the metabolic rate from 0.5 met to 2 met, the predicted temperature for thermal comfort will decrease by 25.6%. Accordingly, the predicted temperature will decrease by 30.7% when I_{cl} is set 0.5 clo; by 35.6% when I_{cl} is 0.7 clo; and by 42.2% when I_{cl} is 1.0 clo. While the corresponding air velocity is always changing in the given range. This shows that the metabolic rate has the most important effect on the predicted air temperature, and little effect on the air velocity. Also, the effect is increasing greatly with the increase of clothing insulation. Thus, the introduction of video camera in our proposed system will help to keep the thermal comfort effectively and flexibly.

(3) With the increase of metabolic rate and clothing insulation, the relative variation of the air temperature Δt_a is increasing except the case when $I_{cl} = 0.3$ clo and M = 0.5 met, which shows that the adjustable scope of air temperature for the thermal control system is enlarged with the increase of metabolic rate and clothing insulation.

(4) The multiple solutions in a certain condition also provide possibility to use the system in the environment with more persons.

5 Conclusions

In this paper, we present a personal thermal comfort control model for indoor environment, which integrates the video camera into conventional sensors into an IOT network for data acquisition. To facilitate the individuality of our model, the system combines personal information including activity and clothing condition from the video camera with environment measurements such as temperature, humidity, and air velocity. And the individual's thermal comfort is kept by continuous calibration of the air temperature and air velocity using PVM model. We deduced the solution optimization based on Cuckoo Search algorithm. Experiment result shows our model optimization process is convergent rapidly, which demonstrates the practicability of our proposed model. Furthermore, the results analysis show the humidity has smaller effect on thermal comfort compared to metabolic rate and clothing, which shows that we could pay less attention to the humidity in the future studies. Also, the multiple solutions for thermal comfort in a certain condition illustrate the potential for energy saving and the possible application of our model in environment with more than one person. For future work, we intend to make use of big data captured from more transducer, and integrate the big data driven cluster [7, 8] into the system to provide more optimal control strategy.

Acknowledgements. This work is supported by Chinese National Natural Science Foundation (61771169), science and technology project of Beijing Municipal Education Commission (KM201510009005) and the excellent youthful teacher project of North China University of Technology (XN019006).

References

1. Klepeis, N.E., Nelson, W.C., Ott, W.R., et al.: The national human activity pattern survey (NHAPS): a resource for assessing exposure to environmental pollutants. J. Expo. Anal. Environ. Epidemiol. **11**(3), 231–252 (2000)
2. Fanger, P.O.: Calculation of thermal comfort: introduction of basic comfort equation. ASHRAE Trans. **73**, III4.1–III4.20 (1967)
3. International Standard Organization. ISO 7730 (2005)
4. Castilla, M., Álvarez, J.D., Normey-Rico, J.E., et al.: Thermal comfort control using a non-linear MPC strategy: a real case of study in a bioclimatic building. J. Process Control **24**(6), 703–713 (2014)
5. Yang, X.S., Deb, S.: Cuckoo search via levy flight. In: Proceedings of World Congress on Nature & Biologically Inspired Computing, pp. 210–214. IEEE Publications, India (2009). Washington
6. Yang, X.S.: Cuckoo search for inverse problems and simulated-driven shape optimization. J. Comput. Methods in Sci. Eng. **12**, 129–137 (2012)
7. Shuai, H., Xu, S., Meng, W., et al.: An agile confidential transmission strategy combining big data driven cluster and OBF. IEEE Trans. Veh. Technol. **66**(11), 10259–10270 (2017)
8. Shuai, H., Xu, S., Meng, W., et al.: Dense-device-enabled cooperative networks for efficient and secure transmission. IEEE Netw. **32**(2), 100–106 (2018)

Context Adaptive Visual Tracker in Surveillance Networks

Wei Feng[1], Minye Li[2], Yuan Zhou[3]($\boxtimes$), Zizi Li[3], and Chenghao Li[3]

[1] Systems Engineering Research Institute of China State Shipbuilding Corporation,
Beijing 100036, China
[2] Unit 61660 of PLA, Beijing 100089, China
[3] Tianjin University, Tianjin 300072, China
zhouyuan@tju.edu.cn

Abstract. CNN-based visual trackers has been successfully applied to surveillance networks. Some trackers apply sliding-window method to generate candidate samples which is the input of network. However, some candidate samples containing too much background regions are mistakenly used for target tracking, which leads to a drift problem. To mitigate this problem, we propose a novel Context Adaptive Visual tracker (CAVT), which discards the patches containing too much background regions and constructs a robust appearance model of tracking targets. The proposed method first formulates a weighted similarity function to construct a pure target region. The pure target region and the surrounding area of the bounding box are used as a target prior and a background prior, respectively. Then the method exploits both the target prior and background prior to distinguish target and background regions from the bounding box. Experiments on a challenging benchmark OTB demonstrate that the proposed CAVT algorithm performs favorably compared to several state-of-the-art methods.

Keywords: Visual tracking · Surveillance network

1 Introduction

Visual tracking is one of the most fundamental problems in computer vision with various applications such as surveillance and vehicle navigation. Despite great progress has been made over the past decade, it remains a challenging problem to design a robust tracker due to factors such as occlusion, illumination changes and geometric deformations, etc.

Recently, CNN-based discriminative tracking methods have been proven to be capable to achieve favorable tracking performance. Particularly, some trackers use sliding-window method to generate candidate samples which is the input of network. Although achieved the encouraging results both in accuracy and robustness, some candidate samples containing too much background regions

© ICST Institute for Computer Sciences, Social Informatics and Telecommunications Engineering 2019
Published by Springer Nature Switzerland AG 2019. All Rights Reserved
S. Han et al. (Eds.): AICON 2019, LNICST 286, pp. 374–382, 2019.
https://doi.org/10.1007/978-3-030-22968-9_33

are mistakenly used for target tracking, which leads to a drift problem. The reason is as follows.

At the initial frame of a video sequence, the patches of a tracking target are sampled from the region which is manually labeled as a target bounding box (a rectangular box). The patches of the tracking target are input to the network to extract the feature of the target, and then the classifier distinguishes the patches as the target or background. The appearance of a tracking target is usually irregular, however, the target bounding box is regular. As a result, the target bounding box contains some background regions. Since the patches are extracted from the bounding box, some of the patches may contain too much background regions, which may cause inaccurate tracking results. Moreover, the inaccurate tracking results may spread to the subsequent frames, thus leading to a drifting problem. Besides, the error produced in tracking process would gradually accumulate and propagate, resulting in poor performance in long-term tracking.

To combat this problem, the paper proposes a context adaptive learning method and for visual tracking. We propose a method to distinguish target and background regions from the bounding box. First, we formulate a weighted similarity function to construct a pure target region that has no background regions. The pure target region is used as a target prior and the surrounding area of a bounding box are used as a background prior. We exploit both the target prior and background prior to distinguish target and background regions from the bounding box. Patches which contain too much background regions could be discard to construct a robust appearance model of tracking targets.

2   The Proposed Context Adaptive Tracker

In this section, we will provide the details of the proposed context adaptive tracker. We use CNN-SVM [1] as baseline. We detail the process of extracting target region from target bounding box. This process is crucial to alleviate the drifting problem caused by inaccurate appearance representation of tracking target.

2.1   Superpixel-Based Pure Target Region Extraction

For a given image, the image domain consists of two parts: the target bounding box region T_r and its surrounding background region B_r. The region T_r could be obtained by the manually labeled ground truth $X = [x, y, w, h] \in \Re_4$ in the initial frame. (x, y) is the center location of the tracking target; w and h denote its weight and height in x-axis and y-axis, respectively.

At the initial frame of a video sequence, we segment the context region (The bounding box of the context region could be represented by $X_r = [x, y, \lambda w, \lambda h] \in \Re_4$. The $\lambda > 1$ is a constant parameter, which controls the size of the context region.) into N superpixels set $S = \{s_1, \cdots, s_n, \cdots, s_N\}$ for further processing. Here any edge preserving superpixel methods can be used and SLIC algorithm is adopted in our paper. The input image is segmented into multiple uniform and compact region. For a certain superpixel S_N, we have:

$$l_n(S_n) = \begin{cases} 1, if & S_n \in T_p \\ 0, if & S_n \in B_r \end{cases} \tag{1}$$

where $l_n(S_n)$ denotes the label of superpixel s_n, the region T_p are set to $\gamma(\gamma < 1)$ time the target bounding box and is a constant parameter which is employed to construct a pure target region. The value of γ should not be set too large to ensure the region T_p to have abundant features of tracking target. However, tracking targets always have irregular sizes, leading to the region T_p still with some outliers which should be classified into background region. For further processing, it is worthy to construct a pure target region without outliers.

Given in the region T_p, we seek the most reliable target superpixels to construct a pure target region by using a weighted similarity function. Compared with the superpixels belonging to the pure target region, the number of outliers which are dissimilar with target in appearance, always occupy a little of proportion. The appearance of outliers always is different with the target superpixels, while several superpixels which are similar to a target superpixel can usually be found in the pure target region. Thus, a method that examines the similarity between each superpixel was proposed to detect outliers based on the Kernelized Correlation Filters.

$$c_i^p \doteq \sum_{S_j \in T_p} \max(F(I(s_i)w_s^p)) \odot F(I(s_j)w_s^p)w_{s_i}^p, s_i \in T_p \tag{2}$$

where c_i^p is defined as a likelihood of the superpixel s_i belonging to the tracking target or the background, F denotes the Fast Fourier Transform function and $\odot$ is the element-wise product, $I(s_i)$ denotes image intensity of a rectangular patch which could contain the superpixel s_i. A spatial weight function $w_{s_i}^p$ is defined by

$$w_{s_i}^p \doteq exp(-\frac{\|z_{s_i} - (x,y)\|^2}{(\sigma^p)^2}) \tag{3}$$

where context location z_{s_i} is the center of superpixel s_i, is a scale parameter of the region T_p.

The N_s number of patches with lowest score of c_i^p computed by Eq. (2) are regarded as outliers. N_s is an integer parameter which is used to control the number of outliers. Due to the outliers are more likely to be background, they should not be used to exploit target prior. A pure target region T_r^* is defined without the outliers. Assume that T_r^* is only composed by a set of superpixels which belong to tracking target, we only need to distinguish the rest of region T_r'. And the $l_n(S_n)$ is updated as

$$l_n(S_n) = \begin{cases} 1, if & S_n \in T_r^* \\ 0, if & S_n \in B_r \end{cases} \tag{4}$$

2.2 Target and Background Likelihood

Assume pure target region as target prior and surrounding of the target bounding box as background prior, the similarity metrics between each superpixel $s_n \in T'_r$, target and background likelihood are calculated for distinguishing the region T'_r, respectively. Given a set of superpixels S, an undirected graph $\zeta = (\nu, \xi)$ is constructed to reveal the connection relationships (similarity metrics) between T'_r, T^*_r and B_r, where $\nu = \{\nu_1, \ldots, \nu_n, \ldots, \nu_N\}$ denotes a set of nodes corresponding to superpixels set S and ξ is a set of undirected edges corresponding to nodes set ν. We define mean feature vectors ν_n^{lab} in the CIELAB color space and geometric center ν_n^{geo} on Euclidean distance for each node. The ν_n^{lab} and ν_n^{lab} are widely used in many algorithms to simplify further processing, due to their advantages of high-efficiency and superior appearance representation.

An initial regular graph where each node is only connected to its immediate neighbors is established by us. The adjacency matrix of the graph ζ is defined to be $A = [a_{ij}]_{N \times N}$. If the nodes ν_i and ν_j are immediate neighbors, then $a_{ij} \doteq 1$, otherwise $a_{ij} \doteq 0$. We subsequently define target and background edges based on the initial regular graph for calculating similarity metrics between T'_r, T^*_r and B_r, respectively.

For each node $\nu_n \in T^*_r$, we consider it as an initial node, and connect it with its immediate and mediate neighbors. These neighbors are restricted to the target bounding box region T_r. The color feature constraint is considered to ensure the similarity between the initial node and its neighbors. Besides, the connections among these nodes are constrained by spatial geometric distance. The rule can be represented as:

$$\xi_i^{T^*_r} \doteq \{(s_i, s_j) | a_{ij} = 1, \nu_{ij}^{lab} \le Th_{ij}^{T^*_r}, s_i \in T^*_r, s_j \in T_r\}$$
$$\cup \{(s_i, s_n) | a_{jn} = 1, \nu_{in}^{lab} \le Th_{in}^{T^*_r}, s_n \in T_r\}$$
$$\cup \{(s_i, s_k) | a_{nk} = 1, \nu_{ik}^{lab} \le Th_{ik}^{T^*_r}, s_k \in T_r\} \qquad (5)$$
$$\cup \{(s_i, s_l) | a_{kl} = 1, \nu_{il}^{lab} \le Th_{il}^{T^*_r}, s_l \in T_r\}$$
$$Th_{ij}^{T^*_r} \doteq \alpha_{T^*_r} \cdot \max \nu_{il}^{lab} \cdot \frac{w_n}{Z_j}, s_i \in T^*_r, s_j, s_m \in T_r$$

where the $\xi_i^{T^*_r}$ is a target edge corresponding to the node $\nu_i \in T^*_r$, $\nu_{ij}^{lab} \doteq \|\nu_i^{lab} - \nu_j^{lab}\|$ is a measure of visual similarity between superpixel s_i and s_j in the CIELAB color space, $\alpha_{T^*_r}$ is a fixed parameter which is used to ensure the similarity between the superpixel corresponding to the initial node and its neighbors, σ_j^{geo} is the variance of all the ν^{geo} corresponding to the set of superpixels $s^{geo} \doteq \{s_j | \nu_{ij}^{lab} \le \alpha_{T^*_r} \cdot \max \nu_{im}^{lab}, s_i \in T^*_r, s_j \in T_r\}$, $\nu_{ij}^{geo} \doteq \|\nu_i^{geo} - \nu_j^{geo}\|$ is spatial geometric distance in euclidean space, $Th_{ij}^{T^*_r}$ is an adaptive threshold to determine whether the superpixel s_i is similar with the superpixel s_j, w_n is a threshold weight function and will be defined in detail in the following paragraphs, Z_j is a normalization factor to ensure that $\sum_{s_i \in s^{geo}} \frac{w_n}{Z_j} \doteq 1$.

Considering in the target bounding box region T_r, the central position of a superpixel which is near to the tracking target center, indicating that the superpixel is more likely to belong to tracking target. Furthermore, the near the geometric distance between the superpixel s_i and s_j is, the more likely that the superpixel s_j is similar to the superpixel s_i. Thus, different weight should be set for the adaptive threshold $Th_{ij}^{T^*}$ at different position of a superpixel. The threshold weight function is defined as:

$$
w_n = \begin{cases} exp(-\dfrac{\nu_{ij}^{geo}}{(\sigma_{c_i^1}^{geo})^2}) & if \quad S_n \in T_r^* \\[4ex] exp(-\dfrac{\min \|\nu_n^{geo} - \nu_{center}^{geo} \pm (\frac{w}{2\gamma}, \frac{h}{2\gamma})\|^2}{(\sigma^{geo})^2}) \\[2ex] \times exp(-\dfrac{\nu_{ij}^{geo}}{(\sigma_{c_i^1}^{geo})^2}) & if \quad S_n \in T_r' \end{cases}
\tag{6}
$$

where σ^{geo} is the variance of all the ν_n^{geo} corresponding to the set of superpixels $s_n \in T_r'$, ν_{center}^{geo} is geometric center of the superpixel which locates to the center of the tracking target, $exp(-\frac{\nu_{ij}^{geo}}{(\sigma_{c_i^1}^{geo})^2})$ measures the spatial variance between the superpixel s_i and s_j. Given a superpixel $s_n \in T_r'$, the larger the value of the threshold weight function, the more probable it will be connected with the superpixel $s_i \in T_r^*$.

We could obtain the each target edge $\xi_i^{T_r}$ through Eq. (5) and define the set of target edges ξ^{T_r} as $\xi^{T_r} \doteq [\xi_1^{T_r} \cdots \xi_i^{T_r} \cdots \xi_{N_T}^{T_r}]$, where N_T is the total number of superpixels which belong to the pure target region T_r^*. In each target edge $\xi_i^{T_r}$, all the superpixels are similar with the superpixel s_i which belongs to the T_r^*. If a superpixel $s_n \in T_r'$ is discovered multiple times in the target edges ξ^{T_r}, it shows that the superpixel is actually quite similar with the pure target region T_r^* and should be categorized into tracking target region. Then we define the target similarity metric Sim_n^T as:

$$
Sim_n^T \doteq \frac{N_n^T}{N_T}, \{n|s_n \in T_r'\}
\tag{7}
$$

where the N_n^T is the number of times that the superpixel $s_n \in T_r'$ appears in the ξ^{T_r}.

Besides target prior, we also exploit background prior for distinguishing the region T_r'. For a robust performance of visual tracking, our purpose is to distinguish the background region from the target bounding box, which may lead to drift problem. The rule can be represented as:

$$\xi_i^{B_r} \doteq \{(s_i, s_j) | a_{ij} = 1, \nu_{ij}^{lab} \leq \alpha_{B_r} \cdot \max \nu_{in}^{lab}$$

$$s_i \in B_r, s_j, s_n \in B_r \cup T_r'\} \tag{8}$$

$$\cup \{(s_i, s_k) | a_{jk} = 1, \nu_{ik}^{lab} \leq \alpha_{B_r} \cdot \max \nu_{in}^{lab}$$

$$s_n, s_k \in B_r \cup T_r'\}$$

where the edge $\xi_i^{B_r}$ is a background edge corresponding to the node $v_i \in B_r$, α_{B_r} is a fixed parameter which promise the visual similarity between superpixel s_i, s_j and s_n in the CIELAB color space.

Similarly, the set of background edges ξ^{B_r} is defined as $\xi^{B_r} = [\xi_1^{B_r} \ldots \xi_i^{B_r} \ldots \xi_{N_B}^{B_r}]$, where N_B is the total number of superpixels which belong to the surrounding background region of target bounding box. Then we define the background similarity metric Sim_n^B as:

$$Sim_n^B \doteq \frac{N_n^B}{N_B}, \{n | s_n \in T_r'\} \tag{9}$$

where the N_n^B is the number of times that the superpixel $S_n \in T_r'$ appears in the ξ^{B_r}.

2.3 Classification for Superpixel

As aforementioned, we calculate the similarity metrics between each superpixel $S_n \in T_r'$, target and background, respectively. Based on these, we could classify the each superpixel $S_n \in T_r'$, to indicate whether it belongs to the target or the background. The label of the superpixel is determined by

$$l_n(S_n) = \begin{cases} 1, if & Sim_T \geq Sim_B \\ 0, if & Sim_T < Sim_B \end{cases} \tag{10}$$

Through Eqs. (4) and (10), we could obtain a complete region of tracking target.

3 Experiments

In this section, extensively experiments are conducted for the proposed CAVT method. We first introduce the details of our experimental setup including parameters, dataset, and evaluation metrics. We then evaluate our method on an online object tracking benchmark with comparisons to state-of-the-art methods.

3.1 Experimental Setup

The constant parameter is set to 1.35, which means that the size of context region is initially set to 1.35 times the size of the ground truth target bounding box. The SLIC algorithm [2] is applied to extract superpixels from the context region where the maximal number of superpixels is set 200. The value of outliers are fixed at 0.8 and 6, respectively, which are used to make sure a purificatus target regions. The threshold α_{Br} and $\alpha_{T_r^*}$ are empirically defined as 0.1 and 0.15, respectively. We note that the parameters are fixed in all the experiments. As for the rest of parameters, we use the default setting of the base CNN-SVM tracker to prove that our method could improve the effectiveness for part-based trackers. Dataset and Evaluation Metrics:

We report the evaluation of our proposed CAVT method on the CVPR2013 Online Object Tracking Benchmark (OOTB) [3] that contains 50 fully annotated sequences with comparisons to state-of-the-art methods. The OOTB is a comprehensive benchmark specifically designed for evaluating tracking performance, which extensively used in the online tracking literature over the past several years. In OOTB, the quantitative evaluation for the effectiveness of different trackers is based on four types of metrics. The first metric is mean Center Location Error (CLE), which is defined as the average Euclidean distance between the center of tracking result and the ground truth for each frame. The second metric is Pascal VOC Overlap Ratio (VOR), which is defined as $VOR \doteq \frac{Area(B_T \bigcap B_G)}{Area(B_T \bigcup B_G)}$, where B_G and B_T denote the bounding box of ground truth and the tracking results, respectively. The rest of metrics are precision plot and success plot which can measure the overall performance of the different trackers. The precision plot demonstrates the percentage of successfully tracked frames on which the CLE of a tracker is within a given threshold. The success plot also illustrates the percentage of successfully tracked frames by measuring the Intersection Over Union (IOU) metrics on each frame. The area under curve (AUC) score is used to rank the tracking algorithms in both the precision plot and success plot.

3.2 Comparison with State-of-the-Arts

In this paper, we compare the proposed tracker on the OOTB with 34 representative tracking methods. Among the competitor trackers, we first consider those 29 popular approaches whose results are available in OOTB including TLD [4], etc. The 29 popular trackers can be referred to [3] in details. And on top of these, other 6 recently published state-of-the-art trackers with their shared source code: CNN-SVM [1], RPT [5], KCF [6], CNT [7], SAMF [8] and MEEM [9].

To quantitatively compare all the 34 trackers, we use the original software provided by [3] to compute both precision and success plots in Fig. 1. Following the setting in [3], we conduct all the experiments using one-pass evaluation (OPE) strategy for fair comparison with the state-of-the-art trackers. The OPE is computed by running a tracker throughout a video sequence with initialization by the ground truth in the initial frame. The performance gap between our tracker and the second best tracker in the literature is 0.3% in tracking precision measure and 2.7% in success measure under OPE; the proposed tracker achieves 85.5% and 62.4% accuracy while the base tracker is 85.2% and 59.7% (CNN-SVM). It is obvious that both the precision and success plots demonstrate that the proposed tracker performs well against the competitors. The precision and success plots

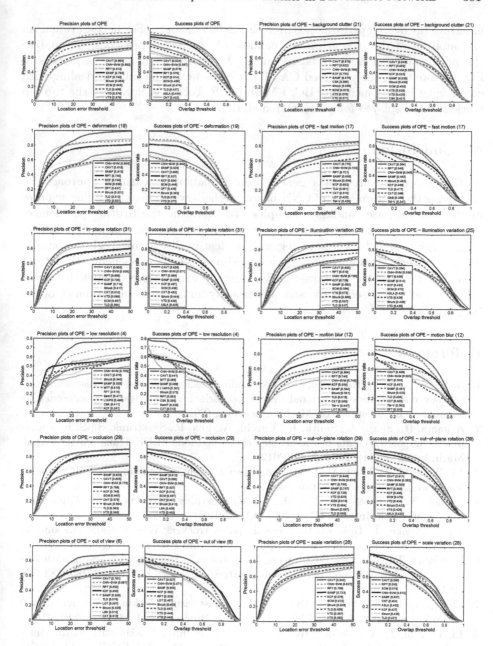

Fig. 1. Precision and success plots of the OPE and Overlap success plots for 11 challenging attributes. The legend contains the AUC score for each tracker. The proposed CAVT method performs favorably against the state-of-the-art trackers when evaluating with 11 challenging factors.

illustrate the overall performance over all the 50 sequences. For better evaluation and analysis of the strength and weakness of tracking approaches, we analyze the performance of trackers based on the 11 attributes of image sequences in Fig. 1. Note that, the proposed CAVT performs well, especially in dealing with challenging factors including BC, FM and IPR. For each plot, only the top ten trackers are displayed for presentation clarity.

4   Conclusion

In this paper, we propose a generic context adaptive learning approach for improving the performance of CNN-based methods which use the sliding-window method to generate candidate samples. To overcome the drifting problem of state-of-the-art CNN-based trackers, we exploit the intrinsic relationship among target regions and background regions to identify distracting regions containing too much background. Extensive experiment results on benchmark dataset demonstrates that the proposed CAVT method can achieve competitive accuracy on challenging sequences and significantly improve the performance of the base tracker.

References

1. Hong, S., You, T., Kwak, S., Han, B.: Online tracking by learning discriminative saliency map with convolutional neural network. In: International Conference on International Conference on Machine Learning (2015)
2. Achanta, R., Shaji, A., Smith, K., Lucchi, A., Fua, P., Süsstrunk, S.: SLIC superpixels compared to state-of-the-art superpixel methods. IEEE Trans. Pattern Anal. Mach. Intell. **34**(11), 2274–2282 (2012)
3. Yi, W., Lim, J., Yang, M.H.: Online object tracking: a benchmark. In: Computer Vision and Pattern Recognition (2013)
4. Zdenek, K., Krystian, M., Jiri, M.: Tracking-learning-detection. IEEE Trans. Pattern Anal. Mach. Intell. **34**(7), 1409–1422 (2012)
5. Yang, L., Zhu, J., Hoi, S.C.H.: Reliable patch trackers: robust visual tracking by exploiting reliable patches. In: Computer Vision and Pattern Recognition (2015)
6. Henriques, J.F., Caseiro, R., Martins, P., Batista, J.: High-speed tracking with kernelized correlation filters. IEEE Trans. Pattern Anal. Mach. Intell. **37**(3), 583–596 (2015)
7. Zhang, K., Liu, Q., Wu, Y., Yang, M.-H.: Robust visual tracking via convolutional networks without training. IEEE Trans. Image Process. **25**(4), 1779–1792 (2016)
8. Li, Y., Zhu, J.: A scale adaptive kernel correlation filter tracker with feature integration. In: Agapito, L., Bronstein, M.M., Rother, C. (eds.) ECCV 2014. LNCS, vol. 8926, pp. 254–265. Springer, Cham (2015). https://doi.org/10.1007/978-3-319-16181-5_18
9. Zhang, J., Ma, S., Sclaroff, S.: MEEM: robust tracking via multiple experts using entropy minimization. In: Fleet, D., Pajdla, T., Schiele, B., Tuytelaars, T. (eds.) ECCV 2014. LNCS, vol. 8694, pp. 188–203. Springer, Cham (2014). https://doi.org/10.1007/978-3-319-10599-4_13

Research on Indoor Localization Based on Joint Coefficient APIT

Min Zhao[1], Danyang Qin[1(✉)] , Ruolin Guo[1], and Lin Ma[2]

[1] Heilongjiang University, Harbin 150080, People's Republic of China
qindanyang@hlju.edu.cn
[2] Harbin Institute of Technology, Harbin 150001, People's Republic of China

Abstract. The APIT algorithm has become a popular technology for indoor localization due to its simplicity and low power consumption. However, the APIT algorithm often has misjudgments of In-to-Out in practical applications. And a large number of nodes cannot be located, when the density of anchor nodes (AN) is low. For this, this paper proposes a joint coefficient triangle APIT localization algorithm (JCTA). First, an effective triangle decision method is proposed. Then, the RSSI localization, the maximum likelihood method, and the weighted triangular coordinate calculation method are introduced and combined. Finally, an iterative co-location idea is used to locate the pending node (NP). The simulation results show that the JCTA algorithm can show good performance in terms of localization coverage rate and localization error about nodes.

Keywords: Indoor localization · Misjudgments of In-to-Out · APIT ·
Iterative co-location

1 Introduction

As the importance of location information in the WSN increases, various nodes localization algorithms emerge continuously. Among them, the location method based on ranging includes: the bias reduction method using the source locating explicit solution of TDOA [1], Received Signal Strength Indicator (RSSI) [2], RSSI-based automatic positioning method [3], etc. Although they can achieve high localization accuracy, they are costly. In contrast, location algorithms based non-ranging are low cost and can meet the requirements of localization accuracy for most applications. Among them, the typical non-ranging algorithms includes: an adaptive location algorithm based on APIT proposed for nodes randomly distributed in WSN [4], three-dimensional localization algorithm of APIT based on tetrahedral centroid iteration [5], and the traditional APIT algorithm [6]. Although the above algorithms can complete the localization of the nodes under certain conditions, the localization accuracy of the

This work is supported by the National Natural Science Foundation of China (61771186, 61571162), Ministry of Education-China Mobile Research Foundation (MCM20170106), University Nursing Program for Young Scholars with Creative Talents in Heilongjiang Province (UNPYSCT-2017125), Distinguished Young Scholars Fund of Heilongjiang University, and postdoctoral Research Foundation of Heilongjiang Province (LBH-Q15121).

S. Han et al. (Eds.): AICON 2019, LNICST 286, pp. 383–390, 2019.
https://doi.org/10.1007/978-3-030-22968-9_34

APIT algorithm depends on the locations of adjacent ANs and is susceptible to the density and distribution of sensor nodes. To this end, a JCTA algorithm is proposed to reduce the localization error and increase the localization coverage rate of nodes.

2 APIT Algorithm

The principle of APIT [7] is to use the ANs around the Pending Node (PN) to determine whether the PN is within a triangle consisting of ANs. And the APIT algorithm is invalid when the number of ANs around the PN is less than 3 or the ANs cannot form a valid triangle. We assume that there are C_N^3 triangles composed of N ANs around the PN, and it is determined by the APIT that there are M effective triangles. And different effective triangles have different roles in the evaluation.

A tricky issue with APIT is the misjudgments of In-to-Out [8]. As shown in Fig. 1, when the node D is in the inner boundary of the $\triangle ABC$, if the node D moves toward the node 4, the node D may be judged to be outside the $\triangle ABC$.

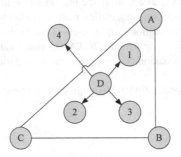

Fig. 1. Misjudgments of In-to-Out in APIT algorithm

The limitation of the APIT algorithm is that it requires a high density of ANs and a large communication radius. If the above requirements are not met, a large number of nodes cannot be located and the localization error will be large.

3 Proposed JCTA Algorithm

Aiming at the problems in APIT application, a JCTA algorithm is proposed. The algorithm includes determining effective triangles, RSSI assisted locating, maximum likelihood coordinate estimations and weighted triangle coordinate calculations, and interactive communication between nodes. Figure 2 depicts the overall flow chart of the JCTA algorithm. The detailed steps are as follows:

Step 1. Define the identification information of the node by $u\_f = 0$ represents a PN that is not located, $u\_f = 1$ represents a known AN, $u\_f = 2$ represents a PN that has been located.

Step 2. The PN collects the transmitted signal power from the neighbor ANs.

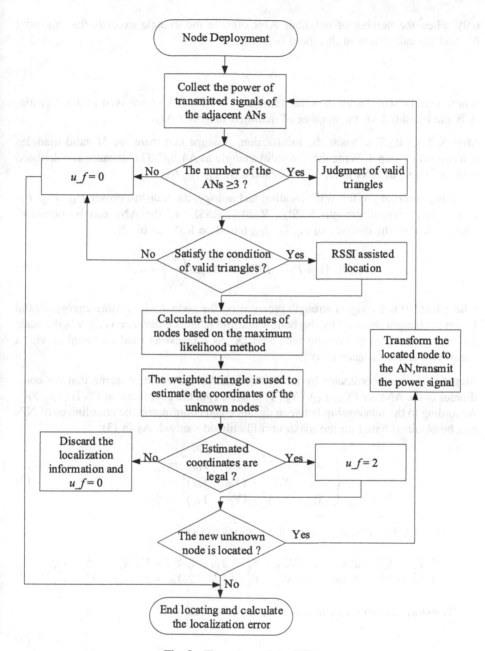

Fig. 2. Flow chart of the JCTA

Step 3. Determine whether the number of ANs is no less than 3. If yes, go to step 4; If no, terminate the locating and set the node ID to $u\_f = 0$.

Step 4. Determine whether the PN is within the triangle by APIT algorithm, and if so, the triangle is a valid triangle. However, the PN is considered to be outside the triangle only when the number of neighbor ANs outside the triangle exceeds the threshold N. And the calculation of threshold is in (1):

$$N = \mu \times n \tag{1}$$

where μ is the scale factor, n is the number of neighbor ANs involved in the decision, N is the threshold for the number of qualified neighbor ANs.

Step 5. Take RSSI to assist the localization. Assume that there are M valid triangles determined by step 4. Write the i-th valid triangle as $\Delta A_i B_i C_i$ The distance is calculated from A_i, B_i, C_i of ANs to D_i of PN denoted by l_{Ai}, l_{Bi}, l_{Ci}.

First, according to the WiFi locating technology, the transmit power P_{A_i}, P_{B_i}, P_{C_i} and received signal strength $RSSI_{A_i}$, $RSSI_{B_i}$, $RSSI_{C_i}$ of the ANs can be obtained. Then, calculate the distance of l_{Ai}, l_{Bi}, l_{Ci}, based on RSSI as in (2).

$$RSSI(l) = P_T - PL(l_0) - 10\rho lg\left(\frac{l}{l_0}\right) + X_\sigma \tag{2}$$

where $RSSI(l)$ is the signal strength received by the node, P_T is sending energy, $PL(l_0)$ is signal strength received by the node when the reference distance is l_0, ρ is the scale factor between path length and path loss, X_σ is a Gaussian random variable with a mean of 0 and a variance of σ^2.

Step 6. Estimate coordinates by maximum likelihood method. Assume that the coordinates of the ANs are (X_{Ai}, Y_{Ai}), (X_{Bi}, Y_{Bi}), (X_{Ci}, Y_{Ci}), the coordinate of PN is (X_{Di}, Y_{Di}). According to the relationship between distance and coordinates, the coordinates of NPs can be obtained based on the maximum likelihood method. As in (3):

$$\begin{cases} (X_{Ai} - X_{Di})^2 + (Y_{Ai} - Y_{Di})^2 = l_{Ai}^2 \\ (X_{Bi} - X_{Di})^2 + (Y_{Bi} - Y_{Di})^2 = l_{Bi}^2 \\ (X_{Ci} - X_{Di})^2 + (Y_{Ci} - Y_{Di})^2 = l_{Ci}^2 \end{cases} \tag{3}$$

Convert (3) to a linear system of equations as (4):

$$\begin{cases} X_{Ai}^2 - X_{Ci}^2 - 2(X_{Ai} - X_{Ci})X_{Di} + Y_{Ai}^2 - Y_{Ci}^2 - 2(Y_{Ai} - Y_{ci})X_{Di} = l_{Ai}^2 - l_{Ci}^2 \\ X_{Bi}^2 - X_{Ci}^2 - 2(X_{Bi} - X_{Ci})X_{Di} + Y_{Bi}^2 - Y_{Ci}^2 - 2(Y_{Bi} - Y_{ci})X_{Di} = l_{Bi}^2 - l_{Ci}^2 \end{cases} \tag{4}$$

Transform (4) into a matrix form of least squares:

$$BX = c \tag{5}$$

$$B = \begin{bmatrix} 2(X_{Ai} - X_{Ci}) & 2(Y_{Ai} - Y_{Ci}) \\ 2(X_{Bi} - X_{Ci}) & 2(Y_{Bi} - Y_{Ci}) \end{bmatrix} \tag{6}$$

$$c = \begin{bmatrix} X_{Ai}^2 - X_{Ci}^2 + Y_{Ai}^2 - Y_{Ci}^2 + l_{Ci}^2 - l_{Ai}^2 \\ X_{Bi}^2 - X_{Ci}^2 + Y_{Bi}^2 - Y_{Ci}^2 + l_{Ci}^2 - l_{Bi}^2 \end{bmatrix} \tag{7}$$

$$X = \begin{bmatrix} X_{Di} \\ Y_{Di} \end{bmatrix} \tag{8}$$

Thus, the location coordinate of the PN can be obtained by (9):

$$\begin{bmatrix} X_{Di} \\ Y_{Di} \end{bmatrix} = (B^T B)^{-1} B^T c \tag{9}$$

Step 7. The weighted triangle location method is used to estimate the coordinates of PNs. The mean value and standard deviation of each effective triangle distance l_{Ai}, l_{Bi}, l_{Ci} are calculated to obtain $E(l_i)$ and $\sqrt{V(l_i)}$, where l_i is the distance from the PN to AN i. Then the mean weighted factor $\beta_{Ei} = \frac{1}{E(l_i)}$ and the standard deviation weighted factor $\beta_{Vi} = \frac{1}{\sqrt{V(l_i)}}$ can be calculated. The mean weighted coordinates and standard deviation weighted coordinates of the M effective triangles are calculated as shown in (10) and (11). Then, the coordinate of the PN are estimated as a linear combination of (X_E, Y_E) and (X_V, Y_V) as shown in (12).

$$(X_E, Y_E) = \left(\frac{\sum_{i=1}^M \beta_{Ei} X_{Di}}{\sum_{i=1}^M \beta_{Ei}}, \frac{\sum_{i=1}^M \beta_{Ei} Y_{Di}}{\sum_{i=1}^M \beta_{Ei}} \right) \tag{10}$$

$$(X_V, Y_V) = \left(\frac{\sum_{i=1}^M \beta_{Vi} X_{Di}}{\sum_{i=1}^M \beta_{Vi}}, \frac{\sum_{i=1}^M \beta_{Vi} Y_{Di}}{\sum_{i=1}^M \beta_{Vi}} \right) \tag{11}$$

$$(X, Y) = \alpha \times (X_E, Y_E) + \gamma \times (X_V, Y_V) \tag{12}$$

where α and γ are the weighted coefficient of the mean and standard deviation coordinates.

Step 8. In this step, the legality should be checked. Suppose node A is an AN and D is a PN, and the distance from node A to node D is calculated. If the distance is within 120% of the communication radius of node D, the estimated coordinate of PN is legal, the coordinate values are recorded and the node's identity is set to $u\_f = 2$; Otherwise, the locating fails, the location information is discarded, and the identification of node is set to $u\_f = 0$.

Step 9. New anchor node will be added through iterative co-location. After each location is completed, it is judged whether the node that is successfully located this time is a new NP. If so, the node ($u\_f = 2$) is changed to AN, the power signal is sent to the neighboring area, and the localization coordinate of the node is broadcast. Then go to Step 2 and participate in the next round of localization calculation; if not, end the locating and calculate the localization error.

4 Simulation and Results Analysis

This paper verifies the localization performance of JCTA algorithm through MATLAB. The localization error rate E_{mean} and localization coverage rate ε of the node are defined as follows:

$$E_{mean} = \frac{\sum_{i=1}^{n} Q_i}{n} = \frac{\sum_{i=1}^{n} \frac{\sqrt{(X_e-X_t)^2 + (Y_e-Y_t)^2}}{R}}{n} \tag{13}$$

where Q_i is the localization error of a single node, n is the number of PNs in the network, (X_t, Y_t) is the actual coordinates of PNs, (X_e, Y_e) is the estimated coordinates of PNs, R is the communication radius of PNs.

The node localization coverage rate ε indicates the ratio of the number of PNs that can be successfully located to the total number of NPs in the network. Suppose there are a total of n PNs in the network, and the localization algorithm can successfully locate z nodes as (14):

$$\varepsilon = \frac{z}{n} \times 100\% \tag{14}$$

In addition, according to (1), μ is set to be 0.2. According to the (12), a plurality of tests are performed by setting $\alpha = 0.25, 0.5, 0.75$, $\gamma = 0.25, 0.5, 0.75$, and it is found that the minimum localization error can be obtained when $\alpha = 0.5$, $\gamma = 0.5$. Therefore, $\alpha = 0.5$, $\gamma = 0.5$ are used in all of the following experiments.

4.1 Localization Coverage Rate

Figure 3 depicts the localization coverage rate ε of the JCTA, RSSI, IAPIT and APIT algorithms as the density of the ANs in the network and the communication radius of the PNs change. It can be seen from Fig. 3(a) that as the density of the AN increases, the ε of the four localization algorithms increases. However, at the same density of ANs, JCTA has the highest ε of nodes, which is basically maintained at 100%. This is because the JCTA algorithm continuously converts the successfully determined PNs into ANs, and guarantees the legitimacy of the new ANs through the maximum likelihood method and the legality test, thereby greatly improving the problem that the node cannot be located when the density of the ANs is small.

4.2 Error of Localization

Figure 4 shows the localization error E_{mean} of the four algorithms as the density of the ANs in the network changes and the communication radius of the PNs changes. Figure 4(a) shows the comparison of E_{mean} generated by four simulated algorithms when

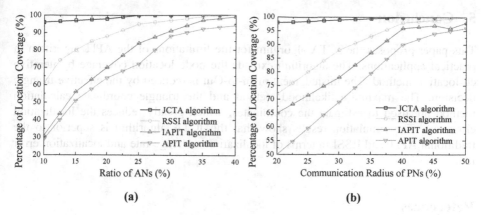

Fig. 3. Comparisons of localization coverage with (a) density of ANs and (b) communication radius of PNs

the communication radius of the PNs is 30 m and the density of ANs varies over a large range. It can be seen that the E_{mean} of JCTA is 15% smaller than that of APIT algorithm, 13% smaller than that of RSSI algorithm, and 8% smaller than that of IAPIT algorithm, showing good localization performance. This is because the JCTA algorithm will introduce a legality test to estimate the PNs so as to achieve better localization accuracy.

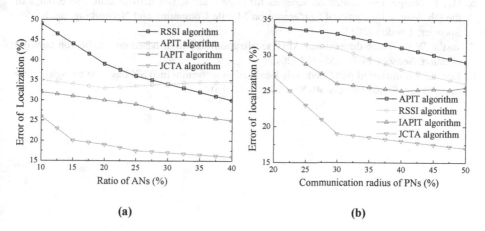

Fig. 4. Comparisons of localization error with (a) density of ANs and (b) communication radius of PNs

390 M. Zhao et al.

5 Conclusion

This paper proposes the JCTA algorithm for the limitations of the APIT algorithm in practical applications. The algorithm extends the node location coverage by iterative co-location method. The misjudgment of In-to-Out is reduced by the effective triangle decision. The maximum likelihood method and the triangle coordinate calculation method are used to estimate the coordinates, which greatly reduces the localization error rate. The simulation results show that the JCTA algorithm is superior to the traditional APIT and RSSI in terms of localization coverage rate and localization error rate.

References

1. Ho, K.C.: Bias reduction for an explicit solution of source localization using TDOA. IEEE Trans. Signal Process. **60**(5), 2101–2114 (2016)
2. Feng, C.: A new node self-localization algorithm based RSSI for wireless sensor networks, pp. 1616–1619 (2018)
3. Kumar, V., Arablouei, R., Jurdak, R., et al.: RSSI-based self-localization with perturbed anchor positions. J. Wirel. Commun. **15**(7), 215–226 (2017)
4. Yong, Z.: An improved APIT node self-localization algorithm in WSN. In: World Congress on Intelligent Control & Automation (2008)
5. Wei, H.U.: Three-dimensional APIT localization algorithm based on tetrahedron centroid iteration. IEEE Access **26**(10), 1432–1436 (2017)
6. He, T.: Range-free localization schemes for large scale sensor networks. In: Proceedings of the 9th Annual International Conference on Mobile Computing and Networking, pp. 81–95. Springer, London (2013)
7. Jestin, W.B.: Three-dimensional APIT localization algorithm based on tetrahedron centroid iteration. Sensors **24**(7), 155–168 (2017)
8. Lee, Z.: An improved APIT node self-localization algorithm in WSN based on triangle-center scan. Trans. Signal Process. **46**(8), 566–574 (2016)

A Cross-Layer Approach to Maximize the Lifetime of Underwater Wireless Sensor Networks

Yuan Zhou[1,2]([✉]), Hui Liu[1], Hai Cao[1], Dan Li[1], Hongyu Yang[2], and Tao Cao[2]

[1] National Ocean Technology Center, Tianjin 300072, China
zhouyuan@tju.edu.cn
[2] Tianjin University, Tianjin 300072, China

Abstract. Efficient usage energy of sensors can lead to prolonged lifetime in underwater wireless sensor networks (UWSNs). This paper addresses maximization of the network lifetime for UWSNs. More specifically, it considers an optimal cross-layer design of transmission schemes. Here we restrict ourselves to the type of time division multiple access schedules in the link layer. In order to balance energy consumption over different nodes, we develop a Mixed Integer Non-Linear Programming formulation to facilitate joint optimization of link schedules, transmission powers and rates of sensors. We have also conducted extensive network simulations to test the proposed algorithm. The results confirm that our approach can prolong overall network lifetime.

Keywords: Cross-layer design · Network lifetime ·
Underwater wireless sensor networks

1 Introduction

Underwater Wireless Sensor Networks (UWSNs) are self-organized systems in which a number of sensors collect and relay useful data in harsh underwater environments. UWSNs are various and promising, including monitoring different areas for security surveillance, monitoring pollution and oil extraction etc. [1,8]. Methods developed for terrestrial wireless sensor networks to maximize their lifetime perform poorly in UWSNs. One of the reasons is that UWSNs usually communicate via underwater acoustic channels with consideration of the properties of underwater environments [2]. Available energy of sensors in UWSNs are limited due to the failure of replacing the batteries of sensors, and unreasonable use of the limited energy may cause a short network lifetime in UWSNs.

The underwater acoustic channels are well studied in [7]. Based on this kind of researches, methods which economize on energy for UWSNs were proposed. Jornet et al. [3] proposed a focused-beam routing (FBR) protocol that determined the most energy-efficient candidates for nodes relaying data. Yan et al. [9]

S. Han et al. (Eds.): AICON 2019, LNICST 286, pp. 391–397, 2019.
https://doi.org/10.1007/978-3-030-22968-9_35

proposed an energy efficient routing based on nodes' depth information. Rhdo-plu et al. [5] proposed an energy optimized MAC protocol. Ponnavaikko et al. [4] focused on computing energy-efficient TDMA-based routes for delay-constrained UWSNs. While they all enjoy high energy efficiency, however, they fail to take the energy balance of nodes into account so that some special nodes with heavy data load might quickly drain their energy in these methods. As a result, the performance in terms of network lifetime are severely compromised.

In our method, we first restrict the link schedules to the type of time division multiple access (TDMA) schedules, so as to eliminate the communication inter-ference among nodes. Then, with considering constraints of nodes and under-water acoustic channels, we define an optimal problem whose objective is to maximize the network lifetime. We find that the optimal problem is a Mixed Inte-ger Non-Linear Programming (MINLP). Finally, we propose the iterative algo-rithm named network lifetime maximization algorithm which alternates adjust-ing TDMA schedules and computation of optimal transmission rates and powers of nodes under a fixed TDMA schedule.

2   Problem Formulation and Network Lifetime Maximization Algorithm

In this section, we formulate an optimization problem, the objective of which is to maximize the network lifetime for UWSNs. Moreover, we restrict the link sched-ules to be some kind of TDMA schedules, and propose an iterative algorithm which optimizes the transmission scheme for network lifetime maximization.

2.1   Optimization Objective: Network Lifetime

We consider UWSNs which consist of a number of common nodes (CN) and one sink node. Common nodes are deployed underwater and measure the environ-mental parameters at a fixed source rate. Let T_i be the lifetime of common node i, $i.e.$, the time span from its deployment to the time it drains its energy, then the network lifetime T_{total} is defined as $T_{total} = min_{i \in I} T_i$, where I represents the set of common nodes. The objective of our design is to maximize the network lifetime T_{total},

$$max \ T_{total} = max \ min_{i \in I} T_i, \tag{1}$$

subject to the following constrains that are used to balance the energy consump-tion among different nodes.

Flow Conservation. During a TDMA cycle period, for each common node (CN) in the network, the transmitted data should be equal to the sum of received data and sensed data, which could be formulated as:

$$\sum_{n \in Send} x_i^n - \sum_{n \in Receive} x_i^n = N \cdot s_i \cdot T_{slot}, \tag{2}$$

where x_i^n is the transmitted bits or received bits of the i-th node in the n-th time slot. *Send* is the set of allocated time slots for the i-th node transmitting data, and *Receive* is the set of time slots for the i-th node receiving data. N is the total amount of time slots during a TDMA period. s_i represents the source rate of the i-th node, i.e., the constant rate of collecting environmental information in bit per second. Both x_i^n and s_i are positive numbers. T_{slot} is the time length of a TDMA time slot. The transmission time $T_{transmit}$ and the propagation time $T_{propagate}$ should be included in a time slot T_{slot}. Let the transmission rate of the i-th node in the n-th time slot be R_i^n. Then, x_i^n can be expressed as:

$$x_i^n = R_i^n \cdot T_{transmit}. \tag{3}$$

Energy Conservation. During the network lifetime, energy consumption of each node should be equal to or less than the initial energy $E_{initial}$ stored in the battery before deployment. We neglect $E_{receive}$ and E_{sense} in our design because $E_{transmit}$ is often 100 times more than both of them [6]. $E_{transmit}$ is computed as the product of the average energy consumption during a TDMA period and the total amount (we assume that it is p) of available TDMA periods during the network lifetime. Then we have:

$$E_{initial} \geq E_{average\_TDMA} \cdot p = \frac{\sum_{n \in Send} P_{transmit,i}^n \cdot T_{transmit}}{N \cdot T_{slot}} \cdot T_{total}, \tag{4}$$

where $P_{transmit,i}^n$ is the transmission power of the i-th node in the n-th time slot. In this paper, the 3dB bandwidth $B_{3dB}(l)$ is used. And we assume the transmitted signal p.s.d. $S(f)$ is flat, *i.e.*, $S(f) = S_l$ for frequencies within the range of $B_{3dB}(l)$ and 0 otherwise, which is also appropriate in practice. Then, we have:

$$P_{transmit,i}^n(l) = \int_{B_{3dB}(l)} S(f)df = B_{3dB}(l) \cdot S_l. \tag{5}$$

Rate Constraints. According to the information theory, the transmission rate of a node at any time should be equal to or less than the available channel capacity C:

$$R_i^n \leq C \approx \int_{B_{3dB}(l)} \log_2\left(\frac{P_{transmit,i}^n(l)/A(l,f)}{N(f) \cdot B_{3dB}(l)}\right)df \tag{6}$$

$$= B_{3dB}(l) \cdot \log_2 P_{transmit,i}^n(l) - \lambda(l)$$

where $\lambda(l)$ is defined as: $\lambda(l) = \int_{B_{3dB}(l)} log_2[A(l,f)N(f)B_{3dB}(l)]df$. We assume that the channel capacity in each transmission process can be adequately used, *i.e.*, R_i^n is equal to C in each transmission, then we have:

$$R_i^n = B_{3dB}(l) \cdot \log_2 P_{transmit,i}^n(l) - \lambda(l) \tag{7}$$

The transmission power $P_{transmit,i}^n$ should be less than the maximum transmission power P_{max} determined by the sensor's hardware.

With the consideration of aforementioned constraints, we can formulate the optimization problem. Let $q_i = 1/T_i$ and $q = 1/T_{total}$. Then the optimization problem Eq. (1) can be re-formulated as the following equivalent:

$$min. \; q$$

$$s.t. \; (\sum_{n \in Send} R_i^n - \sum_{n \in Receive} R_i^n) \cdot T_{transmit} = N \cdot s_i \cdot T_{slot}$$

$$q_i N T_{slot} E_{initial} \geq \sum_{n \in Send} 2^{\frac{R_i^n + \lambda(l)}{B_{3dB}(l)}} \cdot T_{transmit} \tag{8}$$

$$q = max_{i \in I} \; q_i$$

$$P_{transmit,i}^n \leq P_{max}$$

The optimization problem is formulated as a Mixed Integer Non-Linear Programming (MINLP). Variables in this optimal problem are TDMA schedules and transmission rates (and powers) of nodes for a fixed TDMA schedule.

2.2 Network Lifetime Maximization Algorithm

In this subsection, a transmission scheme optimizing algorithm which maximizes the network lifetime for UWSNs is proposed. The algorithm alternately adjusts the TDMA schedules and computation of the optimal transmission powers and rates of nodes in all time slots for a fixed TDMA schedules. Steps of the proposed algorithm are shown as follow:

(1) Initialize from a transmission scheme with an uniform TDMA schedule where all links are allocated with the same number of time slots. Common nodes transmit data in allocated slots, and receive data or idle in other slots.
(2) Compute the optimal transmission powers and rates of nodes under the TDMA schedule in this iteration by solving the optimal problem. Compare the calculated q value in this iteration with q value at the last iteration. If q in this iteration is decreased, turn to (3), otherwise, turn to (4).
(3) Update the TDMA schedule. When we adjust the TDMA schedule without changing data load of nodes which is calculated in the step (2), if the q value of the network decreases, the adjusted TDMA schedule is feasible for the next iteration. The adjusted TDMA schedule is regarded as the TDMA schedule in the next iteration.
(4) The transmission scheme in the last iteration is regard as the optimal transmission scheme for the network.

3 Simulation Results

3.1 Simulation Setup

Here, we will compare the performance of our algorithm with that of transmission scheme with an uniform TDMA schedule. We simulate in a linear topology, in which common nodes $CN = \{CN_1, CN_2, \ldots, CN_M\}$ and a sink are deployed in a line, and the geographic distance between adjacent nodes l is a constant. We avoid the transmission loop problem by restricting that each node only selects nodes nearer to the sink as its next hops. For each node, we assume that it transmits data by hops and only its adjacent nodes are in its communication range.

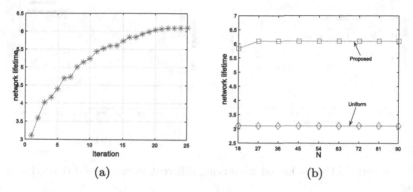

(a)   (b)

Fig. 1. Network lifetime with varying N. (a) Network lifetime in each iteration when $N = 90$, (b) comparison of our algorithm with transmission schemes with an uniform TDMA schedule under different N

3.2   Numerical Results

We first simulate with $M = 9$, $L = 5\,\mathrm{km}$, $s_i = 0.10\,\mathrm{kb/s}$, $N = 90$ and $T_{slot} = 5\,\mathrm{s}$. Figure 1(a) shows that, when $N = 90$, the network lifetime roughly converges after 20 iterations.

Figure 1(b) shows the network lifetime achieved by our proposed algorithm and transmission schemes with an uniform TDMA schedule under different numbers of nodes. Note that the network lifetime achieved by the proposed algorithm when $N = 18$ is a little lower than those of other values of N. The reason is that, when $N = 18$, the most energy-consumption nodes still have potential to raise its lifetime even if the network is under the optimal transmission schedule. In other words, when the number of time slot is small, it not enough for the network to allocate an appropriate number of time slots to the most energy-consumption node, thus resulting in the reduction of the network lifetime.

Figure 2(a) shows the network lifetime achieved by our algorithm and transmission schemes with an uniform TDMA schedule under different s_i (ranges from $0.05\,\mathrm{kb/s}$ to $0.25\,\mathrm{kb/s}$) in the linear topology when $N = 27$. The network lifetime decreases with the source rate increasing because of the increasing data load in the network. The results show that our algorithm outperforms transmission schemes with an uniform TDMA schedule.

Figure 2(b) shows how the maximal network lifetime achieved by our algorithm changes with L under different s_i. We set $N = 27$, and L are respectively 4 km, 5 km and 6 km. We find that the network lifetime decreases with L increasing.

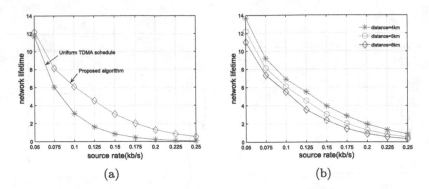

(a)   (b)

Fig. 2. Network lifetime achieved by varying different parameters. (a) varying s_i, (b) varying l.

4   Conclusion

We consider a cross-layer approach to maximize the network lifetime for energy-constrained UWSNs. An optimization problem is defined when we restrict the link schedules to be the kind of TDMA schedules, which is formulated as a mixed integer non-linear programming. Then, the algorithm is proposed to solve the optimal problem. Simulation results show that our algorithm constantly outperforms transmission schemes with an uniform TDMA schedule.

References

1. Akyildiz, I.F., Pompili, D., Melodia, T.: State-of-the-art in protocol research for underwater acoustic sensor networks. In: The Workshop on Underwater Networks, WUWNET 2006, Los Angeles, CA, USA, September, pp. 7–16 (2006)
2. Farr, N., Bowen, A., Ware, J., Pontbriand, C.: An integrated, underwater optical/acoustic communications system. In: OCEANS, pp. 1–6 (2010)
3. Jornet, J.M., Stojanovic, M., Zorzi, M.: Focused beam routing protocol for underwater acoustic networks. In: The Workshop on Underwater Networks, WUWNET 2008, San Francisco, California, USA, September, pp. 75–82 (2008)
4. Ponnavaikko, P., Yassin, K., Wilson, S.K., Stojanovic, M.: Energy optimization with delay constraints in underwater acoustic networks. In: Global Communications Conference, pp. 551–556 (2013)
5. Rodoplu, V., Min, K.P.: An energy-efficient MAC protocol for underwater wireless acoustic networks. In: OCEANS, vol. 2, pp. 1198–1203 (2005)

6. Sendra, S., Lloret, J., Jimenez, J.M., Parra, L.: Underwater acoustic modems. IEEE Sens. J. **16**(11), 4063–4071 (2016)
7. Stojanovic, M., Preisig, J.: Underwater acoustic communication channels: propagation models and statistical characterization. IEEE Commun. Mag. **47**(1), 84–89 (2009)
8. Wang, K., Gao, H., Xu, X., Jiang, J.: An energy-efficient reliable data transmission scheme for complex environmental monitoring in underwater acoustic sensor networks. IEEE Sens. J. **16**(11), 1 (2015)
9. Yan, H., Shi, Z.J., Cui, J.-H.: DBR: depth-based routing for underwater sensor networks. In: Das, A., Pung, H.K., Lee, F.B.S., Wong, L.W.C. (eds.) NETWORKING 2008. LNCS, vol. 4982, pp. 72–86. Springer, Heidelberg (2008). https://doi.org/10.1007/978-3-540-79549-0_7

An Efficient Indoor Localization Method Based on Visual Vocabulary

Ruolin Guo, Danyang Qin[(⊠)] [iD], Min Zhao, and Guangchao Xu

Key Lab of Electronic and Communication Engineering,
Heilongjiang University, Harbin 150080, People's Republic of China
qindanyang@hlju.edu.cn

Abstract. This paper proposes a new efficient indoor localization method based on visual vocabulary. The special feature of this method is that no additional components are needed, but only mobile devices equipped with cameras. By matching the query image with a visual vocabulary constructed by a Bag of Self-Optimized-Ordered Visual Vocabulary (BoSOV), the user's position can be accurately determined. In addition, the efficiency of our scheme is compared with that of other schemes, and simulation results reveal that our method has higher indoor positioning efficiency, especially when the amount of image data is large. Simulation results show that our method can well achieve efficient visual indoor positioning when the data volume is relatively large.

Keywords: Self-optimization · Visual vocabulary · Feature selection · AP clustering · Indoor localization

1 Introduction

Nowadays, there is a growing demand for Location-based Services (LBS) in smartphones, which are provided by external positioning methods such as the Global Positioning System (GPS) or radio communication networks such as the GSM network. Therefore, most LBSs are only suitable for outdoor environments, and the research on indoor localization has received wide attention.

The typical indoor positioning solutions mainly use Wi-Fi technology [1], which performs positioning tasks in indoor environments through Wireless Local Area Networks (WLAN), but it depends on the location of wireless access points. If not taking surrounding Wi-Fi signal into account, errors such as floor positioning wrong are likely to occur. Moreover, the coverage of the wireless access point is limited, the signal is also unstable and it is susceptible to interference. Another solution is to apply Simultaneous Localization and Mapping (SLAM) [2] to locate in an indoor environment. Its process can be described as the machine moving in the environment to be

This work is supported by the National Natural Science Foundation of China (61771186), University Nursing Program for Young Scholars with Creative Talents in Heilongjiang Province (UNPYSCT-2017125), Distinguished Young Scholars Fund of Heilongjiang University, and postdoctoral Research Foundation of Heilongjiang Province (LBH-Q15121).

S. Han et al. (Eds.): AICON 2019, LNICST 286, pp. 398–406, 2019.
https://doi.org/10.1007/978-3-030-22968-9_36

located, and creating a map according to the data recorded by the sensors. Its shortcoming is that it requires complex external facilities to record the relative position of the machine and the ground, and the requirements for the landmarks are very high, but it is difficult to extract the landmarks that meet the requirements by the camera of the mobile phone alone.

This paper proposes a novel vision-based indoor localization scheme that constructs a visual vocabulary through a visual vocabulary bag called BoSOV (Bag of Self-Optimized-Ordered Visual Vocabulary). The difference in this scheme is that the resulting visual vocabulary does not have to be recorded by an additional machines, it has location information itself and can automatically optimize the constructed vocabulary. The method we proposed only requires a smartphone with a camera, which is more cost effective than the previous solution. Moreover, our method is more efficient and accurate in indoor positioning than in Wi-Fi based or SLAM based methods.

The rest of the paper will be organized as follows. Some of the main processes of our proposed indoor positioning solution will be introduced in Sect. 2. The three main processes of our program in the implementation phase will be described in Sect. 3. Section 4 will compare our plan with other programs and evaluate our plan and the full text will be summarized in Sect. 5.

2 Methods

This section introduces some main processing procedures of our proposed indoor localization scheme, which are image processing and clustering methods. The most important step in the image processing is introduced, which is the feature selection and extraction of images. We are also introduced two clustering methods.

2.1 Image Processing

At present, in image processing, feature selection [3] and extraction of the target is a more appropriate method. Because under the BoVW framework, there are many features that are useless for image recognition, so the selection of features with statistical significance from a large number of original features can reduce the amount of calculation and improve the efficiency of image recognition.

One popular algorithm is SURF [4], which consists of three steps: feature point selection, feature point description, and descriptor pairing. Since the selected feature points have the property of rotation invariance in the process of image recognition, a descriptor is generally given to the feature points in order to maintain this property and make them easy to be distinguished. SURF algorithm has the problem of too much computation, because all feature points extracted by the algorithm need to be stored to describe the image. In addition, when descriptors are paired, a large amount of computation will be generated, and there is also a great demand for storage space.

BoVW (Bag of Visual Word), however, can just solve this problem. It only needs to retain variable descriptors and can represent images with fixed length feature vectors, thus reducing the storage pressure. Therefore, the process of our scheme is to extract the SURF descriptor from the original feature set under the BoVW framework, then cluster and quantize it to generate visual vocabulary, thus forming a fixed-length visual vocabulary for the vocabulary. The number of occurrences of each word in the statistic is counted to represent the image as a numerical vector.

2.2 Clustering Method

For the image representation process, the most important step is to cluster the SURF descriptors into clusters. The commonly used clustering method is to use the K-means algorithm [5], which uses the idea of iteration to aggregate the descriptors into their own specifications. The K cluster makes all the data in the cluster have higher similarity, and the similarity between the cluster and the cluster is low.

Initially, K values are randomly selected as the center of the cluster, the distance from each descriptor to the K centers is calculated, and it is divided into the clusters where the nearest center is located. The iteration is repeated until the center value is unchanged or reached the maximum number of iterations, the clustering process is shown in Fig. 1. Eventually, each graph becomes a numerical vector corresponding to the visual vocabulary. But one of the biggest problems with the K-means algorithm is that the K value is difficult to estimate. Since the number of clusters needs to be specified in advance, the user does not know at first that these descriptors should be classified into several categories.

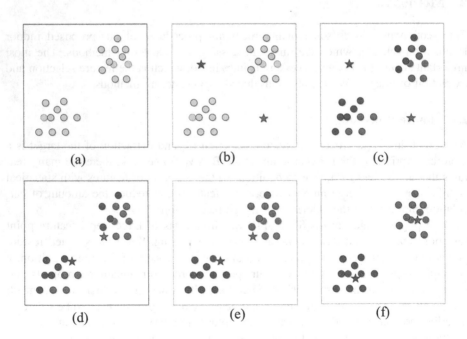

Fig. 1. K-means clustering process

The clustering method used in our scheme is affinity propagation (AP) clustering [6]. Its advantage is that it does not need to determine the number of clustering clusters by itself like the K-means algorithm, nor does it need to take newly generated data as the center of the cluster. It can be selected from existing data points, and the result has small squared error. The basic idea of AP clustering [7] is to treat all descriptors as nodes of a network, and each cluster center is calculated by the information transmitted by each edge of the network. In the clustering process, the attribution degree and the attraction degree are transmitted as the main information between the nodes, and the two values are iteratively updated until a high-quality cluster center is generated. Then the remaining descriptors are allocated to the corresponding clusters.

3 Proposed BoVW and Localization

In the execution phase, three main processes in our scheme are introduced: feature selection and extraction, clustering and visual vocabulary generation and matching of reference images.

3.1 Feature Selection and Extraction

SURF algorithm is adopted for feature extraction with some preparatory work before extraction. The original SURF feature is generally 64-dimensional or 128-dimensional. We choose 64-dimensional and then insert two elements describing relative spatial information, which becomes a descriptor containing 66 elements. We also need to unify the standard for extracting SURF features, and set the resolution of the image to 1200 m $\times$ 1600 m. In addition, remove the feature points whose brightness is higher than the threshold, because these points are generally derived from light and are not useful for image recognition. The descriptor is as Eq. (1):

$$V = (v_0, v_1, \ldots, v_n, q(x)q(y)) \tag{1}$$

where $q(x)$ and $q(y)$ are quantization functions.

3.2 Clustering and Visual Vocabulary Generation

Affinity propagation (AP) clustering is applied to cluster SURF descriptors into clusters. The algorithm flow is as follows:

Attraction Information Update. The attraction information of the similar matrix should be updated first, as shown in Fig. 2(a). The updating process can be written as Eq. (2).

$$r(i,k) \leftarrow s(i,k) - \max\{a(i,k') + s(i,k')\} \tag{2}$$

where $a(i,k')$ indicates the attribution value of points other than k for point i; $s(i,k')$ represents the attraction of other points except k to i; $s(i,k)$ is a similarity matrix (Euclidean distance) between the descriptors i and k; and $r(i,k)$ represents the extent to which the descriptor k is suitable as the clustering center for the descriptor i, and describes the message from i to k.

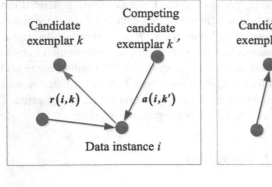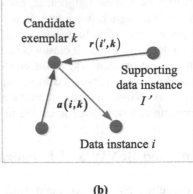

(a)   **(b)**

Fig. 2. Updating process for (a) the attraction information and (b) attribution information

Attribution Information Update. After the attraction information of the similar matrix updated, it turns to attribution information to perform the similar process, as in Fig. 2(b). Such process can be modelled by Eq. (3):

$$
\begin{cases}
a(i,k) \leftarrow \min\left\{0, r(k,k) + \sum_{i' \subsetneq \{i,k\}} \max[0, r(i',k)]\right\}, & i \neq k \\
a(k,k) \leftarrow \sum_{i' \subsetneq \{i,k\}} \max[0, r(i',k)], & i = k
\end{cases}
\tag{3}
$$

where $r(i',k)$ represents the similarity value of point k as the clustering center of other points except i; $a(i,k)$ indicates the degree to which descriptor i selects descriptor k as its clustering center, and describes the messages from k to i.

Summation and Detection. Now it should sum the attraction information [8, 9] and the attribution [10] information. Moreover, the selected cluster center should be detected. If the cluster center remains unchanged or reaches the maximum number of iterations after several iterations, the algorithm ends. The overall process of Affinity Propagation (AP) clustering is shown in Fig. 3.

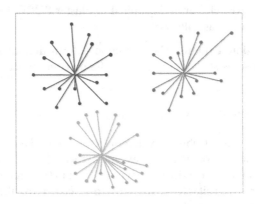

Fig. 3. Affinity propagation clustering process

Suppose there are n segment $\{Seg_1, Seg_2, \ldots, Seg_n\}$s, for the kth fragment, it contains m images as $\{Img_1, Img_2, \ldots, Img_m\}$. For the ith image, a total of $p(i)$ individual feature descriptors are extracted as $\{D_{i1}, D_{i2}, \ldots, D_{ip(i)}\}$. Then, the affinity propagation of the kth segment is clustered using the feature descriptors as the combination of $\{(D_{11}, \ldots, D_{1p(1)})(D_{21}, \ldots, D_{2p(2)})\ldots(D_{n1}, \ldots, D_{np(n)})\}$.

After clustering all the elements into m clusters, a visual vocabulary can be generated from each cluster as ξ. Assume that all p descriptors are assigned to set $i(i \leq n)$ and are represented as $x = (x_1, x_2, \ldots, x_p)$. Then perform 1-mean clustering on x to get the corresponding visual word. We find the visual vocabulary W such as the follows Eq. (4):

$$\xi = arg\ min_W \sum_{i=1}^{p} \|W - x_i\| \qquad (4)$$

After applying 1-means clustering in the clustering of each segment, all the visual words sorted by segment number can be added to construct an intermediate visual vocabulary. The segment and visual vocabulary with high mutual information content constitute the final visual vocabulary. The process is shown in Fig. 4. For ith segment, there have $m(i)$ visual vocabularies.

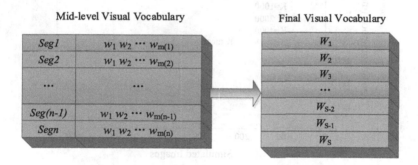

Fig. 4. Generation of the visual vocabulary

3.3   Reference Image Matching

After matching the query image with all the segments and finding the segment S that is most similar to it, we then searched all the images in it to find the image of the visual vector T_{query} closest to the T distance. Suppose the S segment image is $\{Img_1, Img_2, \ldots, Img_m\}$ and its corresponding visual vector is $\{T_1, T_2, \ldots, T_m\}$, the goal is to find Img_i for any i:

$$i = arg\ min_{k \in \{1,2,\ldots,m\}} \|T_{query} - T_k\| \qquad (5)$$

4 Performance Evaluation and Analysis

This section studies and analyzes the efficiency at the construction stage and the efficiency with or without feature selection respectively, and compares our scheme with the scheme using K-means clustering.

4.1 Image Matching Efficiency

The higher efficiency and accuracy is the main focus in the research, in which the large amount of image data matching is the most important foundation. Simulations are performed on the indoor image mating efficiency with large amount of images being sampled at offline phase. Time consumptions are evaluated and recorded cost by comparing the image database and the collecting images in online phase. The comparison results between the proposed algorithm and the typical K-means are shown in Fig. 5.

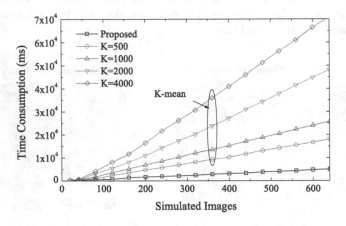

Fig. 5. Comparison of matching efficiency in the constructing phase

From Fig. 5, we can clearly see that no matter what the size of image data is, the scheme using K-means clustering consumes much more time in the execution stage than our scheme. When the number of images is 640, the time consumption of our scheme is 5.059 s, while when there are 640 collecting images, the time required by K-means is 19.778 s at least, which is almost four times more than that of the BoVW.

To achieve high execution efficiency will make the practical application available, especially when the image data volume is large. The relationship between the data volume and the execution speed should be analyzed deeply. We take $k = 2000$ as an example to study. When the number of images is 160, it will the K-mean clustering scheme 7.927 times as long as the proposed scheme. And when the collecting images increase to 640, it will take K-mean clustering scheme 9.469 times more duration as long as the proposed scheme.

4.2 Performance of Feature Selection

In the above introduction, we mentioned that under the BoVW framework, nearly half of the features that are useless for image recognition increase the computational load of execution. Therefore, selecting the features with statistical significance from the original features can reduce the computational load and improve the efficiency of image recognition. Moreover, feature selection is time-consuming and efficient. Figure 6 shows the time consumption of feature selection and non-feature selection in the proposed scheme, and is compared with the scheme using K-means clustering.

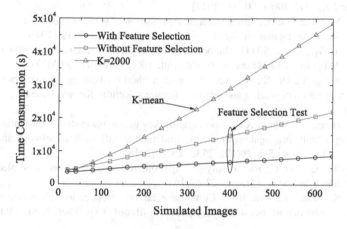

Fig. 6. Comparison of efficiency with/without feature selection

It can be seen from Fig. 6 that no matter how large the image data volume is, without feature selection always takes longer than use feature selection, and it becomes more and more obvious with the increase of data volume. In comparison with the K-means clustering scheme, we find that the efficiency of our scheme is much higher than that of the K-means clustering scheme, no matter whether the feature selection is adopted or not.

5 Conclusions

In this paper, a new high-precision indoor positioning method based on affinity clustering is proposed, which is compared with the K-means clustering method. According to the performance analysis, our method has higher indoor positioning efficiency, especially when the amount of image data is large. When the amount of image data is greater than 40, the query time consumption of K-means clustering scheme is greater than 4 times that of our method, and the proportion is inversely proportional to the increase of the size of image database. Moreover, our method does not require additional components to record the location, but only requires a smartphone with a camera, which is more cost-effective than previous solutions.

References

1. Xiao, C., Zou, S.: Improved Wi-Fi indoor positioning based on particle swarm optimization. IEEE Sens. J. **99**, 1–10 (2017)
2. Wang, X., Zhang, C., Liu, F.: Exponentially weighted particle filter for simultaneous localization and mapping based on magnetic field measurements. IEEE Trans. Instrum. Meas. **66**(7), 1658–1667 (2017)
3. Li, J., Cheng, K., Wang, S.: Feature selection: a data perspective. ACM Comput. Surv. **50** (6), 89–99 (2016)
4. Pan, J., Hao, J., Zhao, J.: Improve algorithm based on SURF for image registration. Remote Sens. Land Resour. **40**(6), 60–74 (2017)
5. Dalmiya, S., Dasgupta, A., Kanti, Datta S.: Application of wavelet based K-means algorithm in mammogram segmentation. Int. J. Comput. Appl. **52**(15), 15–19 (2016)
6. He, S., Lin, W., Chan, S.H.G.: Indoor localization and automatic fingerprint update with altered AP signals. IEEE Trans. Mob. Comput. **16**(7), 1897–1910 (2017)
7. Wei, Z., Wang, Y., He, S.: A novel intelligent method for bearing fault diagnosis based on affinity propagation clustering and adaptive feature selection. Knowl.-Based Syst. **116**(1), 1–12 (2017)
8. Jiang, J., Huang, J., Wang, X.R.: Investigating key genes associated with ovarian cancer by integrating affinity propagation clustering and mutual information network analysis. Eur. Rev. Med. Pharmacol. Sci. **20**(12), 2532–2540 (2016)
9. Sun, L., Guo, C., Liu, C.: Fast affinity propagation clustering based on incomplete similarity matrix. Knowl. Inf. Syst. **51**(3), 1–23 (2016)
10. Chen, Q.S., Dan, W., Liu, B.L.: Combining affinity propagation clustering and mutual information network to investigate key genes in fibroid. Exp. Ther. Med. **14**(1), 251–259 (2017)

Realization and Performance Simulation of Spectrum Detection Based on Cyclostationarity Properties

Zhiqun Song[1,2(✉)], Yujing Lv[2], and Zhongzhao Zhang[1]

[1] School of Electronics and Information Engineering,
Harbin Institute of Technology, Harbin 150080, China
zhiqunsy@163.com
[2] The 54th Research Institute of CECT, Shijiazhuang 050081, China

Abstract. With the wide application of radio technology, spectrum resources are becoming more and more important. Cognitive radio is a new subject that is used to make full use of spectrum resources. The paper studies the spectrum sensing in cognitive radio and focuses on non-cooperative detection method. Based on the energy detection and analysis of the principle of feature detection in periodic stationary process. Using MATLAB for simulation analysis, making comparison of performance between the two methods. The detection performance of the periodic stationary process feature method is 5–7 dB better than the energy detection performance. And the system overhead is about an order of magnitude higher than energy detection.

Keywords: Cognitive radio · Smooth cycle · Energy detection method · Periodic stationary process feature detection method

1 Introduction

With the widespread use of radio technology, modern society is increasingly dependent on radio spectrum resources, radio spectrum resources have become an important resource in today's society, and the scarcity of spectrum resources is becoming more and more obvious. In addition, the average utilization of spectrum resources is very low and extremely unbalanced [1]. Some unlicensed bands are overused, at the same time, the usage rate of some licensed frequency bands is at a low level. Since the current spectrum allocation policy is based on a fixed frequency, most of the spectrum is allocated to licensed band applications (e.g. TV broadcasts). The spectrum resources of unlicensed bands are much less. Most emerging radio applications operate on unlicensed bands, making spectrum occupancy overcrowded on unlicensed bands.

The US Federal Communications Commission have made a large number of studies which shown that some unlicensed bands, such as industrial, scientific, medical bands, and licensed bands around 2 GHz for land mobile communications are overcrowded while some licensed bands are often idle. This is clearly contradictory to the shortage of spectrum resources that are currently of widespread concern. It can be assumed that if the system can automatically sense the spectrum environment in which

S. Han et al. (Eds.): AICON 2019, LNICST 286, pp. 407–416, 2019.
https://doi.org/10.1007/978-3-030-22968-9_37

it is located, intelligently learn to adjust the transmission parameters such as modulation, coding, channel protocol and bandwidth in real time; or use the idle frequency band outside the original designated frequency band to realize the access of the spectrum in the multi-dimensional space. This will undoubtedly greatly improve spectrum utilization. So a revolutionary intelligent spectrum sharing technology, cognitive radio, has the original idea [2].

The core idea of cognitive radio is to realize dynamic spectrum allocation and spectrum sharing through spectrum sensing and intelligent learning ability of the system [3]. Cognition provides the ability to sense and reset spectrum so that the radio can operate dynamically according to the wireless environment, greatly improving spectrum utilization [4]. In this sense, cognitive radio meets the increasing demand for radio spectrum resources in today's society.

Spectrum sensing is the basic function of cognitive radio systems and is the prerequisite for spectrum management and spectrum sharing. The so-called "perception" means that in the time domain, frequency domain and airspace multidimensional space, the spectrum is allocated to the primary user (authorized user) and detect whether the primary user works in these frequency bands, thereby obtaining spectrum usage. If the band is not used by the primary user, it is under "spectral hole" state [5], and the cognitive user (unauthorized user) can use it temporarily. The purpose of spectrum sensing is to discover spectral holes without causing harmful interference to the primary user.

This paper studies the spectrum sensing in cognitive radio, focusing on non-cooperative detection methods, including energy detection and periodic stationary process feature detection. Firstly, the energy detection method and the signal detection method of the signal are introduced. Then the actual analysis method and simulation implementation of the cyclostationary process are carried out. The performance of the two detection methods was then compared and analyzed by MATLAB simulation.

The rest of this article is as follows: The first part briefly introduces the energy detection method and the periodic characteristic detection method of the signal; The second part introduces the actual analysis method and simulation implementation of the cyclostationary process; The third part compares and analyzes the two methods. Finally, the fourth part summarizes the full text.

2 Non-cooperative Detection

The source detection (i.e., non-cooperative detection) is based on cognitive radio to detect the weak signal emitted by the first user transmitter, which is low in complexity mature in technology and easy to implement. The source detection is further divided into energy detection and periodic stationary process feature detection [6].

2.1 Energy Detection

This method assumes that the power is different depending on whether or not the signal is present. Since this detection method is independent of the prior information of the input signal. Therefore there is no strict limit to the type of signal. The main idea of the energy detection method.

The energy detection method is a relatively simple signal detection method and belongs to signal incoherent detection. The detection method is to directly sample and model the time domain signal and then square it. In addition, it is also possible to convert the signal from the time domain to the frequency domain by using a Discrete Fourier Transform, and then modulo square the frequency domain signal. The main advantage of the energy detection method is that it does not require any prior knowledge of the detected signal [7].

In practical applications, the energy detection method is to accumulate energy in a certain frequency range. If the accumulated energy is greater than a preset threshold, the signal exists; If it is less than this threshold, the signal does not exist and only noise exists. The starting point of energy detection is that when there is additive noise on the channel, the energy of the signal plus noise is greater than the energy of the noise. The energy detection method is quite a blind detection algorithm. This method is applicable to any signal, but in addition to obtaining the approximate frequency band of the signal, this detection method cannot give other parameters of the signal more accurately, which brings trouble to the next processing. The input signal is averaged over a period of time and compared with a preset threshold to determine whether an input signal is present.

2.2 Periodic Characteristics Detection of Signals

In a communication system, the statistical characteristics of the signal are periodically changed due to modulation, sampling, encoding, and the like of the signal. Such a random signal is a cyclostationary signal and also becomes a periodic stationary signal. The periodic stationary process feature detection can be performed by extracting characteristic features of the modulated signal, such as carrier, modulation type, symbol rate, and the like. These characteristics are detected by analyzing the spectral correlation property function [8].

The main advantage of spectral correlation function detection is that it can distinguish noise energy from the modulating signal power. Compared with energy detection, the system robustness of periodic stationary process feature detection is better than energy detection, but the complexity is much larger than the energy detection method.

If the statistical mean of the signal has periodicity, its statistical mean can be expanded into a Fourier series.

$$m_X(t) = \sum_{m=-\infty}^{\infty} m_X^\alpha \exp(j2\pi\alpha t) \tag{1}$$

$$m_X^\alpha = \frac{1}{T} \int_{-\frac{T}{2}}^{\frac{T}{2}} m_X(t)\exp(j2\pi\alpha t)dt \tag{2}$$

Defined $\alpha = m/T_0$ as the cycle frequency, which m_X^α is the cycle average. The cyclic mean corresponds to the time average after the left shift of the signal spectrum by α.

Define a cyclic autocorrelation function $R_X^\alpha(\tau)$ when the signal $x(t)$ has loop ergodicity. The Wiener-Sinqin theorem shows that the result of the Fourier transform of the autocorrelation function $R_X^\alpha(\tau)$ is the spectral density function, which is denoted as $S_X^\alpha(f)$.

Analysis of the cyclic autocorrelation function, available

$$R_X^\alpha(\tau) = \lim_{T\to\infty} \frac{1}{T} \int_{-\frac{T}{2}}^{\frac{T}{2}} u\left(t + \frac{\tau}{2}\right) v^*\left(t - \frac{\tau}{2}\right) dt = R_{UV}(\tau) \tag{3}$$

$$u(t) = x(t)\exp(-j\pi\alpha t) \tag{4}$$

$$v(t) = x(t)\exp(j\pi\alpha t) \tag{5}$$

Hypothesis $U(f)$ and $V(f)$ are the Fourier transform results of $u(t)$ and $v(t)$, respectively. $X(f)$ is the Fourier transform result of the original signal $x(t)$. According to the characteristic of the frequency shift of the Fourier Transform. $U(t) = X(f + \alpha/2)$ and $V(f) = X(f - \alpha/2)$. Therefore, $u(t)$ and $v(t)$ are equivalent to the signals obtained by shifting the original signal $x(t)$ to $\pm\alpha/2$ respectively. The spectral density function $S_X^\alpha(f)$ reflects the degree of correlation of the signal $x(t)$ at the frequency shift component $f \pm \alpha/2$, as can be seen from the above analysis. From the above analysis, $S_X^\alpha(f) = S_{UV}(f)$, the spectral density function $S_X^\alpha(f)$ is also called the spectral correlation density function.

When the signal is actually detected, since the length Δt of the received data cannot be extended indefinitely, the usual concern is how to obtain a valid estimate of the spectral density function from the finite-length data. The Fourier transform with a time length of T_0 is obtained for the signal.

$$X_{T_0}(t,f) = \int_{t-T_0/2}^{t+T_0/2} x(\xi)\exp(-j2\pi f\xi)d\xi \tag{6}$$

The estimated value of the cyclic spectral density function at this time is

$$\hat{S}_X^\alpha(f) = \lim_{T_0\to\infty \Delta t\to\infty} \frac{1}{\Delta t} \int_{-\Delta t/2}^{\Delta t/2} S_{X_{T_0}}^\alpha(t,f)dt \tag{7}$$

$$S_{X_{T_0}}^\alpha(t,f) = \frac{1}{T_0} X_{T_0}\left(t,f + \frac{\alpha}{2}\right) X_{T_0}^*\left(t,f - \frac{\alpha}{2}\right) \tag{8}$$

$S_{X_{T_0}}^\alpha(t,f)$ is called a cycle diagram. The method of estimating the cyclic spectral density function is usually a time domain smoothing period diagram method and a frequency domain smoothing period diagram method.

Time domain smoothing period graph method: Let $T_0 = 1/\Delta f$, the cyclic spectral density function can be described as:

$$\hat{S}_X^\alpha(f) = \lim_{\Delta f \to 0 \Delta t \to 0} \frac{1}{\Delta t} \int_{-\Delta t/2}^{\Delta t/2} \Delta f X_{\Delta f}\left(t, f + \frac{\alpha}{2}\right) X_{\Delta f}^*\left(t, f - \frac{\alpha}{2}\right) dt \qquad (9)$$

$$X_{\Delta f}(t, v) = \int_{t-1/2\Delta f}^{t+1/2\Delta f} x(u) \exp(-j2\pi uv) du \qquad (10)$$

Therefore $X_{\Delta f}(t, v)$ is the result of $x(t)$ short-time Fourier transform. Center frequency is v, the approximate bandwidth is Δf. When $\Delta f \to 0$, $\hat{S}_X^\alpha(f)$ represents the time-dependent limit between the two spectral components at frequencies $(f + \alpha/2)$ and $(f - \alpha/2)$.

Frequency domain smoothing period diagram method:
If $T_0 = \Delta t$, then

$$\hat{S}_X^\alpha(f) = \lim_{\Delta f \to \infty \Delta t \to \infty} \frac{1}{\Delta t} \int_{f-\Delta f/2}^{f+\Delta f/2} \frac{1}{\Delta t} X_{\Delta f}\left(t, v + \frac{\alpha}{2}\right) X_{\Delta f}^*\left(t, v - \frac{\alpha}{2}\right) dv \qquad (11)$$

When Δt is large enough, the time domain smoothing period graph method is roughly the same as the frequency domain smoothing period graph method. In order to achieve high reliability, the cyclic frequency resolution must be much smaller than the traditional Fourier frequency resolution [9].

The use of periodic stationary process feature detection utilizes a spectral correlation function to distinguish between signal energy and noise energy from the power of the modulated signal. The noise is a generalized incoherent stationary signal, and the signal is periodic and spectrally coherent. The detection stability of the periodic stationary process feature detection is better than the energy detection, but the implementation complexity is higher than the energy detection. The energy detection only needs to calculate the result of the discrete Fourier transform, and the periodic stationary process feature detection also needs to calculate the mutual dryness of the discrete Fourier transform results.

3 Practical Analysis Method and Simulation Implementation of Cyclostationary Process

In the theoretical analysis, the mean value of the signal studied and the time value of the autocorrelation function are derived from it, so it is impossible to implement in practice because the length of the received data cannot be infinitely long. Therefor it is possible to estimate with a limited length sequence. There are N data in the actual sampled sample, which can be regarded as a real sequence of length, and the estimated value of the autocorrelation function is

$$\hat{R}(m) = \frac{1}{N} \sum_{n=0}^{N-|m|-1} x(n)x(n+|m|) \qquad (12)$$

Assume that the actual signal is a band-limited signal, that is, when the signal is Fourier transformed and then expressed in the frequency domain, it is not 0 in the range of the lower limit frequency b and the upper limit frequency B, that is,

And then there is: $X(f) \neq 0 (b \leq |f| \leq B)$

$$S_X^\alpha \neq 0 \left(\left| |f| - \frac{|\alpha|}{2} \right| \leq b \right) \bigcup \left(\left| |f| + \frac{|\alpha|}{2} \right| \geq B \right) \tag{13}$$

Then, the area which is not 0 in the plan view is a region of four diamonds (as shown in Fig. 1(a)).

If the signal is in the form of a simple sine wave, i.e. $s(t) = \cos(2\pi f_0 t + \theta)$, then the cyclic autocorrelation function of the signal is found to be:

$$R_S^\alpha(\tau) = \cos(2\pi f_0 \tau)/2 \ \alpha = 0 \bigcup \exp(\pm j2\theta)/4 \ \alpha = \pm 2f_0 \tag{14}$$

Finding the spectral correlation function of sine wave signal by Fourier transform

$$S_S^\alpha(f) = \frac{\delta(f - f_0)}{4} + \frac{\delta(f + f_0)}{4} (\alpha = 0) \bigcup \frac{\exp(j2\theta)\delta(f)}{4} (\alpha = \pm 2f_0) \tag{15}$$

On the three-dimensional graph of the spectral correlation function, four impulse functions can be seen, the impulse intensity is 1/4 unit, and the frequency points are at $(\pm f_0, 0)$ and $(0, \pm 2f_0)$. As shown in Fig. 1(b)

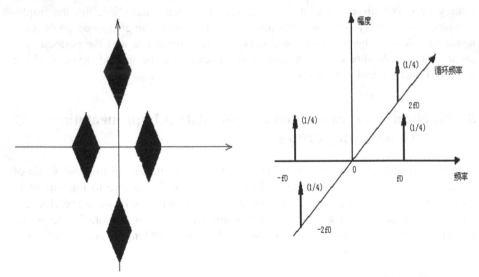

(a) Three-dimensional cross-section of the cyclic spectrum of a wideband signal.

(b) Three-dimensional map of the cyclic spectral density of a single frequency signal

Fig. 1. Theoretical analysis of the three-dimensional map of the cyclic spectrum

4 Simulation Results and Analysis

In order to analyze and compare the performance of different spectrum detection methods, it is necessary to unify the external conditions, such as the time domain waveform of the signal, the sampling point, the number of accumulations, and the accumulated bandwidth. The above problem will be described before actually comparing the detection performance of different detection methods. After determining the detection performance of different detection methods, it involves how to select a reasonable detection method to achieve full utilization of system resources.

4.1 Relationship Between the Number of Sampling Points and the Noise Performance of the Detection Signal

For the same signal, the number of different sampling points will cause the noise characteristics of the actual analysis results to be very different. Since the power of the noise is calculated according to the accumulation in the entire frequency band, when the sampling time is constant and the number of sampling points is larger, the wider the frequency band to be referred to, the larger the noise power is (Fig. 2).

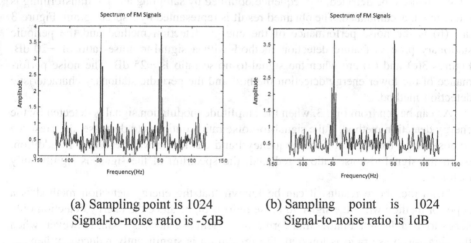

(a) Sampling point is 1024   (b) Sampling point is 1024
Signal-to-noise ratio is -5dB   Signal-to-noise ratio is 1dB

Fig. 2. Relationship between the number of sampling points and signal noise performance

Theoretical analysis shows that the power spectral density of Gaussian white noise is the same at each frequency. Therefore, the power of the Gaussian white noise in a certain frequency band is calculated to be proportional to the width of the frequency band. In the above actual signal analysis, it can be found that for the same signal, when the sampling point is increased from 256 points to 1024 points, the noise performance is significantly improved. The noise performance of 1024-point sampling at SNR −5 dB can be comparable to the noise performance of 256-point sampling analysis of the same signal at a signal-to-noise ratio of 1 dB. The theoretical value shows that $\log_{10} 4 = 6.02...$, that is to say, for every 4 times increase in the number of sampling points, the energy of the signal is constant, and the energy of the noise is four times that of the original. That is, when the signal-to-noise ratio of the detection signal is increased by 6 dB, the resolution of the detection is substantially the same as the original. The actual analysis is close to the theoretical analysis value. The following analysis can approximate that when the number of sampling points is multiplied by 4, the experimental analysis value of the detection signal-to-noise ratio needs to be added by 6 dB, which is comparable with the original analysis result.

4.2   Performance Comparison Between Energy Detection Method and Periodic Stationary Process Feature Detection Method

In the performance comparison, 15 independent test results were used for accumulation. At the sampling point, in order to accurately estimate the noise of the signal, the signal is analyzed by 1024 point sampling. If the actual number of sampling points is not 1024, the noise performance of the signal detection can be converted using the conclusions in the previous section.

The following is 15 times of independent sampling of the amplitude modulated signal. Using the principle of energy detection and periodic stationary process feature detection, the sequence after each sampling is calculated. Then, according to the frequency band to be detected, the sequence obtained by sampling and the transforming is intercepted, accumulated. The obtained result is represented by a spectrogram. Figure 3 (a), (b) is the noise performance of the energy detection method and the periodic stationary process feature detection method with a signal-to-noise ratio of −20 dB. Figures 3(c) and (d) are when the signal-to-noise ratio is −25 dB. The noise performance of the lower energy detection method and the periodic stationary characteristic detection method.

As can be sen from Fig. 3, when the amplitude modulation signal is detected by the energy detection method, if the signal-to-noise ratio continues to decrease, the presence or absence of the signal on the frequency band cannot be well resolved. In addition, when the signal-to-noise ratio is reduced, the spectrum of the signal is significantly distorted.

From the above results, it can be known that the energy detection method is a superior method when the signal to noise ratio is high. Since the energy detection only needs to do a discrete Fourier transform, the system overhead is small. However, when the signal-to-noise ratio is lowered, the resolution is significantly reduced. When the signal-to-noise ratio close to −15 dB, the amplitude modulated signal can only see the spectrum of the carrier signal, and the spectrum of the modulated signal can not be resolved. When the signal-to-noise ratio drops below −20 dB, it is completely unresolvable whether the spectrum to be detected is already occupied.

When using the periodic stationary process feature detection method, it can be seen that the noise fluctuation of the spectrum diagram is significantly smaller than that of the energy detection method when the signal-to-noise ratio is the same. In addition, the distortion of the signal frequency domain is more than the energy detection method at the same signal-to-noise ratio. In general, the noise performance of signal detection when using periodic stationary process feature detection is about 5–7 dB higher than that of energy detection.

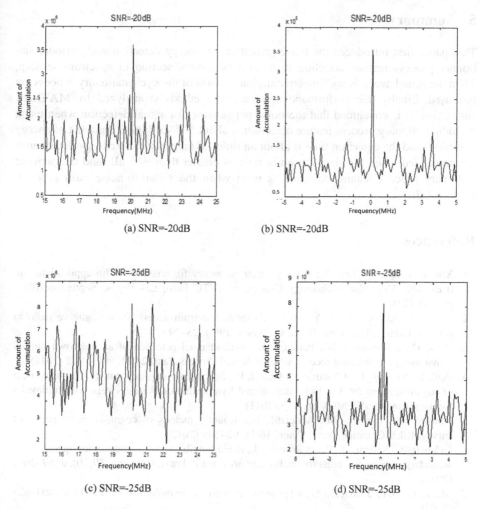

Fig. 3. Noise performance of energy detection method and periodic stationary process feature detection method

However, the periodic stationary process feature detection method is much more computationally intensive. From the time of simulation calculation, the time taken by the system when using the energy detection method is about 2.5 s, and the time calculated by the periodic stationary process feature detection method is about 24 s, which is about one order of magnitude.

5 Summary

This paper first introduces the basic principles of energy detection and periodic stationary process feature detection in non-cooperative detection in spectrum sensing. Then the actual analysis and implementation method of the cyclostationary process are proposed. Finally, the performance of the two methods is analyzed by MATLAB simulation. It is concluded that the noise performance of signal detection when using periodic stationary process feature detection is about 5–7 dB higher than that of energy detection, and the detection time is about an order of magnitude. So energy detection is recommended when the signal-to-noise ratio is greater than −15 dB, and the periodic stationary process feature detection is used when the signal-to-noise ratio is lower than −15 dB.

References

1. Xue, J., Feng, Z., Chen, K.: Beijing spectrum survey for cognitive radio applications. In: IEEE 78th Vehicular Technology Conference (VTC Fall), Las Vegas, September 2013, pp. 1–5 (2013)
2. Song, M., Xin, C., Zhao, Y., et al.: Dynamic spectrum access: from cognitive radio to network radio. IEEE Trans. Wirel. Commun. 19(1), 23–29 (2012)
3. Hack, D.E., Rossler, C.W., Patton, L.K.: Multichannel detection of an unknown rank-N signal using uncalibrated receivers. IEEE Signal Process. Lett. 21(8), 998–1002 (2014)
4. Patil, K., Skouby, K., Chandra, A., Prasad, R.: Spectrum occupancy statistics in the context of cognitive radio. In: The 14th International Symposium on Wireless Personal Multimedia Communications (WPMC), pp. 1–5 (2011)
5. Youssef, M., Ibrahim, M., Abdelatif, M.: Routing metrics of cognitive radio networks survey. IEEE Commun. Surv. Tutor. 16(1), 92–109 (2013)
6. Gelabert, X., Sallent, O., Perez-Romero, J., et al.: Flexible spectrum access for opportunistic secondary operation in cognitive radio networks. IEEE Trans. Commun. 59(10), 2659–2664 (2011)
7. Ma, J., Li, G.Y., Juang, B.: Signal processing in cognitive radio. Proc. IEEE 97(5), 805–823 (2009)
8. Wang, B., Liu, K.J.R.: Advances in cognitive radio networks: a survey. IEEE J. Sel. Top. Signal Process. 5(1), 5–23 (2011)
9. Axell, E., Leus, G., Larsson, E.G., et al.: Spectrum sensing for cognitive radio: state-of-the-art and recent advances. IEEE Signal Process. Mag. 29(3), 101–116 (2012)
10. Lee, J.: Cooperative spectrum sensing scheme over imperfect feedback channels. IEEE Commun. Lett. 17(6), 1192–1195 (2013)

AI-Enabled Network Layer Algorithms and Protocols

An Improved TDoA Localization Algorithm Based on AUV for Underwater Acoustic Sensor Networks

Kaicheng Yu[1], Kun Hao[1($\boxtimes$)], Cheng Li[1], Xiujuan Du[2], Beibei Wang[3], and Yonglei Liu[1]

[1] School of Computer and Information Engineering, Tianjin Chengjian University, Tianjin 300384, China
ykc888@qq.com, littlehao@126.com,
licheng.mun@gmail.com, sanxiong_l@163.com
[2] School of Computer Science and Technology, Qinghai Normal University, Xining 810008, Qinghai, China
dxj@qhnu.edu.cn
[3] School of Control and Mechanical Engineering, Tianjin Chengjian University, Tianjin 300384, China
wbbking@163.com

Abstract. Now localization is one of the major issues in underwater environment work. In terrestrial application, time different of arrival (TDoA) localization algorithm has been widely used. However, most localization systems rely on radio or optical signals while they cannot propagate well in water. Therefore, with complicated environment in underwater acoustic sensor networks (UASNs), traditional TDoA localization algorithm suffers various unstable factors, such as they can only work in a finite region or need clock synchronization. In this paper, we propose an improved TDoA localization algorithm (ITLA) based on AUV for UASNs. The mobile AUV first finds its own accurate three-dimensional coordinates in the surface with the help of GPS or other terrestrial location systems. Then we deployed AUV at predefined depth in underwater as reference nodes. AUV periodically sends packets with coordinates information to unlocalized nodes in different positions. After receiving data and a series of calculation, we quantify the conditions for unique localization and propose another condition to evaluate the reliability of results. This algorithm can achieve relatively higher accuracy with relatively smaller calculation and overcome some traditional localization drawbacks. We demonstrate the trade-offs between location coverage, the cost in placing reference nodes, and energy consumption.

Keywords: Underwater acoustic sensor networks (UASNs) ·
Time different of arrival (TDoA) · Autonomous underwater vehicles (AUVs) ·
AUV-aided localization

S. Han et al. (Eds.): AICON 2019, LNICST 286, pp. 419–434, 2019.
https://doi.org/10.1007/978-3-030-22968-9_38

1 Introduction

Over the years, we have observed underwater wireless sensor networks are getting more attention [1]. They have been widely used in both military and civilian applications such as natural disaster warning system, oceanic navigate assistance, and biological environment monitoring, etc. To achieve these goals in complicated environment in underwater, the common method is to deploy some ordinary sensor nodes in networks.

For traditional devices, they collect data from their surroundings and need exchange information with the vessel on surface. However, these devices can be replaced by sensor nodes with relatively small in shape and less expensive in cost.

In underwater, sensor nodes continuously collect data, sense the environment and transmit to surface vessel or onshore stations. However, the traditional propagation medium such as radio and optical signals attenuate rapidly and scatter due to adverse environment in underwater [2]. Consequently, acoustic signals have been widely used in recent years as they attenuate less and travel far.

In reality, once sensor nodes have been deployed, recycling work will become very difficult. The position of sensor nodes will be greatly affected by the currents of water and the accurate position of sensor nodes will randomly change. Therefore, localization scheme now has been considered as a crucial mission in network composition, marking the collected messages, detecting the position of target and network routing protocol [3]. Range measurements in localization can be based on time of arrival (ToA) [4], time different of arrival (TDoA) [5], received signal strength (RSS) [6, 7], and direction of arrival (DoA) [8]. Most sensor nodes are equipped with pressure sensors to measure their depth. Hence, the coordinates of sensor nodes can be simplified into x-y coordinates.

The development of AUVs began to attract interest in the use of AUVs in localization [9]. AUVs are now being used in various tasks. The mobility of AUVs makes it possible to locate the position of sensor nodes in large scale. But some AUV-aided location methods also suffer time delay problem.

The structure of the paper is as follows: Sect. 2 introduces several related UASN localization techniques. Section 3 describes the improved localization algorithm based on the methods mentioned above in Sect. 2. We compare the ordinary localization algorithm in several aspects and the effects if we take AUVs to replace traditional anchor nodes in Sect. 4. Finally, we draw some conclusions and present the future research in Sect. 5.

2 Related Work

A lot of researches have been updated in localization algorithms in the past few years [1]. Many localization algorithms have been proposed to solve the unique situation of underwater acoustic environment for UASNs. In this section, we briefly provide a review of localization techniques that proposed in UASNs.

A silent positioning range-based system named Underwater Positioning System (UPS) has been proposed for UASNs in [10, 11] as is shown in Fig. 1. It is a basic

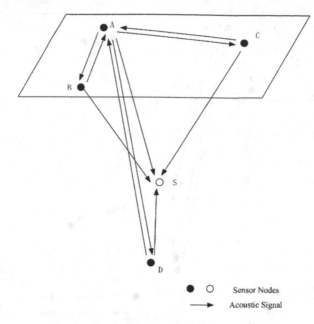

Fig. 1. Underwater Positioning System (UPS)

TDoA range-based measurement algorithm. By exchanging beaconing signals with reference nodes deployed on seabed, UPS estimates the location of a sensor node before localization schemes begin or surface buoys with GPS. However, using the method mentioned above, three-dimensional space will need at least four reference nodes and two-dimensional space will need at least three reference nodes to locate. It assumes the reference nodes cover the entire UASN area, therefore constrain the coverage area of interest. And the sensor nodes in underwater are moving freely with currents. Another drawback is the successful localization highly depends on the successful communication among fixed nodes. Time-delay is also a major issue to discuss.

To overcome the drawbacks mentioned above, like the limit of location area, in [12], the authors present more sensor nodes in localization schemes named Wide Coverage Positioning System (WPS). Four sensor nodes will be needed whenever four nodes attain unique localization, else five nodes will be needed in [13] (see in Fig. 2). But the cost of deploying sensor nodes in underwater is still too expensive. And the schemes still suffer time-delay error because of transmission error.

Hence at the first time, people prompted a method that using AUVs to replace traditional fixed sensor nodes in [14, 15]. This is an algorithm for a hybrid, three-dimensional UASN where AUVs moving in the same region with anchor nodes fixed nearby. AUVs will periodically send wake up messages to anchor nodes and calculate the range by receive response packets. The main drawback is that two-way ranging requires high synchronization which is hard to achieve in underwater environment. And too many AUVs also lead to high system cost [16].

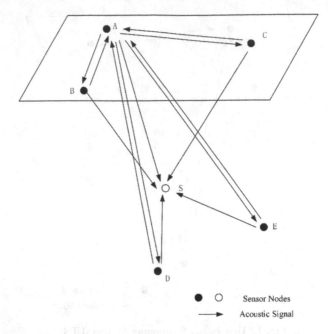

Fig. 2. Wide Coverage Positioning System (WPS)

3 An Improved TDoA Localization Algorithm

3.1 Main Innovations

Compared with classical TDOA algorithm, ITLA use AUVs as reference nodes which means a single AUV is used instead of too many anchor nodes in positioning scheme. This change solves the problems of high network cost and complexity of deployment. Besides, we add a result correction process in algorithm which improved the accuracy and at the same time, decreased the cost of deploying more sensor nodes. The movement of AUV also extend the location area.

3.2 Background and Assumptions

We assume a three-dimensional underwater sensor networks area. There are randomly deployed ordinary sensor nodes that without their positions only to sense the network. These sensor nodes are all capable to determine their depth and their transceivers can cover the entire interest space. AUVs are deployed from the surface and get their coordinates by GPS. We assume that AUVs periodically accelerate to predefined positions and send wake up messages to anchor node. There are at least four non-coplanar positions we predefined and no three of them are collinear. We propose an efficient localization algorithm by using mobile AUVs. To simplify the localization process, we present only one AUV to locate one anchor nodes that can extend to locate more anchor nodes with more AUVs. Network architecture we proposed is presented (see in Fig. 3).

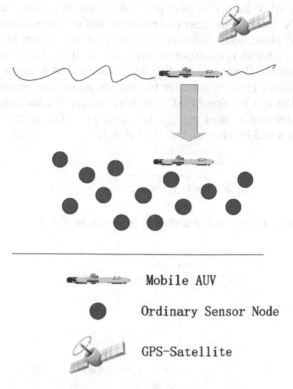

Mobile AUV

Ordinary Sensor Node

GPS-Satellite

Fig. 3. Network architecture

Besides, the coordinates of AUV is got by GPS, the GPS positioning error may influence the accuracy of node location. But in our algorithm, to introduce ITLA better and clearly, we assume the errors in GPS positioning can be temporarily ignored.

3.3 Implementation

We assume every ordinary sensor node communicate with AUV and each other by acoustic waves. The mobile AUVs form a channel with GPS satellite via radio waves and use acoustic waves to communicate with underwater ordinary nodes. AUV will move to different position and send messages to anchor nodes.

3.4 Algorithm Operations

There are two main phases in our algorithm.

1. Localization message broadcasting and receiving
2. Location computation and results correction.

In the first phase, AUV dives into predefined depth and sends requesting message to anchor node S. If S receive the wake-up message, it will answer and send an answer packet to AUV. AUV moves to next position during this packet transmitting. By analogy, the AUV moves to the next two positions and continues to send packets to S.

In the second phase, when S receives all the information sent by the AUV from various positions, it begins to calculate its own position. But the location of S might not be uniquely localized. Hence, we let S send a new request to allow AUV move to another new position. Then we continue to start the positioning process.

We assume the first location of AUV is $A(x_1, y_1, z_1)$. We have other positions of AUV can be expressed as $B(x_2, y_2, z_2)$, $C(x_3, y_3, z_3)$, $D(x_4, y_4, z_4)$. Let d_{ab} be the distance between a and b, where $a, b \in (1, 2, 3, 4, s)$.

We have

$$d_{s1} = \sqrt{(x - x_1)^2 + (y - y_1)^2(z - z_1)^2} \tag{1}$$

The mathematical model we established is shown in Fig. 4.

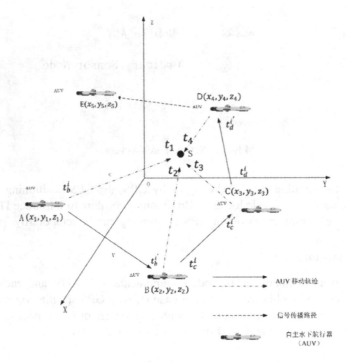

Fig. 4. Mathematical model

AUV sends wake-up messages to sensor node S from position A and initiates a localization cycle every T seconds. Each cycle begins when AUV transmits a signal from position A. S receives packets sent by AUV from position A in t_1^i.

We assume in t_b^i, AUV begins to move from position A to B and sends wake-up messages. The time of arrival at position B is $t_b^{i\prime}$. We have the time difference of AUV arrival Δt_b^i is

$$\Delta t_b^i = t_b^{i\prime} - t_b^i \tag{2}$$

We can get the velocity of AUV from the accelerometer, and assume v is the velocity and distance between A and B is:

$$d_{12} = \Delta t_b^i \times v \tag{3}$$

In the meantime, S receives packets sent by AUV from position B in t_2^i.

By analogy, AUV successively begins to move to next two positions $C(x_3, y_3, z_3,)$, $D(x_4, y_4, z_4)$ at t_c^i, t_d^i and arrive at $t_c^{i\prime}, t_d^{i\prime}$. The same as mentioned above, we can get Δt_c^i and Δt_d^i.

During its moving, AUV continues to send packets to the $S(x, y, z)$ at these two positions. Then we can conclude that S receives packets at t_j^i, $i,j \in \{1,2,3,4\}$, respectively. And clearly, based on triangle inequality,

$$t_1^i < t_2^i < t_3^i < t_4^i \tag{4}$$

We assume

$$\Delta t_1^i = t_2^i - t_1^i \tag{5}$$

$$\Delta t_2^i = t_3^i - t_1^i \tag{6}$$

$$\Delta t_3^i = t_4^i - t_1^i \tag{7}$$

Since the speed of ultrasound is c, we obtain

$$d_{12} + d_{s2} - d_{s1} + v \times \Delta t_b^i = c \times \Delta t_1^i \tag{8}$$

$$d_{13} + d_{s3} - d_{s1} + v \times \Delta t_c^i = c \times \Delta t_2^i \tag{9}$$

$$d_{14} + d_{s4} - d_{s1} + v \times \Delta t_d^i = c \times \Delta t_2^i \tag{10}$$

Which gives us

$$d_{s2} = d_{s1} + c \times \Delta t_1^i - d_{12} - d_{12} = d_{s1} + \emptyset_1^i \tag{11}$$

$$d_{s3} = d_{s1} + c \times \Delta t_2^i - d_{13} - d_{23} = d_{s1} + \emptyset_2^i \tag{12}$$

$$d_{s4} = d_{s1} + c \times \Delta t_2^i - d_{14} - d_{34} = d_{s1} + \emptyset_3^i \tag{13}$$

Where d_{12}, d_{13}, d_{23}, d_{14}, and d_{34}, are positive real numbers; and averaging $\emptyset_1^i$, $\emptyset_2^i$ and $\emptyset_3^i$ over I intervals gives

$$\emptyset_1^i = \frac{c}{I} \times \sum_{i=1}^{I} \Delta t_1^i - 2d_{12} \tag{14}$$

$$\emptyset_2^i = \frac{c}{I} \times \sum_{i=1}^{I} \Delta t_2^i - (d_{13} + d_{23}) \tag{15}$$

$$\emptyset_3^i = \frac{c}{I} \times \sum_{i=1}^{I} \Delta t_3^i - (d_{34} + d_{14}) \tag{16}$$

In the next step, the algorithm applies trilateration with $\emptyset_1$, $\emptyset_2$, and $\emptyset_3$ to calculate coordinates of S.

From (11)–(13) and (14)–(16), based on trilateration, we obtain four equations with four unknowns x, y, z, and d_{s1}, where $d_{s1} > 0$, like

$$(x - x_1)^2 + (y - y_1)^2 + (z - z_1)^2 = d_{s1}^2 \tag{17}$$

$$(x - x_2)^2 + (y - y_2)^2 + (z - z_2)^2 = (d_{s1} + \emptyset_1)^2 \tag{18}$$

$$(x - x_3)^2 + (y - y_3)^2 + (z - z_3)^2 = (d_{s1} + \emptyset_2)^2 \tag{19}$$

$$(x - x_4)^2 + (y - y_4)^2 + (z - z_4)^2 = (d_{s1} + \emptyset_3)^2 \tag{20}$$

Solving these four equations, we have

$$d_{s1}^{(1)} = \frac{-B - \sqrt{B^2 - 4AC}}{2A} \tag{21}$$

$$d_{s1}^{(2)} = \frac{-B + \sqrt{B^2 - 4AC}}{2A} \tag{22}$$

$$x = A_x d_{s1} + B_y \tag{23}$$

$$y = A_y d_{s1} + B_y \tag{24}$$

$$z = A_z d_{s1} + B_z \tag{25}$$

where

$$A = A_x^2 + A_y^2 + A_z^2 - 1 \tag{26}$$

$$B = 2(A_x B_x + A_y B_y + A_z B_z) \tag{27}$$

$$C = B_x^2 + B_y^2 + B_z^2 \tag{28}$$

$$A_x = -\frac{\emptyset_1}{x_2} \tag{29}$$

$$B_x = \frac{x_2^2 - \emptyset_1^2}{2x_2} \tag{30}$$

$$A_y = \frac{\emptyset_1 x_3}{x_2 y_3} - \frac{\emptyset_2}{y_3} \tag{31}$$

$$B_y = \frac{x_3^2 + y_3^2 - x_2 x_3 + \frac{x_3 \emptyset_1^2}{x_2} - \emptyset_2^2}{2y_3} \tag{32}$$

$$A_z = \frac{\emptyset_1 x_4}{x_2 z_4} - \frac{\emptyset_3}{z_4} - \frac{y_4 \left(\frac{\emptyset_1 x_3}{x_2} - \emptyset_2 \right)}{y_3 z_4} \tag{33}$$

$$B_z = \frac{x_4^2 + y_4^2 + z_4^2 - x_2 x_4 + \frac{x_4 \emptyset_1^2}{x_2} - \emptyset_3^2 - \frac{y_4 x_3^2}{y_3}}{2z_4} + \frac{-y_3 y_4 + \frac{x_2 x_3 y_4}{y_3} - \frac{\emptyset_1^2 x_3 y_4}{x_2 y_3} + \frac{\emptyset_2^2 y_4}{y_3}}{2z_4} \tag{34}$$

The result is interesting that only when S is not close to or behind any position of AUV sending messages, (21) presents a unique feasible solution. Therefore, we add a result correction in the last step.

3.5 Result Correction

If we now substituting for x, y, z into (2), d_{s1} has to satisfy the following condition:

$$d_{s1}^2 A + 2B d_{s1} + C = 0 \tag{35}$$

According to (26), we assume

$$\lambda_A - 1 = A_x^2 + A_y^2 + A_z^2 - 1 = A \tag{36}$$

The uniqueness of d_{s1} depends on the value of λ_A, as follows:

$$d_{s1}^{(1)} = d_{s1}^{(2)}, \lambda_A = 1; \tag{37}$$

$$d_{s1}^{(1)} \cdot d_{s1}^{(2)} < 0, \lambda_A < 1; \tag{38}$$

$$d_{s1}^{(1)} \cdot d_{s1}^{(2)} > 0, \lambda_A > 1; \tag{39}$$

If $\lambda_A > 1$, then there will be two solutions and we cannot uniquely localize the position of S. Then we ask AUV to move to position $D(x_5, y_5, z_5)$.

We can get:

$$d_{s1}^2 A + 2(\lambda_{AB} - \emptyset_4)d_{s1} + \lambda_{BB} - \emptyset_4^2 = 0 \tag{40}$$

Where $B_{nn} = B_n - n_5, n \in \{x, y, z\}$, and

$$\lambda_{BB} = B_{xx}^2 + B_{yy}^2 + B_{zz}^2 \tag{41}$$

$$\lambda_{AB} = A_x B_{xx} + A_y B_{yy} + A_z B_{zz} \tag{42}$$

(35) and (40) have the same solutions under the following conditions:

$$\lambda_{AB} - \emptyset_4 = A_x B_x + A_y B_y + A_z B_z \tag{43}$$

$$\lambda_{BB} - \emptyset_4^2 = B_x^2 + B_y^2 + B_z^2 \tag{44}$$

These conditions can be transformed as follows:

$$A_x x_5 + A_y y_5 + A_z z_5 = \emptyset_4 \tag{45}$$

$$B_x x_5 + B_y y_5 + B_z z_5 = \frac{x_5^2 + y_5^2 + z_5^2 - \emptyset_4^2}{2} \tag{46}$$

We assume $\lambda_A > 1$, then S will be unique localization by adding position E and satisfy conditions in (46); else, the value of d_{s1} is determined by the solution of the following equation:

$$2d_{s1}(A_x^2 + A_y^2 + A_z^2 - 1 + \emptyset_4) + (d_{15}^2 - 2B_x x_5 - 2B_y y_5 - 2B_z z_5) + \emptyset_4^2 = 0 \tag{47}$$

Where d_{15}^2 can be measured by AUV. Then S can be uniquely localized. Pseudocode is shown below.

```
Improved TDoA Localization Algorithm: Pseudocode for S
procedure ITLA
1: t=0
2: position = A
3: pkts = 0
4: Position of S = 0
5: Start localization beaconing sequence
6: while Position of S == 0 do
7: if (receive new beacon) then
8: pkts += 1
9: end if
10: if (pkts == 4 & λ_A ≤ 1)|( pkts == 5 & condition(46)=
FALSE) then
11: Position of S =1
12: end if
13: end while
end procedure
```

4 Experiments and Discussions

4.1 Performance Metrics

In this section, we discuss the performance of ITLA and traditional TDoA localization algorithm like UPS and WPS in terms of localization time, localization error, and localization coverage. The complete positioning flow chart is shown in Fig. 5.

Besides, in many practical situations, the Doppler effect is also an important aspect to consider. When acoustic waves travel in shallow water, there are many factors that cause Doppler shifts, but there are two main factors:

The relative motions between signal reception and emission position cause a Doppler effect. We assume the frequency of a single acoustic signal is f_s, the moving speed of the transmitter is $\bar{v}_s$, and the moving speed of the receiver is $\bar{v}_r$, the frequency change of the received signal is expressed as follows:

$$f_r = f_s \cdot (c - \bar{v}_r)/(c - \bar{v}_s) \tag{48}$$

We assume the direction from transmitter to the receiver is the forward direction. $\bar{v}_s$ and $\bar{v}_r$ are vectors of unit m/s. The unit of f_s and f_s is Hz. c is the speed in water which could be considered as 1500 m/s.

When there is no relative motion between the receiver and the transmitter, the movement of the transmission medium will also cause Doppler effects such as waves and turbulence. These two factors are the main cause of the Doppler effect, which are closely related to the wind speed in surface. If the water wave is in the form of a sinusoid, the acoustic wave will be modulated by the forward scattering of the water wave during the propagation process, and the frequency of the acoustic wave received by the receiver will change. The Doppler effect caused by the waves can be given by the Carson rule.

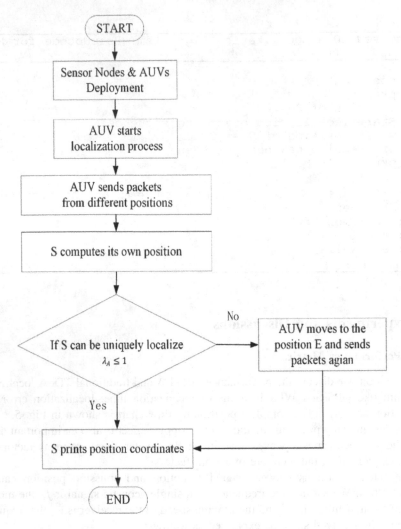

Fig. 5. Flow chart of complete localization process

$$f_d = 2f_w(1 + 2w\cos\theta_0 h_w/c) \tag{49}$$

Where f_w is the frequency of water wave, h_w is the mean square value of wave height, w is the wind speed (m/s), θ_0 is the nominal incident angle in the receiving end.

Certainly, the accuracy is affected by the Doppler effect caused by the motion of the transmission medium. Therefore, to improve the positioning accuracy, we need to do some frequency compensation, but the amount of compensation can be determined in advance, so in this paper, we temporarily ignore the Doppler shift caused by the motion of the transmission medium.

4.2   Simulation Environment and Discussion

We assume the mobility of AUV parameter varying from 2.0 m/s ($\approx$3.887688 kn) to 5.0 m/s ($\approx$9.71922 kn). The entire underwater area is 1000 m * 1000 m * 100 m water volume and filled with randomly deployed sensor nodes vary from 0 to 200. We use only one AUV to localize all sensor nodes.

The experiment results of different localization time are represented in Fig. 6. Due to the use of AUVs, the traditional localization algorithm cost much more time than ITLA. The extra time is mostly spent in the positioning process between different nodes. While AUV is used, the velocity of AUV movement in underwater also influences the speed of localization time. If AUV moves as fast as possible, then a positioning cycle ends sooner. AUV in 2.0 m/s cost nearly more 5 s than in 5.0 m/s in our simulation, but still better than UPS and WPS which the latter two spend more than 30 s in total. Besides, with more sensor nodes needs to be localized, the gap becomes bigger.

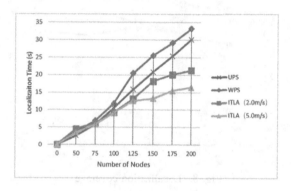

Fig. 6. Localization time

The localization error is represented in Fig. 7. With the distance between the unlocalized nodes and AUV and numbers of nodes increases in underwater, the error also increases. Owing to the efficient use of mobile AUV as the reference node, the localization error has been controlled into an acceptable situation. As is shown below, the accuracy of nodes coordinates improves nearly 1 m than traditional ways. This is mainly due to we add a result correction at last and the lateration of calculation. These differences are becoming more obvious with the increase of sensor nodes need to be localized.

The localization coverage is shown in Fig. 8. UPS only localized 66% of nodes while WPS reach to nearly 80% in the end. Due to AUV floating nearby, more sensor nodes can be localized by using ITLA. On the other hand, the localization coverage area is determined by the transmission range of nodes. As the transmission range of these nodes increases, more nodes get their accurate coordinates. Obviously, due to the wider range of AUV movement, the positioning coverage is larger than traditional ways and its coverage is nearly close to 90%. More unlocalized nodes will be in transmission range by the movement of AUV.

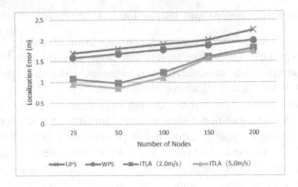

Fig. 7. Localization error

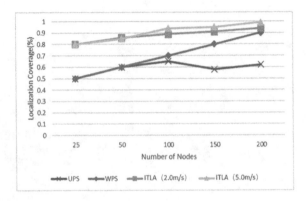

Fig. 8. Localization coverage

5   Conclusion

We propose an improved TDoA localization algorithm based on AUV. Comparing with traditional TDoA algorithm, we take AUV as reference nodes to locate the unlocalized anchor nodes. Our algorithm consists of two steps, localization message broadcasting and receiving and location computation and results correction. AUVs are deployed from the surface into underwater, it is equipped with accelerate and gyroscope to get their coordinates and direction by GPS and dive into predefined depth. Then AUV broadcast wake-up messages to unlocalized anchor nodes. After receiving position messages from AUV sent in different positions, anchor node computes its own coordinates by applying various mathematical techniques. And preliminary computation results will be corrected by results correction for more accurate positioning. Due to the use of mobile AUV in underwater, the localization coverage is improved, results in less localization error and localization time relatively shortened.

Acknowledgments. This research was supported by Tianjin Natural Science Fund Project 18JCYBJC85600, Qinghai Key Laboratory of Internet of Things Project (2017-ZJ-Y21), Tianjin Enterprise Science and Technology Commissioner Project 18JCTPJC60500, Infrared Radiation Heating Intelligent Control and Basic Ventilation Auxiliary Engineering System Development of No. 2 Section of Changchun Metro Line 2 (hx 2018-37).

References

1. Erol-Kantarci, M., Mouftah, H.T., Oktug, S.: A survey of architectures and localization techniques for underwater acoustic sensor networks. IEEE Commun. Surv. Tutor. **13**(3), 487–502 (2011)
2. Bahcebasi, A., Gungor, V.C., Tuna, G.: Performance analysis of different modulation schemes for underwater acoustic communications. In: 2018 3rd International Conference on Computer Science and Engineering (UBMK), pp. 396–401 (2018)
3. Hao, K., Shen, H., Liu, Y., Wang, B., Du, X.: Integrating localization and energy-awareness: a novel geographic routing protocol for underwater wireless sensor networks. Mob. Netw. Appl. **23**(5), 1427–1435 (2018)
4. Gong, Z., Li, C., Jiang, F.: AUV-aided joint localization and time synchronization for underwater acoustic sensor networks. IEEE Signal Process. Lett. **25**(4), 477–481 (2018)
5. Liang, Q., Zhang, B., Zhao, C., Pi, Y.: TDoA for passive localization: underwater versus terrestrial environment. IEEE Trans. Parallel Distrib. Syst. **24**(10), 2100–2108 (2013)
6. Park, D., Kwak, K., Chung, W.K., Kim, J.: Development of underwater short-range sensor using electromagnetic wave attenuation. IEEE J. Oceanic Eng. **41**(2), 318–325 (2016)
7. Beaudeau, J.P., Bugallo, M.F., Djurić, P.M.: RSSI-based multi-target tracking by cooperative agents using fusion of cross-target information. IEEE Trans. Signal Process. **63**(19), 5033–5044 (2015)
8. Peters, D.J.: A Bayesian method for localization by multistatic active sonar. IEEE J. Oceanic Eng. **42**(1), 135–142 (2017)
9. Paull, L., Saeedi, S., Seto, M., Li, H.: AUV navigation and localization: a review. IEEE J. Oceanic Eng. **39**(1), 131–149 (2014)
10. Cheng, X., Shu, H., Liang, Q., Du, D.H.C.: Silent positioning in underwater acoustic sensor networks. IEEE Trans. Veh. Technol. **57**(3), 1756–1766 (2008)
11. Cheng, X., Shu, H.S.H., Liang, Q.: A range-difference based self-positioning scheme for underwater acoustic sensor networks. In: International Conference on Wireless Algorithms, Systems and Applications, WASA 2007, pp. 38–43 (2007)
12. Tan, H.P., Gabor, A.F., Eu, Z.A., Seah, W.K.G.: A wide coverage positioning system (WPS) for underwater localization. In: 2010 IEEE International Conference on Communications (ICC), pp. 1–5 (2010)
13. Tan, H.P., Eu, Z.A., Seah, W.K.: An enhanced underwater positioning system to support deepwater installations. In: MTS/IEEE Biloxi-Marine Technology for Our Future: Global and Local Challenges, OCEANS 2009, pp. 1–8 (2009)
14. Erol, M., Vieira, L.F.M., Gerla, M.: AUV-aided localization for underwater sensor networks. In: International Conference on Wireless Algorithms, Systems and Applications, WASA 2007, pp. 44–54 (2007)

15. Maqsood, H., Javaid, N., Yahya, A., Ali, B., Khan, Z.A., Qasim, U.: MobiL-AUV: AUV-aided localization scheme for underwater wireless sensor networks. In: 2016 10th International Conference on Innovative Mobile and Internet Services in Ubiquitous Computing (IMIS), pp. 170–175 (2016)
16. Waldmeyer, M., Tan, H.P., Seah, W.K.: Multi-stage AUV-aided localization for underwater wireless sensor networks. In: 2011 IEEE Workshops of International Conference on Advanced Information Networking and Applications (WAINA), pp. 908–913 (2011)

Fuzzy Probabilistic Topology Control Algorithm for Underwater Wireless Sensor Networks

Wenhao Ren[1], Kun Hao[1(✉)], Cheng Li[1], Xiujuan Du[2], Yonglei Liu[1], and Li Wang[1]

[1] School of Computer and Information Engineering, Tianjin Chengjian University, Tianjin 300384, China
1090387132@qq.com, littlehao@126.com,
licheng.mun@gmail.com, Sanxiong_l@163.com,
liwang_tjcj@qq.com
[2] School of Computer Science and Technology, Qinghai Normal University, Xining 810008, Qinghai, China
dxj@qhnu.edu.cn

Abstract. Aiming at the problem that the underwater wireless sensor network is limited in energy and the underwater topology is susceptible to the dynamic environment, this paper designs an AUV-assisted fuzzy probability power topology control (FPPTC) algorithm by introducing AUV nodes and clusters generated by clustering. Head node communication reduces power consumption of low energy nodes. According to the data deviation value between the current data value of the AUV node and the target parameter, the adjustment probability of the transmission power is determined, and the transmission power of the AUV node is adjusted to an optimal value to reduce the underwater topology energy consumption, prolong the network life cycle, and improve the network. The purpose of communication quality. The simulation results show that the FPPTC algorithm can improve network coverage, slow down node failure speed and extend network life cycle.

Keywords: Underwater wireless sensor networks (UWSNs) ·
Topology control · Autonomous underwater vehicle (AUV) ·
Fuzzy power control

1 Introduction

The underwater world has a tremendous impact on the development of human beings. It is not only closely related to people's living environment, but also contains a large amount of minerals and natural resources under the water, which is also inextricably linked with economic development. With the emphasis on underwater environment and resources, underwater wireless sensor networks have been widely used in various fields such as underwater pollution monitoring, gas leakage monitoring and navigation [1].

The underwater wireless sensor network topology is mainly composed of a large number of wireless sensor nodes randomly scattered in the target water area. Unlike the

S. Han et al. (Eds.): AICON 2019, LNICST 286, pp. 435–444, 2019.
https://doi.org/10.1007/978-3-030-22968-9_39

terrestrial wireless sensor network, the underwater wireless sensor network is subject to more restrictions. The underwater node has limited energy and can't be charged, and its life is short. Because the Radio Frequency (RF) wave is seriously attenuated in the underwater environment [2], the communication quality is degraded. Therefore, in UWSNs, the underwater acoustic mode is mainly used for communication [3], The acoustic channel has limited bandwidth and is not suitable for large-scale communication. Secondly, the underwater node is easy to change with the influence of ocean currents and the like, and the topology is damaged.

Faced with the problems faced by the current underwater wireless sensor network topology, many solutions have been proposed, which can be mainly divided into two categories: node power control and cluster topology control [4]. Although traditional wireless sensor networks propose many topological control algorithms, their application to underwater environments is still limited. With the development of technology, AUV has been applied to underwater wireless sensor networks. As proposed in the literature [5], the AUV collaborative control strategy consists of multiple AUV nodes participating in the underwater network to improve network performance. However, AUV is costly and large-scale use is not realistic. In the traditional network topology control algorithm, when there is a deviation between the transmission power and the calculation power based on the optimal algorithm, the node needs to adjust the transmission power. This method is effective for network resource rich or static network, because the node energy is limited and topology in UWSN. The structure changes dynamically, and the effect of this method is not obvious. At the same time, in the AUV assisted underwater network topology, when there is a deviation between the AUV transmission power and the transmission power based on the optimal algorithm, adjusting the power may not be the best strategy, so consider balancing between network performance and network functions.

Aiming at the limitations of the above underwater wireless sensor network topology, this paper proposes a fuzzy probability power topology control (FPPTC) algorithm. Add AUV as a secondary node in UWSNs. On the basis of the residual energy of AUV node and ordinary node, the optimal algorithm based on factors such as transmission power and degree of enumerated list. Reference fuzzy logic control algorithm, In accordance with the current value and the deviation between the target parameters, output probability to adjust the parameters, such as transmission power, he greater the difference, the greater the probability of adjustment. The cluster head node is selected by the adaptive clustering method, and the AUV mainly exchanges data with the cluster head node to reduce the communication frequency of the low energy node. The mobility of AUV can realize dynamic link of underwater wireless sensor network, comprehensively consider parameters such as common node and AUV node transmission power, optimize network topology control, reduce energy consumption of underwater nodes, extend network life cycle, and improve communication quality.

2   Related Work

In recent years, many control algorithms have been proposed for underwater wireless sensor network topology. According to the underwater topology features, they are mainly divided into three categories [6]: energy control, mobile assisted technology and radio mode management. In the topology control process, based on different transmission power, it can be used to improve localization [7]. For dynamic topology control, AUV assistance or depth adjustment of some nodes can be used [8].

In the literature [9], two topology control algorithms, improved distributed topology control (iDTC) and power adjustment distributed topology control are proposed for underwater wireless sensor networks. These two methods can improve network communication capabilities while reducing energy consumption. The method mainly guarantees data transmission through the communication of geographic information opportunity routing. Then, according to the topology control strategy of complex network theory, a dual clustering structure is constructed, including two cluster head nodes, to ensure the coverage of the network connectivity nodes. However, in the underwater environment, it is not realistic to use the Global Positioning System (GPS) method. The wire is used to anchor the sensor node in the underwater environment, and the sensor node is offset around the anchor point, which causes the node to move in the horizontal direction. The node location is not accurate. In [10], an energy control underwater wireless sensor network topology control algorithm EFPC is proposed. This algorithm optimizes the node transmission power through a certain limited Nash equilibrium function to avoid underwater biological interference. It can better implement network topology, improve network performance, and avoid underwater biological interference. However, game theory equilibrium cannot fully guarantee network coverage and node connectivity, while other factors affecting energy consumption are not considered. In [11], the R-ERP^{2}R algorithm makes decisions based on the distance between nodes and residual energy, performs data transmission, and adds connection quality metrics and retransmission mechanisms to increase reliability.

3   FPPTC Algorithm

The FPPTC algorithm draws on the idea of fuzzy control theory to adjust the output power in FCTP [12] algorithm. Meanwhile, according to the fuzzy probability adjustment method, the transmission power of the AUV node is adjusted to ensure the underwater topological communication quality, and the average energy consumption of the node is reduced. The FPPTC algorithm is mainly composed of four stages: they are topological clustering, solving data deviation values, calculating power adjustment probability, and fuzzy power control.

3.1   Topological Clustering

The underwater wireless sensor nodes are randomly scattered in the target waters, and then the nodes are clustered. The selection of the cluster head node N_i is mainly based on the residual energy of the underwater topology node. The time required for the topology to complete the clustering is T_c. The time interval for the next clustering process is T_n. The underwater topology triggers the cluster every $T_c + T_n$ seconds (this process is a network cycle), reselect cluster head, simultaneous multiple iterations in the clustering process. Set the initial cluster head percentage for all underwater topology nodes, i.e. C_p (e.g. 6%), Where C_p is limited to the notification of the initial cluster head, no direct influence on the formation of the final cluster. Set the node to cluster head probability to CH_p, as shown in Eq. (1):

$$CH_p = \frac{C_p \times E_{residual}}{E_{max}} \tag{1}$$

Where $E_{residual}$ is the current remaining energy of the node, E_{max} is the maximum energy of the node (generally the energy when the node is fully charged), However, the value of the node is not allowed to be lower than a certain value Pim (such as 10^{-4}). The probability that a node is selected to be a cluster head is proportional to $E_{residual}$.

3.2 Solving Data Deviation Values

In order to realize UWSNs communication, there is a deviation between the current data of the AUV node and the target. According to this, the ratio of the difference between the data optimal solution and the current time parameter to the optimal solution is defined as the data deviation value. In order to ensure the communication quality and network connectivity of the underwater topology. In this paper, the data deviation analysis of the node's transmission power, neighbor node degree and residual energy value provides a reliable basis for AUV transmission power control.

According to the definition of the data deviation value above, the data deviation value is solved for the AUV transmission power, as shown in formula (2).

$$D_p = \frac{\left| \frac{\sum_{i=1}^{n} (P_a + P_{vi})}{n} - P^* \right|}{P^*} \tag{2}$$

The number of AUV communication nodes is n, P_a is the current transmission power of the AUV node, P_{vi} is the transmission power of the communication node, P^* is the best transmission power of AUV when communication is realized, and D_p is the data deviation value of transmission power. Similar to the transmission power, the data deviation value is calculated for the neighbor list degree (defined herein as the number of one-hop nodes in the AUV node communication range). Let the AUV node realize that the maximum neighbor node degree is Q^*, and the current neighbor list degree of the AUV node is Q, then the neighbor node degree deviation value is as shown in formula (3):

$$D_Q = \frac{|Q - Q^*|}{Q^*} \tag{3}$$

For the residual energy deviation value, similar to the transmission power, not only the remaining energy of the AUV node but also the remaining energy of the cluster head node V_i with the AUV communication. Let the total energy of the AUV node and the communication node be E^*, the remaining energy of the AUV node be E_a, and the remaining energy of the communication node be E_{vi}, then the residual energy deviation value is as shown in formula (4):

$$D_E = \frac{\left| \frac{\sum_{i=1}^{n}(E_a + E_{vi})}{n} - E^* \right|}{E^*} \tag{4}$$

From the above definition of the data deviation value, the magnitude of the deviation value and the difference between the current value of the data and the optimal solution value are proportional to each other. The larger the difference, the larger the data deviation value.

3.3 Fuzzy Adjustment Probability

According to the data deviation value calculated in Sect. 3.2, the fuzzy logic algorithm is used to solve the adjustment probability of the transmission power. The larger the deviation, the greater the adjustment probability. However, there is no clear relationship between the data bias value and the adjustment probability. Therefore, in order to realize the correlation between them, this paper adopts the fuzzy logic algorithm to adjust them. According to the conclusions of the literature [10]. Using cross-layer parameters as the input value of the fuzzy logic system, i.e. the data deviation value. Give each cross-layer parameter a dynamic weight. The more fuzzy rules, the more output. Therefore, the accuracy is higher, the number of fuzzy rules set in this paper is 7, as shown in Table 1:

Table 1. The fuzzy rules

Input	Output
Very Small (VS)	Very Small (VS)
Medium Small (MS)	Medium Small (MS)
Small (S)	Small (S)
Medium (M)	Medium (M)
Large (L)	Large (L)
Medium Large (ML)	Medium Large (ML)
Very Large (VL)	Very Large (VL)

According to Table 1, the input and output membership function is shown in Fig. 1:

According to the above fuzzy rule input and output, the transmission power adjustment probability is proportional to the data deviation value. The data deviation values have been solved for AUV transmission power, neighbor list degree and residual energy respectively in Sect. 3.2. Three adjustment probabilities are output from the above fuzzy rules, respectively, the transmission power adjustment probability ρ_P, the adjustment probability of the neighbor list degree is ρ_Q, and the adjustment probability of the remaining energy is ρ_E. In order to improve network performance, it is necessary to determine the probability of adjusting the transmission power. Since the performance determined by a large deviation value cannot be guaranteed with a small probability,

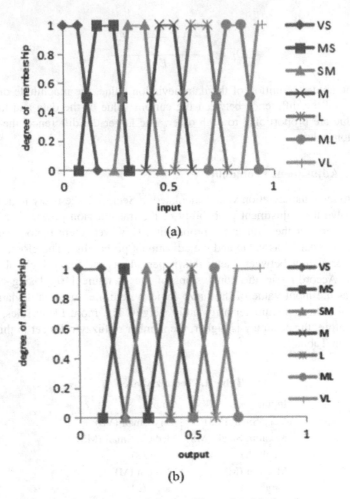

Fig. 1. Input (a) and Output (b) membership function

the maximum adjustment probability should be selected. The AUV transmission power adjustment probability is shown in formula (5):

$$\rho = \max\{\rho_P, \rho_Q, \rho_E\} \tag{5}$$

Through Eq. 5, the adjustment probability of the transmission power is determined by the worst performance parameter, and the network performance can be improved by this method.

3.4   Power Control

When calculating the transmission power deviation, it is necessary to solve the optimum transmission power to determine the magnitude of the deviation. When the AUV needs to adjust the power, adjust it to the optimal transmission power. Therefore, the optimal transmission power plays a crucial role in the overall network topology.

In this paper, the calculation of the optimal transmission power is based on the FCTP algorithm proposed in [12]. Most nodes are between 4 and 7, with an average node degree of around 5.89.

This method is a power control method based on fuzzy logic. The power adjustment method uses closed-loop control, as shown in Fig. 2. Define Ed as the expected neighbor list degree, and Td as the current node degree of the AUV node. All nodes are running under the same rules. Closed-loop working mode: The AUV node has an initial power and the AUV node periodically broadcasts its uniquely represented message Msg. All cluster head nodes that receive Msg send a feedback confirmation message FBMsg to reply. Calculate the number of FBMsg received during the period before the node sends the next Msg. Its the Td of the current cycle, When there is a gap between Td and Ed, the TP value of the AUV is output through the fuzzy logic control algorithm. The fuzzy power control of the FPPTC algorithm based on the improved FCTP algorithm is shown in Fig. 2:

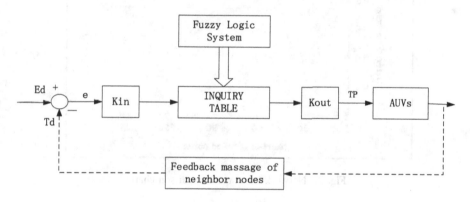

Fig. 2. Power control

4 Performance Analysis

FCTP algorithm is a traditional fuzzy logic topology control method. In order to verify the performance of the FPPTC algorithm, the simulation tool NS-3 was used to evaluate and compare with FCTP and R-ERP^{2}R under the same parameter settings. The simulation configuration parameters are shown in Table 2:

Figure 3 is a comparison of the coverage of underwater wireless sensor networks. as can be seen from the simulation results, compared with R-ERP^{2}R algorithm and FCTP algorithm, FPPTC algorithm coverage is higher. When the number of node failures is small (less than 20), the gap in network coverage is not obvious. As the number of failed nodes increases (when the failed node exceeds 61), network coverage declines faster. Due to the introduction of AUV node assistance in the underwater network topology, utilizing its autonomous mobility and expanding transmission

Table 2. Simulation configuration

Parameter	Value
Simulation area	300 m × 300 m
Number of nodes	150
Depth	15 m
Sound speed	1475 m/s
Communication radius	30 m
Initial energy	1000 J
Data rate	2000 bit/s
Transmission power	2.8 W
Receive power	1.5 W

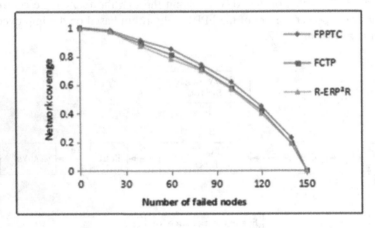

Fig. 3. Network coverage comparison chart

power, improve network coverage and communication quality of underwater acoustic networks.

Figure 4 shows the relationship between the operating cycle of the reaction node and the average remaining energy. As can be seen from the figure, the average residual energy of the FPPTC algorithm is slightly larger than the other two algorithms. Since the FPPTC algorithm needs to consume a certain amount of energy when initial clustering, the average energy of the node is slightly lower than the FTC algorithm when the number of running rounds is less than 10. As the number of running rounds increases, the average remaining energy is improved compared to the other two algorithms. This is because the FPPTC algorithm adjusts the AUV transmission power according to the probability, reduces the adjustment frequency (about 30%), and saves energy.

Figure 5 is a comparison of the number of algorithm nodes and the network life cycle of the three algorithms. As can be seen from the figure, as the number of deployed nodes increases, the FPTTC algorithm network lifetime is greater than the FCTP algorithm. This indicates that the FPTTC algorithm network runs more

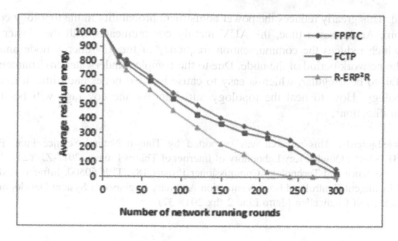

Fig. 4. Residual energy comparison chart

efficiently as the number of deployed nodes increases. Compared with R-ERP²R, although the clustering process is carried out, the auxiliary of AUV significantly reduces the energy consumption of cluster head node communication. Thus extending the network life cycle.

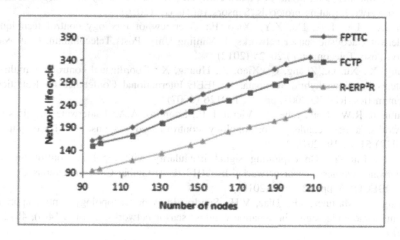

Fig. 5. Network life cycle comparison chart

5 Conclusion

Based on the FCTP algorithm, this paper proposes an AUV-assisted fuzzy probability power adjustment topology control algorithm. The FPPTC algorithm is characterized by the combination of AUV and underwater acoustic network topology. When the AUV transmission power and the optimal transmission power are not equal, it is determined according to the fuzzy rule whether the transmission power needs to be adjusted. This greatly reduces the power adjustment probability in the topology control algorithm. At the same time, the AUV mainly communicates with the cluster head node, which reduces the communication frequency of the low energy node and prolongs the network period of the node. Due to the complex underwater environment, the nodes fail to be irregular, which is easy to cause isolated nodes and difficult to repair the topology. How to heal the topology and improve the coverage will be further research directions.

Acknowledgments. This research was supported by Tianjin Natural Science Fund Project 18JCYBJC85600, Qinghai Key Laboratory of Internet of Things Project (2017-ZJ-Y21), Tianjin Enterprise Science and Technology Commissioner Project 18JCTPJC60500, Infrared Radiation Heating Intelligent Control and Basic Ventilation Auxiliary Engineering System Development of No. 2 Section of Changchun Metro Line 2 (hx 2018-37).

References

1. Tuna, G., Gungor, V.C.: A survey on deployment techniques, localization algorithms, and research challenges for underwater acoustic sensor networks. Int. J. Commun. Syst. **30**(17), e3350 (2017)
2. Benson, B., et al.: Design of a low-cost, underwater acoustic modem for short-range sensor networks, pp. 1–9 (2010)
3. Li, N., Martínez, J.F., Meneses Chaus, J.M., Eckert, M.: A survey on underwater acoustic sensor network routing protocols. Sensors **16**(3), 414 (2016)
4. Sun, L.J., Liu, L.F., Du, X.Y., Xiao, F.: Overview of topology control techniques in underwater acoustic sensor networks. J. Nanjing Univ. Posts Telecommun. (Nat. Nanjing Univ. Posts Telecommun.) 20–25 (2012)
5. Xiang, X., Xu, G., Zhang, Q., Xiao, Z., Huang, X.: Coordinated control for multi-AUV systems based on hybrid automata. In: IEEE International Conference on Robotics and Biomimetics, ROBIO 2007, pp. 2121–2126 (2007)
6. Coutinho, R.W., Boukerche, A., Vieira, L.F., Loureiro, A.A.: Underwater wireless sensor networks: a new challenge for topology control-based systems. ACM Comput. Surv. (CSUR) **51**(1), 19 (2018)
7. Liu, L., Liu, Y.: On exploiting signal irregularity with topology control for mobile underwater wireless sensor networks. In: 2013 IEEE Global Communications Conference (GLOBECOM), pp. 522–527 (2013)
8. Huang, Y., Martínez, J.F., Díaz, V.H., Sendra, J.: A novel topology control approach to maintain the node degree in dynamic wireless sensor networks. Sensors **14**(3), 4672–4688 (2014)
9. Nasir, H., Javaid, N., Mahmood, S., Qasim, U., Khan, Z.A., Ahmed, F.: Distributed topology control protocols for underwater sensor networks. In: 2016 19th International Conference on Network-Based Information Systems (NBiS), pp. 429–436 (2016)
10. Li, N., Martinez, J.F., Diaz, V.H.: The balanced cross-layer design routing algorithm in WSNs using fuzzy logic. Sensors **15**, 19541–19559 (2015)
11. Wahid, A., Lee, S., Kim, D.: A reliable and energy-efficient routing protocol for underwater wireless sensor networks. Int. J. Commun. Syst. **27**, 2048–2062 (2014)
12. Zhang, J., Chen, J., Sun, Y.: Transmission power adjustment of wireless sensor networks using fuzzy control algorithm. Wirel. Commun. Mob. Comput. **9**, 805–818 (2009)

Naive Bayes Classifier Based Driving Habit Prediction Scheme for VANET Stable Clustering

Tong Liu[(✉)], Shuo Shi, and Xuemai Gu

Harbin Institute of Technology, Harbin 150001, China
liutongsasa@hotmail.com

Abstract. Vehicular ad hoc networks (VANETs) is a promising network form for future application on road, like arriving automatic driving and in-vehicle entertainment. Compare with traditional mobile ad hoc networks (MANETs), its advantages are multi-hop communication without energy restriction and relative regular moving pattern. However, the high mobility of nodes raises many challenges for algorithm designers such as topology changing, routing failures, and hidden terminal problem. Clustering is an effective control algorithm provides efficient and stable routes for data dissemination. Efficient clustering algorithms became challenging issues in this kind of distributed networks. In this paper, a novel machine learning based driving habit prediction scheme for stable clustering is proposed, briefly named NBP. In the scheme, vehicles are divided into two alignments with opposite driving habit from which stable cluster design could benefit. Naive Bayes classifier is introduced to estimate the alignment of vehicles by several factors, such as relative speed, vehicle type, number of traffic violations and commercial vehicle or not. Combined with clustering design, the proposed method has been proven effective for stable clustering in VANET.

Keywords: Naive Bayes classifier · VANET clustering · Driving habit

1 Introduction

As a research focus of intelligent transportation system (ITS), auto-driving attracts tremendous attention. It is an enormous and complicated project supported by stable communication system, quality sensors, deep data mining and so on. The most important part is stable communication which provide a foundation for safety application, assistant to the drivers and emergency warning. VANET is an architecture design for vehicles to exchange data with other neighbor vehicles. It is derived from MANET whose characteristic is multi-hop communications and no-infrastructures. Generally, communication in VANET is divided into two parts: vehicle-to-vehicle (V2V) and vehicle-to-infrastructure (V2I). On board units (OBUs) are installed on vehicles to make vehicles as a message sender, router and receiver. Road side units (RSUs) are assembled along the roads to provide Internet access and relaying. Compare with traditional MANET, nodes in VANET have relative regular mobility patterns on account of road restrictions, and energy consumption is no longer taken into

S. Han et al. (Eds.): AICON 2019, LNICST 286, pp. 445–452, 2019.
https://doi.org/10.1007/978-3-030-22968-9_40

consideration [1]. At the same time, the high speed makes network topology change rapidly than before.

Such characteristics raised new challenge in VANET, like hidden terminal in high dynamic topology and message congestion in high density network. Associating mobile vehicles into groups is a reasonable solution, that is clustering. According some rule set, it groups nodes to enhance communication efficiency. Cluster head (CH) is selected as a center of the cluster to host the whole cluster. In order to avoid congestion and meet quality of service (QoS) criteria, cluster also can be used for frequency reuse [2]. Recent years, widely study and discuss are focus on it. [4] provide a comprehensive and comparative survey of clustering technique. Vehicle communication benefit a lot from clustering, such as high communication efficiency, routing scalability and frequency resource sharing [5].

Dynamic topology of VANET make stable cluster a hard stuff. Therefore, the stability is one of the most important performance criteria. It means a stable cluster needs a long lifetime of CH and cluster members (CM) to decrease overhead. Fewer numbers of changes in vehicles states and fewer CH changes also can be take into consideration [6]. The recent designs of clustering algorithms are based on velocity of nodes, running lanes, nodes density, moving pattern and communication range. These methods are aim to ensure cluster stability by analyzing dynamic elements around vehicle. A well-design clustering algorithm need keep stable cluster and have integrated member joining and leaving procedures, and control overheads at the same time [7, 8]. Recently Seyhan Ucar proposed a new stable cluster based message dissemination method in [9]. VMaSC choosing relative mobility as the metric for CH selection. Relative mobility is calculated between neighboring vehicles. In order to reduce overheads, it introduces a direct connection from CM to CM. Periodic hello packets and CM information broadcasting maintain the cluster structure.

In this paper, the proposed novel machine learning based scheme aims to predict driving habit for stable clusters constructions. In this scheme, vehicles are divided into two alignments with opposite driving habit from which stable cluster design could benefit. Naive Bayes classifier is introduced to estimate the alignment of vehicles by several factors, such as relative speed, vehicle type, number of traffic violations and commercial vehicle or not.

The rest of the paper is arranged as follows: Sect. 2 introduces how the prediction scheme works, including vehicle alignments definition, Naive Bayes classifier and driving habit prediction system. Then, it describes CH selection method with the result from proposed scheme. In Sect. 3, simulation set-up scenarios, results and discussions are presented. At last, we conclude our algorithm and raise some future works in Sect. 4.

2 Driving Habit Prediction Scheme

2.1 Vehicle Alignments

Driving habit of drivers are decided by many personal factors, such as character, education, and life experience. The habit is developed from long time accumulation and will be relatively stable. It is believed that certain vehicles have fixed drivers on certain roads in most cases. We can infer that a vehicle keeps same driving habit in a certain route. Based on this conclusion, vehicles are divided into opposed alignments: Law Vehicles (LVs) and Chaos Vehicles (CVs). Originally the law and chaos axis were defined as the distinction between "the belief that everything should follow an order, and that obeying rules is the natural way of life", as opposed to "the belief that life is random, and that chance and luck rule the world". In this Scheme, the characteristics of alignments are only restricted in driving habit category. Vehicles in different alignments follow totally opposite driving patterns.

Most of the time, LVs keep moving at a constant speed which is around the average speed running on the road. When meeting vehicles ahead with similar speed on the same lane, LVs will slow down and stay uniform speed without changing lane. The rate of changing lanes is low for LVs. On the contrary, CVs always keep moving with higher speed than average, even beyond the speed limits on road sometimes. When meeting vehicles ahead, CVs will change lane immediately and overtake them with acceleration. Therefore, the rate of changing lanes is high for CVs.

2.2 Naive Bayes Classifier

In machine learning, naive Bayes classifiers are probabilistic classifier based on applying Bayes theorem with strong independence assumptions. Despite the simple design of naive Bayes classifier, naive Bayes classifiers have worked well in many area, such as medicine, economics and so on.

Bayes' theorem is stated as follows:

$$P(b|x) = \frac{P(b)P(x|b)}{P(x)} \tag{1}$$

where $P(b|x)$ is a conditional probability: the likelihood of event b occurring given that x is true, $P(b)$ and $P(x)$ is the prior probability.

When the "naive" conditional independence assumptions come into play, we assume that each feature x_i is conditionally independent of every other feature x_j for $i \neq j$, given the category b. The formula can be rewritten as follows:

$$P(b|x) = \frac{P(b)}{P(x)} \prod_{i=1}^{d} P(x_i|b) \tag{2}$$

The naive Bayes classifier combines this model with a decision rule. One common rule is to pick the hypothesis that is most probable; this is known as the maximum a posteriori rule.

$$h_{nb}(x) = \arg\max_{c \in y} P(b) \prod_{i=1}^{d} P(x_i|b) \tag{3}$$

2.3 Driving Habit Prediction Framework

It is easy to judge the alignment of a vehicle on a specific road by monitoring its driving record. The number of lanes changing and the proportion of acceleration time can be used to draw a conclusion. In the process of vehicle clustering, we need to predict the vehicle motion pattern to establish a stable cluster. However, vehicles did not complete the driving on this section when choosing CHs. It is impossible to judge their camp according to the method just mentioned. It means that we need to judge which alignment the vehicle belongs to according to its current inherent properties before the vehicle completes the whole driving process on the road. As introduced before, Naive Bayes Classifier is suitable for this occasion. Relative independent features of vehicles are required to design the prediction method. Here four vehicle characteristics that may be relevant to driving habit have been selected: relative speed, vehicle size, number of violations and whether commercial vehicles.

- Relative speed: the speed difference between the vehicle and the traffic. Traffic speed is defined as the average speed of neighbor vehicles. This feature represents whether the speed of vehicles in this section is higher than the average level. The higher the relative speed is, the higher possibility of belonging to the chaotic alignment is. The formula of relative speed is stated as follows:

$$v_i^r = v_i - \frac{\sum_{j \in N} v_j}{n} \tag{4}$$

where v_i^r means the relative speed of vehicle i, N is the set of neighbor vehicles, and v_j is the speed of neighbor vehicle j.
- Vehicle size: distinguished by the length of vehicles. In this scheme, vehicles are divided into two categories, small and large. A small car is less than six meters long, such as cars, jeeps, minivans, light buses, and light trucks. A large car is with a length of 6 m or more, such as ordinary buses, medium-sized and large trucks.
- Number of violations in the past three years: we believe that the more violations, the more barbaric the driving habits of drivers, that is, the more inclined to the chaotic camp.
- Whether commercial vehicles or not: commercial vehicle means a vehicle engaged in road transport business activities for the purpose of making a profit. It is believed that the commercial vehicles focus on driving safety, because profit risk need to be taken into account. That is, a higher probability of belonging to the law alignment.

It is assumed that the velocity of vehicles has a normal distribution [10]. According the formula 4, we can easily infer that the relative speed also follows a normal distribution.

$$p(x = v_i^r | c) = \frac{1}{\sqrt{2\pi}\sigma_i} \exp\left(-\frac{(v_i^r - \mu_i)^2}{2\sigma_i^2}\right) \tag{5}$$

Where μ_i and σ_i^2 denote the average value and the variance of relative velocity for the vehicle i.

The other three characteristics are all discrete variable. The conditional probability of these features can be calculated as follows:

$$P(x_i|c) = \frac{|D_{c,x_i}|}{|D_c|} \qquad (6)$$

where D_c denotes the training set of category c, and $|D_{c,x_i}|$ denotes the elements number of the set. D_{c,x_i} is the set of elements whose value is x_i in category c.

Combined with formulas 3, 5 and 6, the vehicles' alignment can be judged. Then the driving pattern of vehicles can be predicted when a clustering process initiate.

2.4 Stable Clustering

The stable clustering process consists of several steps: start, joining, CH selection, leaving procedure and merging procedure. The proposed scheme is working on the CH selection step. For the reason that the speed of CVs changes frequently, CVs are excluded from CH candidates in the algorithm. In traditional method, the metric is unique without an evolving view. The following moving pattern of vehicles make great difference to the cluster stability. For example, when the CH election start, a CV just happen to meet the requirement of CH. After becoming a CH, CV overtake the front car and keep acceleration as its moving pattern. The cluster will expire after CV driving out of the communication range. It can be avoided with the proposed Naive Bayes Classifier based driving prediction method.

The procedures of cluster formation are described below:

- Start: Every node is marked as an uncertain node. It does not receive any joining message (JM) or hello message (HM) after running on the street from beginning.
- Join: CHs disseminate JM periodic when they running on the road. If an uncertain node which is not belong any cluster receives the JM, and it is running on the same direction with this CH, this node will send a reply message (RM) to the relevant CH. After the CH receives the RM, it will allocate the node a unique cluster member number and send it to the new CM. If the uncertain node does not receive any reply from the CH after a certain period, it will broadcast a joining request (JR) for seeking a cluster.
- CH selection: If an uncertain node still does not receive any (JM) after several period, CH selection procedure will start. It will calculate relative speed between neighbor nodes, and select the center of the graph as the new CH. Then using the result of NBP, if the new CH is LV, continue to build the cluster. Or else, restart the CH selection procedure and exclude the CVs.
- CM Leaving: When a CM fails to receive any packets from CH over some periods, this node will change itself to an uncertain node role. It means this CM may be out of the communication range of its CH. At the same time, the CH will also remove this CM from the membership list.
- Cluster Merging: When a CH receive a JM from another CH, that means two CHs are within communication range. Cluster merging procedure need be executed.

Both of the CHs will give up the role of CH and come to CH selection procedure to build a new cluster.

3 Simulation Results

The simulations are running on the Network Simulator 2 platform. In order to simulate realistic mobility of vehicles, Simulation of Urban Mobility (SUMO) is employed combined with ns2. It is an open-source traffic simulator which can mode drivers' behavior. Driving habit of LVs and CVs are adjusted in the SUMO. For example, the acceleration and overtaking decision of the vehicles is determined by the driving habit which is obtained from designed prediction scheme. The road is designed two lanes and two-way. The simulation time is 500 s. The maximum speed of the vehicles is a variable ranging from 60 to 120 km/h.

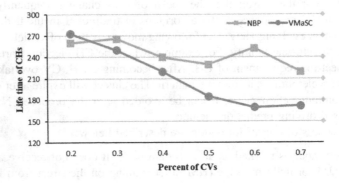

Fig. 1. Lifetime of CHs with the percent of CVs

A simplified VMsSC which only adopts its CH election strategy is compared with proposed scheme in this paper. Figure 1 states relationship between the lifetime of the CHs with the percent of CVs. With larger proportion of CVs, the CH lifetime decrease rapidly. That is because there is more CVs selected as CH, which is an unstable factor. The outcome of simulation also illustrates that NBP has longer CHs lifetime than VMaSC.

Figure 2 shows the lifetime of the cluster head between NBP and VMaSC with transmission range. The simulation result shows the lifetime of the clusters is prolonged by using NBP. That is because CVs is exclude from CH candidates. The unstable factor of node moving pattern is almost from CVs. On another hand, the result demonstrated wide transmission range will provide stability of clusters. Cluster stability benefits from longer transmission range.

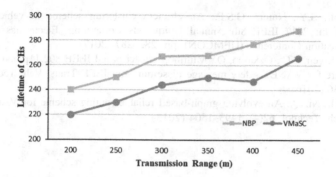

Fig. 2. Lifetime of CHs with its transmission range

4 Conclusions

In order to construct stable clusters, a novel machine learning based driving habit prediction scheme is proposed in this paper. In this scheme, vehicles are divided into two alignments with opposite driving habit from which stable cluster design could benefit. Naive Bayes classifier is introduced to estimate the alignment of vehicles by several factors, such as relative speed, vehicle type, number of traffic violations and commercial vehicle or not. The proposed technique has been proven effective for stable clustering in VANET.

References

1. Karagiannis, G., et al.: Vehicular networking: a survey and tutorial on requirements, architectures, challenges, standards and solutions. IEEE Commun. Surv. Tutor. **13**(4), 584–616 (2011)
2. Eze, E.C., Zhang, S., Liu, E.: Vehicular ad hoc networks (VANETs): current state, challenges, potentials and way forward. In: Proceedings of the 20th International Conference on Automation and Computing: Future Automation, Computing and Manufacturing, ICAC 2014, pp. 176–181 (2014)
3. Shea, C., Hassanabadi, B., Valaee, S.: Mobility-based clustering in VANETs using affinity propagation. In: GLOBECOM - IEEE Global Telecommunications Conference, pp. 1–6 (2009)
4. Cooper, C., Franklin, D., Ros, M., Safaei, F., Abolhasan, M.: A comparative survey of VANET clustering techniques. IEEE Commun. Surv. Tutor. **19**(1), 657–681 (2017)
5. Azizian, M., Cherkaoui, S., Hafid, A.S.: DCEV: a distributed cluster formation for VANET based on end-to-end realtive mobility. In: 2016 International Wireless Communications and Mobile Computing Conference, IWCMC 2016, pp. 287–291 (2016)
6. Ren, M., Khoukhi, L., Labiod, H., Zhang, J., Vèque, V.: A mobility-based scheme for dynamic clustering in vehicular ad-hoc networks (VANETs). Veh. Commun. **9**, 233–241 (2017)
7. Rawashdeh, Z.Y., Mahmud, S.: A novel algorithm to form stable clusters in vehicular ad hoc networks on highways. EURASIP J. Wirel. Commun. Netw. **2012**(1), 15 (2012)

8. Kannekanti, S.Y., Nunna, G.S.P.: An efficient clustering scheme in vehicular ad-hoc networks. In: 2017 IEEE 8th Annual Ubiquitous Computing, Electronics and Mobile Communication Conference (UEMCON), pp. 282–287 (2017)
9. Ucar, S., Ergen, S.C., Ozkasap, O.: Multihop-cluster-based IEEE 802.11p and LTE hybrid architecture for VANET safety message dissemination. IEEE Trans. Veh. Technol. **65**(4), 2621–2636 (2016)
10. Eiza, M.H., Ni, Q.: An evolving graph-based reliable routing scheme for VANETs. IEEE Trans. Veh. Technol. **62**(4), 1493–1504 (2013)

Path Optimization with Machine-Learning Based Prediction for Wireless Sensor Networks

Jianxin Ma[✉], Shuo Shi, and Xuemai Gu

Harbin Institute of Technology, Harbin 150001, Heilongjiang, China
hrbmjx@126.com, crcss@hit.edu.cn

Abstract. The trajectory scheduling of the mobile nodes is a critical research problem in rechargeable wireless sensor networks. In this paper, we propose a machine-learning based energy consumption prediction (ML-ECP) approach, which uses machine-learning to predict the energy consumption rates in wireless sensor networks. Based on the prediction, the sensor nodes are partitioned into multiple clusters and the optimal trajectories are obtained for mobile nodes. We compare the proposed approach with the existing approach, the results show that the ML-ECP improves the energy efficiency for sensor nodes recharging and data collection, and the mobile nodes collect information and recharge sensor nodes periodically in the network.

Keywords: Path optimization · Machine-learning · Wireless sensor networks

1 Introduction

Due to the characteristics of low cost and small size, sensor nodes can monitor and record the physical conditions of the environment and have the ability for data processing and wireless communication [2]. For the most existing sensor networks, they are powered by batteries, and their lifetime is limited by the battery capacity. In recent years, the energy provisioning problem is noticed by many researchers. [5] decouples the energy recharging problem into a node deployment problem and a charging and activation scheduling problem. They propose an algorithm and prove that it achieves the optimal solution under a mild condition. [7] develops the joint downlink energy assignment and uplink power control scheme with the heterogeneous statistical QoS provisioning (HeP) for wireless powered sensor networks (WPSNs). In [8], the authors propose a novel energy synchronized mobile charging (ESync) protocol, which simultaneously reduces the charger travel distance and the charging delay.

For this case, mobile nodes have the delay to visit the sensor nodes and the sensor nodes have the limited battery capacity. The task scheduling for sensor

© ICST Institute for Computer Sciences, Social Informatics and Telecommunications Engineering 2019
Published by Springer Nature Switzerland AG 2019. All Rights Reserved
S. Han et al. (Eds.): AICON 2019, LNICST 286, pp. 453–459, 2019.
https://doi.org/10.1007/978-3-030-22968-9_41

nodes in the network plays a critical role in achieving a high charging and information collecting efficiency [12]. If we consider the delay of the mobile node and the diversity of sensor nodes energy consumption, one mobile node is not enough for a large-scale network. The multiple traveling salesman problem (mTSP) is a scheduling problem, which is a generalization of the traveling salesman problem (TSP), and which aims to determine a set of routes for m salesmen who start from and return to a home [1]. It has been widely studied in recent years, and how to schedule the traveling trajectories of mobile nodes and how to reduce the energy-hole are two crucial topics in this field.

However, most of the previous works focus on the location of sensor nodes [3,4] and ignore the different energy consumption for each sensor node. In a traveling tour, some sensor nodes are visited when it do not need to be recharged. This increases the traveling distance of mobile nodes and prolongs the waiting time of the energy-hungry sensor nodes [8]. To address this issue, we propose a machine-learning based energy consumption prediction (ML-ECP) approach that considers both the location of sensor nodes and the energy consumption diversity of sensor nodes. Based on the energy consumption rate prediction, the sensor nodes are partitioned in the first step. Then, the sensor nodes search neighbors within its cluster. In the last step, the traveling trajectories and the meeting point locations of mobile nodes are scheduled.

The remainder of this paper is organized as follows. Section 2 proposes energy consumption prediction approach and presents the traveling tour optimization approach. Section 3 provides a particular case of our approach and compares the results of our approach with the existing approach. Finally, Sect. 4 concludes this paper.

2   Proposed Work

We assume the case that N immobile and rechargeable sensor nodes are randomly deployed in a region $\mathcal{R}$. The locations of them are known *a priori*. Each of them has a fixed communication range which is a circular area with radius of r and a unique identification (ID). The energy consumption of a sensor node mainly comes from the information monitoring and data transmission and is different with each other. Based on this difference, we propose ML-ECP approach which construct a set of nested TSP tours to balance the energy provisioning.

2.1   Machine-Learning Based Energy Consumption Prediction

First of all, all sensor nodes are fully charged. The different kinds of sensor nodes may have the different consumption rates and the energy consumption rates of the same sensor node may vary over time [8]. We assume the mobile nodes have certain knowledge on the energy consumption conditions of all sensor nodes. Based on this assumption, the prediction on their energy consumption rates is feasible [11]. ML-ECP solves the issue by three steps.

In the first step, we use fuzzy machine-leaning clustering algorithm to partition the network based on the different energy consumption rates of sensor nodes. Instead of the hard clustering algorithm, the fuzzy clustering algorithm is less likely to get stuck in the certain energy consumption rate in iteration through the use of membership values, and a sensor nodes can belong to more than one cluster. For high energy consumption sensor nodes, this is a effective method to avoid the sensor nodes death before the mobile nodes recharge them.

The most classic fuzzy clustering algorithm is the fuzzy c-means algorithm that is proposed by [6,10]. The algorithm provides a degree of membership for each data point to a given cluster. The values of the degrees of membership are between 0 and 1. When it close to 0, the data point has the low probability to be assigned to the corresponding cluster. Conversely, the data point has the high probability to be assigned to the cluster when the value close to 1. In this paper, based on the differences of the energy consumption rates, the clustering issue is based on minimization of the following objective function:

$$\sum_{i=1}^{N}\sum_{j=1}^{C} u_{ij}^{m} |e_i - e_{c_j}|^2 \quad 1 < m < \infty \tag{1}$$

where m is any real number greater than 1, u_{ij} is the degree of membership of the sensor node i in the cluster j, e_i is the energy consumption rate of the sensor node i, e_{c_j} is the mean value of the energy consumption rate of the cluster j, and $|\cdot|$ is the difference between any sensor node energy consumption rate and the mean value of the energy consumption rate.

Initially, the mean values of the energy consumption rate are randomly selected. Every sensor nodes will be assigned to the similar mean value cluster. Fuzzy clustering is carried out through an iterative optimization of the objective function, with the update of membership u_{ij} and the mean value of the energy consumption rate e_{cj} by:

$$u_{ij} = [\sum_{k=1}^{C} (\frac{|e_i - e_{c_j}|}{|e_i - e_{c_k}|})^{\frac{2}{m-1}}]^{-1} \tag{2}$$

$$e_{c_j} = \frac{\sum_{i=1}^{N} u_{ij}^{m} e_i}{\sum_{i=1}^{N} u_{ij}^{m}} \tag{3}$$

This process will stop when it satisfies the Eq. (4), where ε is a termination criterion, U_l is the matrix of the degree of membership in the lth iteration.

$$|U_{l+1} - U_l| \leq \varepsilon \tag{4}$$

Therefore, we have the clusters $G_1, G_2, ..., G_j, ..., G_C$.

2.2 Path Optimization for Mobile Nodes

In the second step, each sensor node finds the neighbors of itself within its cluster. The mobile nodes know the serial numbers and the location information of sensor

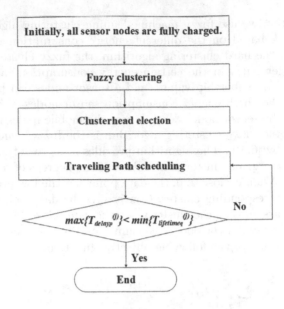

Fig. 1. The flow of the ML-ECP approach.

nodes. Only the sensor nodes that belong to the same cluster and is within its 1/2 communication radius can become the neighbors. Through several iterations, based on the location information, the neighbors become the child nodes and belong to only one clusterhead. The sensor node that has more neighbors is more likely to become a clusterhead, and the sensor node that has no neighbors becomes the clusterhead of itself.

After we obtain a series of clusterheads, in the third step, the traveling paths are scheduled for each cluster based on these clusterheads, and the mobile node will stop at the meeting point that is at the circle of clusterheads' 1/2 communication radius. This can be formulated as a traveling salesman problem, which is NP-hard. We adopt the two-step solver [9] to solve it. After running the solver, each cluster will obtain an optimized path and the meeting points information.

Then, the mobile nodes need to estimate whether the number of sensor nodes within its cluster are more than the threshold. That can be judged by the following function:

$$max\{T_{delay_p}(j)\} < min\{T_{lifetime_q}(j)\} \tag{5}$$

where $max\{T_{delay_p}(j)\}$ is the maximum delay in the cluster j, and min $\{T_{lifetime_q}(j)\}$ is the minimum lifetime in the cluster j.

If the number of sensor nodes in this cluster cannot satisfy the above function, this means there are some sensor nodes will stop work before the mobile node recharge them. To avoid this situation, for this cluster, there are more than one mobile nodes will be assigned to visit it, and the extra mobile nodes will be selected from the waiting mobile nodes. Figure 1 shows the procedure of the proposed approach.

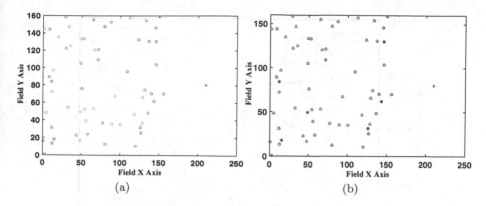

Fig. 2. The simulation results of the first two steps in a synthetic example of ML-ECP. (Color figure online)

3   Performance Evaluation

In this section, we present the procedure by applying ML-ECP to a synthetic example. In order to show the outstanding performance of our approach, we compare the performance of our approach with the existing approach.

3.1   An Example of ML-ECP

To illustrate our approach, we first randomly generate 60 sensor nodes in the size of $160 \times 160 \, \text{m}^2$. Then we use fuzzy algorithm to partition these sensor nodes into 3 clusters based on the different energy consumption rates. The result is shown in Fig. 2a where different clusters are labeled with different colors and the red five-pointed star represents the sink point. Figure 2b shows the simulation result when the clusterheads have been elected in the second step. The red plus sign icons represent the sensor nodes have been elected to the clusterheads and the blue asterisks show the sensor nodes have become the child nodes.

3.2   Investigating the Traveling Distance

We invistigate the traveling distance with different network scales in this section. Based on the same sensor nodes' location, we utilize TSP and our ML-ECP approach to calculate the traveling trajectories when the number of sensor nodes varies from 20 to 140 and the size of network is $160 \times 160 \, \text{m}^2$. The results is shown in Fig. 3. We can see the traveling distances of ML-ECP for each mobile node are obviously shorter than the results of TSP.

3.3   Investigating the Traveling Delay

We analyze the effects of the number of the sensor nodes on the traveling delay of mobile nodes. From 20 to 140 sensor nodes are randomly deployed in the size

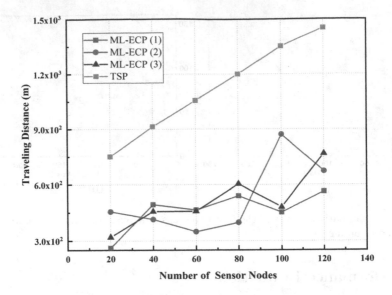

Fig. 3. Effects of the network scale on the traveling distance.

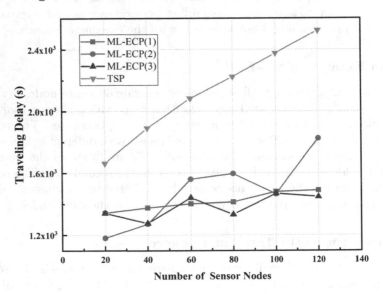

Fig. 4. Effects of the network scale on the traveling delay.

of $160 \times 160\,\mathrm{m}^2$. We assume $t_0 = 900\,\mathrm{s}$ and each sensor node generates a data packet at every $1\,\mathrm{s}$. The movement speed of mobile nodes is $1\,\mathrm{m/s}$. In Fig. 4, the yellow line shows the delay results of TSP and the others represent the delay results of ML-ECP for each mobile node. The results represent ML-ECP has obvious advantage over TSP.

4   Conclusion

This paper mainly focused on the optimization of the traveling tour for multiple mobile nodes in rechargeable wireless sensor networks. To improve the efficiency of recharging, we use machine-learning to predict the energy consumption rates of sensor nodes in the network. Then, the mobile nodes can visit these sensor nodes based on the prediction periodically. We evaluate and compare the proposed approach by extensive simulations. The results show that the performance of the energy efficiency and the traveling delay have been improved significantly.

References

1. Bektas, T.: The multiple traveling salesman problem: an overview of formulations and solution procedures. Omega **34**(3), 209–219 (2006)
2. Boyinbode, O., Le, H., Takizawa, M.: A survey on clustering algorithms for wireless sensor networks. Int. J. Space-Based Situated Comput. **1**(2–3), 130–136 (2011)
3. Ding, K., Yousefi'zadeh, H.: A systematic node placement strategy for multi-tier heterogeneous network graphs. In: 2016 IEEE Wireless Communications and Networking Conference (WCNC), pp. 1–6. IEEE (2016)
4. Ding, K., Yousefi'zadeh, H., Jabbari, F.: A robust advantaged node placement strategy for sparse network graphs. IEEE Trans. Netw. Sci. Eng. **5**(2), 113–126 (2018)
5. Du, R., Xiao, M., Fischione, C.: Optimal node deployment and energy provision for wirelessly powered sensor networks. IEEE J. Sel. Areas Commun. **37**, 407–423 (2018)
6. Dunn, J.C.: A fuzzy relative of the ISODATA process and its use in detecting compact well-separated clusters (1973)
7. Gao, Y., Cheng, W., Zhang, H., Li, Z.: Heterogeneous statistical qos provisioning over wireless powered sensor networks. IEEE Access **5**, 7910–7921 (2017)
8. He, L., et al.: ESync: an energy synchronized charging protocol for rechargeable wireless sensor networks. In: Proceedings of the 15th ACM International Symposium on Mobile Ad Hoc Networking and Computing, pp. 247–256. ACM (2014)
9. Jianxin Ma, S.S., Gu, X.: An optimization-based MTSP-CR mobile data gathering algorithm for large-scale wireless sensor networks. In: Vehicular Technology Conference, VTC Fall 2018. IEEE (2018)
10. Peizhuang, W.: Pattern recognition with fuzzy objective function algorithms (James C. Bezdek). SIAM Rev. **25**(3), 442 (1983)
11. Wang, Y., Vuran, M.C., Goddard, S.: Stochastic analysis of energy consumption in wireless sensor networks (2010)
12. Zhou, Z., Du, C., Shu, L., Hancke, G., Niu, J., Ning, H.: An energy-balanced heuristic for mobile sink scheduling in hybrid WSNs. IEEE Trans. Ind. Inform. **12**(1), 28–40 (2016)

Research on the Maximization of Total Information Rate Based on Energy Allocation in Multi-user SWIPT Relaying System

Jianxiong Li[1,2], Xuelong Ding[1,2], Xianguo Li[1,2(✉)], Kunlai Li[1,2], Ke Zhao[1,2], and Weiguang Shi[1,2]

[1] School of Electronics and Information Engineering,
Tianjin Polytechnic University, Tianjin 300387, China
{lijianxiong, lixianguo, shiweiguang}@tjpu.edu.cn,
1206737984@qq.com, 2493936832@qq.com,
1140350591@qq.com

[2] Tianjin Key Laboratory of Optoelectronic Detection Technology and Systems,
Tianjin 300387, China

Abstract. With the rapid development and wide application of the wireless communication network, the communication network based on the simultaneous wireless information and power transfer (SWIPT) technology has attracted more and more extensive research. This technology solves the problem of frequent charging or replacement of the device battery very well, has greatly extended the working hours of the device, and can be adapted to some special communication environments such as high temperature and high pressure. This paper studies the effect of the energy allocation in multi-user SWIPT relaying system on the information rate. Thereinto, the relay uses the energy harvested in the energy harvesting mode to amplify and forward the information of the users. The total information rate maximization model is proposed and the corresponding energy allocation scheme is derived. The simulation results show that the proposed energy allocation scheme can maximize the total information rate of all users.

Keywords: Simultaneous wireless information and power transfer (SWIPT) · Multi-user relaying system · Amplify-and-forward · Information rate

1 Introduction

With the rapid development of human civilization, people gradually realize the importance of green energy. The sun and the wind can produce green energy. In addition, the radio frequency (RF) signals can not only transmit information, but also carry energy. The energy harvesting (EH) technology based on RF signals plays an important role in the field of communication. In recent years, there has been an upsurge of research interests in RF-EH technique [1]. As a promising wireless technology, RF-EH technique is getting more and more research. The EH networks based on RF have found their applications quickly in various forms, such as wireless sensor networks [2], wireless body networks [3], and wireless charging systems [4].

S. Han et al. (Eds.): AICON 2019, LNICST 286, pp. 460–471, 2019.
https://doi.org/10.1007/978-3-030-22968-9_42

Since Varshney first proposed the concept of simultaneous wireless information and power transfer (SWIPT) [5], this technique has attracted increasing interest. In [5], the authors investigated the fundamental tradeoff between the information transmission rate and power transfer. The SWIPT can provide a controllable and efficient allocation scheme of on-demand wireless information and energy [6].

The key of the SWIPT technology is the design of the receiver. The reason is because information reception and RF-EH work on very different power sensitivity (e.g., -10 dBm for energy harvesters versus -60 dBm for information receivers) [7]. In [7], due to the potential limitation that practical energy harvesting receivers are not yet able to decode information directly, the authors investigated two practical designs for the co-located receiver, namely, time switching (TS) and power splitting (PS). For the TS architecture, the receiver divides a time block into two parts, one for transmitting information and the other for harvesting energy. For the PS architecture, the receiver splits the received signal into two parts, one for transmitting information and the other for harvesting energy.

The existing research on the structure of the receiver is mostly based on TS or PS, and the research on the operation strategy of the receiver is mainly focused on single-input-single-output (SISO) channel. In [8], Liu L et al. studied the optimal switching strategy of EH/information decoding (ID) mode under a SISO channel subject to the time-varying interference. In [9], Zhou et al. summarized the strategy based on TS and PS as a dynamic PS strategy. This strategy dynamically splits the RF signal into two arbitrary proportion signal streams according to the change of the time.

The relaying technology can extend the coverage of communication. Combining the relaying technology with the SWIPT technology can further improve the performance of the system containing energy-constrained nodes. The relaying system based on SWIPT has also attracted the attention of scholars [10–15]. In [10], the authors studied a two-way decoding and forwarding relaying network based on the SWIPT technology, in which the relay is an energy-constrained node, but can obtain energy from the RF signals transmitted from the source node. Based on this network, the authors first analyzed the total information rate that could be achieved by the PS-based relaying transmission protocol, and then determined the PS ratio at the maximum total information rate, i.e., the optimal signal flow split ratio for EH and ID. In [11], the authors studied the outage probability of a cooperative network, in which the relay is a cooperative node capable of harvesting RF energy. The outage probabilities of amplify-and-forward (AF) and decode-and-forward (DF) were derived.

In this paper, we investigate the relaying energy allocation scheme in the multi-user SWIPT relaying system based on the TS operation strategy, in which a source transmits its signals to K $(K \geq 2)$ destinations via the help of an energy-constrained relay. The relay uses the energy harvested in the energy harvesting mode to decode, then amplify and forward the information of each user one by one. This paper will study the energy allocation scheme of the "total information rate maximization" model.

The rest of this paper is organized as follows. Section 2 describes the system model. Section 3 discusses the information rate of user. Section 4 discusses the energy allocation scheme and simulation. Finally, the conclusions are given in Sect. 5.

Notation: The notation $CN(0, N_0)$ denotes a circularly symmetric complex Gaussian random variable with zero mean and variance N_0. $E[\cdot]$ and $|\cdot|$ denote the mathematical expectation and modulus value, respectively.

2 System Model

As shown in Fig. 1, this paper considers a multi-user SWIPT relaying system including a transmitter (Tx), a relay and K $(K \geq 2)$ receivers (Rx). The Tx and the Rx are equipped with single antenna. The relay is equipped with two antennas, one for receiving signals and the other for forwarding signals. It should be specially noted that the Tx and the Rx have energy supply devices, i.e., they have no energy limit. However, the relay has no energy supply devices, i.e., it is energy-constrained and operates by converting collected RF signals into electricity. The distance between the Tx and the relay is denoted as D_0, and the distance between the relay and the Rx of the i-th $(i = 1, \cdots, K)$ user is denoted as D_i.

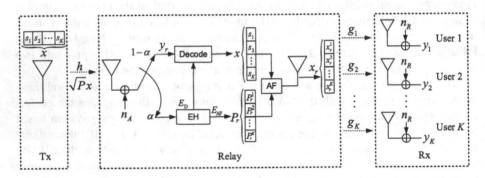

Fig. 1. System model

The Tx sends the information of all users to the relay. The relay decodes the received information, separates the information of each user, and then amplifies and forwards them to the receiver of each user. For the sake of discussion, we assume that the information of all users are correct after decoded and verified by the relay, and the relay will forward the information of all users. The receiver of the relay employs the TS strategy to receive signals. This paper considers a block-based transmission [16] of duration T. Thus, in the time of a transmission block, α proportion of time, i.e., αT, is used for EH, and $(1 - \alpha)$ proportion of time, i.e., $(1 - \alpha)T$, is used for information transmission. Correspondingly, the Tx transmits the energy signal (without the information of the user) within αT time, and the information signal (with the information of the user) within $(1 - \alpha)T$ time. After completing the EH process of a transmission block, the relay uses a part of the harvested energy for the circuit consumption in the information decoding process and the remaining energy to amplify and forward the information of each user.

The working states of two antennas of the relay for the information signals are shown in Table 1. Except for the first transmission block at the beginning of communication, the information transmitted by the transmitting antenna is the information received by the receiving antenna in the previous transmission block. It is assumed that the amount of information at the relay is conserved, i.e., the transmitting module can forward the information processed by the receiving module in real time, and there will be no situation that the transmitting module has no information to send or the information is accumulated in the transmitting module. It can be achieved by adjusting the transmitting power of the Tx and the time slot switching coefficient at the relay. This paper will mainly study the information rate of the relay to the receiver of the user.

Table 1. Working states of the relay antennas for the information signals.

Transmission block	Receiving antenna	Transmitting antenna
1	Receive the information of transmission block 1	free
2	Receive the information of transmission block 2	Transmit the information of transmission block 1
3	Receive the information of transmission block 3	Transmit the information of transmission block 2
...	...	...

As shown in Fig. 1, the Tx sends signal x to the relay, and x contains information sent to all users. s_i $(i = 1, \cdots, K)$ is baseband signal, and represents the information sent to the i-th user. The RF band signal is expressed as $\sqrt{P}x$ with the average transmitting power P. y_r is the information signal received by the relay and n_A represents the noise introduced by the receiving antenna of the relay, $n_A \sim CN(0, \sigma_A^2)$. Before forwarding information, the relay decodes x and separates the information of each user. At the Rx side, the signal received by the i-th user is expressed as y_i. Similarly, n_R represents the noise introduced by the receiving antenna of the Rx, $n_R \sim CN(0, \sigma_R^2)$. The link from the Tx to the relay is referred to as the downlink with channel gain $h > 0$, and the link from the relay to the Rx of the i-th user is referred to as the uplink with channel gain $g_i > 0$.

3 Information Rate

As shown in Fig. 1, the information signal x transmitted by the Tx is expressed as

$$x = \sum_{i=1}^{K} s_i \qquad (1)$$

where x satisfies $E[|x|^2] = 1$.

The information signal received by the relay is expressed as

$$y_r = \sqrt{h} \cdot \sqrt{P}x + n_A = \sqrt{hP} \cdot \sum_{i=1}^{K} s_i + n_A \tag{2}$$

During a transmission block time, the energy harvested by the relay is expressed as

$$E_{EH} = \eta hQ \cdot \alpha T \tag{3}$$

where η represents the energy conversion efficiency and Q represents the average power of the energy signal.

Defining the energy consumed by the relay for decoding information as E_D and the energy used for amplifying and forwarding signal as E_{AF}, we have

$$E_{EH} = E_D + E_{AF} \tag{4}$$

This paper assumes that E_D is a fixed value, i.e., $E_D = z \cdot \eta hQT$, where z is a fixed coefficient, and $z \in (0, \alpha)$.

Figure 2 shows the time and energy allocation schematic of the relay in the multi-user relaying system. The receiving module of the relay harvests energy E_{EH} during αT time and receives information signal during $(1 - \alpha)T$ time. Decoding information consumes the energy E_D. After decoding, the AF energy E_{AF} is divided into K parts by the transmitting module in a block T to forward the information signal of each user. The energy proportion of the i-th user is expressed as τ_i. In addition, this paper assumes that the relay sends signals to the receiver of the user by time division multiple address (TDMA), i.e., a transmission block (T) is divided into K time slots and the relay forwards the amplified signals to each user one by one. For the sake of discussion, it is assumed that the relay averagely divides the time of a transmission block (T) according to the number of users (K), i.e., the time for the relay to forward information of each user is $t_i = T/K$.

Therefore, the amplification power of the i-th user information signal is

$$P_r^i = \frac{\tau_i \cdot E_{AF}}{t_i} \tag{5}$$

The energy allocation proportions τ_i meets the following conditions,

$$\sum_{i=1}^{K} \tau_i \leq 1 \tag{6}$$

By substituting (3) and (4) into (5), we obtain

$$P_r^i = \frac{\tau_i \cdot \eta hQT(\alpha - z)}{T/K} = \tau_i \cdot \eta hKQ(\alpha - z) \tag{7}$$

After amplification, the signal sent to the i-th user can be expressed as

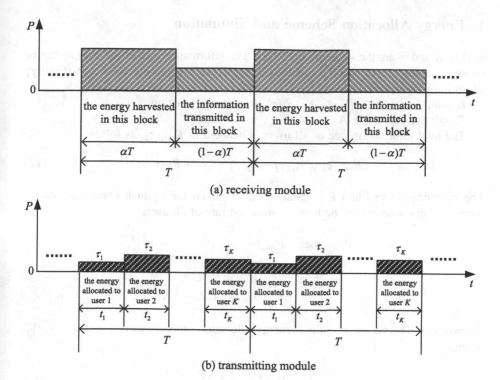

Fig. 2. Schematic of time and energy allocation

$$x_r^i = \sqrt{P_r^i} \cdot s_i = \sqrt{\tau_i \cdot \eta h K Q(\alpha - z)} \cdot s_i \tag{8}$$

The signal received by the i-th user from the relay can be expressed as

$$y_i = \sqrt{g_i} x_r^i + n_R = \sqrt{g_i \cdot \tau_i \cdot \eta h K Q(\alpha - z)} \cdot s_i + n_R \tag{9}$$

The signal to noise ratio (SNR) received by the i-th user is

$$SNR_i = \frac{\left(\sqrt{g_i \cdot \tau_i \cdot \eta h K Q(\alpha - z)}\right)^2}{\sigma_R^2} = \frac{g_i \cdot \tau_i \cdot \eta h K Q(\alpha - z)}{\sigma_R^2} \tag{10}$$

Therefore, the information rate of the i-th user receiving information is expressed as

$$R_i = \frac{1}{K} \cdot \log_2\left(1 + \frac{g_i \cdot \tau_i \cdot \eta h K Q(\alpha - z)}{\sigma_R^2}\right) = \frac{1}{K} \cdot \log_2(1 + \gamma_i \tau_i) \tag{11}$$

where $\gamma_i = \frac{g_i \eta h K Q(\alpha - z)}{\sigma_R^2}$.

4 Energy Allocation Scheme and Simulation

In (11), K and γ_i are the system parameters. The information rate of the user R_i can be viewed as a function of τ, and denoted as $R_i(\tau)$, where τ represents the vector of energy allocation proportions, i.e., $\tau = [\tau_1, \cdots, \tau_K]$.

Lemma: For any $i \in [1, \cdots, K]$, $R_i(\tau)$ is a convex function.

Proof: See Appendix A.

The total information rate of all users is denoted as $R_{sum}(\tau)$, as follows

$$R_{sum}(\tau) = R_1(\tau) + R_2(\tau) + \cdots + R_K(\tau) \tag{12}$$

The optimization problem P is established to obtain the optimal energy allocation scheme τ^* that maximizes the total information rate of all users.

$$\text{P}: \quad \max_{\tau} \quad R_{sum}(\tau)$$

$$\text{s.t.} \quad \sum_{i=1}^{K} \tau_i \le 1,$$

$$\tau_i \ge 0, \quad i = 1, 2, \cdots, K.$$

Proposition: The vector of optimal energy allocation proportions is $\tau^* = [\tau_1^*, \cdots, \tau_K^*]$, where

$$\tau_i^* = \frac{1}{K} - \frac{K-1}{K\gamma_i} + \frac{1}{K} \sum_{\substack{j=1 \\ j \ne i}}^{K} \frac{1}{\gamma_j} \tag{13}$$

Proof: See Appendix B.

In practical application, $h \propto D_0^{-\kappa_{sr}}$ ($\propto$ represents a proportional relationship), $g_i \propto D_i^{-\kappa_{rd}}$, $i = 1, 2, \cdots, K$, where $\kappa_{sr} (\kappa_{sr} \ge 2)$ and $\kappa_{rd} (\kappa_{rd} \ge 2)$ represent the path fading index of the downlink and the uplink, respectively. Therefore, according to (11), we have $\gamma_i \propto h g_i$.

In this simulation, we set $K = 2$, $D_2 = 2D_1$, $\kappa_{sr} = \kappa_{rd} = 2$, so the relationship between γ_1 and γ_2 is

$$\frac{\gamma_1}{\gamma_2} = \frac{g_1}{g_2} = \left(\frac{D_2}{D_1}\right)^{\kappa_{rd}} = 4 \tag{14}$$

Further, for convenience, γ_1 and γ_2 is set to 22 dB and 16 dB, respectively.

Figure 3 shows the information rates of the users for different energy allocation proportions in a two-user SWIPT relaying system. It is observed that the information rate increases with the increase of the energy allocation proportion.

Figure 4 is the schematic of the total information rates of the system corresponding to different energy allocation proportions. As shown in Fig. 4, along the direction of the arrow, the total information rate of the system increases. This is because when $0 < \tau_1 + \tau_2 < 1$, the relay does not fully allocate the energy to all time slots. According to (11), for each user, R_i increases with the increase of τ_i, which it can also be seen in

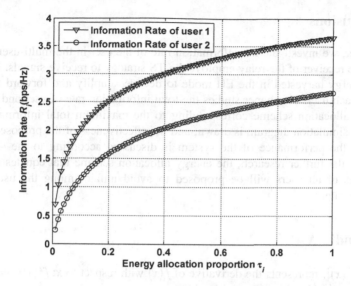

Fig. 3. Information rate (in bps/Hz) of the user versus energy allocation proportion

Fig. 3. Therefore, the maximum value of the total information rate of the system is obtained at $\tau_1 + \tau_2 = 1$. In Fig. 4, the point P represents the energy allocation proportions corresponding to the maximum total information rate of the system, i.e., $\tau^* = [0.5094, 0.4906]$. At the optimal value τ^*, $R_{sum}(\tau^*) = 5.356\,\text{bps/Hz}$; according to (11), $R_1(\tau^*) = 3.176\,\text{bps/Hz}$ and $R_2(\tau^*) = 2.180\,\text{bps/Hz}$.

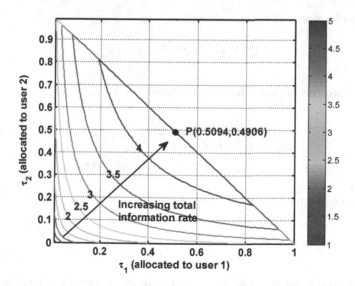

Fig. 4. Total information rate (in bps/Hz) versus energy allocation proportion

5 Conclusions

In this paper, we investigate the information rate of the user in the multi-user relaying system. The receiver of the relay employs the TS strategy to receive signals. The relay uses the energy harvested in the EH mode to decode, amplify and forward the information of each user. This paper studies the total information rate of user and proposes the energy allocation scheme corresponding to the maximum total information rate. Finally, the simulation diagram is drawn, and the effectiveness of the proposed scheme to improve the performance of the system is discussed according to the simulation diagram. In the further research, the energy allocation scheme that equates the information rates of all users will be proposed to avoid unfair among the users in the information rate.

6 Appendix A

Notation: $f^1(x)|_x$ represents the derivative of $f(x)$ with respect to x; $f^2(x)|_x$ denotes the derivative of $f^1(x)|_x$ with respect to x.

In (11), taking the first and second derivatives of $R_i(\tau)$ with respect to τ_i, we obtain

$$\nabla R_i(\tau) = \frac{1}{K} \cdot \frac{1}{\ln 2} \cdot \frac{\gamma_i}{1 + \gamma_i \cdot \tau_i} \tag{15}$$

$$\nabla^2 R_i(\tau) = \frac{1}{K} \cdot \frac{1}{\ln 2} \cdot \frac{-\gamma_i^2}{(1 + \gamma_i \cdot \tau_i)^2} \tag{16}$$

The Hessian matrix of $R_i(\tau)$ is defined as

$$\nabla^2 R_i(\tau) = \left[d_{jj}^{(i)} \right], \quad 1 \le j \le K \tag{17}$$

where $d_{jj}^{(i)}$ represents the entry for row j, column j of $\nabla^2 R_i(\tau)$, and

$$d_{jj}^{(i)} = \begin{cases} \dfrac{1}{K} \cdot \dfrac{1}{\ln 2} \cdot \dfrac{-\gamma_i^2}{(1 + \gamma_i \cdot \tau_i)^2} &, \quad j = i \\ 0 &, \quad \text{others} \end{cases} \tag{18}$$

For any real vector $v = [v_1, \cdots, v_K]^T$, we have

$$v^T \nabla^2 R_i(\tau) v = \frac{1}{K \cdot \ln 2} \cdot \frac{-\gamma_i^2}{(1 + \gamma_i \cdot \tau_i)^2} \cdot v_i^2 \le 0 \tag{19}$$

i.e., $\nabla^2 R_i(\tau)$ is a negative semidefinite matrix for any i; therefore, $R_i(\tau)$ is a convex function of $\tau = [\tau_1, \cdots, \tau_K]$.

7 Appendix B

The Lagrangian of the problem P can be expressed as

$$L_{sum}(\tau, \upsilon) = R_{sum}(\tau) - \upsilon\left(\sum_{i=1}^{K} \tau_i - 1\right) \tag{20}$$

where υ represents the lagrangian multiplier. Taking the first derivative of $L_{sum}(\tau, \upsilon)$ with respect to υ and τ_i, respectively, we have

$$L_{sum}(\tau, \upsilon)^1\big|_{\upsilon} = \sum_{i=1}^{K} \tau_i - 1 \tag{21}$$

$$L_{sum}(\tau, \upsilon)^1\big|_{\tau_i} = \frac{\partial}{\partial \tau_i} R_{sum}(\tau) - \upsilon, \quad i = 1, \cdots, K \tag{22}$$

Making $L_{sum}(\tau, \upsilon)^1\big|_{\upsilon} = 0$ and $L_{sum}(\tau, \upsilon)^1\big|_{\tau_i} = 0$, we have

$$\sum_{i=1}^{K} \tau_i - 1 = 0 \tag{23}$$

$$\frac{1}{K} \cdot \frac{1}{\ln 2} \cdot \frac{\gamma_i}{1 + \gamma_i \cdot \tau_i} - \upsilon = 0, \quad i = 1, \cdots, K \tag{24}$$

According to (23), we can get

$$\sum_{i=1}^{K} \tau_i = 1 \tag{25}$$

According to (24), we can get

$$\frac{\gamma_i}{1 + \gamma_i \cdot \tau_i} = K\upsilon \cdot \ln 2 = \text{constant} \tag{26}$$

So, we have

$$\frac{\gamma_1}{1 + \gamma_1 \cdot \tau_1} = \frac{\gamma_2}{1 + \gamma_2 \cdot \tau_2} = \cdots = \frac{\gamma_K}{1 + \gamma_K \cdot \tau_K} \tag{27}$$

According to $\frac{\gamma_1}{1+\gamma_1 \cdot \tau_1} = \frac{\gamma_2}{1+\gamma_2 \cdot \tau_2}$, we have

$$\tau_2 = \frac{1}{\gamma_1} - \frac{1}{\gamma_2} + \tau_1 \tag{28}$$

Similarly, we can obtain

$$\tau_i = \frac{1}{\gamma_1} - \frac{1}{\gamma_i} + \tau_1, \quad i = 2, \cdots, K \tag{29}$$

Combined with $\sum_{i=1}^{K} \tau_i = 1$, we can get

$$\tau_1 + \left(\frac{1}{\gamma_1} - \frac{1}{\gamma_2} + \tau_1\right) + \cdots + \left(\frac{1}{\gamma_1} - \frac{1}{\gamma_K} + \tau_1\right) = 1 \tag{30}$$

Further, we have

$$K\tau_1 + \frac{K-1}{\gamma_1} - \sum_{j=2}^{K} \frac{1}{\gamma_j} = 1 \tag{31}$$

So, we obtain

$$\tau_1 = \frac{1}{K} - \frac{K-1}{K\gamma_1} + \frac{1}{K}\sum_{j=2}^{K}\frac{1}{\gamma_j} \tag{32}$$

By substituting (32) into (28), we obtain

$$\tau_2 = \frac{1}{K} - \frac{K-1}{K\gamma_2} + \frac{1}{K}\sum_{\substack{j=1 \\ j \neq 2}}^{K}\frac{1}{\gamma_j} \tag{33}$$

Similarly, we can get

$$\tau_i = \frac{1}{K} - \frac{K-1}{K\gamma_i} + \frac{1}{K}\sum_{\substack{j=1 \\ j \neq i}}^{K}\frac{1}{\gamma_j}, \quad i = 1, \cdots, K \tag{34}$$

Acknowledgments. This work was supported by the National Natural Science Foundation of China (Grant No. 51877151, 61372011), and Program for Innovative Research Team in University of Tianjin (Grant No. TD13-5040).

References

1. Visser, H.J., Vullers, R.J.M.: RF energy harvesting and transport for wireless sensor network applications: principles and requirements. Proc. IEEE **101**(6), 1410–1423 (2013)
2. Nishimoto, H., Kawahara, Y., Asami, T.: Prototype implementation of ambient RF energy harvesting wireless sensor networks. In: 2010 IEEE Sensors Conference, pp. 1282–1287 (2010)

3. Zhang, X., Jiang, H., Zhang, L., Zhang, C., Wang, Z., Chen, X.: An energy-efficient ASIC for wireless body sensor networks in medical applications. IEEE Trans. Biomed. Circuits Syst. **4**(1), 11–18 (2010)
4. Lu, X., Niyato, D., Wang, P., Kim, D., Han, Z.: Wireless charger networking for mobile devices: fundamentals, standards, and applications. IEEE Wirel. Commun. **22**(2), 126–135 (2015)
5. Varshney, L.R.: Transporting information and energy simultaneously. In: 2008 IEEE International Symposium on Information Theory, pp. 1612–1616 (2008)
6. Lu, X., Wang, P., Niyato, D., Kim, D., Han, Z.: Wireless networks with RF energy harvesting: a contemporary survey. IEEE Commun. Surv. Tutor. **17**(2), 757–789 (2015)
7. Zhang, R., Ho, C.K.: MIMO broadcasting for simultaneous wireless information and power transfer. IEEE Trans. Wirel. Commun. **12**(5), 1989–2001 (2013)
8. Liu, L., Zhang, R., Chua, K.C.: Wireless information transfer with opportunistic energy harvesting. IEEE Trans. Wirel. Commun. **12**(1), 288–300 (2013)
9. Zhou, X., Zhang, R., Ho, C.K.: Wireless information and power transfer: architecture design and rate-energy tradeoff. IEEE Trans. Commun. **61**(11), 4754–4767 (2013)
10. Peng, C., Li, F., Liu, H.: Optimal power splitting in two-way decode-and-forward relay networks. IEEE Commun. Lett. **21**(9), 2009–2012 (2017)
11. Zhong, S., Huang, H., Li, R.: Outage probability of power splitting SWIPT two-way relay networks in Nakagami-m fading. Eurasip J. Wirel. Commun. Netw. **1**, 11 (2018)
12. Li, D., Shen, C., Qiu, Z.: Sum rate maximization and energy harvesting for two-way of relay systems with imperfect CSI. In: 2013 IEEE International Conference on Acoustics, Speech and Signal Processing, pp. 4958–4962 (2013)
13. Li, Q., Zhang, Q., Qin, J.: Secure relay beamforming for simultaneous wireless information and power transfer in nonregenerative relay networks. IEEE Trans. Veh. Technol. **63**(5), 2462–2467 (2014)
14. Krikidis, I., Timotheou, S., Sasaki, S.: RF energy transfer for cooperative networks: data relaying or energy harvesting? IEEE Commun. Lett. **16**(11), 1772–1775 (2012)
15. Krikidis, I., Sasaki, S., Timotheou, S., Ding, Z.: A low complexity antenna switching for joint wireless information and energy transfer in MIMO relay channels. IEEE Trans. Commun. **62**(5), 1577–1587 (2014)
16. Assanovich, B.A.: Two schemes for block-based transmission of variable-length codes. In: 2008 IEEE Region 8 International Conference on Computational Technologies in Electrical and Electronics Engineering, pp. 253–256 (2008)

Optimization of AODV Routing Protocol in UAV Ad Hoc Network

Jianze Wu[1(⊠)], Shuo Shi[1,2], Zhongyue Liu[1], and Xuemai Gu[1,2]

[1] Harbin Institute of Technology, Harbin 150001, Heilongjiang, China
wujianze_hit@163.com, crcss@hit.edu.cn
[2] Pengcheng Laboratory, Shenzhen, China

Abstract. According to high-speed mobile nodes in unmanned aerial vehicles (UAV) Ad Hoc network to bring the network topology changes frequently, link time is short, and node energy is limited, this paper puts forward an optimized AODV protocol (EV-AODV) based on residual energy and relative movement speed of nodes. Simulation results show that EV-AODV routing protocol proposed improves the packet delivery ration and network life time compared with traditional AODV protocols. It is better suitable for the networks environment with UAV Ad Hoc network.

Keywords: UAV · AODV · High-speed mobile nodes · Link stability · EV-AODV

1 Introduction

The UAV ad hoc network developed by the vehicle self-organizing net-work completes the communication between the drones through dynamic networking, and has the characteristics of high dynamic topology, self-organization, no center and multi-hop, but the link is easy to break and it is difficult to meet the network performance requirements of military drones [1–4]. In the process of establishing a link in the AODV routing protocol, the established link between the two nodes is easily broken due to the mobility and energy consumption of the nodes in the network, and the link survival time is short.

There have been many improvements to the problem of unmanned self-organizing network routing. The energy-improved AODV-E routing protocol [5] selects links with few hops and high node energy for data transmission to avoid the fracture problem, but does not fundamentally reduce the node energy consumption. The cognitive-based AODV routing protocol [6] selects links with a large average number of neighbor nodes to transmit data to improve the success rate of link repair, but in-creases the storage space. The AODV routing protocol based on local route repair [7] uses a two-hop local repair mechanism to save resources and reduce end-to-end delay, but the link repair mode is limited by the location of the break, and the repair speed is slow. These improvements are mainly for networks with low node movement speeds, not for fast moving speeds.

In this paper, an improved AODV (EV-AODV) routing protocol is proposed for the problems of high node mobility, fast network topology change and unstable link

S. Han et al. (Eds.): AICON 2019, LNICST 286, pp. 472–478, 2019.
https://doi.org/10.1007/978-3-030-22968-9_43

connection. EV-AODV considers the energy and relative moving speed factors, and makes some improvements to the routing process to achieve efficient energy utilization, improve the quality of the selected link, and achieve the purpose of prolonging the network lifetime.

2 Optimization of AODV Routing Protocol

2.1 Link Stability

The stability of the link in the UAV ad hoc network is affected by many factors. UAV nodes move faster, and each node has different load and power consumption conditions, and the stability of links between nodes is different. Therefore, it is difficult to establish a stable and long-lasting link, and the broken chain the probability of road reconstruction is not high. The traditional AODV routing protocol uses the hop count as the metric to select the transmission path. It does not consider the link state. It is easy to select the path with unstable links. Especially in an environment where the network topology changes rapidly, the route is frequently interrupted, affecting the network performance. For the scenario where the node moves faster and the network topology changes drastically, the traditional AODV protocol is obviously not applicable. For this reason, we propose an improved AODV protocol (EV-AODV). It defines routing stability in the UAV ad hoc network and selects in the routing process with the routing stability as the metric.

We define E_0 as the initial energy of the node, generally a fixed value, and E_i is the residual energy of the node i, so the energy residual ratio η_i of the node i can be expressed as:

$$\eta_i = \frac{E_i}{E_o} \tag{1}$$

To measure the relative mobility of the two nodes, we define V_{ij} as the relative velocity between node i and node j, which can be expressed as:

$$V_{ij} = \sqrt{(v_{ix} - v_{jx})^2 + (v_{iy} - v_{jy})^2} \tag{2}$$

In Eq. (2), v_{ix} and v_{jx} represent the velocity components in the horizontal direction representing node i and node j, v_{iy} and v_{jy} represent the velocity components in the vertical direction representing node i and node j. Normalize the relative movement speed between nodes, we define σ_{ij} as the relative movement rate between node i and node j:

$$\sigma_{ij} = \frac{V_{ij}}{V_{ijmax}} = \frac{\sqrt{(v_{ix} - v_{jx})^2 + (v_{iy} - v_{jy})^2}}{|v_i| + |v_j|} \tag{3}$$

The EV-AODV routing protocol proposed in this paper comprehensively considers the node energy residual rate and the relative mobility of the nodes. On the basis of the normalization process, the energy consumption rate and the relative mobility rate are weighted, and the route cost of node i is defined as:

$$EV_i = \alpha(1 - \eta_i) + \beta\sigma_{ij} = \alpha\frac{E_0 - E_i}{E_0} + \beta\frac{V_{ij}}{V_{max}} \tag{4}$$

In formula (4), EV_i is the route cost of node i, $1 - \eta_i$ represents the energy consumption rate of node i, α and β are the weighted parameters, and they satisfy $\alpha + \beta = 1$. We choose the appropriate weighting coefficient for different network. The more residual energy of a node, the smaller the relative mobility, the higher the stability of the node. Therefore, the smaller the value of EV_i, the higher the stability of node i.

$$EV = \sum_{i=0}^{N} EV_i = \sum_{i=0}^{N} [\alpha(1 - \eta_i) + \beta\sigma_{ij}] \, j \in [i+1, N] \tag{5}$$

EV is the stability of the entire path, N is the number of nodes on the path. According to Eq. (5), we define the function of selecting the best route for the EV-AODV protocol as

$$PathSelect\langle source, dest\rangle = \min[EV(k)] \, k \in [1, M] \tag{6}$$

In formula (6), M is the number of available paths. We choose the path with the smallest EV value as the best transmission path.

2.2   Improvements in Route Discovery

The traditional AODV protocol finds routes based on hop count and network delay. The intermediate node and the destination node only forward and respond to RREQ packets with short delay and few hops. However, the route constructed according to this standard has a big problem in a highly dynamic network, and a route interruption or destruction may occur in a short time in the future. Therefore, the improved AODV protocol takes into account the stability factor of the link. For the received RREQ, the power of the received signal of the node, the hop count of the link, the remaining energy of the node, and the stability of the forwarding link are considered. Construct a stable path based on it.

When the source node wants to send a packet to the destination node, if there is no valid route to the destination node, the source node will initiate the route discovery process. In the route discovery process, the source node obtains its own horizontal split speed, vertical split speed, and remaining energy into the new data field of the RREQ message, and makes the initial value of the *EV* in the message 0, and then the message The broadcast is sent to the neighboring node; each node that receives the RREQ message first obtains its own horizontal and vertical speeds, and after calculating the previous route stability coefficient by the formula (1) to formula (4), Then use formula (5) to accumulate it in the new data field *EV*. After the RREQ packet arrives at the destination node, the destination node sends back a RREP packet along the original route, and the packet records the final *EV* value of the link. The source node receives multiple RREP packets within a specified time. After discovering multiple routes, according to formula (6), the path with the smallest *EV* is selected as the transmission route.

3 Simulation Analysis

3.1 Simulation Environment

The experiment uses network simulation software NS to simulate and compare the traditional AODV and the EV-AODV routing protocol. The topology environment of the network is composed of 100 mobile nodes according to the random waypoint model. The nodes are randomly distributed in the simulation area of 1500 m × 1500 m. The moving speed of the nodes is between 5 and 30 m/s, and the dwell time is 0, the attenuation law of the wireless signal conforms to the dual-ray ground reflection model, the wireless bandwidth is 2Mbps, the effective wireless transmission range is 250 m, and the link layer protocol uses IEEE 802.11 DCF (Distributed Coordination Function). The initial energy of the node is 10 J, the transmission power is 0.6 W, the receiving power is 0.3 W, the simulation time is 600 s, and the average value of 10 simulation results is taken.

3.2 Simulation Results and Performance Analysis

We evaluate the impact of EV-AODV on reliability and effectiveness by comparing the difference in average packet arrival rate between AODV and EV-AODV protocols, and evaluate the improvement of EV-AODV by simulating average node lifetime. In this simulation, we take the weight coefficient of *EV* as $\alpha = \beta = 0.5$.

It can be seen from Fig. 1 that as the node moves faster, the packet delivery rate decreases. At the same rate, the EV-AODV packet delivery rate is higher than that of AODV, because EV-AODV considers the relative mobility of nodes and the relative mobility between nodes, increasing the probability of participation of high-energy nodes and relatively stable nodes, and routing requests. The response is not blindly performed, effectively reducing the probability of link disconnection and improving the packet delivery rate.

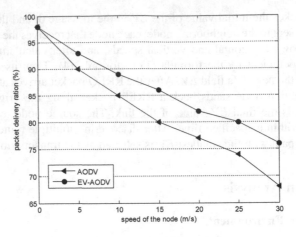

Fig. 1. Packet delivery ration

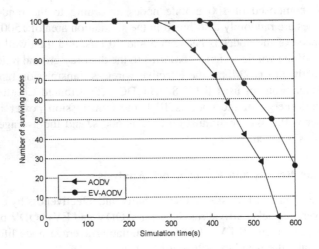

Fig. 2. Number of surviving nodes

As can be seen from Fig. 2, the classic AODV routing protocol begins to have the first node failure around 280 s, while the EV-AODV routing protocol takes about 380 s to appear the first failed node. At the simulation time of 600 s, the EV-AODV routing protocol has 25 surviving nodes, while the classic AODV routing protocol has no remaining nodes.

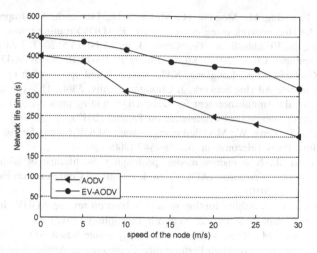

Fig. 3. Network life time

It can be seen from Fig. 3 that the network lifetime decreases with the increase of the node rate, but the EV-AODV route improvement scheme adopts the energy threshold and the route request forwarding rule to avoid the probability of participation of lower energy nodes, so that the established route is established. The probability of link breakage is reduced, which effectively prolongs network lifetime.

4 Conclusions

Aiming at the instability of UAV ad hoc network, a new EV-AODV protocol algorithm is proposed. In the process of link establishment, we comprehensively consider the residual energy of the node and the relative mobility between the nodes, and define the parameter *EV* that measures the stability of the route, by selecting the link with the lowest *EV* value and the link is stable. The simulation results show that EV-AODV has higher packet delivery rate when the node has higher mobility, which improves the link life and significantly prolongs the network lifetime. In addition, EV-AODV can flexibly adjust the weighting factors to meet more network environments.

References

1. Yadav, M.K., Kant, C.: Selective flooding based improved AODV routing protocol in MANETs: analysis & implementation. Wirel. Commun. **3**, 245–253 (2012)
2. Lin, L., et al.: A geographic mobility prediction routing protocol for Ad Hoc UAV Network. In: Globecom Workshops (2012)
3. Pu, C.: Link-quality and traffic-load aware routing for UAV Ad Hoc networks. In: 2018 IEEE 4th International Conference on Collaboration and Internet Computing (CIC) (2018)
4. Mallapur, S.V., Terdal, S.: Enhanced ad-hoc on demand multipath distance vector routing protocol. Int. J. Comput. Sci. Inf. Secur. **7**(3), 21–30 (2010)

5. Faouzi, H., Er-rouidi, M., Moudni, H., Mouncif, H., Lamsaadi, M.: Improving network lifetime of Ad Hoc network using energy Aodv (E-AODV) routing protocol in real radio environments. In: El Abbadi, A., Garbinato, B. (eds.) NETYS 2017. LNCS, vol. 10299, pp. 27–39. Springer, Cham (2017). https://doi.org/10.1007/978-3-319-59647-1_3
6. Liang, J., Xiaoliang, M.A., Longlong, X.U.: Research and optimization of AODV routing protocols in mobile Ad Hoc network. J. Chongqing Univ. **38**(4), 152–158 (2015)
7. Saadi, Y.A., et al.: An enhancement for DH-AODV routing protocol by using local route repair. In: Fourth International Conference on Parallel (2017)
8. Zhang, Z., Pei, T., Zeng, W.: Modified energy-aware AODV routing for Ad Hoc networks. J. Nanjing Inst. Posts Telecommun. **3**, 338–342 (2004)
9. Malek, A.G., et al.: New energy model: prolonging the lifetime of ad-hoc on-demand distance vector routing protocols (AODV). In: International Conference on Future Computer & Communication (2010)
10. Yang, H., Li, Z.Y.: A stablity routing protocols base on reverse AODV. In: International Conference on Computer Science & Network Technology (2012)
11. Kumar, R., Gupta, M.: Route stability and energy aware based AODV in MANET. In: International Conference on High Performance Computing & Applications (2015)

A KFL-TDOA UWB Positioning Method Based on Hybrid Location Algorithm

Shuo Shi[✉], Meng Wang, and Kunqi Hong

Harbin Institute of Technology, Harbin 150001, Heilongjiang, China
crcss@hit.edu.cn, wangmeng_hit@163.com,
neverlietoyourself@foxtail.com

Abstract. For the improvement of accuracy and efficiency of indoor positioning in complex environment, this paper proposed a new positioning method, which combined Ultra-Wide Band (UWB) based on time difference of arrival (TDOA) with linearized Kalman filters (KFL-TDOA), in order to obtain more accurate and stable positioning results. On this basis, two classic location algorithms, Chan and Taylor series expansion algorithm, were integrated to get lower Root Mean Square Error (RMSE) and better anti-interference performance under non-sight-of-light (NLOS) and multipath effect, compared with using them separately. The proposed method considered interference both in ranging phase and positioning phase caused by complex indoor environment. Simulation case studies were conducted to demonstrate how the proposed method was implemented and the simulation results showed that compared with traditional TDOA based positioning method, the proposed method has improvement in positioning accuracy and stability both in ideal environment and interference environment if the parameters were set reasonable.

Keywords: UWB indoor positioning · Kalman filtering · TDOA · Chan algorithm · Taylor series expansion algorithm

1 Introduction

Global Positioning System (GPS) is the most widely used positioning method in outdoor positioning, however, due to the blocking of buildings, especially multiple walls, satellite signals cannot piece through indoors, which leads to the development of indoor positioning [1]. In recent years, there is a wide range of needs for indoor positioning in various areas, including security, smart cities, medical, factories and so on. Currently, popular indoor positioning technology includes WiFi, Bluetooth, UWB and so on [2]. Among them, UWB positioning has its advantage of high accuracy and anti-interference because of its strong signal penetration and wide bandwidth, however under an environment with serious interference, the performance of positioning will still be greatly affected [3].

Compared with outdoor environment, the indoor environment is more complex. Obstacles and walls will reflect or even block the transmission of the positioning signal results in NLOS and multipath effect, which will reduce the accuracy of position results. At present, TDOA is the most extensive technology in wireless location system,

S. Han et al. (Eds.): AICON 2019, LNICST 286, pp. 479–487, 2019.
https://doi.org/10.1007/978-3-030-22968-9_44

on the basis of base station clock synchronization, the main error comes from the weaken of signal [4]. Traditional TDOA based location algorithm such as Chan algorithm and Taylor expansion algorithm and so on, only when the measurement error obeys zero mean Gaussian distribution can these algorithms have high precisions [5]. [6, 7] propose a hybrid location algorithm based on Chan and Taylor series expansion, however, in a real indoor environment, NLOS errors and multipath effects are often unavoidable, the simulation conditions is too ideal to reflect real systems.

Aiming at proposing a high-precision positioning algorithm that is practical to the actual environment, and improving the stability to external disturbances, this paper comes up with a TDOA based UWB indoor positioning method combined with Kalman filtering, using a hybrid location of Chan and Taylor expansion algorithm. The method considers noises in both the measurement phase and the positioning phase with its advantages of high stability and accuracy. To verify the algorithm, we build a UWB positioning system of 4 anchors with a target doing linear motion. Since measurement error exists during the process of mobile station (MS) and base station (BS) ranging, Kalman filtering is used to filter out mutation measurement data and fluctuation noise. To have a stable performance, we combine the Chan algorithm with Taylor series expansion algorithm. The simulation results shows that compared with traditional positioning method, the RMSE lows and the positioning performance in strong interference improves significantly.

The rest of paper is organized as follows: Sect. 2 gives a basic description of TDOA based UWB Positioning Theory. The KFL-TDOA positioning method is given in Sect. 3. Section 4 elaborates the hybrid positioning algorithm. Field evaluation on both positioning accuracy and precision are presented in Sect. 5 in the form of MATLAB simulation results. The paper is briefly summarized in Sect. 6.

2   TDOA Based UWB Positioning Principle

The TDOA principle determined the target coordinates by computing the difference in propagation time of a signal from a MS to a BS. Each time propagation difference corresponding to a distance difference, so that a hyperbolic equation with the focus of two corresponding BSs can be obtained. In order to get the position of the MS, at least two sets of TDOA differences should be measured, which means at least three BSs are needed. The intersection of the two hyperbolars is the estimated position of the target [8]. [9] presents that the position accuracy increases as the number of BSs increases. Let (x, y) be the unknown MS position, and (X_i, Y_i) be the position of different BSs. The distance between MS and BSi R_i is given by:

$$R_i = \sqrt{(X_i - x)^2 + (Y_i - y)^2} \tag{1}$$

The distance difference refer to BS1 is given by:

$$R_{i,1} = c\tau_{i,1} = R_i - R_1 \tag{2}$$

where c is the speed of light, $\tau_{i,1}$ is the TDOA value.

A variety of positioning algorithms are based on the study of the speciality of TDOA hyperbolic equations. Figure 1 shows the basic principles of TDOA.

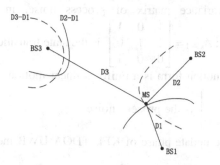

Fig. 1. TDOA positioning schematic

Current mainstream positioning methods based on TDOA principle, such as Chan algorithm, Taylor series expansion algorithm can have high precision only under low interference environment. In practical systems, noise and measurement errors is unavoidable, on the aim of targeting an algorithm which performs well in harsh environment, this paper use Kalman filter to reduce measurement error caused by noise.

3 KFL-TDOA Positioning Method

The real indoor environment is normally complex and full of noise and interference, which will cause the loss of positioning precision. Kalman filtering is used in this paper to restore the state of the real system from measurement noise, making this positioning method practical.

It is assumption that UWB indoor positioning's motion mode is linear. We set the state vectors as follows:

$$X_K = (x_k, y_k, v_k)^T \tag{3}$$

The fundamental equations of Kalman filtering include state equation and observation equation. The following state transition equations can be established:

$$\begin{bmatrix} x_k \\ y_k \\ v_k \end{bmatrix} = \begin{bmatrix} 1 & 0 & 1 \\ 1 & 1 & 0 \\ 0 & 0 & 1 \end{bmatrix} \begin{bmatrix} x_{k-1} \\ y_{k-1} \\ v_{k-1} \end{bmatrix} + \begin{bmatrix} 1 & 0 \\ 0 & 1 \\ 0 & 0 \end{bmatrix} \begin{bmatrix} w_{x/k-1} \\ w_{y/k-1} \end{bmatrix} \tag{4}$$

where $w_{x/k-1}$ and $w_{y/k-1}$ are the process noise in x and y directions respectively, the standard form of Kalman filter prediction equation is given as follows:

$$X_{k+1/k} = A_{k+1}X_{k/k} + W_{k+1} \tag{5}$$

$$P_{k+1/k} = A_{k+1}P_{k/k}A_{k+1}^T + Q_w \tag{6}$$

where $X_{k+1/k}$ is the predicted state estimate; $P_{k+1/k}$ is the predicted estimate covariance; Q_w is the covariance matrix of process noise, in this paper, we take

$Q_w = \begin{bmatrix} 10 & 0 & 0 \\ 0 & 10 & 0 \\ 0 & 0 & 20 \end{bmatrix}$; $A_{k+1} = \begin{bmatrix} 1 & 0 & 1 \\ 1 & 1 & 0 \\ 0 & 0 & 1 \end{bmatrix}$ is the state transition model which means

in the ideal state, the motion form is a uniform linear motion in the direction of 45°;

$W_{k+1} = \begin{bmatrix} 1 & 0 \\ 0 & 1 \\ 0 & 0 \end{bmatrix} \begin{bmatrix} w_{x/k-1} \\ w_{y/k-1} \end{bmatrix}$ is the process noise.

The formulas in the update phase of KFL-TDOA UWB method is:

$$K_{k+1} = P_{k+1/k}H_{k+1}^T(H_{k+1}P_{k+1}H_{k+1}^T + R_k) \tag{7}$$

$$X_{k+1/k+1} = X_{k+1/k} + K_{k+1}(Z_{k+1} - H_{k+1}X_{k+1/k}) \tag{8}$$

$$P_{k+1/k+1} = (I - K_{k+1}H_{k+1})P_{k+1/k} \tag{9}$$

where K is the Kalman gain; $X_{k+1/k+1}$ is updated state estimate; $P_{k+1/k+1}$ is updated estimate covariance; R_k is covariance matrix observation noise; $H = \begin{bmatrix} 1 & 0 & 0 \end{bmatrix}$ is the observation model.

The KFL-TDOA UWB positioning method executes the formulas in every loop, simulation results shows that under harsh environment the output data is stable and smooth, effectively reduces the impact of measurement errors and noise.

4 Hybrid Positioning Algorithm

Currently, two classical positioning algorithms based on TDOA equations are being widely used, one is Chan algorithm, the other is Taylor series expansion algorithm. These two algorithms have different characteristics, Chan algorithm has low complexity, only need two iterations can it derive the target position and the result does not depend on the selection of the initial value [10]. Taylor series expansion algorithm has a higher positioning accuracy, but depends on the selection of the initial value. In previous literature, the two algorithms are integrated on the aim of obtaining respective advantages. Use Chan algorithm to obtain initial coordinates, then use Taylor series expansion algorithm to iterates the final positioning results.

The Chan algorithm has two iterations, by linearizing the TDOA equations, past work has proved that take R_1 as unknown, the equation can be transformed into linear equations on x, y and $R = \sqrt{x^2 + y^2}$. When the number of BSs is larger than 4, the first estimated position is given as:

$$Z_a \approx (G_a^T Q^{-1} G_a)^{-1} G_a^T Q^{-1} h \tag{10}$$

where

$$G_a = - \begin{bmatrix} x_{2,1} & y_{2,1} & R_{2,1} \\ x_{3,1} & y_{3,1} & R_{3,1} \\ \cdot & \cdot & \cdot \\ \cdot & \cdot & \cdot \\ \cdot & \cdot & \cdot \\ x_{m,1} & y_{m,1} & R_{m,1} \end{bmatrix}; \quad h = \frac{1}{2} \begin{bmatrix} R_{2,1}^2 - x_2^2 - y_2^2 + x_1^2 + y_1^2 \\ R_{3,1}^2 - x_3^2 - y_3^2 + x_1^2 + y_1^2 \\ \cdot \\ \cdot \\ \cdot \\ R_{m,1}^2 - x_m^2 - y_m^2 + x_1^2 + y_1^2 \end{bmatrix}$$

Q is the covariance matrix of TDOA, (x_i, y_i) is the i-th BS's coordinates, $(x_{i,1}, y_{i,1})$ is the difference of the i-th BS and the first BS, $R_{i,1}$ is MS to the distance difference between the i-th and the first BS. The second estimated position is given as:

$$Z_a' = (G_a'^T \varphi'^{-1} G_a')^{-1} G_a'^T \varphi'^{-1} h' \tag{11}$$

where $G_a' = \begin{bmatrix} 1 & 0 \\ 0 & 1 \\ 1 & 1 \end{bmatrix}$; $\varphi' = 4B' \text{cov}(z_a) B'$; $B' = diag\{x^0 - X_1, y^0 - Y_1, R_1^0\}$; $\text{cov}(z_a) = E[\Delta z_a \Delta z_a^T] = (G_a^{0T} \varphi^{-1} G_a^0)^{-1}$, the final result is given as follows:

$$Z_P = \sqrt{Z_a'} + \begin{bmatrix} X_1 \\ Y_1 \end{bmatrix} \tag{12}$$

Take Z_P as the initial value of Taylor series expansion algorithm.

The Taylor sequence expansion is a recursive algorithm that requires an initial estimated position, and the estimated position is improved by solving the local least squares (LS) solution of the TDOA measurement error in each recursion. For a set of TDOA measurements, the algorithm first performs Taylor expansion on the selected MS initial position (x0, y0), ignoring the second order component, which translates to:

$$M = G\Delta + \varepsilon \tag{13}$$

$$G = \begin{bmatrix} (X_1 - x)/R_1 - (X_2 - x)/R_2 & (Y_1 - y)/R_1 - (Y_2 - y)/R_2 \\ (X_1 - x)/R_1 - (X_3 - x)/R_3 & (Y_1 - y)/R_1 - (Y_3 - y)/R_3 \\ \cdot & \cdot \\ \cdot & \cdot \\ \cdot & \cdot \\ (X_1 - x)/R_1 - (X_m - x)/R_m & (Y_1 - y)/R_1 - (Y_m - y)/R_m \end{bmatrix}$$

$$M = \begin{bmatrix} R_{2,1} - (R_2 - R_1) \\ R_{3,1} - (R_3 - R_1) \\ \cdot \\ \cdot \\ \cdot \\ R_{m,1} - (R_m - R_1) \end{bmatrix}; \Delta = \begin{bmatrix} \Delta x \\ \Delta y \end{bmatrix}; \varepsilon \text{ is the error of the algorithm.}$$

According to the weighted least squares algorithm, the covariance matrix Q of the TDOA measurement error is approximated by the approximation matrix of the error ε to obtain the estimate result, given as follows:

$$\Delta = (G^T Q^{-1} G)^{-1} G^T Q^{-1} M \qquad (14)$$

In the next iteration, take $x = x_0 + \Delta x$, $y = y_0 + \Delta y$ the algorithm stops when $|\Delta x| + |\Delta y| < \sigma$, σ is a threshold value. The final (x, y) is the positioning result. Figure 2 shows the complete process of the positioning method proposed in this paper.

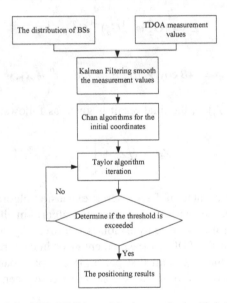

Fig. 2. The process of the KFL-TDOA positioning method with hybrid location algorithm

5   Simulation Verification

In this section, the MATLAB simulation results is given to verify the performance of the algorithms mentioned above. Considering that indoor positioning objects do approximate linear motion in most cases, we use a uniform linear motion along a 45-degree angle as a mathematical model. The simulation condition is followed: The coordinates of 4 anchors is set in advance, $BS1(0,0)$, $BS2(750,433)$, $BS3(750,-433)$,

$BS4(500, 500)$. Start coordinates is $(x_0 = 100, y_0 = 100)$, $v_x = v_y = 5$. Different levels of noises is considered in both the measurement phase and the positioning phase to better simulate the actual environment. The results are given as follows.

In Fig. 3, the number of sample points $N = 500$, the initial value of the state matrix $X_0 = \begin{bmatrix} 100 & 100 & 10 \end{bmatrix}^T$, system noise matrix $Q_w = \begin{bmatrix} 10 & 0 & 0 \\ 0 & 10 & 0 \\ 0 & 0 & 20 \end{bmatrix}$. The original data is interfered by noise, the figure shows that Kalman filtering can reduces measurement and system errors.

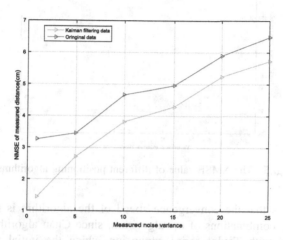

Fig. 3. The performance of Kalman filtering

In Fig. 4, the number of sample points $N = 100$, the rest of the parameters are set as Sect. 4. From the figure, it is obvious that the hybrid method's trajectory is smoother.

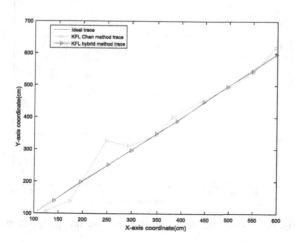

Fig. 4. The simulated paths of different methods

In Fig. 5, the number of sample points $N = 500$. Compared with traditional Chan algorithm, Chan algorithm with Kalman filtering, hybrid positioning algorithm without Kalman filtering, Fig. 5 shows that the method this paper proposed has lower NMSE value, and when noise interference in the environment is serious, it has stronger anti-interference ability than Chan algorithm.

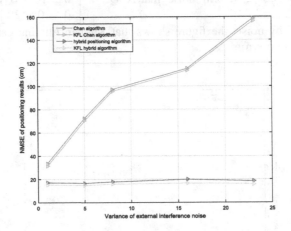

Fig. 5. The NMSE value of different positioning algorithms

Figure 6 shows that the convergence speed of the algorithm is not significantly slower due to the combinations of the algorithm, since Chan algorithm needs 2 iterations. Compared with Taylor series expansion which the initial value is chosen arbitrarily, the proposed algorithm has a better performance.

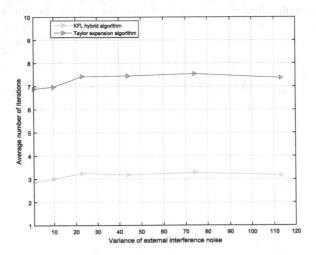

Fig. 6. Average iterations of different positioning algorithms

6 Conclusion

In view of the simulation conditions of the current positioning algorithms are too ideal, the results are often cannot reflect the actual system. A KFL-TDOA positioning method based on hybrid location algorithm is proposed in this paper. The proposed method adds noise interference to both measurement process and the positioning process. The method first use Kalman filtering in order to smooth the measurement error, then combine Chan algorithm with Taylor series expansion algorithm to obtain a precision positioning result. Simulation results are given to verify the performance of the algorithm in positioning accuracy, anti-interference and iteration speed.

References

1. Davidson, P., Piché, R.: A survey of selected indoor positioning methods for smartphones. IEEE Commun. Surv. Tutor. **19**(2), 1347–1370 (2017)
2. Khalajmehrabadi, A., Gatsis, N., Akopian, D.: Modern WLAN fingerprinting indoor positioning methods and deployment challenges. IEEE Commun. Surv. Tutor. **19**(3), 1974–2002 (2017)
3. Mazhar, F., Khan, M., Sällberg, B.: Precise indoor positioning using UWB: a review of methods, algorithms and implementations. Wirel. Pers. Commun. **97**(3), 4467–4491 (2017)
4. Tiemann, J., Eckermann, F., Wietfeld, C.: Multi-user interference and wireless clock synchronization in TDOA-based UWB localization. In: International Conference on Indoor Positioning and Indoor Navigation (2016)
5. Xia, B., Liu, C.P., Sun, W.Z., et al.: Localization algorithm based on multivariable Taylor series expansion model. J. Univ. Electron. Sci. Technol. China (2016)
6. Yang, J.F., Zhang, P.Z.: Time difference of arrival localization based on Chan algorithm and Taylor series algorithm. Nucl. Electron. Detect. Technol. **33**, 480–482 (2013)
7. Zhang, L., Tan, Z.: A new TDOA algorithm based on Taylor series expansion in cellular networks. Front. Electr. Electron. Eng. China **3**(1), 40–43 (2008)
8. Boccadoro, M., De Angelis, G., Valigi, P.: TDOA positioning in NLOS scenarios by particle filtering. Wirel. Netw. **18**(5), 579–589 (2012)
9. Jianwu, Z., Chenglei, Y., Yingying, J.: The performance analysis of Chan location algorithm in cellular network. In: World Congress on Computer Science and Information Engineering. IEEE (2009)
10. Gholami, M.R., et al.: Hybrid TW-TOA/TDOA positioning algorithms for cooperative wireless networks. In: IEEE International Conference on Communications (2011)

Simultaneous Wireless Information and Power Transfer Protocol Under the Presence of Node Hardware Impairments

Yanlin Liu[1], Juan Li[1], Fengye Hu[1(⊠)], and Qiao Qiao[2]

[1] College of Communication Engineering, Jilin University, Changchun, China
hufy@jlu.deu.cn
[2] ChangChun University, Changchun, China

Abstract. Hardware impact to the wireless sensor network node can reduce the life cycle and communication quality of the energy harvesting network. In this paper, we use a three-node network communication model to derive the exact closed form and asymptotic expression of the outage probability and through the Rayleigh fading channel. Then, we study the outage probability and throughput of the wireless sensor network from the hardware impact of the source node and the destination node. In addition, we provide numerical results to demonstrate the correctness of the simulation. The hardware impact of the node physical transceiver is unavoidable, but we can minimize the impact on the network by selecting configuration parameters, which is of great significance to engineering practice.

Keywords: Amplify-and-forward · Energy harvesting ·
Hardware impairments · Outage probability · Throughput ·
Wireless power transfer

1 Introduction

Using energy harvesting to prolong the lifetime of wireless networks has received widespread attention [1]. The wireless sensor node can collect energy from the radio frequency signal in the surrounding environment to supply the node to operate, and at the same time can transmit the radio frequency information [2, 3]. In [4], the author proposes a time-switching-relay (TSR) protocol and a power-switching-relay protocol (PSR) protocol for the energy harvesting network. Then, as discussed in [5], the TS scheme energy harvesting relay network analyzes the throughput of the network using decoding-forwarding (DF) and amplification-forwarding (AF) relay methods, respectively. Due to the limitation of the transmit power of the relay node, the authors in [6] considered the cooperative communication model under the hardware impact of the relay node to analyze the network performance index. In [7], the authors analyse the outage performance of multi-relay cooperative networks subject of wireless communications. For the specific application of node damage, the research in [8] introduced a wireless energy harvesting two-way relay (TWR) network, considering the impact of relay node impairment on the networks TSR protocol and PSR protocol, and

S. Han et al. (Eds.): AICON 2019, LNICST 286, pp. 488–496, 2019.
https://doi.org/10.1007/978-3-030-22968-9_45

comparing the situation under different conditions. The authors quantify the impact of transceiver impairments in a two-way amplify-and-forward configuration and then obtain the effective signal-to-noise-ratios at both transmitter nodes [9]. In [10], the authors studied the performance of communication systems with both wireless information and power transfer capabilities under non-ideal transmitter hardware. The author analyzes the impact of relay node impairment on the simultaneous transmission of wireless information energy in single-point communication [11].

The remainder of the paper is organized as follows. The second section explains the wireless sensor network system model. In the third section, we derive the outage probability and throughput for node impairments based on the TSR protocol. The fourth section verifies the experimental results by simulation. Finally, Sect. 5 summarizes the main contributions of this paper.

2 Guidelines for Manuscript Preparation

We analyze the three-node network, source node S, relay node R and destination node D to complete the information transmission of the entire network. In the subsequent analysis and derivation, we consider the following assumptions for the network: The source node S and the destination node D have continuous power supply, and the relay node R as an energy-limited node can only supply energy by collecting energy from the radio frequency signals in the surrounding environment, but the relay node R does not limit the received signal, minimum power, energy harvesting and information transfer for each received data block. Due to the impact of the node hardware in the manufacturing process or in the harsh environment, we only consider the source node S and the destination node D to be impacted, which will have a serious impact on the overall network communication quality. To simple derive the data, we assume that the two nodes have the same degree of impact. Figure 1 below shows the system model for the considered system.

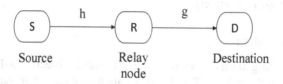

Fig. 1. The relay auxiliary communication system model between the source node and the destination node of hardware damage

2.1 Time Switching-Based Relaying (TSR) Protocol

Figure 2 depicts the key parameters in the TSR protocol for simultaneous energy and information processing at the relay node. It is the block time of transmitting a certain information block from the source node to the destination node, and is a time allocation parameter of the relay node receiving the energy block. The relay node collects energy of the received signal during the time and transmits the information within the time. In the information transmission process, time is used by the source node to transmit information to the relay node, and the relay node transmits information to the destination node. We assume that the energy collected during the energy harvesting phase is all consumed by the relay node. The time allocation parameter for collecting energy at the relay node is the research key of the whole protocol. Reasonable allocation time will reduce the network outage probability and improve the achievable throughput of the network.

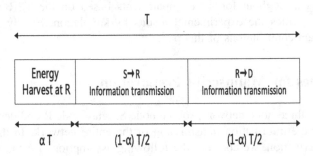

Fig. 2. Illustration of the key parameters in the TSR protocol for energy harvesting and information processing at the relay.

2.2   Channel Model

We assume that the communication link between the source node S and the destination node D is not available, so the network needs the relay node R to assist the source signal S in signal transmission to the destination node D. The fading coefficients are constant within one block and independent and identically distributed (i.i.d.) from one block to the next. Let h and g denote the channel coefficients between S and relay R, between R and D, respectively. Hence, $|g|^2$ and $|h|^2$ follow the exponential distribution with mean λ_g and λ_h, respectively.

2.3   Energy Harvesting

The energy harvesting receiver rectifies the RF signal directly and gets the direct current to charge up the battery. The details of such an energy harvesting receiver can be found in [5]. It first harvests energy from the source signal. Then, it uses the harvested energy as a source of transmit power to forward the source information to the destination. During the energy harvesting time aT at the relay node can be expressed as

$$E_h = \frac{\eta P_S |h|^2}{d_1^m} \alpha T \tag{1}$$

Where $0 < \eta < 1$ is the energy conversion efficiency, P_S is the transmitted power from the source, d_1 is the distance of the source and relay node, m is the loss of channel. The transmission power of relay node is

$$P_r = \frac{E_h}{(1-\alpha)T/2} = \frac{2\eta P_S |h|^2 \alpha}{d_1^m (1-\alpha)}. \tag{2}$$

3   Performance Analysis

This section analyzes the performance of the proposed TSR protocol. The received signal at the relay node, $y_r(t)$ is given by

$$y_r(t) = \frac{1}{\sqrt{d_1^m}} \sqrt{P_S} h(s(t) + w_1(t)) + n_1(t) + n_2(t) \tag{3}$$

$s(t)$ is the normalized information signal from the source, i.e., $E\left\{|s(t)|^2\right\} = 1$, where E $\{\cdot\}$ is the expectation operator and $|\cdot|$ is the absolute value operator. $w_1 \sim CN\left(0, k_1^2 P_S\right)$ is the aggregate distortion affecting noise caused by hardware impact at the source, k_1 characterize the level of impairments of the source hardware, $n_1 \sim CN\left(0, \sigma_r^2\right)$ and $n_2 \sim CN\left(0, \sigma_r^2\right)$ is the noise at the relay node, $CN(\cdot)$ stands for complex circularly symmetric Gaussian distributions.

In the case of high SNR, we choose the amplification and forwarding scheme. The magnification factor G at the relay is

$$G = \sqrt{\frac{P_S |h|^2}{d_1^m} (1 + k_1^2 P_S) + \sigma_r^2} \tag{4}$$

Relay amplifies the received signal and the transmitted signal is

$$x(k) = G y_r(k) \tag{5}$$

At the destination, the received signal from relay node can be expressed as $y_d(k)$ is given by

$$y_d(k) = \frac{1}{\sqrt{d_2^m}} \sqrt{P_r} g x(k) + w_2(k) + n_d(k) \tag{6}$$

$w_2 \sim CN\left(0, k_2^2\right)$ is the aggregate distortion affecting noise caused by HI at the D, k_2 characterize the level of impairments of the destination, $n_d \sim CN\left(0, \sigma_d^2\right)$ is the noise at the destination node.

Substituting (3), (4), (5) to (6), the received signal at the destination, $y_d(k)$ is given by

$$y_d(k) = \frac{\sqrt{2\eta|h|^2\alpha P_s h g s(k)}}{\sqrt{(1-\alpha)d_1^m d_2^m}\sqrt{P_s|h|^2 + d_1^m \sigma_r^2}} + \frac{\sqrt{2\eta|h|^2\alpha P_s h g w_1(k)}}{\sqrt{(1-\alpha)d_1^m d_2^m}\sqrt{P_s|h|^2 + d_1^m \sigma_r^2}}$$

$$+ \frac{\sqrt{2\eta|h|^2\alpha P_s g n_r(k)}}{\sqrt{(1-\alpha)d_2^m}\sqrt{P_s|h|^2 + d_1^m \sigma_r^2}} + w_2(k) + n_d(k) \tag{7}$$

The outage probability can be expressed as $P_{\text{out}} = p[Y_D < Y_0]$, where Y_D is the received SNR at the destination and Y_0 denotes the SNR threshold. Y_D can be expressed as

$$\gamma_D = \frac{|y_d signal|^2}{|y_d noise|^2} \tag{8}$$

Substituting $y_d(k)$ from (7) into (8), Y_D is given by formula (9).

$$\gamma_D = \frac{2\eta\alpha P_s^2|h|^4|g|^2}{2\eta\alpha P_s^2 k_1^2|h|^4|g|^2(k_1^2|h|^2) + 2d_1^m\eta\alpha P_s|h|^2|g|^2\sigma_r^2 + \left[(1-\alpha)d_1^m d_2^m(P_s|h|^2 + d_1^m\sigma_r^2)\right](k_2^2 + \sigma_d^2)} \tag{9}$$

The outage probability of the destination node of TSR protocol is

$$P_{\text{out}} = p(\gamma_D < \gamma_0) = p(|g|^2 < \frac{a|h|^2 + b}{c|h|^4 - d|h|^2}) \tag{10}$$

Where

$$a = \gamma_0[(1-\alpha)d_1^m d_2^m P_s](\sigma_d^2 + k_2^2) \tag{11}$$

$$b = \left[(1-\alpha)d_1^{2m}d_2^m\sigma_r^2\right](\sigma_d^2 + k_2^2)\gamma_0 \tag{12}$$

$$c = 2\eta P_s^2\alpha(1 - k_1^2\gamma_0) \tag{13}$$

$$d = 2\eta P_s\alpha\sigma_r^2 d_1^m\gamma_0 \tag{14}$$

Then, we find through formula that the value of b is about equal to 0 in the case of high SNR. So we can get a simpler formula for the outage probability

$$P_{\text{out}} \approx 1 - e^{-\frac{d}{c\lambda_h}} \int_{x=0}^{\infty} e^{-(\frac{x}{\lambda_h c} + \frac{a}{x\lambda_g})} dx \tag{15}$$

$$= 1 - e^{-\frac{d}{c\lambda_h}} \mu K_1(\mu)$$

$K_1(\cdot)$ is the first-order modified Bessel function of the second kind.

Where

$$u(k) = \sqrt{\frac{4a}{c(k)\lambda_h\lambda_g}} \qquad (16)$$

The throughput, τ, at the destination is given by

$$\tau = (1 - P_{out})(1 - \alpha)R/2 \qquad (17)$$

4 Numerical Results and Discussion

In this section, we use the simulation data to prove the correctness of the throughput expression for the above derivation formula. Since in the formula derivation process, the first-order modified Bessel function and the analytical expressions of various variables are involved, we use the offline optimization numerical evaluation algorithm, simulation and numerical results to verify our derivation and evaluate various parameters. Table 1 shows the parameters we used during the simulation.

Table 1. Numerical analysis of network parameters

Parameter	R	P_S	d_1	d_2	η	m
Numerical value	3	1	1	1	0.8	2.7

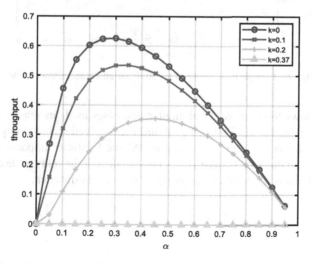

Fig. 3. Throughput at the destination node with respect to α for the TSR protocol

We set the hardware impact parameters to $k_1 = k_2 = k_3 = \{0.1, 0.2 \text{ and } 0.37\}$. We also add simulation plots when $k = 0$ for comparative analysis in [4].

In Fig. 3, we present the effect of a on throughput for TSR protocol. The throughput increases as α increases from 0 to the optimal α but later, it starts decreasing as α increases from its optimal value. It can be notice that, there exists a maximum value for throughput with the increase of α, and the value of α that maximize throughput with different distortion level k sets. When the hardware impact parameter is 0, 0.1, 0.2 and 0.37, the optimal α of the network is 0.28, 0.33, 0.44 and none.

Figure 4 shows the throughput as a function of the transmit power PS. Depending on the degree of hardware impact to the nodes, we use the corresponding optimal α value. When the node hardware has a large degree of influence, the source node needs more transmission power to achieve the maximum network throughput. However, when the node transmission power increases indefinitely, the throughput of the network reaches a certain threshold.

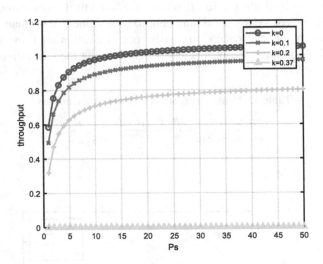

Fig. 4. Comparison between throughput and transmission power

Figure 5 shows the optimal throughput τ decreases as d_1 increases. By increasing d_1, energy harvested for the TSR protocol and the received signal strength at the relay node decrease due to the larger path loss, m. As the hardware impairments increases, the communication distance between the source node and the relay node decreases. It is very important practical significance on the transmission distance.

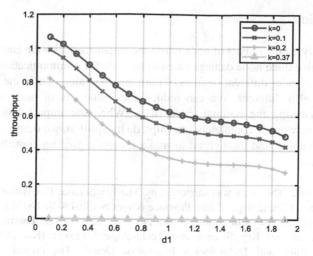

Fig. 5. Optimal throughput for the TSR protocol for different values of source to relay distance

Figure 6 plots the optimal throughput τ for the TSR protocol, η. In the different hardware impact parameters, the $k = 0$ outperforms the other impact parameter for all the values of η. We can conclude that the throughput of the network continues to increase with the energy conversion efficiency, while considering the influence of the rectifier circuit, we finally set the energy conversion efficiency to 0.8.

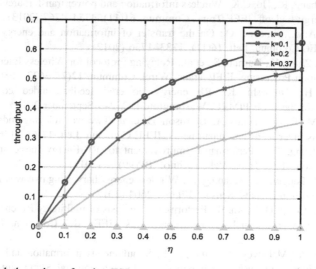

Fig. 6. Optimal throughput for the TSR protocol for different values of energy harvesting efficiency

5 Conclusion

This paper analyzes the impact of node hardware impairments on the energy harvesting network. We give three node damage cases to analyze the communication performance of the network. Under different degrees of damage, the value of α in the TSR protocol we chosen is also different. We can reduce the influences of node impact on the network by selecting the optimal value of α. When the impact level reaches the threshold, the network is completely interrupted. In addition, we derive the expression of outage probability and throughput to make a certain guiding contribution to engineering practice.

Acknowledgement. This work was supported by The key Science Foundation of the Department of Science and Technology of Jilin Province (Grant No. 20180201081SF), Jilin Provincial Special Funding for Industrial Innovation (Grant No. 2017C031-1), Jilin Provincial Science and Technology Department Key Science and Technological Project (No. 20190302031GX), Changchun Scientific and Technological Innovation Double Ten Project (No. 18SS010), National Natural Science Foundation of China (No. 61671219), and Jilin Province Development and Reform Commission Project (No. 2017C046-3).

References

1. Xu, J., Zhang, R.: Throughput optimal policies for energy harvesting wireless transmitters with non-ideal circuit power. IEEE J. Sel. Area. Commun. (2013, accepted). http://arxiv.org/abs/1204.3818
2. Zhou, X., Zhang, R., Ho, C.K.: Wireless information and power transfer: architecture design and rate-energy tradeoff. IEEE Trans. Commun. **61**(11), 4754–4767 (2013)
3. Fouladgar, A.M., Simeone, O.: On the transfer of information and energy in multi-user systems. IEEE Commun. Lett. **16**(11), 1733–1736 (2012)
4. Nasir, A.A., Zhou, X., Durrani, S., et al.: Relaying protocol for Wireless Energy Harvesting and Information Processing. IEEE Trans. Wirel. Commun. **12**(7), 3622–3636 (2012)
5. Kawabata, H., Ishibashi, K.: RF energy powered feedback-aided cooperation. In: Proceedings of the IEEE PIMRC, Washington, DC, 2–5 September 2014
6. Matthaiou, M., Papadogiannis, A., Bjornson, E., et al.: Two-way relaying under the presence of relay transceiver hardware impairments. IEEE Commun. Lett. **17**(6), 1136–1139 (2013)
7. Liu, K.H., Kung, T.L.: Performance Improvement for RF Energy-Harvesting Relays Via Relay Selection. IEEE Trans. Veh. Technol. **PP**(99), 1 (2017)
8. Chunling, P., Fangwei, L., Huaping, L.: Wireless energy harvesting two-way relay networks with hardware impairments. Sensors **17**(11), 2604 (2017)
9. Do, N.T., da Costa, D.B., An, B.: Performance analysis of multirelay RF energy harvesting cooperative networks with hardware impairments. IIEEE IET Commun. **10**, 2551–2552 (2016)
10. Ozcelikkale, A., Mckelvey, T., Viberg, M.: Simultaneous information and power transfer with transmitters with hardware impairments. In: International Symposium on Wireless Communication Systems. IEEE (2016)
11. Huynh, T.P., Nguyen, H.S., Do, D.T., et al.: Impact of hardware impairments in AF relaying network for WIPT: TSR and performance analysis. In: International Conference on Electronics. IEEE (2016)

An Improved A* Algorithm Based on Divide-and-Conquer Method for Golf Unmanned Cart Path Planning

Yi Chen[✉], Liangbo Xie, Wei He, Qing Jiang, and Junxing Xu

School of Communications and Information Engineering,
Chongqing University of Posts and Telecommunications, Chongqing, China
751796746@qq.com

Abstract. Path planning based on A* algorithm has been widely used in various engineering projects, but the time cost of A* algorithm for large-scale road networks is expensive, which is proportional to the square of node N. This paper proposes an improved A* algorithm based on the divide-and-conquer method for the golf unmanned cart path planning requirements, which splits the global optimal path into several local optimal paths and greatly reduces the time cost of the traditional A* algorithm with the more data space needs. Experiment results show that the proposed algorithm can decrease the time cost by at least 46% compared with the traditional A* algorithm. The real-time performance is stronger and the global optimizing path is smoother.

Keywords: Path planning · A* algorithm · Golf unmanned cart · Divide-and-conquer method

1 Introduction

With the fast advancement of science and technology, the human desire for the intelligentization of all things is becoming stronger. Unmanned robots are the direct products of such demand, such as driverless cars, unmanned factory and so on. For mobile robots, path planning is one of the most important requirements [1]. Path planning is planning an optimal path in time or distance in a certain environment model. When gives the source node and destination node information of the robot, it can guide the robot to complete the planning mission. Common path planning algorithms include A* algorithm [2], Dijkstra algorithm [3], Lazy Theta* algorithm [4], RRT algorithm [5] and some intelligent optimization algorithms such as genetic algorithm [6] and ant colony algorithm [7]. Among them, A* algorithm is an optimal path planning algorithm based on map search, which uses an inspiring idea to search along the direction of the target, avoiding blind, time-consuming and useless search effectively. This heuristic search algorithm is now widely used in path planning [8].

As one of the most classical path planning algorithms, A* algorithm has attracted great attractions of a large number of scholars and has achieved many research achievements. Chen et al. [9] use the direction vector as the heuristic search function of A* algorithm and introduce the parallel search method to search both the source node

S. Han et al. (Eds.): AICON 2019, LNICST 286, pp. 497–505, 2019.
https://doi.org/10.1007/978-3-030-22968-9_46

and the destination node simultaneously, which greatly improves the efficiency of the algorithm. In [10], the method of A* algorithm with time cost is proposed to achieve efficient and collision-free path planning of multiple AGVs for the parking scenario. In [11], a smooth A* algorithm is proposed. When the front and back nodes of the intermediate node meet the obstacle-free condition, the intermediate node on the extension line can be deleted, which can get better path planning at the expense of part of the time efficiency. In [12], the optimal path is obtained by simplifying the A* algorithm in the indoor positioning environment, and the rotation direction and the minimum rotation angle at the inflection node are obtained from the vector theory. Cui et al. [13] extend the A* algorithm from the traditional 8 domain to the 24 domain, increasing the search directionality, and selecting the optimal fscore and the sub-optimal fscore when expanding the node, thereby increasing the search flexibility. The number of turning nodes of planning path is reduced and the planning path becomes smoother. Huang et al. [1] combine distance transform and line-of-sight algorithms to make the planning path smoother and farther away from obstacles.

The above algorithms optimize the A* algorithm from a certain aspects. In order to solve certain environments, the time efficiency of some algorithms has to be sacrificed. For complex scenarios or large-scale road networks, the real-time performance is insufficient and the above algorithms are only theoretically simulated, which lacks certain engineering practice. Therefore, this paper proposes an improved A* algorithm with divide-and-conquer method that aims to improve the time cost of optimal path for the golf unmanned cart. First, establish a precise two-dimensional grid map of the golf course environment. Second, based on the A* algorithm, the divide-and-conquer method which splits the global optimal path into several local optimal paths is used to optimize the algorithm which reduces the time cost of the traditional A* algorithm and improves the real-time performance.

The rest of the paper is organized as follows. In Sect. 2, a precise two-dimension grid map model of golf environment is introduced. In Sect. 3, we describe the detailed theories of improved A* algorithm. The experiment results show the algorithm efficiency in Sect. 3. And Sect. 4 concludes this paper.

2   Environment Map Model

The environment map extracts the position, state and other information of objects in the real environment into a map model, which is the first step of all map-based search algorithms. The common map model representation methods mainly include grid maps and topological maps. The former uses the way of the coordinate system to be occupied by obstacles or not to describe the environmental features. The method is simple and the environment description ability is strong; the second is the use of topology nodes to establish map information which is mainly for environmental maps with large-scale road networks [14]. In this paper, based on the characteristics of the golf environment, a grid map is used to represent the golf environment characteristics.

A grid map breaks down the real environment into a series of discrete grid nodes and all grid nodes are uniformly and evenly distributed which are described according to whether they are occupied by obstacles. If the grid cell is occupied by an obstacle, it is a barrier grid, and vice versa is a free grid.

The construction process of the golf environmental model is mainly as follows. Firstly, the anchor nodes are identified on the four corners of the golf course, the real position information of the golf course is collected by RTK equipment, and then the aerial image technology is used to obtain an environmental picture with high resolution; The node can use the interpolation algorithm to obtain the real position information of each node in the environment, and then match the high-resolution environment picture one by one, and finally establish a two-dimensional grid map, the map not only has environment specific information, and each grid has real location information, which greatly facilitates the path planning algorithm and the automatic control of golf cart. Figure 1 shows an aerial view of a 75×120 m^2 golf course. Figure 2 shows a two-dimensional grid map with an interval of 1 m, white is a feasible area and red is an obstacle.

Fig. 1. Golf aerial image (Color figure online)

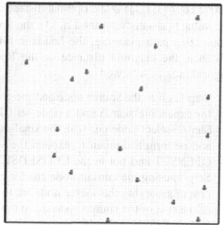

Fig. 2. Grid map (Color figure online)

3 Algorithm Description

3.1 A* Algorithm

The A* algorithm is a heuristic search algorithm which is similar to breadth-first search (BFS) and depth-first search (DFS) algorithm. They are based on certain principles to determine how to expand the node tree structure that needs to be searched [15], A* algorithm can be considered as a search algorithm based on "advantage nodes".

The core part is to design an estimation function for each road node, as shown in Eq. (1):

$$f(s) = g(s) + h(s) \tag{1}$$

where $f(s)$ represents the estimated length from the starting node through the node s to the goal node; $g(s)$ represents the known path length from the starting node to the current node, which is calculated by Eq. (2).

$$\sum_{i=start}^{k-1} \cos t(s_i, s_{i+1})(k \le goal) \tag{2}$$

In the Eq. (1), the heuristic function $h(s)$ is the estimated value of the current node to the goal node, and the precondition that A* algorithm can get the optimal path must be able to satisfied Eq. (3).

$$h(s) \le \cos t^*(s, s_{goal}) \tag{3}$$

where $\cos t^*(s, s_{goal})$ is the optimal distance from current node to goal node. The larger the value $h(s)$ satisfying the Eq. (3), the fewer the extension nodes. In order to get the optimizing path planning, the heuristic function is usually chosen as the Manhattan distance, the diagonal distance or the Euclidean distance [16]. The process of A* algorithm is as followed.

- Step 1: given the source node and the goal node, and establish a node set OPENSET for expanding search and a node set CLOSEDSET for completed search node;
- Step 2: select node cur with the smallest cost from OPENSET, that is min{f(cur)} and perform 8 domain to expand the search. If the extended node u is not in the OPENSET and not in the CLOSEDSET, then add it to the OPENSET.
- Step 3: using the current node cur for cost update, the update criterion is when the cost of satisfying the source node src to the extended node u is greater than the sum of the cost of the source node src to the current node cur and the cost of the current node cur to the extended node u;
- Step 4: after the current node cur is expanded, put it into CLOSEDSET, indicating that the node has found the shortest distance and does not need to join OPENSET for search and update again;
- Step 5: loop through step 2, step 3 and step 4 until the goal node is found.

3.2   Improved Algorithm

The time cost of traditional A* algorithm is $O(N^2)$ [17], which means its computational complexity is proportional to the square of the grid number in the two-dimensional grid map, so its cost is very large for some scenes having many grids. For example, in a 2D game, the game map is at least 88×88. Using A* algorithm to find the optimal path, it is necessary to traverse all the nodes in the worst case, and the time cost is $n = 88 \times 88 = 7744$. Therefore, this paper uses the divide-and-conquer method to improve the A* algorithm, which can increase the efficiency of A* algorithm and reduce its time complexity.

Classic physics theories prove that the straight line between point A and point B is the shortest. Therefore, the optimal path searched by A* algorithm is a straight line when there is no obstacle. Their middle point C obtained by using the line drawing algorithm must be in the optimal path. If the optimal path from A to B is divided into two segments AC and BC, respectively, we can get their local optimal path planning with traditional A* algorithm. Finally, according to the dynamic programming idea, the global optimal path planning is achieved by put their local optimal path together with more space cost. For the previous example, the algorithm complexity at this time can be calculated as $n = (44 * 44) + (44 * 44) = 3872$, so the time cost decrease 50% at least.

Figure 3 is the logic block diagram of the improved A* algorithm. First given the segment number N, source node SRC, destination node DST and grid map MAP, and then we use the line drawing algorithm to get the $N - 1$ middle point. If there is an obstacle, take the neighboring point with the shortest heuristic distance as an alternative. Secondly, use the A* algorithm to find the local optimal path of each segment, and then connect them to obtain the global optimal path. The improved A* algorithm pseudo code is as follows.

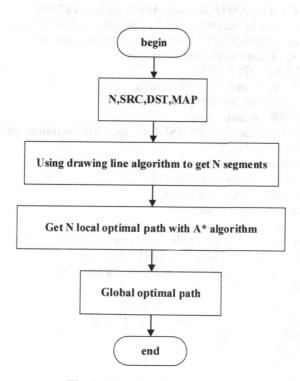

Fig. 3. Algorithm block diagram

function globalOptimizingPath = ImprovedAstar(MAP, SRC, DST, N)
1.   create globalOptimizingPath
2.   create POINT_SET
3.   create stepX, stepY, index
4.   stepX = (DST.x – SRC.x) / N
5.   stepY = (DST.y – SRC.y) / N
6.   index = 1
7.   // find N – 1 middle points without obstacles
8.   POINT_SET = getMiddlePoint(SRC, DST, stepX, stepY, N)
9.   **while all points from POINT_SET**
10.   curSrc = POINT_SET(index)
11.   curDst = POINT_SET(index+1)
12.   **localBestPath = AStar_Routing(MAP, curSrc, curDst)**
13.   **add localBestPath into globalOptimizingPath**
14. **end**
    end fucntion

function best_path = AStar_Routing(MAP, curSrc, curDst)
15. create vertex set CLOSEDSET // set of already visited nodes
16. create vertex set OPENSET   // set of nodes to be expanded
17. create gScore, fScore with default value inf
18. insert curSrc into OPENSET
19. gScore[src] = 0, fScore[src] = h(src, dst)
20. create pre_path with default value **nullptr**
21. **while** OPENSET **is not** empty:
22.   current = the node v in OPENSET s.t. fScore[v] is minimum in OPENSET
23.   **if** current == curDst
24.   return reconstruction_best_path(pre_path, current)
25.   remove current from OPENSET
26.   insert current into CLOSEDSET
27.   **for each** neighbor u of current:
28.   **if** u is in closeSet:
29.   continue;   // ignore the neighbor who has already been evaluated
30.   candidate_score = gScore[current] + h(current, u)
31.   **if u not in** OPENSET: // discovered a new node
32.   insert u into OPENSET
33.   **else if** candidate_score >= gScore[u]:
34.   **continue;**   // this is not a better path
35.   pre_path[u] = current
36.   gScore[u] = candidate_score
37.   fScore[u] = gScore[u] + h(u, dst)
38. **end fuction**

4 Experiment Results

In order to verify the efficiency of the improved algorithm, WINDOWS10 education version is used as the platform and the algorithm is simulated and verified by MATLAB software. The experimental hardware platform is Intel Core i5-3230M processor, 2.6 GHz and 8 GB memory. Under the same platform conditions, we have the comparison experiment between the proposed algorithm and the traditional A* algorithm. For the two-dimensional grid map of the golf course, different source nodes and destination nodes are given respectively to verify their algorithm time cost.

As shown in Fig. 4, three different source nodes and destination nodes are selected respectively. The optimal path obtained by the traditional A* algorithm and the proposed algorithm is compared, the green path and the black path are the result of traditional A* algorithm and the improved A* algorithm, respectively. We can find that the proposed algorithm is smoother and the path length is shorter than the traditional A* algorithm.

Table 1 is the cost time of the traditional A* algorithm and the proposed algorithm at different source and destination nodes when N is 2. The time cost of three group data using the traditional A* algorithm is 0.1583 s, 0.1246 s, 0.1736 s, respectively, and the time cost of the proposed algorithm is 0.0800 s, 0.0633 s, 0.0928 s, respectively. The increase efficiency is 49%, 49%, and 46%, respectively, so the proposed algorithm is at least 46% better in time efficiency than the traditional A* algorithm. In addition, it is known from Table 2 that under different N values (N = 2, 4, 6), we can find that the time cost of the three group data decreases as the value of N increases, as shown in Fig. 5.

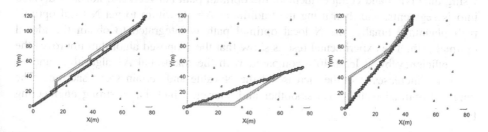

Fig. 4. Algorithm comparison (black is improved A*, green is traditional A*) (Color figure online)

Table 1. Algorithm comparison

Group	Source	Destination	A* cost (s)	Improved A* cost (s)	Efficiency
1	(1, 1)	(75, 90)	0.1583	0.0800	49%
2	(1, 1)	(75, 40)	0.1246	0.0633	49%
3	(1, 1)	(45, 90)	0.1736	0.0928	46%

Table 2. N efficiency comparison

Group	Source	Destination	N = 2	N = 4	N = 6
1	(1, 1)	(75, 90)	49%	55%	64%
2	(1, 1)	(75, 40)	49%	53%	62%
3	(1, 1)	(45, 90)	46%	62%	71%

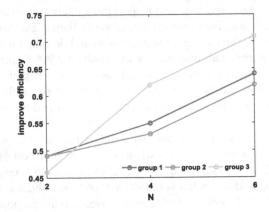

Fig. 5. Different N increase efficiency

5   Conclusions

This paper proposes a method to reduce the time cost of the traditional A* algorithm. Using the divide-and-conquer method, the optimal path between two nodes is divided into N segments, and then using the traditional A* algorithm to get N local optimal path planning. Finally, the N local optimal path is integrated to obtain the global optimal path. The experimental results show that the proposed algorithm improves the time efficiency by at least 46% compared with the traditional A* algorithm, and its efficiency increases with the increase of the N value and certain space sacrifice. The obtained optimal path is also smoother and shorter, which has a strong engineering practice.

References

1. Huang, L., Zhou, F.: Path planning of moving robot based on path optimization of D* lite algorithm. Control Decis. J. (2018)
2. Bundy, A., Wallen, L.: A* algorithm. In: Bundy, A., Wallen, L. (eds.) Catalogue of Artificial Intelligence Tools. SYMBOLIC, p. 1. Springer, Heidelberg (1984). https://doi.org/10.1007/978-3-642-96868-6_2
3. Johnson, D.B.: A note on Dijkstra's shortest path algorithm. J. ACM **20**(3), 385–388 (1973)

4. Firmansyah, E.R., Masruroh, S.U., Fahrianto, F.: Comparative analysis of A* and basic Theta* algorithm in android-based pathfinding games. In: International Conference on Information & Communication Technology for the Muslim World. IEEE (2017)
5. Song, J.Z., Dai, B., Shan, E.Z., et al.: An improved RRT path planning algorithm. Acta Electron. Sin. (2010)
6. Tsai, C.C., Huang, H.C., Chan, C.K.: Parallel elite genetic algorithm and its application to global path planning for autonomous robot navigation. IEEE Trans. Ind. Electron. 58(10), 4813–4821 (2011)
7. Fan, X., Xiong, L., Sheng, Y., et al.: Optimal path planning for mobile robots based on intensified ant colony optimization algorithm. In: IEEE International Conference on Robotics (2003)
8. Chen, H., Xiong, G.: Theory and Design of Unmanned Ground Vehicle. Beijing Institute of Technology Press, Beijing (2018)
9. Chen, H., Li, Y.: Research of mobile robot path planning based on improved A* algorithm optimization. Autom. Instrum. 12 (2018)
10. Zhang, Y., Chen, Y., Wei, L.: AGV intelligent parking algorithm based on improved A* algorithm. Comput. Syst. Appl. 28(1) (2019)
11. Wang, H., Ma, Y.: Path planning for mobile robots based on smoothing A* algorithm. J. Tongji Univ. (Nat. Sci. Ed.) 38(11), 1647–1650 (2010)
12. Wang, D.: Indoor mobile robot path planning based on improved A* algorithm. J. Tsinghua Univ. (Nat. Sci. Ed.) 8, 1085–1089 (2012)
13. Cui, B., Wang, M., Duan, Y.: Algorithm a path planning based on searchable 24 neighborhoods. J. Shenyang Univ. Technol. 40(2), 180–184 (2018)
14. Liu, S.: First Book on Driverless Technology. Electronic Industry Publisher (2017)
15. Hart, P.E., Nilsson, N.J.: A formal basis for the heuristic determination of minimum cost paths in graphs. IEEE Trans. Syst. Sci. Cybern. (SSC) 4(2), 100–107 (1968)
16. Bander, J.L., White, C.C.: A heuristic search algorithm for path determination with learning. Int. J. Imaging Syst. Technol. 16(5), 154–161 (1998)
17. Feng, Q., Gao, J., Deng, X.: Path planner for UAVs navigation based on A* algorithm incorporating intersection. In: 2016 IEEE Chinese Guidance, Navigation and Control Conference (CGNCC). IEEE (2016)

Power Allocation Method for Satellite Communication Based on Network Coding

Jin Liu[1], Zhuoming Li[1(✉)], and Gongliang Liu[2]

[1] School of Electronics and Information Engineering,
Harbin Institute of Technology, Harbin 150001, China
Zhuoming@hit.edu.cn
[2] School of Information Science and Engineering,
Harbin Institute of Technology at Weihai, Weihai 264209, China

Abstract. With the development of aerospace technology, more and more application tasks require satellite communications for information transmission. In space communication, the resources on the star are very precious, and it is particularly urgent to improve the utilization of resources on the star. The application of network coding in satellite communication can not only solve the traditional routing problem, but also greatly improve the reliability and efficiency of communication. So the power allocation method on satellite based on network coding is proposed. Two power allocation algorithms can improve the utilization of inter-satellite resources, and the network coding of relay nodes can reduce the bit error rate and the packet loss rate of the communication system. The simulation results show that network coding can reduce the bit error rate of the system and the impact of different power allocation algorithms on the bit error rate of the system.

Keywords: Network coding · Satellite communications · Game theory · Water injection method

1 Introduction

Inter-satellite communication is one of the hottest issues in the field of satellite communication. Although there are many satellites in the sky, most of them are self-contained and it is difficult to achieve resource sharing. However, it is difficult for a single satellite to meet various needs. The realization of multi-point communication between satellites is an inevitable trend in the development of satellite communications. Network coding is a new technology of network communication, which can optimize the transmission performance of the network. Research shows that the application of network coding in satellite communication can not only solve the traditional routing problem, but also greatly improve the reliability and efficiency of communication.

In terms of satellite resource allocation methods, Literature 2 designs a bandwidth and power allocation algorithm to ensure efficient use of satellite resources. In the third paper, considering the QoS requirement, the Lagrangian heuristic algorithm is used to solve the subcarrier allocation problem of low-orbit satellite networks. Literature 4 considers the impact of delay on real-time services, and proposes a power and

S. Han et al. (Eds.): AICON 2019, LNICST 286, pp. 506–521, 2019.
https://doi.org/10.1007/978-3-030-22968-9_47

bandwidth resource allocation method to achieve a balance between throughput and delay. Document 5 proposes a power and bandwidth allocation method for a multi-beam satellite network to improve the fairness of the capacity among beams. The above method is mainly for downlink resources and is not suitable for inter-satellite links. The application of network coding technology in satellite communication can not only solve the traditional routing problem, but also greatly improve the reliability and efficiency of communication.

Aiming at the problem of high bit error rate of satellite communication, considering the application of network coding to satellite communication, two power optimization methods on satellite based on network coding are proposed. With the goal of reducing the bit error rate, the network coding satellite communication system is optimized for power, and the bit error rates of the two methods are compared.

The following is a brief introduction to the contents of each section. The second part introduces the concept of network coding. The third part introduces three kinds of satellite communication system based on network coding. The fourth part introduces a satellite communication system combined with network coding and power allocation algorithm.

2 Network Coding

Taking the "butterfly net" model as an example, the basic concepts of network coding are analyzed. As shown in the following figure: assume that the capacity of each link is 1, y and z are both sink nodes, s is the source node, and the rest are intermediate nodes. In Fig. 1(a), the traditional route transmission mode is used. Node w is only responsible for the operation of storage and forwarding. Figure 1(b) uses the network coding method. The node w is mainly responsible for encoding the input information, and then adding module 2 to b1 and b2, and transmitting the operation result b1 $\oplus$ b2 to the node x. The result of the operation is finally transmitted to the nodes y and z through the links xz and xy. After the node y receives the information b1 and the information b1 $\oplus$ b2, it can decode the b1 $\oplus$ (b 1 $\oplus$ b2), so that the information b2 can be solved. Similarly, the node z can decode the complete information in this way, and the resulting transmission has a capacity of 2. It can be seen that the application of network coding to satellite communication can theoretically achieve the maximum amount of information transmission. At the sink node, this can be done by performing the inverse of the decoding and will eventually be able to be sent from the source of the original data.

Based on the characteristics of satellite communication networks, network coding is particularly suitable for the field of satellite communication networks. If a node generates interest in different data packets of neighboring nodes, it can effectively save satellite communication by encoding these different data packets so that it and all neighboring nodes can receive information of the data packets in them. Therefore it effectively saves satellite communication resources. In addition, the application of network coding in the satellite communication network can also significantly reduce the times of transmitting data packets, so that the transmission energy is greatly reduced.

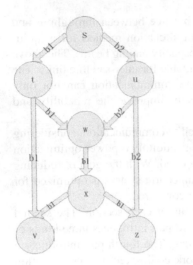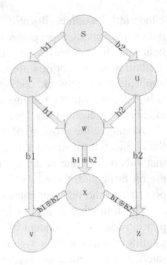

Fig. 1. (a) Traditional routing. (b) Network coding method.

And we will briefly introduce two power allocation algorithms which include game theory and water injection method in the forth section.

3 Satellite Communication System Simulation Based on Network Coding

3.1 ARQ Mechanism Based on Network Coding

System Model and Principle

In recent years, many scholars at home and abroad have been concerned about the problem of service transmission performance in satellite communications. However, the environment in which satellite channels are located is very complex, and these complex environments can significantly reduce the communication quality of satellite channels. Due to the particularity of satellite channels, many terrestrial protocols are often inefficient when applied to satellite networks. In order to overcome this problem, the researchers have made in-depth analysis and improved the ARQ for the satellite environment based on the idea of terrestrial ARQ. ARQ mainly has three modes: stop waiting, backward N step and selective retransmission. In addition, network coding has been widely used in the field of wireless communications. A large number of studies have shown that network coding in wireless communication can reduce the number of packet retransmissions and packet loss rate. In order to further reduce the transmission delay and the number of packet loss of the satellite channel, the network coding is applied to the ARQ of the satellite network, and a network coding-based ARQ (Sat-NC-ARQ) mechanism suitable for the satellite network is proposed. In Sat-NC-ARQ, in addition to transmitting the data packets of the real service terminal, the satellite terminal also creates a virtual service terminal to send the network coded data packets, so that the receiving terminal can decode the data packets as long as it receives enough data packets. So it can reduce the number of retransmissions.

As shown in Fig. 2, the source service terminals S1 and S2 are connected to the source satellite terminal through the terrestrial link, and the destination service terminals D1 and D2 are connected to the destination satellite terminal through the terrestrial link, and the source satellite terminal connect with the destination satellite terminal through satellite link.

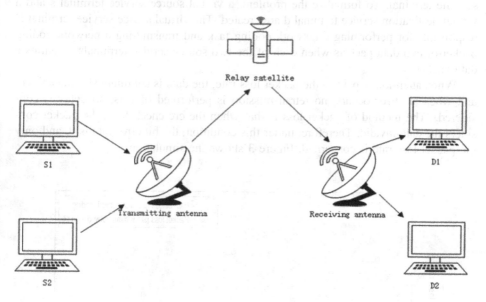

Fig. 2. System model of ARQ mechanism.

It is assumed that the source service terminal S1 is to send the data packet 1101 to the destination service terminal D1, and the source service terminal S2 is to send the data packet 1001 to the destination service terminal D2. First, S1 and S2 respectively send data packets to the source satellite terminal through the terrestrial link. When the source satellite terminal receives the data packets of S1 and S2, it can perform network coding on the data packets of S1 and S2, that is XOR, i.e. 1101 XOR 1001 = 0100; then the data packets 1101, 1001 and the network coded packet 0100 are sent together to the destination satellite terminal. When the destination terminal receives any two of the three data packets, the original data packet can be decoded by using the network coding. For example, it is assumed that the destination satellite terminal receives the data packet 1101 of S1 and the network coded data packet 0100, and the data packet 1001of S2 is lost, and the destination satellite terminal can decode the data packet of S2 by XOR operation 1101XOR0100 = 1001. The destination satellite terminal can then send the packets of S1 and S2 to D1 and D2 respectively. It can be seen from the example that when the packet of S2 is lost, the Sat-NC-ARQ mechanism does not need to retransmit the packet data by S2, so the transmission delay and the number of lost packets of the satellite network can be reduced.

Simulation Analysis

To simplify system processing, we can adjust the length of the packet to send one packet every 1 ms. At the same time, it can be assumed that each source service terminal polls the packets at each moment in turn. In order to introduce the network coding, after the source satellite terminal receives the data packets of the two source service terminals, the two data packets are network coded (XOR operation), and then the two data packets and the network coding packets are sequentially sent to destination satellite terminal. To formalize the problem, a virtual source service terminal s and a virtual destination service terminal d are created. The virtual source service terminal is responsible for performing a network coding task and transmitting a network coding packet of two data packets when each of the two source service terminals transmits a data packet.

When attention is paid to the packet loss rate, the data is continuously transmitted, and when an error occurs, no retransmission is performed (that is, no delay is considered). The method of packet loss is that when the crc check fails, the packet considers the data invalid. Therefore, under this condition, the bit error rate is 0, and only the packet loss rate is concerned. Figure 3 shows the simulation.

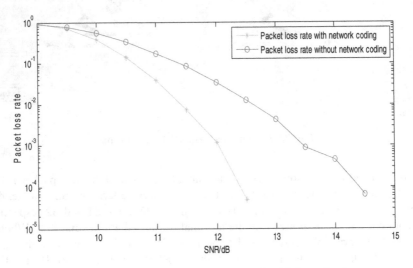

Fig. 3. Comparison of packet loss rate under ARQ mechanism.

The ARQ mechanism based on network coding achieves the goal of reducing the number of packet loss on the satellite channel by reducing the number of retransmissions of data packets. The simulation results also show that network coding can reduce the packet loss rate of satellite networks.

3.2   Satellite Physical Layer Network Coding System

System Model and Principle

Two low-orbit satellites are used as the data source of the system, and the schematic diagram of the satellite physical layer network coding system is shown in Fig. 4. In the MAC phase, the source nodes S1 and S2 simultaneously transmit data to the ground relay node R and the destination node within the respective coverage area, wherein the source node S1 covers the relay node R and the destination node T1, and the source node S2 covers the relay node R and destination node T2. In the BC phase, after the relay node R is processed in the forwarding mode, the superposed signal is broadcasted to the destination nodes T1 and T2.

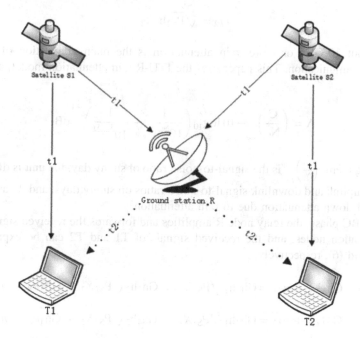

Fig. 4. Satellite physical layer network coding system model.

System Description: The transmission process of the system data is divided into two phases: one is the multiple access phase (MAC), in which the satellite source node transmits its own data to the destination node and the relay node; the second is broadcast phase (BC). After the relay node uses the function to process the superimposed signal, the signal is broadcasted to the two destination nodes, and the destination node uses the known information of the destination as the reference information to extract the transmitting information of the other end to complete the decoding process.

In the MAC phase, the signals of the relay node R receiving the signals X_1 and X_2 from S1 and S2 can be expressed as:

$$Y_R = \sqrt{P_{S1}} h_1 X_1 + \sqrt{P_{S2}} h_2 X_2 + n_g \tag{1}$$

Among them, P_{S1} and P_{S2} are the transmission powers of the source nodes S1 and S2, h_1 and h_2 are the channel gains between the source nodes S1 and S2 and the ground relay R, and X_1 and X_2 are the transmission information of the source nodes S1 and S2, and n_g is the relay node R receives the superimposed noise of the signals X_1 and X_2.

In the case of a sunny day, it is assumed that the channel gains between the nodes in the same coverage area and the satellite are the same, so the signals the terminal nodes T1 and T2 receive are represented by Eqs. (2) and (3), respectively.

$$Y_{T1} = \sqrt{P_{S1}} h_1 X_1 \tag{2}$$

$$Y_{T2} = \sqrt{P_{S2}} h_2 X_2 \tag{3}$$

At about 10 GHz or more, rain attenuation is the main attenuation of satellite wireless communication. This paper uses the ITU-R rain attenuation model, as shown in Eq. (4):

$$A = \left(\frac{C}{N_0}\right)_{t.e} - 10 \log_{10} \left(\frac{1}{10^{\frac{S_u - A_u}{10}}} + \frac{1}{10^{\frac{S_d - A_d}{10}}}\right)^{-1} dB \tag{4}$$

Among them, $\left(\frac{C}{N_0}\right)_{t.e}$ is the signal-to-noise ratio of sunny day, the unit is dB, S_u and S_d are the uplink and downlink signal-to-noise ratios on sunny days, and A_u and A_d are the up and down attenuation due to rain attenuation.

In the BC phase, the relay node R amplifies and forwards the received signal to the two destination nodes, and the received signals of T1 and T2 can be expressed as Eqs. (5) and (6), respectively.

$$Y_{T1} = Gh_3 Y_R + n_{T1} = Gh_3 h_1 \sqrt{P_{S1}} X_1 + Gh_3 h_2 \sqrt{P_{S2}} X_2 + Gh_3 n_R + n_{T1} \tag{5}$$

$$Y_{T2} = Gh_4 Y_R + n_{T2} = Gh_4 h_1 \sqrt{P_{S1}} X_1 + Gh_4 h_2 \sqrt{P_{S2}} X_2 + Gh_4 n_R + n_{T2} \tag{6}$$

While G is the amplification gain, h_3 and h_4 are the channel gains of the relay node R and the destination nodes T1 and T2, and n_{T1} and n_{T2} are the additive white Gaussian noise of the destination node, $n_{T1}, n_{T2} \sim CN(0, \sigma_T^2)$.

$$G = \sqrt{\frac{P_R}{P_{S1}|h_1|^2 + P_{S2}|h_2|^2 + \delta_R^2}} \tag{7}$$

Simulation Analysis

Two low-orbit satellites are used as data sources, one ground station is used as a relay node, two destination nodes are base stations in the respective coverage areas of two satellites, and the channel between the satellite and the relay node uses a wireless channel, and the channel from the relay node to the destination node uses a wired channel. The wireless channel noise n of the source node to the node in the coverage domain is set as additive white Gaussian noise, and the channel gain is a Gaussian random variable with a mean of 0 and a variance of 1. Refer to Feng Yun No.3 Constellation, the satellite constellation parameters are shown in Table 1. The orbital height is 836.4 km, two orbital planes. The two satellites will send data to the ground synchronously in six equal time segments within 24 h. It is assumed that the two satellite communication bands adopt the Ka band, and the satellite downlink transmission power is the same and the system is completely synchronized. The Ka band frequency range is 37.5–40.5 GHz. When the Ka band is transmitted, the channel performance is greatly affected by the rainfall environment, and the ITU-R rain attenuation model is used in the simulation. The modulation and demodulation method are BPSK.

Table 1. Satellite parameter.

Parameter	Parameter value
Track height/km	836.4
Orbital inclination/degree	98.753
Cycle/min	101
Number of satellites	2
Number of tracks	2
Constellation type	Feng Yun No.3 Constellation

Figure 5 shows the error rate simulation.

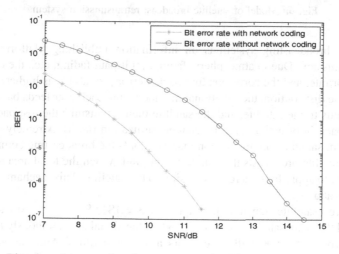

Fig. 5. Bit error rate comparison between network coding and no network coding.

As can be seen from the figure, network coding can significantly reduce the system's bit error rate.

3.3   Network-Coded Satellite Broadcast Retransmission System

System Model and Principle
Figure 6 shows a model of a satellite broadcast retransmission system.

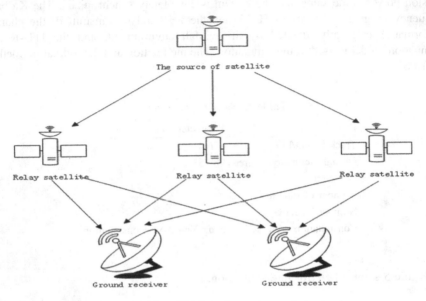

Fig. 6. Model of satellite broadcast retransmission system.

The satellite broadcasting system is an information publishing platform based on packet transmission. Due to atmospheric fading, multipath fading, etc., the channel has a higher error rate, and the corresponding packet error probability is higher. In order to ensure reliable distribution, the traditional method is that each user feeds back his or her receiving status to the satellite, and the satellite then retransmits the lost packets based on the feedback information, and the channel utilization rate is extremely low.

At present, satellite communication mainly adopts the broadcasting communication mode. The satellite broadcasts the data to the ground. When the local area receives the error, it needs to apply for data retransmission to the satellite. This mechanism is shown in the figure above.

The source satellite transmits the signal of S = [S1, S2, S3 .... Sn] to the relay satellite, and the relay satellite forwards it. When the signal is continuously transmitted, the signal ground receives will have errors at different times. And the wrong frame numbers different ground receiving devices receive may be different due to the uncertainty of satellite communication transmission during actual reception. For example, the first ground receiving device has an error in the S1 frame, and the second one is in the S2 frame. In the original broadcast mode, any frame error in any device needs to be retransmitted, which brings great obstacles to satellite communication. The network coded retransmission can wait for each device to appear up to two frames of error before retransmission. It is assumed that during the retransmission process, the receiving node can receive the data packet broadcast by the source node without error.

Simulation Analysis

In order to verify the superiority of network coding, we carried out simulation comparison of packet loss rate. Figure 7 shows the comparison of packet loss rates.

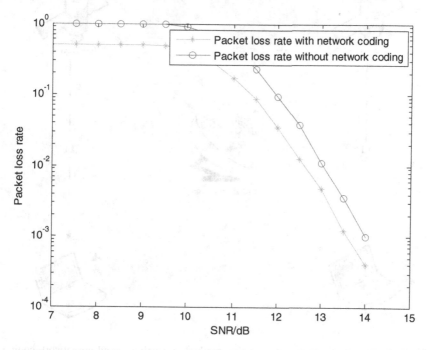

Fig. 7. Comparison of packet loss rate with and without network coding.

It can be seen from the above figure that network coding can significantly reduce the packet loss rate of the satellite broadcasting system.

3.4 Summary

Through the analysis and simulation of three kinds of satellite communication methods using network coding, and observing the optimization effect of network coding on satellite communication, it can be seen that the application of network coding to satellite communication can improve the data transmission rate and improve the robustness of communication. When the satellite communication delay is large and the bit error rate is high, the network coding can effectively reduce the bit error rate of the satellite broadcast communication system and reduce the times of retransmission.

4 Power Allocation Method on Satellite Based on Network Coding

4.1 System Model and Basic Description

We used the same satellite model as the second case in the previous section. Figure 8 shows the system model.

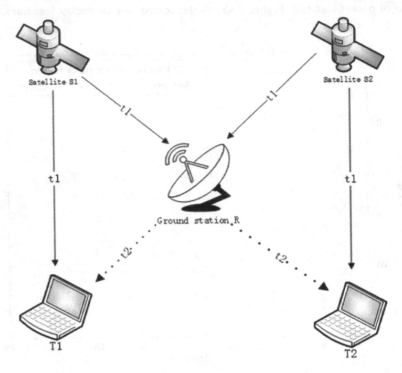

Fig. 8. System model of power allocation method on satellite based on network coding.

The model and the basic principle are exactly the same as the second case of the previous part. The difference is that two resource allocation algorithms are added to further optimize the system performance. The power of S1 is $P1$, the power of S2 is $P2$, the power of R is $P3$ and $P1+P2+P3<$ P_all. P_all is the maximum total power.

The transmission method without network coding is as follows:

Divided into four time gaps, in t1, the information of S1 is sent to R, in t2, R broadcasts the information it receives to T2, in t3, the information of S2 is sent to R, in t4, R broadcasts the information it receives to T1.

The transmission method with network coding is as follows:

Divided into three time gaps, in t1, the information of S1 is sent to R, in t2, the information of S2 is sent to R, in t3, R broadcasts network coded information to T1and T2.

The power allocation method adopts the game function-based utility function optimal method and the greedy water injection method:

The utility function allocation method based on game theory adopts the game theory. Under the condition of fixed total power and total transmission bandwidth, the lowest bit error rate T1 and T2 receive is the target utility function, that is, the utility function is:

$$U = \frac{err_{T1} + err_{T2}}{data_{T1} + data_{T2}} \tag{8}$$

In order to achieve the minimum utility function, the power of T1 and T2 are distributed by means of game distribution to achieve the result of Nash equilibrium, and the utility function is minimized.

The greedy water injection method is based on the greedy resource allocation method. The independent target criterion is adopted for different receiving sources. The error rate of each of T1 and T2 which reaches a target threshold is regarded as the judgment condition to adjust the power allocation. No adjustments are made when the target value is reached.

4.2   Simulation Analysis

It is assumed that S1 is to send the data packet 1101 to the destination service terminal T1, and S2 is to send the data packet 1001 to the destination service terminal T1. First, S1 and S2 need to send data packets to the ground station through the satellite link. When R receives the information of both, it can perform network coding on the data packets of S1 and S2, that is, XOR operation. It is 1101 XOR 1001 = 0100. Then it directly broadcasts a coded data result.

If network coding is not used, the dual-worker network needs to adopt the method of time division multiplexing or frequency division multiplexing to achieve the dual power effect, so that the required transmission power is twice as much as the original. Therefore, pay attention to the difference in the bit error rate between the two when the transmission power is the same.

Game-Based Power Allocation Without Network Coding

In the case of no network coding, when the power distribution of S1 and S2 is optimal, the bit error rate is the lowest, and the game is used for resource optimization. As shown in Fig. 9, when there is no network coding, the relationship between BER and the power of S1 and S2 are both convex function, so the optimal solution in the figure below is:

P1 = 0.165
P2 = 0.150
P3 = 0.185
Lowest bit error rate is 1.01×10^{-3}.

In the game mode, S1 and S2 respectively increase the power. After each additional power increase, the error rate is checked. If the bit error rate decreases, the power

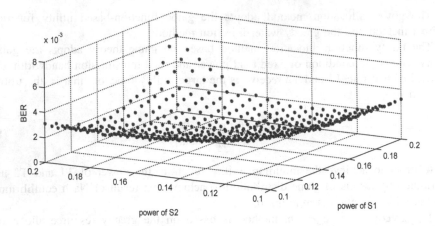

Fig. 9. Relationship between game-based power allocation and bit error rate without network coding.

operation is continued. If not, the previous step is returned, and the power of the other end is adjusted.

Water-Based Power Allocation Without Network Coding

Without the network coding, the resource allocation of S1 and S2 adopts the water injection mode. Under the greedy water injection mode, S1 and S2 only care about the error rate they receive, so they will continuously increase their power to achieve the expected result of the error. Due to S1 and S2 is uncorrelated, a single power is used as the abscissa. As shown in Fig. 10, when there is no network coding, the optimal solution in the following figure is:

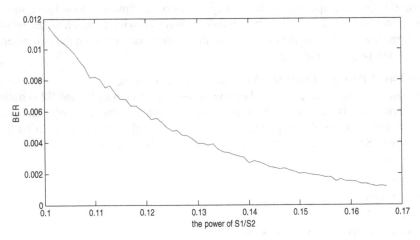

Fig. 10. Relationship between power distribution based on water injection and bit error rate without network coding.

P1 = 0.167
P2 = 0.167
P3 = 0.167
Bit error rate is 1.22×10^{-3}.

In the water injection mode, S1 and S2 increase power at the same time, and when the power is increased, it is checked whether its error rate has reached the expected value. Since the error rate setting in the program is expected to be 1×10^{-4}, in this state, S1 and S2 will continue to improve their own power.

Game-Based Power Allocation with Network Coding

After the network coding is used, the output data R broadcasts is changed from the original 1000 bit to 500 bit, and the Eb/n0 is increased by 3 dB under the same power. So the optimal solution of the resource allocation is changed. Figure 11 shows the error rate simulation.

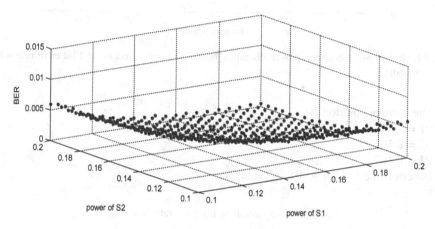

Fig. 11. The relationship between power allocation and bit error rate based on game theory with network coding.

From Fig. 11, the optimal solution is:

P1 = 0.1900
P2 = 0.1950
P3 = 0.1150
Bit error rate is 4.9×10^{-4}.

Due to the use of network coding, the bit error rate is reduced under the limit of the same maximum power.

Water-Based Power Allocation with Network Coding

With the network coding, the output data R broadcasts is changed from the original 1000 bit to 500 bit, and the Eb/n0 is increased by 3 dB under the same power. However, under the water distribution mode, the power allocation of the optimal solution has not changed because the expected bit error rate is not achieved, but the bit error rate has been reduced. Figure 12 shows the error rate simulation.

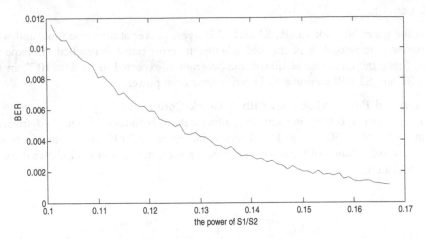

Fig. 12. Relationship between power allocation based on water injection and bit error rate with network coding.

The optimal solution is:
P1 = 0.167
P2 = 0.167
P3 = 0.167
Bit error rate is 1.00×10^{-3} (Table 2).

Table 2. Comparison of bit error rate in 4 ways.

Bit error rate	Game theory	Water injection
Network coding	4.9×10^{-4}	1.0×10^{-3}
No network coding	1.01×10^{-3}	1.22×10^{-3}

4.3   Summary

Through the comparison of the bit error rates in the above four cases, it can be seen that the network coding rate in the resource allocation mode is lower than that in the case of no network coding, that is, the performance is improved. The superiority of network coding is illustrated. The bit error rate of game-based resource allocation method in this particular satellite scenario is lower than that of the water injection-based system. So the game theory has certain advantages.

5 Conclusion

By analyzing and simulating three common satellite communication methods with network coding, and observing the optimization effect of network coding on satellite communication, it can be seen that network coding applied to satellite communication can improve data transmission rate and improve communication robustness. At the same time, in the case of satellite communication delay and high bit error rate, the use of network coding can effectively reduce the number of retransmissions and reduce the bit error rate of satellite broadcast communication system. In addition, by comparing the two types of resource allocation methods with or without network coding in a specific satellite scenario, that is, the comparison of the bit error rates in four cases, it can be seen that the network coding is better than the case of no network coding in any resource allocation mode. The bit error rate has been reduced to a certain extent, that is, the performance has been improved, indicating the superiority of network coding. The bit error rate of power allocation method based on the game theory is lower than that of power allocation method based on the water injection. The game theory has certain advantages, that is, the choice of resource allocation method also has a certain impact on system performance.

References

1. Nakahira, K., Abe, J., Mashino, J.: Novel channel allocation algorithm using spectrum control technique for effective usage of both satellite transponder bandwidth and satellite transmission power. IEICE Trans. Commun. **95**(11), 3393–3403 (2012)
2. Wu, X.L., Chen, Y.Y., Gao, L.Q., et al.: A utility-based OFDM resource allocation scheme for LEO small satellite system. In: International Conference on Cyberspace Technology, pp. 68–73. IET, Stevenage
3. Ji, Z., Wang, Y.Z., Feng, W., et al.: Delay-aware power and bandwidth allocation for multiuser satellite downlinks. IEEE Commun. Lett. **18**(11), 1951–1954 (2014)
4. Wang, H., Liu, A.J., Pan, X.F.: Optimization of joint power and bandwidth allocation in multi-spot-beam satellite communication systems. Math. Probl. Eng. **20**(4), 1–9 (2014)
5. Kaveh, A., Bakhshpoori, T., Afshari, E.: An efficient hybrid particle swarm and swallow swarm optimization algorithm. Comput. Struct. **14**(3), 40–59 (2014)
6. Fujii, H., Asai, T., Okumura, Y., et al.: Capacity achievable by spectrum sharing with adaptive transmit power control: based on field measurements. In: 2009 4th International Conference on Cognitive Radio Oriented Wireless Networks and Communications, CROWNCOM 2009, pp. 1–6. IEEE (2009)
7. Cheung, K., Lau, C., Lee, C.: Link analysis for space communication links using ARQ protocol. In: Aerospace Conference, pp. 1–8. IEEE
8. Fong, S.L., Yeung, R.W.: Variable-rate linear network coding. In: Proceedings of IEEE Information Theory Workshop (ITW), Chengdu, pp. 409–412
9. Jaggi, S., Sanders, P., Chou, P.A., et al.: Polynomial time algorithms for multicast network code construction. IEEE Trans. Inf. Theory **51**(6), 1973–1982 (2005)
10. Bahramgiri, H., Lahouti, F.: Robust network coding using diversity through backup flows. In: 4th Workshop on Network Coding. Theory and Applications, NETCOD 2008, Hongkong, pp. 1–6
11. Eritmen, K., Keskinoz, M.: Improving the performance of wireless sensor networks through optimized complex field network coding. IEEE Sens. J. **15**(5), 2934–2946 (2015)

Seamless Positioning and Navigation System Based on GNSS, WIFI and PDR for Mobile Devices

Yuanfeng Du[✉] and Dongkai Yang

Shandong Orientation Electronic Technology Co. Ltd.,
Postdoctoral Workstation of Jining Hi-Tech Industry Development Zone,
Beihang University, Beijing, China
yfdu1989@163.com

Abstract. As the rapid development of mobile Internet, many location-based services (LBS) have emerged for commercial cooperation, entertainment, security, and so forth. All of these require accurate and real time positioning of mobile devices with seamless indoor-outdoor transition in high dense urban regions. While satisfactory outdoor location services are achieved based on the global navigation satellite system (GNSS) technology, a really ubiquitous location system for both indoor and outdoor scenarios is not yet available. To cope with this challenge, we propose a hybrid location system, which makes the best of WIFI reference signal strength index (RSSI) fingerprinting technique for indoor positioning, traditional GNSS for the outdoor positioning, and pedestrian dead reckoning (PDR) technology for supplement. An environment-adaptive positioning handover module is proposed to perform positioning technology switching as environment changes. Moreover, a novel algorithm based on continuous hidden Markov model (CHMM) is proposed for the navigation in the indoor regions. Extensive tests for the seamless system proposed have been performed with satisfactory results and effectiveness.

Keywords: Seamless positioning · RSSI fingerprinting · CHMM · GNSS · PDR

1 Introduction

People are more and more concerned about their precise location information, for the purpose of positioning and navigation in daily life. GNSS, as an effective way of outdoor positioning, has become a necessary tool for traveling. Developed systems include global position system (GPS) of USA, GLONASS of Russia, BeiDou navigation satellite system of China, and Galileo system of Europe. Besides, combination of these positioning systems will also enhance the positioning accuracy.

Unfortunately, for an indoor mobile device, the satellite signal will be disrupted or blocked. Consequently, the device will be located with poor accuracy, or even unable to be located [1]. Meanwhile, indoor positioning is highly desirable since 70% of daily life is indoors. Several indoor positioning technologies have emerged, such as infrared-based positioning, ultra-wideband (UWB), radio frequency identification (RFID)

S. Han et al. (Eds.): AICON 2019, LNICST 286, pp. 522–540, 2019.
https://doi.org/10.1007/978-3-030-22968-9_48

positioning, and WIFI, most of which require modification of existing equipment or additional equipment, and are too costly to be used in large areas [2, 3]. With the development of wireless networks, a large amount of WIFI access points (APs) have been installed, which create a convenient condition for WIFI positioning. In addition to the good availability, a unique advantage of WIFI positioning technology is that WIFI chips have been equipped in most kinds of mobile devices. WIFI positioning systems based on the fingerprint method have been developed with accuracy between 1–5.4 m [4, 5].

Even though a sequence of technologies has been developed and infrastructures have been constructed, none of them are prospective to be accurate and efficient in both indoor and outdoor scenarios [6]. Thus, in order to provide effective location services for mobile users at anytime and anywhere, different technologies should be combined to supply an adaptive and dynamic solution, which can perform the handover between different technologies and adopt the best one available based on the environment together with the user requirements [4, 7].

The aim of this paper is to investigate the infrastructure of a seamless positioning system used in the urban region. We propose a seamless positioning system based on the GNSS, WIFI and PDR technologies. Detailed modules and self-management processes, including the signaling for communication between different modules, are discussed.

The remainder of this paper is organized as follows. After drawing state of the art in Sect. 2, we propose a hybrid positioning system in Sect. 3 followed by a handover algorithm in Sect. 4. Section 5 concerns the indoor and semi-outdoor navigation approach. Experimental and simulation results are detained in Sect. 6 and a conclusion is given in Sect. 7.

2 State of the Art

As aforementioned, most of studies on positioning have been performed for indoor and outdoor scenarios separately. Only a little attention has been paid to the seamless positioning for both scenarios.

Existing approaches include independent positioning technologies, such as ray tracing method [8], and combination of different technologies, such as GSM assisted GPS. LACB, a navigation prototype, is demonstrated in [9] to be capable of seamless outdoor-indoor navigation using RFID, WLAN, GPS, GSM, and Bluetooth. The combination of positioning systems, including satellite, UWB, RFID, and inertial measurement unit (IMU), is proposed for reliable positioning in [10–12].

In the combined systems above, not only different technologies are used to obtain positioning results, but also information fusion is used as the mobile devices move, such as Monte Carlo localization [13] for fusion of different sensory data and KF [14] for fusing WLAN, Bluetooth, and highly sensitive GPS positioning results with accelerometer. Moreover, some systems need modification on the device or additional equipment [15–17], which is difficult for mass market application.

On the other hand, an effective handover algorithm between different technologies is quite important in the seamless system, which has been thoroughly researched.

In [18], the method of combining GPS and WIFI networks is put forward to achieve seamless positioning and navigation, with the switching strategy according to GPS satellite number, WIFI signal number and geometric dilution of precision (GDOP) value. For environment matching, a weighted sum algorithm and a zone identification method based on media access control (MAC) address are introduced for system selection in [19]. In [20], key aspects of the seamless handover between outdoor and indoor positioning in StreamSpain are addressed. Result of GPS is superior to that of WIFI if GPS reports position every second out of 5 s. In addition, the user can switch the system from an outdoor to an indoor environment with only a simple vocal command [21]. Most of the existing positioning handover algorithms require the GNSS and WIFI modules are always working, which is power-consuming.

3   Seamless Positioning System

The seamless system with superior property selects the proper positioning technology to provide location information in both indoor and outdoor scenarios. Besides, in order to minimize power consumption, the switching state of positioning modules, including the GNSS module and WIFI module, should indicate a corresponding technology and environment.

The system has the ability to run in both the manual and non-manual mode. While the environment information can be imported directly by the user for positioning module and technology choosing, the proposed scenario-adaptive architecture is in charge of seamless positioning in the non-manual mode.

To realize this, a new scenario detection module is proposed, which obtains changes of the environment and triggers the handover between different positioning modules and technologies. The proposed architecture could be categorized into five layers: sensor, algorithm, hardware, data, and application, denoted by L1 to L5, respectively (shown in Fig. 1).

As the sensor layer, L1 consists of three modules, the user requirement module, the scenario module, and the state module. According to the user requirement, the best technology available should be chosen in terms of cost, processing time, and accuracy. When the scenario module detects an environmental change, a flag indicated handover will be sent to the handover module. Additionally, the motion state classification is performed by the state module to provide extra information for determining the update rate and improving the navigation performance [22].

L2 is the algorithm layer. All candidate technologies used for positioning are included in this layer, such as the GNSS positioning, WIFI fingerprint, PDR and so on. L3 is the hardware layer, which opens or closes the GNSS or WIFI modules according to the instruction from the handover modules Data collected from L3 will be processed for positioning in data layer: L4, by positioning algorithms and data fusion methods.

Afterwards, the location of the interested target will be showed on the map or used for other LBS applications in the application layer: L5.

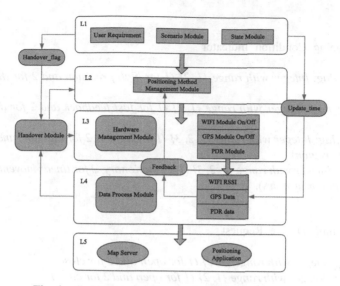

Fig. 1. Architecture of the seamless positioning system

To realize the self-management of the system, each layer should have the ability to exchange information with each other. A set of communication signaling based on the above architecture is proposed for applications. The signaling between the first five layers is shown in Fig. 2 and the detail parameters are as follows:

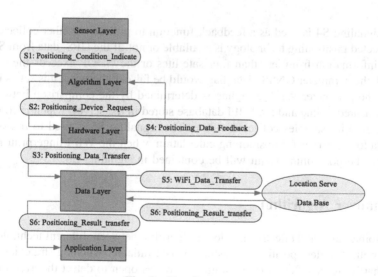

Fig. 2. Signaling structure

S1: Positioning_Condition_Indicator
{
  Accuracy_flag: Integer with range {1, 2} (1 for high precision and 2 for the general accuracy);
  Timedelay_flag: Integer with range {1, 2} (1 for fast feedback and 2 for the normal delay);
  Scenario_flag: Integer with range {1, 2, 3} (1 for indoor, 2 for outdoor, and 3 for the intermediate region);
  State_flag: Integer with range {1, 2, 3} (1 for stationary, 2 for linear movement, and 3 for downstairs or upstairs).
}

S2: Positioning_Device_Request
{
  WIFI_flag: Integer with range {1, 2} (1 for open and 2 for close);
  GNSS_flag: Integer with range {1, 2} (1 for open and 2 for close).
}

S3: Positioning_Data_Transfer
{
  WIFI_data: Numeric vector (RSSI from nearby APs);
  GPS_data: Numeric vector (information from visible satellites);
  PDR_data: Numeric vector (measurement from sensors).
}

The signaling S4 is used as a feedback function to indicate whether collected data of the selected positioning technology is available or not. If the GPS_data from S3 only contains information from less than four satellites or the GDOP exceeds the required threshold, the parameter GNSS_data_flag would be false. Otherwise, it is set as true. In addition, the parameter WIFI_data_flag is determined by the comparison between the AP set measured online and the WIFI database stored in the server, which is composed by the fingerprint samples collected offline. The signaling S5 is used to transmit the WIFI data to the server for positioning calculation, when the WIFI fingerprint method is chosen. The positioning result will be contained in signaling S6.

4 Handover Algorithm

An autonomic, fast, and effective handover algorithm between different technologies is crucial for the seamless positioning system. Most available switching strategies require that the hardware of different technologies is always open to detect the availability of data at the cost of large power consumption of mobile devices [18–21]. Here, we propose an environment adaptation handover algorithm, which can perform the handover intelligently based on the information of environmental change obtained by the scenario module.

4.1   Scenario Detector and Handover Requirement

The basic premise of the proposed algorithm is an accurate and efficient scenario detector. Existing methods for detection of indoor and outdoor environment are mostly based on the image recognition technology, which is too complicated to be used in mobile devices.

Light detectors are equipped in almost all mobile devices to adjust the lightness of screens. It has been shown in [23], by monitoring the light sensor, the strength of base stations and the measurement of magnetization, IODetector achieves a high accuracy rate of distinguishing indoor and outdoor scenarios. Because the intensity of sunlight within the visible spectrum is normally much higher than that from ordinary lighting lamps, the light intensity inside buildings is typically lower than that in either outdoor or semi-outdoor scenarios even in cloudy or rainy days. However, when a mobile device in the pocket or hold by hand is passed through areas around indoor windows, a miscarriage of justice might happen. Moreover, as environment changes, it becomes difficult to determine the detection threshold since change of cellular signal strength and magnetic flux can provide very limited help.

When a mobile device is in the outside and close to a building, the signal from APs both indoors and nearby environment can be received. If several received APs are not included in the offline WIFI database of the first floor of the building, the mobile device will be confirmed out of the building to a great extent.

Consequently, we consider using the matching of WIFI AP set together with the light detector to make a distinction between indoor and outdoor scenarios. Furthermore, we prefer to detect change of environment rather than the environment itself, as it is much easier and more accurate.

Let P be the matching degree between the detected AP set and that in the database

$$P = \sum_{i=1}^{N} t_{AP_i}, \quad t_{AP_i} = \begin{cases} 1 & if\ AP \in \Theta \\ -b & if\ AP \notin \Theta \end{cases} \tag{1}$$

with Θ the AP set in the database and t_{AP_i} the matching degree of each AP. Here b is the penalty factor whose value increases as the number of all APs in the area increases, with the typical value $\{2, 4\}$.

The pseudocode of detecting scenario change is as follows:

Assume the existing light intensity is L_0 and AP matching degree is p_0. The following judgments will be processed after each time increment T_0 with T_{total} the total time.

The proximity sensor firstly checks whether the light sensor is available for detection or not. If not, the information from light sensor ($\Delta L_t = |L_{t+1} - L_t|$) will not be considered.

$$Initially\ Handover\_flag = 0$$
$$For\ t = 0 : T_0 : T_{total}$$
$$\quad If\ present\ is\ daytime$$
$$\quad Detected\ the\ light\ intensity\ and\ proximity\ sensor$$
$$\quad\quad If\ \Delta L_t = |L_{t+1} - L_t| > thr_1$$
$$\quad\quad Matching\ the\ AP\ set$$
$$\quad\quad\quad If\ \Delta P_t = |P_{t+1} - P_t| > thr_2$$
$$\quad\quad\quad\quad Handover\_flag = 1$$
$$\quad\quad\quad End$$
$$\quad\quad End$$
$$\quad Else$$
$$\quad Only\ use\ the\ AP\ set\ matching\ in\ the\ nighttime$$
$$\quad\quad If\ \Delta P_t = |P_{t+1} - P_t| > thr_2$$
$$\quad\quad\quad Handover\_flag = 1$$
$$\quad\quad End$$
$$\quad End$$
$$Return\ Handover\_flag$$

As the detection of light intensity is very simple and accurate in some specific scenarios, the light detector is used as the main factor. Then the AP set matching algorithm is used to confirm the environment change especially in the building with large windows or nighttime scenario. To decrease the communication between the device and database, the AP set indoor Θ should be downloaded and stored in advance.

If the mobile device is inside of the building, the WIFI module is always open for indoor positioning and AP collection matching. On the other hand, when the device is in outside environment, the WIFI module would be switched on in the semi-outdoor area once the GNSS signal is not available. So the AP set matching for scenario change detection works well without extra power consumption from the WIFI module.

4.2   Handover Procedure

When the seamless positioning system initializes for the first response, if the user imports the information of indoors or outdoors to the system as manual mode, only the proper positioning module will be powered on. On the other hand, the system processes in the non-manual mode will execute and both GNSS and WIFI modules are powered on. After the system collects GNSS data and WIFI signal strength, the proper positioning technology module is chosen depending on their availability, with another one closed. The cellular network positioning can serve as a supplement in the case neither of the above two are available. Moreover, the A-GNSS technology is adopted to reduce the first response time if possible.

After initialization, the scenario module is used to monitor the environmental change. The handover module is then in charge of all the procedures related to the technology switching as illustrated in Fig. 3.

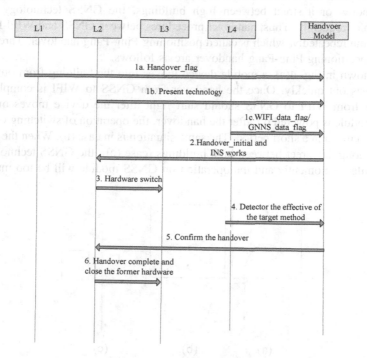

Fig. 3. Handover procedure

The handover_flag is sent out by the scenario module or the user requirement, and the handover module will be aware of the current technology from L2. Meanwhile, the data analysis result WIFI_data_flag or GNSS_data_flag from L4 will confirm the necessity of switching. The WIFI_data_flag is obtained based on the AP matching degree, while the GNSS_data_flag is obtained by the number of satellites detected.

Then, the PDR technology is used and the positioning technology management module will choose the candidate technology and asks the hardware management module to turn on the related modules in L3. If the measurement in L4 indicates the candidate technology is effective, the handover module will send out a confirmation signaling to L2; Otherwise, PDR or other reserved technologies will be selected. At last, the positioning technology module associated to the previous technology will be turned off.

As the stage of checking the availability of both present positioning technology and the candidate positioning method by the measurement exists, the wrong handover indication from the scenario detector will hardly impact the seamless system. For example, if the GNSS measurement can still works for the positioning, the handover would be stopped by the handover module.

4.3   Positioning Ping-Pang Handover Issues

The above handover procedure could perform technology switching effectively and provide location information seamlessly. However, if a user is walking along a large glass window or a street between high buildings, the GNSS technology may be unavailable frequently. Thus, handover procedures between GNSS and WIFI functions will execute repeatedly, which is called positioning Ping-Pang handover. Three typical cases of positioning Ping-Pang handover are as follows.

As shown in Fig. 4(a), a mobile device moves into the building from outside and then moves out quickly. Once the handover from GNSS to WIFI is completed, the handover from WIFI to GNSS should start right after the device moves out. If the related module is powered off after the handover, the operation of switching on and off will be too much in a short period. The same situation is in case (b). When the device is moving along the street between high buildings (case (c)), the GNSS technology will be unavailable momently and the operation on GNSS module will be too much.

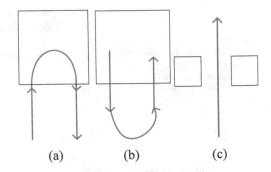

(a)   (b)   (c)

Fig. 4. Ping-Pang handover scenarios

To avoid the frequent switching, two timekeepers are employed. The first one records the working time of current environment, denoted by T1, and the second one indicates the unavailable duration of the former technology, denoted by T2. Only if T1 and T2 satisfy certain thresholds (30 s used in the experiments), the former positioning module would be powered off.

According to the proposed approach, both GNSS and WIFI modules are online for continuous operation over complex scenarios, with PDR positioning technology as backup. The number of positioning handover will be greatly reduced and the seamless position system will run more effectively.

5   Seamless Positioning

Besides indoor and outdoor scenarios, there exist semi-outdoor regions, where the GNSS signals are not available with high SNR and the WIFI fingerprint database is not exit. Seamless positioning can be achieved by taking the three scenarios into account.

5.1 Outdoor Positioning

GNSS has been developed for many years, and is the simplest and most precise method for outdoor positioning. It is widely equipped in smart phone or mobile devices. GNSS receiver calculates the real time positioning information through obtaining, tracking navigation signals with multiple channels each for one satellite. Its update rate could be set as one Hz or more.

5.2 Indoor Positioning

Nowadays, WIFI APs are popular and accessible in many public places, such as airports, offices, hotels. These APs are used for WIFI fingerprinting positioning technology, containing offline and online phases. In the offline phase, the positioning region is divided into many grids and fingerprint samples of each grid are collected to form a radio map. Information stored in this map includes the signal strength, and the number of detected APs, together with the location of grids. In the online phase, the real time data is collected and compared with samples in the radio map. The grid with the highest similarity is considered as the location of the mobile device. Although the technology needs a lot of time for collected samples, the matching algorithm has been well developed, based on interference eliminating and machining learning.

In indoor environment, the continuous positioning has drift result for the time-variant WIFI channel and signal strength. To overcome this problem, a new tracking method: Coherent matching (CM) method is proposed, which is based on several consecutive strength vectors received in the continuous receiving. Take the case of two continuous samples for example. Let S_{T_1} and S_{T_2} be two coherent vectors during the movement of a mobile device, and $S_{T_1 T_2}$ be the augmented vector which is the combination of these two vectors.

$$S_{T_1} = (rssi_{11}, rssi_{12}, \ldots, rssi_{1n}) \tag{2}$$

$$S_{T_2} = (rssi_{21}, rssi_{22}, \ldots, rssi_{2n}) \tag{3}$$

$$S_{T_1 T_2} = (rssi_{11}, rssi_{12}, \ldots, rssi_{1n}, rssi_{21}, rssi_{22}, \ldots, rssi_{2n}) \tag{4}$$

T1 and T2 are time when a vector is collected and n is the number of the APs.

Due to limitations of network hardware and software processing, the time period to receive each signal strength vector is almost 1.4 s [24]. The online interval for information collection is $T_{interval}$, which is assumed as 2 s to ensure real-time tracking.

$$L > T_{interval} \times V_0 \tag{5}$$

Because the normal speed of a walking person V_0 is 0.6 m/s, the inequality (5) above is satisfied when the grid size L $\geq$ 1.2 m. After movement of the mobile device over interval $T_{interval}$, only two cases could happen. The device either stays in the same grid, or moves to a next grid.

Since the positioning region has been equipped with grids for offline collection, the spatial continuity can be used to change fingerprints of the two adjacent grids into a series of combined vectors. The online vector $S_{T_1 T_2}$ is then matched with combined database to obtain the positioning result.

As time evolves, change of location from one grid to another can be treated as a dynamic state changing process. To analyze its series pattern, the CHMM is adopted, which models a Markov process with parameters as a stochastic finite state machine. In this situation, the underlying process is the user's sequential changes in location, with the hidden internal states, and measured signal strengths are observables. More precisely, we define a CHMM on the location-state space χ and the observation space ϕ. The CHMM consists of a radio map $\lambda = \{P(s_i|l_j)\}$, a location-state transition matrix $A = \{P(l_i|l_j)\}$, and an initial state distribution $\pi = \{P(l_i)\}$. The radio map λ is a set of conditional probabilities which give the likelihood of obtaining measured signal strength. The transition matrix A indicates the possible movements in the state space. Consider the case that the mobility of the device is limited and it can only move to adjacent grids. For example, a mobile device can only move in the hallway but not across the wall. Thus, only a few elements in matrix A are nonzero. Moreover, the transition matrix A should be trained by a series of labeled traces with the Baum-Welch method [25].

Given a coherent observation sequence V_{T1T2}, the well-known Viterbi algorithm [26] can be used to infer the most possible hidden state sequence in CHMM, which is a sequence of changes of the user's location. Detailed steps are as follows:

$$Initialization: \quad \begin{aligned} \delta_1(i) &= \pi_i b_i(S_1), \quad 1 \le i \le N \\ \phi_1(i) &= 0, \quad 1 \le i \le N \end{aligned} \tag{6}$$

$$Recursion: \quad \begin{aligned} \delta_t(j) &= \max_{1 \le i \le N} [\delta_{t-1}(i) a_{ij}] b_j(S_i), \quad t = 2, 1 \le j \le N \\ \phi_t(j) &= \arg\max_{1 \le i \le N} [\delta_{t-1}(i) a_{ij}], \quad t = 2, 1 \le j \le N \end{aligned} \tag{7}$$

$$Finalization: \quad \begin{aligned} p^* &= \max_{1 \le i \le N} [\delta_T(i)] \\ q_T^* &= \arg\max_{1 \le i \le N} [\delta_T(i)] \end{aligned} \tag{8}$$

$$Sequence\,solving: \quad q_t^* = \phi_{t+1}(q_{t+1}^*), \quad t = 2, 1 \tag{9}$$

Here $\delta_T(i)$ is the maximum value at time T, $b_i(S_i)$ is the probability of S_j in location i, a_{ij} is the transition probability from location i to location j, and q_T^* is the obtained sequence. p^* and $\phi_t(i)$ are intermediate variables.

5.3 Semi-outdoor Positioning

When a positioning service is requested in the semi-outdoor region for initialization, the positioning result can only be provided by the positioning based on cellular network. Positioning results will not be updated until the device moves to indoor or outdoor scenarios.

Besides, the semi-outdoor region plays an important role as an intermediate connection for the seamless indoor and outdoor. With the PDR technology, the user's location can be easily updated over time, since accelerometers and electronic compasses are equipped in most mobile devices [27].

In order to explain the above process, let us take a route from one building to a nearby bus station for example. After the WIFI technology directs the user to the exit of the building, the positioning technology will switch to the PDR technology and the location of the exit is consider as the starting point. Through the acceleration sensor and magnetic sensor, the step number and heading can be computed separately. Displacement is then calculated by multiplying step number and step length. Adding the last position information to the displacement produces the current position.

However, results from accelerometers and electronic compasses in mobile devices are highly noisy. The good news is that the dimension of semi-outdoor regions is always small and the time duration is short. A simplified PDR technology is proposed to solve the problem and the detection of step number and step length is avoided. Firstly, a fairly accurate walking speed can be obtained when the WIFI or GNSS technology works effectively. Then, an initial segment is obtained by the time duration of location updating T_{update} multiplying the average velocity v. After a set of segments perform the angular deflection obtained from the magnetic sensor, they are connected from one point to another. If the component of accelerometer measurement in Z axis indicates no change in the body's center of gravity, the mobile device is considered as static in the updating interval and no segment will be added [6]. Thus, the tracing route will be extended periodically until another accurate positioning technology is available to replace this method.

$$\bar{v} = s/t \tag{10}$$

$$(x_i, y_i) = (x_{i-1}, y_{i-1}) + \bar{v} \times T_{update} \times (\cos(\alpha), \sin(\alpha)) \tag{11}$$

where (x_{i-1}, y_{i-1}) and (x_i, y_i) are the previous and current locations, respectively. α is obtained from the measurement of the compass and compensated by the difference between the geomagnetic south pole and geographic north pole.

6 Experimental Evaluation

To evaluate proposed algorithms and modules in the system, both experiments and simulations are performed for the scenario detection module, the handover module, and the indoor tracing algorithm. The experiment is taken out in the New Main Building block E in Beihang University (shown in Fig. 5), with more the 20 APs around. The area in the first floor is about 12 m * 8 m, with a large glass door. During the offline phase, 50 RSS time samples are collected for each of the 40 RPs. The RPs are evenly distributed with an average grid spacing of 2 m.

Fig. 5. Experiment scenario

Firstly, we collect the AP set $\Re_{indoor}$, $\Re_{semi-out}$ and $\Re_{outdoor}$ for indoor, semi-outdoor and outdoor scenarios, respectively. Then, a series of samples collected from the whole area are compared with the AP set from different scenarios. As shown in Figs. 6 and 7, each cylindrical represent the number of same APs in one AP set sample. Outdoor samples match $\Re_{outdoor}$ to a high extent, and indoor samples match $\Re_{indoor}$ better, which provides a good foundation for the scenario detected algorithm.

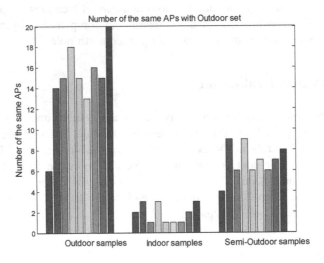

Fig. 6. Number of matched APs with $\Re_{outdoor}$

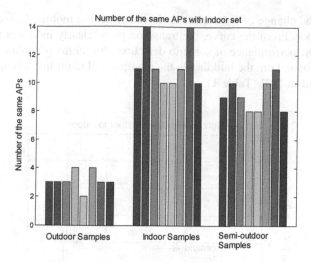

Fig. 7. Number of matched APs with $\Re_{indoor}$

In practice, only $\Re_{indoor}$ is collected and stored in the fingerprint database and the proposed P is the matching degree between the detected AP set and those in the database. When the mobile device move from indoor to outdoor, the matching result is obtained in Fig. 8 and the decreasing trend becomes obvious as b changes between {2, 4}.

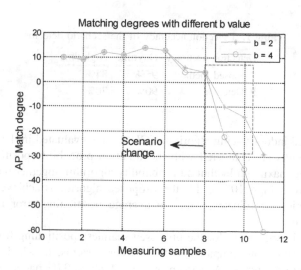

Fig. 8. Matching degrees with different b value

In Fig. 9, the change of light intensity is shown as the mobile device moves from outdoor to indoor. From the curve, the transition point clearly indicates the change of the scenario. The performance of scenario detection algorithms is evaluated through 20 traces walking in and out the building in the daytime and nighttime, compared with the IODetector used in [18] (Table 1).

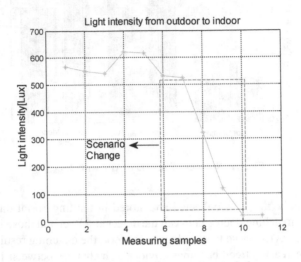

Fig. 9. Light intensity from outdoor to indoor

Table 1. Detection accuracy of the scenario detector

Detection accuracy	Daytime	Nighttime
Proposed method	95%	84%
IODetector	90%	70%

The proposed indoor tracing algorithm (CHMM) is evaluated in the following and experimental results are compared with the tradition probability positioning method, which adopts the maximum likelihood probability algorithm together with the Kalman filter. As shown in Figs. 10 and 11, the proposed algorithms achieve better performances in location coordinates, with the average positioning error improved from 1.45 m to 0.98 m.

The biggest improvement for the proposed seamless positioning framework is the less battery consumption compared to the former systems, in which the WIFI and GNSS devices are always on. As shown in Fig. 12, about 37% battery is saved due to the handover algorithm proposed in this paper.

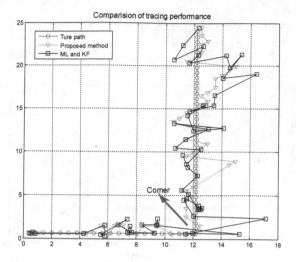

Fig. 10. Comparisons of location error computed by different algorithms

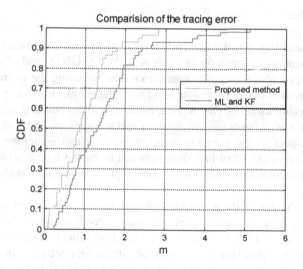

Fig. 11. Comparisons of tracing error

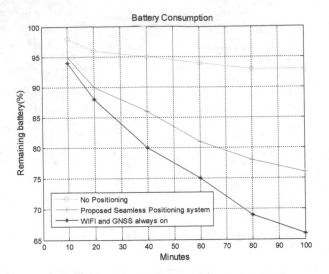

Fig. 12. Battery consumption

7 Conclusion

We present a seamless positioning and navigation system for inferring indoor and outdoor user location information by means of WIFI, GNSS and PDR positioning technologies. It provides a complete organic system, including the overall hierarchical structure, the environment adaptation handover algorithm, and the positioning and navigation algorithm used in different area, especially in the building and semi-outdoor region. In such a way, various optimization technologies can be seamlessly implemented with respect to the scenario detection module and switching of the related hardware. These provide a fast handover between using the best available positioning technology and minimizing the power consumption associated with the usage of mobile devices.

A careful evaluation of the proposed system in more general situations will of great interest, including different environment and users' speeds of motion, building layer or altitude information, which will provide a fully operational 3D positioning picture. Another challenging problem is to combine fusion technologies from indoor and outdoor maps for seamless switching and providing excellent user experiences since single outdoor or indoor maps can only provide a coarse granularity positioning and navigation results within limited regions.

References

1. Liu, H., Darabi, H., Banerjee, P., Liu, J.: Survey of wireless indoor positioning techniques and systems. IEEE Trans. Syst. Man Cybern. Part C Appl. Rev. **37**, 1067–1080 (2007)
2. Fang, S.-H., Lin, T.-N., Lin, K.-C.: A novel algorithm for multipath fingerprinting in indoor WLAN environments. IEEE Trans. Wirel. Commun. **7**, 3579–3588 (2008)

3. Luo, Y., Law, C.L.: Indoor positioning using UWB-IR signals in the presence of dense multipath with path overlapping. IEEE Trans. Wirel. Commun. **11**, 3734–3743 (2012)
4. Alshamaa, D., Mourad-Chehade, F., Honeine, P.: Tracking of mobile sensors using belief functions in indoor wireless networks. IEEE Sens. J. **18**, 310–319 (2018)
5. Gan, X., Yu, B., Heng, Z., Huang, L., Li, Y.: Ubiquitous Positioning, Indoor Navigation and Location-Based Services (UPINLBS), pp. 1–7 (2018)
6. Mozamir, M.S., Bakar, R.B.A., Din, W.I.S.W.: Indoor localization estimation techniques in wireless sensor network: a review. In: 2018 IEEE International Conference on Automatic Control and Intelligent Systems (I2CACIS), pp. 148–154 (2018)
7. Yuan, Y., Melching, C., Yuana, Y., et al.: Multi-device fusion for enhanced contextual awareness of localization in indoor environments. IEEE Access **6**, 7422–7431 (2018)
8. Wang, C., Luo, J., Zheng, Y.: Optimal target tracking based on dynamic fingerprint in indoor wireless network. IEEE Access **6**, 77226–77239 (2018)
9. Zundt, M., Ippy, P., Laqua, B., Eberspächer, J.: LACBA - a location – aware community – based architecture for realizing seamless adaptive location-based service. In: 12th European Enabling Technologies for Wireless Multimedia Communications, pp. 1–7 (2006)
10. Kruppa, M.: Emergency indoor and outdoor user localization. In: Wichert, R., Eberhardt, B. (eds.) Ambient Assisted Living, pp. 239–256. Springer, Heidelberg (2011). https://doi.org/10.1007/978-3-642-18167-2_17
11. Di Flora, C., Ficco, M., Russo, S., Vechio, V.: Indoor and outdoor location based services for portable wireless devices. In: IEEE International Conference on Distributed Computing Systems Workshops, pp. 244–250 (2005)
12. Sakamoto, Y., Ebinuma, T., Fujii, K., Sugano, S.: GPS-compatible indoor-positioning methods for indoor-outdoor seamless robot navigation. In: Advanced Robotics and its Social Impacts (ARSO), pp. 95–100 (2012)
13. Fernadez-Madrigal, J.A., Cruz-Martin, E., Gonzalez, J., Galindo, C., Blabco, J.L.: Application of UWB and GPS technologies for vehicle localization in combined indoor-outdoor environments. In: International Symposium on Signal Processing and Its Applications, pp. 1–4 (2007)
14. Kuusniemi, H., Chen, L., Ruotsalainen, L., Pei, L., Chen, Y., Chen, R.: Multi-sensor multi-network seamless positioning with visual aiding. In: International Conference on Localization and GNSS, pp. 146–151 (2011)
15. Nord, J., Synnes, K., Parnes, P.: An architecture for location aware applications. In: Proceedings of the 35th Hawaii International Conference on System Science (2002)
16. Peng, J., Zhu, M., Zhang, K.: New algorithms based on sigma point Kalman filter technique for multi-sensor integrated RFID indoor/outdoor positioning. In: Indoor Positioning and Indoor Navigation (IPIN), pp. 21–25 (2011)
17. Johannes, L., Degener, J., Niemeier, W.: Set-up of a combined indoor and outdoor positioning solution and experimental results. In: Indoor Positioning and Indoor Navigation (IPIN), pp. 1–6 (2010)
18. Yan, M., Yubin, X., Xiuwan, C.: Wireless local area network assisted GPS in seamless positioning. In: Computer Science Electronics Engineering (ICCSEE), pp. 612–615 (2012)
19. Khan, M.S.Z., Tan, C.-W., Silvadorai, T., Ramadass, S.: Novel algorithm to ensure smooth and unobtrusive handover among positioning systems. In: Information Retrieval & Knowledge Management (CAMP), pp. 229–234 (2012)
20. Hansen, R., Wind, R., Jensen, C.S., Thomsen, B.: Seamless indoor/outdoor positioning handover for location-based services in StreamSpin. In: Proceedings of the 10th International Conference on Mobile Data Management Systems, Services and Middleware, pp. 267–272 (2009)

21. Ran, L., Helal, S., Moore, S.: Drishti: an integrated indoor/outdoor blind navigation system and service. In: Proceeding of the Second IEEE Annual Conference on Pervasive Computing and Communications, pp. 23–30 (2004)
22. Bancroft, J.B., Garrett, D., Lachapelle, G.: Activity and environment classification using foot mounted navigation sensors. In: Indoor Positioning and Indoor Navigation (IPIN), pp. 1–6 (2010)
23. Zhou, P., Zheng, Y., Li, Z., Li, M., Shen, G.: IODetector: a generic service for indoor outdoor detection, SenSys 2012, Toronto, Canada (2012)
24. Bullock, J.B., Chowdhary, M., Rubin, D., Leimer, D., Turetzky, G., Jarvis, M.: Continuous indoor positioning using GNSS, Wi-Fi and MEMS dead reckoning. In: ION GNSS, pp. 2408–2416 (2012)
25. Rabiner, L.R.: A tutorial on hidden Markov models and selected applications in speech recognition. Proc. IEEE **77**, 257–286 (1989)
26. Viterbi, A.: Error bounds for convolutional codes and an asymptotically optimum decoding algorithm. IEEE Trans. Inf. Theory **13**, 260–269 (1967)
27. Kealy, A., Roberts, G.: Evaluating the performance of low cost MEMS inertial sensors for seamless indoor/outdoor navigation. In: Position Location and Navigation Symposium (PLANS), ION, pp. 157–167 (2010)

Adaptive Routing Protocol for Underwater Wireless Sensor Network Based on AUV

Yuying Ding[1], Cheng Li[1(✉)], Kun Hao[1], Xiujuan Du[2], Lu Zhao[1], and Qi Liu[3]

[1] School of Computer and Information Engineering,
Tianjin Chengjian University, Tianjin 300384, China
1076545117@qq.com, licheng.mun@gmail.com,
Kunhao@tcu.edu.cn, zhaolu6892@163.com
[2] School of Computer Science and Technology, Qinghai Normal University,
Qinghai 810008, China
dxj@qhnu.edu.cn
[3] Computation Center, Tianjin Chengjian University, Tianjin 300384, China
liuqicj@126.com

Abstract. Underwater Wireless Sensor Networks (UWSNs) have the characteristics of high energy consumption, low transmission rate, and narrow bandwidth. How to extend the lifespan of UWSNs is a research hotspot of underwater routing protocols. An adaptive routing protocol (ARPA) based on autonomous underwater vehicle (AUV) is proposed in this paper. In the phase of network layering, ARPA takes AUV as the sink node to dynamically layer the network. In the data transmission stage, the next hop forwarding node that meets the requirements is selected based on the horizontal and vertical mechanism. In this paper, the ARPA is verified by the network simulator NS-3. The simulation results show that compared with the existing underwater routing protocols, the ARPA not only guarantees the efficient and stable data transmission rate but also reduces the network delay and improves the energy utilization rate.

Keywords: UWSNs · AUV · Dynamic layering · Adaptive routing

1 Introduction

With the deepening of ocean exploration and research, underwater wireless sensor networks (UWSNs) [1, 2] have attracted extensive attention, and they are mainly applied in ocean management, auxiliary navigation, disaster monitoring, military activities and other fields [3, 4]. In practice, due to the particularity of underwater environment, common underwater nodes usually use acoustic communication for data transmission. However, the acoustic communication network has such characteristics as narrow bandwidth, high bit error rate and low transmission rate [5–7]. Therefore, compared with the traditional terrestrial sensor network, the implementation of UWSNs will face more difficulties and challenges.

In addition, the battery capacity of underwater nodes is limited, and battery replacement is difficult and expensive. Therefore, extending the network lifespan [8] is

S. Han et al. (Eds.): AICON 2019, LNICST 286, pp. 541–553, 2019.
https://doi.org/10.1007/978-3-030-22968-9_49

one of the important contents of the research of UWSNs. In the current three-dimensional UWSNs, mobile AUV [9, 10] is mostly used to coordinate and operate with underwater nodes, surface base stations, and other equipment. AUV can change the depth its own depth in underwater, send various control information to underwater nodes, and forward the collected data to the surface base station, which effectively improve the transmission reliability of data packets.

To solve the above problems, some scholars have proposed the following routing protocols. Literature [11] proposes a vector-based forwarding protocol (VBF). When receiving a packet, the node will determine whether to forward the packet according to the distance of the forwarding vector and transmit the packet along the preset virtual "routing pipe". However, in areas with a small number of network nodes, appropriate next-hop forwarding nodes may not exist in the virtual "routing pipe", which leads to routing void problem, thus additional network delay increases, the service life of UWSNs reduces and energy consumption increases. Literature [12] proposes a depth-based routing protocol (DBR). DBR obtains the current depth of each node through the depth sensor. When forwarding data, it compares the depth of nodes for forwarding and uses the depth threshold to control excessively redundant forwarding. However, one packet may be repeatedly forwarded by multiple nodes, which may easily lead to packet conflict and increase network energy consumption. Literature [13] proposed void-aware pressure routing (VAPR) protocol. In VAPR, nodes use periodic beacons to establish a directed path to the surface and obtain the location information that can reach the sink node, then the nodes perceive the routing void by greed-forwarding packets. However, in order to avoid routing void, nodes need to periodically maintain and update the directed path to the surface, which leads to serious congestion of packets and rapid energy consumption. Literature [14] proposed a level-based adaptive geo-routing for UWSNs (LBAGR). Different routing decisions are adopted for different flows, and the optimal routes were determined according to the compound forwarding factors of the candidate nodes. Moreover, the upstream flows were unicast to reduce collision and energy consumption. However, the sender may send the last frame multiple times because it does not receive the acknowledgment (ACK) packet, resulting in an increase in the hierarchy of underwater nodes to infinity. In addition, after a long time of data packet transmission, sink node may fail to broadcast and receive data packets, resulting in state deadlock of sink node.

Aiming at the above shortcomings, this paper proposes an adaptive routing protocol based on AUV (ARPA) for UWSNs. ARPA mainly includes network layering and data transmission phase. In the phase of network layering, ARPA takes AUV as the sink node, compares the distance between the underwater sensor node and AUV with the distance threshold, and forms a dynamic layering structure centering on AUV. In the data transmission stage, the source node introduces the vertical mechanism according to the vertical distance and vector angle between candidate nodes and AUV to choose the best the next-hop node, when energy consumption of the selected candidate nodes is greater than the predetermined threshold, the node performs level mechanism, and selects a replacement node from the list of candidate child nodes to replace the forwarding function of the node. Simulation results show that ARPA not only ensures efficient and stable data transmission rate but also reduces network delay and prolongs network lifespan.

The remainder of the paper is organized as follows. Section 2 introduces the network model and energy consumption model of ARPA. Section 3 describes the design of ARPA. Section 4 evaluates the performance. Section 5 concludes the paper.

2 Network Model and Energy Consumption Model

2.1 Network Model

In the three-dimensional UWSNs model, various nodes in the network mainly include ordinary underwater nodes, AUV, surface nodes and monitoring center. The network model of ARPA is shown in Fig. 1. Each ordinary underwater node is randomly distributed in the underwater area. It obtains its depth information through the depth sensor and has a unique ID. It is mainly responsible for collecting underwater data and storing the monitoring data into its buffer zone. As a sink node, AUV is responsible for collecting and transmitting data information in the task area to form a dynamically self-organizing sensor network. The transmission of data information from the source node to AUV marks the success of data transmission, then AUV sends the data information along the fixed or dynamic transmission path to the surface node distributed in the specified range. Then the underwater routing is completed.

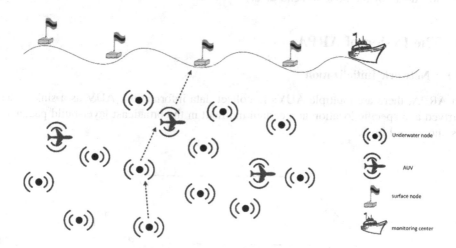

Fig. 1. Network model of ARPA

2.2 Energy Consumption Model

In UWSNs, the energy consumption of nodes mainly includes the consumption when sending data and receiving data. The energy consumption of data transmission depends on the length of the transmission path. The longer the transmission distance is, the energy consumption becomes the greater. The energy consumption of receiving data is constant regardless of the transmission distance. Therefore, in the process of data transmission, the energy consumption of sending data is used to measure the energy consumption of the entire network. In the attenuation model of underwater acoustic signal [15], let $A(x)$ be the attenuation factor of power and transmission distance, x represents the transmission distance of transceiver node, then the attenuation factor is:

$$A(x) = x^k \alpha^x \tag{1}$$

$$\alpha = 10^{\frac{\alpha(f)}{10}} \tag{2}$$

The energy absorption coefficient is:

$$\alpha(f) = \frac{0.11f^2}{1+f^2} + \frac{44f^2}{4100+f^2} + 2.75 \times 10^{-4}f^2 + 0.003 \tag{3}$$

The energy used by the node to send L bit data is:

$$E = T_P P_0 A(x) = 10^{\frac{\alpha f(x)}{10}} P_0 T_P x^3 \tag{4}$$

Where, k is the spread spectrum factor with a value of 1.5, f is the signal frequency, P_0 is the minimum power required for the node to receive data, and T_P is the transmission delay of the node to send data.

3   The Design of ARPA

3.1   Network Initialization

In ARPA, there are multiple AUVs to collect data information. AUV as a sink node, arrived at a specific location at a certain moment in the broadcast layer-build package, as shown in Fig. 2.

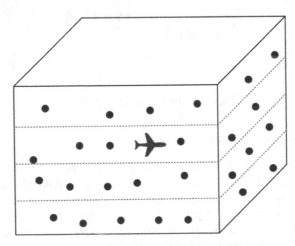

Fig. 2. Schematic diagram of dynamic layering structure centered on AUV

AUV will broadcast data collection information to each node, after the node receives signals, the distance x between it and AUV is calculated according to the signal strength (from formula 1–3), and compared with threshold distance D. If the distance x is less than the distance threshold D, the node defines itself as the first layer node of the AUV, and then the first layer node floods again to establish the entire layering network in turn.

3.2 Data Transmission

In UWSNs, with the increase of communication distance, packet forwarding frequency increases, network energy consumption increases and packet transmission rate decreases. Therefore, in order to improve packet transmission rate and save energy consumption, when the next-hop forwarding node is selected in this protocol, the source node introduces a vertical mechanism based on the vertical distance and vector angle between candidate nodes and AUV to determine the optimal next-hop node. When the energy consumption of the selected candidate node is greater than the pre-determined threshold, the node executes the horizontal mechanism and selects the replacement node from the list of candidate child nodes to replace the forwarding function of the node.

Vertical Mechanism

AUV broadcasts the control package to the entire underwater node. After the underwater node receives this broadcast, the source node i looks for the next hop candidate node within the communication range R. As is shown in Fig. 3:

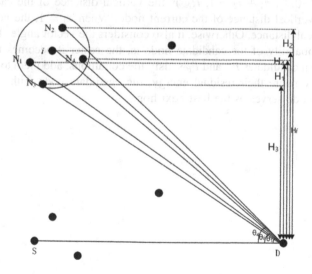

Fig. 3. Schematic diagram of vertical mechanism searches for candidate nodes

N_1, N_2, N_3, and N_4 are neighbor nodes on the first floor of i. Firstly, the vertical distance H_i between i and AUV node D is established. H_i can be obtained by the depth sensor. The vertical distance between N_2 and D is H_2. Since $H_2 > H_i$, N_2 does not meet the requirements of being a candidate node, so the candidate nodes that meet the requirements are N_1, N_3 and N_4. Therefore, in order to reduce the filtering range in regions with more candidate nodes, the vector angle θ_i is established in i and AUV, which represents the angle formed by the two vectors. Among them, $\overrightarrow{sD}$ represents the horizontal vector of AUV, and $\overrightarrow{iD}$ represents the vector of i and AUV, $\theta_i \in [0, 2\pi]$.

$$\theta_i = \arccos \frac{\left|\overrightarrow{iD}\right|^2 + \left|\overrightarrow{sD}\right|^2 - \overrightarrow{iD} \cdot \overrightarrow{sD}}{2\left|\overrightarrow{iD}\right|\left|\overrightarrow{sD}\right|} \tag{5}$$

θ_4 as the vector angle between node N_4 and AUV, due to $\theta_4 > \theta_i$, So N_4 is not eligible. The candidate next hop nodes that meet the requirements are N_1 and N_3.

The forwarding probability of candidate nodes is:

$$P = \alpha_1 P_H + \alpha_2 P_\theta = \alpha_1 \left(1 - \frac{H_N}{H_i}\right) + \alpha_2 \left(1 - \frac{\theta_N}{\theta_i}\right) \tag{6}$$

Where, P_H, P_θ are respectively the forwarding probability of candidate nodes considering the vertical distance and the vector angle. α_1, α_2 are called coefficient factors, $\alpha_1 \alpha_2 \in [0, 1]$, $\alpha_1 + \alpha_2 = 1$. H_N is the vertical distance of the candidate node, and H_i is the vertical distance of the current node. When $\alpha_1 = 1$, the node only considers the vertical distance. Otherwise, it also considers the vector angle. The higher the forwarding probability of the candidate node is, the easier it becomes the ideal next hop. And if both candidates P_H and P_θ satisfy the conditions, add them to the candidate list of i, and compare their residual energy, the candidate node with larger residual energy of the node serves as the best next hop.

Algorithm 1 ARPA protocol Vertical mechanism
Inputs:
1: H_N: the vertical distance between node N and AUV.
2: θ_N: the angle between node N and the vector AUV.
3: E_N: the residual energy of node N.
4: P_N: the forwarding probability of node N.
5: P_{θ_N}: node N only considers the forwarding probability
6:     when the vector angle is included.
7: P_{H_N}: node N only considers the forwarding probability of
8:     vertical distance.
9: if $(H_1 = H_3)$ {
10:   if $(\theta_1 = \theta_3)$ {
11:     if $(E_1 = E_3)$
12:           $P_1 = 1$;
13:   else
14:           $P_3 = 1$; }
14:   else $\{P_1 = P_{\theta_1}; P_3 = P_{\theta_3}; \}\}$
15: else {
16:     if $(\theta_1 = \theta_3)$ {
17:           $P_1 = P_{H_1}; P_3 = P_{H_3}; \}\}$

Horizontal Mechanism

When the energy consumption of the selected candidate node is greater than the pre-determined threshold, the node performs the horizontal replacement mechanism and selects the replacement node from the list of candidate child nodes to replace the forwarding function of the node. Where, the predetermined threshold:

$$T = \frac{E}{X \cdot L} \tag{7}$$

$$L = \lceil x/R \rceil \tag{8}$$

E is the residual energy of the node, X is the predefined positive number, L is the ideal minimum level for the node to send packets to AUV, R is the communication distance of the node, and x is the distance between the node and its nearest node. In order to reduce the impact of node replacement on other parts of the network, the protocol should consider selecting the node with the highest probability of data transmission as the replacement node.

The average SNR with distance d [15] is:

$$\tau(d) = \frac{E_b/A(d,f)}{N_0} = \frac{E_b}{N_0 d^k a(f)^d} \tag{9}$$

Where, E_b and N_0 are constants, respectively representing the average energy consumption per unit bit and the noise power density.

Rayleigh fading modeling is adopted, and the probability distribution of SNR is as follows:

$$P_d(X) = \int_0^\infty \frac{1}{\tau(d)} e^{-\frac{X}{\tau(d)}} \tag{10}$$

The probability of bit error $P_e(d)$ can be calculated as:

$$P_e(d) = \int_0^\infty P_e(X) P_d(X) dX \tag{11}$$

This protocol adopts BPSK modulation mode, and the bit error rate of any pair of nodes with distance d is:

$$P_e(d) = \frac{1}{2} \left(1 - \sqrt{\frac{\tau(d)}{1 + \tau(d)}} \right) \tag{12}$$

Therefore, the probability $p(d, m)$ of packet transmission of m bit transmitted by any pair of nodes with distance d is:

$$p(d, m) = (1 - P_e(d))^m \tag{13}$$

In conclusion, if the probability of packet delivery of the node in the list of candidate child nodes is higher, the node will be horizontal replacement nodes of the current node.

The source node selects the next hop and sends the packet according to the horizontal-vertical mechanism. At this time, the forwarding node turns into a new source node and continues to look for the optimal path to select the best next hop node until AUV is found within the broadcast range of the source node and the packet is successfully transmitted to AUV. The overall flow chart of ARPA is shown in Fig. 4.

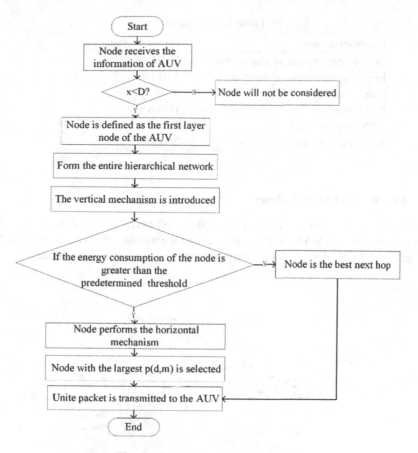

Fig. 4. Overall flow chart of ARPA

4 Performance Evaluations

In this paper, we use NS-3 as the simulator of a routing protocol to verify the performance of ARPA, and the performance parameters such as average end-to-end delay, packet transmission rate, and average energy consumption is compared and analyzed with VBF and LB-AGR. Experimental parameter selection is shown in Table 1:

Table 1. Experimental parameters list

Parameter names	Parameter value
Area size of three-dimensional water	2500 m * 2500 m * 2500 m
Number of ordinary nodes	1000
Initial energy of the nodes	100 J
Acoustic signal frequency	25 kHz

(continued)

Table 1. (*continued*)

Parameter names	Parameter value
Energy consumption of transmitting data	60 μJ/bit
Energy consumption of receiving data	3 μJ/bit
Number of AUV	2
Packet size	100kB
AUV moving speed	1 m/s
Simulation run time	2000 s

4.1 Average End-to-End Delay

Figure 5 shows the change curve of the end-to-end average time delay of the three routing protocols in UWSNs with the increase of the number of nodes. Compared with VBF and LB-AGR, ARPA significantly reduces the average end-to-end delay.

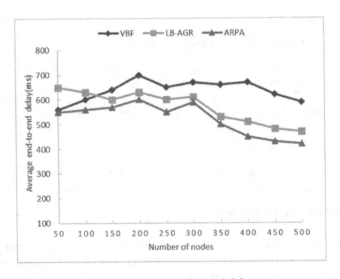

Fig. 5. Average end-to-end delay

The reason is that when the nodes in UWSNs change dynamically, the trajectory motion controllability of AUV makes the end-to-end delay fluctuation of ARPA smaller than the other two protocols. In addition, the vertical distance from node to AUV may be taken into consideration during data transmission to determine the next-hop forwarding node, which greatly improves the packet transmission rate and reduces the network delay.

4.2   Packet Transmission Rate

As shown in Fig. 6, packet transmission rates of the three protocols vary with the number of nodes, among which ARPA is the best and LB-AGR has a higher packet transmission rate than VBF. This is because the ARPA adopted based on vertical distance, the Angle of the vector, residual energy and packet transmission rate factors, namely the vertical - horizontal mechanism to determine the optimal under a forwarding nodes, making increased when the number of network nodes, node density is more and more big, the ARPA is easier to determine the next hop node, network connectivity, data transmission rate is also improved.

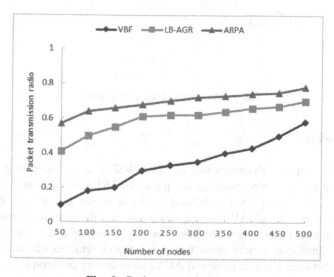

Fig. 6. Packet transmission rate

4.3   Average Energy Consumption

As shown in Fig. 7, when the number of nodes participating in the network increases, the total energy consumption increases. The average energy consumption of the network in this paper is lower than the other two protocols. Compared with VBF and LB-AGR, the average energy consumption of ARPA is reduced by 26.7% and 11.3% respectively. This is because the nodes in ARPA transmit data directly to AUV along the direction of the hierarchy ladder, avoiding the increase of transmission number when the data packet is transmitted along the node path with unsatisfied conditions, thus achieving better energy saving effect. And the inactive nodes are dormant to save energy.

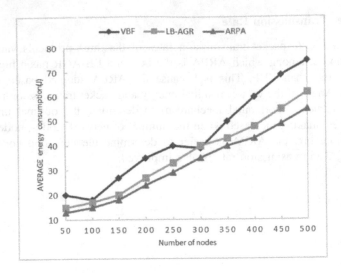

Fig. 7. Average energy consumption

5 Conclusion

Aiming at the dynamic characteristics of 3D UWSNs, an adaptive routing protocol (ARPA) based on AUV is proposed in this paper. In ARPA, the data in the network are transmitted to AUV along the hierarchical ladder direction through the dynamic layering structure formed with AUV as the sink node, and the next-hop forwarding node that meets the conditions is selected based on the horizontal and vertical hierarchical mechanism. Simulation results show that the protocol achieves efficient data packet transmission between a source node and AUV, saves energy consumption and prolongs network lifespan.

Acknowledgments. This research was supported by Tianjin Natural Science Fund Project 18JCYBJC85600, Qinghai Key Laboratory of Internet of Things Project (2017-ZJ-Y21), Tianjin Enterprise Science and Technology Commissioner Project 18JCTPJC60500, Infrared Radiation Heating Intelligent Control and Basic Ventilation Auxiliary Engineering System Development of No. 2 Section of Changchun Metro Line 2 (hx 2018-37).

References

1. Akyildiz, I.F., Pompili, D., Melodia, T.: Underwater acoustic sensor networks: research challenges. Ad Hoc Netw. **3**(3), 257–279 (2005)
2. Xu, W., et al.: Marine information gathering, transmission, processing, and fusion: current status and future trends. Scientia Sinica Informationis **46**(8), 1053–1085 (2016)
3. Alfouzan, F., Shahrabi, A., Ghoreyshi, S.M., Boutaleb, T.: Efficient depth-based scheduling MAC protocol for underwater sensor networks. In: 2017 Ninth International Conference on Ubiquitous and Future Networks (ICUFN), pp. 827–832 (2017)

4. Alfouzan, F., Shahrabi, A., Ghoreyshi, S.M., Boutaleb, T.: Performance comparison of sender-based and receiver-based scheduling MAC protocols for underwater sensor networks. In: 2016 19th International Conference on Network-Based Information Systems (NBIS), pp. 99–106 (2016)
5. Souiki, S., Hadjila, M., Feham, M.: Energy efficient routing for mobile underwater wireless sensor networks. In: 2015 12th International Symposium on Programming and Systems (ISPS), pp. 1–6 (2015)
6. Souiki, S., Hadjila, M., Feham, M.: Clustering combined with bio inspired routing in underwater wireless sensor networks. In: Proceedings of the International Conference on Intelligent Information Processing, Security and Advanced Communication (ACM), p. 62 (2015)
7. Hao, K., Shen, H., Liu, Y., Wang, B., Du, X.: Integrating localization and energy-awareness: a novel geographic routing protocol for underwater wireless sensor networks. Mob. Netw. Appl. 23(5), 1427–1435 (2018)
8. Su, R., Venkatesan, R., Li, C.: An energy-efficient asynchronous wake-up scheme for underwater acoustic sensor networks. Wirel. Commun. Mob. Comput. 16(9), 1158–1172 (2016)
9. Khan, J.U., Cho, H.S.: Data-gathering scheme using AUVS in large-scale underwater sensor networks: a multihop approach. Sensors 16(10), 1626 (2016)
10. Ghoreyshi, S.M., Shahrabi, A., Boutaleb, T.: An efficient AUV-aided data collection in underwater sensor networks. In: 2018 IEEE 32nd International Conference on Advanced Information Networking and Applications (AINA), pp. 281–288 (2018)
11. Xie, P., Cui, J.H., Lao, L.: VBF: vector-based forwarding protocol for underwater sensor networks. In: Boavida, F., Plagemann, T., Stiller, B., Westphal, C., Monteiro, E. (eds.) NETWORKING 2006. LNCS, vol. 3976, pp. 1216–1221. Springer, Heidelberg (2006). https://doi.org/10.1007/11753810_111
12. Yan, H., Shi, Z.J., Cui, J.H.: DBR: depth-based routing for underwater sensor networks. In: Das, A., Pung, H.K., Lee, F.B.S., Wong, L.W.C. (eds.) Ad Hoc and Sensor Networks, Wireless Networks, Next Generation Internet, NETWORKING 2008. LNCS, vol. 4982, pp. 72–86. Springer, Heidelberg (2008). https://doi.org/10.1007/978-3-540-79549-0_7
13. Noh, Y., Lee, U., Wang, P., Choi, B.S.C., Gerla, M.: VAPR: Void-aware pressure routing for underwater sensor networks. IEEE Trans. Mob. Comput. 12(5), 895–908 (2013)
14. Lan, S., Du, X., Liu, F., Feng, Z.X.: Level-based adaptive geo-routing for underwater sensor network. Appl. Res. Comput. 31(1), 236–238 (2014)
15. Sozer, E.M., Stojanovic, M., Proakis, J.G.: Underwater acoustic networks. IEEE J. Oceanic Eng. 25(1), 72–83 (2000)

Performance Analysis of Energy-Efficient Cell Switch off Scheme for CoMP Networks

Fei Ding[1,2], Yan Lu[3], Jialu Li[4], Ruoyu Su[1,2(✉)], Dengyin Zhang[1,2], and Hongbo Zhu[1,2]

[1] Jiangsu Key Laboratory of Broadband Wireless Communication and Internet of Things, Nanjing University of Posts and Telecommunications, Nanjing 210003, China
{dingfei,suruoyu,zhangdy,zhuhb}@njupt.edu.cn
[2] Jiangsu Key Laboratory of Wireless Communications, Nanjing University of Posts and Telecommunications, Nanjing 210003, China
[3] China Mobile Group Jiangsu Co., Ltd., Nanjing 210029, China
[4] The 28th Research Institute of China Electronics Technology Group Corporation, Nanjing 210007, China

Abstract. In this paper, a joint power and subcarrier optimization problem to minimize the network energy consumption with considerations of dynamic Coordinated Multipoint Transmission (CoMP) clustering, user quality of service (QoS) requirement and base station (BS) load is formulated for cell switch off in CoMP transmission scenario. Since the complexity of such optimization problem is prohibitive in practical application, following the manner of dynamic programming (DP), the original problem is decomposed to a sequence of subproblems on cell switch off with dynamic CoMP clustering and system transmit power optimization. Then the Cluster Load Search, User Sum SINR and Cell Sum Load Based Clustering Schemes are proposed for cell switch off evaluation. The simulation results show that the proposed schemes achieve competitive network energy-efficient performance compared with benchmark optimization scheme while at the same time save up to 40% of the overall overhead.

Keywords: Coordinated Multipoint · Cell switch off · Energy efficiency

1 Introduction

It is widely accepted that switching off the Evolved NodeB (eNB) which is not fully loaded is an effective way to improve system energy efficiency [1]. However, in current cell switch off schemes, neighboring cells are usually required to increase transmit power to enlarge their coverage and handover the traffic of the switched off cells [2], and thus result in degradation of energy saving performance from the view of the whole network.

Coordinated Multipoint (CoMP) technology has been noticed for its advantage in interference avoidance and spectrum efficiency enhancement [2–6]. Naturally, the combination of CoMP and cell switch off in cellular network is a promising approach for energy saving [7] without increasing the transmit power of the active cells.

S. Han et al. (Eds.): AICON 2019, LNICST 286, pp. 554–562, 2019.
https://doi.org/10.1007/978-3-030-22968-9_50

However, detailed power consumption models for eNB with CoMP transmission was missing until the contribution of [8] and [9]. Compared with power consumption model from Energy Aware Radio and neTwork TecHnologies (EARTH) project [10], the power consumption for additional signal processing and backhauling were introduced by [8] and [9] and thus made these models more accurate for CoMP application. Based on these power consumption models, [11] studied the improvement of energy saving gain and energy consumption ratings (ECR) for CoMP and Non-CoMP systems. The comparison of energy efficiency performance between different cooperative modes (dynamic cell selection (DCS), joint transmission (JT) and coordinated beam forming (CB)) are presented in [12] and JT is suggested as the most energy efficient mode among all CoMP modes under the same transmit power constraint due to its diversity gain. However, most previous works only discussed the cases with fixed CoMP cluster size and thus limited their application in realistic network. If dynamic CoMP clustering is introduced, the variety of CoMP clustering configuration and discontinuous allocation of subcarriers will render the joint optimization problem a combinatorial optimization problem involving integer variables, and thus requires exhaustive search to find the optimal solution. In most cases, the complexity brought by such exhaustive search is prohibitive and hard for realistic implementation.

The rest of this paper is organized as follows: Sect. 2 describes the cellular network system model. Section 3 introduces the cell switch-off based energy minimization schemes and Sect. 4 illustrates the simulation results. Section 5 gives a conclusion.

2 System Model

2.1 CoMP Transmission

Only joint transmission (JT) mode is considered in this paper for its better energy efficiency performance according to [12, 13, 16]. In JT, the downlink traffic data and payload is available at each point in the CoMP cooperating group and transmitted via Physical Downlink Shared Channel (PDSCH) from multiple eNBs in the CoMP group [2].

Assumes that an M-cell cellular network with base-stations $BS_1 ... BS_M$ of omnidirectional antennas and random user equipment (UE) location are configured. Let's define set $M = \{1,2,3...M\}$, for non-CoMP scenario, the SINR of user u in serving cell T is:

$$SINR_u = \frac{P_{tx,T} h_{u,T}}{\sum\limits_{q \in M, q \neq T} P_{tx,q} h_{u,q} + P_{Noise}} \tag{1}$$

Where $P_{tx,T}$ is cell transmit power, $h_{u,T}$ is the large scale channel gain from BS_T to user u. $P_{tx,q} h_{u,q}$ is the received power of the co-channel interfering cells q. P_{Noise} is the noise power.

For CoMP cell switch off scenario as shown in Fig. 1, when a cell T is switched off, one or more of its neighboring cells (i, j, k, for example) enable CoMP transmission to serve UEs in the switched off cell T. Assume that total L neighboring cells participate in this cooperative transmission cluster, which is denoted as CoMP cluster C_T with cluster size L_{C_T}. Assumes the impact of intra-cell interference could be eliminated by cyclic prefix (CP) of OFDM symbols, according to the definition of CoMP JT, received signals from cells belong to C_T are considered as desired signal, while received signal other than this CoMP cluster are interference. Then the SINR for CoMP scenario is

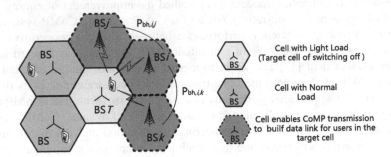

Fig. 1. CoMP Transmission after cell switched off. After switching off the light loaded cell T, the neighboring cells i, j, k enable CoMP transmission to build data link for users original in cell T.

$$SINR_{u,CoMP} = \frac{\sum\limits_{i \in C_T} P_{tx,i} h_{u,i}}{\sum\limits_{j \in \mathcal{M}, j \notin C_T} P_{tx,j} h_{u,j} + P_{\text{Noise}}}$$ (2)

2.2   Power Consumption Model for Cooperative Cells

As in [9], for macro eNB, the overall power consumption can be divided into several parts. Among them, the radio frequency (RF) transmit power and baseband signal processing are most significant ones. Besides, the cooling loss, battery backup and backhauling power consumption between base stations under CoMP transmission should also be considered. Hence, the overall power consumption for eNB macro base station under CoMP transmission is,

$$P_{\text{BS\_CoMP}} = \left(\frac{P_{tx}}{\mu_{\text{PA}}} + P_{sp}\right) \cdot (1 + C_c) \cdot (1 + C_{\text{PSBB}}) + P_{bh}$$ (3)

where μ_{PA} stands for the power amplifier efficiency, power cooling loss and battery backup loss are denoted as C_c and C_{PSBB}. The eNB transmit power is denoted as P_{tx}, power consumption for signal processing is denoted as P_{sp} while P_{bh} represents the backhauling power consumption.

3   Cell Switch off Based Energy Minimizing Schemes

In this section, the optimization problem for minimum network energy consumption is presented. Since this optimization problem is often very high complexity, it is decomposed into a sequence of dynamic CoMP clustering and cluster energy optimization sub-problems with cell switch off. Finally, three low complexity schemes are proposed for solving the sub-problems.

3.1   Optimization Problem

The optimization problem for minimum network power consumption is given by:

$$\min_{P_{tx},S_f,W} P_{\text{network}} = \sum_{i=1}^{M} P_{\text{BS},i} \tag{4}$$

$$s.\ t.\ R_{u,i} = \begin{cases} W_{u,C_T}^{S_f,C_T,L_{C_T}} \log_2\left(1 + SINR_{u,T,CoMP}\right) \geq D_{u,i}, \forall u \in K_T \\ W_{u,i} \log_2\left(1 + SINR_{u,i}\right) \geq D_{u,i},\ \forall u \in K_{C_T} | \forall u \notin K_T \end{cases} \tag{4a}$$

$$\sum_{u=1}^{K_i} N_{u,S_f,C_T,L_{C_T}} \leq N_{w,i},\ \forall\, i \in M \tag{4b}$$

$$L_{C_T} \in Z^+ \text{ for } \forall\, C_T \tag{4c}$$

In order to avoid any coverage issue, constraints (4a) and (4b) are proposed, where (4a) represents the achievable user data rate for user u of cell i should be no less than its demanded rate $D_{u,i}$ in both CoMP and non-CoMP cells, to fulfill the user QoS requirement. The notion $S_{f,C_T,L_{C_T}}$ defines the cell combination set of CoMP cluster C_T with size L_{C_T} (4b) set a limitation that the total TFRB requirements from all K_i users in cell i should be no more than the overall available TFRB resource for the cell. (4c) guarantees that the CoMP cluster size is a positive integer for all clusters.

The optimization problem (4) is a combinatorial optimization problem not only because finding the optimal cell combination set $S_{f,C_T,L_{C_T}}*$ for cluster C_T is an NP-hard problem but also the allocation for discontinuous subcarrier $W_{u,C_T}^{S_f,C_T,L_{C_T}}$ for user u and real continuous variable of transmit power $P_{tx,i}$ for cell i.

As a result, one approach to solve problem (4) is exhaustive search with iteration on $P_{tx,i}$, $W_{u,C_T}^{S_f,C_T,L_{C_T}}$ and all possible cluster configurations. However, the complexity of such search is not acceptable for most systems. In order to reduce the complexity, some algorithms, like that in [14], relaxed $W_{u,C_T}^{S_f,C_T,L_{C_T}}$ to continuous variable and fixed the CoMP cell combination $S_{f,C_T,L_{C_T}}$ with few constant L_{C_T} categories, and converts the power-frequency allocation problem to convex problem. But fixed CoMP cluster size will limit the algorithm's application in real network. Hence, dynamic CoMP cell clustering is proposed in this paper.

In order to reduce the complexity of (4), according to DP, the optimization problem is decomposed to several sequential sub-problems (also known as DP stages) each, with single cell switch off. In each of them, dynamic CoMP clustering and BS transmission power optimization is considered. Then assumes $W_{u,C_T}^{S_f,C_T,L_{C_T}*}$ a continuous real variable that can be allocated based on user rate requirement and received SINR. Since in the original problem, $W_{u,C_T}^{S_f,C_T,L_{C_T}}$ is an integer number, there is certain degradation caused by rounding error when mapping the obtained $W_{u,C_T}^{S_f,C_T,L_{C_T}*}$ to $W_{u,C_T}^{S_f,C_T,L_{C_T}}$ in (4). However, if suppose the total available frequency subcarrier resource is much larger than the number of users, then the allocated number of subcarriers for each user is significantly larger than the rounding error, the degradation is acceptable.

Therefore, problem (4) is reformulated as a DP problem with time sequentially subproblems (5) on minimizing cluster energy consumption as:

$$\min_{P_{tx},S_f,W} P_{cluster} = \sum_{\substack{i=1 \\ i \in C_T}}^{L} P_{BS,i} \tag{5}$$

$$s.\ t.\quad R_{u,i} = \begin{cases} W_{u,C_T}^{S_f,C_T,L_{C_T}*} \log_2\left(1+SINR_{u,T,CoMP}\right) \geq D_{u,i}, \forall u \in K_T \\ W_{u,i} \log_2\left(1+SINR_{u,i}\right) \geq D_{u,i},\ \forall u \in K_{C_T}|u \notin K_T \end{cases} \tag{5a}$$

$$\sum_{u=1}^{K_i} N_{u,S_f,C_T,L_{C_T}} \leq N_{w,i}\quad \forall i \in M \tag{5b}$$

$$L_{C_T} \in Z^+ \quad \text{for } \forall C_T \tag{5c}$$

Problem (5) can be further decomposed to an integer optimization problem on the combination of $S_{f,C_T,L_{C_T}}$ and L_{C_T}, and a convex problem on the allocation of $W_{u,C_T}^{S_f,C_T,L_{C_T}*}$ and $P_{tx,i}$. The convex problem can be solved by power and subcarrier optimization with efficient tools from [15], while for the integer optimization problem, three low complexity cell switch off schemes are proposed in this paper to obtain the optimal $S_{f,C_T,L_{C_T}}$ with dynamic L_{C_T} for each sub-problem.

The energy saving performance of proposed schemes are impacted by parameters such as subscriber scale, user rate demands, cell transmit power, bandwidth and cluster size. For the convergence consideration, cell load as well as user rate demand are checked during each iteration. During the optimization iteration of cell switch off, if the cell load limit is reached, the iteration will break and a test of smaller cluster size will be initiated. If all the cluster sizes are not applicable for the current sub-problem, a new target cell will be obtained and corresponding cell switch off problem will be initiated. If the proposed schemes are not applicable for any cell in the pre-set network, it will get terminated.

4   Simulation Results

The parameters are listed in Table 1 in accordance with [8, 14]. Assume perfect channel information sharing among CoMP cells and Zero-Forcing Beamforming (ZF) is employed in CoMP-JT downlink transmission, which is widely used with low complexity [14]. The wrap-around technique is applied in our simulation.

Table 1. Simulation parameters.

Parameter	Value
No. of subscribes per cell	2, 4, 6, ... 60
Network configuration (Size and BS type)	19 cells with Macro BS
Cell diameter	500 m
BS Maximum RF output power $P_{tx, max}$	46 dBm
Minimum user rate	256 kbps
Maximum user rate	1.5 Mbps
eNB signal BW	10 MHz
No. of CoMP cluster size L_{C_T}	2, 3, 4, 5, 6
Power density of thermal noise P_{noise}	−174 dBm/Hz
Shadow Fading	Log-Normal, $\sigma = 6$dB
Propagation & Pathloss mode	$PL_{LOS}(dB) = 131 + 42.8 \lg d$, d in km
Power amplifier efficiency μ_{PA}	38.8%
Power supply and battery backup factor P_{PSBB}	11%
Cooling factor C_c	23%
Baseline signal processing power consumption p_{sp}	58 W
Backhauling efficiency μ_{BH}	0.5 W/Mbps
Signal power fractions $\gamma_1 = \gamma_2$	0.001
Backhauling additional pilot density fraction p	8/168
Backhauling additional signaling fraction q	8

The normalized network energy saving performance is shown in Fig. 2 for different clustering schemes after a single cell switches off. Thanks to the exhaustive search for all the possible cell combinations for CoMP cluster C_T, CLS cell switch-off scheme results in better performance compared with sum-LOAD and sum-SINR schemes. On the contrast, the sum-SINR based cell switch-off scheme achieves comparative energy saving performance with CLS but less complexity. The sum-LOAD scheme results in the worst energy saving performance due to the introduction of user QoS requirement to the clustering scheme and that makes the $S_{f, C_{T, L_{CT}}} *$ estimation affected much more by the user behavior.

The average network energy saving gain after a single cell switch off under different L_{C_T} are compared in Fig. 2. The result shows that in a typical homogeneous network with macro eNB, the network energy saving decreased largely with more users in each cell due to user QoS requirement and backhauling between CoMP cells. It is also found that larger CoMP cluster has advantage for applications with fewer users per cell. With the increase of user density, the energy consumption by additional signal processing and backhauling between CoMP cells degrade the power saving performance of larger CoMP clusters.

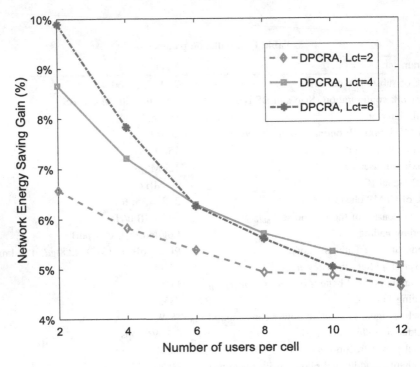

Fig. 2. Network energy saving gain with different L_{C_T}, User rate = 256 kbps.

As illustrated in Fig. 3, the energy efficiency performance after a single cell switch off is compared for different average user rate requirements, which reveals that it's harder to support more users or higher average data demands within the same cluster. This figure also clearly shows that outage points are reached after the increase of users per cell and therefore the iteration stops with no upgrade. In Fig. 3, the switch off scheme of sum-SINR with fixed eNB power is also simulated, which provides a lower EE performance until the outage points are reached.

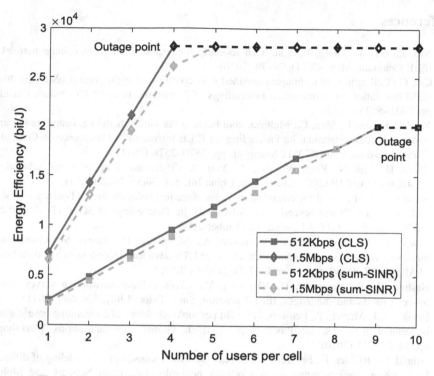

Fig. 3. Energy Efficiency (EE), average user rate = 512 kbps, 1.5 Mbps.

5 Conclusions

In this paper, in order to reduce the complexity of the combinatorial problem of CoMP clustering in each DP stage, three low complexity clustering schemes are proposed in this paper. Simulation results show the Cluster Load Search Based Scheme (CLS) has the best energy saving performance but the worst in complexity. The sum LOAD based scheme requires lower complexity but worst in the energy saving performance. The sum SINR based scheme has a competitive energy saving performance with CLS while has the lowest complexity. The following work based on the proposed schemes could be the study of its effectiveness under different network scenarios, such as HetNet and Hyper-dense network.

Acknowledgements. This work is partially supported by the Ministry of Education-China Mobile Research Foundation, China (No. MCM20170205), the Scientific Research Foundation of the Higher Education Institutions of Jiangsu Province, China (No. 17KJB510043), Six talent peaks project in Jiangsu Province (No. DZXX-008), and the Research Foundation for Advanced Talents of Nanjing University of Posts and Telecommunications (No. NY217146).

References

1. Niu, Z., Wu, Y., Gong, J., et al.: Cell zooming for cost-efficient green cellular networks. IEEE Commun. Mag. **48**(11), 74–79 (2010)
2. Cili, G.: Cell switch off technique combined with coordinated multi-point (CoMP). In: 2012 IEEE International Conference on Proceedings of Communications (ICC), Ottawa, Canada, pp. 5931–5935 (2012)
3. Yu, W., Kwon, T., Shin, C.: Multicell coordination via joint scheduling, beamforming and power spectrum adaptation. In: Proceedings of IEEE International Conference on Computer Communications (INFOCOM), Shanghai, pp. 2570–2578 (2011)
4. Wang, H., Liu, N., Ping, W., Pan, Z., You, X.: Three novel opportunistic scheduling algorithms in CoMP-CSB scenario. Sci. China Inf. Sci. **56**(8), 1–12 (2013)
5. Nakamura, T.: Proposal for candidate radio interface technologies for IMT-advanced based on LTE release 10 and beyond (LTE-Advanced). In: Proceedings of 3GPP ITU-R WP 5D 3rd Workshop on IMT-Advanced, 15 October 2009
6. Sawahashi, M., Kishiyama, Y., Morimoto, A., Nishikawa, D., Tanno, M.: Coordinated multipoint transmission/reception techniques for LTE-advanced [coordinated and distributed MIMO]. IEEE Wirel. Commun. J. **17**(3), 26–34 (2010)
7. Hashmi, Z., Boostanimehr, H., Bhargava, V.: Green cellular network: a survey, some research issues and challenges. IEEE Commun. Surv. Tutor. **13**(4), 524–540 (2011)
8. Fehske, A.J., Marsch, P., Fettweis, G.P.: Bit per joule efficiency of cooperating base stations in cellular networks. In: Proceedings of IEEE Global Communications Workshops, pp. 1406–1411 (2010)
9. Arnold, O., Richter, F., Fettweis, G., Blume, O.: Power consumption modeling of different base station types in heterogeneous cellular netwroks. In: Future Network and Mobile Summit (2010)
10. EARTH Project: D2.3 V2 - Energy efficiency analysis of the reference systems, areas of improvements and target breakdown (2012). https://www.ict-earth.eu/publications/publications.html
11. Eluwole, O.T., Lohi, M.: Coordinated multipoint power consumption modeling for energy efficiency assessment in LTE/LTE-advanced cellular networks. In: 2012 19th International Conference on Proceedings of Telecommunications (ICT), pp. 1–6 (2012)
12. Huq, K.M.S., Mumtaz, S., Rodriguez, J., Aguiar, R.L.: Comparison of energy-efficiency in bits per joule on different downlink CoMP techniques. In: 2012 IEEE International Conference on Proceedings of Communications (ICC), Ottawa, Canada, pp. 5716–5720 (2012)
13. Han, S., Xu, S., Meng, W., Li, C.: Dense-device-enabled cooperative networks for efficient and secure transmission. IEEE Netw. **32**(2), 100–106
14. Han, S., Yang, C., Wang, G., Lei, M.: On the energy efficiency of base station sleeping with multicell cooperative transmission. In: Proceedings of the 22nd IEEE International Symposium on Personal, Indoor and Mobile Radio Communications, pp. 1536–1540 (2011)
15. Boyd, S., Vandenberghe, L.: Convex Optimization. Cambridge University Press, Cambridge (2004)
16. Han, S., Huang, Y., Meng, W., Li, C., Xu, N., Chen, D.: Optimal power allocation for SCMA downlink systems based on maximum capacity. IEEE Trans. Commun. **67**(2), 1480–1489

An Energy-Efficient Routing Protocol for Internet of Underwater Things

Ruoyu Su[1,2], Fei Ding[1,2], Dengyin Zhang[1,2]([✉]), Hongbo Zhu[1,2],
and Xiaohong Wang[3]

[1] Jiangsu Key Laboratory of Broadband Wireless Communication and Internet of
Things, Nanjing University of Posts and Telecommunications, Nanjing 210003, China
{suruoyu,dingfei,zhangdy,zhuhb}@njupt.edu.cn
[2] Jiangsu Key Laboratory of Wireless Communications,
Nanjing University of Posts and Telecommunications, Nanjing 210003, China
[3] State Grid Jiangsu Economic Research Institute, Nanjing 210008, China
hxwang@163.com

Abstract. By using underwater acoustic sensor networks (UWSNs) as a
backbone, Internet of Underwater Things (IoUT) have developed rapidly
due to their applications, such as environmental monitoring, marine
resources development, and geological oceanography. Frequently changing or recharging the batteries of underwater sensor nodes may not be
realistic due to the harsh marine environment and high cost of underwater equipment. In this paper, we propose an energy-efficient routing
protocol for IoUT for marine environmental monitoring. Our simulation
results show that the proposed routing protocol can prolong the network
lifetime for IoUT compared with other published routing protocols.

Keywords: Routing metric · Internet of Underwater Things ·
Residual energy

1 Introduction

By using underwater acoustic sensor networks (UWSNs) as a backbone, Internet
of Underwater Things (IoUT) have developed rapidly due to their applications,
such as environmental monitoring, marine resources development, and geological
oceanography [1–8]. Unlike the conventional wireless sensor networks (WSNs),
IoUT has several distinct features. First of all, underwater nodes utilize limited
battery power to collect data and to communicate with each other. It is difficult to frequently recharge the batteries. Furthermore, a fairly high transmitting

Supported by the Ministry of Education-China Mobile Research Foundation, China
(No. MCM20170205), the Scientific Research Foundation of the Higher Education
Institutions of Jiangsu Province, China (No. 17KJB510043), Six talent peaks project in
Jiangsu Province (No. DZXX-008), and the Research Foundation for Advanced Talents
of Nanjing University of Posts and Telecommunications (No. NY217146).

power may required when the distance between a source node and a destination node is large. Therefore, underwater communications with multiple hops is always used in IoUT [9–14], efficient underwater communication is a challenging issue when designing routing scheme. In this paper, we proposed an energy-efficient routing protocol for IoUT by jointly considering the power levels of the acoustic modem and the residual energy of each sensor node. We demonstrate the novel performance of the proposed routing protocol by comparing with other published routing protocols.

2   Routing Protocol

In this section, we propose a routing protocol for IoUT. Specifically, a sensor node send data to the sink by using different paths and different transmitting power levels. As we know, the energy consumption during underwater communications is controlled by the transmitting and receiving power levels in IoUT. Only using the minimum cost paths results in quick batteries depletion. An efficient route between a source node to a destination node should contain underwater acoustic link with lower transmitting power with underwater sensor nodes with relatively high residual energy. Denote $\mathbb{E}_r^{(u)}$ and $\mathbb{E}_r^{(v)}$ as the residual energies of node u and v, respectively. Suppose p_{tmax} as the maximum transmitting power. We express the cost of an underwater acoustic link $\mathbb{C}$ between u and v as:

$$\mathbb{C}^{(u,v)} = w_p \frac{t \times (p_t^{(u,v)} + p_r)}{t \times (p_{tmax} + p_r)} + w_e \left(\frac{\mathbb{E}_0^{(u)} - \mathbb{E}_r^{(u)}}{\mathbb{E}_0^{(u)}} + \frac{\mathbb{E}_0^{(v)} - \mathbb{E}_r^{(v)}}{\mathbb{E}_0^{(v)}} \right), \qquad (1)$$

where t is the transmission time of a data packet, w_p and w_e are the weights for power level and energy consumption, respectively. The latter in Eq. (1) represents the energy consumption of nodes u and v.

3   Performance Evaluation

3.1   Simulation Settings

We consider the IoUT with grids topology to evaluate the performance of the proposed routing protocol. We suppose that 600 m is the average distance between any two adjacent sensor nodes. At the beginning of simulation, each underwater sensor node's battery energy is $(N^2 - 1) \times 10^6$ J, where N is the number of sensor nodes in IoUT. The traffic intensity is 100 packets per day per node. In our simulation, data packets are collected by underwater sensor nodes and then are transmitted to the sink node. The sink node will send the collected data to the sea surface. To evaluate the proposed routing scheme under different energy consumption, we employ the operation parameters of the EvoLogics modem. In general, we suppose three transmitting power with to different efficient range [15]. The energy consumption can be calculated as follows [7].

$$\mathbb{E}_t = p_t^{(u,v)} \times t, \qquad (2)$$

where $\mathbb{E}_t$ is the energy consumption of node u when it transmits a data packet to node v. Equation (2) is employed to compute the energy consumption when sensor nodes are in receiving and idle listening. The data rate of the acoustic modem is 13900 bit/s.

Parameter settings are presented in Table 1.

Table 1. Simulation parameters of the proposed routing protocol

Parameters	Value
Network size	11×11, 13×13, 15×15, and 17×17
Initial energy of node u $\mathbb{E}_0^{(u)}$	10^6 J
Data rate	13900 bit/s
Distance between two closest adjacent nodes d_c	600 m
Traffic $i^{(u)}$	100 packets/day
Transmitting power $p_t^{(u,v)}$	2.8 W, 8 W, and 35 W
Corresponding transmission range	1000 m, 2000 m, and 3500 m
Receiving power p_r	1.1 W
Idle listening power p_l	0.08 W
Sleeping power p_s	0 W
Packet size	1200 bytes

3.2 Routing Protocol Performance with Different Weights of Power and Energy Consumption

In this section, we consider two sets of transmitting power. One set has two transmitting power, i.e., 2.8 W, 8 W. The other set includes three transmitting power, i.e., 2.8 W, 8 W, and 35 W. The network size is set to a 11×11 grid IoUT to present the performance of the proposed routing protocol. As shown in Fig. 1(a) and Fig. 2(a), for both two sets of transmitting power, we can obtain the best ratio of w_p to w_e to generate the maximum received number of data packets in the sink node. When the weight of energy consumption increases and the weight of transmitting power decreases, the number of received packets by the sink node appears at 0.6:0.4 for the set of two transmitting power and 0.5:0.5 for the set of three transmitting power.

In Figs. 1(b) and 2(b), we observe that, for two or three transmitting power, according to the proposed routing metric (as shown in Eq. (1)), the transmitting power and the residual energy mainly control the performance of the proposed routing protocol. As the ratio of the weights of power and energy, i.e., $w_p:w_e = 1 : 0$, the number of times using the lowest transmitting power reaches the maximum value, which represents that the nodes frequently select routes with lowest transmitting power. It is worth to note that these nodes close to the sink

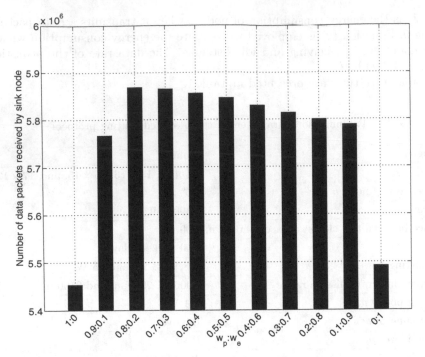

(a) Number of received data packets vs. $w_p : w_e$

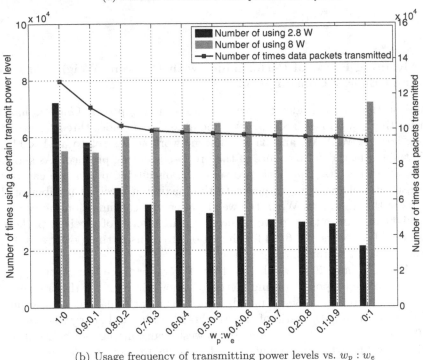

(b) Usage frequency of transmitting power levels vs. $w_p : w_e$

Fig. 1. Two transmitting power levels, network size: 11×11

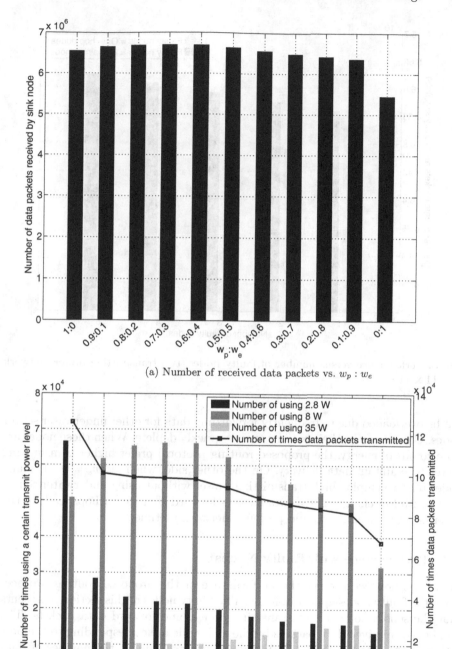

(a) Number of received data packets vs. $w_p : w_e$

(b) Usage frequency of transmitting power levels vs. $w_p : w_e$

Fig. 2. Three transmitting power levels, network size: 11×11

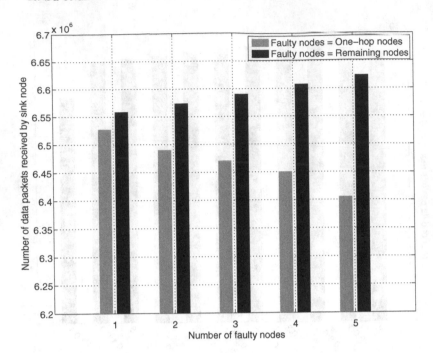

Fig. 3. Performance versus number of faulty nodes: two transmitting power, network size: 11×11

can be overloaded due to frequently forwarding data for other underwater sensor nodes. Consequently, their battery energy quickly deplete. When those nodes are close to out of energy, the proposed routing protocol prefer higher transmitting power to maintain data delivery. On the other side, when $w_p:w_e = 0 : 1$, many nodes tend to employ high transmitting power without using underwater sensor nodes with low energy. Thus, data packets forwarded via fewer hops leads to the lower energy consumption and prolongs network lifetime.

3.3   Performance with Faulty Nodes

In this section, we present the performance of the proposed routing protocol when the faulty nodes appear in IoUT. The faulty nodes in this section represents that the sensor node cannot transmit, receive, and forward data packets. The numbers of received data packets by the sink node are corresponding to the best ratios as presented in Sect. 3.2. As shown in Figs. 3 and 4, the number of data packets decreases with the increasing of number of faulty one-hop nodes. The reason is that the sensor nodes (except the one-hop nodes) have to use more hops to report data to the sink node when the faulty one-hop nodes appear. The remaining one-hop nodes (which can transmit, receive, and forward data) must forward a larger amount of data compared with that without faulty one-hop nodes. Additionally, we observe that the number of data packets received by the

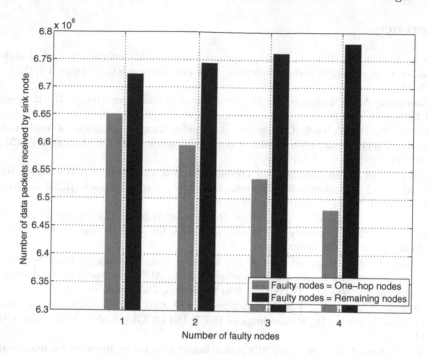

Fig. 4. Performance versus number of faulty nodes: three transmitting power, network size: 11×11

sink node increases when the number of faulty nodes increases. The reason is that the amount of forwarding data decreases when the number of faulty nodes increases. The one-hop nodes can transmit their own data to the sink node directly and reduce energy consumption.

4   Conclusions

In this paper, we propose a routing protocol for IoUT. The simulation results show that the network lifetime can be prolonged under different network sizes. Furthermore, we can get the best ratio of the weight for the transmitting power to the weight for the energy consumption, which can lead to the maximum number of received data packets by the sink node. We also evaluate the performance of the proposed routing protocol when the faulty nodes appears in IoUT. In the future, we will consider the scenario of dynamic network topology of IoUT to evaluate our proposed routing protocol and will figure out any possible improvement.

References

1. Kao, C., Lin, Y., Wu, G., et al.: A comprehensive study on the internet of underwater things: applications, challenges, and channel models. Sensors **17**(7), 1–20 (2017)
2. Nordrum, A.: A language for the internet of underwater things. IEEE Spectr. **54**(9), 9–10 (2017)
3. Petroccia, R., Petrioli, C., Potter, J.: Performance evaluation of underwater medium access control protocols: at-sea experiments. IEEE J. Ocean. Eng. **43**(2), 547–556 (2018)
4. Caiti, A., et al.: Linking acoustic communications and network performance: integration and experimentation of an underwater acoustic network. IEEE J. Ocean. Eng. **38**(4), 758–771 (2013)
5. Mohapatra, A., Gautam, N., Gibson, R.: Combined routing and node replacement in energy-efficient underwater sensor networks for seismic monitoring. IEEE J. Ocean. Eng. **38**(1), 80–90 (2013)
6. Jornet, J., Stojanovic, M., Zorzi, M.: Focused beam routing protocol for underwater acoustic networks. In: Proceedings of the ACM international workshop on Underwater Networks, WuWNeT, San Francisco, California, pp. 75–82 (2008)
7. Park, V., Corson, M.: A highly adaptive distributed routing algorithm for mobile wireless networks. In: Proceedings of IEEE INFOCOM, Kobe, Japan, pp. 1405–1413 (1997)
8. Xie, P., Cui, J.-H., Lao, L.: VBF: vector-based forwarding protocol for underwater sensor networks. In: Boavida, F., Plagemann, T., Stiller, B., Westphal, C., Monteiro, E. (eds.) NETWORKING 2006. LNCS, vol. 3976, pp. 1216–1221. Springer, Heidelberg (2006). https://doi.org/10.1007/11753810_111
9. Tiansi, H., Fei, Y.: QELAR: a machine-learning-based adaptive routing protocol for energy-efficient and lifetime-extended underwater sensor networks. IEEE Trans. Mob. Comput. **9**(6), 796–809 (2010)
10. Chang, J., Tassiulas, L.: Maximum lifetime routing in wireless sensor networks. IEEE/ACM Trans. Netw. **12**(4), 609–619 (2004)
11. Huang, C., Ramanathan, P., Saluja, K.: Routing TCP flows in underwater mesh networks. IEEE J. Sel. Areas Commun. **29**(10), 2022–2032 (2011)
12. Madan, R., Lall, S.: Distributed algorithms for maximum lifetime routing in wireless sensor networks. IEEE Trans. Wirel. Commun. **5**(8), 2185–2193 (2006)
13. Gatzianas, M., Georgiadis, L.: A distributed algorithm for maximum lifetime routing in sensor networks with mobile sink. IEEE Trans. Wirel. Commun. **7**(3), 984–994 (2008)
14. Vazifehdan, J., Prasad, R., Niemegeers, I.: Energy-efficient reliable routing considering residual energy in wireless ad hoc networks. IEEE Trans. Mob. Comput. **13**(4), 434–447 (2014)
15. Evologics. http://www.evologics.de/en/products/acoustics/s2cm_series.html

Author Index

Printed in the United States
By Bookmasters